SENTENCING AND SANCTIONS IN
WESTERN COUNTRIES

Sentencing and Sanctions in Western Countries

Edited by
Michael Tonry
& Richard S. Frase

UNIVERSITY PRESS

2001

OXFORD
UNIVERSITY PRESS

Oxford   New York
Athens   Auckland   Bangkok   Bogotá   Buenos Aires   Calcutta
Cape Town   Chennai   Dar es Salaam   Delhi   Florence   Hong Kong   Istanbul
Karachi   Kuala Lumpur   Madrid   Melbourne   Mexico City   Mumbai
Nairobi   Paris   São Paulo   Shanghai   Singapore   Taipei   Tokyo   Toronto   Warsaw

and associated companies in
Berlin   Ibadan

Copyright © 2001 by Oxford University Press, Inc.

Published by Oxford University Press, Inc.
198 Madison Avenue, New York, New York 10016

Oxford is a registered trademark of Oxford University Press.

Library of Congress Cataloging-in-Publication Data
Sentencing and sanctions in western countries / edited by Michael Tonry and
Richard S. Frase.
　　p.　cm.
　　Includes bibliographical references.
　　ISBN 0-19-513053-7; 0-19-513861-9 (pbk.)
　　1. Sentences (Criminal procedure)   2. Punishment.   I. Tonry, Michael H.   II. Frase,
Richard S.
K5121 .S26 2000
345'.0772—dc21   99-054690

9 8 7 6 5 4 3 2 1

Printed in the United States of America
on acid-free paper

Preface

Because crime and punishment are basic human problems, policy makers and analysts charged with formulating better solutions ought to look widely for relevant knowledge both within and beyond national borders. In practice, barriers of language and parochialism have long been obstacles. But they should be no longer.

There has been little genuinely cross-national or comparative scholarship on sentencing and sanctions, though there are domestic literatures within countries that can be compared. Our aim was to contribute to the development of such a body of scholarship by persuading leading scholars in several countries to discuss sentencing and punishment in their countries and the causes and consequences of major recent changes, and by persuading others to look across national boundaries at international developments and at issues that arise in every country. In doing this, we follow the lead of Chris Clarkson and Rod Morgan, who edited a similar book, *The Politics of Sentencing Reform* (Clarendon Press, 1995), based on papers presented at a conference in Bristol, England, in 1993. We have extended their efforts by including more civil law countries within the scope of this volume and by commissioning essays on explicitly international subjects.

The chapters in this volume were initially prepared for a May 1998 conference in Minneapolis entitled "Sentencing Policy in Comparative International Perspective: Recent Changes within and across National Boundaries." The conference was sponsored by the University of Minnesota Law School and the Max Planck Institute for International and Comparative Criminal Law in Freiburg, Germany. The tactical aim was to bring together researchers from the United States and other Western countries to discuss current knowledge about sentencing and sanctions in individual countries, and also what is known or knowable about the effectiveness of particular practices. The strategic aim was to consider whether practices that appear to achieve important public purposes in some countries can or should be adopted by others and whether the spread of ineffective or failed practices can be prevented.

Preparation of a volume such as this involves much work by many people. The writers prepared initial drafts, willingly subjected themselves to public reaction and criticism, and good-naturedly accepted further suggestions from the editors. Barbara Damchik-Dykes put the manuscripts and references into standard formats, no small job with writers from several disciplines and six countries, managed the extensive communications over editorial questions and proofs that a multi-author volume entails, and in general coordinated its production. We are grateful to the writers, and to Barbara, and also to Dean E. Thomas Sullivan of the University of Minnesota Law School and Professor Hans-Jörg Albrecht, director of the Max Planck Institute, who provided the funding and institutional support that made the venture possible. Finally, we express our gratitude to all who attended the Minnesota conference. A not-so-hidden personal agenda was to bring together people whose work we knew and respected, so that we could learn from them. People argued, questioned, and explained, and all participants went away knowing more than when they arrived. The book is much the better as a result. These in addition to the authors of the essays in this volume were our instructors: David Boerner (Seattle University), Craig Bradley (Indiana University School of Law, Bloomington), Francis Carney (Massachusetts Sentencing Commission), Debra Dailey (Minnesota Sentencing Guidelines Commission), Nora Demleitner (St. Mary's University of San Antonio School of Law), Walter Dickey (University of Wisconsin Law School), Pat Dowdeswell (Home Office, England and Wales), J. Fiselier (University of Gröningen), Daniel J. Freed (Yale Law School), Richard Gebelein (Superior Court, Wilmington, Delaware), Sally Hillsman (National Institute of Justice), Neil Hutton (University of Strathclyde), James B. Jacobs (New York University School of Law), Michael Kilchling (Max Planck Institute), Roxanne Lieb (Washington Institute for Public Policy), Austin Lovegrove (University of Melbourne), Marc Miller (Emory University), Neil Morgan (University of Western Australia), Norval Morris (University of Chicago Law School), Stephan Parmentier (University of Leuven), Julian Roberts (University of Ottawa), Michael Smith (University of Wisconsin Law School), Edward Tomlinson (University of Maryland School of Law), Tom Vander Beken (University of Ghent), Anton van Kalmthout (Tilburg University), Dirk van Zyl Smit (University of Cape Town), Kate Warner (University of Tasmania), Edward Wise (Wayne State University), Ronald Wright (Wake Forest University), David Yellen (Hofstra University), Warren Young (Victoria University of Wellington), Li-ling Yue (University of Beijing), and George Zdenkowksi (University of New South Wales).

Our hope in initiating the venture was to continue the effort started in Bristol to build a genuinely multinational and comparative literature on sentencing and sanctions in Western countries. Whether this volume usefully advances that project, readers will decide for themselves.

Minneapolis, Minnesota   M. T.
October 2000   R. S. F.

Contents

Contributors

Hans-Jörg Albrecht is director of the Max Planck Institute for International and Comparative Criminal Law, Freiburg.

Andrew Ashworth is Vinerian Professor of English Law, All Souls College, Oxford University.

Richard S. Frase is Benjamin N. Berger Professor of Criminal Law, University of Minnesota.

Arie Freiberg is head, Department of Criminology, and professor of criminology, University of Melbourne.

Leena Kurki is senior research associate, Minnesota Council on Crime and Justice.

Tapio Lappi-Seppälä is director of the National Research Institute of Legal Policy, Helsinki.

Rod Morgan is professor of law, University of Bristol.

Kevin R. Reitz is professor of law, University of Colorado.

Peter J. Tak is professor of law, University of Nijmegen.

Michael Tonry is director, Institute of Criminology, Cambridge University, and Sonosky Professor of Law and Public Policy, University of Minnesota.

Andrew von Hirsch is Honorary Professor of Penal Theory and Penal Law, Cambridge University.

Thomas Weigend is director, Institute on International and Comparative Criminal Law, and professor of law, University of Cologne.

SENTENCING AND SANCTIONS IN
WESTERN COUNTRIES

MICHAEL TONRY

Punishment Policies and Patterns in Western Countries

W e can learn things about crime and punishment by looking across national boundaries. For despite many important similarities in how Western nations respond to crime, and in the values that underlie those responses, sentencing and punishment policies vary greatly. U.S. Supreme Court Justice Louis Brandeis observed, in *New State Ice Co. v. Liebmann*, 285 U.S. 262, 311 (1932), that "it is one of the happy incidents of the federal system that a single, courageous state may, if its citizens choose, serve as a laboratory and try social and economic experiments without risk to the rest of the country." Countries likewise can learn from one another's experiments if they will.

The formal similarities are great. Among the Western countries, at least, there is widespread commitment to democratic values and Enlightenment ideals, and the institutions of criminal justice are everywhere much the same. These include professional police, public prosecutors' offices, an independent judiciary, and reliance on imprisonment as the primary sanction for very serious crimes and chronic criminals and on various community penalties for others. There is much more similarity than difference in the content of criminal law doctrine, rules of evidence, and procedural safeguards.

Nonetheless, and despite broad similarity in most countries in crime trends over the past thirty years, sentencing and punishment policies and patterns vary enormously. In the United States, England, and the Netherlands and many other western European countries, crime rates rose rapidly from the mid-1960s until the late 1980s or early 1990s and have been declining since (see, e.g., Downes and Morgan 1997; van Dijk 1997; Mirrlees-Black et al. 1998; Pfeiffer 1998; Bureau of Justice Statistics 1999b). Similarity in crime trends, however, has not been paralleled by similarity in policy or institutional responses. At least four areas for comparison stand out.

First, prevailing beliefs vary greatly among policymakers about the causes of crime and the capacity of criminal justice policy changes to affect crime rates. In the United States and more recently in England and some Australian states, many policymakers believe that crime is primarily the result of bad or irresponsible people, not criminogenic conditions and inadequate socialization, and that harsher and more restrictive punishments will reduce crime rates through deterrent and incapacitative processes. As a result, as U.S. crime rates went up for two decades and penalties steadily became harsher, little thought was given to the possibility that crime rates may not be much affected by punishment policies. More recently, as crime rates have fallen in many countries, newly adopted harsh polices have been retained in the United States, England, and Australia, possibly because of a belief that declining crime rates are attributable to them. By contrast, the absence of steadily increasing imprisonment rates in many western European countries suggests that crime rates and patterns are not regarded as something easily controlled or necessarily much affected by punishment policies. The polar case is the widespread Finnish view that sentencing and punishment play an important backup role in norm-reinforcement, but that primary institutions, such as the family, the church, and the school, play the primary roles in socializing people into law-abiding habits. Accordingly, though punishment should be certain, it need not be harsh. Such premises, Patrik Törnudd observes, do not imply that "changes in policy, such as increases in the severity of punishment, would be widely seen as an appropriate or cost-effective means of controlling the level of crime" (Törnudd 1997, p. 190).

Second, relationships between crime and imprisonment patterns vary greatly. Against the backdrop of similar crime trends, imprisonment rates and prisoner numbers increased continuously in the United States after 1973 and in the Netherlands after 1975, decreased continuously in Finland after 1976, fluctuated widely in France and Italy, fluctuated slightly in Germany, Sweden, and Denmark, and followed other patterns elsewhere. In the 1990s, imprisonment rates have increased in many but not all countries. Whatever else these data show, they refute the existence of any inexorable or even general relationship between crime rates and imprisonment, directly, or, through intermediate effects on public fears, opinions, or policies, indirectly.

Third, policies governing types and amounts of punishment vary greatly. The most dramatic difference is between the United States, which continues to use the death penalty and life sentences without possibility of parole and where prison sentences exceeding ten years are common, and the rest of the Western world, which has renounced the death penalty and where prison sentences longer than a few years are uncommon. But there are many more differences than this. In some countries, for example, Germany and Austria, prison sentences shorter than six months are regarded as destructive and serving no valid penal purpose and are therefore strongly discouraged. In others, including Sweden and Finland, certainty of punishment is seen as important, but not severity, and as a result many sentences to days or weeks of imprisonment are imposed. And there are wide divergences in the use of community punishments. Community service is a commonly used prison alternative in England, Scotland, and the Netherlands, but is seldom used as a primary punishment in many other countries. Day fines are an oft-imposed punishment in Germany and much of Scandinavia but are used not at all in the

English-speaking countries and many others (e.g., the Netherlands) and only sparingly in still others (e.g., France). Electronic monitoring has been common in the United States for a decade but has only recently begun to catch on in most other countries (chap. 8, this volume).

Fourth, though nearly all Western countries attempt to insure use of fair procedures for determining guilt or innocence at and before adjudication of guilt (see, e.g., Weissbrodt and Wolfrum 1997), they vary greatly in whether, how, and how seriously they try to achieve just outcomes at the sentencing stage. Put differently, countries vary greatly in what they do to minimize unwarranted disparities in sentencing and to insure horizontal and vertical equity among sentences imposed. The approaches range from use of numerical guidelines for sentencing in many U.S. jurisdictions (and for prosecutors' sentence recommendations in the Netherlands), guideline judgments in England issued by the Court of Appeal, sentencing information systems in Scotland and New South Wales (and earlier in several Canadian provinces), and statutory sentencing principles enunciated in the Finnish and Swedish criminal codes to the approach of most European countries, Canada, Australia, New Zealand, and large parts of the United States that leaves the matter in the hands of sentencing judges.

Most of the chapters in this volume concern sentencing policies and practices in individual countries, and a few concern more general cross-cutting issues that arise in all countries. The chapters speak for themselves and I see no point in summarizing them or in commenting on them except in passing. Instead, I approach the subject from the back, from punishment policies and patterns, and suggest some of their implications for thinking about sentencing policies in individual countries and comparatively.

Some might think this gets things backwards, since punishment is the outcome of sentencing, and the populations and flows of offenders in prisons and subject to other criminal penalties are merely the outcome of sentencing in the aggregate. Many judges and prosecutors firmly assert the irrelevance to them of such things as prison capacity and correctional resources. Their jobs, they say, are to see that just punishments are imposed and public safety interests are advanced; handling sentenced offenders is someone else's business. In a small minority of jurisdictions in the United States, legislators and corrections officials believe that correctional resources and capacities should influence sentencing policies, and a few jurisdictions have incorporated "prison capacity constraints" into their sentencing policies and required that sentencing commissions develop guidelines whose application is not projected to produce larger numbers of inmates than can be housed within the jurisdiction's existing prison capacity. That is important and has helped shape the details of sentencing policy in those jurisdictions (chap. 6, this volume), but it reflects the wholesale views of people with systemic interests and not the retail views of front-line practitioners.

Several lessons for comparative understanding of sentencing stand out if one thinks from punishment to sentencing rather than from sentencing to punishment. First, the punishment backdrop has important implications for assessing the merits of proposed innovations in particular places. In countries, such as Finland and Sweden, with relatively low incarceration rates and a tradition of imposing sentences measured in days or months, strong sentencing standards are less desirable than in countries, such as the United States, eastern Europe, and increasingly England and Australia, with higher incarceration rates and a tradition of imposing sentences measured in years and decades. Sentencing standards must try to reconcile both parts of the equality principle. That is, they must be concerned to treat like cases alike and to treat different cases differently. U.S. federal guidelines, three-strikes laws, and mandatory sentences, for example, prescribe sentences for offenders who are like situated in terms of their crimes, but at the cost of ignoring differences in their lives and circumstances that many judges (and others) believe ethically relevant to thinking about just punishments. Indeterminate sentencing, as in Australia and Canada and some U.S. states, by contrast, allows ample latitude to differentiate sentences to take account of offenders' biographies, but critics argue that they often produce unwarranted disparities in relation to offense severity. No system of sentencing standards can perfectly reconcile the two parts of the equality principle, but approaches can make one or the other kind of injustice more likely. Concerns about unwarranted disparities, for example, may be less important in Scandinavia, and hence the case for detailed sentencing standards less strong, than in the United States. When judges' human idiosyncrasies result in disparate two-, three-, and four-month sentences for like-situated offenders in Sweden, the stakes are much lower than in the United States, where the same idiosyncrasies might yield one-, three-, and five-year prison sentences. Many U.S. sentencing policies, in Arie Freiberg's terms (chap. 1, this volume), risk unwarranted parities in the interest of treating formally like cases alike, and Sweden may risk unwarranted disparities in the interest of treating factually different cases differently. Against their different punishment backdrops, both those acceptances of risk may make sense, and the cases for Swedish adoption of numerical guidelines or U.S. adoption of Swedish-style statutory sentencing principles be correspondingly weak. Thus one major implication for sentencing policy of comparisons of punishment polices and patterns is diagnostic: one size does not fit all. Sentencing reforms need to be sensitive to the problems to which they can serve as (partial) solutions.

Second, comparative assessment of punishment policies and patterns supports a strong case for development of international and cross-national human rights conventions concerning sentencing and punishment. The enormous differences in punishment patterns in Western countries cannot be justified in human rights terms. International human rights conventions have long enunciated minimum standards concerning defendants' pretrial and trial rights but not concerning sentencing and punishment. In Europe, the European Convention on Human Rights increasingly is being used to override national laws and practices in trial and pretrial settings (Weissbrodt and Wolfrum 1997) but so far only at the furthest margins of sentencing and punishment (chap. 9, this volume). The European Torture Convention is increasingly effective as an extra-legal device (i.e., acting through moral suasion and publicity rather than court orders) for improving conditions in prisons, jails, and police lockups (chap. 10, this volume). There is, of course, a chicken-and-egg problem that the cultural and political forces that produce inhumanely harsh practices also prevent countries from subscribing to international conventions that ban or repudiate such practices (e.g., the U.S. and Chinese refusals to ratify without qualification international conventions against the death penalty [see chap. 8, this volume] and the same two countries' opposition to creation of an International Criminal Court to handle war crimes, genocide, and crimes against humanity). However, moral example and suasion often matter. Many eastern European countries have abolished the death penalty in order to join the Council of Europe, and the United States continues to try to influence the development of the International Criminal Court. Widely endorsed international human rights standards, even if they are solely precatory, can in the long term influence the evolution of sensibilities, policies, and practices in all countries, including those that initially reject them.

This introduction consists of three main sections. The first looks at crime and punishment trends in many countries to ask and answer the question whether differences in crime rates and patterns explain punishment differences between countries. Because imprisonment is the punishment everywhere mostly used for serious crimes, the focus is on imprisonment. Somewhat parochially, the issue is approached by using claims about U.S. experience as an example, and using data from other countries to test those claims. The evidence is clear; national differences in imprisonment rates and patterns result not from differences in crime but from differences in policy.

The second section accordingly looks at national differences in policies about crime. The major differences relate to whether crime policy has become a major contested issue in partisan and ideological politics, whether moral notions about the need to punish wrongdoers are dominantly influential, and whether policy makers appear to believe that punishment policies and practices are likely importantly to influence crime rates. The answers to these questions provide explanations for punishment trends and also set the conditions that determine what sentencing injustices — unwarranted disparities or parities, "undue leniency," racial, class, or gender-bias — are perceived as important problems. Here, too, the evidence is clear: there are stark differences in the political salience of crime and punishment issues in various countries and those differences fundamentally shape sentencing policies and punishment practices.

The third section then surveys approaches taken in various countries to achieve consistency in sentences imposed. Discussions are short since many of the chapters in this volume discuss developments in particular countries in detail. Approaches vary, but their value and significance also vary greatly depending on punishment politics and conventions. The overriding lesson to be learned is that the feasibility and desirability of a system of sentencing standards depends crucially on the environment in which it is introduced. U.S.-style numerical guidelines, for example, may be the best among several undesirable choices in a punitive country like the United States but would likely do more harm than good in a northern European country in which crime policy has not been heavily politicized and in which punishment severity is restrained.

I. Comparative Imprisonment Trends

The relations between crime and imprisonment are complex and diverse. Stunning dissimilarity in imprisonment trends between countries becomes apparent when longitudinal data are examined. This dissimilarity is not as widely recognized as it might be because longitudinal data are generally well known only within countries and international comparisons are typically based on cross-sectional data on prisoners per 100,000 population in a given year. Thus, in the United States, it is well known that imprisonment rates have been increasing for twenty-five years, (see figure I.1) and that the United States has imprisonment rates four to twelve times those of other countries with which it is ordinarily compared (see table I.1). From these comparisons come arguments over whether the U.S. rates are too high, whether rising crime rates justified the initial increased use of imprisonment, and whether subsequently declining crime rates justify continued increased use of imprisonment. These, however, are at best oversimplified arguments, and at most naive, as quickly becomes evident when better international comparisons are made.

Looking only at one country's trend data misleads because it invites parochial reactions either that local experience is "normal" and need not be examined closely or critically, or that unique local crime problems and trends explain local differences (e.g., Wilson and Herrnstein 1986; Bennett, DiIulio, and Walters 1996). Both of these claims are made in explanation of why U.S. imprisonment

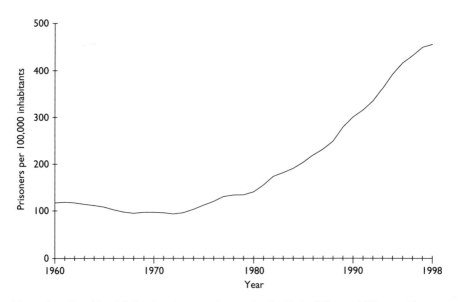

Figure I.1. Combined federal and state prisoners in the United States, 1960 to mid-year 1998 (per 100,000 population). *Sources:* Maguire and Pastore (1998); Bureau of Justice Statistics (1999c).

Table I.1: Various Western Countries Ranked by Incarceration Rate per 100,000, 1997–1998

	Total in Penal Institutions (Including Pretrial Detainees)	Date	Prison Population per 100,000 National Population
United States	1,725,842	6/30/97	645
New Zealand	5,236	1997	145
Portugal	14,336	3/15/98	145
England and Wales	65,906	9/30/98	125
Canada	34,166	1997–98	115
Spain	42,827	9/1/97	110
Australia	17,661	1997	95
France	53,259	10/1/98	90
Germany	74,317	9/1/97	90
Austria	6,946	9/1/97	85
Italy	49,477	9/1/97	85
Netherlands	13,618	9/1/97	85
Belgium	8,342	9/1/97	80
Denmark	3,508	11/6/98	65
Sweden	5,221	9/1/97	60
Greece	5,577	9/1/97	55
Finland	2,798	9/1/97	55
Norway	2,318	9/1/97	55

Source: Walmsley (1999).

rates are so much higher than in other countries: U.S. crime rates are higher and long rose more sharply than other countries' and higher imprisonment rates are the result; or U.S. crime is more serious than elsewhere and that explains the difference. Both of those assertions could be true. However, the first is completely untrue and the second is mostly untrue but with an important qualification.

A. Do Imprisonment Rate Changes Track Crime Rate Changes?

There is nothing inherently implausible in claims that rising crime rates drive rising imprisonment rates and that crime rates in the 1970s and 1980s rose faster in the United States than elsewhere and imprisonment rose with them. Without international comparisons, there is no way to assess those claims. But international comparisons can be made that shed some light on both crime rate trends and absolute levels. The available data, of course, are not perfect but they are good enough to undermine the crime-driven explanations for U.S. imprisonment patterns.

Because countries define and record crimes differently, statements about absolute differences in rates based only on official crime data inevitably are suspect. In figures I.2, I.3, and I.4 for example, U.S. homicide data include completed murders and non-negligent homicides, while the Finnish data also include at-

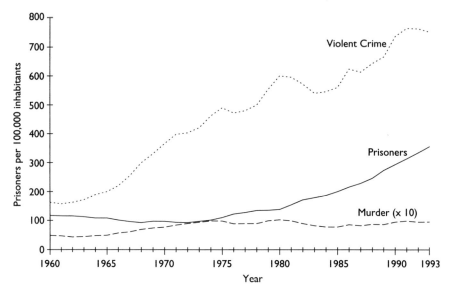

Figure I.2. Imprisonment, violent crime, and murder rates in the United States, 1960–1993 (per 100,000 population). *Note:* Crime rates are somewhat differently calculated in the United States than in Finland and Germany; U.S. incarceration rates do not include jail inmates. *Sources:* Bureau of Justice Statistics, Prisoners, various years (Washington, D.C.: U.S. Department of Justice, Bureau of Justice Statistics); Federal Bureau of Investigation, *Crime in the United States*, various years (Washington, D.C.: U.S. Government Printing Office).

tempts. Definitional differences should not matter, however, because the comparison is not between absolute crime rates but between trends in each country in events that country counts as violent felonies and homicides. The trend is what is important.

Two things stand out. First, in all three countries, violent crime and homicide rates increased a great deal and nearly continuously through the early 1990s. (The ending date was chosen because it precedes recent declines in crime rates.) The upward curves are comparably steep in each country. Second, the imprisonment rate patterns in the three countries are very different. In the United States, imprisonment rates increased steeply and continuously after 1972, tripling in the following twenty years. In Finland, imprisonment rates fell significantly and continuously after 1975, declining 38.2 percent in the following fourteen years (Törnudd 1993). In Germany, imprisonment rates fell from 1968 to the mid-1970s, rose for a few years, fell again in the early 1980s, and then roughly stabilized (Weigend 1997).

There is no necessary relationship between crime rates and imprisonment rates. The three figures refute both the notion that crime rate increases directly cause imprisonment to rise (more people to lock up) and the notion that rising crime rates necessarily indirectly cause imprisonment to rise (increased public fear, anx-

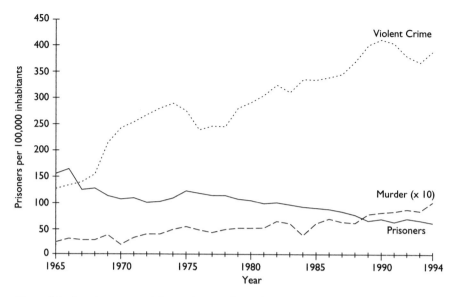

Figure I.3. Imprisonment, violent crime, and murder rates in Finland, 1965–1994 (per 100,000 population). *Note*: Violent crime and murder rates are somewhat differently calculated in Finland than in the United States; the Finnish imprisonment rate includes pretrial detainees. *Source*: Finnish Ministry of Justice (unpublished data provided to author).

iety, and anger compel harsher policies). Imprisonment patterns are not immune to influence from changes in crime rates and patterns, but they are at least as much and often more the consequences of conscious policy choices made by public officials. In the United States, many elected officials wanted punishments made harsher and more people to be sent to prison and to be held there longer (during periods of both rising and falling crime rates), and they were (Tonry 1998; chap. 6, this volume). In Finland, officials and others wanted imprisonment rates to decline, and they did, despite very large crime rate increases (Törnudd 1993, 1997; chap. 3, this volume). In Germany, officials wanted fewer people sentenced to prison and especially wanted the use of prison sentences under six months drastically curtailed, and they were, and imprisonment rates fell, despite rising violent crime rates (Weigend 1997; chap. 5, this volume).

B. Higher Imprisonment Rates Result from Higher Crime Rates

If crime rate trends do not drive imprisonment rates, it would be surprising if absolute levels of crime did. Comparisons between Finland in 1960, 1970, 1980, and 1990 provide a strong counterexample; if those data were thought of as if they were cross-sectional data from different countries at the same time rather than from the same country at different times, the absence of a causal relationship

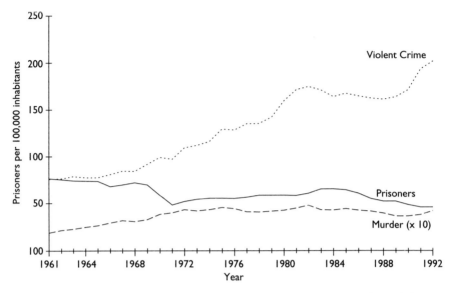

Figure I.4. Imprisonment, violent crime, and murder rates in Germany, 1961–1992 (per 100,000 population). *Note*: Violent crime and murder rates are somewhat differently calculated in Germany than in the United States; the German imprisonment rate excludes pretrial detainees. *Source*: German Ministry of Justice (unpublished data provided to author).

would be clear. Nonetheless, it is commonly said in the United States that U.S. crime rates are much higher than those elsewhere and that is why so relatively many more people are in prison and jail (e.g., Wilson and Herrnstein 1986; Bennett, DiIulio, and Walters 1996). The corollary would be that places with lower or low crime rates would have low levels of imprisonment. Because of the near impossibility of making comparative statements about crime trends based on official data (Lynch 1995), it is not easy to offer strong conclusions about this based on reliable data, but findings from the International Crime Victimization Survey (Mayhew and van Dijk 1997) suggest that U.S. imprisonment rates cannot be explained in this way.

The International Crime Victimization Survey (ICVS) has been carried out in Western countries three times since 1989. Designed to avoid the problems involved in trying to compare official data, the ICVS uses standard questionnaires employing common definitions of crimes to collect data from randomly selected residents of various countries. Table I.2 summarizes findings from the latest survey on self-reported victimizations per 1,000 residents aged 16 and over in eleven countries. For no offense are U.S. rates the highest, though they are among the highest for some violent offenses, and for some property crimes U.S. rates are among the lowest. As with any survey, methodological issues can be raised concerning the ICVS, particularly sample sizes, variable nonresponse rates, and cul-

Table I.2: Victimization Rates per 1,000, by Country and Offense, 1995

Country	Burglary	Robbery	Car Theft	Personal Theft[1]	Sexual Incidents	Assaults and Threats	Eleven Specific Crimes[2]
England and Wales	3.0	1.4	2.5	5.0	2.0	5.9	30.9
Scotland	1.5	0.8	1.7	4.5	1.3	4.2	25.6
Northern Ireland	1.5	0.5	1.6	2.5	1.2	1.7	16.8
Netherlands	2.6	0.6	0.4	6.8	3.6	4.0	31.5
Switzerland	1.3	0.9	0.1	5.7	4.6	3.1	26.7
France	2.4	1.0	1.6	4.0	0.9	3.9	25.3
Finland	0.6	0.5	0.4	3.2	2.6	4.1	18.9
Sweden	1.3	0.5	1.2	4.6	2.9	4.5	24.0
Austria	0.9	0.2	0.2	5.1	3.8	2.1	18.9
United States	2.6	1.3	1.9	3.9	2.5	5.7	24.2
Canada	3.4	1.2	1.5	5.7	2.7	4.0	25.2

Source: Kurki (1997).

[1]Thefts of personal property.
[2]Based on eleven crimes standard across sweeps, omitting thefts from garages.

tural differences in willingness to discuss embarrassing subjects, that caution against unqualified acceptance of findings, but there are several indications that the findings are broadly reliable. First, the patterns of between-country comparisons in the latest survey in 1997 replicate those in the two earlier rounds. That is, the relative rank ordering of countries by reported victimization rates for various crimes is fairly stable. Second, more important and persuasive, for individual countries the victimization trends shown in the three surveys parallel those shown in official data and victim surveys in the same countries (van Dijk 1997). For the United States, for example, the ICVS shows a rise in victimization rates between 1988 and 1992 and a fall between 1992 and 1995, which is the same pattern shown by official data from the FBI's Uniform Crime Reports (Federal Bureau of Investigation 1999) and by victimization data from the Department of Justice's National Crime Victimization Survey (Bureau of Justice Statistics 1999a).

An important qualification needs to be made. The ICVS does not and could not measure homicide rates, and U.S. violence rates involving firearms are higher than elsewhere. Even after recent declines, the 1998 U.S. homicide rate of 6.3 per 100,000 residents is two to four times higher than those of most Western countries. Franklin Zimring and Gordon Hawkins in *Crime Is Not the Problem* (1997) show that violence rates are considerably higher in U.S. cities than in comparable cities elsewhere. To a considerable extent both these patterns are entangled in U.S. cultural attitudes about guns and gun control. Assaults, robberies, and attempts to kill people are substantially more likely to result in death when guns are involved than otherwise (Zimring 1972), so to some extent the higher U.S. homicide rates are a product of higher rates of gun use in crime and, compared with most other countries, higher levels of gun availability and ownership. Nonetheless, U.S. homicide rates remain higher than those in other developed countries even when only data on nongun homicides are compared (but not so much higher; the 1998 nongun homicide rate in the U.S. was 4.1 per 100,000 and that in England was well under 1 per 100,000), and violent crime, though probably no more common in the United States, is more violent.

This contradictory pattern within a pattern—lower violent crime rates overall than in some other developed countries, but a higher fraction (and absolute rates) of those involving death, guns, and serious violence—no doubt is a partial explanation for high U.S. imprisonment rates. Two trends, however, cut in the opposite direction. The percentage of people sentenced to U.S. prisons for violent crimes is low (29.5 percent in 1996) (Bureau of Justice Statistics 1999b, table 1.23) and has not increased since 1991, so it is hard to attribute rising prison populations to violent offenders. Moreover, much the largest component of recent prison population growth has been a vast increase in admissions of people convicted of drug crimes (Blumstein and Beck 1999).

Prison population levels and trends, accordingly, do not happen automatically or as the result of simple relations between crime and punishment. They happen because people will them to happen or because people decide not to take action to control them when they begin to increase. As the chapters in this volume on Australia (chap. 1), England (chap. 2), the Netherlands (chap. 4), and the United States (chap. 6) show, recent increases in prison populations in Australia, England, and the Netherlands, and the longer-term increases in the United States, happened because politicians willed it.

II. Comparative Crime Policy Trends

In every country and at every time there is a range of views about punishments for crime that range from classic Kantian arguments that wrongdoers must be punished because they deserve it to classic Benthamite views that wrongdoers must be punished only so much and in such ways as will maximize net public benefit. Likewise in every country and at every time there are individuals who see some punishments of some offenders as unduly lenient and coddling and individuals who see some punishments as unduly severe and cruel. Over time the balances of such views change and both general policies and particular policies change with them.

Prevailing attitudes about punishment set limits on sentencing policy. Where attitudes are harsh and moralistic, the bounds for development of principled, humane policies are narrow, but the stakes are high. Where attitudes are less stereotyped and moralistic, the potential for innovation may be greater but the need less. As in the preceding section, I explore this subject by using the United States as an example and use data and experience from other countries to demonstrate that the United States is atypical and that the prospects for humane policy innovations elsewhere may therefore be greater.

For the past twenty-five years, many people in the United States have called for harsher punishments. In the 1970s at the beginning of the modern "sentencing reform movement," many proponents of change were conservatives and law enforcement officials who urged adoption of determinate and fixed sentencing laws in order to prevent lenient judges from coddling criminals (Messinger and Johnson 1978). In the early 1990s, one Republican gubernatorial candidate in Virginia, George Allen, campaigned primarily on a platform to toughen sentences by abolishing parole and when elected oversaw changes that make Virginia's among the harshest sentencing laws in the United States. In many states, conservatives launched campaigns for "truth in sentencing," by which they meant abolition or restriction of parole release and remission or time off for good behavior. By 1994, those campaigns had become so effective that the U.S. Congress authorized $8 billion in subsidies for prison building to states that would enact truth-in-sentencing laws requiring designated violent, drug, and other offenders to serve at least 85 percent of the announced sentence in prison. By 1999, more than thirty states had changed their laws to qualify for the federal money.

Thus there seems in the United States to be a widespread vicarious interest in ensuring that offenders are severely punished or, at least, that they experience all the punishment ordered. Many proponents of harsh sentencing policies appear to worry that offenders may not be punished enough, but not to worry that they may be punished too much. Put differently, certainty and severity are seen as governing values, with proportionality and parsimony being given much less weight. Such sentiments impose significant limits on efforts to reduce the prison population, repeal or amend harsh laws, or in other ways reduce sentencing severity. Some three-strikes laws, for example, most infamously California's, require minimum twenty-five-year sentences, and sometimes life sentences without possibility of parole, for third-time felons convicted of minor property offenses or trafficking in marijuana (Dickey and Hollenhorst 1998). One recurring criticism of the federal sentencing guidelines is that they often result in imposition of harsh mandatory minimum five-, ten-, and twenty-year sentences on low-level drug traffickers or on drug couriers while other provisions of the guidelines allow for imposition of much slighter sentences on large-scale traffickers and importers (Stith and Cabranes 1998). Andrew von Hirsch (chap. 11, this volume) tries to account for the development of such policies, now common in many U.S. jurisdictions, and the principled justifications, assuming there are some, for removing considerations of fairness to offenders from among the important values to be served by sentencing policies.

Are U.S. punishment policies harsher than those of other countries? The answer is yes, though reaching it is not simple. That then raises the question why (the answer is that U.S. officials want punishments to be severe, and with the passage of time have wanted them made more severe). In at least some other Western countries, the popular and political cultures seem less resolute in their determination that offenders be punished in full measure, as can be shown in a number of ways. This difference between U.S. moralism and other countries' lesser commitment to seeing that offenders suffer their full desert provides an important backdrop to sentencing policy formulation.

In terms of conventional categories, the United States has the most punitive crime policies in the Western world and various Scandinavian countries probably have the least punitive. There are several bases for such a claim. First, U.S. incarceration rates per 100,000 residents, as presented in table I.1, are four to twelve times higher than those of other Western countries. This comparison is not de-cisive, of course, as various people have shown (Young and Brown 1993; Pease 1994; Kommer 1994), because it assumes that prisoners per population is the right way to compare punitivism. Other possibilities include prisoners per crime, arrest, or conviction. Warren Young and Mark Brown (1993), using United Nations and Council of Europe data, show that punitiveness rankings change significantly when the denominator used in the calculation changes. Or, as table I.3, adapted from Kommer 1994, shows, punitiveness rankings change substantially when an-nual admissions to prison per 100,000 population are compared, rather than prison population on an average or given day per 100,000. Although from the perspective of an individual offender, a U.S.-style ten- or fifteen-year sentence must be more punitive than a Dutch- or Swedish-style one- or two-year sentence for the same offense, reasonable people could differ over whether a society like Sweden with a high rate of prison admissions but short sentences is more punitive than a society with a much lower admissions rate but longer sentences. Nonetheless, the im-prisonment rate is vastly higher in the United States than in any other country and cannot be attributed to commensurately higher crime rates.

Second, some penalties in the United States are harsher than the harshest in other Western countries. The most striking evidence is that the United States is the only major Western country that retains the death penalty. But also striking are the mandatory minimum ten-, twenty-, and thirty-year sentences required by federal and some state laws; three-strikes laws in states such as California, which requires life sentences without possibility of parole for some felons and lengthy minimums for others; and the proliferation of life-without-possibility-of-parole laws in many states. Some other countries allow unqualified life sentences, though they are seldom imposed (the European Human Rights Convention does not forbid such sentences; chap. 9, this volume). However, many European countries have established ten to fifteen years as the maximum prison sentence that can be im-posed (Kyvsgaard 1998; Larsson 1999; chap. 3, this volume), and the German Constitutional Court has set fifteen years as the longest sentence that may be imposed without eligibility for release consideration (chap. 8, this volume).

Third, although lack of careful comparative analyses makes this a more tentative assertion, it appears that the average severity of sentences in the United States is greater than elsewhere (e.g., Tonry 1996, table 7.1). Probably the most honest way to explore this question is to provide reasons for believing U.S. practice is more severe than elsewhere and then summarize the objections that can be made to such a claim. The clear weight of the evidence supports the conclusion of greater U.S. severity.

One argument is that greater severity can be inferred from the vastly higher U.S. incarceration rates. A response, however, is that we lack data for making such a claim since it would have to be based on a comparison disaggregated by offense type and taking account of differences in average offense severity. Substantially higher U.S. homicide rates combined with substantially greater use of guns in U.S. violent crime probably makes the average violent U.S. crime a more serious crime than are crimes of the same generic type in other developed countries.

Table I.3: Prison Statistics for Various European Countries, 1990

	Imprisonment Rate per 100,000	Convicted Prisoner Rate	Admission Rate per 100,000	Average Duration of Detention
Netherlands	44.4 (1)	27.2 (1)	137.8 (2)	3.9 (3)
Norway	56.5 (2)	44.9 (4)	237.1 (6)	2.7 (1)
Italy	56.6 (3)	33.6 (2)	—	—
Sweden	58.0 (4)	58.8 (9)	591.5 (8)	3.0 (2)
Denmark	63.0 (5)	46.3 (5)	—	—
Belgium	66.1 (6)	35.2 (3)	184.4 (4)	4.5 (5)
Switzerland	76.9 (7)	47.0 (6)	—	—
FRG	77.8 (8)	57.3 (8)	149.6 (3)	6.7 (7)
France	82.2 (9)	48.7 (7)	135.3 (1)	6.9 (8)
England and Wales	90.3 (10)	70.3 (10)	226.7 (5)	5.1 (6)
Northern Ireland	109.5 (11)	84.4 (11)	314.4 (7)	4.3 (4)

Source: Adapted from Kommer (1994), table 1.

Note: Figures in parentheses = rank number.

However, as noted above, well under one-third of prison admissions are for violent crimes.

Another argument is that comparisons of data on lengths of sentences imposed typically show that only a few percent of prison sentences in most countries are for terms longer than one year (e.g., Sweden: Jareborg 1995; Finland: chap. 3, this volume; Germany: chap. 5, this volume; Netherlands: chap. 4, this volume; Australia: chap. 1, this volume), while, by contrast, in 1994, the most recent year for which U.S. data are available, the mean average maximum sentence of persons committed to U.S. state prisons was seventy-one months (Bureau of Justice Statistics 1997, table 7). An important response here, however, is that the U.S. federal system makes such cross-national comparisons impossible. Data on federal and state prisoners include only prisoners receiving sentences of one year or longer, so sentence-length averages exclude nearly all sentences under one year. Such sentences are typically served in local jails, about which national aggregate data on sentence lengths are not readily available. However, data are available on sentences imposed. In 1994, combining state and federal data, of persons convicted of murder or manslaughter, rape, robbery, and aggravated assault, the percentages sentenced to state or federal prisons were 95, 71, 78, and 48 percent, respectively, and jail sentences represented an additional 2, 11, 17, and 27 percent of cases (Bureau of Justice Statistics 1997, table 5.52). Thus while the U.S. distinction between prison and jail exaggerates severity of prison sentence lengths in comparative analyses, because other countries' data on mean average sentence lengths are "diluted" by inclusion of data for less serious offenses that might receive jail sentences in the United States, the effect is not likely to be large since nearly all of the sentences for serious violent crimes are to prisons.

A final argument is that average sentences of people in U.S. prisons at any one time are vastly longer than those elsewhere. In 1991, the average length of sentence being served by a state prisoner was 108 months (Beck et al. 1993) and, as just noted, the mean average sentence of people admitted to state prisons in 1994 was 71 months (Bureau of Justice Statistics 1998). As the chapters on particular European countries in this volume (and table I.3) show, the averages in European countries are much shorter. There are several qualifications to be considered in addition to the inflation that results from excluding jail sentences. They are also inflated by long sentences. People serving lengthy sentences accumulate, whereas those serving short sentences cycle in and out. Thus the average sentence of prisoners as calculated on a given day will contain an overrepresentation of long sentences and thus exaggerate average sentence length. Finally, though this is less true than in earlier times, nominal sentence lengths can be misleading since parole release eligibility was broader in the United States than elsewhere and the important comparison would be between sentences actually served rather than between nominal sentence lengths.

Overall, despite the qualifications, there is little reason to doubt that sentence lengths in the United States are longer than elsewhere, at least for more serious crimes. Why might that be so? The answers probably include some combination of American moralism, distinctive features of the U.S. historical experience, and peculiarities of modern America that have caused crime and punishment to become major issues in partisan and ideological politics (Caplow and Simon 1999; Tonry 1999a, 1999b; Garland 2000).

Punitive sentiments exist in all countries. An influential article by Anthony Bottoms (1995) discusses the causes and consequences of "populist punitivism" in England and Wales and elsewhere, and most writers on punishment policy now cite Bottoms's analysis in reference to their own countries. There is evidence in many countries that ordinary people, when asked whether criminal punishments are too harsh, too lenient, or just about right, by large majorities answer, "too lenient" (Hough and Roberts 1997; Roberts and Stalans 1997). In many countries, crime is receiving increasing attention in political discussion (Kyvsgaard 1998; Larsson 1999; chaps. 1 and 4, this volume). Incarceration rates in the Netherlands, long renowned for its progressive penal policies, have been increasing since the mid-1970s and between 1988 and 1998 increased by two and one-half times (as rapidly as in the United States) (Junger-Tas 1998).

Nonetheless, the force of punitivist populism seems nowhere else to be as powerful and monolithic as in the United States. This can be shown in several ways. In England and Australia, for example, crime control politics have most resembled those in the United States (especially in England where Tony Blair, like Bill Clinton, apparently resolved always to be to the right of conservatives on crime issues) (Downes and Morgan 1997). Yet, as is shown in this volume by Ashworth on England (chap. 2) and Freiberg on Australia (chap. 1), the relevant legislation in those countries is typically much less severe than in the United States and often contains escape clauses that provide flexibility. England's controversial, recently enacted "mandatory life sentences for murder," for example, do not affect an offender's eligibility for parole or pardon. U.S. sentences of "life without possibility of parole" mean exactly that. Similarly, recently enacted English mandatory minimum sentence laws, for selected drug crimes and burglaries, contain provisions allowing judges in unusual circumstances to impose some other sentence. U.S. mandatory minimum laws seldom include such provisions.

Widespread opposition to softening, weakening, or shortening sentences, which underlay U.S. truth in sentencing, does not appear to be as prevalent or as powerful in most other countries. Unlike incarceration rates for Finland, Germany, and the United States, shown in figures I.2, I.3, and I.4, the French incarceration rate, shown in figure I.5, varies erratically. The explanation for this variation is the many large-scale pardons and amnesties granted by every government of the past thirty years, combined with enactments of legislation designed to reduce prison numbers by creation of alternatives to incarceration. If there were important political prices to be paid in France for releasing large numbers of people from prison early, or if it were deeply unpopular with a large fraction of the population, such practices could not be put into effect. Similar patterns have occurred in Spain and Italy in recent decades (Kuhn 1999).

A similar limited influence of popular punitivism can be seen in a Dutch (chap. 4, this volume), Danish (Kyvsgaard 1998), and Norwegian (Larsson 1999) method for dealing with prison crowding. When in the 1980s and 1990s a combination of rising crime rates and harsher sentences overburdened prison capacity, officials in those countries dealt with the problem by creating prison entrance queues. Convicted, sentenced prisoners for whom space was unavailable would be told as much and would be informed when and where they should appear to begin serv-

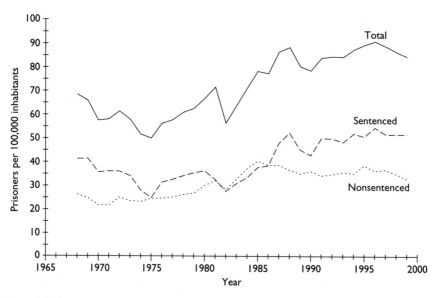

Figure I.5. Incarceration rate in France, 1969–1999 (per 100,000 population). *Source*: Kuhn (1999).

ing their sentences. The Dutch also developed detailed policies for determining, on the basis of offense seriousness, which categories of convicted offenders should be immediately admitted to prison and which categories of current prisoners should be released early to open up space (chap. 4, this volume). Sometimes in the United States, courts have created population caps for unconstitutionally over-crowded prisons, thereby effectively requiring prisons to offset front-door entries with back-door releases. Such orders have been deeply unpopular and resented by state officials and have resulted in massive prison building and in pressure for truth-in-sentencing laws designed to prevent such ad hoc releases in the future.

Thus, there do seem to be fundamental differences between countries in attitudes toward punishment and offenders. These attitudes create political and cultural pressures for greater or lesser harshness in general and in individual cases. They also set a context for thinking about alternate sentencing policy choices.

III. Comparative Sentencing Policies

Most judges, and most thoughtful people who have closely considered the subject, believe that justice in sentencing depends on ever-provisional resolutions between the injunctions to treat like cases alike and different cases differently. Few people disagree fundamentally with the proportionality ideas at the core of Andrew von Hirsch's influential works (e.g., 1976, 1985, 1993): more serious crimes, all else equal, should be more severely punished than less serious crimes, and comparably serious crimes, all else equal, should be comparably severely punished. At the same time, though more people may disagree, at least most judges believe that sentences to be just must be individualized to the particular circumstances of the crime and the convicted offender before the court. It is easy to tease judges about the rhetoric in which they express that belief, for example, the Australian appellate courts' celebration of the "intuitive synthesis" by which judges should fashion sentences or the Austrian "existential conversation" (Tonry 1996, chap. 7, pp. 178–79), but it is hard not to admire the conviction that justice must be decided not in general but in relation to the individual human being whose liberty and well-being are in the court's hands.

The like-cases-alike intuition gives rise to various attempts to reduce or eliminate sentencing disparities. The different-cases-differently intuition gives rise to calls for individualized and indeterminate sentencing. Both intuitions have caused excesses and injustice. U.S. federal guidelines or mandatory minimum laws may require that all persons convicted of a particular crime receive the same lengthy prison sentence and thereby treat like cases alike in terms of current crimes and past criminal records, but they are often decried for prohibiting judges from taking account of ethically important differences between offenders (e.g., Stith and Ca-branes 1998). Indeterminate U.S. sentencing laws of the 1960s and earlier permitted judges and parole authorities to tailor every sentence to the offender's cir-cumstances and thereby treat different cases differently, but they were decried for giving little if any weight to proportionality concerns (American Friends Service Committee 1971; von Hirsch 1976).

Efforts have been made in many countries to reconcile the equality and difference principles in sentencing. Various of the chapters in this book discuss some of the better known such efforts. All are premised on the equality principle's goal of reducing unwarranted sentencing disparities. They can be arrayed in a continuum of concerns from avoidance of unwarranted disparities to avoidance of unwarranted parities. In the following paragraphs, I canvass them briefly, leaving detailed discussion and exploration of relevant literatures to other chapters. I review most of the literature on which these assertions are based elsewhere (Tonry 1996, chap. 5), and do not repeat references here.

A. Mandatory Standards

Only in the United States have large numbers of mandatory sentencing laws been enacted. All are premised on notions that legislation should precisely prescribe the sentence, or the minimum sentence, to be imposed for designated crimes (typically homicide, designated violent or sexual crimes, firearms offenses, and many drug trafficking offenses) or on types of offenders (typically, second- or third-time felons). Such laws include habitual-offender laws first enacted in the 1920s and 1930s (though seldom applied between ca. 1970 and 1990), mandatory minimum sentencing laws (mostly enacted between 1975 and 1985 though often subsequently amended and toughened), three-strikes laws (mandatory lengthy or life sentences for qualifying third-felony convictions), and life-without-possibility-of-parole laws (variously for homicide, other designated violent crimes, some drug trafficking, and some repeat felons).

The three mandatory minimum sentencing laws that recently took effect in England (chap. 2, this volume), in various ways allow for discretionary exceptions to how they are applied.

Because such laws, especially in their U.S. forms, do not allow for different cases to be treated differently openly, often they are treated differently surreptitiously. Techniques include plea bargaining practices that enable the defendant to be convicted of an offense different from one governed by the mandatory law, various forms of "swallowing the gun" in which counsel stipulate to facts other than those that actually happened, and willful disregard of a literally applicable sentencing standard by tacit or overt agreement of the judge and counsel. However, patterns of circumvention are generally ad hoc and idiosyncratic with the result that sentencing disparities are often extreme: among like situated offenders, some will be sentenced to the ten- or twenty-year minimum sentence and others, benefiting from circumventions, will receive much less severe sentences.

B. Presumptive Numerical Judicial Guidelines

Presumptive sentencing guidelines typically specify types (prison or not; occasionally a specific community penalty) and amounts (e.g., twenty-four months) or ranges (e.g., twenty-four to thirty months) of presumptively applicable sentences for designated cases. The presumption can be rebutted but judges must provide reasons for believing the presumptively applicable sentence inappropriate. The persuasiveness of those reasons may be appealed, typically by the defendant or the state, to a higher court.

Guidelines of this sort exist only in the United States. They are in effect in approximately fifteen jurisdictions (chap. 6, this volume), and they vary substantially in format (matrices, narrative statements, offense-specific scoring sheets), in scope (all felonies and misdemeanors, all felonies, only some felonies), in specificity (e.g., narrow ranges, such as twelve to fifteen months, to broad ranges, such as three to six years), and in the degree to which appellate courts carefully scrutinize sentence appeals (from nearly not at all as in Pennsylvania to excruciatingly closely as in the federal system).

A modest evaluation literature shows that, compared with predecessor indeterminate sentencing systems, well-designed presumptive guidelines systems backed up by meaningful appellate sentence review, as in Minnesota, Oregon, and Washington, can reduce sentencing disparities in general and in relation to race, gender, and geography in particular and, by making sentencing more predictable, can be used to tie sentencing and corrections policies more closely together than theretofore.

Few presumptive guidelines systems, however, are well-designed and reviewed and as a result few realize the goals just described. At one extreme, the federal guidelines, by statute "presumptive" but in the U.S. Sentencing Commission's publications "mandatory," are detailed and rigid and suffer all the problems of mandatory sentencing generally. At the opposite extreme, Florida's presumptive guidelines were so little respected and so little backed up by appellate courts that they were little more than voluntary and thus achieved none of their aims.

C. Presumptive Numerical Administrative Guidelines

Numerical sentencing guidelines have been used by parole agencies in the United States since the mid-1970s (e.g., Gottfredson, Wilkins, and Hoffman 1978) and by the Netherlands Public Prosecution Service since 1999 (Schurer and van Loon 1999). Evaluation research in the 1970s and 1980s in the United States showed that guidelines in an administrative parole agency could successfully reduce disparities in prison sentences and execute policies governing criteria to be used in setting release dates and conditions (Blumstein et al. 1983, chap. 3). Probably a majority of surviving U.S. parole systems now use parole guidelines, but they are not glamorous and receive relatively little attention from researchers or lawmakers. As systems of sentencing standards, their great drawback in the United States is that they apply only to offenders sentenced to state prisons and therefore can have no effect on disparities in type of sentence (community penalty, local jail, state prison) or lengths of jail sentences.

Dutch numerical prosecution guidelines for sentence recommendations are of much broader scope because they can potentially apply to all offenders and offenses. Because they are used within an administrative agency, they are potentially subject to the kinds of internal administrative controls, to insure reasonable consistency of application, that helped some parole guidelines systems succeed. Because, however, they concern sentence recommendations rather than sentences, their effects are subject to the independent discretion of judges, so risks of overly rigid application are reduced. Pilot studies conducted for the Dutch Prosecution Service showed significant reduction of disparities compared with earlier periods. The current guidelines, however, which replaced previous guidelines adopted in the 1970s and generally adjudged ineffective, took effect only on April 1, 1999, and it is much too early to say how they are working.

D. Voluntary and Informative Sentencing Guidelines

Two separate developments—voluntary sentencing guidelines systems in the United States (Wilkins et al. 1978; Kress 1980) and sentencing information systems in Canada, Australia, and Scotland—derive from the same hypothesis (Doob and Park 1987; Hogarth 1988; Tata and Hutton 1997). That is that knowledge of a court's past sentencing patterns, its going rates, will influence the sentences judges impose. One rationale is that courts have going rates, often vaguely understood and loosely recognized, and that empirical research on sentencing patterns will bring the going rates to light. A second rationale is that conscientious judges will want to sentence even-handedly and to minimize the chances that their own idiosyncrasies will produce sentences significantly different from those of other judges, and that knowledge of the going rates will help them do that. A third, minimalist, rationale is that descriptive data on sentencing patterns will identify anomalous outliers and reduce the incidence of aberrantly severe sentences.

The difference between voluntary guidelines and information systems is primarily semantic. They involve the same kind of underlying empirical efforts to document a court's past or ongoing sentencing decisions. Voluntary guidelines present the resulting data in grid format that sets out the ranges of sentence within which the middle 80 or 90 percent of sentences fall for various crime and criminal record combinations. Sentencing information systems have evolved gradually but essentially provide the raw data in aggregate and case-by-case formats from which guidelines would be developed.

Unfortunately, the evidence on their effectiveness so far is not promising. Most of the early U.S. voluntary guidelines systems were abandoned in the face of evaluation research findings showing that they had few or no discernible effects on sentencing patterns (Blumstein et al. 1983, chap. 3). The earliest information systems in Canada in the 1980s (Doob and Park 1987; Hogarth 1988) atrophied and fell into disuse. A system developed in New South Wales in the mid-1980s continued operating well into the 1990s, but no evaluations or scholarly writings document its operation. The newest system, in Scotland, has been in operation for several years and benefits from technological advances that make it much easier to use than earlier systems, but no impact evaluations have been published (Tata and Hutton 1997).

E. Appellate Guideline Judgments

The English Court of Appeal has been issuing decisions on sentencing appeals since early in the twentieth century and since the early 1980s has been issuing guideline judgments that set out starting points for consideration of sentence for generic categories of cases. So far as I am aware, there is no credible evaluation literature that demonstrates that adoption and elaboration of guideline judgments has reduced sentencing disparities in general or that patterns of sentences for particular kinds of cases change after issuance of a pertinent new judgment. However, many English judges and some informed observers believe that guideline judgments do influence sentencing patterns. The most formidable criticism is that they are narrow in scope and deal only with the relatively small numbers of serious violent cases, while providing no guidance for high-volume offenses, such as shoplifting, simple assault, and unaggravated burglary, or for the mine-run of minor offenses (e.g., chap. 2, this volume). The verdict appears to resemble that for well-designed parole guidelines—useful as far as they go, but they do not go nearly far enough.

F. Statutory Sentencing Principles

Finland in 1975 (chap. 3, this volume) and Sweden in 1988 (Jareborg 1995) adopted systems of statutory sentencing principles that provide detailed guidance about the considerations that should guide sentencing in general (proportionality notions) and in particular (the relevance of prior record, various personal characteristics, etc.). In a system like the American in which sentences are typically long and judges and prosecutors are politically selected, there would be grounds for skepticism that the effects of statutory sentencing principles would be any greater than those achieved by voluntary guidelines. In Scandinavian systems characterized by professional, career judges and prosecutors and relatively short sentences, the prospects are much rosier.

IV. Conclusion

The preceding litanies of differences could overwhelm, but they are provided to make two main points. First, the desirability and prospects of various approaches for bringing consistency and predictability to sentencing depend on the sentencing traditions and politics of a jurisdiction. Dangers of unwarranted disparities and unwarranted parities vary greatly and proponents of rational, humane sentencing policy changes should be clear about which is the greater danger and choose their weapons accordingly.

Second, in Western countries that share a common history, values, and commitments to human rights, there should not be such great differences in punishment practices and policies as now exist. Existing international covenants, conventions, and declarations contain few enforceable provisions that relate to the nature and amount of criminal punishments (the most notable exception being the European Convention on Human Rights' prohibition of capital punishment), but they should and some day they will.

The stock objection is that such proposals ignore important cultural differences that are made manifest in national policy through democratic processes, and that such normative differences should be respected. But this misleads. There is already broad agreement among Western countries about values and principles that just sentencing should respect, and there is growing congruence in policy. At least three examples can be offered as demonstration. Within countries and some regional groups, human rights standards forbid particular policy choices (the death penalty in member states of the Council of Europe, whipping and other corporal punishments throughout the United States and most other Western countries). In some countries, particularly in northern Europe, human rights ideas have led to enactment of laws creating upper limits on prison sentences that may be imposed; with very few exceptions, ten to fifteen years is the longest prison sentence that may be imposed in Norway, Finland, Denmark, and Germany for the most serious offenses. Finally, the vertical proportionality proposition that more serious crimes should, all else equal, be punished more severely than less serious crimes, and the horizontal equity proposition that comparably serious crimes, all else equal, should be punished comparably severely, are increasingly influential in sentencing systems as diverse as U.S. guidelines, English guideline judgments, and Scandinavian sentencing principles. Formal concerns for respecting national sovereignty have so far prevented adoption of many enforceable international standards concerning sentencing and the imposition of punishment, but their creation is inevitable.

That human rights concerns will eventually trump national sovereignty interests (and claims about respect for cultural differences) is suggested by sentencing policy trends in the United States, a country among the most zealous in protecting its autonomy. Every time a U.S. sentencing commission, including in the federal system, has discovered substantial differences in sentencing practice in different areas or regions of the jurisdiction, the uncontroversial policy decision has been made that such differences are unjust and that an offender's loss of liberty or property should not depend greatly on where within a state he is sentenced. No one doubts that there may be significant regional and cultural differences in assessments of the gravity of offenses, but few disagree that equal treatment values require that sentencing policies be uniform throughout a jurisdiction. Though at present there are no applicable authoritative international standards, it is difficult to understand why human rights values should not require compliance with substantive standards (e.g., proportionality requirements and absolute limits on punishments in general and for particular crimes) whenever a person is sentenced, wherever a person is sentenced. The important question is the frame of reference, and for human rights questions, the answer should be the international community of (at least) developed Western states.

REFERENCES

American Friends Service Committee. 1971. *Struggle for Justice*. New York: Hill & Wang.
Beck, Allen, Darrell Gilliard, Lawrence Greenfeld, Caroline Harlow, Thomas Hester, Louis Jankowski, Tracy Snell, James Stephan, and Danielle Morton. 1993. *Survey of State Prison Inmates, 1991*. Washington, D.C.: U.S. Department of Justice, Bureau of Justice Statistics.
Bennett, William J., John J. DiIulio, and John P. Walters. 1996. *Body Count: Moral Poverty and How to Win America's War against Crime and Drugs*. New York: Simon & Schuster.

Blumstein, Alfred, and Allen Beck. 1999. "Population Growth in U.S. Prisons, 1980–1996." In *Prisons*, edited by Michael Tonry and Joan Petersilia. Vol. 26 of *Crime and Justice: A Review of Research*, edited by Michael Tonry Chicago: University of Chicago Press.

Blumstein, Alfred, Jacqueline Cohen, Susan E. Martin, and Michael Tonry, eds. 1983. *Research on Sentencing: The Search for Reform*. 2 vols. Washington, D.C.: National Academy Press.

Bottoms, Anthony. 1995. "The Philosophy and Politics of Punishment and Sentencing." In *The Politics of Sentencing Reform*, edited by C. M. V. Clarkson and Rod Morgan. Oxford: Clarendon Press.

Bureau of Justice Statistics. 1997. *Felony Sentences in the United States, 1994*. Washington, D.C.: U.S. Department of Justice, Bureau of Justice Statistics.

———. 1998. *Prisoners in 1997*. Washington, D.C.: U.S. Department of Justice, Bureau of Justice Statistics.

———. 1999a. *Criminal Victimization 1998*. Washington, D.C.: U.S. Department of Justice, Bureau of Justice Statistics.

———. 1999b. *Correctional Populations in the United States, 1996*. Washington, D.C.: U.S. Department of Justice, Bureau of Justice Statistics.

———. 1999c. *Prison and Jail Inmates at Midyear 1998*. Washington, D.C.: U.S. Department of Justice, Bureau of Justice Statistics.

Caplow, Theodore, and Jonathan Simon. 1999. "Understanding Prison Policy and Population Trends." In *Prisons*, edited by Michael Tonry and Joan Petersilia. Vol. 26 of *Crime and Justice: A Review of Research*, edited by Michael Tonry. Chicago: University of Chicago Press.

Dickey, Walter, and Pam Stiebs Hollenhorst. 1998. "Three-Strikes Laws: Massive Impact in California and Georgia, Little Elsewhere." *Overcrowded Times* 9(6):2–8.

Doob, A., and N. Park. 1987. "Computerised Sentencing Information for Judges: An Aid to the Sentencing Process." *Criminal Law Quarterly* 30:54.

Downes, David, and Rod Morgan. 1997. "Dumping the 'Hostages to Fortune': The Politics of Law and Order in Post-War Britain." In *The Oxford Handbook of Criminology*, 2d ed., edited by Mike Maguire, Rod Morgan, and Robert Reiner. Oxford: Oxford University Press.

Federal Bureau of Investigation. 1999. *Crime in the United States: Uniform Crime Reports 1998*. Washington, D.C.: U.S. Government Printing Office.

Garland, David. 2000. "The Culture of High Crime Societies: The Social Precondition of the New Politics of Crime Control." *British Journal of Criminology* 40 (forthcoming).

Gottfredson, Don M., Leslie T. Wilkins, and Peter B. Hoffman. 1978. *Guidelines for Parole and Sentencing*. Lexington, Mass.: Lexington Books.

Hogarth, J. 1988. *Sentencing Database System: User's Guide 4th Draft*. Vancouver: University of British Columbia.

Hough, Michael, and Julian Roberts. 1997. *Attitudes to Punishment: Findings from the British Crime Survey*. Home Office Research Study no. 179. London: Home Office.

Jareborg, Nils. 1995. "The Swedish Sentencing Reform." In *The Politics of Sentencing Reform*, edited by C. M. V. Clarkson and Rod Morgan. Oxford: Clarendon Press.

Junger-Tas, Josine. 1998. "Dutch Penal Policies Changing Direction." *Overcrowded Times* 9(5):1, 14–20.

Kommer, Max. 1994. "Punitiveness in Europe: A Comparison." *European Journal on Criminal Policy and Research* 2:29–43.

Kress, Jack M. 1980. *Prescription for Justice: The Theory and Practice of Sentencing Guidelines*. Cambridge, Mass.: Ballinger.

Kuhn, André. 1999. "Incarceration Rates across the World." *Overcrowded Times* 10(2):1, 12–20.
Kurki, Leena. 1997. "International Crime Survey: American Rates about Average." *Overcrowded Times* 8(5):1, 4–7.
Kyvsgaard, Britta. 1998. "Penal Sanctions and the Use of Imprisonment in Denmark." *Overcrowded Times* 9(6):1, 9–10.
Larsson, Paul. 1999. "Norway Prison Use Up Slightly, Community Penalties Lots." *Overcrowded Times* 10(1):1, 11–13.
Lynch, James. 1995. "Crime in International Perspective." In *Crime*, edited by James Wilson and Joan Petersilia. San Francisco, Calif.: Institute for Contemporary Studies.
Maguire, Kathleen, and Ann L. Pastore, eds. *Sourcebook of Criminal Justice Statistics, 1997.* Washington, D.C.: U.S. Department of Justice, Bureau of Justice Statistics.
Mayhew, Pat, and Jan van Dijk. 1997. *Criminal Victimisation in Eleven Industrialized Countries*. The Hague: Dutch Ministry of Justice.
Messinger, Sheldon, and Phillip Johnson. 1978. "California's Determinate Sentencing Laws." In *Determinate Sentencing: Reform or Regression?* Washington, D.C.: U.S. Government Printing Office.
Mirrlees-Black, Catriona, Tracey Budd, Sarah Partridge, and Pat Mayhew. 1998. *The 1998 British Crime Survey, England and Wales*: London: Her Majesty's Stationery Office.
Pease, Ken. 1994. "Cross-National Imprisonment Rates: Limitations of Method and Possible Conclusions." *British Journal of Criminology* 34 (special issue):116–30.
Pfeiffer, Christian. 1998. "Juvenile Crime and Violence in Europe." In *Crime and Justice: A Review of Research*, vol. 23, edited by Michael Tonry. Chicago: University of Chicago Press.
Roberts, J. V., and L. J. Stalans. 1997. *Public Opinion, Crime, and Criminal Justice*. Boulder, Colo.: Westview.
Schurer, Gerrit, and Reinier van Loon. 1999. "The Netherlands Adopts Numerical Prosecution Guidelines." *Overcrowded Times* 10(3):1, 4–7.
Stith, Kate, and José A. Cabranes. 1998. *Fear of Judging: Sentencing Guidelines in the Federal Courts*. Chicago: University of Chicago Press.
Tata, Cyrus, and Neil Hutton. 1997. "Scottish High Court Develops Sentencing Information System." *Overcrowded Times* 8(6):1, 14–20.
Tonry, Michael. 1996. *Sentencing Matters*. New York: Oxford University Press.
———. 1998. "Introduction: Crime and Punishment in America." In *The Handbook of Crime and Punishment*, edited by Michael Tonry. New York: Oxford University Press.
———. 1999a. "Rethinking Unthinkable Punishment Policies in America." *UCLA Law Review* 46:1751–91
———. 1999b. "Why Are U.S. Incarceration Rates So High?" *Crime and Delinquency* 45(4): 419–37.
Törnudd, Patrik. 1993. *Fifteen Years of Declining Prisoner Rates*. Research Communication no. 8. Helsinki: National Research Institute of Legal Policy.
———. 1997. "Sentencing and Punishment in Finland." In *Sentencing Reform in Overcrowded Times: A Comparative Perspective*, edited by Michael Tonry and Kathleen Hatlestad. New York: Oxford University Press.
van Dijk, Jan J. M. 1997. "Towards a Research-Based Crime Reduction Policy." *European Journal on Criminal Policy and Research* 5(3):13–26.
von Hirsch, Andrew. 1976. *Doing Justice: The Choice of Punishments*. New York: Hill & Wang.
———. 1985. *Past or Future Crimes?* New Brunswick, N.J.: Rutgers University Press.
———. 1993. *Censure and Sanctions*. Oxford: Clarendon Press.

Walmsley, R. 1999. *World Prison Population List*. Research Findings no. 88. London: Home Office Research, Development and Statistics Directorate.

Weigend, Thomas. 1997. "Germany Reduces Use of Prison Sentences." In *Sentencing Reform in Overcrowded Times: A Comparative Perspective*, edited by Michael Tonry and Kathleen Hatlestad. New York: Oxford University Press.

Weissbrodt, David, and Rüdiger Wolfrum. 1997. *The Right to a Fair Trial*. Berlin: Springer.

Wilkins, Leslie T., Jack M. Kress, Don M. Gottfredson, Joseph C. Calpin, and Arthur M. Gelman. 1978. *Sentencing Guidelines: Structuring Judicial Discretion—Report on the Feasibility Study*. Washington, D.C.: U.S. Department of Justice.

Wilson, James Q., and Richard J. Herrnstein. 1986. *Crime and Human Nature: The Definitive Study of the Causes of Crime*. New York: Simon & Schuster.

Young, Warren, and Mark Brown. 1993. "Cross-National Comparisons of Imprisonment." In *Crime and Justice: A Review of Research*, vol. 17, edited by Michael Tonry. Chicago: University of Chicago Press.

Zimring, Franklin E. 1972. "The Medium Is the Message: Firearms Caliber as a Determinant of Death from Assault." *Journal of Legal Studies* 1:97–123.

Zimring, Franklin E., and Gordon Hawkins. 1997. *Crime Is Not the Problem*. New York: Oxford University Press.

Three Strikes and You're Out— It's Not Cricket

Colonization and Resistance in Australian Sentencing

In *Sentencing Matters*, Michael Tonry comments that sentencing in 1995 in the United States would be unrecognizable to a judge of 1970 (Tonry 1996, p. 6). The same could not be said of sentencing in Australia, where change is a constant but its magnitude is not large. An Australian judge of a quarter-century ago would most likely feel comfortable with today's sentencing process. Though he or she (the latter would be an innovation) might feel more constrained by the plethora of legislative provisions introduced to guide and shape his or her discretion and powers, the landscape would be relatively familiar. Assisted by a wider range of appellate cases, access to which would be facilitated by a new range of textbooks, encyclopedias, law reports, and, in some states, on-line access to the judgments, the modern sentencing judge can choose from a wider range of sentencing options: the smorgasbord would be richer, but not totally foreign or unknowable. Parole systems would still be in place, though not in identical forms. Although subjected to greater pressures from the media and politicians, and more sensitive to the role of the victim in the criminal justice system, yesterday's judge, presiding today (and there are still some), would remain fortified and comforted by the fact that he or she, whether as a judge at first instance or on appeal, was still the center of the Australian sentencing universe, relatively free of grids, guidelines, or graphs and indeed of administrative or legislative committees to create or impose such guidelines.

Until recent decades, Australia's legal history has been derived from, been modeled upon, or run parallel to English law. With colonization in the late eighteenth century came the English statute book and common law. Many of the innovations of the late nineteenth and twentieth centuries were drawn directly or indirectly from England, though some of the English innovations had been, in turn, influenced by events in the United States. To that extent, Australia has never been an insular jurisdiction.

In recent years, however, the range of international influences on law in general, and sentencing in particular, has increased. The process of globalization seems to have gathered pace. Australia, as a net importer of ideas, has been particularly exposed to such influences, in particular to those of the United States, whose language and ideas, expressed through television, films, books, the Internet, newspapers, and academic journals tend to permeate and possibly eclipse local cultures, including legal and sentencing regimes and practices.

This chapter outlines some of the external historical influences on Australian sentencing and then attempts to locate present Australian law and practice within an international context. It examines some of the major changes in Australian sentencing that have taken place over the last quarter century such as the consolidation of sentencing laws, attempts to control discretion and disparity, and the changing role of the principles of just deserts and proportionality. It discusses the development of intermediate sanctions and the emerging role of the victim and the movement toward restorative justice. After noting Australia's conformity to the international trend of steadily increasing imprisonment rates, it argues that a distinctive Australian contribution to sentencing can be identified but laments that in an age of global communication, franchised correctional systems, and transnational corporations, national differences are more likely to diminish than they are to be accentuated.

I. Historical Influences

The direct and indirect influences of English and U.S. legislation have always been evident throughout Australian statute books (for the sake of convenience, most examples are drawn from Victorian law). The nascent Australian penalty structures and sanctions were an adoption of the values, attitudes, and approaches of the colonial parent (Fox and Freiberg 1985, p. 4). The origins of Australian probation can be traced to both England and the United States. Although the rudiments of probation can be found in the common-law practice of binding over to keep the peace, Massachusetts claims the credit for coining the word *probation* in 1878 and the first statute. England followed with the Probation of First Offenders Act 1887 and then the Probation of Offenders Act 1907, whose authors were attracted to the U.S. system of probation under statutory supervision. The 1907 act was influential throughout Australia and formed the basis of many probation and quasi-probation statutes. This act was, in turn, replaced by the Criminal Justice Act 1948 (U.K.), which led to creation of the adult probation service in Victoria in 1956 through the Penal Reform Act 1956 (Vic.) (Fox and Freiberg 1985, p. 288). Similarly, in Victoria, the Juvenile Offenders Act 1887 (Vic.) drew heavily upon the Probation of First Offenders Act 1887 (U.K.).

Laws dealing with habitual criminals, in particular, indeterminate sentencing laws, were introduced in many jurisdictions in Australia in the early part of the twentieth century and were regarded as a modern and progressive step in penal reform, having recently been introduced in England and New Zealand as well as the United States. The Indeterminate Sentences Act 1907 (Vic.), for example, drew upon these models, but pressure for the introduction of such sentences had been building since the late 1880s by penal administrators who were much taken by these overseas innovations (Murphy 1996).

The criminal appeal structure in Victoria, introduced in 1914, was modeled directly upon the Criminal Appeal Act 1907 (U.K.) (Fox and Freiberg 1985, p. 15) allowing defendant appeals against sentence. Prosecution appeals against sentence were introduced in Victoria in 1970, well in advance of England, which introduced a limited form of appeal in the Criminal Justice Act 1988 (U.K.).

Parole grew out of the colonial ticket of leave system and, in Victoria, from the early-twentieth-century legislation governing indeterminate sentences. The modern Victorian parole system grew out of a 1951 report of Alex Whatmore, the inspector-general of penal establishments, which was based upon his observations of the latest in overseas developments, particularly those of the United States, which had introduced forms of parole some decades earlier. The title of Whatmore's report indicates its scope and influences: *Report of the Inspector-General of Penal Establishments on Developments in Penal Science in the United Kingdom, Europe, and the United States of America; Together with Recommendations Relating to Penal Administration* (Fox and Freiberg 1985, p. 339).

Australian sentencing jurisprudence during the 1970s was consciously modeled upon David Thomas's work of the period (Thomas 1970; Daunton-Fear 1977). The range of noncustodial options that became fashionable in the early 1980s were copied from, or were modified versions of, English schemes. Attendance center orders, introduced in Victoria in the early 1980s, were derived from an English scheme of 1950 under sec. 19 of the Criminal Justice Act 1948 (U.K.), which applied to offenders under the age of 21 (Fox and Freiberg 1985, p. 312). Community service orders made their appearance in England in 1973 following a Californian lead in the 1960s. The Victorian Sentencing Alternatives Committee recommended them in 1979 and they came into operation in 1981 (Victoria, Sentencing Alternatives Committee 1979). By the mid-1980s, changes tended to be more indigenous: the Victorian community-based order, which amalgamated probation, community service orders, and attendance center orders in 1985, was well in advance of the English combination order of 1991, though the causal relationship is unclear. Australian ideas for criminal injuries compensation schemes, introduced in the early 1970s, drew from earlier models in England and New Zealand.

Duncan Chappell, an expatriate Australian who had worked in the United States for many years, returned in the late 1970s and chaired a major federal review of sentencing, whose influences were clearly American rather than English. This particularly applied to the debate over the purposes of punishment (Australian Law Reform Commission 1980). This report marks the start of the more recent trends in sentencing in which the dominant influence appears to be that of the United States.

More recently, economic rationalism has seen the dismantling of the social and criminal justice policies developed in the postwar period (O'Malley 1994). The concept of the market has assumed a dominant role and with it such ideas as privatization, deregulation, small government, and competition (O'Malley 1994, p. 285). Just as the state retreats from economic interventionism, so it does at the individual level: rehabilitative models give way to atomistic theories of personal responsibility for action and punishment. The fiction of *homo economicus*, the rational, wealth-maximizing individual upon whom the economy is modeled is extended to *homo criminalicus*, the rationally calculating criminal, similarly seeking to maximize wealth through crime. Prison, not welfare, is seen as the solution to crime.

The transformation of economies is a powerful and fundamental force. As Pat O'Malley has noted, this is not just a retreat to conservatism, with its "comfortable familiarities," but a "specific and radical shift centered on the dismantling of welfarist, interventionist and socialized state managerialism" (O'Malley 1994, p. 286). It is, he observes, "breathtakingly reformist." In Victoria, for example, the structure of the state is rapidly being dismantled, with many state institutions, authorities, and activities being contracted out or privatized. Over 45 percent of Victorian prisoners are now housed in private prisons. State bureaucracies have shrunk in size and the nature of administration itself has been transformed. Conforming to international trends, managerialism in all its forms, systemic, consumerist, and actuarial (Bottoms 1995, p. 24), has come to dominate the discourse of government in Australia. This postdates England, the United States, and Canada by around a decade. As elsewhere, these social and economic trends have manifested themselves in the criminal justice system, which is similarly becoming internationalized, globalized or, perhaps, colonized, but not necessarily without resistance.

II. International Sentencing Trends

Michael Tonry in his recent writings has sketched the broad outlines of U.S. sentencing changes (Tonry 1996; Tonry and Hatlestad 1997). If it is true, as Tonry suggests, that "America's today could be other countries' tomorrow" (Tonry and Hatlestad 1997, p. 3), then the rest of us should pay attention to the agenda he has articulated. The issue for a country like Australia is whether it is possible to ignore or resist these trends.

Sentencing reform in the United States emerged from the sustained attacks on disparity, partly attributable to the indeterminate sentencing regimes then in place in most jurisdictions. The renaissance of retributive or just deserts theory resulted in the reduction or elimination of the discretion exercised by judges and parole boards in favor of more or less rigorous guidelines. Administrative modifications of sentence such as parole and remissions were narrowed or removed, but executive input into the sentencing process by means of sentencing commissions or councils was increased. Partly as a result, discretion appears to have moved to the prosecutorial, rather than the dispositional stages of the process. Offender-based sentencing changed to offense-based. By the 1990s, Tonry identifies a move beyond just deserts to incapacitative, preventive, or public safety rationales, possibly heralding a returning to offender-oriented considerations. One-, two- and three-strikes laws proliferated, as did mandatory and minimum sentences, many of which overrode or displaced carefully crafted sentencing guidelines. Capital punishment continues to gain in popularity.

Intermediate, or noncustodial sanctions, never as prominent in the United States as in England, Australia, or Canada, became even more problematic under the just deserts model. To an increasingly punitive population they appeared to be an inadequate response to their fear or their desire for punishment. As a means of reducing an increasing prison population, they failed because they were never capable of fulfilling that mandate. Nonetheless, American ingenuity persevered, with the development of such schemes as intensive supervision orders, house arrest, electronic monitoring, boot camps, public shaming or humiliation rituals, and others. Fines and other minimalist orders continue to be severely under used in comparison with other Western jurisdictions.

In England, Barbara Hudson (1993) identifies similar themes, but with different emphases. The decline of rehabilitation is noted, but the move to desert-based sentencing is less pronounced because the abandonment of classical theory was never as dramatic. Intermediate sanctions, always more widely accepted and used, proliferated: suspended sentences, community service orders, attendance center orders, fines and discharges (see also Ashworth 1995). Their basis in social work practice, rather than in psychiatry or technology, may have made them more widely available, acceptable, and adaptable. More problematic than their under use is the modern problem Hudson identifies as "sanction stacking" or penal inflation, that is, the aggregation or combination of various sanctions that result in noncustodial sanctions that are effectively more severe than the short terms of imprisonment they are meant to replace (Hudson 1993, p. 134). Overall, Hudson identifies a number of major trends: a bifurcation of sentences—fewer sentences but for longer periods for the most problematic offenders; an increase in informalism, expressed through diversion, deinstitutionalization, decarceration, reparation, or mediation schemes; and an increase in individualism over corporatism: more particularly, a move away from collective responsibility of the state to personal responsibility of the individual.

III. Australia

Looking broadly at the past quarter century or so, but concentrating on the past decade, what major changes have occurred in Australian sentencing?

A. Consolidation of Sentencing Statutes

Until recently Australian sentencing laws were scattered in a mosaic of state and federal acts, full of duplications and inconsistencies. Legislation rarely specified factors that should be taken into account when determining whether a particular sanction was appropriate or provided for priorities in the imposition of sentences. There was no declaration of the purposes of sentencing nor a ranking of their importance. Statutory maximum penalties were inconsistent and incoherent.

Following decades of criticism that the legislature had failed in its duty to provide courts with a rational and coherent legislative and policy framework for sentencing, major legislative reforms have taken place at federal and state levels. This process commenced with the Sentencing Act 1991 (Vic.) and was followed by the Penalties and Sentences Act 1992 (Queensland), Sentencing Act 1995 (Northern Territory), Sentencing Act 1995 and Sentence Administration Act 1995 (Western Australia), and finally the Sentencing Act 1997 (Tasmania). In New South Wales, the most populous jurisdiction, the Law Reform Commission recently recommended the introduction of two sentencing acts along the lines of the Western Australian structure: one act dealing with sentencing principles and policies and the other with the administration of sentences (New South Wales Law Reform Commission 1996, p. 324). In that state, a small amount of progress toward consolidation has been made by the passing of the Fines Act 1996 (N.S.W.), which regulates the administration of fine payment and fine enforcement.

The New South Wales Law Reform Commission saw the advantages of consolidation of sentencing powers as being ease of understanding and access for the community, judicial officers, and the legal profession (New South Wales Law Reform Commission 1996, p. 326). In addition, it was argued that it would decrease the risk of error in sentencing. The commission stressed, however, that such a legislative process should be, in strict legal terms, a consolidation rather than a codification. In that vein, the Sentencing Act 1997 (Tas.), sec. 6 states firmly:

> This Act is a consolidation, not a codification, of the State's sentencing law and does not derogate from the powers that a court may exercise, or the rights that a person may have, under any other enactment or law for or in relation to the sentencing of offenders.

The New South Wales commission went further and recommended strongly against the incorporation of common-law principles because they were likely to stultify the development of the law, were likely to make the task of sentencing more time consuming, and, finally, because the common law did not need restatement (New South Wales Law Reform Commission 1996, p. 333).

Nonetheless, the various acts have attempted to give some direction in relation to sentencing policy in matters that had previously been wholly left to the courts. Thus, various acts list the purposes for which sentences can be imposed. For example, section 5(1) of the Sentencing Act 1991 (Vic.) specifies just punishment, deterrence, rehabilitation, denunciation, community prosecution, or a combination of two or more of these purposes. Some jurisdictions also specify some of the factors that a court must have regard to in sentencing. Sentencers may be provided with the legislatively preferred hierarchy of sanctions and a direction to observe the common-law principle of parsimony, that a court is "not to impose a sentence that is more severe than that which is necessary to achieve the purpose or purposes for which the sentence is imposed."[1] The legislation may also provide guidance in relation to the exercise of the discretion whether or not to record a conviction (Sentencing Act 1991 [Vic.], sec. 8), or include directions regarding the use of the various orders such as indefinite sentences, community-based orders, and dismissals, discharges, or adjournments. In some instances, for example in Victoria, the legislature has spelled out its policy on the relationship between particular sentencing orders, so that a court is now directed to give priority to restitution or compensation over a fine (Sentencing Act 1991 [Vic.], sec. 50(4)) and is obliged to take into account the total impact of a combination of financial sanctions (sec. 50(3)). The legislation also directs courts to have regard to the interests of victims (sec. 5(2)(da)).

When forms of statutory sentencing guidance of this sort are introduced, courts sometimes object that they are being "over-governed." Thus, in *Young* [1990] V.R. 951, 954 the Victorian Court of Criminal Appeal referred to the substantial amount of legislation that a sentencing judge must bear in mind and complained that statutory instructions, generally speaking, "make the task of the sentencing judge more difficult, if for no other reason than that he must keep in mind a number of provisions which are not invariably clearly expressed."

However, the guidance offered within the legislative framework is couched in terms of such generality as to leave sentencers flexibility in interpreting their meaning and ample residual discretion in relation to the type and quantum of penalty. Australian federal and state sentencing legislation does not even slightly approximate the extremely specific and rigid legislative controls placed on judicial discretion under federal law and some states in the United States.

B. Discretion and Disparity

Despite the overwhelming evidence of unjustifiable disparity that persuaded so many U.S. jurisdictions to curtail judicial discretion, Australian legislatures and courts have rejected both the definition of the "problem" and its proposed solution. The epistemology of Australian criminology in general, and sentencing in particular, may partly account for this rejection. Australian criminology grew out of a legal, rather than sociological, framework. Norval Morris, an early contributor, was a lawyer and most current commentators are legally trained. Quantitative data are rare, rudimentary, and generally regarded with suspicion. Lawyers and the judiciary have retained control of the various parliamentary inquiries, law reform commissions, and ad hoc investigations of crime and punishment in Australia.

Australian courts remain firmly of the view that the retention of a wide judicial discretion is necessary and that individual justice is possibly more important than some more abstract notion of systemic fairness. The New South Wales Law Reform Commission rejected any reforms that would constrain the exercise of discretion by codification of common law principles, creation of sanction hierarchies, or specification of tariffs for each offence (New South Wales Law Reform Commission 1996, p. 7). Indeed, reference to the U.S. experience confirmed them in that view, citing with approval Anthony Doob's analysis (Doob 1995) that the federal sentencing guidelines were "nothing short of a disaster" (New South Wales Law Reform Commission 1996, p. 12), although it was recognized that there had been "mixed success" in other jurisdictions.

Responding to the U.S. experience of overcrowded and expensive prisons, the extensive use of short prison terms, and mandatory prison sentences, the commission probably sums up the Australia-wide reaction to these American innovations:

> The context of sentencing in the United States is very different from that in Australia, and resort to such techniques has been consistently rejected by judicial officers in

Australia as inappropriate to the Australian context. (New South Wales Law Reform Commission 1996, pp. 12–13)

Michael Tonry's admonition that not every jurisdiction should attempt to learn from the U.S. experience and establish guidelines to structure sentencing discretion has been taken to heart. His conclusion, that the cure may be worse than the ailment (Tonry 1996, p. 187), is given credibility, particularly when examples of unjust parity, of different cases being treated alike, are cited (Tonry 1996, p. 14).

Even relatively moderate attempts to structure judicial discretion have met with a lukewarm response. Since 1995, the Supreme Court of Western Australia has had the power to hand down guideline judgments, that is, judgments which provide sentencing judges with general guidance, in terms of both quantum and the aggravating and mitigating factors that might be taken into account, for particular types of offenses (see chap. 2, this volume). For example, Sentencing Act 1995 (W.A.), sec. 143 states:

(1) The Full Court of the Supreme Court or the Court of Criminal Appeal may give a guideline judgment containing guidelines to be taken into account by courts sentencing offenders.

(2) A guideline judgment may be given in any proceeding considered appropriate by the court giving it, and whether or not it is necessary for the purpose of determining the proceeding.

(3) A guideline judgment may be reviewed, varied or revoked in a subsequent guideline judgment.

According to Neil Morgan (1996, p. 368), even prior to the enactment of this provision, the Court of Criminal Appeal had been prepared to describe in very general terms the range of sentences for particular offenses, but refused to use the power, for example, to guide sentencers in the use of various noncustodial sentencing options. Since 1995, the Supreme Court has avoided the question of guideline judgments and has made little use this power, citing the problems of lack of experience, wide fact variation, and the unnecessary restrictions that guidelines may place upon sentencers (Morgan and Murray 1999).

Unhappy with the courts' response to public and political concerns with sentencing practices, in late October 1998 the government introduced a bill to amend the sentencing legislation. This bill will provide for a "sentencing matrix," in effect, the beginnings of a numerical guidelines regime. It is intended to make the sentencing process clearer, more consistent, and more understandable to the public and ultimately to give the Parliament more control over sentences imposed by the courts. Courts are to be made more accountable to Parliament through a system of information gathering and publication of benchmark sentences and, finally, through the legislative prescription of "presumed" sentences, deviation from which will create an automatic right of appeal.

Appellate courts do not need a statutory warrant to lay down a guideline judgment. In October 1998, in New South Wales, a Full Bench of five Supreme Court justices presided over by a new Chief Justice, Spigelman C J, handed down the state's first guideline judgment. The Court, aware of growing public dissatisfaction with sentencing, particularly with lenient sentences for the offense of dangerous driving causing death, brought down a judgment the intention of which was to lift sentencing levels for this offense as well to decrease sentence disparities (*Jurisic*, October 12, 1998). In its judgment, the court drew heavily from the practice and experience of the United Kingdom but expressly rejected U.S. style "grid" systems or minimum penalties. It emphasized that the guidelines were not binding in any formal sense and that judges would retain the ultimate discretion in sentencing.

The judgment drew national attention and provoked intense debate about the role and independence of the courts, the role of discretion, and the relationship between the courts and the community. The attorney general of the state responded immediately by foreshadowing legislation that would permit the prosecution to ask the court to issue guideline judgments for particular crimes (*The Australian*, October 14, 1998).

The essence of the Australian approach is that the courts should adopt a "consistency of approach in the sentencing of offenders" (*Sentencing Act* 1991 [Vic.], sec. 1(a); New South Wales Law Reform Commission 1996, p. 13). Thus:

> Wide discretion which, properly, allows individualization and broad choice of rationales for punishment should be accompanied by accountability. In our view this is best achieved by a clear statement from the sentencing court as to the sentencing rationale chosen, the relevant factors and the reasons for adopting them. This makes the position clear to the offender, improves community and media understanding of the process (including apparent superficial inconsistencies) and provides an unequivocal platform for appellate review. (New South Wales Law Reform Commission 1996, p. 14)

As long as the sentences imposed are not outside the "acceptable range," as determined from time to time by the appellate courts, sentencing discretion will be upheld. Though there are few studies of the number of appeals and their outcomes, a recent study of appeals to the Victorian Court of Appeal between the years 1993 and 1995 found that some 24 percent of all sentences imposed by the Supreme and County Court were appealed and, of these, 36 percent resulted in the sentence being varied. That a sentence is "manifestly excessive" or "manifestly inadequate" is by far the most common ground of appeal in cases coming before the Victorian Court of Appeal. Approximately 80 percent of all appeals contain at least one ground relating to excessiveness or inadequacy, and in 38 percent of appeals, it is the sole ground (Fox and Freiberg 1999, paras. 13.201, 13.225).[2]

Innovations such as the New South Wales Judicial Commission's Sentencing Information System, now emulated in Scotland (Tata and Hutton 1997), aim to improve the consistency of sentencing by making available to sentencers, on line, sentencing law, statistics, information about correctional facilities, and a sentencing calculator. Although there is some evidence that the use of this system is increasing, there have been no evaluations of whether, or to what extent, it has affected sentencing behavior.

My own reading of Victorian sentencing law and practice following the introduction of the Sentencing Act 1991 (Vic.) leads me to believe that, although all of the structural and other innovations outlined above have simplified the sentencing task and clarified the conceptual frameworks, they have not improved the quality or consistency of sentencing outcomes.

C. Proportionality

The principle of proportionality remains the keystone of Australian sentencing, albeit that it finds expression in a Morrisonian form, as a restraint upon excessive punishment, rather than in a von Hirschian form, as a precise measure or calibration of punishment. It has been consistently affirmed by the High Court (*Veen* (*No. 2*) (1988) 164 C.L.R. 465; see Fox 1988) and by appellate courts in most Australian jurisdictions (Fox and Freiberg 1999, para. 3.501). However, as Fox has observed, it is a concept that carries an implicit claim of greater precision in its formulation and operation than it actually possesses (Fox 1994).

In broad terms the rule is that except where overridden by competent legislation, the common law of sentencing in Australia prohibits judges or magistrates from awarding sentences exceeding that which is commensurate to the gravity of the crime then being punished. It is impermissible at common law for any punishment to be extended above this limit in an effort to isolate potentially dangerous persons or to punish offenders with criminal histories more severely than the offence itself warrants or to provide for medical, psychiatric, or other treatment for convicted persons in penal or other settings or to enhance special or general deterrence through exemplary sentences or to promote other "educative" purposes or to force cooperation, restitution, or compensation irrespective of whether fulfillment of these ancillary objectives would protect the community against further crime. The rule applies to sentences of imprisonment (including the nonparole period) whether immediate or deferred and, arguably, to all other forms of sentence.

Proportionality operates to define the lower as well as the upper reaches of punishment, thus containing excessively lenient as well as overly severe responses to crime. It attempts to ensure that the sanction imposed falls within boundaries that are commensurate with the crime. The requirement of some minimal level of deterrence also helps to define the lower limits of the penalty, particularly if it is thought that the undue leniency will provide no special deterrent for the offender and will also undermine the public's confidence in the legal system. Other principles, such as mitigation and mercy, are accepted as allowing some forbearance from punishment. The problem of determining the community's retributive expectations has concerned the courts, and they are conscious that sentences regarded as unduly lenient may undermine their role and legitimacy in the sentencing process.

Australian legislation may now incorporate the concept of proportionality in a number of separate ways: first, by listing "just" punishment as one of the purposes of the act,[3] and second, by the obligation imposed upon sentencers to have regard to the "nature and gravity" of the offense and the "offender's culpability and degree of responsibility for the offence" (Sentencing Act 1991 [Vic.], sec. 5(2)(b) and (d)). The Sentencing Act 1995 (W.A.), sec. 6(1) specifically states that "a sentence must be commensurate with the seriousness of the offence." Finally, Australian legislation may incorporate proportionality by grading the different types of sanction allowed under the act into levels of severity and by including the instruction that no sentence more severe than is necessary to achieve its purpose be imposed (Sentencing Act 1991 [Vic.], sec. 5(3)–(7)).

At the federal level, the main statutory directive regarding proportionality is to be found in the Crimes Act 1914 (Commonwealth), sec. 16A(1). It states that in determining the sentence to be passed, or the order to be made, in respect of any person for a federal offense, a court must impose a sentence or make an order that is of a severity appropriate in all the circumstances of the offense. There is also a reference to the need for "adequate" punishment in section 16A(2)(k). In determining the adequacy of a federal sentence, the sentencer must also have regard to the severity of any conditions that may be attached to a sentence or ancillary order (Crimes Act 1914 [Cth.], sec. 16A(3)).

D. Statutory Departures

Though the proportionality principle remains central at common law, legislatures have made numerous attempts to modify or overturn it. These attempts have met with little success; some even have evoked judicial hostility (Freiberg 2000). From the early twentieth century, special legislation was introduced at state and federal levels permitting the preventive detention of habitual criminals, usually minor but persistent property offenders (Pratt 1997). The legislation was based on the concept that in sentencing an offender who had at least two serious previous convictions, a court should be allowed to award an extended sentence on convicting the offender for any similar subsequent crime. The legislation was little used. Most provisions fell into desuetude or were repealed. However, the concept of some form of preventive detention has maintained its appeal to legislators and has, over recent years, seen a revival especially in relation to violent and dangerous offenders (Fairall 1995; Parke and Mason 1995; Pratt 1995; Meek 1995; Thomas 1995).

In recent years the proportionality principle has been ousted by a series of provisions that have attempted to revamp or revive the use of indefinite or indeterminate sentences.[4] In 1990 Victoria introduced special preventive detention legislation, the Community Protection Act 1990 (Vic.), to deal with a single notorious offender, Gary David (see *Attorney-General v. David* [1992] 2 V.R. 46), but this legislation lapsed upon his death in 1993. It was eventually replaced by more generally applicable legislation in that year, the Sentencing (Amendment) Act 1993 (Vic.), modeled upon the Penalties and Sentences Act 1992 (Qld.), pt. 10, which reintroduced the concept of indeterminate sentences into Victorian law (see Victoria Social Development Committee 1992; Fairall 1993).

The 1993 Victorian legislation was aimed at extending the prison terms of serious sexual and serious violent offenders and created the new indefinite sentence of imprisonment for serious sexual and serious violent offenders (Sentencing Act 1991 [Vic.], secs. 6A, 18A). In 1997, these provisions were extended to serious drug and serious arson offenders. Now, when a Victorian judge is considering imprisoning a "serious offender' " as defined in Sentencing Act 1991 (Vic.), sec. 6B(3), a reorientation of the statutory purposes of sentencing takes place. The court is directed to regard the protection of the community as the principal purpose for which the sentence is imposed. The new legislation expressly declares that the sentencer may, in order to achieve that purpose, impose a custodial sentence "longer than that which is proportionate to the gravity of the offence considered in the light of its objective circumstances."[5]

However, the courts have held that the discretion given by such provisions should be confined to "very exceptional cases" (*Connell* [1996] 1 V.R. 436). For these provisions to be invoked, a court must first be satisfied that it is necessary for the protection of the community that a disproportionately long sentence be imposed. If that objective can equally be achieved by a proportionate sentence, particularly since such a sentence may be quite lengthy if the accused has been found guilty of multiple serious crimes, then it will be unnecessary to impose a longer sentence (*Robertson* (1995) 82 A.Crim.R. 292, 298). In emphasizing that the legislation does not overturn the principle of proportionality in its entirety when one of the special classes of "serious" offenders is being sentenced, a judge of the Victorian Court of Appeal, Charles J. A., stated in *Connell*:[6]

> [T]he section requires the sentencing judge to regard the protection of the community, which was already "one of the most important results that the criminal law is designed to secure" [*Pedder*, Unreported CCA Q, 29/5/64] as the principal purpose. Proportionality remains, in my view, a very important consideration for the judge. . . . If the judge decides to act under s 5A(b) and deprive the prisoner of the benefit of the long-established and entrenched principle of proportionality, the judge should provide adequate reasons for so doing. . . . For it must have been established, to the satisfaction of the judge, that the prisoner will remain a danger to the community beyond the period that the principle of proportionality would permit his detention to last.

When dealing with anyone over twenty-one convicted of "a serious offence," judges are now also empowered to impose an indefinite term of imprisonment regardless of the maximum penalty prescribed for the offense (Sentencing Act 1991 [Vic.]v, sec. 18A(6)). A "serious offence" includes at least fifty different crimes varying greatly in gravity (Sentencing Act 1991 [Vic.], sec. 3). Because the measure amounts to an indefinite extension of what would normally be a determinate conventional custodial sentence,[7] it necessarily means the imposition of disproportionately long sentences in all but the worst cases.

The antipathy that Australian judges have shown to such legislation is indicated by the cautious approach they have enunciated, linking proportion to protection and totality, as exemplified by the judgment in *Connell*. It is also demonstrated by their reluctance, and that of prosecution authorities, to invoke the indefinite sentence legislation.

Although Queensland introduced provisions for indefinite sentences for serious sexual and serious violent offenders in 1992, to date no such sentences have been imposed. In Victoria only three indefinite sentences have been imposed, but each was for an offender who, despite any new provision, would have received an extremely long sentence. Though highly symbolic, the practical effect of these provisions has been extremely limited and they cannot be said to have contributed to the rising rates of imprisonment.[8]

The antipathy of the courts is also evident through the striking down of a New South Wales law, the Community Protection Act 1994 (N.S.W.), an ad hominem law that was intended to allow the imprisonment of a single allegedly dangerous offender following civil proceedings, without the need for charges to be laid. Following the offender's release after some six months of preventive detention, the act was struck down by a majority of the High Court on the tenuous and narrow ground that it improperly attempted to invest the state court with a nonjudicial power (*Kable* (1996) 138 A.L.R. 577).[9] The legislation was enacted just prior to the offender's release from a long term of imprisonment after fears had been raised over his potential for future violence based on a series of threats made by him whilst in prison (Zdenkowski 1997).

More recent measures, which seem to draw their inspiration from U.S.-style "three-strikes" legislation and which have the potential for producing disproportionate sentences, have been introduced in New South Wales, the Northern Territory, and Western Australia. This kind of legislation probably has less to do with risk, dangerousness, and public safety than with the emergence of another rationale for punishment, which might be termed the "forfeiture" theory of punishment. This is found not in the statutes or in the common law but in public expressions of anger and frustration, which are then picked up and amplified by politicians more attuned to such emotions. Although Andrew Ashworth (1995) has argued that the imposition of punishment requires justification, and that therefore we "should not be satisfied with the proposition that anyone who commits any offence forfeits all rights, and may be dealt with by the State in whatever manner the courts decree" (p. 59), he does not accept that the concept of forfeiture itself may, in the minds of some, provide its own justification.

The "forfeiture" theory, for want of a better term, seems to hold that each citizen is given a defined supply of liberty that can somehow be exhausted by the commission of illegal acts. Thus, for a first offense, an offender may be required to surrender some of his or her liberty in exchange for the right to commit that offence. The measure of punishment may well be proportionate to the instant offence. This equation may also hold true for the second offense, or the second sentence may be slightly increased on deterrence, proportionality, or other grounds. But by the third or subsequent offense, the offender has "forfeited," in some cases permanently, his or her right to remain in the community. This massive loss of liberty no longer has to be justified on the basis of the gravity of the precipitating offense or on the basis of the offender's predicted future conduct but can be justified simply on the basis that the implicit social contract has been fundamentally breached by the offender, thus bringing that contract to an end. No more social exchange is desired by the community. Nigel Walker 1996, p. 7) has recently well encapsulated this new justification:

> Someone who has harmed, or tried to harm another person, can hardly claim a right to the presumption of harmlessness: he has forfeited that right, and given society the right to interfere in this life. . . . The justification [of the right to interfere] is not a duty based on retribution but the offender's forfeiture of an immunity.

In the Northern Territory, amendments to the Sentencing Act 1995 (N.T.) and the Juvenile Justice Act 1983 (N.T.) introduced what effectively amounted to "one-strike" legislation (Flynn 1997). The legislation requires a court to impose a mandatory minimum term for persons convicted of a range of property offenses: fourteen days for adult first offenders; ninety days for an adult with one prior property conviction, and twelve months for an adult with two or more prior property convictions. A juvenile (15–17 years old) with one or more prior property convictions must be sentenced to twenty-eight days in a detention center.

In Western Australia, just ten days after the Sentencing Act 1995 (W.A.) came into force, the Criminal Code Amendment Act (No. 2) 1996 (W.A.) introduced provisions that require the courts to impose a mandatory twelve-month prison sentence upon a person classified as a repeat burglar. This legislation, which was designed to deal with a spate of "home invasions," is directed at offenders with at least one prior conviction for burglary and is expected to increase the number both of juveniles and of adults in the prison system, particularly indigenous offenders (Morgan 1996). It follows earlier legislation to the same effect, the Crimes (Serious and Repeat Offenders) Sentencing Act 1992 (W.A.), which Richard Harding and his colleagues have condemned as a failure on almost every criminological criterion upon which they were measured, namely, that they failed to incapacitate offenders, failed to decrease overall crime rates, had little deterrent effect, and fell short of international standards and obligations (Harding 1995).

E. Maximum Penalties

Adjustments and distortions of the proportionality principle take forms other than statutory interventions of this kind. Australian legislatures, like those abroad, are ready to respond to the periodic crises of confidence that crime waves, or crime-reporting waves, tend to precipitate. Whether it be carnage on the road (Crimes [Dangerous Driving] Amendment Act 1994 [N.S.W.]), rape, aggravated burglaries, or home invasions (Crimes [Home Invasions] Amendment Act 1994 [N.S.W.]), arson (Bush Fires Amendment Act 1994 [N.S.W.]), or crime in general,[10] maximum penalties can be, and often are, increased to assuage the current moral panic. The trend to create what Neil Morgan (1995) has termed "UPPIES" (Upwardly Mobile Penalty Provisions) (p. 299) has become more frequent and pervasive. The fragmentation of the maximum penalty structure has meant that, to date, these interventions have been sporadic and relatively specific, dealing with individual offenses or small groups of offenses.

Victoria is one state that has allowed spurious opinion polls to drive a wholesale increase in maximum penalties despite having earlier rationalized and simplified sentencing by the creation of a sentencing scale (see Fox and Freiberg 1990; Fox 1991; Freiberg 1995). The Sentencing and Other Acts (Amendment) Act 1997 (Vic.) reformed the scale and, in the process, increased maximum penalties for sixty-eight serious offenses and reduced them for only twelve. This episode indicates the danger of introducing highly connected systems and the possible unintended or untoward consequences of applying a strict logic to sentencing. Neat, coherent, and highly focused sentencing systems are more prone to capture than those that are disorganized, chaotic, and dispersed.

F. The Factual Basis of Sentencing

Whatever attraction U.S. sentencing practices may have to Australian legislators, they do not extend to an adoption of the process of fact finding that is exemplified in the U.S. federal system. The danger of disproportionality that may arise from the sentencing of offenders for offenses they may not have committed is far lower in Australia than in the United States. As described by Doob (1995, p. 216; see also Reitz 1993), the "relevant conduct" provisions that permit federal courts to take into account a host of matters beyond the offense of conviction stand in marked contrast to Australian rules, which are punctilious in this regard. Despite the absence of a bill of rights, it could be argued that, at least in this respect, Australian legalism has accorded greater respect for due process at sentencing than U.S. constitutionalism, at least at the federal level.

It is a cardinal principle of Australian law that no one should be punished for an offense of which he or she has not been found guilty. This means that the offender should not be sentenced on the basis of facts that constitute a more serious charge that has been withdrawn or has resulted in an acquittal. Nor should the offender be sentenced on the basis of circumstances of aggravation that could have been the subject of a distinct charge but that were not. Some circumstances of aggravation (e.g., serious injury, breach of trust, use of firearms, or commercial quantities of drugs) are specifically added to a provision creating an offense for the purpose of increasing the applicable penalty if those elements are present. These will be read as creating a separate aggravated form of the offense with a higher penalty.

Aggravated forms of offenses differ from a general list of aggravating factors that sentencers may be directed to take into account when imposing sentence but that do not alter any maximum statutory penalty. If an aggravated form of the offense has been created, the aggravating circumstances must be alleged in the indictment and, unless admitted, must be proven beyond reasonable doubt by the prosecution, together with all the elements of the substantive offense charged. If an enhanced offense has not been created and the aggravating elements are listed only for the purpose of helping the sentencer exercise the sentencing discretion,[11] they need not be charged in the indictment, and, if they are not admitted, it is for the sentencer to decide whether they exist beyond reasonable doubt. If not so proved, the offender must be sentenced on the basis that the circumstance of aggravation has not been shown to exist (Anderson (1993) 177 C.L.R. 520, 536, High Court of Australia). Circumstances of aggravation that in themselves amount to a discrete and serious crime that could have been made the subject of a separate charge but were not so charged cannot be relied upon as aggravating factors in fixing sentence.

The courts have conceded that the lines between chargeable, uncharged, and unchargeable conduct is a fine one, and courts have allowed an exception to the above rules where the act or omission by which the offense charged took place also produced an immediate injury. If the offense was committed and the resultant injury was produced by a single act or omission, the consequences of that conduct may be taken into account in determining sentence, either at common law[12] or under statute[13] without being separately charged.

The importance attached to these rules is indicated by the fact that in the past decade appellate courts around Australia have carefully reviewed the issue of the factual basis of sentencing in an attempt to obtain greater clarity and consistency in these rules.[14]

IV. Restoration of Victims and Others

Although once it may have been true that the victim was the forgotten party in the criminal justice system, it no longer is true. Victims now play an important role at several stages in the system, particularly sentencing. Victims' rights legislation is becoming more common (e.g., Victims Rights Act 1996 [N.S.W.]), encompassing such matters as statutory charters of rights for victims and victims' bureaus and advisory boards, and providing victims with a say in parole-release decisions (Sentencing Amendment [Parole] Act 1996 [N.S.W.]).

Victim impact statements are now common.[15] Despite fears that they would lead sentencers to give disproportionate weight to the effect of the crime on the victim to the detriment of other considerations, such as rehabilitation of the offender, victim impact statements have not been shown to have had significant effects upon sentence lengths or sentencing patterns generally (Hinton 1995; Erez and Roger 1995).

Paradoxically, the success of the victim's movement has resulted in what appears to be the start of a movement to restrict victims' rights. Schemes to compensate victims of crime for personal injuries have been in effect in Australia since the early 1970s. They provided limited compensation for a range of injuries, but as victims became more aware of their rights and came to assert them more frequently and aggressively, state budgets came under increasing strain. The open-ended nature of the state's commitment to providing compensation has come to be regarded as untenable and in response some jurisdictions have now legislated to transform the compensatory system from financial compensation to therapeutic intervention.

In Victoria, the Victims of Crime Assistance Act 1996 (Vic.) removed the right of victims to claim for pain and suffering and replaced it with vouchers for psychological counseling. Although this legislation advances the interests of victims in many respects, in particular, by establishing an improved infrastructure of support and advice, it is clear that the imperative is financial rather than supportive.

In a further initiative, the legislation reprivatizes the victim compensation mechanism by requiring a victim who seeks compensation under this head to do so directly from the offender by an application under Sentencing Act 1991 (Vic.), sec. 86(1) for a compensation order. If the offender has no means, such an order will be of no assistance to the victim. Other jurisdictions are now taking a close look at this initiative (Freckelton 1997).

Possibly more influential than developments concerning victims per se, and surprisingly omitted from Tonry's discussion of sentencing matters, is the movement toward restorative justice at the juvenile and adult levels. Many scholars see restorative justice, diversionary conferencing, family group conferencing, or community conferencing as a major alternative to traditional sentencing forms. Drawing upon a variety of theoretical and historical bases (Braithwaite 1989; Moore 1993; Alder and Wundersitz 1994; Hudson et al. 1996; Blagg 1997, p. 482) these programs seek to create pre- or postsentencing alternatives bringing victims and offenders together. The aim is for the latter to take responsibility for their actions and make reparation to the former as part of an agreed outcome.

Various conferencing, mediation, community justice, and similar schemes have been tried in New South Wales, especially in what became known as the Wagga Wagga experiment (New South Wales Law Reform Commission 1996, p. 296; Young Offenders Act 1998 [N.S.W.]), South Australia (Young Offenders Act 1993 [S.A.]), Victoria, and Western Australia (Young Offenders Act 1994 [W.A.]). Both Western Australia and Tasmania have introduced new provisions for "mediation reports," which permit a court, before passing sentence on an offender, to adjourn proceedings and order a mediation report. The report, by a mediator, may be oral or written and may advise the court about the attitude of the offender to mediation and to the victim, the effects on the victim of commission of offense, and any agreement between offender and victim about actions to be taken by the offender by way of reparation (Sentencing Act 1997 [Tas.], sec. 84; Sentencing Act 1995 [W.A.], secs. 27–30).

The largest, and most important, of these experiments is taking place in Canberra, in the Australian Capital Territory, and is known as RISE, the Reintegrative Shaming Experiment (Sherman, Braithwaite, and Strang 1994; Jarrett 1997) and is based upon Braithwaite's theory of reintegrative shaming. The experimental scheme, conceived of and evaluated by John Braithwaite of the Australian National University and Lawrence W. Sherman of the University of Maryland, randomly assigns offenders into a court stream and a conference stream. The majority of offenders are drunk drivers and youthful property-and-violence offenders. The preprosecution conferences, convened by police officers, bring together the offender and his or her family, friends, victims, or community representatives. Although the ultimate test of the trial may be the rate of recidivism, preliminary results of interviews with over five hundred offenders indicate, perhaps unsurprisingly, that diversionary conferences (taking on average seventy-one minutes compared with six minutes for court cases) give offenders more respect for the legal system because they felt that they were listened to more, given more chance to correct factual errors, had their rights explained to them, were treated with equal rights, and were accorded more respect and courtesy. The emerging conclusion seems to be that independent of, or in addition to, the effects of shaming, affording better procedural justice to an offender through a conference is more likely to result in law-abiding behavior than the usually perfunctory traditional court process of trial and sentence (see also Tyler 1990).

V. Intermediate Sanctions

In 1990 Morris and Tonry argued in favor of a sentencing system in which sanctions could be regarded as interchangeable and used in combination (Morris and Tonry 1990). However, in the United States, "intermediate" sanctions have had only moderate success and, according to one commentator, "no U.S. jurisdiction has succeeded in materially altering its sentencing patterns through the use of alternative punishments" (Reitz 1996, p. 159).

Australian and U.S. conceptions of what amount to intermediate sanctions differ, not only in the extent of use, but in their conceptions of the scale of "intermediacy." The United States Department of Justice (1990, cited in Junger-Tas 1994, p. 1) defines an intermediate sanction as "a punishment option that is considered on a continuum to fall between traditional probation supervision and traditional incarceration." In contrast, an intermediate sanction in Australia would be regarded as falling between dismissals, discharges, and adjournments or bonds, at the lower end of the sentencing scale, and immediate imprisonment at the other. The United States' conception of where the intermediate sanction commences is already regarded as a mid-range sanction in Australia. This difference may also say something about the overall scale of punishments in the two cultures. Australian sentencing is very much weighted toward the lower end of the scale, toward fines and bonds, and sentences of imprisonment, when they are imposed, tend to be relatively short. In the United States, although comparative data are difficult to evaluate, it would appear that overall sentence lengths are greater, and more use is made of imprisonment as a sanction (Tonry 1996, p. 128).

The multiplicity of intermediate sanctions gives rise to the danger of "sanction stacking," to which Hudson (1993, p. 134) has drawn attention in England. Courts are groping their way toward the concept of "sanction packages" that create a proportionate mix of sentences. The problem of sentencing on breach of multiple sanctions vexes courts, torn between the need to maintain the credibility of such sanctions in the eyes of the public, on one hand, and the requirements of individual justice and flexibility, on the other. Australian legislatures have generally adopted the option of allowing courts to resentence on breach, rather than requiring them automatically to impose a further sanction or to execute the breached sentence. This loosely coupled system has acted as a restraint on prison numbers, especially where the intermediate sanctions have been inappropriately imposed through penalty escalation.

Now that the "experiments" of the 1980s and 1990s with "alternative to imprisonment," such as community service, periodic detention, attendance centers, and intensive probation, have run their course, with moderately little impact upon sentencing patterns, a new wave of experimentation is under way. Intensive correction or supervision orders intended as front- or back-end diversions have been introduced in Western Australia, South Australia, Queensland, and the Northern Territory, some allied with electronic monitoring or surveillance (Morgan 1996, p. 381). Home detention has since 1992 been piloted in New South Wales, where legislation, the Home Detention Act 1997 (N.S.W.), was introduced to regularize its status. This scheme, which in effect imprisons the offender in the home, is available for a sentence of up to eighteen months for a range of nonserious offences but has been slow to be accepted (Liverani 1998). Other experiments are taking place with new sanctions, such as curfews and "area restriction orders," in Western Australia (Morgan 1996, p. 378), but these are still in their early stages.

A. Boot Camps

Australia's flirtation with an American-style innovation, the boot camp, seems to have come and gone. Following a by-election win in 1994, the conservative Western Australian government opened a form of boot camp designed to administer discipline to hard-core repeat offenders aged 16 to 21. Boot camps are as indigenous and authentic to Australian conditions as boot-scooting and line dancing. The Western Australian government drew its inspiration from shock incarceration camps in the United States and opened a rural facility designed to accommodate thirty inmates who would otherwise have gone to prison. It was intended that half of the inmates would be Aboriginal offenders.

After a mere eighteen months, the facility was closed after a scathing report by a judge revealed that the facility was too remote, that it was culturally inappropriate for the intended participants, that it provided poor training and services, and that, anyway, the young people referred there would not have received a prison sentence. The daily occupancy of the facility was ten offenders, one-third of its capacity, no juveniles were sent, and only one Aboriginal offender was referred. In all, some $2.8 million was spent on what the report described as a "fiasco" (Newman 1996).[16] Reviewing the U.S. literature and example and the short Australian experience, Lynne Atkinson (1995, p. 6) presciently concluded:

> The boot camp context is inappropriate and arguably alien to Australian history and cultures. . . . [Boot camps are] inappropriate and dangerous to Aboriginal offenders. . . . Boot camps have not taken firm root in Australia. They do not have the public profile, or relentless momentum of the U.S. example.

B. Suspended Sentences

Suspended sentences, which have been available for some years in South Australia, have now been introduced in Queensland, the Northern Territory, Western Australia (up to five years), Tasmania (for any period of time and subject to such conditions as the courts think necessary or expedient)[17] and have been recommended for introduction in New South Wales (New South Wales Law Reform Commission 1996). The conditions that can be attached to them vary from jurisdiction to jurisdiction and include supervision and community service, though in the majority of jurisdictions no restrictions other than good behavior and no further offending can be attached.

In Victoria, the suspended sentence was reintroduced in 1985 after a brief existence in the early part of century to provide a substitute for sentences of imprisonment of under twelve months. This was extended to twenty-four months in 1991 and thirty-six months in 1997 because of its popularity. In fact, in Victoria the suspended sentence has had a greater impact upon the pattern of sentencing in Victoria than any other newly introduced sentencing option (Tait 1995). Within three years of the reintroduction of this sanction in 1985, some 14 percent of offenders in the higher courts were given a suspended sentence, by 1991–92, the figure was up to 24 percent, and by 1994, 35 percent of sentences for principal offenses in the higher courts were suspended sentences of imprisonment (Freiberg and Ross 1999).

The evidence in Victoria appears to be that the suspended sentence has diverted some sentences of imprisonment but also some intermediate sentences. Although it has also had an impact upon lower-order sanctions such as fines and bonds, the patterns are variable and very much offense-sensitive. It is also clear that Victorian breach rates are lower than those reported in England, as are the execution rates (Freiberg and Ross 1999). This may change, however, with the increases in the length of possible suspensions, as well as a tightening of the rules relating to sentencing on breach introduced in 1997.

VI. Prisons and Prison Populations

In March 1998, 18,459 prisoners were held in Australian prisons, an increase of 6,771 or approximately 60 percent over 1987. Table 1.1 sets out the changes in Australian prison populations and imprisonment rates between 1987 and March 1998.

A. State-by-State Variation

The imprisonment rate increased from 72.3 per 100,000 of the population to 98.9 per 100,000 or by 36.8 percent and with it a disturbing increase in deaths in custody, both Aboriginal and non-Aboriginal. Table 1.1 also reveals a complex picture of regional variation in the use of imprisonment.

Between 1987 and 1998, the New South Wales imprisonment rate per 100,000 of the population jumped from 72.8 to 99.7 (37 percent), most of which occurred between 1989 and 1995, a period following a major sentencing reform that included both the abolition of remission and a restructuring of the method by which prison sentences are imposed by the courts (see Freiberg 1995). A slight downward trend in full-time custody appeared between 1994 and 1998. The New South Wales government intends to commission a nine-hundred-bed remand and reception center and hopes that the commencement of a home detention program will divert minor offenders from full-time custody (Australia Steering Committee for the Review of Commonwealth State Service Provision 1998, p. 436).

In Victoria, since the abolition of remissions in April 1992, the actual number of offenders imprisoned jumped from 2,240 in mid-1993 to 2,722 in March 1998. Between 1987 and 1998 the imprisonment rate increased by 22.5 percent. The explanations for the changes in Victoria's prison population are complex. Victoria abolished remissions in mid-1992, but, unlike in New South Wales, the prison population did not immediately increase. This effect may be due partly to legislative directions to sentencers to compensate for their removal but is more likely to be due to a significant contemporaneous decrease in the number of offenders coming before the court.[18] Since the sentencing reforms of the early 1990s, sentence lengths have slowly increased and offenders serving longer terms of imprisonment are accumulating in the prisons. While the number of prisoners serving short terms (under twelve months) fell by around 30 percent, the numbers in all

Table 1.1. Prisoners in Custody in Australia, 1987–1998

Year	N.S.W.	Vic.	Qld.	W.A.	S.A.	Tas.	N.T.	A.C.T.	Aust.
	Average Number of Prisoners Rate per 100,000 Population								
1987	4,077	1,970	2,311	1,625	878	269	467	91	11,688
	72.8	47.0	87.6	110.2	63.5	59.6	311.3	33.7	72.3
1988	4,190	2,049	2,400	1,631	820	297	384	70	11,841
	73.8	48.1	88.1	116.1	53.5	65.8	239.4	26.0	71.9
1989	4,627	2,235	2,463	1,543	869	242	360	89	12,428
	80.0	51.8	87.7	97.2	61.1	53.9	232.3	31.7	74.0
1990	5,322	2,298	2,206	1,804	935	229	403	114	13,322
	91.6	52.6	75.6	110.2	65.1	50.6	258.3	40.6	78.0
1991	5,771	2,299	2,220	1,885	1,013	256	473	118	14,045
	98.1	51.8	74.5	112.7	69.7	57.5	299.4	40.5	81.0
1992	6,102	2,247	NA	1,947	1,131	254	440	92	NA
	102.2	50.3	NA	114.9	76.8	54.7	275.0	30.6	NA
1993	6,305	2,240	2,061	1,995	1,133	255	421	98	14,508
	104.8	50.0	66.5	118.9	77.2	53.9	249.1	32.8	82.0
1994	6,438	2,481	2,459	2,065	1,316	250	459	107	15,576
	106.3	55.4	77.0	121.6	89.7	52.7	271.1	35.3	87.3
1995	6,400	2,482	2,879	2,200	1,370	245	460	113	16,063
	104.7	55.1	87.8	127.1	98.9	51.9	264.3	37.1	89.0
1996	6,273	2,450	3,539	2,257	1,485	280	488	126	16,806
	101.9	54.2	106.7	129.2	100.6	59.1	276.1	50.2	92.5
1997	6,375	2,543	4,077	2,258	1,496	259	574	160	17,622
	102.6	57.4	113.2	127.1	101.9	55.0	312.2	50.9	94.9
1998*	6,277	2,722	4,856	2,262	1,447	270	593	153	18,459
	99.7	57.6	141.6	127.4	96.5	57.0	334.7	49.1	98.9

Source: Australian Bureau of Statistics, various years.

Note: Daily average number of persons held in custody during June of each year, except for 1995, which are July data.

*Data for 1998 are as of March 1998. Imprisonment rates are estimates only.

sentence-length categories over two years have risen substantially (Freiberg and Ross 1999). I argue that these changes are due as much to a changing social and legal culture as they are to changes in sentencing law.

Steadier but consistent increases in imprisonment rates have occurred in South Australia and Queensland. In South Australia the rate jumped from 63.5 per 100,000 in 1987 to 96.5 in 1998 (an increase of 52 percent). The increase has been attributed partly to significant increases in average sentence lengths and non-parole periods (the latter being more important in terms of actual time spent in prison) arising from a series of problematic changes in laws relating to parole and remissions (Roeger 1993), but prison numbers have now stabilized and are, if anything, declining.

The most spectacular changes have occurred in the state of Queensland. Between 1987 and 1997 prison numbers increased from 2,311 to 4,856, or by 110 percent. The rate increased from 87.6 per 100,000 to 141.6, or by 61.6 percent. Most of this change occurred between June 1993 and March 1998, when the Queensland prison population increased from 2,061 to 4,856, a 135 percent increase. According to the Queensland Criminal Justice Commission (1999), the increase in prison numbers was not due to an increase in crime rates, which have remained stable since 1984, or to increasing sentence lengths but to increased throughput in the courts. The number of persons dealt with by the higher courts increased by 58 percent while, in addition, the number of persons sentenced to imprisonment by the Magistrates' Court increased by 41 percent, because of both increased numbers and an increased use of imprisonment as a sanction. In the court system, whereas 55 percent of sex offenders were sentenced to imprisonment in 1992, 78 percent were being imprisoned in 1997. There was also a marked increase in the number of persons imprisoned for breaching orders, such as suspended sentences, home detention orders, probation, parole, and community service orders.

Between 1986 and 1996, the nature of Australian prison populations changed (see Australian Bureau of Statistics 1997). The average age of prisoners rose from 29.9 years to 31.8 years; the proportion of prisoners aged 25 years or less decreased from 36.5 percent to 28.6 percent and the proportion of female prisoners rose from 4.8 percent to 5.3 percent. Sex offences increased from 9.1 percent of offenses by most serious offense category to 13.6 percent, as did assaults, from 5.9 percent to 12 percent. Property offenses, however, declined.

The reasons for variations in imprisonment rates are complex. To some extent, the differences may be due to differences in crime rates, which, like the differences in imprisonment rates, have been long standing. Crime rate data indicate, for example, that Victoria and Tasmania have generally low rates of recorded crime across all of the common offense types. Victoria's assault rate, for example, is nearly half the Australian average, its robbery rate is less than half the national average and about 25 percent of that of New South Wales, its sexual assault rate is 20 percent below the average, and the unlawful entry rate is 30 percent below the national average and half that of Western Australia. To some extent, therefore, there is some relationship between crime rates and imprisonment rates. However, there appears to be far less variation in aggregate crime rates than in imprisonment rates. The state with the highest crime rate (Western Australia) has 1.7 times as much crime as the state with the lowest (Victoria). In contrast, the highest imprisonment rate (for the Northern Territory) is 6 times higher than that of the lowest (for Tasmania). An analysis of the relationship between imprisonment rates and crime rates seems to indicate that some jurisdictions are more punitive than others in that they imprison more offenders or for longer periods than do other jurisdictions for the same number of crimes (Freiberg and Ross 1999, chap. 4).

B. Indigenous Imprisonment Rates

The number of indigenous persons in a jurisdiction and the indigenous imprisonment rate are certainly contributing factors to differences in imprisonment rates. Approximately one in five Australian prisoners is identified as Aboriginal or Torres

Strait Islander (ATSI). The imprisonment rate was 1,820 per 100,000 ATSI adults, a rate that was twelve to seventeen times that for the general population except in the Northern Territory and Tasmania, where rates were three to six times higher. Aboriginal offenders comprise 70 percent of the Northern Territory prison population, 33 percent of the Western Australian prison population, and 26.6 percent of the Queensland population but only 4.6 percent of the Victorian prison population. As a consequence, in jurisdictions such as the Northern Territory, Queensland, and Western Australia that have relatively large indigenous populations, the high level of indigenous imprisonment is a significant contributing factor to their high general imprisonment rates. However, to the extent that states that have higher imprisonment rates also tend to have higher rates of crime, especially serious crime and proportionally larger indigenous male populations, the relationship among imprisonment, race, and crime is rendered more complex (Michalowski and Pearson 1990, p. 68).

Concerned by high Aboriginal crime rates, courts wrestle with the problem of the role of Aboriginal customary law in sentencing. Although race, color, and ethnicity are not, in themselves, permissible grounds of discrimination in the sentencing process, cultural background can be taken into account. The Crimes Act 1914 (Cth.), sec. 16A(1)(m), for example, requires a court sentencing a federal offender to take into account, among other factors, the "cultural background" of the offender. Though ethnicity or Aboriginality, of themselves, cannot be aggravating or mitigating factors (Australian Law Reform Commission 1987, para. 270), "in imposing sentences courts are bound to take into account, in accordance with those principles, all material facts including those facts which exist only by reason of the offender's membership of an ethnic or other group."[19] Courts, in dealing with identifiable racial or ethnic groups, particularly with persons of Aboriginal background, have tried to make allowance for "ethnic, environmental and cultural matters."[20] These matters relate not necessarily to the offender's race but to his or her actual circumstances, such as background, education, cultural outlook, and life experiences.[21] On one hand, courts in jurisdictions such as the Northern Territory, Western Australia, South Australia, and Queensland have considered such matters as the high level of alcohol consumption and substance abuse in Aboriginal settlements, and the reasons for such abuse, in arriving at sentence.[22] On the other hand, the courts do not wish to deprive Aboriginal victims of violent crimes of the protection of the law.[23]

The particular impact of a sanction upon an offender[24] and the question whether an offender will suffer legal sanctions other than those awarded by the sentencing court are relevant to sentence. In the context of dealing with Aboriginal offenders, the question whether it is proper to take mitigating account of the likelihood of parallel punishment under Aboriginal customary law or other local communal reaction has arisen. In *Minor*,[25] the Supreme Court of the Northern Territory, in considering an appeal against the leniency of a sentence that had taken into account that the offender would inevitably be subject to "payback" by the relatives of the victims, supported the legitimacy of taking the possibility of future payback punishment into account. In doing so, it was not giving its approval to forms of punishment that it did not recognize itself and that might be unlawful but was recognizing that some form of retribution might be exacted by the offender's own community.[26] The decision also takes account of the principle that a person should not be punished twice for the same offense. Furthermore, the Court also recognized that the sentencing judge was influenced by the fact that the infliction of payback would be of benefit to a community that considers that, once inflicted, payback wipes out any feuds arising out of the original offense. However, the tension between majority and minority law remains unresolved and no federal Australian government has yet had the courage to take action on the Australian Law Reform Commission's report (1986) on Aboriginal customary law, which recommended that the mainstream legal system should take more account of Aboriginal customary law.

Modern Australian governments seem to be ambivalent about imprisonment numbers and rates. They encourage more and longer sentences by increasing maximum penalties, exhorting sentencers and parole boards to be "tough on crime," and introducing measures that limit judicial discretion. Low imprisonment rates are not causes for self-congratulation. However, the cost of these measures is of concern each budget time, and so these governments introduce measures to curb the use of imprisonment. Thus, Western Australia has recently abolished sentences of imprisonment of less than three months, except in limited circumstances (Sentencing Act 1995 [W.A.], sec. 86; see Morgan 1996, p. 366) and requires written reasons for custodial sentences of under twelve months (Sentencing Act 1995 [W.A.], sec. 35). Parole has been maintained, in one form or another, in every jurisdiction, and New South Wales even toyed briefly with the idea of reintroducing remissions on management grounds (New South Wales Law Reform Commission 1996, p. 174).

C. Privatization

The managerialist and competitive environment in which governments now operate has affected the delivery of correctional services. In 1997 there were 111 prison and periodic detention facilities in Australia, including 6 privately operated facilities in four jurisdictions, New South Wales, Victoria, Queensland, and South Australia. There were 1,862 prisoners, or 11 percent of the total population, in private facilities, compared with 2 percent in the United States (Australia Steering Committee for the Review of Commonwealth State Service Provision 1998, p. 408). In Victoria in 1997, 40 percent of prisoners were held in private facilities, compared with 32 percent in Queensland.

Private prisons were another U.S.-inspired initiative, which, proportionately, Australia seems to have taken further than any other jurisdiction (Russell 1997). Australian private prisons are part subsidiaries of U.S. and English corporations, such as Wackenhut, Corrections Corporation of America, and Group 4, and, in some instances, have brought with them overseas personnel and practices.

The organization of correctional services has been transformed in Victoria and Queensland through the corporatization of correctional services, the purpose of which is to separate "purchasers" and "providers" of correctional services, steerers from rowers, in order to provide competition. In Victoria, government providers of prison and community correctional services operate under a corporate structure and they, like the private providers, are now responsible to the commissioner of Correctional Services, who has oversight of, and responsibility for, the whole correctional system. The implications of this system, in terms of accountability to the public, are profound (Harding 1997; Freiberg 1997). And despite privatization of over 40 percent of the prison system in Victoria, the cost per prisoner has not decreased (Australia Steering Committee for the Review of Commonwealth State Service Provision 1998, p. 437). To date there have been no published evaluations of Australia's experiment with privatization, in terms of relative costs, speed, and flexibility of deployment and other important issues.

Attempts to outsource or to privatize 40 percent of community corrections in Victoria commenced in 1997 but apparently foundered on the rock of cost: it was found that the private sector could not deliver the same or better service at a lower cost than the public sector. Although Australia's community corrections are delivered through the public sector, specialized services, such as drug treatment, education, and skills training, have always been delivered by both private and public agencies. However, community corrections in Australian states are generally public, statewide, and in the main, well managed. This may, to some degree, account for the greater use of such intermediate sanctions in Australia than in the United States.

VII. Conclusion

Despite our common heritage as British colonies, Australian and U.S. legal histories have traveled widely divergent paths. Whereas the United States achieved its independence in 1778, Australia's separation was much slower and was not born of revolution. The Australian colonies federated in 1901 and the country achieved full legal independence only with the abolition of appeals to the Privy Council as recently as 1975. Where the United States treads boldly, rapidly, and sometimes foolishly, Australia tiptoes carefully, slowly, and most times reluctantly. And if the nineteenth century was the century of Pax Britannicus, then the latter half of the twentieth century emerged as Pax Americanus. This is an empire founded on economic, cultural, and intellectual vibrancy, a domination of capital markets, and supremacy in the media, telecommunications, and technology. In a world characterized by an unequal distribution of power, globalization probably results in cultural hegemony.

Although, as Michael Tonry (1996, chap. 7) argues, we can learn from successes across national and state boundaries, we should, as Jerome Skolnick (1995) suggests, also learn "what not to do about crime." In summing up developments in Australia, identifying what we have *not* done should be as important as what we have. Thus, for example, in addition to resisting a return to capital punishment, we have not embraced boot camps, we have kept imprisonment rates at a comparatively low level, rejected numerical sentencing grids and guidelines, and kept the number of mandatory sentences to a minimum.

Within Australia, governments have sporadically borrowed from one another but in the sentencing arena have tended to remain relatively insular. Before deciding to adopt truth-in-sentencing legislation, Victoria looked carefully at the New

South Wales experience and crafted its legislation to avoid what appeared to be the consequence of that action, a large increase in the prison population. A later evaluation of the Victorian response indicates that that initiative was only partially successful. Other states have also abolished remissions,[27] some without compensating legislation. Victoria borrowed the indefinite sentence provisions from Queensland, while other states have adopted a legislative structure similar to Victoria's Sentencing Act 1991.

Unlike state and federal government initiatives in the area of the substantive criminal law, which have seen an attempt to establish a model penal code for Australia, there has been no similar cooperative national initiative in sentencing. The ill-fated Australian Law Reform Commission's 1980 attempt to reform federal sentencing law resulted in probably the worst of Australia's sentencing statutes, though little of the responsibility for that can be laid at the feet of the commission.

Informal liaison exists between governments. Information is exchanged, law reform and parliamentary commissions criss-cross the country, and the world looks for successful and unsuccessful ideas. The Tasmanian Parliament, having enacted its new Sentencing Act 1997, established an upper house committee with broad terms of reference.[28] With a staff of one, and membership of three parliamentarians, one can only wish them well.

From New Zealand, we have learned much about family group conferences (Hudson et al. 1996). These powerful ideas, picked up and developed by Braithwaite (1989), have taken root in Australia as well as Canada (La Prairie 1995; Immarigeon 1996; Longclaws et al. 1996) and, to a lesser extent, in the United States (Graber, Keys, and White 1996). We tend to learn less from non-English-speaking countries, possibly because of our limited linguistic frame. This force may be weaker now in England because of that nation's membership in the European Community but probably still applies to the United States and Australia.

However, powerful as are the forces of propinquity, collegiality, and comity between states, especially among public servants, academics, and consultants, for the politicians, they are eclipsed by the powerful cultural and political forces of England and the United States. Zero tolerance is becoming increasingly tolerated. The idea of boot camps seems to play as well in Perth as in Peoria. Three strikes seem to capture the Australian imagination better than three wickets.

Internationally, what is more important and more intangible than the importation of specific sentencing laws or sanctions is the hegemony of U.S., and, to a lesser extent, English, ideas about the structure and functioning of societies. The sentencing manifestations of individualism, privatization, managerialism, economism, and technology are merely variations of wider themes that play themselves out in commercial and industrial organizations, in the changing role of government, and in the forms of law. In *Punishment and Modern Society*, David Garland (1990, p. 287) suggests that punishment should be regarded as:

a "total social fact," which on its surface appears to be self-contained, but which in fact intrudes into many of the basic spheres of social life. . . . Punishment is a distinctive social institution which, in its routine practices, somehow contrives to condense a whole web of social relations and cultural meanings.[29]

Elsewhere he has written (1991, pp. 142–43):

> The ways in which we punish depend not just on political forces, economic interests, or even penological considerations but also on our conceptions of what is or is not culturally and emotionally acceptable. Penal policy decisions are always taken against a background of mores and sensibilities that, normally at least, will set limits to what will be tolerated by the public or implemented by the penal system's personnel.

This complex interplay between the global and local seems to hold the key to understanding the changes in sentencing in Australia. More important than the specific examples of new sanctions or statutes are the major global (or Western) changes in economic, political, and social formations that have influenced the mood, sensitivities, and sensibilities of the public, legislators, and judges. To the extent that we are a part of the global economy and the global marketplace of ideas will we continue to be influenced by events elsewhere.

Now that I have identified Australia as a colonial country and identified some of the influences upon current Australian sentencing laws and practices, is there anything that can be identified as a particularly Australian contribution to sentencing, something that would distinguish it, for example, from England, Canada, or the United States?

One feature worth noting is formal rather than functional, the sentencing legislation itself. The sentencing statutes of the 1990s are more streamlined, clearer, and more consistent than their predecessors or the hodgepodge of acts that govern, for example, English sentencing. Some articulate the objectives of sentencing, the identification of aggravating and mitigating circumstances, some means of determining offense seriousness, the purposes of particular sanctions, and the power to hand down guideline judgments, and some contain sanction hierarchies that are aimed at guiding sentencers' discretion. I am doubtful that the achievement of a clear, accessible, and coherent sentencing act is an end in itself, but in view of the endemic disagreement about what "good" sentencing should be, it is a start.

Notwithstanding legislative attempts to overturn them in relation to dangerous offenders, the common law principles of parsimony and proportionality still remain central to sentencing practice, especially in retaining some upper limits on sentences. Unlike federal courts in the United States, which employ "real offense" sentence enhancements, Australian courts have maintained strict control of the factual foundations of sentence. These limits appear to be much greater than those of conviction offense-based U.S. state guideline systems and certainly far greater than indeterminate sentencing systems, which appear to grant almost unfettered discretion to courts to increase sentences up to the statutory maximum.

Other features worth noting may be the development of a powerful appellate jurisdiction and a common law that does not exclude ethically relevant factors in the same way as do the U.S. federal guidelines (cf. Tonry 1996, p. 11). Nonetheless, it is clear that the appellate courts have neither increased nor decreased unjustifiable disparity, if we could even agree about its nature and extent. Finally, there is evidence that family group conferencing, originally imported from New Zealand and given new emphasis through Braithwaite's theory of shaming, is being franchised for re-exportation abroad, especially to the United States. The appro-

priateness of the New Zealand model to Australia, let alone its re-exported desti-
nations, has been questioned (Blagg 1997).

The reality is that in an age of global communications, franchised merchandise,
and transnational corporations, national differences diminish in the face of a ho-
mogenization of culture, commerce, and law. The "carpet bombing" of culture
precedes the three pinpoint strikes. Resistance may not be useless, but it is difficult.
From baseball to boot camps, from Macy's to macing, the process of Coca-
colonizing Australian criminal justice, while not yet a fait accompli, has more
than a little commenced. In the new Australian fashion, we could say, it has just
got to first base!

ACKNOWLEDGMENTS

My thanks to John Brigham, Richard Fox, Richard Frase, Neil Morgan, Monica Pfeffer,
Michael Tonry, and George Zdenkowski for their valuable comments on earlier drafts.
Malcolm Feiner was, as always, of great assistance in providing statistical and bibliographical
data.

NOTES

1. Sentencing Act 1991 (Vic.), sec. 5(3)–(7), s.7; Crimes Act 1914 (Commonwealth),
sec. 16A(2); cf. recent amendments to Queensland laws that state that imprisonment is no
longer a penalty of last resort for serious violent offenders.

2. These figures were kindly supplied by L. T. Hill from his unpublished study of appeals to the Court of Appeal for the years 1993 to 1995, inclusive.

3. E.g., Sentencing Act 1991 (Vic.), sec. 5(1)(a); cf. the Sentencing Act 1997 (Tas.),
sec. 1, which omits this clause. Sentencing Act 1997 (Tas.), sec. 3(b) not only does not
restate the common law principles of sentencing but declares that "the purpose of the Act
is to promote the protection of the community as a primary consideration in the sentencing
of offenders."

4. Criminal Code 1924 (Tas.), sec. 392; Criminal Code Amendment (Life Prisoners
and Dangerous Criminals) Act 1994 (Tas.), secs. 13–16; Sentencing Act 1997 (Tas), sec.
19; see *Hueston* (1995) 5 Tas. R. 210; *Read* (1994) 3 Tas. R. 387; *Criminal Code* (Qld.)
sec. 659; Penalties and *Sentences Act* 1992 (Qld.), secs.162–79; Sentencing Act 1995
(W.A.), secs. 98–101; Criminal Code (W.A.), secs. 662; *Gooch* (1989) 43 A.Crim.R. 382;
Clinch (1994) 72 A.Crim.R. 301; Crime (Serious and Repeat Offenders) Sentencing Act
1992 (W.A.); see S *(A Child)* (1995) 12 W.A.R. 392; Criminal Law (Sentencing) Act 1988
(S.A.), sec. 21; see also *South Australia v. O'Shea* (1987) 73 A.L.R. 1, 4–5; Sentencing Act
1995 (N.T.), secs. 65–78.

5. Sentencing Act 1991 (Vic.), sec. 6D(b). Similar legislation is now in place in Queensland, where serious violent offenders must now serve at least 80 percent of their sentence
before being eligible for parole.

6. [1996] 1 V.R. 436, 443 per Charles J. A.; see also *Cowburn* (1994) 74 A.Crim.R. 385.
These principles apply also when considering the totality of sentences in multiple offending.

7. Interestingly, the Victorian, Queensland, and Western Australian legislation all require a court to impose a "nominal" sentence, based on proportionality, followed by the
possibility of indeterminate detention.

8. See also Habitual Criminals Act 1957 (N.S.W.), still on the statute book but last used in 1973.

9. An attempt to strike down the more general Victorian indefinite sentence on similar constitutional grounds failed. See *Moffatt* (1997) 91 A.Crim.R. 557.

10. Criminal Law Amendment Act 1997 (Qld.). In conjunction with these changes, the Queensland government distributed a pamphlet entitled "Our New Laws: Getting Tough on Criminals."

11. E.g., factors listed in the sentencing guidelines found in Sentencing Act 1991 (Vic.), sec. 5(2).

12. *Sessions* (1997) 95 A.Crim.R 151. In this case, a child victim of vaginal rape suffered internal injuries, which were caused by the act of penetration itself. It was held not necessary to charge the offense of recklessly inflicting serious bodily harm for the sentence to reflect the nature of the injuries occasioned by the rape.

13. Sentencing Act 1991 (Vic.), sec. 5(2)(db) (sentencer to have regard to any injury, loss, or damage resulting directly from the offense).

14. E.g., *Bresnehan* (1992) 1 Tas. R. 234; *Anderson* (1993) 177 C.L.R. 520 (High Court of Australia); *Turnbull* (1994) 4 Tas. R. 216 (Tasmania); *Nardozzi* [1995] 2 Qd.R. 87 (Queensland); *Storey* (1996) 89 A.Crim.R. 519 (Victoria); *Langridge* (1996) 87 A.Crim.R. 1 (Western Australia); *Isaacs* (1997) 90 A.Crim.R. 587 (New South Wales).

15. See, e.g., Victims of Crime Act 1994 (W.A.); Sentencing (Victim Impact Statement) Act 1994 (Vic.); Victims Rights Act 1996 (N.S.W); Crimes Act 1900 (A.C.T.), pt. 12, div. 1.

16. Apparently the same fate has befallen the first English boot camp at Colchester, for many of the same reasons. See "The Boot for Boot Camp," *The Guardian*, March 18, 1998.

17. Criminal Law (Sentencing) Act 1988 (S.A.), sec. 38; Penalties and Sentences Act 1992 (Qld.), ss. 143–51A; Sentencing Act 1995 (N.T.), secs. 40–43; Sentencing Act 1995 (W.A.), sec. 76; Sentencing Act 1997 (Tas.), sec. 24.

18. My earlier conclusions about the efficacy of legislative directions may have overstated the case, in the light of data that later became available to explain the remarkable stability of the prison population in the eighteen months following the commencement of the Sentencing Act 1991 (Vic.). See Freiberg 1995.

19. *Neal* (1982) 149 C.L.R. 305, 326 per Brennan J. However, sentencers have been reminded that not all of the problems ascribed to certain groups apply equally to all persons in that group, *Russell* (1995) 84 A.Crim.R. 386, 392 per Kirby P.

20. *Rogers* (1989) 44 A.Crim.R. 301, 305. The literature and case law on the general issue of Aborigines and the criminal justice system is extensive; see for example Australian Law Reform Commission 1986, chap. 21; 1988, p. 107; McKillop 1992; Roeger 1993; Lofgren 1997.

21. *Gibuma and Anau* (1991) 54 A.Crim.R. 347, 349; *Harradine* (1992) 61 A.Crim.R. 201; *Fernando* (1992) 76 A.Crim.R. 58, 62–63 per Wood J.

22. *Davey* (1980) 50 F.L.R. 57; *Rogers* (1989) 44 A.Crim.R. 301; *Juli* (1990) 50 A.Crim.R. 31; *Fernando* (1992) 76 A.Crim.R. 58.

23. *Fernando* (1992) 76 A.Crim.R. 58, 62–63 per Wood J.

24. For example, whether imprisonment will be unduly harsh on an Aborigine because of the foreigness of the environment: *Fernando* (1992) 76 A.Crim.R. 58, 62–63 per Wood J.

25. (1992) 79 N.T.R. 1. See also *Jadurin* (1982) 44 A.L.R. 424.

26. *Minor* (1992) 79 N.T.R. 1, 11; see also *Munugurr* (1994) 4 N.T.L.R. 63; *Wilson* (1995) 82 A.Crim.R. 270; *Miyatatawuy* (1996) 87 A.Crim.R. 574 (resolution of dispute

under traditional law a factor to be taken into account when sentencing Aboriginal offender).

27. See, e.g., Statutes Amendment (Truth in Sentencing) Act 1994 (S.A.), which requires the courts to take into account the abolition of remissions.

28. The terms are: (1) privatization of prisons including design, financing, construction, and administration; (2) sentencing involving the deprivation of liberty; (3) rehabilitation and parole of persons serving terms of imprisonment an allied matters; and (4) matters incidental thereto.

29. See also Doob and Marinos 1995, pp. 423–24.

REFERENCES

Alder, C., and J. Wundersitz, eds. 1994. *Family Conferencing and Juvenile Justice: The Way Forward; or, Misplaced Optimism.* Canberra: Australian Institute of Criminology.

Ashworth, A. 1995. *Sentencing and Criminal Justice.* 2d ed. London: Butterworths.

Atkinson, L. 1995. *Boot Camps and Justice: A Contradiction in Terms?* Trends and Issues in Crime and Criminal Justice no. 46. Canberra: Australian Institute of Criminology,

Australian Bureau of Statistics. 1997. *Prisoners in Australia.* Canberra: Australian Bureau of Statistics.

———. Various Years. *Correctional Services Australia.* Sidney: Australian Bureau of Statistics.

Australian Law Reform Commission. 1980. *Sentencing of Federal Offenders.* Report no. 15. Canberra: Australian Law Reform Commission.

———. 1986. *The Recognition of Aboriginal Customary Law.* Report no. 31. Canberra: Australian Government Australian: Printing Service.

———. 1987. *Sentencing Discussion Paper No. 30.* Sydney: Australian Law Reform Commission.

———. 1988. *Sentencing.* Report No. 40. Sydney: Australian Law Reform Commission.

Australia Steering Committee for the Review of Commonwealth State Service Provision. 1988. *Report on Government Services.* Vol. 1. Canberra: Australian: Government Printing Service.

Blagg, H. B. 1997. "A Just Measure of Shame? Aboriginal Youth and Conferencing in Australia." *British Journal of Criminology* 37: 481–501.

Bottoms, A. E. 1995. "The Philosophy and Politics of Punishment and Sentencing." In *The Politics of Sentencing Reform,* edited by C. Clarkson and R. Morgan. Oxford: Clarendon Press.

Braithwaite, J. 1989. *Crime, Shame, and Reintegration.* Melbourne: Cambridge University Press.

Daunton-Fear, M. 1977. *Sentencing in Western Australia.* Brisbane, Australia: University of Queensland Press.

Doob, A. N. 1995. "The United States Sentencing Commission Guidelines: If You Don't Know Where You Are Going, You Might Not Get There." In *The Politics of Sentencing Reform,* edited by C. Clarkson and R. Morgan. Oxford: Clarendon Press.

Doob, A. N., and V. Marinos. 1995. "Reconceptualizing Punishment: Understanding the Limitations on the Use of Intermediate Punishments." *University of Chicago Law School Roundtable* 2:413–33.

Erez, E., and L. Roger. 1995. "The Effect of Victim Impact Statements on Sentencing Patterns and Outcomes: The Australian Experience." *Journal of Criminal Justice* 23: 363–75.

Fairall, P. A. 1993. "Violent Offenders and Community Protection in Victoria: The Garry David Experience." *Criminal Law Journal* 17:40–54.

———. 1995. "Imprisonment without Conviction in New South Wales: Kable v Director of Public Prosecutions." *Sydney Law Review* 17:573–80.

Flynn, M. 1997. "One Strike and You're Out." *Alternative Law Journal* 22:72–76.

Fox, R. G. 1988. "The Killings of Bobby Veen: The High Court on Proportion in Sentencing." *Criminal Law Journal* 12:339–66.

———. 1991. "Order Out of Chaos: Victoria's New Maximum Penalty Structure." *Monash University Law Review* 17:102–31.

———. 1994. "The Meaning of Proportionality in Sentencing." *Melbourne University Law Review* 19:489–511.

Fox, R. G., and A. Freiberg. 1985. *Sentencing: State and Federal Law in Victoria*. Melbourne: Oxford University Press.

———. 1990. "Ranking Offence Seriousness in Reviewing Statutory Maximum Penalties." *Australian and New Zealand Journal of Criminology* 23:165–91.

———. 1999. *Sentencing: State and Federal Law in Victoria*. 2d ed. Melbourne: Oxford University Press.

Freckelton, I. 1997. "A New Victim Rhetoric in Victoria." *Alternative Law Journal* 22:302–3.

Freiberg, A. 1995. "Sentencing Reform in Victoria: A Case Study." In *The Politics of Sentencing Reform*, edited by C. Clarkson and R. Morgan. Oxford: Clarendon Press.

———. 1997. "Commercial Confidentiality, Criminal Justice, and the Public Interest." *Current Issues in Criminal Justice* 9:125–52.

———. 2000. "Guerillas in Our Midst?—Judicial Responses to Governing the Dangerous." In *Dangerous Offenders: Punishment and Social Order*, edited by M. Brown and J. Pratt. London: Routledge.

Freiberg, A., and S. Ross. 1999. *Sentencing Reform in Victoria, 1850–1997*. Melbourne: Department of Criminology, University of Melbourne.

Garland, D. 1990. *Punishment and Modern Society: A Study in Social Theory*. Oxford: Clarendon Press.

———. 1991. "Sociological Perspectives on Punishment." In *Crime and Justice: A Review of Research*, vol. 14, edited by Michael Tonry. Chicago: University of Chicago Press.

Graber, L., T. Keys, and J. White. 1996. "Family Group Decision-Making in the United States: The Case of Oregon." In *Family Group Conferences: Perspectives on Policy and Practice*, edited by J. Hudson, A. Morris, G. Maxwell, and B. Galaway. Sydney: The Federation Press.

Harding, R. 1997. *Private Prisons and Public Accountability*. London: Open University Press.

———. ed. 1995. *Repeat Juvenile Offenders: The Failure of Selective Incapacitation in Western Australia*. 2d ed. Perth: University of Western Australia Crime Research Center.

Hinton M. 1995. "Expectations Dashed: Victim Impact Statements and the Common Law Approach to Sentencing in South Australia." *University of Tasmania Law Review* 14:81–99.

Hudson, B. 1993. *Penal Policy and Social Justice*. London: Macmillan.

Hudson, J., A. Morris, G. Maxwell, and B. Galaway, eds. 1996. *Family Group Conferences: Perspectives on Policy and Practice*. Sydney: The Federation Press.

Immarigeon, R. 1996. "Family Group Conferences in Canada and the United States: An Overview." In *Family Group Conferences: Perspectives on Policy and Practice*, edited by J. Hudson, A. Morris, G. Maxwell, and B. Galaway. Sydney: The Federation Press.

Jarrett, J. 1997. "ACT Region Trial to Stop Repeat Crime Shows Good Interim Results." *Platypus* 56:17.

Junger-Tas, J. 1994. *Alternatives to Prison Sentences: Experiences and Developments*. Amsterdam: Kluger.

La Prairie, C. 1995. "Altering Course: New Directions in Criminal Justice: Sentencing Circles and Family Group Conferences." *Australian and New Zealand Journal of Criminology* 28 (special issue):78–99.

Liverani, M. R. 1998. "Slow Take-up for Home Detention." *Law Society Journal* (N.S.W.) 36:42–48.

Lofgren, N. 1997. "Aboriginal Community Participation in Sentencing." *Australian and New Zealand Journal of Criminology* 21:127.

Longclaws, L., B. Galaway, and L. Barkwell. 1996. "Piloting Family Group Conferences for Young Aboriginal Offenders." In *Family Group Conferences: Perspectives on Policy and Practice*, edited by J. Hudson, A. Morris, G. Maxwell, and B. Galaway. Winnipeg: The Federation Press.

McKillop S., ed. 1992. *Aboriginal Justice Issues*. Canberra: Australian Institute of Criminology.

Meek J. 1995. "The Revival of Preventive Detention in New Zealand, 1986–93." *Australian and New Zealand Journal of Criminology* 28:225–57.

Michalowski, R. J., and M. A. Pearson. 1990. "Punishment and Social Structure at the State Level: A Cross-Sectional Comparison of 1970 and 1980." *Journal of Research in Crime and Delinquency* 27:52–78.

Moore, D. B. 1993. "Shame, Forgiveness, and Juvenile Justice." *Criminal Justice Ethics* 12: 3–26.

Morgan, N. 1995. "Criminal Law Reform, 1983–1995: An Evaluation." *University of Western Australia Law Review* 25:283–300.

———. 1996. "Non-Custodial Sentences Under WA's New Sentencing Laws: Business as Usual or a New Utopia?" *University of Western Australia Law Review* 26:364–88.

Morgan, N., and B. Murray. 1999. "What's in a Name? Guideline Judgments in Australia." *Criminal Law Journal* 23:90–107.

Morris, N., and M. Tonry. 1990. *Between Prison and Probation: Intermediate Punishments in a Rational Sentencing System*. New York: Oxford University Press.

Murphy, P. 1996. "Indeterminate Sentences: The Victorian Experience." Master's thesis, University of Melbourne.

Newman, K. 1996. *Report of His Honour Kingsley Newman into the Kurli Murri Work Camp, Laverton, Western Australia, and the Management of Young Offenders*. Perth: State of Western Australia.

New South Wales Law Reform Commission. 1996. *Sentencing*. Report 79. Sydney: New South Wales Law Reform Commission.

O'Malley, P. 1994. "Neo-Liberal Crime Control: Political Agendas and the Future of Crime Prevention in Australia." In *The Australian Criminal Justice System: The Mid 1990s*, edited by D. Chappell and P. Wilson. Sydney: Butterworths.

Parke, J., and B. Mason. 1995. "The Queen of Hearts in Queensland: A Critique of Part 10 of the Penalties and Sentences Act 1992 (Qld)." *Criminal Law Journal* 19:312–31.

Pratt, J. 1995. "Dangerousness, Risk, and Technologies of Power." *Australian and New Zealand Journal of Criminology* 28:3–31.

———. 1997. *Governing the Dangerous*. Sydney: The Federation Press.

Queensland Criminal Justice Commission. 1999. "Prisoner Numbers in Queensland." Preliminary Report. Unpublished manuscript.

Reitz, K. R. 1993. "Sentencing Facts: Travesties of Real-Offense Sentencing." *Stanford Law Review* 45:523.

——. 1996. "Michael Tonry and the Structure of Sentencing Laws." *Journal of Criminal Law and Criminology* 86:1585–602.

Roeger, L. S. 1993. *Supreme and District Court Imprisonment, 1981–1992.* Adelaide, Australia: Office of Crime Statistics.

Russell, S. 1997. "Private Prisons for Private Profit." *Alternative Law Journal* 22:7–9.

Sherman, L. W., J. Braithwaite, and H. Strang. 1994. "Reintegrative Shaming of Violence, Drink Driving, and Property Crime." Technical proposal. Canberra: Research School of Social Sciences, Australian National University.

Skolnick, J. H. 1995. "What Not to Do about Crime." *Criminology* 33:1–15.

Tait, D. 1995. "The Invisible Sanction: Suspended Sentences in Victoria, 1985–1991." *Australian and New Zealand Journal of Criminology* 28:143–62.

Tata, C., and N. Hutton, N. 1997. "Scottish High Court Develops Sentencing Information System." *Overcrowded Times* 8(6):1, 14–20.

Thomas, D. A. 1970. *Principles of Sentencing.* London: Heineman.

——. 1995. "Sentencing the Dangerous Offender." *Judicial Officers Bulletin* 7: 60.

Tonry, M. 1996. *Sentencing Matters.* New York: Oxford University Press.

Tonry, M., and K. Hatlestad, eds. 1997. *Sentencing Reform in Overcrowded Times: A Comparative Perspective.* New York: Oxford University Press.

Tyler, T. R. 1990. *Why People Obey the Law.* New Haven, Conn.: Yale University Press.

Victoria Sentencing Alternatives Committee. 1979. *Sentencing Alternatives Involving Community Service.* Melbourne: University of Melbourne Law Department.

Victoria Social Development Committee. 1992. *Inquiry into Mental Disturbance and Community Safety.* Melbourne: University of Melbourne Law Department.

Walker, N. 1996. *Dangerous People.* London: Blackstone Press.

Zdenkowski, G. 1997. "Community Protection through Imprisonment without Conviction." *Australian Journal of Human Rights* 3:8–520.

The Decline of English Sentencing
and Other Stories

So significant have been the changes in sentencing in England and Wales[1] since the early 1970s that it is not easy to pick out the principal developments. There are now more than three times as many recorded indictable offenses[2] as there were in 1971; the average daily prison population in 1998 was some 70 percent higher (65,298, compared with 38,040 in 1971); and sentencing law is vastly more complicated, in that in 1971 there was little reported case law and there were few statutes. However, I attempt to provide an overview of a quarter of a century's developments in English sentencing policy and practice through a detailed consideration of five changes.

I begin by discussing in section I the decline of English sentencing, by which I mean the increasing tendency to divert indictable offenders from the criminal courts, which actually produced the surprising result that the English courts sentenced fewer offenders in 1996 than they did in 1971. I then describe in section II the revival of community sentences, by which I mean noncustodial sentencing options that involve some element of supervision or surveillance over offenders. The trend began in the early 1980s, but a repackaging of the sentences in 1991 has led to a further resurgence in their use. Over the same period a notable English invention has been the guideline judgment, now developed by the Court of Appeal into a reasonably successful and judge-friendly method of structuring judicial discretion in various fields of sentencing, discussed in section III. Indeed, this success may have contributed to the growing resentment among judges and magistrates about the increasingly frequent "interference" of the legislature in sentencing matters, discussed in section IV. When Parliament passed the Criminal Justice Act 1991, intended to provide the first coherent legislative structure for English sentencing, vocal sections of the judiciary revolted. What many commentators regarded as a veritable feast of sentencing law was devoured by the judiciary as if a rather insignificant amuse-bouche, with the Court of Appeal destroying some provisions through wrecking interpretations, and other judges and magistrates calling

for retraction of certain provisions so loudly that the government inserted amendments into the Criminal Justice Act 1993 to overturn three pillars of the 1991 act's
scheme. Section V demonstrates that this unanimity of sentencers and the government was short-lived, and the story of the mid-1990s was a ferocious public
struggle between the Home Secretary and the Lord Chief Justice over the introduction of mandatory and mandatory minimum sentences into English law. Victory went to the Home Secretary, in the sense that mandatory provisions were
enacted in the Crime (Sentences) Act 1997, but there were some concessions to
judicial reservations about this approach.

For those unfamiliar with the English sentencing system, it may be appropriate
to begin by sketching some salient features (see, further, Ashworth 1997). This
chapter is concerned with indictable offenses, the category that contains all serious
offenses and many others, including all thefts (irrespective of value). Most indictable offenses are actually dealt with in the magistrates' courts, the lower level of
criminal courts in England and Wales. Over 90 percent of defendants plead guilty
there, and the maximum sentence is six months' imprisonment (or a total of twelve
months for two or more offenses). If the magistrates think their sentencing powers
inadequate, they can commit the offender for sentence in the Crown Court. Trials
in the Crown Court are by judge and jury, but around 60 percent of defendants
plead guilty[3] and so the judge's only function then is to pass sentence. Since the
Crown Court deals with the most serious offenses, around half of those convicted
are sent to prison. The system of remission and parole has been much changed
in the past two decades. The present position, briefly, is that there are no remissions. Prisoners sentenced to terms under four years serve one-half of their term
and are then conditionally released (with liability to be reimprisoned if convicted
of another offense before the expiry of the sentence). Prisoners sentenced to four
years or longer must be released conditionally after three-quarters but may be
released by the Parole Board after two-thirds.

With this general background in mind, we turn to the first of the five major
themes—the growth of diversion from prosecution.

I. The Decline of English Sentencing

Rising crime rates have been reported the world over in recent decades, even
though they are now leveling off and falling in some countries. Even victim surveys
in England and Wales suggest that there have been considerable real increases as
well as increased reporting of some types of crime (Mirrlees-Black, Mayhew, and
Percy 1996), although the recorded crime rate in England has begun to fall slightly
in the past few years. Yet the number of indictable offenders dealt with by the
courts between 1971 and 1996 did not keep pace with the higher rates of recorded
crime over the twenty-five years, and indeed the number of indictable offenders
convicted in 1996 was lower than the number in 1971. What has been going on?

The figures are presented in table 2.1. Column 1 shows that indictable offenses
recorded by the police increased more than threefold in twenty-five years. Column
2 indicates the "clear-up rate" for the relevant years, in effect the percentage of
offenses traced to an offender (not necessarily someone against whom official ac-

Table 2.1. Recorded Crime, Convictions, and Cautions in England and Wales, 1971–1996, All Ages

Year	(1) Indictable Offenses Recorded by the Police	(2) CUR[1]	(3) Indictable Convictions	(4) Discharges[2]	(5) Indictable Cautions	Total of (3) and (5) Combined
1971	1,646,081	45	321,836	12	72,414	394,250
1976	2,135,700	43	415,503	15	97,681	513,184
1981	2,794,000	38	464,600	12	104,000	568,600
1986	3,847,410	32	384,000	14	137,000	521,000
1991	5,276,173	29	337,600	19	179,900	517,500
1996	5,036,550	26	300,600	18	190,800	491,400

Source: Data are from relevant annual volumes, 1971–96, of Criminal Statistics, England and Wales; 1996 is the last year for which full statistics are available.

[1]Percentage "clear-up rate" of offenses by the police.
[2]Discharges, absolute and conditional.

tion was then taken: the offender could be very young, or in prison following conviction for one or more other offenses). The clearance rate declined, but 45 percent of the 1971 figure for recorded crimes is still only about half as many offenses as 26 percent of the 1996 figure. In other words, the change in clearance rates cannot explain what we find in column 3—a dramatic decline in the proportion of offenders brought to court after the early 1980s. One explanation for that decline is evident in column 5: the use of formal police cautions rose considerably after the early 1980s. Thus, as we find in column 6, if one adds together the numbers of convictions and cautions, the overall numbers of those against whom official action was taken have shown rather less variation over the years. However, it must not be inferred that those who are prosecuted and convicted in the courts are necessarily a "hard core" of really serious criminals. Column 4 indicates that the rate at which the courts granted an absolute or conditional discharge to offenders (the lowest available penalty) actually shows a rise rather than a fall, suggesting that a significant proportion of those who were brought to court as indictable offenders were not heinous criminals.

What is a police caution? A police caution is the principal means of diverting from prosecution in England and Wales, and it takes the form of a warning to the offender about his or her offending conduct, usually delivered by a senior police officer in uniform. Strictly speaking, a caution may be administered only if the recipient has admitted to the offense, although a person who is "offered" a caution might be tempted to accept even though the offense is denied. In a gloriously English fashion the police caution has no legal basis whatsoever; it is simply a practice that has grown up. It survives because, under the English prosecution system, the police retain the initial decision whether to prosecute a person. Only if the police decide to prosecute is the case handed over to the Crown Prosecution Service (see, further, Sanders 1997; Ashworth 1998). If instead the police decide on a caution, the case proceeds no further. However, a caution can be cited in court as part of a prior record, and this is common practice for young offenders. A minor revolution has recently taken place in this area: police cautioning of young offenders has been restructured and placed on a statutory basis in the Crime and Disorder Act 1998 (see Fionda 1999). There are now two kinds of caution (known as a "reprimand" and a "final warning"), which are intended to form part of a more rigorous system for dealing with young offenders. But the glory of old England is to be preserved, in that cautions for offenders aged 18 and over will continue to be totally unregulated by law.

Why was cautioning encouraged in the 1980s? Three reasons are stated in the "National Standards for Cautioning," issued by the Home Secretary as guidance to the police (Home Office 1990a, 1994a). The first is "to deal quickly and simply with less serious offenders," a rationale that suggests that there are some offenders for whom court action is too severe and too slow a response. Further examination of the cautioning guidelines shows that old age, youth, mental or physical disability, and a mistake about the law are factors pointing towards a caution rather than prosecution. The second reason is "to divert them from the criminal courts": insofar as it differs from the first reason, this seems to be a cost-related argument. Taking a case to court is expensive, and cautioning is a cheaper option that should be considered where the offense is nonserious. If a court would be likely to pass a small or nominal sentence, the guidelines favor a caution. The third reason is "to reduce the chances of their reoffending." This is a reference to research findings that suggest a lower reconviction rate for young offenders who have been cautioned than for those who have been prosecuted and convicted (Home Office 1994b). The foremost initiative on cautioning in the 1980s was directed at young offenders, and it was argued that sparing them the stigma (or even the cachet) of a court appearance would also contribute to the prevention of their reoffending. Criminologists were naturally suspicious that the drive to caution more young offenders might lead to "net-widening," with some offenders being cautioned when they might otherwise have been let off without formal action. However, this does not appear to have taken place on any significant scale. The figures for indictable cautions and indictable offenses shown in table 2.1 (which, admittedly, covers all ages) certainly do not suggest any net-widening, and there is evidence that some police forces actively encourage the use of "informal cautions" for those whose offending is not considered serious enough for a formal caution (Evans and Ellis 1997). Indeed, there is a kind of mini-tariff of diversionary measures operating in the English system (although "system" would be too strong a word). The least response is to take no further action; then there is an informal warning or caution; a formal caution; and what is termed "caution plus," which counts as a caution but is accompanied by some other obligation, which may involve participating in some form of scheme or making reparation to the victim or entering into a form of mediation if the victim is willing. Moreover, these are only the options available to the police; it would be wrong to overlook the various forms of diversion employed by the tax authorities, Her Majesty's Customs, local councils, and the many inspectorates (health and safety, pollution, etc.) that have the power to prosecute.

If we return to formal police cautions, we can see how the cautioning rate (i.e., the proportion of all those cautioned or prosecuted, who are cautioned) increased rapidly in the 1980s. The starting point was the issue of a Home Office circular in 1983, urging police forces to use cautions rather than to prosecute in the categories mentioned earlier. The cautioning rate for adult males had been static at 4 percent throughout the 1970s and into the early 1980s, but the approach began to change soon after 1983 (see table 2.2). For young offenders the caution was advocated strongly, and the 1980s was a decade of spectacular transformation: cautions soared and convictions declined, so that by 1990 some three-quarters of male offenders under 17 and almost nine out of ten female offenders under 17 were cautioned rather than prosecuted.[4]

In 1994 the Home Secretary took the view that the trend had gone too far and issued a new circular to police forces, under the catch phrase "Your first chance is your last chance," instructing them not to use repeat cautions save in exceptional circumstances (see, further, Ashworth 1998, chap. 5). But this change of policy has had little more than a steadying effect on the cautioning rate. The figures are difficult to compare precisely, because the statistics from 1993 onward (table 2.2c)

Table 2.2. Cautioning Rate in England and Wales, 1983–1996

A. 1983–1988

Year	M 10–16	M 17+		F 10–16	F 17+	
1983	52	4		77	12	
1984	55	5		79	14	
1985	60	7		84	17	
1986	62	10		85	24	
1987	66	12		87	28	
1988	67	13		84	29	

B. 1989–1992

Year	M 10–16	M 17–20	M 21+	F 10–16	F 17–20	F 21+
1989	71	17	14	86	31	31
1990	75	22	16	89	38	34
1991	76	26	18	90	45	40
1992	78	33	23	92	55	46

C. 1993–1996

Year	M 10–17	M 18–20	M 21+	F 10–17	F 18–20	F 21+
1993	69	32	26	87	52	46
1994	66	34	25	85	50	44
1995	64	35	26	84	51	44
1996	60	35	26	80	50	44

Source: Criminal Statistics, England and Wales, annual volumes, 1983–96.

Note: "Cautioning rate" represents the percentage of offenders, cautioned or prosecuted, who are cautioned. M = Male; F = Female.

lump together all offenders aged 10 to 17 inclusive, whereas those for earlier years (tables 2.2A–B) classify offenders aged 10 to 16 together, and it is probably the inclusion of the 17-year-olds as much as the 1994 circular that produced the post-1993 dip in the cautioning rate for boys and girls. However, the cautioning rate is still far in excess of the rate for the early 1980s, particularly for adults. Despite the 1994 changes, it is still possible to represent the twenty-five years from 1971 to 1996 as a period marked by the decline of sentencing in England and Wales.

II. The Revival of Community Sentences

At the start of our twenty-five-year period, in the early 1970s, the fine was by far the most frequent sentence for indictable offenders, accounting for well over one-half of all males and all females aged 21 and over convicted of such offenses. In contrast, what later came to be termed "community sentences" (i.e., those requiring some kind of intervention from a probation officer or some other restrictions or duties on the offender) stood at their lowest point for many years. Probation orders were the only community sentence available at this time, and in 1971 only 7 percent of male indictable offenders aged 21 and over received probation. The percentage for female indictable offenders aged 21 and over was 15, double that for males and in the tradition of the more pathological view taken of female offending.

There was no great optimism about the rehabilitative effect of probation orders. An attempt was made by the Home Office to test whether a more intensive form of supervision would be more effective than "normal" probation, but the results were largely discouraging (Folkard, Smith, and Smith 1975). Great hope rested, however, on the community service order, introduced as an experiment in the Criminal Justice Act 1972 and made available to all courts in 1975. A community service order (CSO) requires an offender to undertake unpaid work for the community for between 40 and 240 hours, as specified by the court. The allocation of tasks and overall supervision of the order are undertaken by the probation service, although much of the unpaid work is carried out with and for voluntary organizations. It was hoped that the community service order would appeal to a whole range of penal philosophies, from the retributive (demanding and hard work) to the reparative (labor for the benefit of the community) and even the rehabilitative (working alongside volunteers, and working with members of the community in need of help and support) (Advisory Council on the Penal System 1970, para. 33). It was proposed as an alternative to short custodial sentences, and indeed the government raised the maximum number of hours from 120 to 240 when introducing the legislation, so as to strengthen its credentials in this respect. In the event the CSO was welcomed by the courts: it quickly came to be used widely for young offenders and, its proportionate use for adult males rose (see table 2.3) so that by the early 1980s it was used as frequently as the probation order.

One of the longstanding difficulties in persuading courts to make a probation order was that it was perceived as "soft" and as placing few demands on offenders. In the Criminal Justice Act 1982 an effort was made to tackle this by introducing two forms of additional requirement (attendance at a day center for up to sixty

Table 2.3. Males Aged 21 and Over Sentenced for Indictable Offenses in England and Wales, by Type of Sentence (%)

Year	Discharge	Fine	Probation	Community Service	Combined Order	Suspended Sentence	Immediate Prison	Total Community Sentences
1971	9	51	7	—	—	14	18	7
1972	9	52	7	—	—	14	18	7
1973	9	55	7	—	—	12	16	7
1974	9	56	6	—	—	12	15	6
1975	9	55	6	—	—	13	16	7
1976	9	53	5	2	—	13	16	7
1977	8	55	5	2	—	13	16	7
1978	7	54	4	3	—	13	17	7
1979	7	54	5	3	—	12	17	8
1980	7	52	5	4	—	12	17	9
1981	8	49	6	5	—	12	18	11
1982	8	47	6	6	—	12	19	12
1983	9	47	6	7	—	11	19	13
1984	9	45	7	7	—	11	20	14
1985	9	43	7	7	—	12	21	14
1986	10	41	7	7	—	12	21	15
1987	10	41	7	7	—	12	21	15
1988	10	41	8	7	—	12	20	15
1989	12	43	8	6	—	11	19	14
1990	13	43	8	7	—	10	17	15
1991	15	39	8	8	—	10	18	16
1992	17	37	9	9	0	8	18	8
1993	18	38	10	11	2	1	18	23
1994	16	36	11	11	2	1	20	25
1995	15	34	11	11	3	1	24	24
1996	14	33	11	10	3	1	24	24

Source: *Criminal Statistics, England and Wales,* annual volumes, 1971–96.

days, or participation in or refraining from specified activities), but there was only a slight upturn in the proportionate use of probation orders during the 1980s. (see tables 2.3 and 2.4).

The government decided that a different approach was needed. Just as a major purpose of the Criminal Justice Act 1972 had been to draw the courts away from imposing so many (short) custodial sentences, so in the late 1980s the government's view was that prison was being used unnecessarily in some cases — although at this time the concern was as much one of economics (prison being much more expensive than probation or community service) as one of effectiveness or humanitarianism. Two important steps were taken in 1988. First, the Home Office

Table 2.4. Females Aged 21 and Over Sentenced for Indictable Offenses in England and Wales, by Type of Sentence (%)

Year	Discharge	Fine	Probation	Community Service	Combined Order	Suspended Sentence	Immediate Prison	Total Community Sentences
1971	20	56	15	—	—	5	3	15
1972	20	57	15	—	—	5	2	15
1973	20	56	15	—	—	5	3	15
1974	20	58	14	—	—	5	2	14
1975	21	58	13	0	—	5	3	13
1976	21	57	12	1	—	6	3	13
1977	19	58	12	1	—	6	3	13
1978	19	57	12	1	—	6	4	13
1979	18	55	13	1	—	7	4	14
1980	18	53	15	2	—	7	4	17
1981	20	49	16	2	—	7	5	18
1982	21	48	16	2	—	7	5	18
1983	21	46	17	2	—	7	5	19
1984	22	43	17	3	—	8	6	20
1985	23	41	18	3	—	8	7	21
1986	24	38	19	3	—	8	7	22
1987	26	36	18	3	—	8	8	21
1988	27	35	18	3	—	8	7	22
1989	28	34	17	3	—	9	7	20
1990	32	32	18	4	—	8	6	21
1991	34	28	17	4	—	8	6	21
1992	36	27	16	5	0	7	6	22
1993	34	31	17	6	1	2	7	24
1994	32	28	19	7	2	2	8	28
1995	30	26	20	7	3	2	10	30
1996	28	25	21	7	3	2	12	31

Source: Criminal Statistics, England and Wales, annual volumes, 1971–96.

issued a consultation paper that began by questioning the need for so many custodial sentences. It argued that, for

> less serious offenders, a spell in custody is not the most effective punishment. Imprisonment restricts offenders' liberty, but it also reduces their responsibility . . . If offenders are not imprisoned, they are more likely to be able to pay compensation to their victims and to make some reparation to the community through useful unpaid work. Their liberty can be restricted without putting them behind prison walls. Moreover, if they are removed in prison from the responsibilities, problems and temptations of everyday life, they are less likely to acquire the self-discipline and self-reliance which will prevent reoffending in future. Punishment in the community would encourage offenders to grow out of crime and to develop into responsible and law-abiding citizens. (Home Office 1988, para. 1.1)

The Green Paper went on to propose more restrictive forms of what were now to be called "community sentences," enforced more rigorously so as to gain the confidence of the courts—a factor identified as a cause of the under use of non-custodial measures in previous years. The second Home Office initiative in 1988 was to require the probation service to produce "Action Plans," targeted particularly on young adult offenders in the 17–20 age group, to tackle their offending behavior through innovative schemes. In the late 1980s the traditional ethos of the Probation Service was under attack from the government, with the veiled threat of privatization being part of the pressure exerted on the service to recognize that it is part of the machinery of state punishment (see, generally, Mair 1997). The government announced its intention to introduce national standards on supervision, with requirements to ensure the proper regulation and enforcement of community sentences.

As these changes began to take effect, the Criminal Justice Act 1991 established the legal and ideological framework for the new regime. Whereas statements of policy in the 1970s and early 1980s referred to probation and community service orders as "alternatives to custody"—a description that left many sentencers unconvinced—the 1990s White Paper used the phrases "punishment in the community" and "community sentences," promoting them as restrictive sentences in their own right.

> Restrictions on liberty [will] become the connecting thread in a range of community penalties as well as custody. By matching the severity of the restrictions on liberty to the seriousness of the offence, the courts should find it easier to achieve consistency of approach in sentencing. The more serious the offence is, the greater the restrictions on liberty which would be justified as a punishment. (Home Office 1990b, para. 4.5)

Thus community sentences were to be placed in a sentencing structure based on desert or proportionality, as part 1 of the Criminal Justice Act 1991 went on to provide. The least serious offenses ought to result in a discharge or a fine. A community sentence should be given only if the offense is serious enough to warrant it. And a custodial sentence should be reserved for those cases that are so serious that only prison could be justified (see section IV below).

Section 6 of the 1991 act attempted to place community sentences within this desert-oriented framework and at the same time to emphasize the value of "matching" the sentence to the offender's needs. It did this by adopting the suggestions of academic commentators[5] and by providing that the level of severity of the sanctions should be settled according to proportionality but the choice of community sentence (i.e., probation, a community service order, or the new combination order)[6] should be "the most suitable for the offender." Thus an offender who needs support or help, particularly with a drug or alcohol addiction, might receive a probation order whereas someone with no such recognized needs might require a CSO of a roughly equivalent length. In one sense these tougher and relabeled forms of sentence, supported by National Standards for the Supervision of Offenders in the Community, have been successful. Whereas in 1986 probation orders and community service orders accounted for 14 percent of adult male indictable offenders and 22 percent of adult female indictable offenders, the figures for 1996 (including the new combination orders) were 24 and 31 percent, respectively. (Curfew orders with electronic monitoring also rank as community sentences: at present they are unavailable in most courts, but their experimental use in certain areas is being expanded gradually by the government).[7]

Attention to other sentencing trends suggests, however, that the success may be far less substantial than the figures initially indicate. The same ten-year period saw a significant decline in the use of the fine: it is possible that some of those who were fined in previous years are now granted an absolute discharge, and we see in table 2.1 that the discharge rate has risen steadily, but it also seems likely that some of them receive a community sentence. No less significant was the severe restriction placed on the use of suspended sentence in the 1991 act: the suspended sentence is at odds with the idea behind community sentences, that sentences just beneath custody should be tough and demanding, since a suspended sentence makes no demands other than law abidance, and so the government decided that it should be limited to cases where there were "exceptional circumstances." The effectiveness of this restriction is evident in the statistics for the 1990s (see table 2.3.), as the suspended sentence dropped away from 10 percent of adult male indictable offenders in 1991 to a negligible 1 percent a year beginning in 1993. Some of these offenders will now be given community sentences, but others will probably go to custody. This heavily restricted use of the suspended sentence stands in marked contrast to its widespread use in continental European countries.

It seems likely, then, that a substantial part of the increase in the use of community sentences in the 1990s can be attributed to the restrictions on suspended sentences and the decline of the fine. Why has the use of the fine continued its downward spiral? The prevailing view in the 1980s was that fining declined because of the increasingly high proportion of offenders who were unemployed when convicted, and this high rate continued into the 1990s.[8] But in its 1990 White Paper the government sought to reverse this trend and argued that, so long as fines were properly adjusted according to the varying incomes of offenders, they could and should be used more widely. "Setting fairer fine levels should lead to the greater use of fines and less difficulty in enforcing them" (Home Office 1990b, para. 5.2). The means for achieving this goal was to be the introduction of "unit fines," an adaptation of the "day fine" system used in various continental European countries (most closely related to the German scheme). The Criminal Justice Act 1991 provided that all fines imposed on individual offenders in magistrates' courts should be unit fines. In simple terms, the seriousness of the offense should be rated on a scale of 1 to 50 units, and then the amount to be paid per unit should depend on the offender's "disposable income," with a minimum of £4 per unit and a maximum of £100 (for fuller details, see Ashworth 1995, pp. 262–66). The new law was introduced in October 1992. Only seven months later, at the beginning of May 1993, the Home Secretary announced the abolition of the unit fine system, subsequently accomplished by the Criminal Justice Act 1993. There were many reasons for this debacle. The unit fine had received a particularly bad press: newspapers would compare the different fines imposed on different offenders, as if these pointed to disparities in sentencing (and without mentioning the aim of achieving equality of impact). The amounts payable per unit had been set rather too high, and even magistrates in favor of unit fines had already proposed a restructuring of the principles for calculating payments. Above all, the higher fines were being borne by the middle classes, and it was their complaints that helped mobilize the opposition to the unit fine. The Home Secretary's decision to abolish unit fines was an extravagant political gesture: the scheme could and should have been altered, and no weight appears to have been given at this stage to the successful use of similar systems in many other European countries. The history of the rise and fall of the English unit fine shows comparative sentencing law at its best (in the importation of a sound idea) and then at its worst (in the abolition of an obviously workable approach).

Both community sentences and custodial sentences had large proportionate increases between 1992 and 1996, for women and for men (see tables 2.3 and 2.4). The figures make it difficult to suggest that the rise in community sentences has fulfilled the government's objective, as stated in the 1988 Green Paper and the 1990 White Paper of dealing in the community with offenders who might otherwise have been sentenced to custody (Rex 1998; see section IV, below, for more about custody). Three further points are relevant here. One is that the increasingly punitive atmosphere of the 1990s may have produced not only the increased use of custody but also a view that the response to many offenders needs to be tougher than a fine. That might contribute to the explanation of the rise in community sentences. A second and related point is that the community sentences of the 1990s are themselves more restrictive and demanding than those of the 1980s: although community service orders are little changed, the combination order is particularly restrictive, and far more probation orders have "additional requirements" than in earlier years. The third point is that, as the total number of indictable offenders coming before the courts dwindles, one might expect those who are convicted and sentenced to be the most serious groups. To give the same number of community sentences and custodial sentences in 1996 as in 1991 would therefore produce higher percentages in both categories, since the total number convicted is lower. The difficulty with this explanation is that the courts are also using more discharges, which suggests that the overall seriousness of the offenders brought to court has not necessarily increased. It is therefore difficult to be confident about the correct interpretation of the recent trends.

III. Appellate Review and Guideline Judgments

In the nineteenth century the role of the legislature in matters of sentencing was considerable. Criminal statutes provided for hundreds of subdivided offenses, each with its maximum penalty, and there were also some minimum sentences (Radzinowicz and Hood, 1990, chap. 22). But the trend in the twentieth century has been for much less legislative involvement. At least until the past few years, the legislature's principal tasks have been to set a maximum penalty for each offense and to introduce new forms of penalty. Indeed, as reforms of the criminal law have led to the replacement of the myriad subdivided offenses of the previous century with new "broad band" offenses with high maxima, the area of sentencing discretion left to the courts has increased (Thomas 1978a). Thus, in general, and apart from a small number of special restrictions relating to young offenders, the legislature's role has simply been to set the outer limits of lawful sentencing, leaving most of the significant decisions to judges and magistrates.

The judiciary has long been conscious of the need to strive for some kind of consistency in the exercise of this wide discretion, at least to the extent of having common starting points for all the major offenses. Following lively public debate exactly one hundred years ago, the Lord Chief Justice and his colleagues drew up in 1901 the "Memorandum of Normal Punishments" for six common categories of offense—a step taken somewhat grudgingly and only because it would be "convenient and of public advantage" (Radzinowicz and Hood 1990, pp. 753–58).

A few years later came the most significant development: the enactment of the Criminal Appeal Act 1907, which created for the first time a regular appellate court in criminal matters. Persons convicted on indictment might appeal against conviction or against sentence. Since the formation of the Court of Criminal Appeal in 1907, a corpus of case law has been built up that now, to a large extent because of the pioneering rationalizations of David Thomas in the 1960s,[9] constitutes a common law of sentencing. It may be said that, in the past twenty-five years, the "rule of law" has arrived in sentencing. The reporting of sentence appeals has increased,[10] consequently the citing of previous decisions has become more regular, and what may be termed a culture of legality is sweeping into sentencing decisions. It is not being claimed that the process is complete—indeed, judges occasionally rail against the citing of precedents and reassert that each case has to be approached "on its own facts" (see Ashworth 1995, pp. 26–31)—but the change of approach during those twenty-five years is striking.

Appellate review has yielded a somewhat unbalanced set of precedents. Because defendants are more likely to appeal against severe sentences, the case law is at its richest for the very serious offenses and relatively thin on the less serious (but more common) types of crime. There is no prosecution right of appeal in English law, but section 38 of the Criminal Justice Act 1988 introduced the procedure of the Attorney-General's Reference. This procedure enables the attorney general to refer to the Court of Appeal any case in which the sentence is thought to be unduly lenient (rather than simply lenient), and the power is used in some fifty or more cases each year. The Court of Appeal has the power to increase the offender's sentence, and the decisions add a new dimension to the store of precedents (Shute 1994).

However, by far the most innovative development in recent years has been the technique of the guideline judgment. The idea of incorporating general guidance into a judgment on appeal against a particular sentence was pioneered by L. J. Lawton, in the 1970s,[11] and it became an established feature of sentencing when adopted by Lord Lane, as Lord Chief Justice, in the 1980s.[12] Although the structures of the various guideline judgments differ, the main feature is that they purport to set out general guidance for the sentencing of a particular type of offense, often indicating one or more starting points, and setting out aggravating and mitigating factors (Ashworth 1995, chap. 4). It appears that they are followed by other judges, for the most part.[13] Their format is narrative, although they do include figures and some of them (such as the guidelines on sentencing drug offenders) can be reduced to a kind of mathematical framework. Not much has been documented about the way in which guideline judgments come to be put together, but it seems likely that the Criminal Appeal Office supplies a summary of all past decisions that are relevant, on which the Lord Chief Justice will then build.

Guideline judgments are an innovation of which the senior judiciary can rightly be proud. They show how guidance can be fashioned, in a judge-friendly way, based on experience, and shaping discretion without constraining it too tightly. It might also be claimed that guideline judgments are capable of changing judicial sentencing practices: some were clearly intended to do so,[14] although where there is a strong judicial culture the guideline judgment may be less than fully successful in altering sentencing practice.[15] Lord Bingham, as Lord Chief Justice, has not only continued the practice of formulating guideline judgments but has increased their number considerably.[16]

But, worthwhile as the mechanism of the guideline judgment is, senior judges seem to believe that there is a technical difficulty in developing them. Those that have been delivered remain clustered around the serious offenses that tend to attract substantial prison sentences. Each time a Lord Chief Justice comes close to an area of everyday sentencing—notably burglary, theft, deception, and handling stolen goods—the cry "impossible" goes out. The need for some proper guideline on burglary sentencing is manifest and may have been one cause of the previous Home Secretary's decision to put a minimum sentence for repeat burglars in the Crime (Sentences) Act 1997 (see section V). But on the two occasions in the 1990s when a Lord Chief Justice tackled burglary, he, in effect, backed off. In *Mussell* (1990)[17] Lord Lane C. J. resorted to listing some common aggravating and mitigating factors and provided no starting points at all. In *Brewster* (1998)[18] Lord Bingham C. J. felt able to do little more than tackle the question whether burgling an empty house is, in general, more or less serious than burgling an occupied house. Both of their Lordships clearly formed the conclusion that there are simply too many variable factors in offenses of burglary, and that any starting points would tend towards undue rigidity and concreteness.

Is this so? How, then, does the individual judge or bench of magistrates approach the sentencing of a burglar? Even if it is said to be a matter of "experience," it is only possible to make sense of one's experience if one develops some kind of rough categorization of types of burglary, their relative seriousness, and the appropriate starting points for sentence.[19] Some judges have claimed that they keep a little book, to remind themselves of appropriate starting points and to adapt them where appropriate (Cooke 1987). It may be surmised that those who do not keep such a book may occasionally misremember their own starting points or unwittingly allow them to drift (Ashworth et al. 1984, pp. 50–56). In terms of policy, since burglary is one of the most frequent indictable offenses for which courts have to pass sentence, it is strange that the judiciary feel unable to make any progress on formulating guidance (the same applies to the common offenses of theft, handling, and deception).

The only concerted attempt to develop sentencing guidance for these common offenses is to be found in the Magistrates' Association's *Sentencing Guidelines*, which have gone through various editions and changes since their first publication in 1989.[20] Each page sets out the maximum penalty, identifies some common factors making the offense more or less serious, proposes a starting point (custody, community sentence, fine), and reminds the court of various statutory and other factors to be considered. The guidelines are hardly a perfect instrument, but they have no smaller significance in sentencing terms than the Court of Appeal's guide-line judgments, since the magistrates' courts deal with about three times as many indictable offenses as the Crown Court. The guidelines not only set out a range of seriousness factors for each type of offense but also indicate an "entry point" for the court—which may be custody, a community sentence, or a fine of a certain amount. There has been no research into the effectiveness of these guidelines in fostering consistency of approach. It is often thought that this is difficult to ensure, in view of the fact that the English system relies on some thirty thousand lay magistrates to pass sentence in the magistrates' courts. It seems likely, however, that the greatest threat to consistency lies not in the large numbers of lay people but in the different traditions of local benches and the influence of "professionals" such as the justices' clerk and the local liaison judge (Hood 1972; Tarling 1979). Recent research shows that, in respect of calculating the amount of fines, the Magistrates' Association's guidelines are adopted in 55 percent of districts, a further 28 percent use the guidelines "with significant local variations," and the remaining 17 percent use other forms of calculation (Charman et al. 1996).

It would be possible to develop the Magistrates' Association's guidelines into a more substantial document, covering a wider group of crimes and offering guid-ance also to judges in the Crown Court who have to pass sentence for the many common crimes (burglary, theft, deception, handling stolen goods) that, as I show, are not covered by existing Court of Appeal guideline judgments. It must be said, however, that this would require some reappraisal of sentence levels in the two levels of courts. A Home Office study that compared the sentencing of in-dictable offenses with similar features, taking account of the offender's age and prior record, found that persons sentenced in the Crown Court were three times as likely to receive custody (and that custodial sentences were on average two and a half times as long) as those sentenced in magistrates' courts. Those who are concerned about overall sentence levels in English courts might well fear that any realignment of sentencing practices would lead to even greater severity, in that magistrates' sentencing might be raised rather than Crown Court sentence levels lowered.[21]

The next phase in the development of judicial sentencing guidance is difficult to predict because of the recent arrival of a new institution: the Sentencing Ad-visory Panel. Sections 80 and 81 of the Crime and Disorder Act 1998 provide for the creation of such a panel to advise the Court of Appeal on sentencing guide-lines. There is little supporting documentation about the functions of the proposed panel, although the origins of the idea can be traced back some fifteen years (Ashworth 1983, chap. 11) and the proposal formed part of Labour Party policy in opposition. The panel, appointed late in 1999, is composed of members from various parts of the criminal justice system and lay persons; it can consider, either on its own motion or on reference from the Home Secretary, whether sentencing guidelines should be created for a particular type of offense and can submit draft guidelines to the Court of Appeal. The panel has no executive authority: it will be for the Court of Appeal, under the Lord Chief Justice, to decide whether to issue guidelines.

IV. Judiciary and Militancy

The past three decades have seen an increasingly powerful judicial presence in public debates over sentencing policy. For judges to enter into public debate is certainly not a new phenomenon (see Radzinowicz and Hood 1990, chaps. 22, 23), and recent battles have been marked by the use of the mass media to put over the judicial argument. In the 1970s and early 1980s it was apparent that there was considerable judicial sensitivity to legislative "interference" in sentencing. More sentencing legislation came to be passed, and it became more restrictive of judicial discretion. A brief survey of legislative developments should establish a context for the discussion that follows.

The Criminal Justice Act 1972, described in section I, was a reforming statute, and it was swiftly followed by a consolidation of sentencing law in the Powers of Criminal Courts Act 1973. There was then a considerable gap before the next major sentencing statute, the Criminal Justice Act 1982. Even in the 1980s many of the changes to the system—the expansion of cautioning, the changes in parole, and remission on custodial sentences[22]—did not involve further legislation. The Drug Trafficking Offenses Act 1986 introduced a mandatory system for the confiscation of the assets of drug traffickers, complex in nature and found irksome by many judges. The Criminal Justice Act 1988 brought a few changes, one of which was to require a court to consider making a compensation order (for the offender to pay compensation to the victim) in every case involving death or injury, loss or damage. Imposing requirements on the courts was not well received by the judges and, as often happens, the legislation was less than perfectly drafted. David Thomas, England's preeminent sentence appeal scholar, began to write disparagingly about the volume and style of sentencing legislation, supporting the judicial view that the best course was to leave ample judicial discretion (see Thomas 1988 and, more constructively, Thomas 1997). Others saw the need to change aspects of the judicial approach and regarded legislation as the proper means of bringing it about.

The watershed came with the Criminal Justice Act 1991. It was the result of a lengthy period of consultation and discussion, initiated when the Thatcher government was still strong (Downes and Morgan 1997). Among the 1991 act's chief aims were to establish a primary rationale for sentencing (desert and proportionality),[23] to ensure that the public was protected from "dangerous" offenders but to encourage the use of tougher "community sentences" for many of those who had previously been sent to prison. Many members of the judiciary did not see the point of passing such a wide-ranging statute and were determined to regard the statute as largely confirming the existing judicial approach. The opening words of an article by David Thomas, who was largely responsible for instructing the judiciary on the 1991 act, are revealing.

> According to one view, Part 1 of the Criminal Justice Act 1991 is a landmark in the history of sentencing; another view is that it is a largely irrelevant exercise in teaching

grandmother to suck eggs. The principle around which the rules relating to custodial sentences are said to have been constructed, the principle of "just deserts", is not new; it has been the basis of judicial practice in the use of custodial sentences for years. (Thomas 1992, p. 232)

This quotation leaves little doubt about the author's view of the 1991 act, and I describe in the coming paragraphs how the judiciary dealt with the statute. For now, the point is that it was the first of several sentencing statutes in the 1990s — the Criminal Justice Act 1993, which amended some provisions of the 1991 act; part 1 of the Criminal Justice and Public Order Act 1994, which changed the powers of the courts to sentence young offenders to custody; and the Crime (Sentences) Act 1997, discussed in section V below.

This torrent of legislation not merely placed demands on judges and magistrates, in their having to become familiar with new legislative restrictions, but was a considerable departure for Parliament. For most of the century it had done little more than set maximum penalties and introduce new penal measures, and the judges had come to expect a wide and unfettered sentencing discretion, with a form of self-regulation (appellate review) to guard against excesses. When in 1981–82 there were suggestions that Parliament might legislate to restrict the use of custodial sentences for young offenders, some judges suggested (and some politicians agreed) that this might undermine the principle of judicial independence (see Ashworth 1983, chap. 2). The issue raised questions, in a country without a written constitution, about the constitutional status of the sentencing function.

There has never been any clear and authoritative doctrine on the respective responsibilities of the legislature and the judiciary in English sentencing (Munro 1992). It would seem difficult to argue that Parliament is not competent to legislate on any aspect of sentencing: nobody has suggested that the mandatory sentence of life imprisonment for murder is unconstitutional, for example, and in the nineteenth century minimum sentences attached to various offenses (Thomas 1978b). Probably it was the abstentionist approach of Parliament, in legislating only on maximum penalties and new forms of penal measure, that emboldened some judges to claim that they had a right to a certain sentencing discretion, and to claim that legislative attempts to structure discretion in statutes such as the Criminal Justice Acts of 1982, 1988, and 1991 went against the principle of judicial independence. But there was never any substance in these arguments. The true meaning of judicial independence is that judges should be able to pass sentence in each case without fear or favor, affection or ill-will. The principle says nothing about the extent of the discretion that ought to be left to judges at the sentencing stage (Home Office 1990b, para. 2.1; Ashworth 1995, chap. 2).

What, then, is the constitutional role of the judiciary in sentencing? The starting point must be that the legislature has supremacy — subject only to higher obligations such as the European Convention on Human Rights, which now forms part of English law under the Human Rights Act 1998.[24] The division of responsibility inherent in the Criminal Justice Act 1991 seemed attractive: the legislature laid down certain general policies, and the courts were left to develop them in detail, with the Court of Appeal laying down guidance on the application of the general policies to specific types of offense. How did this fare in practice?

In what appears, in retrospect, to have been a sentiment based on naivete and miscalculation, the Home Office declared in 1990:

> The legislation will be in general terms. It is not the Government's intention that Parliament should bind the courts with strict legislative guidelines. . . . The Government hopes that the Court of Appeal will give further guidance, building on the legislative framework. (Home Office 1990b, paras. 2.16–2.17)

The Court of Appeal's handling of three provisions in the Criminal Justice Act 1991 shows how the judiciary responded to the government's trust.

First let us consider section 2(2)(a) of the act, which lays down that the length of prison sentences "shall be . . . commensurate with the seriousness of the offense." A fair reading of the 1990 White Paper makes it clear that the act was intended to give prominence to sentencing based on proportionality or desert. Thus the White Paper criticized the assumptions behind deterrent sentencing and stated that "injustice is more likely if courts do not focus on the seriousness of the offence" (Home Office 1990 para. 2.1a). Yet when the case of *Cunningham* came before the Court of Appeal, and Lord Taylor C. J. formulated guidance for the lower courts, he twisted the meaning of the words in section 2(2)(a). By declaring that "commensurate with the seriousness of the offense" means "commensurate with the punishment and deterrence that the seriousness of the offense requires," he effectively undermined one of the primary purposes of that provision, even though he did go on to rule out exemplary deterrent sentences in individual cases (*Cunningham* (1993) 14 Cr.App.R.(S) 444). Thus *Cunningham* made it acceptable for judges to base sentences on deterrence when the intention of Parliament was to exclude this rationale in favor of proportionality to the seriousness of the offense.

Why did Lord Taylor take this approach? One might speculate on various possible explanations. He might have made a genuine attempt to interpret the statute: but it was hardly a purposive interpretation, since it ignored the various passages in the 1990 White Paper that clearly indicated an intention to give primacy to desert. Moreover, the judgment contains no analysis of the White Paper. Or perhaps he was so confident that deterrence is the right policy that he decided to give a creative interpretation to the statutory wording. This would have been strange, given his subsequent lambasting of the government's assumption that high sentences would act as a deterrent—on the basis that the risk of detection is much more powerful than the penalty imposed in the event of being caught (Taylor 1996, p. 10). So that leaves the further possibilities that he was unaware that he was making a fundamental departure from the act's intentions, or that he was aware of what he was doing and the aim was to ensure that the judicial sentencing tariff survived the legislation intact. My belief is that the last explanation is the most probable: the judges were announcing "business as usual," despite the small inconvenience of a statutory intrusion.

Second, let us consider the judicial handling of section 1(2)(a), which states that no offender should be given a custodial sentence unless the offense is so serious that only custody could be justified. A similarly worded restriction on custodial sentences for young offenders had been introduced by the Criminal Justice Act 1982, in the face of arguments that this incursion into sentencers' discretion was both unnecessary and contrary to the principle of judicial independence. In the event, it appeared that this provision contributed to a reduction in the use of custody in that age group in the 1980s (Allen 1991), which encouraged the government to introduce the provision applicable to offenders of all ages into the 1991 act (Home Office 1990b, paras. 2.6–3.9). Unfortunately, the test adopted by the courts in the 1980s — the test of the "right thinking member of the public"[25] — soon showed its lack of substance in the 1990s, when one judge was able solemnly to declare that right-thinking members of the public would expect a man who obtained a £35 car alarm from a superstore by deception, and who had one previous conviction, to receive a prison sentence.[26] The test has become a substitute for reasoning and was certainly not having the intended effect of reducing the use of short prison sentences. Thus in 1993 some 23,901 offenders were sentenced to custodial sentences of up to six months, whereas in 1996 the number had gone up to 38,952. It is to the credit of Lord Bingham C.J. that he responded to criticism of the "right-thinking-member-of-the-public" test (Ashworth and von Hirsch 1997) by abolishing it in 1998, although the judgment in which he accomplished this fails to give clear guidance to courts on the approach to be taken.[27]

Third, we should also consider section 2(2)(b). This provision sets out the only circumstances in which courts should depart from the proportionate sentence, that is, where it is thought that a sexual or violent offender needs to be sentenced to a longer term in order to protect the public from serious harm from him. This provision, like section 1(2)(a) just considered, fails to give many indications of the way in which the courts should develop the criteria. However, the Court of Appeal has made considerable efforts to develop criteria to guide the judges about when longer-than-proportionate sentences may and may not be appropriate, even if there are a few respects in which the criteria might be improved (von Hirsch and Ashworth 1996). Why did this provision receive a rather sympathetic reading when sections 1(2)(a) and 2(2)(a) did not? The answer to that question is unknown, but it may have something to do with judicial belief in the need for some such provision as section 2(2)(b) and their skepticism about the need for the other two subsections.

Inasmuch as there is substance in this analysis, it suggests that the judges adopted a "pick and choose" approach to the 1991 act, aiming so far as possible to preserve their existing practices. Or, to put it another way, they have had little compunction about neutralizing those parts of the 1991 act that they least like — not merely by exercising their discretion in ways that fail to advance the purpose of the act (as under sec. 1(2)(a)) but also by placing an untenable interpretation on a key provision (sec. 2(2)(a)) that might otherwise have stood in their way. This points to the conclusion that the judiciary has arrogated to itself the power, effectively, to override the legislature in certain respects, where it disagrees with the provisions — a power that is not unlimited, of course, but that is antidemocratic in the sense that it is used to circumvent legislation that has passed through Parliament.

V. Repression and Discretion

In respect of a few provisions of the 1991 act to which some judges and magistrates objected strongly, a more direct, public, and "democratic" approach was taken. This opposition centered on the unit-fine system (see section II above), and on the sections of the act dealing with previous convictions (a complicated provision) and multiple offenses (courts were permitted to rely on only two offenses, even if the offender was convicted of several, in deciding whether a case was serious enough for imprisonment). Whatever the rights and wrongs of these judicial criticisms,[28] they happened to coincide with the arrival in 1992 of a government with a perilously small majority, and of a Home Secretary (Kenneth Clarke) who was not averse to making grand gestures. So in May 1993 he announced the abolition of unit fines, the reversal of the provision on multiple offenses, and a new section on previous convictions. These changes were accomplished by the 1993 act, and for a short period the judges and the politicians were marching in step.

But 1993 was a crucial year in other respects. For one thing, it was the year in which there was heightened media interest in law and order, following the killing of 2-year-old James Bulger. For another, Michael Howard succeeded Kenneth Clarke as Home Secretary and immediately declared his intention to bring about major reforms of the criminal justice system. He began to pronounce that "prison works" and to call for tougher sentences (see Sparks 1996). It soon became apparent that, among other imports from the United States such as electronic tagging and boot camps, he wanted to introduce some form of mandatory sentences similar to "three strikes and you're out." No doubt the politically shrewd Mr. Howard, as Home Secretary, was trying to outflank the judiciary by implying that their sentencing was in some spheres too lenient and that for this reason mandatory sentences were needed. Mr. Howard was trying to enlist public opinion in support, but the senior judiciary began to use the mass media effectively in order to put the opposite case. Lord Taylor, as Lord Chief Justice, swiftly condemned the Home Secretary's proposal on the same day that it was announced, arguing (among other things) that mandatory sentences would not deter offenders because detection rates are so low, and he and other senior judges kept up the criticism through public lectures and House of Lords debates (e.g., Taylor 1996).

When the Crime (Sentences) Bill was introduced into Parliament in 1996, the judicial criticism intensified, but the Labor Party did not oppose the bill and it went through with only a few late but significant amendments to the mandatory sentencing provisions. The principal provision of the Crime (Sentences) Act 1997 is section 2, which requires courts to impose a sentence of life imprisonment for a second serious sexual or violent offense. The judge sets the minimum tariff period to be served, after which the release date is determined on public protection grounds by the Home Secretary. The only way of avoiding the mandatory sentence is for the court to find "exceptional circumstances," and it seems unlikely that the judges will take a broad view of this proviso (cf. Thomas 1998, pp. 87–88). The 1997 act also introduces a prescribed sentence of seven years' imprisonment for the third offense of class A drug dealing. This is a strange provision, because most third-time drug dealers would receive a sentence in excess of seven years, but the relevant point here is that it was emasculated in Parliament (largely through the efforts of Law Lords, serving and retired, speaking in the House of Lords in its legislative capacity), to the effect that a court need not impose the prescribed sentence if it would be "unjust in all the circumstances." This leaves the courts with ample discretion to impose a sentence below the prescribed minimum, should the occasion arise. The 1997 act contains a third prescribed minimum sentence—three years' imprisonment for a third offense of domestic burglary—which is subject to the same qualification that courts need not impose it if this would be "unjust in all the circumstances." Implementation of this provision was postponed for lack of prison accommodation, but the government declared its intention to bring it into force at the end of 1999.

Another battleground between the government and the senior judiciary in the 1990s has been the mandatory sentence of life imprisonment for murder. In 1989 a House of Lords Select Committee called for abolition of the mandatory life sentence, in favor of judicial discretion (House of Lords 1989). An influential committee headed by Lord Lane, the former Lord Chief Justice, also reported in 1993 in favor of abolition of the mandatory life sentence for murder (Prison Reform Trust 1993). Life imprisonment in English law does not necessarily mean detention for the whole of one's natural life (although that may occur) but does mean that, after expiry of the tariff period based on "retribution and deterrence," release is governed by perceptions of risk and public safety, and release may be followed by recall. In effect, the life sentence transfers the sentence-setting function from the judiciary to the executive, and so the main issue is control over the prisoner's release. For those convicted of murder, it is the Home Secretary (a politician) who ultimately determines the minimum "tariff" period to be served and the time of release, and this practice is criticized as wrong in principle. It has been challenged under Article 5(4) of the European Convention on Human Rights, but the European Court held that for the mandatory life sentence for murder (unlike discretionary life sentences) it is acceptable that the Home Secretary determines the date of release.[29] This is regrettable, since it is too tempting for a politician to pander to public opinion, as expressed through the mass media or otherwise. Recently an action for judicial review was brought against the Home Secretary, to question his decision on the "tariff" period to be served by the two boys who killed James Bulger in 1993. The House of Lords held that the Home Secretary had acted wrongly in taking account of public petitions presented to him.[30] Speaking extra-judicially, Lord Bingham, as Lord Chief Justice, has repeated the judicial call for the abolition of the mandatory life sentence for murder, in favor of judicial discretion, but the Labor Home Secretary, Jack Straw, has reasserted the argument that it is his task to ensure that members of the public are adequately protected.[31]

These political battles, unusually open as they were, form only one part of the story of sentencing in the 1990s. Another important development is that steadily, and with relatively little legislative encouragement,[32] the courts increased their use of imprisonment to the extent that between early 1993 and early 1997 the prison population rose by 50 percent, from 40,000 to 60,000. The increases continued, so that at the end of September 2000 the prison population was 65,100. To put this sudden development into context, we need to look at the twenty-five years documented in table 2.5.

Table 2.5 traces the unprecedented rapid rise in the prison population in the mid-1990s (and tables 2.3 and 2.4 show the increased rate of custodial sentencing). Table 2.5 differentiates the figures for all males and females in prison (much affected by the numbers held pending trial, and thus on court waiting times, etc.), from the numbers of male and female sentenced prisoners. The figures for male sentenced prisoners show a remarkable stability until the mid-1990s, although for much of the 1980s this stability was the result of manipulation of the rules on remission and parole. Nonetheless, the steep rise in the past few years is of extraordinary dimensions, and the 1997 figures show a further 11 percent rise. Since, as I argue, the mid-1990s saw no significant legislative requirements to impose more custodial sentences, the question arises: why have the courts used "their" discretion in order to impose more and longer prison sentences?

At first sight there appears to be a clear self-contradiction here. Three major inquiries into the use of prison in recent years have all been chaired by judges and have all reported strongly in favor of reducing the number and length of prison sentences (May 1979; Carlisle 1988; Woolf 1991). At the very point when the new wave of repression was beginning to dominate the mass media, several leading judges publicly expressed reservations about the value of imprisonment.[33] Yet in the mid-1990s the judiciary initiated a sudden and marked escalation in prison sentences, the like of which has never been experienced in this country before (Morgan 1997). According to the Lord Chief Justice, the escalation was a response to what was taken to be "public opinion": the judges felt that they had to try to stay in touch with an increasingly punitive public mood (Bingham 1997).

To what extent this is the proper role of the judiciary may be debated. A related question is how the judges knew that this was the public mood. When a small number of judges were questioned in the early 1980s, they were careful to distinguish between opinions expressed in the media and what they termed "informed public opinion" (Ashworth et al. 1984, pp. 33–34). In 1993 and thereafter the clamor for greater severity came from both leading politicians and large sections of the television and newspaper industries. There is little doubt that during this period the mass media reported and commented on many cases that, in previous years, would not have received publicity. In speculating on the reasons why so many people appear to be receptive to reporting that assumes the wisdom of severity and repressive measures against offenders, Tony Bottoms has argued that deeper social insecurities may hold the key.

> The tendency of modern politicians occasionally to resort to populist punitiveness is relatively easy to understand. The disembedding processes of modernity . . . have not only probably increased the crime rate, they have also led to a fairly widespread sense of insecurity, especially among older people, as former social certainties are eroded. . . . In such a context, a politician can reasonably easily tap into the electorate's insecurities by promising tough action on "villains"—even if . . . the public are actually rather less punitive when confronted with real situations of criminality. (Bottoms 1995, p. 47)

Table 2.5. Average Daily Prison Population, England and Wales, 1971–1996

Year	Male Prisoners	Sentenced Males	Female Prisoners	Sentenced Females
1971	38,673	33,780	1,035	796
1972	37,348	32,372	980	762
1973	35,747	30,879	1,027	786
1974	35,823	30,638	1,044	758
1975	38,601	32,821	1,219	912
1976	40,161	34,852	1,282	986
1977	40,212	34,595	1,358	1,064
1978	40,409	34,480	1,387	1,081
1979	40,762	34,461	1,458	1,130
1980	40,748	34,783	1,516	1,198
1981	41,904	34,940	1,407	1,082
1982	42,381	34,926	1,326	1,002
1983	42,072	34,638	1,390	1,045
1984	41,822	33,212	1,473	1,109
1985	44,706	35,165	1,532	1,140
1986	45,241	35,358	1,648	1,213
1987	47,191	36,234	1,772	1,297
1988	48,160	37,006	1,789	1,276
1989	46,843	36,599	1,767	1,293
1990	44,039	34,322	1,597	1,209
1991	44,336	34,274	1,561	1,166
1992	44,240	34,230	1,577	1,190
1993	43,005	32,183	1,561	1,135
1994	46,983	34,505	1,811	1,292
1995	49,068	37,593	1,979	1,464
1996	53,019	41,346	2,262	1,697

Source: Prison Statistics, England and Wales, annual volumes, 1971–96.

As Bottoms implies, what we know about the opinions of the public on sentencing paints a more complex picture. Research has long suggested that members of the public will readily agree that sentencing in general is too lenient, but that when confronted with a particular set of facts their sentence choice will be no more severe than court practice. A recent British Crime Survey report confirms this finding (Hough and Roberts 1997) and goes on to show that the reason people nevertheless tend to criticize court sentencing is that they are grossly misinformed about it. In brief, people think that sentencing is much more lenient than in fact it is. Thus the judges, in responding to "public opinion," may merely be shadowboxing. What is presented as public opinion is false, but the falsehood is widely accepted because of the high level of misinformation about sentencing practice (see further Walker and Hough 1988; Roberts and Stalans 1997).

What has been constant about the judicial response to the sentencing reforms of the 1990s is their insistence on maximum discretion. The thread that connects their opposition to the 1991 and 1997 acts is simply that: both statutes attempted, to some degree, to curtail or structure judicial discretion. Vocal sections of the judiciary not only thought that some of the structures were wrong but, more fundamentally, thought them unnecessary and inappropriate. The theme is that justice can be done only if courts are left with wide discretion. The typical judicial defense of discretion is that each case is different and that the sentence needs to be tailored to the particular facts. But it is wrong to imply that, in the process of arriving at sentence, the court makes no assumptions about the relevant principles or the appropriate starting point. It would be absurd to suggest that the facts, of themselves, indicate a suitable sentence: they can be said to do so only in conjunction with various principles and established sentence levels. This is recognized, of course, when the Court of Appeal delivers a guideline judgment (see section III above) or when the Court of Appeal gives its authority to a general principle (e.g., that the sentence discount for pleading guilty need not be given where the offender was caught "red-handed" and has no viable defense).[34] Thus it is possible to set out serviceable general principles and starting points for sentencing. But the English judges want to keep this task for themselves and, even if they have now forsaken the "judicial independence" argument, they are fortified in their preference for wide discretion by the technically incompetent efforts at legislation in recent years. "Leave it all to us" remains the prevailing judicial view.

VI. Conclusions: Sentencing as Art?

My discussion in this chapter focuses on five developments in sentencing in England and Wales. The overall trends may appear confused. A strong movement towards diversion has led to a considerable reduction in the number of indictable offenders sentenced by the courts, and this movement survived into the 1990s simultaneously with a steep rise in the prison population and in punitiveness towards those who commit offenses of medium and high seriousness and repeat offenders. This produces a twin-track approach to criminal justice,[35] suggesting that nonpunitive responses at one end of the sentencing scale are acceptable only in tandem with heavily punitive measures at the other end. Repressive elements may also be found in less obvious places: the rise in the use of community sentences in the 1990s may represent an increase in penal severity for offenders who might otherwise have been fined, and many community sentences are significantly more demanding than in previous years. The judiciary and the legislature have continued to vie for supremacy in sentencing, especially in the 1990s: while Parliament appears to have won the day over mandatory and minimum sentences, in the Crime (Sentences) Act 1997, the only consistent thread in the prevailing judicial approach is a desire for maximum discretion and minimum legislative "interference." In the past three decades the Court of Appeal has developed the technique of the guideline judgment to good effect. But on the question of prison use, the courts appear to be no less willing to see an escalation in penal severity than are politicians.

These developments in England and Wales prompt a number of questions for further discussion in an international comparative context. I conclude by setting four hares running.

First, the mass media (television, popular newspapers) have played a considerable role in recent sentencing policy and practice in this jurisdiction. Of course they take their place among a number of influences, often intertwined with politicians who are able to use the media for their own electoral purposes. It may not be pure chance that the period of greatest penal repression in England (1992–97) coincided with the term of a weak government with a slender majority, anxious to exploit any means of political survival. The problem is how to escape from the repressive mentality that has now become entrenched: the present government has a massive parliamentary majority but shows little inclination to retreat from the penal policies of the previous administration. Is it politically possible to de-escalate the level of penal response? Would it be necessary to "package" such a policy so as to minimize opposition and, if so, who is to be feared—the media, the electorate, or both? How can an alternative mentality, or "replacement discourse," be developed and nurtured into a position of some prominence and influence?

Second, one feature I have not analyzed here is the resurgence of reparative and restorative approaches to criminal justice. Although developments in England and Wales have been slower and more limited than those in New Zealand and some Australian states, restorative justice is firmly on the agenda and several schemes are being put in place. This is not the place to attempt a survey of theory and practice (see von Hirsch and Ashworth 1998, chap. 7), but some general questions can be raised. Are forms of restorative justice, such as Family Group Conferences, capable of gaining wide (political) acceptability or are they destined to remain confined to certain spheres (minor offenders, young offenders) while the predominant approach remains unchanged? To what extent can and do restorative approaches ensure proper safeguards for offenders, in terms of procedure and in terms of limits on the sentences that may be imposed? Insofar as victims and their families have an influence on the outcomes for offenders, is it right that the obligations imposed on offenders should reflect the disposition of the victim (vengeful, forgiving) rather than "objective" features of the offense?

Third, what has happened to values and principles in sentencing during the recent repressive turn in penal politics? At the time of the Criminal Justice Act 1991, politicians and others were prepared to discuss rationales for sentencing. By the time of the Crime (Sentences) Act 1997, political expediency had taken over. Even those who pointed out the lack of empirical support for the assumptions about deterrence and incapacitation that underpinned the new mandatory sentences were not acknowledged: political symbolism was more important than mere evidence and argument (von Hirsch and Ashworth 1998). What mattered was how the new laws would look to the public, media, and other politicians, not whether they would actually "work" as claimed. One feature of the past three decades has been the disappearance of official advisory bodies on penal policy. In the 1970s there was a standing body called the Advisory Council on the Penal System. It was abolished by the Thatcher government, along with similar bodies in other areas of social policy. Whether the new Sentencing Advisory Panel makes any difference remains to be seen. It may at least succeed in drawing into penal policy making a wider range of experts and perhaps in ensuring that proper regard is given to international obligations. In particular, the British government in 1992 signified acceptance of the report of the Council of Europe's Select Committee of Experts entitled *"Consistency in Sentencing"* (Council of Europe 1993). That report recommends that each member state articulate the primary rationale for sentencing, and that sentences should remain in proportion to the seriousness of the offense. It contains several other recommendations on matters of principle in sentencing. I have never once seen or heard any reference to it by any British official or politician.

This leads to my fourth question, and to the idea of sentencing as art. In 1980, when blocking the further progress of an empirical research project into sentencing by English judges, Lord Lane, then Lord Chief Justice, used the phrase that sentencing is "an art and not a science" (Ashworth et al. 1984, p. 64). Many postmodern writers might take a similar view, arguing that the application of the so-called Enlightenment project to sentencing—the search for rational principles, for consistency, and for logical sentencing systems—was always bound to fail, and that we would do better to recognize that it is inevitably a matter of value pluralism and political compromise (e.g., Gray 1995). On this view, the contribution of science, rationality, or liberal principles to issues such as sentencing policy is severely limited. I find this view both depressing and unconvincing and believe that the latter can be established without reliance on the former. This is not the place to develop that theme fully (for some beginnings, see von Hirsch and Ashworth 1998, chap. 8), but I would argue that the indeterminacy, contingency, and contestability that critical sentencing theorists identify do not undermine the case for protecting individuals by ensuring that state power is exercised fairly in response to criminal offenses. No doubt some academic writings on sentencing policy do appear too doctrinaire and too remote from the myriad considerations pressed upon courts in individual cases: both judges and critical sentencing theorists would argue that point, and it has some substance. If anyone claimed that sentencing is or should be a science, they would be wrong. But to regard it as an art is to move to an equally untenable extreme position, echoing the idea that the sentence somehow arises out of the facts of the case or that it involves a kind of "instinctive synthesis."[36] There are principles that can and should be brought to bear on the sentencing decision, and they should be set in the context of a system that declares a primary rationale for sentencing and then offers justifications for departing from that in certain groups of cases. This kind of framework has been all but forgotten amidst the debates in England in the mid-1990s, and the challenge is to rekindle it as soon as possible.

NOTES

1. It is customary to remind non-British readers that England and Wales is a separate jurisdiction from Scotland and from Northern Ireland, which have different sentencing

laws and traditions. This chapter is confined to England and Wales and, for brevity, I use "England" and "English."

2. "Indictable offenses" is the most convenient statistical category for the purposes of this chapter. It means those crimes that it is possible to try on indictment, that is, in the Crown Court, and therefore includes all the most serious offenses. However, most of these offenses are actually tried in the magistrates' courts, and all crimes of theft, deception, and handling stolen goods are indictable no matter how small the value of the goods.

3. A sentence discount of one-third can be expected for a timely guilty plea: Criminal Justice and Public Order Act 1994, sec. 48.

4. It might be mentioned that the use of custody for offenders under 17 also fell dramatically, from a peak of 7,900 in 1981 to 2,400 in 1989; see Allen 1991.

5. Notably an article by Wasik and von Hirsch (1988), with adaptations proposed by Bottoms (1989).

6. Combination orders combine elements of probation and community service within a single order and were intended as the most restrictive community sentence, appropriate for fairly serious cases. On their history and use, see Mair 1997, pp. 1213–14.

7. The relevant law is in sec. 12 and 13 of the Criminal Justice Act 1991. For the latest research, see Mortimer and May 1997.

8. A Home Office study in 1993 found that 69 percent of sentenced offenders were unemployed, 17 percent in employment, and the other 14 percent in full-time education or status unknown: Home Office 1994c.

9. Culminating in his *Principles of Sentencing* (1st ed. 1970; 2d ed. 1979).

10. Since 1979 there has been a set of law reports devoted entirely to sentencing cases: *Criminal Appeal Reports (Sentencing)*, cited as *Cr.App.R.(S)*.

11. First in *Willis* (1974) 60 Cr.App.R. 146 (homosexual offenses against boys), and then in *Taylor, Roberts and Simons* (1977) 64 Cr.App.R. 182 (unlawful sexual intercourse with girls).

12. Lord Lane's first guideline judgment was *Aramah* (1982) 4 Cr.App.R.(S) 407 on drug offenses.

13. For the Court of Appeal's rebuke to a judge who took a different view, see *Johnson* (1994) 15 Cr.App.R.(S) 827.

14. E.g., *Billam* (1986) 82 Cr.App.R. 347 on rape; *Stewart* (1987) 9 Cr.App.R.(S) 135 on social security fraud.

15. For example, the guideline judgment in *Boswell*.

16. E.g., *Ronchetti* [1998] Crim.L.R. 227 (cannabis), *Wijs* [1998] Crim.L.R. 587 (amphetamines), *Avis* [1998] Crim.L.R. 428 (firearms), *Martin* [1999] Crim.L.R. 91 (possessing explosives).

17. (1990) 12 Cr.App.R (S) 607.

18. (1998) 1 Cr.App.R. (S) 181.

19. A point well made by Roger Hood in his pioneering study *Sentencing in Magistrates' Courts* (1962, p. 16), when confronted by magistrates who claimed that sentencing was all a matter of experience.

20. The guidelines have no legal standing. The Magistrates' Association is a voluntary body, to which virtually all magistrates belong. The guidelines have been commended by the Lord Chancellor and the Lord Chief Justice.

21. Without entering into too much detail, it is apposite to mention that a new system of "plea before venue," introduced by the Criminal Procedure and Investigations Act 1996, is designed to ensure that a higher proportion of defendants who intend to plead guilty to an indictable offense are sentenced in the magistrates' courts (and therefore, receive lower sentences); see Ashworth 1998, chap. 8.

22. The changes are too complex to set out briefly and were reversed in 1991 when the system described in section I above was introduced. For a brief history, see Ashworth 1995, pp. 243–47.

23. It is probable that the basic structure of the 1991 act was somewhat influenced by the new Swedish sentencing law, passed in 1988 and publicized in England by von Hirsch and Jareborg (1989). For a fuller description, see Jareborg 1995.

24. When the Human Rights Act comes into force (probably in late 2000), English judges will have the power to issue a "declaration of incompatibility" if they find that a statutory provision is contrary to the European Convention. Although likely to be rare in general and very rare in sentencing, the declaration (which does not affect the validity of the law) exposes the injustice and allows the government to use a fast-track procedure to amend the law so as to conform with the European Convention.

25. First stated by L. J. Lawton in *Bradbourn* (1985) 7 Cr.App.R.(S) 180 and repeated by Lord C. J. Taylor in *Cox* (1993) 14 Cr.App.R.(S) 479 and *Baverstock* (1993) 14 Cr.App.R.(S) 471 when interpreting section 1(2)(a).

26. L. J. Hirst in *Keogh* (1994) 15 Cr.App.R.(S) 279.

27. *Howells* [1998] Crim.L.R. 836.

28. I have urged that most of the criticisms were wrong; see Ashworth 1995, pp. 81, 160–62, 262–66.

29. *Wynne v. United Kingdom* (1994) 19 E.H.R.R. 333. The European Court of Human Rights found against the United Kingdom in a case brought by three prisoners serving discretionary life sentences *(Thynne, Wilson, and Gunnell v. United Kingdom* (1991) 13 E.H.R.R. 666), after which the law was changed. It is now the Parole Board that determines the release of discretionary lifers. Cf. also *Hussain and Singh v. United Kingdom* (1996) 21 E.H.R.R. 1, in respect of young offenders, and also the ongoing appeal in *Thompson and Venables v. United Kingdom* [1998] E.H.R.L.R. 484.

30. *R. v. Secretary of State for the Home Department, ex parte Venables and Thompson* [1997] 3 W.L.R. 23.

31. *The Times*, March 14, 1998. For a detailed and fascinating discussion of developments in this area between 1993 and 1995, see Windlesham 1996, chap. 9.

32. A few scattered provisions might be mentioned: the Criminal Justice Act 1993 doubled the maximum penalty for causing death by dangerous driving and causing death by careless driving whilst intoxicated, from five to ten years, and it also reworded the provision on previous convictions and abolished the restrictions on sentencing for multiple offenses. The Criminal Justice and Public Order Act 1994 doubled the maximum sentence of detention in a young offender institution that can be imposed on offenders aged 15, 16, and 17 from one to two years.

33. See the six judges interviewed in *The Observer*, October 17, 1993, p. 3.

34. On which see, e.g., *Landy* (1995) 16 Cr.App.R. (S) 908.

35. Or what Tony Bottoms precisely identified as "bifurcation" some twenty years ago; Bottoms 1977.

36. The famous phrase from the Australian case of *Williscroft* [1975] V.R. 272, at pp. 299–300.

REFERENCES

Advisory Council on the Penal System. 1970. *Non-Custodial and Semi-Custodial Penalties*. London: Her Majesty's Stationery Office.

Allen, R. 1991. "Out of Jail: The Reduction in the Use of Custody for Male Juveniles, 1981–88." *Howard Journal of Criminal Justice* 30:30–42.

Ashworth, A. 1983. *Sentencing and Penal Policy*. London: Weidenfeld and Nicolson.

———. 1995. *Sentencing and Criminal Justice*. London: Butterworths.

———. 1997. "Sentencing." In *Oxford Handbook of Criminology*, edited by M. Maguire, R. Morgan, and R. Einer. Oxford: Oxford University Press.

———. 1998. *The Criminal Process*. 2d ed. Oxford: Oxford University Press.

Ashworth, A., E. Genders, G. Mansfield, J. Peay, and E. Player. 1984. *Sentencing in the Crown Court: Report of an Exploratory Study*. Occasional Paper no. 10. Oxford: Centre for Criminological Research.

Ashworth, A., and A. von Hirsch. 1997. "Recognizing Elephants: The Problem of the Custody Threshold." *Criminal Law Review*, 187–200.

Bingham, Lord. 1997. Annual Police Foundation Lecture. *The Times*, July 11.

Bottoms, A. E. 1977. "Reflections on the Renaissance of Dangerousness." *Howard Journal* 16:70–97.

———. 1989. "The Concept of Intermediate Sanctions and Its Relevance for the Probation Service." In *The Criminal Justice System: A Central Role for the Probation Service*, edited by R. Shaw and D. Haines. Cambridge: Institute of Criminology.

———. 1995. "The Philosophy and Politics of Punishment and Sentencing." In *The Politics of Sentencing Reform*, edited by C. Clarkson and R. Morgan. Oxford: Clarendon Press.

Carlisle, Lord. 1988. *Report of the Review Committee: The Parole System in England and Wales*, Cm 532. London: Her Majesty's Stationery Office.

Charman, E., B. Gibson, T. Honess, and R. Morgan. 1996. *Fine Impositions and Enforcement Following the Criminal Justice Act 1993*. Home Office Research Findings no. 36. London: Home Office.

Cooke, Judge. 1987. "The Practical Problems of the Sentencer." In *The Psychology of Sentencing*, edited by D. Pennington and S. Lloyd-Bostock. Oxford: Centre for Socio-Legal Studies.

Council of Europe. 1993. "Consistency in Sentencing," Recommendation no. R (92) 17. Strasbourg: Council of Europe.

Downes, D., and R. Morgan. 1997. "Dumping the 'Hostages to Fortune': The Politics of Law and Order in Post-War Britain," in *Oxford Handbook of Criminology*, 2d ed., edited by M. Maguire, R. Morgan, and R. Reiner. Oxford: Oxford University Press.

Evans, R., and D. Ellis. 1997. *Police Cautioning in the 1990s*. Home Office Research Findings no. 52. London: Home Office.

Fionda, J. 1999. "New Labour, Old Hat: Youth Justice and the Crime and Disorder Act 1998." *Criminal Law Review*, 36–47.

Flood-Page, C., and A. Mackie. 1998. *Sentencing Practice: An Examination of Decisions in Magistrates' Courts and the Crown Court in the Mid-1990s*. Home Office Research Study no. 180. London: Home Office.

Folkard, S., D. E. Smith, and D. D. Smith. 1975. *IMPACT volume II*. Home Office Research Study no. 36. London: Her Majesty's Stationery Office.

Gray, J. 1995. *Enlightenment's Wake*. London: Routledge.

Hedderman, C., and D. Moxon. 1992. *Magistrates' Court or Crown Court? Mode of Trial Decisions and Sentencing*. Home Office Research Study no. 125. London: Her Majesty's Stationery Office.

Home Office. 1985. *The Cautioning of Offenders*. Home Office Circular 14/1985. London: Home Office.

————. 1988. *Punishment Custody and the Community*. Cm 424. London: Her Majesty's Stationery Office.

————. 1990a. *The Cautioning of Offenders*. Home Office Circular 59/1990. London: Home Office.

————. 1990b. *Crime Justice and Protecting the Public*. Cm 965. London: Her Majesty's Stationery Office.

————. 1992. *National Standards for the Supervision of Offenders*. London: Home Office.

————. 1994a. *The Cautioning of Offenders*. Home Office Circular 18/1994. London: Home Office.

————. 1994b. *The Criminal Histories of Those Cautioned in 1985, 1988, and 1991*. Home Office Statistical Bulletin 8/94. London: Home Office.

————. 1994c. *Monitoring of the Criminal Justice Acts 1991 and 1993: Results from a Special Data Collection Exercise*. Statistical Bulletin 20/94. London: Home Office.

————. 1995. *National Standards for the Supervision of Offenders*. London: Home Office.

Hood, R. 1962. *Sentencing in Magistrates' Courts*. London: Tavistock.

————. 1972. *Sentencing the Motoring Offender*. London: Heinemann.

Hough, M., and J. Roberts. 1997. *Attitudes to Punishment: Findings from the British Crime Survey*. Home Office Research Study no. 179. London: Home Office.

House of Lords. 1989. *Report of the Select Committee on Murder and Life Imprisonment*. H.L. Paper 78, Session 1988–89. London: Her Majesty's Stationery Office.

Jareborg, N. 1995. "The Swedish Sentencing Reform." In *The Politics of Sentencing Reform*, edited by C. Clarkson and R. Morgan. Oxford: Clarendon Press.

Mair, G. 1997. "Community Penalties and the Probation Service." In *Oxford Handbook of Criminology*, edited by M. Maguire, R. Morgan, and R. Reiner. Oxford: Oxford University Press.

May, Mr. Justice. 1979. *Report of the Inquiry into the United Kingdom Prison Services*. Cmnd 7673. London: Her Majesty's Stationery Office.

Mirrlees-Black, C., P. Mayhew, and A. Percy. 1996. *The 1996 British Crime Survey*. Home Office Statistical Bulletin 19/91. London: Home Office.

Morgan, R. 1997. "Imprisonment: Current Concerns and a Brief History since 1945." In *Oxford Handbook of Criminology*, edited by M. Maguire, R. Morgan, and R. Reiner. Oxford: Oxford University Press.

Mortimer, E., and C. May. 1997. *Electronic Monitoring in Practice: The Second Year of the Trials of Curfew Orders*. Home Office Research Study no. 177. London: Home Office.

Moxon, D. 1988. *Sentencing Practice in the Crown Court*. Home Office Research Study no. 103. London: Her Majesty's Stationery Office.

Munro, C. 1992. "Judicial Independence and Judicial Functions." In *Sentencing Judicial Discretion and Training*, edited by C. Munro and M. Wasik. London: Sweet and Maxwell.

Prison Reform Trust. 1993. *The Penalty for Homicide*. London: Prison Reform Trust.

Radzinowicz, L., and R. Hood. 1990. *The Emergence of Penal Policy in Victorian and Edwardian England*. Oxford: Oxford University Press.

Rex, S. 1998. "Applying Desert Principles to Community Sentences: Lessons from Two Criminal Justice Acts." *Criminal Law Review*, 381–91.

Roberts, J. V., and L. J. Stalans. 1997. *Public Opinion, Crime, and Criminal Justice*. Boulder, Colo.: Westview.

Sanders, A. 1997. "From Suspect to Trial." In *Oxford Handbook of Criminology*, edited by M. Maguire, R. Morgan, and R. Reiner. Oxford: Oxford University Press.

Shute, S. 1994. "Prosecution Appeals against Sentence: The First Five Years." *Modern Law Review* 57:745–61.

Sparks, R. 1996. "Penal Austerity: The Doctrine of Less Eligibility Reborn." In *Prisons 2000: An International Perspective on the State and Future of Imprisonment*, edited by R. Matthews and P. Francis. Aldershot: Macmillan.

Tarling, R. 1979. *Sentencing Practice in Magistrates' Courts*. Home Office Research Study no. 56. London: Her Majesty's Stationery Office.

Taylor, Lord. 1996. "Continuity and Change in the Criminal Law." *King's College Law Journal* 5:1–15.

Thomas, D. A. 1978a. "Form and Function in Criminal Law." In *Reshaping the Criminal Law*, edited by P. R. Glazebrook. London: Sweet & Maxwell.

———. 1978b. *The Penal Equation*. Cambridge: Institute of Criminology.

———. 1979. *Principles of Sentencing*. 2d ed. London: Heinemann.

———. 1988. "Sentencing: Some Current Questions." *Current Legal Problems* 41:115–28.

———. 1992. "The Criminal Justice Act 1991: Custodial Sentences." *Criminal Law Review*, 232–42.

———. 1997. "Sentencing Legislation: The Case for Consolidation." *Criminal Law Review*, 406–17.

———. 1998. "The Crime (Sentences) Act 1997." *Criminal Law Review*, 83–92.

von Hirsch, A., and A. Ashworth. 1996. "Protective Sentencing under Section 2(2)(b): The Criteria for Dangerousness." *Criminal Law Review*, 175–83.

———, eds. 1998. *Principled Sentencing: Readings in Theory and Policy*. 2d ed. Oxford: Hart Publishing.

von Hirsch, A., and N. Jareborg. 1989. "Sweden's Sentencing Statute Enacted." *Criminal Law Review*, 275–82.

Walker, N., and M. Hough, eds. 1988. *Public Attitudes on Sentencing: Surveys from Five Countries*. Aldershot: Cower.

Wasik, M., and A. von Hirsch. 1988. "Non-Custodial Penalties and the Principles of Desert." *Criminal Law Review* 555–66.

Windlesham, Lord. 1996. *Responses to Crime*. Volume 3. Oxford: Oxford University Press.

Woolf, Lord Justice. 1991. *Prison Disturbances April 1990: Report of an Inquiry by the Rt. Hon. Lord Justice Woolf (parts I and II) and His Honour Judge Tumim (part III)*. Cm 1456. London: Her Majesty's Stationery Office.

Sentencing and Punishment
in Finland

The Decline of the Repressive Ideal

The Nordic countries share a long legal and cultural history. The connection between Finland and Sweden has been exceptionally close. For centuries, the same laws were in force in both because Finland was part of Sweden up to 1809. Between 1809 and 1917 Finland remained an autonomous grand duchy of the Russian Empire (but still maintaining its own laws). Finland declared independence from Russia in 1917. During the twentieth century, Finland experienced three wars (the 1918 Civil War and the two wars against Russia between 1939 and 1944). The exceptional wartime and postwar conditions made their mark on Finnish criminal policy. For instance, dire economic circumstances were reflected in the prison administration of the time. There was little scope for the treatment ideology, so prevalent in Denmark and Sweden, to catch on in Finnish policy at mid-century. Instead, the postwar crime increases led to stiffer criminal legislation in the 1950s. In general terms, the criminal justice system of Finland in the 1950s and 1960s was less resourceful, less flexible, and more repressive than those of its Nordic counterparts.

In the 1960s, the Nordic countries experienced heated social debate on the results and justifications of involuntary treatment in institutions, both penal and otherwise (such as in health care and in alcoholism treatment). The criticism found a particularly apt target in the Finnish system. Even though it is difficult to establish that treatment was actually abused (since genuine treatment was hard to find in any event), there was ample evidence of excessive use of incarceration. Also other features of criminal legislation were vulnerable to severe criticism. Most of the provisions of the Criminal Code of 1889 were still in force, representing a sharp contradiction between the values of the class-based society of the nineteenth century and the rapidly developing social welfare state of the 1960s. During the late 1960s, not only did flaws in the treatment ideology become more evident but demands for more adequate and less repressive criminal law grew louder.

In Finland the criticism of the treatment ideology was in a sense merged with that directed against an overly severe criminal code and excessive use of custodial sentences. The outcome was a political ideology for criminal justice policy— "humane neoclassicism"—that stressed legal safeguards against coercive care and less repressive measures in general.[1] During the past twenty-five years, all the main parts of the Finnish criminal legislation have been reformed from these "anti-treatment and anti-repression" starting points. The first reforms of the sanction system were carried out in the early 1970s. In 1972, a total reform of the criminal code was launched. (The old code of 1889 is still formally in force, but few of its provisions are in their original form.) In 1981, a task force was appointed by the Ministry of Justice to carry out the concrete reform work. This work was still under way in 2000—confirming once again the old experience that a total reform of a "continental" corpus of criminal law will take approximately thirty years.

The most significant reform in Finnish criminal policy in the past decades has been the purposeful movement toward a more lenient system of sanctions, and especially toward reduction in the use of custodial sentences. The tangible results can be seen in the consistent and, at times, spectacular fall in prisoner rates in Finland. Over the past twenty-five years, the number of prisoners in Finland has fallen to half the starting rate. One central focus of this chapter is the exploration of this phenomenon, exceptional as it is in an international context.

The other central focus is guidance of sentencing practices. The basic problems are to a large extent similar in different jurisdictions. However, the chosen techniques and the applied substantive principles vary. In 1976, Finland carried out a sentencing reform based on the neoclassical principles of predictability, proportionality, and equality, with an express aim of reducing unwarranted disparity in sentencing.[2] This chapter examines some of the basic solutions and some of the practical experiences of the model applied in Finland.

Section I presents the basic structure of the Finnish sanction system with a brief statistical overview. Section II examines in more detail the long-term (and still continuing) fall of the Finnish prisoner rate. The section examines the ideological factors and the judicial practices and legislative reforms behind this change. The main objective is to answer the question: what made the change possible? The supplementary objective is to present a broader look into those aims and values that still underlie the Finnish penal policy and sentencing law. Section III deals with sentencing law and the question of guidance of the sentencing judge. It discusses the form of legal regulation, the material principles of sentencing, and some of the practical results. Finally, section IV draws general conclusions and takes a brief look at the future.

I. The Structure of the Finnish Penal System

Under the present law, the general criminal punishments are the fine, conditional imprisonment, community service, and unconditional imprisonment. Capital punishment is prohibited.

A. The System of Sanctions

The Finnish constitution forbids the use of the death penalty—as well as any other sort of degrading and inhuman punishments. The last execution in Finland during peace time took place in 1823. After that capital punishment has been imposed only when Finland has been at war. Capital punishment even during wartime was abolished by legislation in 1972.

Fines

A fine is imposed as day fines. According to the system of day fines, which was adopted in Finland in 1921, the number of day fines is determined by the seriousness of the offense, while the amount of a day fine depends on the financial situation of the offender. The number of day fines varies between 1 and 120. The amount of the day fine is determined mainly by the offender's income. One day fine equals roughly one-third of the offender's daily income. Also other factors affecting the financial situation of the offender may have an effect (such as the period of employment or the number of children). If the fine is not paid, it may be converted through separate proceedings into imprisonment. Two day fines correspond to one day of imprisonment. However, imprisonment for nonpayment of fines is imposed for at least four and at most ninety days.

A fine may be imposed either in an ordinary trial or, for certain petty offenses, through simplified summary penal proceedings (penalty orders). The vast majority of fines are ordered in a summary process. Since 1994 the power to order summary fines was transferred from the court to the prosecutor. In addition, for minor traffic offenses there is a specific monetary penalty that is set at a fixed amount (petty fine) and is imposed by the police.

Imprisonment

A sentence of imprisonment may be imposed either for a determinate period (at least fourteen days and at most twelve years for a single offense and fifteen years for several offenses) or for life. A life sentence may be imposed for a relatively restricted number of offenses, such as murder, treason, and genocide. It is a mandatory sentence for murder, which also is the only offense in practice punishable by a life sentence. At present there are about 60 persons serving a life sentence. Those serving such a sentence actually spend approximately ten to twelve years in prison. After this they are normally released by a pardon from the President of the Republic.

Imprisonment may be either conditional or unconditional. Sentences of imprisonment of at most two years may be imposed conditionally, provided that "the maintenance of general respect for the law" does not require an unconditional sentence. In the younger age groups, the presumption in favor of a conditional sentence has been strengthened by a special provision that allows the use of an unconditional sentence for those who committed the offense under the age of 18 only if certain extraordinary reasons call for it. In practice this means either that the offense is especially serious or that the offender has several prior convictions.

An offender who is sentenced conditionally is placed on probation for one to three years. For adults, such probation does not involve supervision. However, a young offender who is sentenced conditionally may be placed under supervision for the period of probation. A conditional sentence may be ordered enforced if, during the probation period, the offender commits a new offense for which he or she is sentenced to imprisonment. Since the changes of 1976, the law no longer contains any other behavioral restrictions or conditions for the offender. As a supplement to a conditional sentence, an offender may be sentenced to an unconditional fine (a supplementary fine) even if the law does not specifically provide for a fine as punishment for the offense in question.

Community Service

Community service was introduced into the Finnish penal system in 1991 as an experiment in four judicial districts. In 1994 the system was extended to cover the entire country and community service became a standard part of the Finnish system of sanctions. Community service is imposed instead of unconditional imprisonment. The prerequisites are that the convicted person consent, that the sentence imposed on the offender not exceed eight months, and that the offender is deemed capable of carrying out the community service order. The offender's ability to carry out the work is evaluated on the basis of a suitability report. This report may be requested by any of the parties, the prosecutor, or the court. The suitability report is prepared by the Probation and After-Care Association (see below).

In order to ensure that community service is used in lieu of unconditional sentences of imprisonment, a two-step procedure was adopted. First the court is supposed to make its sentencing decision by applying the normal principles and criteria of sentencing, without considering the possibility of community service. If the result is unconditional imprisonment (and certain requirements are fulfilled), then the court may commute the sentence to community service. In principle, therefore, community service may be used only in cases where the accused would otherwise receive an unconditional sentence of imprisonment. In commuting imprisonment into community service, one day in prison equals one hour of community service. Thus, two months of custodial sentence should be commuted into roughly sixty hours of community service. If the conditions of the community service order are violated, the court normally imposes a new unconditional sentence of imprisonment (for details, see Lappi-Seppälä 1992a; Takala 1992).

Community service involves unpaid work for the good of the community, for at least twenty hours and at most two hundred hours during the offender's leisure time. Only work for a non-profit organization is allowed. The Probation and After-Care Association supervises for the sole purpose of ensuring that the order is being carried out properly. Unlike in the other Nordic countries, community service does not contain any extra supervision aimed, for example, at controlling the offender's general behavior. The supervision is strictly confined to his or her working obligations.

Specific Provisions on Juveniles

The age limit for criminal responsibility is 15 years. Thus, children under 15 years of age at the time of the offense may not be subjected to criminal punishment. Young offenders (between 15 and 17 years of age) receive the benefit of a mitigated sentence. The court may always go below the prescribed minimum. In addition, the maximum sanction that the court may impose is reduced by one-fourth. The conditions for the waiving of measures and for the imposition of a conditional sentence are much less restrictive for young offenders. The third major difference concerns the imposition of imprisonment. Juveniles may be released after they have served only one-third of their sentence. A fourth major difference is that, unlike adults, young offenders may be placed under supervision during the probation period.

In 1994 a new sanction for those between the ages of 15 and 17 years (juvenile penalty) was introduced experimentally. It has two elements: supervision for a period of four months to one year, and a work order for community service or other similar activity for a ten to sixty hours. On the penalty scale, this new sanction is located on the level of the conditional sentence.

Waiver

The law recognizes a specific disposition called the "waiving of measures." The provisions in question give the police, the prosecutor, or the judge the power to waive further measures under certain circumstances that are set out in law. Accordingly, the law speaks of nonreporting in respect of the police, nonprosecution in respect of the prosecutor, and waiving the sentence in respect of the court. In all of these cases, the guilt of the suspect should be ascertained. The waiving of measures does not relieve the offender of liability for any damage caused by the offense.

Mediation

Experiments with mediation started in Finland during the early 1980s. For the same reason mediation was tried everywhere else, the idea was to provide an alternative to the official criminal justice system. At the moment, mediation is conducted in about one-third of Finnish cities and municipalities. Each year about five thousand offenders participate in the process (by comparison, some six thousand persons are sentenced to imprisonment each year). Since all major cities are involved, more than 70 percent of the population could have a case involving them dealt with through mediation. Mediation has not been integrated into the criminal justice system as a form of "specific penal measure." This would have destroyed its original idea and appeal. The system is based on voluntary participation by all sides. Despite its informal character, mediation has been recognized in the penal legislation as grounds for nonprosecution and the waiving of sentence. Thus the legal system encourages people to enter into negotiations, while at the same time it seeks to exercise control over whether mediation is all that is needed in cases where an offender has breached the provisions of criminal law (see, in more detail, Grönfors 1989; Lappi-Seppälä 1996).

B. The Sentencing System

The sentencing discretion of the courts is guided by several statutory provisions. Those of greatest importance are gathered in chapter 6 of the Criminal Code. The general provision in chapter 6, section 1 contains the leading principles of sentencing and the general sentencing criteria. The other provisions of the act (chap. 6, sec. 2–4 of the Criminal Code) describe specific criteria for aggravation and mitigation of the sentence. The discretion of the courts is also controlled and guided by appellate review and the decisions of the Court of Appeals and the Supreme Court. Both courts have power to examine all aspects of the cases brought before them.

The Discretion of the Courts

The Finnish Criminal Code establishes a punishment range for each offense. Normally, sentencing takes place within the limits set by the penalty scale for the specific offense. In certain circumstances the court may pass a sentence that is below the prescribed minimum. The first concerns the general grounds of reduction. This arises if the offender was between 15 and 17 years of age at the time of the offense, and in some cases of diminished responsibility, aiding, attempt, excessive self-defense, and necessity. When these grounds apply, the court may go below the prescribed minimum. The maximum penalty is reduced by one-fourth. The effect varies (as do the background reasons and principles of each of these factors). In addition, the courts have general authority in exceptional circumstances (other than those mentioned above) to impose a sentence that is less than the prescribed minimum (Criminal Code, chapter 3, sec. 5(2)). There are no circumstances under which the court may exceed the prescribed maximum.[3]

The courts are generally obliged to give their reasons in sentencing. However, before the enactment of chapter 6 of the Criminal Code, judges were very reluctant to give specific reasons concerning the type or severity of sentences. The sentencing reform brought a marked change in this practice. The Supreme Court played a key role. Encouraged by a series of decisions by the Supreme Court in the 1980s, the Magistrate Courts and the Courts of Appeal started to develop their own practices.

Supreme Court decision 3864/1982 serves as an example of a reasoned choice between conditional and unconditional prison sentences in aggravated tax evasion (one year's conditional sentence plus one hundred day fines):

> In considering whether A's sentence shall be conditional or not, the Court establishes that there are weighty reasons that speak both in favor of and against the suspension of sentence. Taken into account the total number of crimes and the degree of premeditation, as well as the fact that A has been in a leading position in a series of criminal activities in which a number of other people have taken part, it is evident

that the maintenance of general obedience to law requires an unconditional sentence in this case. On the other hand A, who was born in the year 1916, is suffering from a serious heart disease and it is likely that the execution of his sentence might worsen the disease and could even in fact endanger his life. These latter arguments give such support for suspension of the sentence that the maintenance of general obedience to the law does not require an unconditional sentence in this case.

The "Ladder Model of Penal Sanctions"

The leading principle in sentencing is "proportionality between the seriousness of the crime and the severity of the sanctions" (Criminal Code, chap. 6, sec. 1). The type and the amount of punishment are determined by the blameworthiness of the act and the culpability of the offender. Thus, penalties can be graded according to their severity in what is in effect a ladder model, with different types of penalties representing different levels of severity. As the blameworthiness of the offense and the culpability of the offender increase (this last element also incorporates the number of prior convictions), one moves step by step up the ladder, closer to the top. At the top is unconditional imprisonment. The other alternatives can be arranged roughly as shown in figure 3.1.

Community service is about at the same level of severity as unconditional imprisonment. Likewise, juvenile penalty and conditional imprisonment are located on the same level. The choice between sanctions of (roughly) similar severity is made on the basis of criteria other than those related to the severity of the sentence and the principle of proportionality.

The Prosecutor

In Finland the principle of legality governs criminal proceedings. The prosecutor has a duty to prosecute when the required evidence of an offense and offender

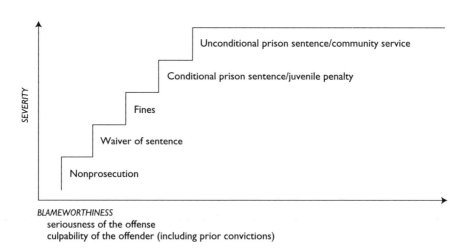

Figure 3.1. Alternatives for sentencing, arranged by severity.

are at hand (the principle of legality in prosecution). This rigidity is softened primarily by two elements: complainant offenses and the statutory rules of non-prosecution.

For complainant offenses, the public prosecutor has power to prosecute only when the complainant requests this. The majority of offenses are classified as noncomplainant offenses. In respect of such offenses, the public prosecutor may bring the suspect to trial regardless of the opinion of the complainant. However, in the case of noncomplainant offenses also, the complainant is a party to the proceedings. He or she must be given the opportunity to express his or her views in court and in every case has the right to claim damages in the same proceedings in which the offense is being tried. The complainant may also bring his or her own charges against the defendant or join the prosecutor's indictment.

For noncomplainant offenses the public prosecutor is obliged to bring charges as soon as there are "reasonable grounds" to suspect that the suspect is guilty of an offense. The rigid requirements of the principle of legality are softened by granting the prosecutor a right of nonprosecution (on other grounds besides lack of evidence). The prosecutor may waive prosecution only on the grounds listed in the Code of Criminal Procedure. The main grounds relate to the seriousness (petty nature) of the offense, the young age of the offender (young offenders under the age of 18), and special reasons of equity or expediency in criminal policy. Because of the strong legalistic tradition, the provisions on nonprosecution have seldom been used, though this is beginning to change. Finnish law does not recognize plea bargaining (on this, see Takala 1997, pp. 115–16).

Probation and Aftercare

Since the treatment model never quite took hold in Finland, the organization for probation and after-care work has remained modest. The basic responsibility for these tasks has been handled by a semiofficial organization, the Probation and After-Care Association. This association has traditionally handled a variety of supporting and aiding activities. The recent expansion of community sanctions has somewhat changed its work. The association now has responsibility for arranging for performance of community service orders. Its duty is to identify appropriate service hosts (and have them approved by the Ministry of Justice), prepare the suitability reports, prepare and confirm a service plan for each offender, supervise performance of the community service order, and inform the prosecutor about possible violations. PACA handles supervision orders of conditionally sentenced young offenders. It carries out juvenile penalties as well.

C. The Prison System

Until 1975, prison sentences were enforced and carried out according to the "principle of progression": the prisoner's status was lowest and his rights were at a minimum at the beginning of the sentence, and as time passed his position improved in accordance with the "progression" made. As a part of the policy shifts of the early 1970s, the aims and objectives of the enforcement were redefined by adopting the "principle of normalization" as the basis for enforcement. According to this principle, conditions should be arranged to correspond as much as possible to living conditions in society in general. According to section 3 of the Penal Custody Decree, "the sentence should be carried out so that the punishment entails only the loss of liberty." The sentence should be enforced so that it does not needlessly hinder, but instead promotes, the integration of the prisoner in society (see, in more detail, Lahti 1977).

Sentences of imprisonment are enforced either in closed prisons or in open institutions. The prison administration decides on the placement in the different prisons. Finnish prisons are not formally classified according to security status, nor are prisoners classified according to any security grading. However, the intensity of supervision varies to some extent between closed prisons.

If a sentence of imprisonment is not longer than two years, it may be implemented in an open institution. A further requirement is that the offender be capable of working or of participating in training offered in the institution and not likely to leave without permission. The open institutions hold about one-fourth of the prison population.

The regime in open institutions is more relaxed than in closed prisons. Prisoners in an open institution receive normal wages for their work, from which they pay normal taxes. One-quarter of their wages goes for their maintenance. Open institutions are in practice prisons without walls: the prisoner is obliged to stay in the prison area, but there are no guards or fences.

The closed prisons are either central or provincial prisons. Prisoners are obliged to work or to take part in vocational training or other activities unless relieved from that duty on grounds of health, schooling, or other reasons. Prisoners may also receive permission to pursue other studies either within or outside the institution. For those serving sentences longer than two months, a prison furlough may be granted. A prisoner may be furloughed from prison for a maximum of six days over a four-month period. Offenders between 15 and 20 years of age at the time of the offense may be placed in juvenile prison.

Release from Prison

All offenders sentenced to a determinate sentence of imprisonment are released on parole by the decision of the board of directors of the prison in question (in accordance with instructions issued by the Ministry of Justice). In general, recidivists are released after they have served two-thirds of their sentence, and first-time prisoners are released after they have served one-half of their sentence. Those placed in juvenile prison are released after they have served one-third of their sentence. In all cases, a further condition is that the prisoner has served at least fourteen days. An offender serving a sentence of life imprisonment may be released only if pardoned by the President of the Republic. Those held in preventive detention (see next subsection) as dangerous recidivists are in practice released on parole once the entire sentence originally imposed by the court has been served.

Release may be postponed beyond these minimum periods in general by one month or, at times, by even more if the grounds for discretion noted in the law are deemed to exist. In practice, release on parole is postponed only for two reasons: the offender either committed a new offense within a very short time of two previous releases or has violated the conditions of furloughs granted during the sentence. Postponement of release on the grounds of the type of offense and a prognosis of dangerousness is very rare. In all, parole is postponed in about 0.3 percent of the cases. Earlier release may be possible for various reasons related to aftercare (education, employment, housing) or general social reasons (illness, family-related reasons). In practice, 2 to 3 percent of offenders are released on parole earlier than usual.

The period of parole is the remaining sentence but lasts at least three months and at most three years. About one-third of those released on parole are placed under supervision. The supervisor may be the Probation and After-Care Association, a private individual, or the police. In principle, supervision involves both control and support. The court decides on revocation of parole if the offender commits an offense during the parole period and on the grounds of a behavioral infraction. In practice, all parole revocations are based on new offenses.

Preventive Detention

Finnish sentencing provisions generally rule out predictive sentencing on the basis of dangerousness. Still, there are some specific arrangements reserved for extreme cases. A small group of dangerous recidivists is held in preventive detention. This system is reserved for those violent offenders who have previously been sentenced for a serious violent offense and who are deemed to present a particular danger to the life or health of another. A dangerous recidivist may be placed in preventive detention if all of the following three requirements are met: the offender is sentenced to prison for a determinate period, at least two years for an offense that involves serious violence or particular danger to the life or health of another (e.g., murder, manslaughter, aggravated assault, rape); during the ten years preceding the offense, the offender had been guilty of similar offenses; on the basis of the evidence, the offender is manifestly to be deemed to present a particular danger to the life or health of another.

The sentences are enforced in "normal" prisons, but prisoners in preventive detention are placed in a special section. In principle, the sentence is enforced like any other longer sentence, with some restrictions concerning furloughs. The principal difference between preventive detention and normal sentences of imprisonment is that preventive detention for dangerous recidivists involves an indeterminate sentence. The offender need not be released even after having served the original sentence, if the Prison Court (a special court for these cases) deems that he or she continues to present a danger in the manner referred to in the law.

Use of preventive detention is quite restricted. Recently, there have been fifteen to twenty prisoners held at any one time in preventive detention and no one has been kept in custody longer than the term of his or her original sentence. In practice, then, the significance of preventive detention is that a small number of prisoners will not receive early release on parole. Even in its limited use, preventive detention contradicts the prevailing Finnish sentencing ideology, which is very reluctant to accept assessments of dangerousness as a basis for criminal sanctions. At the moment, the existence of this system is uncertain. Under a recent proposal, the entire system of preventive detention should be abolished. The dangerousness of the offender could be taken into account through normal rules of release on parole.

D. Statistics

Space constraints do not allow full discussion of sentencing, crime rate, and prison-rate trends in Finland. This subsection offers a brief overview. A comparison of these three data sources reveals that, while crime rates increased significantly over the past quarter-century, relative use of imprisonment and absolute rates of imprisonment declined.

Sentencing Statistics

The fine has been the principal punishment throughout the whole period (see table 3.1) partly because there is no general administrative penal law in Finland. Practically all offenses are classified as crimes and treated under the label of criminal punishments. Among those penalties imposed by the courts, the most striking feature is in the increase in the number of conditional sentences. Another important change is the decrease in the number of unconditional prison sentences in 1990–95.

Reported Crime

A steep increase in reported crime occurred between 1965 and 1975 (see table 3.2). Another period of increased criminality occurred from 1980 to 1990. Behind these changes were deep structural, social, and economic changes, rapid urbanization, and the development from a stable agricultural society into a highly developed postindustrialized information society in a period of some forty to fifty years. These changes are reflected especially in the number of traditional property offenses that dominate the overall picture of crime rate.

Prison Statistics

Between 1975 and 1997 the total number of prisoners fell from 5,469 (116 per 100,000 in population) to 2,974 (58 per 100,000 in population)(see table 3.3). During the 1990s, prisoner admissions continued to decrease, while the average number of prisoners seems almost to have stabilized. An explanation for this is that the average length of time served in prison has increased. This is not surprising because petty property offenses and cases of drunken driving have largely been

Table 3.1. The Use of Different Sentencing Alternatives in Finland, 1970–1995

	1970 N	1980 N	1990 N	1995 N
Offenses leading to a sentence*	208,441	321,476	462,807	390,747
Penalties imposed by courts	(57,675)	(72,282)	(81,627)	(61,208)
Unconditional prison sentence	10,212	10,326	11,657	6,754
Community service	—	—	—	2,803
Conditional prison sentence	5,215	14,556	17,428	13,624
Fine by the court	42,248	47,401	52,542	38,027
Summary proceedings				
Fine by a penalty order,	150,542	249,006	311,889	277,530
of these, traffic violations	129,140	189,752	252,239	234,977
Petty fine (traffic violations)	—	—	69,291	52,009
*Waiving of Penal Measures***				
Nonprosecution	—	1,692	3,170	6,209
Waiving of the sentence	1,259	1,236	1,049	415
Young offenders	691	529	599	733

Source: Statistics Finland, various years.

Note: The population of Finland is 5 million.
*If the offender has been convicted of several offenses the statistics are based on the main offense.
**Excluding traffic offenses.

Table 3.2. Offenses Reported to the Police in Finland, 1950–1995 (per 100,000 in population)

Offense	Year									
	1950	1955	1960	1965	1970	1975	1980	1985	1990	1995
Homicide	—	26	24	16	12	31	23	24	29	29
Assault	148	133	126	128	246	279	292	335	414	434
Rape	—	32	50	70	71	80	77	61	76	87
Fraud	179	163	161	562	632	202	627	321	786	379*
DWI	—	44	96	145	204	380	428	434	597	413
Theft	507	435	700	984	1,359	2,319	2,280	2,726	3,648	4,275
All offenses against the Criminal Code	1,279	1,139	1,472	1,784	2,696	4,069	4,144	5,449	8,056	6,995

Source: von Hofer (1997).

*A change in statistical classifications (related especially to credit-card frauds).

Table 3.3. Prisoners in Finland, 1975–1997

	1975	1980	1985	1990	1995	1997
A. Prisoners						
Serving their sentence	4,521	4,387	3,784	2,962	2,773	2,543
Fine defaulters	120	135	113	95	173	119
Remand prisoners	808	546	500	372	289	295
Preventive detention	7	6	12	12	13	17
Life sentence	—	—	—	28	34	43
15–17 years of age	117	60	36	33	11	7
Total number of prisoners	5,469	5,085	4,411	3,441	3,248	2,974
Prisoner admissions	13,347	10,114	9,307	8,831	7,755	6,201
B. Prisoners per 100,000 in Population						
All prisoners	116	106	90	69	63	58
Remand prisoners	18	11	10	7	6	6
*C. Type of offense**						
Robbery	411	473	326	254	305	274
Violent crimes	513	668	712	698	972	916
Drugs	—	—	65	98	213	362
Drunken driving	1,038	483	621	599	240	260
Property offenses	1,785	2,031	1,497	1,006	901	692
Other**	711	620	469	360	134	170

Source: Ministry of Justice, various years.

Note: Data represents annual averages.
*Figures in column 1 are for 1976.
**Figures for 1976–80 also include drug offenses.

removed from the prison statistics. In turn, the proportion of serious criminality and longer sentences has grown. The number of prisoners in preventive detention and those serving life sentences indicate the same phenomena.

Finnish Prison Figures in an International Comparison

In international comparisons, the Finnish imprisonment rates were among the lowest in the 1990s (see figure 3.2; for more detail see Kuhn 1998).

A similar comparison some twenty-five years earlier would have revealed interesting results (see figure 3.3 also Proband 1997). Between 1971 and 1995, the imprisonment rate per 100,000 residents increased in six of the ten countries compared in figure 3.3, stayed constant in three (Sweden, Denmark, and Germany), and fell in one (Finland). The developments in two countries are strikingly different: while the per capita prison rate fell in Finland from about 110 to 60, the numbers in the Netherlands rose from about 20 to over 60. Extending the period of comparison further would reveal even more dramatic changes.

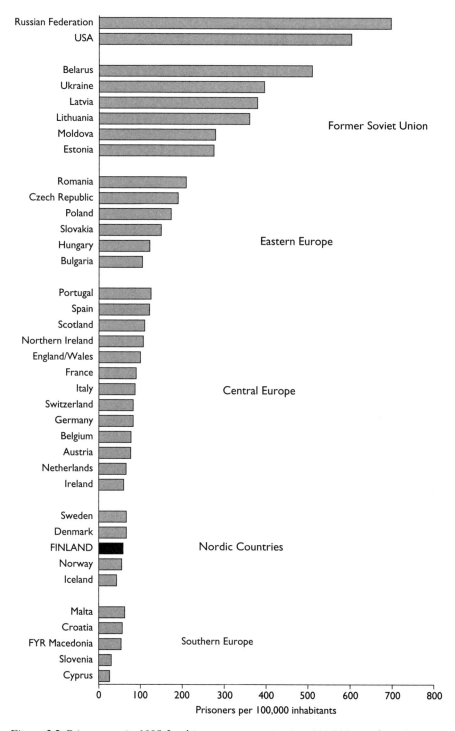

Figure 3.2 Prison rates in 1995 for thirty-seven countries (per 100,000 population).
Source: Kuhn (1998).

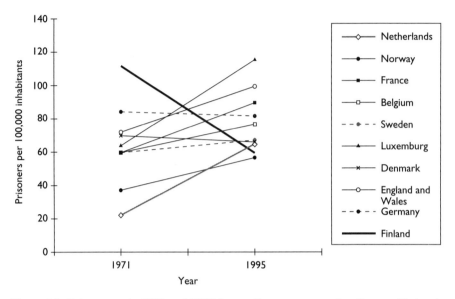

Figure 3.3. Prison rates in 1971 and 1995 for ten European countries. *Sources*: National Correctional Administration (1972); Kuhn (1998).

II. The Long-Term Decline in the Finnish Prison Population

At the beginning of the 1950s, the imprisonment rate in Finland was four times higher than in the other Nordic countries. Finland had some 200 prisoners per 100,000 inhabitants, while the figures in Sweden, Denmark, and Norway were around 50. Even during the 1970s, Finland's prisoner rate continued to be among the highest in Europe. However, the steady decrease that started soon after the Second World War has continued. Slowly, without dramatic changes (see figure 3.4), Finland reached the Nordic level. Between 1990 and 1995 the rate remained stable, and there continues to be a remarkable similarity among the Nordic countries in imprisonment rates.

A. The Change

To explain these trends and changes, we should start by asking why Finland initially adopted a policy that was so strikingly different from the policies of the other Nordic countries. One probable explanation relates to Finland's harsh history, including the Civil War of 1918 and the hardships of the two wars with the Soviet Union between 1939 and 1944. According to Nils Christie, these wars created a cultural climate in which severity was not measured by the same scale used in the other Nordic countries (Christie 1968, p. 171). In Christie's terms, the "penal value" of imprisonment was less (or experienced as being less) in Finland than in the other countries. This argument is consistent with the fact that turn-of-the-

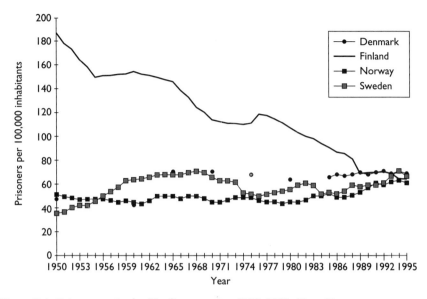

Figure 3.4. Prison rates in the Nordic countries, 1950–1995. *Note*: Data represent annual averages (including remand prisoners). *Sources*: von Hofer (1997); Lappi-Seppälä (1998).

century imprisonment rates in Finland were on the same level as those in other Nordic countries. Another and more technical reason for the initial difference in Finland's policy was the rigidity of the country's penal system. A high minimum penalty for aggravated theft introduced in 1889 (and abolished in 1972) made it difficult for judicial practice to adapt to changing perceptions of the gravity of theft offenses in a prospering society (cf. Lång 1989, p. 84). A third explanation may be found in severe sentencing practices for drunken driving, which kept the figures high as late as the 1960s and the early 1970s.

But what changed the situation? Why did the Finnish numbers go down at the same time as most European countries were experiencing rising prison populations? There is no simple explanation. The development in Finland resulted from several factors, including changes in penal legislation, in sentencing, and in prison policies. But behind these changes, there were changes in penal theory and thinking relating to criminal policy.

B. The Ideology of Criminal Policy

In the Nordic countries, criticism against "coercive treatment" (rehabilitation) became a central theme in public discussions in the mid-1960s. During the 1960s and 1970s a series of reforms were carried out that reduced the powers of the welfare authorities to use methods of coercive treatment and of the agencies of criminal justice to restrict liberty on rehabilitative grounds.[4]

This change reflects more than just a concern over the lack of legal safeguards. Behind this shift in strategies in criminal policy were more profound changes in the way the entire problem of crime was conceived. During the following decade the entire theoretical framework relating to the definition of the aims and the means of criminal justice policy underwent a profound change, as the social sciences and planning strategies merged with criminal justice policy analysis (Anttila and Törnudd 1992). This had its effects in the ways the aims of policy were conceived and conceptualized. The aims of criminal policy were defined so that they were in accordance with the aims of general social policy. Cost-benefit analysis was introduced; in making choices between different strategies and means, the probable policy effects and costs (in a wide sense, including also immaterial costs) were to be assessed. One result was that the arsenal of possible means of criminal justice policy expanded in comparison with the traditional (punitive or rehabilitative) penal system. Furthermore, the possibilities of environmental planning and situational crime prevention in controlling crime were discussed. This new ideology was crystallized in slogans such as "Criminal policy is an inseparable part of general social development policy" and "Good social development policy is the best criminal policy."

The Aims and Means of Criminal Policy

The emergence of the new planning strategies, the functionalistic approach to the problem of crime, the necessity doctrine, and a general mistrust of the effectiveness of penalties (punitive, deterrent, or treatment-oriented), all formed a theoretical background for the redefinition of the aims and strategies of criminal justice policy. The traditional main goals (such as simple prevention, the elimination of criminality, and the protection of society) were replaced by more sophisticated formulae. Beginning in the 1970s, the aims were usually expressed in two parts: first, the minimization of the costs and harmful effects of crime and of crime control (the aim of minimization), and second, the fair distribution of these costs among the offender, society, and the victim (the aim of fair distribution).[5]

The first aim emphasizes the minimization (not "elimination") of the costs and harmful effects of crime and criminal behavior rather than of the number of crimes. In so doing, it also draws attention to means that perhaps do not affect the level of criminality (something that is often extremely difficult to achieve), but which do affect the harmful effects crime has on different parties. By stressing not only the costs of criminality but also the costs in monetary and human terms of the control of crime, the formula draws attention to tangible and intangible losses that are felt, for example, through the operation of the system of sanctions. The aim of fair distribution brings into daylight the delicate issues of who should be responsible, and to what extent, for the tangible and intangible costs involved in crime and crime control. The analysis of the different parties (society, the potential or actual offender, the potential or actual victim) offers a framework for reasoned choices, identification of whom it would be fair and just to burden with the costs of different types of offenses and situations, and whether existing practices should be changed in the name of fairness and social justice.

Conceptualization of the aims of criminal justice policy and conscious cost-benefit thinking also had practical effects extending far beyond the criminal justice system. One result was that punishment, once regarded as the primary means of criminal policy, came to be seen as only one option among many.

Indirect General Prevention

After the fall of the ideal of rehabilitation, the aim of and the justification for punishment were also re-evaluated. A shift was made once again toward general prevention, but this time it was to be reached not through fear (deterrence) but through the morality-creating and value-shaping effects of punishment.[6] According to this idea, the disapproval expressed in punishment influences values and moral views. The norms of criminal law and the values they reflect are internalized; people refrain from illegal behavior not because such behavior would be followed by unpleasant punishment but because the behavior itself is regarded as morally blameworthy.

This hypothesis is based on different assumptions about why, how, and through what kind of mechanisms various features of the legal system influence social values and compliance with the law (see, in more detail, Lappi-Seppälä 1995).[7]

Compliance through personal morality. When punishment is seen as a form of society's disapproval, it can affect moral valuations through the emotive and suggestive force of moral language. This was one of the original ideas of the old Uppsala School (which laid the foundations of this theory, see Ekelöf 1942). But something other than mere "propaganda" may also be involved. People are often ready to reason in matters of morality, and the criminal law may also be taken as a reasoned argument in a moral discourse and in communication. Punishment could be understood as a response to a person's wrongdoing, a response that aims to persuade him or her to accept the moral judgment of the wrongdoing that it expresses (see Duff 1996, p. 32). Furthermore, criminal law may also be able to contribute to a change in attitudes simply by functioning as a means of focusing attention, as a "moral eye-opener" (Andenaes 1974, p. 116). Thus, the law may have a direct suggestive (emotional) effect without our conscious reflection on our valuations. It might lead to more genuine moral reasoning, or it might be only a means of focusing attention.[8] Whatever its effect, the moral disapproval (blame) expressed by criminal law has a central role in the prevention hypothesis.

Compliance through legitimacy. Law and its rules may be followed also because "fair play" requires it. Compliance is explained by the underlying feelings of solidarity towards a system of norms that is appreciated and accepted and that is perceived to be fair and just.[9]

Compliance through obedience and formal authority. Empirical studies confirm that conformity with the law is most often explained by conventional motives. Rules are followed for their own sake. Law is law, and as such, it must be obeyed.[10] This means that for many people the mere fact that an act is forbidden is enough to prevent them from committing it.

The difficulties involved in empirical testing of the effectiveness of general prevention are well known (see, e.g., Beyleveld 1980). These difficulties become even greater once we move from the simple hypothesis of direct deterrence to a more subtle model of indirect influence and of the relations between criminal law and social morality. The role of legitimacy and compliance with the law is documented in research conducted by Tom Tyler (1990). Survey results also support the assumption that to a great extent law-abiding behavior is based on mere habit and respect for formal authority. The few existing studies on the relationship between social values and the content of the criminal law present no clear conclusion (see the studies reported in Schumann 1989), perhaps because most of the research has been done on disputed subjects about which people have strong feelings, such as suicide, drugs, prostitution, and pornography. One cannot expect that the effects of legislative reforms in controversial areas can be measured a year after the reforms are carried out. The intended impact on social values takes place slowly, if ever. Nigel Walker's notion, "the legislation of one generation may become the morality of the next," reminds us of the necessary temporal perspective (Walker and Argyle 1964).[11] Furthermore, to explain a change in social values, one should look not only at criminal legislation but also at the educational work that has been conducted in the media, at schools, in homes, and so on during these years. In this process criminal law has clearly (in Johannes Andenaes's terms) also shaped the framework for moral education practiced in and by other social institutions.[12]

This view of the functions of the penal system has important policy implications. Compliance through personal morality requires that punishment have a moral overtone. Punishment must be regarded as an expression of the disapproval of society. A morality-creating effect requires moral talk. Morally neutral rehabilitation and treatment programs would not have a morality-creating force in the minds of the people. This notion also explains why criminal law has to remain as something unpleasant.[13] The system of sanctions must therefore remain as something that takes a moral stand on matters and confers blame. Compliance through legitimacy requires that the system of punishments is regarded as just and legitimate. Compliance with the law also becomes a matter of procedural justice. It is not only the outcome (the type of sanction) that matters but also the feeling of equal respect in the face of criminal law. And finally, compliance on the basis of respect for authority requires that the system maintain a minimum level of effectiveness. From time to time there must be evidence that the system works and is still in force. Punishments and their enforcement serve as a "reminder" or "convincer." To put it briefly: the aim of indirect prevention is best served by a system of sanctions that maintains a moral character (i.e., disapproval) and that is directed towards the act (i.e., demonstrates the blameworthiness of the act). The mechanisms require a system that is enforced with "fair effectiveness" and that follows procedures that are perceived as being fair and just. It also requires a process that respects the rights and intrinsic moral value of those involved and grants the parties (both offenders and victims) a chance to participate and express their views on the matter.

Policy Conclusions

The general policy conclusions drawn from these ideological changes can be briefly summarized. In crime prevention, criminal law is only one means among many. Other means are often far more important. This does not mean that we could do without criminal law. It still is of vital importance, but its mechanisms are subtle and indirect. The effective functioning of the criminal law is conditioned not necessarily by severe punishments but by legitimacy and perceived fairness. Certainly sentence severity and direct general prevention (deterrence) have a place. But we should not overestimate the deterrent potential and we should be more aware of the subtle mechanisms of indirect prevention in order to pursue both rational and humane penal policy. All in all, we should be realistic about the possibilities of achieving short-term effects in crime control by tinkering with our penal system. And what is most important, we should always weigh the costs and benefits of applied or proposed strategies of criminal policy. These were the tests that the earlier Finnish policy of imprisonment failed to pass. There was no convincing answer to the question why Finland should have three to four times more prisoners than its Nordic neighbors.[14] This realization was the premise for the series of legislative and criminal justice policy reforms that started during the shift of the 1960s and 1970s.

C. Legislative Reforms and Sentencing Policies

One may distinguish among three main types of legislative reforms that influence the imprisonment rate: those that shape the structure of the penal system and sentencing alternatives and principles, those that change the penal value and the level of sanctions for certain offense categories, and those that concern the enforcement of sentences of imprisonment and the system of parole. Of course, there are also other ways to reduce the prisoner rate. In 1967, the number of prisoners was reduced through an amnesty that shortened sentences of imprisonment by one-sixth. In 1969, the decriminalization of public drunkenness reduced the number of default prisoners (prisoners serving a sentence for unpaid fines) from a daily average of eight hundred to fewer than one hundred. However, the following observations concentrate on the reforms and changes that deal with the general structure of the system of sanctions. A more complete list of the criminal law reforms that have been carried out in Finland since 1967 can be found in table 3.4.

The System of Preventive Detention

The first reform in this series of legislative acts was the restriction of the use of preventive detention. The Finnish criminal justice system includes a provision for holding chronic recidivists in preventive detention after the completion of the sentence, if both the sentencing court and a special court so decide. Even during the 1960s, the large majority of these detainees had been guilty of repeat property

Table 3.4. Legislative Reforms, 1967–1991, That Have Affected the Number of Prisoners in Finland

Year	Reform
1967	The amnesty on the occasion of the fiftieth anniversary of Finland's independence reduced the length of all fixed-time prison sentences.
1968	The abolition of the offense of public drunkenness in conjunction with an amendment to the law on converting fines to imprisonment dramatically reduced the number of fine-default prisoners.
1971	The reform of the law allowing detention of dangerous recidivists entered into force in August. Since then only dangerous perpetrators of repeated offenses of violence can be placed in detention. The number of persons held in preventive detention was reduced from over two hundred to about a dozen.
1973	A law reform prescribing that the time spent in pretrial detention shall in its entirety be deducted from the sentence was enacted July 2.
1975	The reform of the legislation on the execution of sentences modernized the law, inter alia, by removing the penalty of imprisonment at hard labour.
1976	The new rules on parole that entered into force February 1 liberalized the parole system, inter alia, by reducing the length of the obligatory time in prison from four to three months.
	The new law on conditional sentences that entered into force April 1 considerably relaxed earlier restrictions associated with this sanction. The option of allowing the combining of a conditional prison sentence with an unconditional fine sentence turned out to be of strategic importance, inter alia, in the sentencing of drunken drivers.
1977	The new chapter of the Penal Code dealing with sentencing entered into force January 1. The earlier rules stipulating special latitudes for recidivists were abolished. (At the same time new provisions of day fines were entered into force).
	The new statutes on drunken driving entered into force April 1. This reform allowed the emergence of new informal sentencing practices introducing a conditional sentence (typically in combination with a fine) as the standard penalty for drunken driving.
1978	The law on converting fines to default imprisonment was revised.
1979	A law reform that entered into force on April 1 made it easier to place serial offenders in remand prison.
1987	A law that removed the special penalty for conscription defaulters for members of Jehovah's Witnesses entered into force.
1989	The reform of the law on the execution of sentences once again reduced the minimum time that must be spent in prison before parole. The new minimum is fourteen days. The parole rules were liberalized in other ways, too.
1990	The new law on pretrial investigation reduced the powers of the police to hold suspects for interrogation.
1991	The statutes on dropping prosecution and absolute discharge were reformed by a law that entered into force January 1. The goal was to considerably increase the use of these methods.
	A trial project involving experimentation with community service as an alternative to unconditional imprisonment was launched by a law that entered into force January 1.
	The first part of the total revision of the Finnish Penal Code entered into force January 1. The latitudes for, inter alia, property offenses were reduced. Prison sentences of up to three months are now measured in days.

Source: Törnudd 1993.

crimes. On the basis of an amendment passed in 1971, the option of preventive detention was restricted to dangerous violent offenders only. The number of persons held in detention as recidivists dropped by 90 percent in one year, from 206 to 24. Since then, the annual average has been between 10 and 20 prisoners. This means fewer than three sentences each year. And, to repeat, those placed in prevention are released, as a rule, once the term of their original sentence has passed.

General Trends in Sentencing, 1950–1995

In an international comparison, Finland's criminal justice system offers relatively few alternatives to imprisonment. The Finnish judge traditionally had the basic options of sentencing the offender to unconditional imprisonment, conditional imprisonment, or a fine. However, the few alternatives to imprisonment have been used fairly effectively.

The fine has been the principal punishment throughout this century. Still, the most effective alternative to imprisonment has been the conditional sentence. The statistics (see table 3.1) show how the popularity of this sentencing option increased throughout the entire period it has been available. From 1950 to 1990 the number of conditional sentences handed down in a year grew from some 3,000 to 17,428. The growth was especially rapid between 1970 and 1980. A closer look at the sentencing patterns of the courts reveals two major changes between 1950 and 1990 (figure 3.5).

The left side of figure 3.5 traces a major change in how the courts mete out unconditional sentences of imprisonment. Between 1950 and 1965, the average length of sentences of imprisonment fell from thirteen months to seven months. The right side illustrates another change. Up to the mid-1960s, two out of three sentences of imprisonment were imposed unconditionally. Beginning in the late 1960s, the proportion of unconditional sentences fell from 70 percent (1966) to 42 percent (1980). These two changes can be explained primarily by changes in sentencing for two distinct crime categories: theft and drunken driving.

Reducing Penalties for Theft

Long custodial sentences imposed for traditional property crimes kept the prison population at its peak level during the early 1950s. High minimum penalties and rigid offense definitions for aggravated forms of theft affected the number of Finnish prisoners as late as the early 1970s. However, in 1972 new definitions and new punishment ranges were introduced. As a result, there was a clear change in sentencing practice. In 1971, 38 percent of offenders sentenced for larceny received a custodial sentence. Twenty years later, in 1991, this had decreased to 11 percent (see Lappi-Seppälä 1998; Törnudd 1993, 1997).

The next amendment that affected sentencing came in 1991. One aim was to limit the use of imprisonment by introducing narrower punishment ranges. Courts were also encouraged to use short sentences of imprisonment by instructing them to mete out the shorter sentences in days instead of months. Furthermore, this

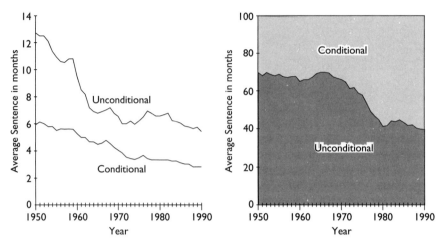

Figure 3.5. Length of sentences of imprisonment imposed by Finnish courts (left) and choice between conditional and unconditional sentences (right), 1950–1990. *Sources*: Statistics Finland, various years; Lappi-Seppälä (1998).

reform increased the use of fines and reduced the average length of sentences of imprisonment.

The changes in the sentencing patterns in cases of theft are dramatic (see figure 3.6.) For example, in 1950 the median length of all sentences of imprisonment imposed for theft was 12 months. In 1971, the median sentence was still 7.4 months, but in 1991 it was only 2.6 months. Of course, one has to take into account that in the long run the typical forms of theft have changed. Crimes against individual victims and households have been replaced in part, for example, by petty shoplifting and more serious forms of theft from the stores.

The effects of the 1991 reform are harder to establish, since in 1992 the sentencing rules for multiple offenders (offenders who are sentenced for more than one offense to a joint punishment) were amended. However, the evidence suggests that the 1991 reform caused an additional "drop" in the already falling trend of penalties. After that, practice seems to have been stabilized.

Drunken Driving and the Sentencing Reforms of the 1970s

Drunken driving plays a special role in Nordic criminal policy, especially in Finland. We have hard drinking habits and many problem users, but at the same time we have a very restrictive and intolerant attitude towards drinking and driving. This combination has kept drunken driving among the key issues in debates on crime policy. A substantial part of our prison problems during the 1960s resulted from fairly long unconditional sentences of imprisonment imposed for drunken driving.

During the 1970s this practice was changed in favor of noncustodial alternatives. The movement was started by the courts themselves, but the development

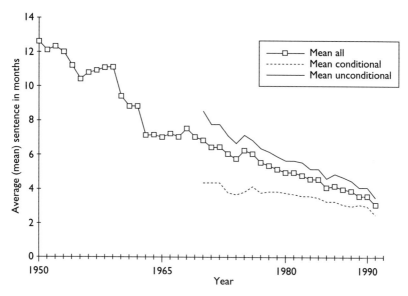

Figure 3.6. Average length of sentences of imprisonment for theft in Finland, 1950–1990. *Sources*: Statistics Finland, various years; Lappi-Seppälä (1998).

was reinforced by separate legislation. The definition of drunken driving was modernized by an amendment to the law in 1977. In this connection, the legislature took a definite stand in favor of conditional sentences and fines.

On the same occasion, three other bills were passed increasing the use of conditional sentences and fines in general (and particularly for drunken driving). Reform of the conditional sentence act created an opportunity for combining a fine with a conditional sentence. Reform of the day-fine system raised the amount of day fines, thus encouraging the court to use fines also in more serious cases. The most important 1977 reform from a principled point of view was, however, enactment of general sentencing rules. These provisions in chapter 6 of the Criminal Code crystallized the aims and values of the new criminal political ideology ("humane neoclassicism"). They gave the courts general guidance in meting out punishments for all offenses. They also provided a framework for further discussions on the proper sentencing level. The first target of such discussions was drunken driving. These discussions were run by the judges with only organizational help from the Ministry of Justice.

The efforts to change sentencing practice regarding drunken driving were a success (see figure 3.7). In 1971, 70 percent of drunk drivers received an unconditional sentence. Ten years later, in 1981, the rate had dropped to 12 percent. Since the reform in 1977, the normal punishment for aggravated drunken driving has been conditional imprisonment together with an unconditional supplementary fine, while "ordinary" drunken driving cases (blood alcohol count under 0.12 percent) are dealt with by fines.

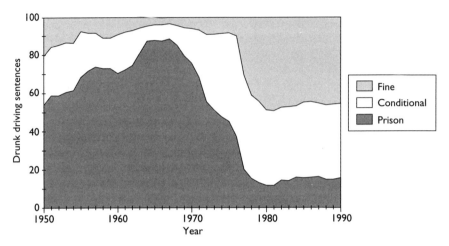

Figure 3.7. Sanctions for drunken driving in Finland, 1950–1990. *Sources*: Statistics Finland, various years; Lappi-Seppälä (1998).

The sentencing reforms of the 1970s have been a policy success. One reason is that these reforms constituted a coherent and consistent approach with clear aims. The handling of drunken driving illustrates a successful legislative strategy: if sentencing patterns are affected by several different elements, one may have to change them all in order to achieve the intended result. On the issue of drunken driving, the legislature first created the opportunity for combining a fine with a conditional sentence, then raised the amount of day fines. After passing a bill on drunken driving, they enacted new provisions on sentencing, and these provided the framework for discussions of sentencing levels and normal punishments. In a way, all these reforms were a part of one big package.

New Sentencing Alternatives: Community Service

The next major change in the penal system was the introduction of community service in the 1990s. In order to avoid "net widening" and to ensure that community service really will be used in lieu of unconditional sentences of imprisonment, a two-step procedure was adopted. In principle community service could therefore be used only in cases where the defendant would otherwise have received an unconditional sentence of imprisonment.

The early experience indicates that on the whole the new sanction has been adopted in the way that the legislators wanted. About nine of ten persons sentenced to community service would have received a custodial sentence. Along with the increase in the number of community service orders, the number of unconditional sentences of imprisonment has decreased (see figure 3.8). In particular, drunken drivers have benefited from the new option.

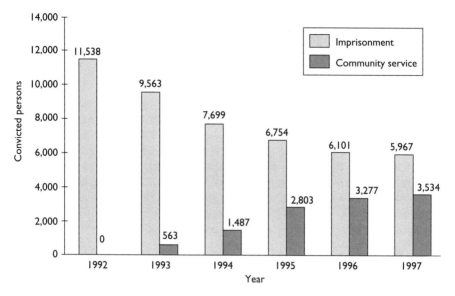

Figure 3.8. Use of unconditional imprisonment and community service in Finland, 1992–1997. *Sources*: Statistics Finland, various years; Lappi-Seppälä (1998).

In 1996, the average daily number of offenders serving a community service order was about one thousand. At the same time there were some three thousand inmates in Finnish prisons. It is therefore fair to argue that within a short period of time community service has proven an important alternative to imprisonment. In practice, community service is seldom used for younger offenders, since relatively few sentences of unconditional imprisonment are imposed on them. Even though no offenses (or offender groups) were intended to have any priority, community service has come to be used especially in cases of drunken driving.

Specific Offender Groups: Juveniles

The age limit for criminal responsibility in Finland is 15 years. Young offenders (between 15 and 17) receive a mitigated sentence. In addition, the conditions for waiver of sanctions (for example, nonprosecution) are much less restrictive for young offenders. Young offenders under 21 who are sentenced to imprisonment are usually released on parole after one-third of the sentence has been served, instead of the normal one-half. Even so, there is no special juvenile criminal system in Finland, in the sense that this concept is understood in the continental legal systems: there are no juvenile courts and the number of specific penalties applicable only to juveniles has been quite restricted. According to the division of labor adopted after the fall of the rehabilitative ideal during the 1970s and the 1980s, the criminal justice system has taken care of punitive measures, while the

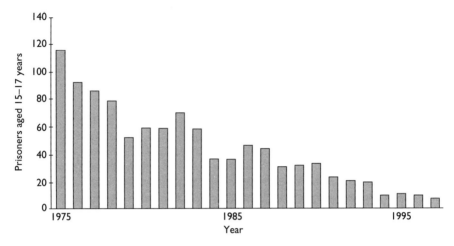

Figure 3.9. Prisoners aged 15–17 years serving sentence in Finland, 1975–1997. *Note*: Data represent annual averages. *Sources*: Ministry of Justice, various years.

child welfare and social policy organizations have supporting, counseling, and aiding roles. This means, for example, that young persons between 15 and 17 years of age are subject both to the criminal justice system and to the child welfare system. The emphasis in the child welfare system lies in its supporting role: finding a job or housing, receiving vocational training, and so on.

The detrimental effects of closed institutions on the lives of young people have been widely acknowledged since the 1960s. Despite the lack of specific measures for juveniles, there has been a deliberate policy preference against the use of imprisonment for the youngest age groups and in favor of relying on the traditional alternatives. The willingness of the courts to impose custodial sentences on young offenders has decreased throughout the entire period. In addition, the Conditional Sentence Act was amended in 1989 by including a provision that allows the use of an unconditional sentence for young offenders only for extraordinary reasons. These changes had a clear impact on practice (see figure 3.9). At the moment there are about one hundred prisoners between the ages of 18 and 20 and fewer than ten in the 15 to 17 age group, while as recently as the 1960s the numbers were ten times higher.

Parole

During the enforcement of sentences of imprisonment the authorities can use the parole system to control the length of time actually spent in prison. Use of this system has also proven to be a very powerful tool in controlling prisoner rates. Any changes in the basic structure of the parole system will have visible effects on prison figures. In Finland all prisoners except those few serving their sentence in preventive detention or serving a life sentence will be released on parole. At present, as the result of a series of reforms, the minimum time to be served before the prisoner is eligible for parole is fourteen days. During the mid-1960s this period was shortened from six to four months, during the mid-1970s from four to three months, and finally in 1989 from three months to fourteen days.

D. Criminality and the Prisoner Rate

The inescapable question remains: has the decrease in the prison figures been reflected in the Finnish crime rate and, if so, in what way? As table 3.2 shows, there has been a steep rise in reported crime especially since the late 1960s. It would, of course, be quite tempting to conclude that this rise resulted from the drop in the prisoner rate. However, a closer analysis does not confirm this hypothesis. There are several ways to approach the issue.

Sentencing Patterns and Criminality in Finland, 1950–1994

The following analysis examines trends in sentencing patterns and reported robbery and drunken driving from 1950 to 1994 (for a more detailed analysis, see Lappi-Seppälä 1995). The severity of sentences (the length of sentences of imprisonment) has decreased, while the level of reported robberies has increased (see figure 3.10). Sanctions and robberies have varied independently.

Between 1950 and 1965, it was possible to halve the sentences of imprisonment for robbery with no effect on the crime rate. During the subsequent period when the length of sentences of imprisonment stayed relatively constant (1965 to 1990), the number of reported robberies first grew five times higher, then decreased by one-quarter, then again almost doubled, and finally decreased by almost 40 percent.

Figure 3.11 contains information on the use of imprisonment for drunken driving and the number of reported (thin line) and actual (thick line) crimes. (The latter figures have been measured on the basis of routine roadside controls; see Lappi-Seppälä 1995, p. 151).

Again, it was possible to decrease the use of unconditional sentences of imprisonment for drunken driving from 50 percent to 20 percent with no effect on the crime rate (1975 to 1978). The severe sentencing practice during the mid-1960s, in turn, coincided with a period of relative stability in reported crime. The main finding illustrated in figure 3.11, however, is that during a period when the use of imprisonment and the average penalties stayed constant, the incidence of drunken driving (short line) was halved (1978 to 1985). This change in the level of criminality is usually explained by a steep increase in the risk of apprehension (as a result of an increase in routine controls).

All of the above indicates that the level of crime is affected primarily by factors other than the severity of sentences. The level of criminality depends primarily on structural, social, and situational factors. In Finland, for example, the consumption of alcohol and the crime rate seem to be much more interrelated than are the level of penalties and the crime rate.

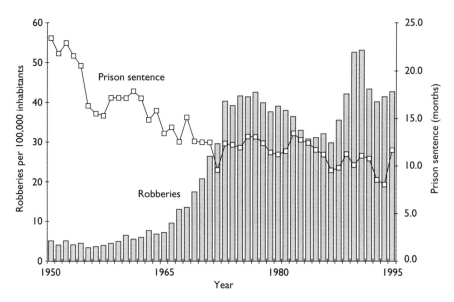

Figure 3.10. Sentencing severity compared to level of reported robberies in Finland, 1950–1995. *Sources*: Statistics Finland, various years; Lappi-Seppälä (1998).

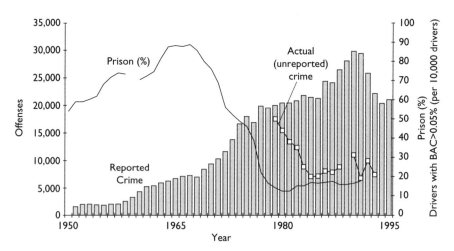

Figure 3.11. Imprisonment for drunken driving compared to reported and actual criminality in Finland, 1950–1995. *Sources*: Statistics Finland, various years; Lappi-Seppälä (1998).

*Imprisonment Rates and Criminality
in the Nordic Countries, 1950–1997*

The analysis still leaves us, however, with the fact that while the total amount of reported crime increased between 1950 and 1995, the number of prisoners fell radically. The commonsense assumption that there *must* be something that ties these two factors together is hard to overcome. Basically, this assumption is correct in the sense that the fall in the prison numbers must have had *some* effect on the crime figures. The point, however, is that there is strong evidence supporting the claim that this effect has been so modest that it would be hard to see the difference in a graphical presentation had the imprisonment rate in Finland remained on its original level since the 1950s. The best test is a comparative analysis of Finland and the other Nordic countries. These countries form an exceptional unity in that they have social and structural similarities but very different penal histories. In this way they provide an opportunity to test how the changes in penal practices have been reflected in the crime rates (see Figure 3.12).

A simple comparison between the Nordic countries reveals a striking difference in the use of imprisonment, and a striking similarity in the trends in recorded criminality. That Finland has heavily reduced its imprisonment rate has not disturbed the symmetry of Nordic crime rates. This result is in line with those estimates of incapacitation that suggest that a 50 percent decrease in the imprisonment rate would lead roughly to a 2 percent increase in the crime rate as a result of the loss of the incapacitative effect. (See, e.g., Tarling 1993, p. 154; these estimates do not take into account possible general preventive effects.)

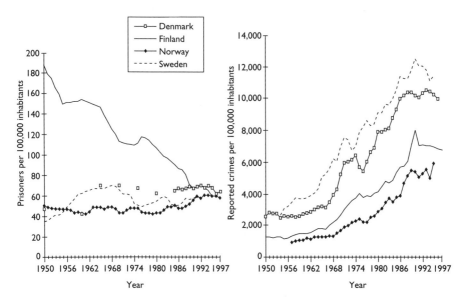

Figure 3.12. Prison rates (*left*) and reported crime (*right*) in the Nordic countries, 1950–1997 (per 100,000 population). *Sources*: von Hofer (1997); Lappi-Seppälä (1998).

The figures also confirm once again the general criminological conclusion that crime rates rise and fall according to laws and dynamics of their own, and sentencing policies in turn develop and change according to dynamics of their own; these two systems are fairly independent of one another.

E. Concluding Remarks

The decrease in the Finnish prison population has been the result of deliberate, long-term, and systematic policy choices. The value of this achievement does not decrease merely because part of this development is explainable also by structural and demographic factors, such as the aging of the large postwar birth cohorts (cf. Aho 1997, p. 272). In addition to the deliberate legislative changes since the mid-1960s, the courts have had an independent role in the change. The courts had already eased their sentencing practice during the 1950s. Later, too, the legislature was strongly supported by the judiciary, especially the courts of first instance.

When we take the crucial importance of sentencing practice into account, it is not surprising that more and more attention has been paid to the regulation and guidance of sentencing. The method of guidance varies from one legal system to another. In European tradition, the guidance is usually based on statutory sentencing yardsticks, such as sentencing principles and criteria, on the control exerted by the appellate courts, and on information systems supporting both these functions. In the Anglo-American legal culture (mainly in the United States), however, guidance has been available through various systems of "sentencing guidelines" (for comparative analyses, see Ashworth 1992b and von Hirsch 1987). Also the level of guidance depends on the motive for it. Stricter guidance may have been necessary, for example, for the implementation of a given substantive approach (such as a change in the relative level of sanctions for a given offense), but the motive may also be nothing more than a reduction in unwarranted disparities in sentencing. A connection can be made also between stricter guidance of sentencing discretion and changes in the aims of criminal punishment. A system tending towards specific prevention requires wide discretion, while a system emphasizing the principle of legality and general prevention is cognizant also of the risks to individual freedom presented by wide powers of discretion.

Finland's sentencing reform of the mid-1970s had multiple objectives. To a large extent, it stressed the neoclassical values of equality and proportionality in criminal law. In addition, it aimed to affect the level of sanctions (e.g., to reduce the increases in severity brought about by recidivism). Connecting the reform to a number of other legislative amendments was an effective method to alter the level of sanctions for traffic drunkenness.

The preceding paragraphs contain a short explanation of the effects of statutory changes (together with other factors) on the imprisonment rates and level of sanctions. What follows is a look into the contents of the legislative guidance given to the sentencing judges (principles and bases of sentencing) and the technical solutions adopted in the Finnish guidance model.

III. Penal Policy and the Law of Sentencing

Sentences are set within minima and maxima prescribed by law. The decision of the court consists of three distinct decisions or steps. First, the court must establish the applicable sentencing ranges. The basic scale is defined in each statutory crime definition. However, in some cases the scale may be reduced. The second decision is usually the choice of the type of the sanction to be applied. For minor offenses the options are a fine and waiver of sanctions. For middle-range and more serious offenses, the additional options are conditional and unconditional imprisonment, community service, and a juvenile penalty. The third decision concerns the amount of punishment (the number of day fines and the amount of the individual day fine, the length of imprisonment, and the number of community service hours). "Sentencing" in its narrowest sense thus refers to the discretion exercised by judges within the given latitude in deciding on the amount of punishment. The widest sense would include also a choice among different types of sanctions, and the establishment of the penal range in cases where there are reasons to adjust it (in other words, to go below the prescribed minimum penalty). In the following, the term is used in the latter, widest, sense.[15]

Finnish law contains provisions on each of these subdecisions. The provisions to be taken into account in deciding on the severity of sanctions (quantity) are gathered together in chapter 6 of the Criminal Code. Those provisions are of fundamental importance also in the choice of sanctions in cases where the choice between different sentencing alternatives is at the same time a decision on the severity of the sentence (as it usually is).

A. Material Principles and Sentencing Criteria

The penal ideology behind the sentencing provisions in chapter 6 of the Criminal Code makes a clear choice among theories of punishment and aims of the criminal justice system. The aim of the penal system is general prevention. The assumption is that this effect is reached not through fear (deterrence) but through the moral-educative effects of punishment. According to this theory, the disapproval expressed in punishment is assumed to influence the values and moral views of individuals. As a result of this process, the norms of criminal law and the values they reflect are internalized. People refrain from illegal behavior not because it is followed by unpleasant punishment but because the behavior itself is regarded as morally blameworthy.

The general policy implications of this theory are discussed above. In general terms, this ideology emphasizes the fairness and justness of sanctions. In sentencing, proportionality, predictability, and equality are the central values. These ideas are also clearly expressed in the basic norm of sentencing (chap. 6, sec. 1 of the Criminal Code).[16]

> In measuring a punishment all the relevant grounds increasing and decreasing the punishment, as well as the uniformity of sentencing practice, shall be taken into

consideration. The punishment shall be measured so that it is in just proportion to the harm and risk involved in the offense and to the culpability of the offender manifested in the offense.

The leading principle in sentencing is proportionality. The foundation of this principle is often sought in retributive notions. But beyond these notions lie the values of liberty and the classical prohibitions against misuse and arbitrariness. The principle of proportionality has its roots in the concept of the rule of law (*Rechtstaat*), legal safeguards, and the guarantees of citizens against the excessive use of force. From this point of view, it is more important to prevent overly harsh and unjustified penalties than it is to prevent overly lenient ones. The main function of the proportionality principle is, thus, to impose the upper limit that the punishment may never exceed. It is much less restrictive when considering the possibilities of imposing sentences that are less severe than the offender's act would prima facie have deserved (see Törnudd 1996, p. 85).

This ordering of priorities and the "asymmetry of the proportionality principle" has been confirmed in several provisions in the Criminal Code. The courts have a general right to go below the prescribed minimum whenever exceptional reasons call for such a deviation. Also, the grading of offenses reflects this same idea: the lists of criteria that make an offense an aggravated one are always exhaustive, while the lists of mitigating criteria are always "open-ended." If a particular feature of the offense would call for a milder assessment, then the courts have the discretionary power to consider the offense one requiring special consideration, even if none of the criteria specified in the law are at hand. Also the sentencing rules in chapter 6 of the Criminal Code embody the same principle, since the phrasing of the mitigating criteria leave somewhat more scope for judicial discretion than does the phrasing of the aggravated factors (see Anttila and Törnudd 1992, p. 15). In addition, the principles guiding the use of community service allow the courts to impose a sentence more lenient than is prima facie required. And, finally, the law recognizes a specific group of sentencing provisions that allow deviation in a more lenient direction on grounds other than those related to "just deserts."

The principle of proportionality raises three types of questions: how can one assess the seriousness and blameworthiness of offenses, how can one assess the severity of sanctions, and how can one link these two together in a manner that respects the requirement of "just proportion"? The provisions in chapter 6 deal primarily with the first issue. The remaining two are the subject of philosophical, policy, and legal theory inquiries, for which the present context allows very little scope.

Assessing Seriousness and Blameworthiness

According to the general provision (chap. 6, sec. 1 of the Criminal Code) the starting points in assessing the seriousness (and blameworthiness) of offenses are, first, harm and risk, and, second, the culpability manifested in the offense. In addition, the law contains (in chap. 6, sec. 2–4 of the Criminal Code) a list of specific aggravating[17] and mitigating criteria. Some of these specify the concept of culpability, and some can be explained by other factors. The list is not, however, exhaustive, and the elaboration and more detailed development of these criteria is left partly to legal doctrine and partly to the courts.

Consequences — harm and the risk of harm. The consequences and their seriousness are determined by the extent to which the crime has in fact either harmed or endangered the interest being protected. The starting points in assessing the harm and risk created by the offense are, thus, to be found in the interpretation of the statutory crime definition and the interests that the criminal prohibition is supposed to protect. Additional guidance is given in the statutory grading criteria (in cases where the legislature has graded the offense into different degrees of seriousness, which is a common practice in Finnish law). Two additional principles govern this assessment. The "principle of endangerment" requires that attention be paid not only to those harms that have already resulted from the act but also to those harms that could have been anticipated before the act. The "principle of subjective coverage" requires that only those consequences that the actor foresaw (intentional crimes) or could (and should) have foreseen (crimes of negligence) may be taken into account.

Assessing the seriousness of the consequences is, in a way, an "offense-internal" matter.[18] The issue may be decided without a need to turn to outside sources or guidance. Accordingly, the Sentencing Act does not contain closer instructions in this respect. The only criteria that deal with the dimension of harm is a provision on organized crime in chapter 6, section 2(2) of the Criminal Code: "the commission of the offense as a member of a group organized for serious offenses" serves as a general ground for aggravation. The provision was motivated with reference to the threat that organized crime poses for security and social order (and, thus, to the exceptionally harmful consequences of this sort of criminality).

Culpability. Culpability focuses basically on the mental state of the actor at the time of the offense. To assess the content and the degrees of culpability, one has to dive into the theory of criminal justice and the principles of substantive criminal law. Sentencing theory makes the following distinctions.

Culpability as act-oriented guilt	The wording of chapter 6, section 1 of the Criminal Code (culpability "manifested in the offense") stresses "act-orientation." The moral evaluation of the reprehensibleness of the actor must be restricted to the concrete offense and it may not be expanded to take account, for example, of the entire personality of the offender or the moral merits and demerits of his or her way of life.
Culpability as desires and/or beliefs	Substantive criminal law theory contains several clues and distinctions regarding the degree of culpability. Direct intent and purpose reflect higher culpability than does mere foresight of consequences; on the other hand, the degree of probability with which the actor

Culpability as an ability to conform with the law

Culpability as acceptable/reprehensible motives

judged that his or her act would constitute an offense has an effect. Also, the firmness of the criminal decision and the decisiveness with which the perpetrator works his or her way towards the desired result help define the degree of culpability. The legislature has taken this dimension into account by confirming the "degree of premeditation" as a general aggravating criterion in sentencing in chapter 6, section 2(1) of the Criminal Code.

Blame presupposes that the actor could have acted (and could have been required to act) otherwise (on the "conformity principle," see esp. Jareborg 1988, p. 75). It is an essential requirement of justice that the amount of blame and punishment must be graded according to the actor's ability to conform with the law. An important part of the legislative sentencing criteria specifies the concept of culpability by describing situations in which the actor's ability to follow the demands of norms is to a greater or lesser level influenced by external or internal impulses or forces (chap. 6, sec. 3(1) and 3(2) of the Criminal Code).

Motives matter. Acts that are committed for respectable and altruistic motives or with the intention to benefit other members of society (compassion, mercy, civil disobedience, social adequacy) incur lesser punishments. This idea is partly reflected in the provision in chapter 6, section 3(1) of the Criminal Code, which allows mitigation for crimes that have been committed because of "strong human compassion." Unacceptable and reprehensible motives (envy, spite, greed, egoism, revenge, racism), in contrast, easily call for harsher punishments. So far the legislature has confirmed only one type of aggravated motive, committing an offense for remuneration (chap. 6, see 2(3) of the Criminal Code). In 1999 the law reform committee was considering whether racist and xenophobic motives should also be included in the law as a general aggravating factor.[19]

Recidivism and Prior Convictions

The role of prior criminality in sentencing is puzzling. The principle that first-time offenders deserve more lenient treatment is generally accepted (see esp. von Hirsch 1981). Almost (but not quite) equally accepted is the principle that the number of prior convictions or previous crimes increases the penalty. The reasons for identifying an offender's prior record as an aggravating factor, however, are far from clear. Much depends on the concept of culpability adopted, general policy considerations, the overall aims in sentencing, and the underlying "crime ideology" (what is essentially "wrong" in any crime; on this, see Jareborg 1988). Use of one's prior record as an aggravating factor may be justified by pointing out that those who repeatedly break the law are likely to do so also in the future (dangerousness). It could be argued, too, that those who still continue committing crimes after having been punished show a clearer lack of respect for the provisions of the law (culpability in the sense of "evil will"). One might also refer to the need to maintain the credibility of the system of criminal justice and the urge to uphold the message that the norms on criminal law are to be taken seriously (general prevention). Since this message is given in the form of a sanction, recidivism requires increased penalties, since otherwise it would be hard to convince anyone that the legislature is seriously concerned with the protection of the interests that had been violated.

The problem is not so much in justifying the use of recidivism as an aggravating factor (there are more than enough competing justifications) but in determining how to keep it in proper limits. In fact, most of the justifying reasons suffer from serious drawbacks. It may well be that repeating an offense shows that the offender is in some way "stubborn" in the face of the norms of society, but whether this really is a result of the offender's free and unrestricted choice is another matter. The effects of imprisonment are well known; prison weakens the offender's ability to live up to the standards of society, and sometimes a relapse into crime is simply the result of lost opportunities. The argument of dangerousness hardly fits with most cases of repeated offending, since the majority of crimes committed by persistent offenders are of a petty nature. Mechanical aggravation of penalties for recidivists has had a long tradition in European criminal codes — and as with so many other traditions in the field of criminal justice, there are good reasons to take a critical look of this practice. One of the achievements of the criminal legislation passed during the twentieth century was a kind of "devaluation" of this aggravation that was accomplished by replacing old casuistic rules with more flexible models of regulation. In Finland this achievement took place with the sentencing reform in 1976. One of the main aims was to limit the significance of prior record in sentencing by replacing old mechanical provisions with a regulation that allowed aggravation only when recidivism implies increased culpability.

According to chapter 6, section 2(4) of the Criminal Code, the previous criminality of the offender may increase the penalty "if the relation between the offenses on the basis of their similarity or for another reason shows that the offender is apparently heedless of the prohibitions and commands of the law." Recidivism should increase punishment only if it indicates greater act-oriented culpability.

Casual or occasional repetition should not increase punishments. Neither should recidivism that is due more to a lack of social possibilities to conform with the law than to the offender's hostile and heedless attitudes towards the norms of criminal law. To find out whether the accused has shown "apparent heedlessness," the judge must compare the new crime with the previous ones and look at the lapse of time between crimes, the amount of premeditation, and the motivational connection between these crimes.[20]

On Mitigation

Mitigating factors fall technically into two subgroups: grounds that justify the use of a reduced penalty scale and grounds that are to be taken into account only within the chosen latitude.

Grounds for reduction. The Criminal Code recognizes six circumstances under which the court may choose the sentence from a reduced penalty scale: young age, diminished responsibility, excessive self-defense, nonexculpatory necessity in certain cases, attempt, and aiding. All these provisions reflect the general principles of liability that separate punishable from nonpunishable behavior. Between the area of total exemption from liability and full responsibility is the intermediate area of diminished blame. Children under the age of 15 are free from all criminal liability, but young offenders between the ages of 15 and 17 years receive a mitigated sentence. Those lacking penal capacity are not punished, and those for whom this capacity is only diminished are less blameworthy and deserve mitigation on the grounds for culpability. (This mitigation may be counter-balanced by prior convictions or evident dangerousness of the offender.) Self-defense and necessity exclude liability (either by justifying the act or by excusing the offender), while self-defense or necessity that are almost justifying or exculpatory may mitigate the sentence. The same idea applies to all defenses (and to the principles of liability, as well). In a way, most mitigating factors carry the job of the general principles and grounds for criminal liability only one step further. They remind us that those very same arguments that dictate whether the offender is to be punished usually are of relevance also after the border between nonpunishable and punishable behavior has been passed. Sentencing law is a "microcosm" not only of the principles of punishment and the aims of criminal justice but also of the principles of substantive criminal law. This sets a rather challenging task for anyone who wishes to condense the principles of sentencing into a nutshell (or into a sentencing grid).

Grounds for mitigation related to culpability. Most of the mitigating criteria in chapter 6, section 3 of the Criminal Code specify the concept of culpability by describing the situations in which the actor's ability to control his or her actions has been diminished by external or internal impulses or forces. According to chapter 6, section 3(1) of the Criminal Code, the punishment may be mitigated if the crime has been committed under "significant pressure, threat or other similar influence on the perpetration of the offense." Pressure may be direct or indirect, physical or psychological. Chapter 6, section 3(2) of the Criminal Code grants the benefit of mitigation when there is "strong human compassion leading to the offense or exceptional and sudden temptation or a similar factor that has been conducive to lowering noticeably the offender's ability to obey the law." Temptation may mitigate the sentence only when it has been both exceptional and sudden. Provocation may be included in a list of the "similar" factors, but self-imposed intoxication may not mitigate the sentence, even if there would be no disagreement that the offender's ability to control his actions has been substantially impaired.

Mitigation on other grounds. The provisions in chapter 6 of the Criminal Code also contain mitigating rules that fall outside the scope of culpability and seriousness of the offense. These "external" arguments are based either on pragmatic reasons of criminal political expediency or on values such as equity and mercy.

The meritorious conduct of the offender belongs primarily in the first category. According to chapter 6, section 3(3) of the Criminal Code, voluntary attempts by the offender to prevent or remove the effects of the offense or to further the clearing up of his or her offense will reduce the punishment. An offender who honestly repents the crime and shows remorse may deserve mitigation also on grounds of culpability. However, the scope of this provision is wider. The point is not so much the offender's moral evaluation but more pragmatic reasons and reasons of criminal justice policy expediency. The promised mitigation in these cases may encourage the offender to compensate the victim for the damage incurred. Also, cooperation with the police may be rewarded. However, the provision refers only to the offender's "own" offense. The law offers no reduction in cases where the offender discloses information that helps to clear up criminal offenses committed by other persons. Finnish law does not recognize the institution of "crown witness," nor does the law recognize any form of plea bargaining.

Another group of "external" factors is based on the principles of equity, mercy, and humanity. The provision concerning the cumulation of sanctions (chap. 6, sec. 4 of the Criminal Code) states: "If the offense has caused or the resultant punishment has imposed on the offender another consequence that together with the punishment imposed on the basis of the application of the grounds mentioned previously in this chapter would lead to a result that is unreasonable in comparison with the nature of the offense, such a situation is to be taken into consideration so far as is reasonable in measuring the punishment." In other words, extra hardship resulting from the consequences of the act (for example, if the offender was injured or lost his or her job) may reduce the penalty from the normal level.

These ideas are reflected also in the provisions on waiver of penal measures. According to chapter 3, section 5(2.4) of the Criminal Code, the court may waive penal measures in case "punishment is to be deemed unreasonable or lacking in purpose, with consideration to (a) reconciliation between the offender and the complainant, (b) other action taken by the offender to prevent or remove the effects of his or her offense, or to further its being cleared up, (c) his or her personal circumstances, (d) the other consequences of the offense to him or her, or (e) actions by the social security and health authorities." Essentially the same provision applies to nonprosecution as well.

On Prevention and Proportionality

Chapter 6 contains a clear statement against aggravation of punishment for the purpose of general prevention (deterrence). In routine cases such a policy would hardly be a sensible option anyway, since the intended marginal preventive effect would remain practically nonexistent. The sentence of a certain drunken driver is of no interest to the general public, and even fewer people would be aware that the judge decided to raise the penalty by one month from the tariff of which the public has, at best, only a vague idea.

No aggravation of punishment for the purpose of general prevention. But what if the case has aroused intensive public interest? Then the cognitive requirements of marginal prevention might be met and there might rise the temptation of a general preventive aggravation in order to give warning examples for potential law-breakers. The counterarguments are well known. It would be a breach of the principles of predictability, equality, and proportionality to sacrifice someone only because his or her case has become "national news." We must first ask, of course, what has made the case so interesting, and then only if this reason has nothing to do with the seriousness and blameworthiness of the case, would aggravation be in conflict with the principle of proportionality. How to solve this conflict depends on how much we appreciate these principles, how serious the deviation would be, and what we expect to achieve by this deviation. For those who would be willing to sacrifice the principle of proportionality in these cases on consequentialist grounds, two points have to be made. First, even if the case has attracted much public interest, it is highly unlikely that the examples given would have long-lasting effects (if any). It might also be wise to stop for a moment to consider what features people really value in the legal system and how the public expects their courts to operate when they are under political and public pressure. Would it really increase public confidence and the legitimacy of the system of criminal justice if the courts every now and then made examples of people and then returned to normal routines? Would it not be more sensible to assume that a system that in such a manner disrespects the basic principles of liberty and justice will in a long run lose its respect and legitimacy and thereby also its positive effects on behavior?

The Finnish penal policy takes a definite position, not only on the relevance of deterrent considerations in routine cases but also on general preventive aggravation in the form of exemplary sentences. However, there remains a third case of general preventive aggravation, based not on examples or on routine decisions in lower courts but on the aim of changing the whole practice also in future cases. But this is another matter. Here we are dealing with "sentencing policy." The subject is not the implementation of certain policies but the content of the underlying principles and norms. The question is, who has and who should have the power to make such decisions? In the continental tradition this is in the hands of the legislature. But whether the legislature or the Supreme Court (or the sentencing commission) has this power, these decisions are of such a general social importance that there are good reasons to demand that they be made only after careful consideration and planning, on the basis of best possible knowledge, and after open discussions. Courtrooms seldom provide the proper framework for this type of planning and decision processes.

Value- and goal-rationality of the sentencing criteria. Nothing that has been said indicates that the system of criminal sanctions would lack motivational or deterrent effect, nor that the aggregate sentencing results from the courts would be irrelevant from the point of view of prevention. Of course, the general level of sanctions and the way these sanctions have been allocated in general is of some preventive significance (albeit a smaller one than the public and politicians usually tend to think). The point is that it is not the task of a single judge to decide on the general level of sanctions, nor is it the task of the judge to establish general rules on how the sanctions are allocated. It is the task of the judge to apply the law in a manner that takes into account legal safeguards and the individual rights of the parties in criminal proceedings; it is the task of the legislator to establish the norms that meet societal requirements and protect vital individual and collective interests. It is also the task of the legislator to formulate these rules in such a manner that the practices that grow out of their concrete application fulfill the utilitarian goals that are being sought in the best possible way, respecting also all the other aims and values to be taken into account while using criminal law as an instrument (among others) for promoting the "good life" and the protection of autonomy (and other goals of criminal law).

This brings us finally to the question of the relation between rational sentencing criteria and political aims involving crime prevention. In order to judge the goal rationality of a single rule or sentencing criterion, one has to draw a distinction between the decisions that concern the whole system (the total amount of available penalties) and decisions that concern the allocation of penalties within the given limits. From this point of view, there is an evident (but often overlooked) link between consequentialist aims (the protection of interests) in the legislative level and value-based argumentation in court decisions. Once we have agreed on the general level of penalties, we have to think what would be the most rational way to allocate those resources. And when we consider this, we find that the very same criteria that are typically justified with reference to the principle of proportionality turn out to be functional—once sentences are seen not as isolated decisions but as aggregated practices. For example, assuming that the preventive effect of punishments at least is grossly related to its severity, it is wise to relate the level of sanctions with the harmfulness of the offense (since it is more important to prevent more harmful offenses than less harmful ones). But it is wise also to save resources when this expenditure would not benefit anyone, for example, in cases where the actor would have been uninfluenced by any motivational threat.[21]

The Choice of Sanction

Sentencing decisions involve not only the amount of punishment but also the type of punishment. Only in the most serious cases is unconditional imprisonment the only alternative available. In more than 95 percent of the sentencing decisions to be made the court has at least two options. Bringing in the qualitative dimension does not obliterate the basic ladder model, consisting of five levels: waiver of sentence, fines, conditional imprisonment, conditional imprisonment combined with a supplementary fine, and unconditional imprisonment (see figure 3.1).

There are no problems in the application in this model to the principles and provisions of chapter 6 of the Criminal Code: they can be applied to the extent that the different sanctions offer alternatives with different degrees of severity. Thus, both the choice between fine and imprisonment and the decision between conditional and unconditional imprisonment are based primarily on the seriousness of the offense (the harm and the risk of harm), culpability, and the previous convictions of the offender, and on other factors described in chapter 6, sections 2–4 of the Criminal Code. However, the recently adopted community sanctions (community service and the juvenile penalty) represent a partial exception to this rule. In these cases, a "third dimension" must be taken into account.

According to section 3 of the Community Service Act, "an offender who is sentenced to imprisonment shall be sentenced to community service instead of a specific, unconditional sentence of imprisonment of at most eight months, unless the unconditional sentences of imprisonment or the earlier community service sentences of the offender or other weighty reasons are to be deemed an obstacle to sentencing him or her to community service." Further prerequisites for sentencing the offender to community service are stipulated in section 4, which requires that the "offender has given his or her consent to performing community service and that it may be assumed that he or she will be able to cope with community service." Section 3 creates a clear presumption in favor of community service over unconditional imprisonment. This presumption may, however, be overturned with reference to the offender's previous criminality, and especially by his or her previous community service orders. An offender who would otherwise be eligible for community service but who has already been sentenced to this punishment several times may lose this benefit. The fundamental criteria to be taken into account in all cases are the consent of the offender and his or her suitability for community service.

According to section 3 of the Juvenile Penalty Act, this sanction, which has been introduced as an experiment in a few jurisdictions, can be imposed for an offense where a fine "in consideration of the seriousness of the offense and the circumstances that led to the offense is to be deemed an insufficient punishment and there are no weighty reasons that demand the imposition of unconditional imprisonment." In other words, if no juvenile penalty would be imposed in this case the offender would in principle be sentenced to conditional imprisonment, which in terms of severity falls between a fine and unconditional imprisonment. A supplementary provision introduced into the act in 1999 clarifies the choice between conditional imprisonment and the juvenile penalty. According to this provision, the offender shall be sentenced to a juvenile penalty rather than conditional imprisonment when "the imposition of a juvenile penalty is to be deemed justified for the prevention of new offenses and for the promotion of the social adjustment of the offender." Through the amendment, the application of the juvenile penalty has been tied more clearly than before to individual-preventive and rehabilitation-oriented goals.

The decision on the selection of the type of sanction is ultimately based on criteria other than the principle of proportionality. However, the principle of proportionality is also present. The question of the imposition of a community service order is raised only in situations where the seriousness of the offense and the culpability of the offender already have led to the selection of unconditional imprisonment. The juvenile penalty, in turn, may be applied only when it has been determined that the seriousness of the crime and the culpability of the offender require a heavier penalty than a fine (but when unconditional imprisonment is still deemed unduly harsh). In other words, community sanctions can also be placed in the ladder model. The special feature is that more than one sanction is situated on the same level of severity, and the selection between them is then based on criteria other than the principle of proportionality.[22]

Summary: Proportionality and Other Values in Court Decisions on Punishment

The principles for the application of sanctions and the relative position of the available sanctions are summarized in figure 3.13. The sanctions are situated on the ladder vertically from the least to the most punitive. In the horizontal dimension, three basic points of departure can be identified: the principle of proportionality, the rehabilitative grounds for applying community-based sanctions, and the general mitigation of sanctions for reasons of expediency and equity (A–C). Moving from left to right within the framework of the principle of proportionality demonstrates an increase in the blameworthiness of the conduct in question. At the same time, moving from the bottom to the top one moves toward more severe sanctions (A). If there is more than one option on the same level of severity, the selection between them takes place on the basis of criteria other than blameworthiness (B). Grounds that are external to an assessment of blameworthiness that also appear are the principles of expediency and equity in general criminal policy (C). These may justify both a change in the amount of a certain sanction and the application of a lower rung on the ladder.

The principle of *ultima ratio* requires that the use of criminal law be restricted to the smallest justifiable minimum. Argument in sentencing should begin at the lowest level of the ladder. The judge must first consider the more lenient options. In borderline cases the principle of *in dubio mitius* applies; this principle advises the judge to choose the least restrictive option.[23]

Arguments of proportionality and sentence severity. In minor cases, the court may first consider the possibility of waiver of sentence, provided that the prosecutor has not employed his or her own right of non prosecution (figure 3.13, steps 1–2). At the second level, the court must decide between fines and imprisonment. This choice is based on the seriousness of the offense and the blameworthiness of the offender. If the offense may be settled by fines, the seriousness of the offense determines the number of day fines while the daily income and financial situation

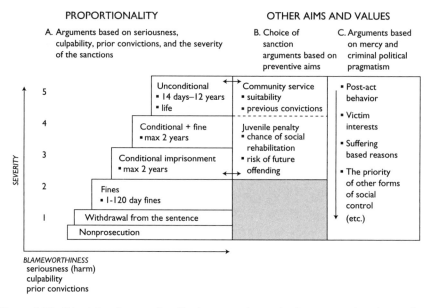

Figure 3.13. Principle of proportionality in sentencing and other sentencing aims and values

of the offender determine the amount of day fines (steps 2–3). If the blameworthiness of the act requires a prison sentence, the court may take a position on both the type (conditional or unconditional) and the length of the sentence.[24] The choice between conditional and unconditional imprisonment is based primarily on harm, culpability, and prior convictions. The age of the offender is also of importance (steps 3/4–5). In borderline cases the court may combine a conditional sentence with a fine (steps 4–5).

Preventive aims and community sanctions. If the court decides in favor of a conditional sentence, and the offender was under 18 at the time of the commission of the offense, the court may order a juvenile penalty. The decision is made primarily (after the 1999 reform) on rehabilitative and preventive grounds (level 3/4). If the court decides on a sentence of unconditional imprisonment that is no more than eight months long, community service may be imposed instead of imprisonment if the offender is deemed to be suitable for community service, and earlier community service orders are not a bar to this (level 5).

Mitigation based on external factors. The meritorious conduct of the offender after the commission of the act—repairing damages, taking part in mediation, or cooperating with the policy—may be grounds for mitigating the sentence on more or less pragmatic grounds. Mitigation on the grounds of reasonableness and equity may be relevant if the offender is of an advanced age, there has been an accumulation of sanctions, or there is another serious reason for this. These factors may justify the use of a more lenient sentence, other mitigation in the sentence, or a waiver of the sentence.[25]

This juxtaposition crystallizes the relationship between the sanctions and the leading principles in their application. However, it does not provide any guidance in concluding what acts would go on which rung of the ladder. Indeed, we need other tools to locate the concrete points of departure for sentencing. The Finnish system does not recognize numeric guidelines. However, the points of departure are provided by the concept of the "normal punishment," which was presented in connection with the drafting of chapter 6 of the Criminal Code.

Reducing Unwarranted Disparity:
The Notion of Normal Punishments

The Sentencing Act also contains a model, usually referred to as the "notion of normal punishments," for the structuring of the sentencing decision. Its purpose is to reduce unwarranted disparity by structuring the decision so that the courts can have a firm starting point for their decisions. This sentencing model is based on a provision in chapter 6, section 1 of the Criminal Code that requires the judge to pay special attention to "uniformity of sentencing practice." Unless special reasons are at hand, the response to the offense should be the penal sanction that is imposed most frequently in similar cases, referred to as "normal punishment."

Sentencing according to the ideology of normal punishments has been outlined as a two-stage process. First, the points of comparison are defined: the most typical cases of the offense in question (the "normal offense") and the relevant punishment (that is, the range or zone of normal punishments). During the second stage, the case at issue is compared with the typical case. The comparison is based on an interpretation of sentencing criteria and arguments.[26]

All in all, the sentencing judge needs three kinds of information. First, statistical information about the penalties (the ranges of normal punishment). What penalties are used most often, for example, in typical cases of drunken driving? Second, information about the typical cases (descriptions of normal offenses). What is the typical case of drunken driving that corresponds with the penalties used most frequently? Third, the criteria that should be taken into account when the case at hand is compared with the normal offense. What aggravating or mitigating features would justify a departure from the normal sentence? Answers to the third (normative) question above are given partly by the legislature, partly by higher court decisions, and partly by the legal doctrine. The judge may receive information concerning questions one and two from several sources. Annual court statistics contain information on the average penalties. In addition, several separate analyses have been made that give a rather detailed picture of the court practice at least in respect of the most common type of offenses. They enable the courts to see what penalties have been imposed for offenses that were committed in an approximately similar manner, in which the consequences have been on about the same level and the offenders had generally the same type of criminal record (see Lappi-Seppälä 1990, 1992b).

Of course, empirical analysis does not relieve the judge of the duty of making normative evaluations. It only provides the relevant information that is needed to give the judge a practical "starting point." The comparison between the case at hand and that described as being the "typical offense" is made by interpreting the normative sentencing criteria (the aggravating and mitigating circumstances) as given by the normal sources of sentencing law and through the accepted principles of legal argumentation. Sentencing is, and remains, an act of the normal application of law. The use of statistical information in sentencing does not turn the decision into mechanical application of statistical average penalties.

The benefit of this method is that the ranges of normal punishments help in the decision-making process by offering a concrete basis for comparisons and by anchoring the scale of crimes and the scale of punishments to each other. One could say that by offering the starting points, the model solves (part of) the problem of cardinal proportionality. What remains is, of course, the comparison between the offense at hand and the "normal offense" (with the corresponding "normal punishment"). This problem of ordinal proportionality is easier to solve, because it is easier to compare entities of the same quality (internal offense seriousness, rather than offenses and sentence severity).

IV. Guiding the Sentencing Judge under a Civil Law Tradition

Guiding the sentencing judge is a highly controversial and delicate matter in any jurisdiction (Ashworth 1992b; Council of Europe 1987). This is also appreciated by Finnish legislators, who offered the model described in section III only as an heuristic tool, not as a binding norm to be followed. However, the 1976 reform means that sentencing no longer lies in the realm of "free" discretion. By demanding that courts pay special attention to uniformity of sentencing practice and that they must give reasons when they deviate from the range of normal punishments, the legislature took a step of principal importance. Critics who pointed towards disparities in sentences could earlier be dismissed with references to "judicial independence" and to the legality of the decision (that the punishment is still within the prescribed scale). After the enactment of chapter 6, judges were legally obliged to take account of decisions of other judges and courts.

The model increases the predictability of the system and promotes equal treatment in similar cases. The normal punishment approach above all offers a tool for enhancing uniformity in sentencing, commenting on it, and ultimately appealing to the Court of Appeal when there is reason to do so. It is not, like most sentencing guidelines in the United States, a system used systematically to oversee the level of punishment and make the changes in this level that are required by an evolving criminal policy. In general, the normal punishment approach does not propose any single and straightforward answer to the question "who should have the actual power, and through what means, to make decisions about the concrete level of sanctions?" There is no simple answer to this question—although the starting point is basically clear. In a civil-law tradition any initiatives in the matter should come from the legislature or be based on a source that has been accepted as an authoritative and valid source of (sentencing) law. The Supreme Court is considered such a source. However, the Supreme Court in Finland has been rather reluctant to give concrete guidance on the level of penalties. Nonetheless, it has pronounced its views on matters concerning the choice between different sentencing alternatives in different situations (conditional sentence, community service, etc.)

Thus, in countries with a civil law tradition the sanction level is determined through something that can perhaps best be described as "a loosely organized process of argumentation." In this discourse the arguments are presented in the form of legislative acts (penalty scales, graded descriptions of offenses) and legislative history that shows the intended direction (while closer guidance or agreement on the concrete level of sentences has to be reached through other means) and in court decisions from higher and lower instances, in legal theoretical analysis, and in research on criminal policy. The discussion is conducted in a rather disorganized manner; mainly in training programs, seminars, and meetings for judges. In other words, the notion of normal punishments is not an "adopt first, then apply" model. It merely provides an orientation model that influences the attitude of the judge and a framework for discussions that have to be conducted again and again. Evidence of existing sentencing disparities has to be presented regularly in order to emphasize the importance of efforts towards more uniform sentencing practice.

This type of open model of regulation can leave unsatisfied any person searching for a clear, concrete approach. However, the civil law tradition has good grounds for providing this model. First, guiding the work of the courts should take place in accordance with constitutional principles and through forms of decision making that have become established and culturally accepted (for an especially well-developed analysis in this respect, see Canadian Sentencing Commission 1987).

Part of the legalistic tradition of the Finnish system is that the courts do not accept instructions from outside. However, the reverse of this tradition is that the courts take seriously all argumentation that is derived from the established sources of law. This is also a sensible way to construct the guidance of sentencing practice. On the basis of, and with the help of, a model of guidance that may look modest from the outside (a few words in a law text and a few comments in legislative history), the courts are ready to discuss the contours of sentencing practice. The practical significance of this is considerably strengthened by the possibility in a small country of assembling all lower court judges to discuss sentencing practice by organizing a dozen seminars in different parts of the country. This is indeed done in connection with every legislative reform that is of the least significance. In addition, the superior courts, including the Supreme Court, regularly organize similar meetings in their own jurisdictions.

One might ask, Should this system be changed in order to get a "stiffer grip" on sentencing practices? Should more detailed regulation be enacted by making the penal scales narrower and by giving more concrete recommendations? Much experience argues against such a development.

In order to set concrete standards for sentencing, the legislature would have to provide very detailed guidance, so detailed that it would be practically impossible.

The level of detail would have to be reduced in a way that would lead to equal treatment of acts that are of a different level of seriousness (which is also a violation of the principle of equality).

There is also another good reason for the legislature to refrain from giving concrete recommendations. Studies on the sense of justice, which measure attitudes towards punishment, have time and again shown how the level of punitiveness increases as the level of the discussion becomes more general. It is easy for a person who looks at the matter from a distance, who has not studied the details and background of the cases, to demand that an unknown miscreant be sentenced to stiff punishment. Such persons compensate for the absence of detailed information by filling in the gaps with distorted images of the offense created by the media. Facts that correspond to the reality and effects of the punishment are replaced by beliefs and hopes. A person who is better acquainted with the matter and who sees the operation of the system in his or her work has a different perspective and is prepared to accept a considerably more lenient treatment. Furthermore, the legislature, which sees matters from a distance, would set the punishment at a considerably higher level of punitivness than would individual Members of Parliament, to say nothing of individual judges, if they had the case before them for judgment.

These reasons for not having the legislature make concrete recommendations about sentencing answer the question whether Finland should move toward using U.S.-style sentencing guideline systems or sentencing commissions. Experiences from these systems demonstrate the dangers involved in restricting the sentencing discretion of the judges by imposing narrow sentencing latitudes decided by political bodies, though some U.S. systems have made it possible to pursue rational and consistent sentencing policies. For someone with a background in the continental tradition, however, a system in which the legislature decides only in broad terms on the ranges, and the rest is at the discretion of the judges seems to be less vulnerable to short-sighted and ill-founded political interventions. What, of course, is needed are statistical information on existing sentencing patterns, reasoned higher court decisions, and open discussions about preferable sentencing levels. But the last word in these matters should be given by the judges who have the facts at their fingertips and who are familiar with the reality of crime (and who unlike the public and the politicians are not dependent on the information given by the media).

V. Conclusions and Discussion

The fall in the prison population in Finland could be described as a "criminal policy triumph." But for a proper sense of perspective, it should be stressed that rather than a massive move toward decarceration, the change could also be described merely as a "normalization" of prison rates: a move from a level that was absurd to a level that can be considered to be a fair Nordic level—albeit one-tenth the present U.S. level.

A. The Conditions of Antirepressive Penal Policy

Still, the Finnish example shows that prisoner rates can be regulated and that decarceration is possible. The question is, By which means and under which conditions can this be achieved?

Proportionality and the Level of Penalties

The simplest answer that can be seen in the Finnish experience is that there is no simple answer. Long-lasting and visible results seem to require a complex combination of several means that should be used simultaneously, as demonstrated by the list of legislative reforms in table 3.4. It is evident, however, in the Finnish experience that the longest-lasting and most effective results can be achieved by influencing sentencing practices of the courts, either by legislative reforms pertaining to particular offenses or by realignment of general sentencing principles.

For some, the idea of having a sentencing reform that involves a list of "nonrepressive law reforms" based on the concepts of justice and proportionality may sound odd. Some of those who opposed the reform ideology of the 1970s argued that sentencing based on the idea of proportionality would favor punitive sentencing policies and thus lead to increased severity of punishments (see Bondeson 1989, pp. 300–301.) However, as applied in Finnish penal policy and sentencing practice, the adoption of proportionality-based sentencing principles has not led to harsher sentences. Rather, the contrary. The principle of proportionality has little effect on the overall level of punishments. Its main function is to ensure that offenses receive just penalties relative to each other and to their relative seriousness ("ordinal proportionality"). The principles of proportionality and equality can insure internal consistency of the system and justice in the same sense that offenses of similar seriousness receive similar punishments and that offenses of different seriousness receive punishments correspondingly ranked in severity. But when we turn to the question of the absolute level within which these comparisons of relative seriousness and severity are made, the principle of (cardinal) proportionality gives much weaker guidance, and other factors become more important. What really matters is the prevailing criminal policy ideology and the social and political contexts in which the sentencing model is to be applied.

Criminal Theory and the Ideology of Crime Policy

A nonrepressive policy must have as its basis a conception of policy that looks beyond crime prevention and takes into account the costs of both crime and crime control and aims for a fair distribution of these costs. What also is necessary is a broad enough conception of the methods of criminal justice policy, putting criminal justice in its proper place among the other (more effective) methods of criminal justice policy. Most important, the doers, movers, shakers, and makers must be aware of all the issues involved. To achieve this, experts and scholars should reach out to the public. The development of convincing crime prevention strategies outside the domain of criminal law reduces political strains on the criminal justice system. Clarifying the (modest) effects of punishments and informing the public of these effects correspondingly reduces unfounded confidence in a punitive penal system. Of course, there are wide cultural differences in this point. As comparative analysis reveals, Finnish judges place much greater reliance on community service than do their colleagues in England and the United States (see Takala 1997). It is difficult to establish how many, if any, of these differences result from differences in the theory and philosophy of crime control. The theory of indirect general prevention has several advantages because it combines pragmatic aims of criminal justice with ideas of fairness and respect for legal safeguards. It may also be backed up by commonsense notions of compliance with the law. For most people, it may appear not at all implausible to assume that laws are usually observed in a civilized democratic society because people feel they are worth following, not because people are afraid of penalties if they violate them.

Political Culture and Legal Professions

Opposition to repressive penal policies is not by itself enough to explain the reforms carried out in Finland. What made this ideology into the official criminal policy? The question has been examined by Patrik Törnudd. He stresses the importance of a political will and a consensus to bring down the imprisonment rate. As he summarizes, "those experts who were in charge of planning the reforms and research shared an almost unanimous conviction that Finland's internationally high prisoner rate was a disgrace and that it would be possible to significantly reduce the amount and length of prison sentences without serious repercussions on the crime situation" (Törnudd 1993, p. 12). This conviction was shared also by civil servants, the judiciary, and the prison authorities and, equally important, by the politicians—to the extent that they did not oppose the reform proposals prepared by officials in the Ministry of Justice.

Finnish criminal policy is exceptionally expert-oriented. Reforms have been prepared and implemented by a relatively small group of experts whose thinking on criminal policy, in basic points, has followed similar lines. The development of Finnish prison policy was for over thirty years deeply influenced by the recently deceased Director-General K. J. Lång, who was the head of the Finnish Prison Administration and a central mover in several important criminal policy reforms. The power of these professionals was reinforced by close personal and professional contacts with senior politicians and with academic researchers. Three ministers of justice during the 1970s and 1980s had direct contact with research work; one of them, Inkeri Anttila, was a professor of criminal law and the director of the National Research Institute of Legal Policy at the time of her appointment. Director-General Lång also served a short but important period as a minister of justice. Consequently, and unlike in many other countries, crime control has never been a central political issue in election campaigns in Finland. None of the "heavyweight" politicians has called for populist policies, such as three-strikes laws or "truth in sentencing."

This leads us to the third element in the Finnish criminal policy composition — the role of the media. The media have taken a sober and reasonable attitude towards issues of criminal policy. In general, the Finns have been saved from low-level populism. But that may be changing. The emergence of a new afternoon newspaper market a few years ago, and an increase in the number of television channels and the resulting intensified competition for viewers have brought crime reports onto Finnish television as well.

"Attitudinal readiness" among the judiciary has been an important factor. It, indeed, would be a misinterpretation to conclude that what happened in Finland during the past decades was just a skillful maneuver by a small group of experts. Collaboration with and assistance from the judiciary was a prerequisite for the changes to happen. In many cases the legislature was strongly supported by the judiciary and especially by the courts of first instance. Quite often, the courts changed their practices even before the legislature changed the law. Of course, the fact that criminology and criminal justice policy are taught in the law faculties to law students — who will later implement the laws — also is part of the big picture. The majority of Finnish local court judges and prosecutors are relatively young, having received their educations during the 1970s and the 1980s in the spirit of liberal criminal policy. In addition, various training courses and seminars arranged for judges (and prosecutors) — in cooperation with the universities — have also influenced sentencing and prosecutorial practices.

Crime and Social Context

The "crime scene" matters. Finland has been, and still is, a peaceful and safe society with a low level of criminality. It has never suffered from the serious drug-related street violence that has troubled some other Western countries; this, of course, makes it easier to adopt liberal policies in crime control. Even so, it may be argued that this factor has a limited explanatory force. Over a period of approximately twenty years, and especially during the 1960s, Finland experienced severe social and structural changes in its development from a rural, agricultural economy into an industrial urban welfare state, and this transition affected crime rates. There was a steep increase in recorded crime from the mid-1960s to the mid-1970s, and again during the 1980s, which, however, did not prevent the prison population from falling (nor is there reason to conclude that this fall had any significant effect in the growth of crime).

B. The Risks of a Return to Repressive Policies

The crime situation in Finland is relatively stable, and the number of offenses is, from an international perspective, rather low (Mayhew and van Dijk 1997). Nonetheless, there are causes for concern. The level of homicide has long been relatively high, and during recent decades has been rising further. The special features of the Finnish alcohol culture play an important role. Drug-related crime is a second category of crime that is increasing. Other types of crime inevitably involve drug trafficking and financing drug abuse as the growing international aspect of crime has brought with it drug-related crime, and new opportunities for economic crime and for certain other types of crime. The opening of the borders has caused demographic changes. Finland must weigh measures designed to avoid cultural conflicts and to facilitate the adjustment of immigrants. Continued urbanization and long-standing high unemployment, with the attendant danger of extensive social marginalization, are likely to lead to an increase in crime. Already, changes in technology and the industrial structure have caused a sharp growth in the opportunity for crime, especially several types of property crime, crime related to means of payment, and economic crime. Furthermore, these changes have created new ways of committing crime.

In the face of such changes, there is every reason to regard crime as a serious problem. How the political system will respond is an open question. Rational and humane policy has a long and quite solid tradition. At the same time, policy is to an exceptional degree dominated by experts and, as Nils Christie (1993) has noted, the power of elites is vulnerable. Elites can change. Indeed, the generation that has been responsible for the long tradition in criminal justice policy is stepping aside (or has already done so). At the same time the risk factors that Christie referred to have become even more apparent. One of these is the general tendency to politicize criminal policy.

The Politicization of Criminal Policy

Criminal justice policy has become more and more "a tool in general politics," and with quite unhappy results. The rule of thumb seems to be that the higher the level of political authority, the more simplistic the approaches advocated. The problems are also connected with forms of political communication. In a world where the message must be squeezed into fifteen-second sound bites, impressions and easy solutions tend to dominate. This is also true of criminal justice politics, which is becoming part of general politics. The results can be seen in programs and slogans that are compressed into two or three words, along the lines of "three strikes," "prison works," "truth in sentencing," "war on drugs," and so on. This leads to the tendency to offer simple solutions to complex problems and to pander to punitive (or presumably punitive) public opinions with harsh law-and-order campaigns. A common feature of such programs is that the solution to social problems is sought in places where it cannot be found, in other words, in the penal system. The model country for this type of politics is (unfortunately) the United States, where criminal policy has repeatedly emerged as a theme even in presidential campaigns. It may be that the prototypes and currents are so strong that it is only a question of time before Finland is caught up in this development.

The most immediate risk factor (from a Finnish point of view) is the increasing cooperation in criminal matters within the framework of the European Union. Criminal law as such, according to the Maastricht Treaty and the Amsterdam Treaty, is an internal matter for the member states. This principle, however, is being eroded by repeated "joint actions," in which member states are obliged to take steps in the area of criminal law. Even if the core area of criminal law could be protected (in part because of strong resistance by Germany and the Nordic countries, among others), it is clear that Finnish criminal justice policy will in the future be increasingly influenced by the European Union. Without denigrating the importance of cooperation in criminal matters as such, there is every reason to fear that criminal justice policy is not being pursued in general European political discussions in a way that satisfies demands of rational and justifiable policy. The measures adopted are often influenced by motives other than pursuit of rational policies, to say nothing of considered analyses of goals and means. In the hands of European politicians, criminal justice policy is just another tool of general politics, a way to transmit "symbolic messages," a way to "take a stand," a way to "make strategic choices," and so on. Instead of careful reasoning based on substantive policy considerations, criminal justice interventions are often determined by a political need to "do something." And it is in this political context that rule-of-law limits on the use of criminal law are regarded by some as more a hindrance than a benefit. At the same time, this is one reason why a large segment of Nordic criminal law scholars are quite skeptical of attempts to harmonize criminal law (see Greve 1995; Träskman 1997).

Topics for Tomorrow

In addition to politicization, one can see other changes in values that have led to a more punitive criminal policy. The social values that emphasize solidarity and joint responsibility (which resonated so strongly during the 1960s) have had to yield to harder values that emphasize individual success. One expression of this is the increasing tendency to speak of personal responsibility rather than social background. In the Finnish debate, criminality is seen not so much as a social problem that is connected with social and structural factors but as a problem caused by individual evil people that can be eliminated by shutting those people away in institutions. Nonetheless, the present concrete legislative reforms in Finland so far do not give cause for any great concern. The total reform of criminal law, which was launched in 1980, should be completed by 2001. The reform has been carried out throughout in the spirit of neoclassical criminal law, with respect for principles of due process. The reassessment of individual offenses has been carried out primarily by reducing penal severity; the primary exception to this has been for some economic crimes. The reform of the penal system has involved the expansion of community-based measures. So far the partial amendments in the reform ideology of the 1970s have been toward increased rehabilitation, not repression. For the time being, it is hard to imagine that the claim that "prison works" will find its way into Finnish political campaigns.

NOTES

1. As Anttila and Törnudd (1992) summarize, the reformers "saw the ideology of coercive treatment and indeterminate sanctions as one of their main foes. But the traditional enemy of any sophisticated crime expert also remained: those who expressively react to all

crime problems with populist demands for stricter punishments. An emphasis on legality, proportionality, predictability and other traditional principles of justice in that situation became the logical weapon on both fronts" p. 13). Trends in Scandinavian criminal policy in the 1960s are analyzed in Anttila 1971. The reform ideology of the 1970s and the 1980s is described in Anttila and Törnudd 1992 and Lahti 1985 and 1993.

2. Sweden also implemented in 1989 an extensive sentencing reform based on similar principles (see von Hirsch and Jareborg 1989; Jareborg 1995). Legislative sentencing provisions, as such, have a long history in European criminal codes.

3. The only exception concerns the situation when offenders are to be sentenced for two or more offenses at one time. In these cases offenders are sentenced to a joint punishment; maximum penalties for the various offenses can be exceeded within the limits prescribed in more detail by the law (chapter 7, Criminal Code on Joint Punishments).

4. The dangers of the ideology of coercive treatment (rehabilitation) are well summarized in a seminal article by Anttila (1971, pp. 14–15):

> But as treatment ideology has increasingly dominated the system and as treatment personnel have gained increasing power, the negative sides of the ideology have become more evident and the criticism against treatment ideology has grown sharper. The parallel of the criminal-sick appears to be false, if one looks for effectiveness of treatment and for the absence of a conflict of interest between the doctor and the doctored. This has led to an acute legal safeguards problem because of the absence of predictability and the absence of proportion between the seriousness of the crime and the strictness of treatment.

5. These were originally introduced into the international discussion at the Sixth International Congress on Criminology 1970 by the Finnish criminologist Patrik Törnudd. This definition of goals was adopted by the Fifth United Nations Congress on the Prevention of Crime and the Treatment of Offenders, where it was embodied in the report of the section dealing with the economic and social consequences of crime. The same report also recommends encouragement of cost-benefit thinking (for a more detailed discussion, see Törnudd 1996; Lahti 1977, p. 145).

6. This "redefinition" of the aim of punishment in the Nordic countries could rely on a long theoretical tradition dating back to the early Scandinavian realism of the Uppsala School of the 1920s and 1930s (Axel Hägerström and Wilhelm Lundstedt), reinforced by the writings of scholars such as Per-Ole Ekelöf (Sweden), Alf Ross (Denmark), Johs. Andenaes and Vilhelm Aubert (Norway) and Klaus Mäkelä and Patrik Törnudd (Finland). See, in general, Andeanes 1974 and Lappi-Seppälä 1995. Since the 1970s German legal theory has discussed these issues under the term "positive" general prevention (or "integration" prevention; see Schünemann, von Hirsch, and Jareborg 1998). See also von Hirsch et al. 1999, pp. 30–40 (on "deterrence and normativity").

7. Andenaes (1974, p. 113) classifies the influence of criminal law on morality as follows—Direct influence: (1) respect for the formal authority (no change in the individual's view of morality), (2) criminal law as a moral eye-opener (a change in moral attitude as a result of personal thinking), and (3) punishment as an authoritative statement (a change in moral attitude as a result of the suggestive influence of laws); Indirect influence: (4) punishment's effect in reducing and neutralizing bad examples (the working mechanism is supposed to be simple deterrence) and (5) criminal law as a framework of moral education.

8. In addition, the moral disapproval expressed in punishment may function also as a direct deterrent factor (unpleasant as it is). In such a case we would be talking of simple deterrence which, of course, also has a role in the criminal justice system.

9. There is a strong intuition in favor of the assumption that legitimacy, trust, and acceptance will have an independent additional value in bringing about compliance. What, then, causes authority to be accepted? The answer given by the procedural school of justice would be "perceived fairness." People value such things as having an opportunity to take part in the decision-making process and they like to believe (in order to regard the system to be fair) that the decision-makers are neutral. People also place great weight on being treated politely and having respect shown for their rights and for themselves as people (on this, see, Tyler 1990, p. 163).

10. In this respect one could make a further distinction between compliance based on authority and conformity as habit (the habituative effect of punishment).

11. British drunken-driving legislation serves as an example of this. Measurements immediately after the reforms showed no change in attitudes. However, after twenty-five years, the picture had changed. See Snortum 1990, p. 484, where the author reports a marked change in the moral assessment of drinking and driving in Great Britain, as well as a significant reduction of driving after drinking since 1967.

12. Andenaes (1974, p. 124) writes:

> The criminal law system may also have indirect effects on a person's moral education during crucial years of his early education and development. This education takes place primarily in the family, in school, and in other small groups, but it is not independent of conditions in society outside these groups. The existence and working of criminal law and its machinery provide a general framework which must necessarily have deep-rooted consequences for the moral climate of society and the moral education to which children are exposed. It would be difficult to teach honesty, nonviolence, and similar positive values in a society where these rules were openly and commonly broken without punishment.

13. But whether there is a need for "hard treatment" is another matter (see, e.g., Feinberg 1970, pp. 99–100 and 115–16 and the discussions in von Hirsch 1993, p. 12). Here the aim is only to point out some of the requirements of indirect general prevention in relation to the system of criminal sanctions. This is not to say that these are the only reasons that support, for example, the principle of proportionality. Nor is this the only connection between value-rational considerations of justice and the goal-rational aim of prevention.

14. In crime policy, cost-benefit analysis has been given a wide interpretation. Costs include also human and immaterial losses (harm and suffering), not just the costs of building and running the prisons.

15. This is, presumably, even narrower than the meaning of this term in the Anglo-Saxon tradition where sentencing covers almost everything from the establishment of guidelines to release on parole. In a civil law tradition, the latter type of issues (such as the types of penalties to be adopted in the criminal law) are deemed part of legislative action and the planning of criminal policy. These are dealt with in sections I and II.

16. The construction of the entire penal structure reflects these same aims. In order to ensure proportionality as well as consistency in sentencing, different offenses are, as a rule, graded into different degrees of seriousness with corresponding specific penalty scales for each subtype of offense. For example, the crime of theft appears in law in three degrees: petty theft (fines), ordinary theft (either a fine or imprisonment up to one year and six months), and aggravated theft (imprisonment for from four months to four years).

17. Aggravating factors are listed in chapter 6, section 2 of the Criminal Code. Grounds that increase punishment are the degree of premeditation; commission of the offense as a member of a group organized for serious offenses; committing the offense for remuneration,

and the previous criminality of the offender if the relation between the offenses on the basis of their similarity or for another reason shows that the offender is apparently heedless of the prohibitions and commands of the law.

18. See also Jareborg 1992. Together with von Hirsch, Jareborg has developed a more general theory of offense seriousness ("living standard" analyses, see von Hirsch and Jareborg 1991 and the comments by Ashworth 1992b, sec. 90 ss).

19. Aggravation based on xenophobic motives (the "hate-crime" concept) has been recognized in several European legal systems in various ways. Usually this has been done in the special part of the Criminal Code (for example, in the definitions of crimes of violence). In Scandinavia, only Sweden has adopted a general sentencing provision on the matter in 1994 (chapter 29, sec. 2, para. 7 the Criminal Code (1994:306)). Also the European Community has undertaken a joint action against crimes committed on racist or xenophobic motives.

20. Despite the reform, prior record is still perhaps the most influental factor in sentencing. It also is true that the guidance given by the legislator is somewhat "elusive" (von Hirsch 1987, p. 54). Still, there is evidence that some of the objectives have been achieved. The mere number of previous convictions is not the only criterion to be taken into account. One sign of the change is that while sentencing a multiple offender, the courts may aggravate the sentence and apply the prior record provision selectively to only some of the crimes.

21. In other words, the same logic applies to culpability-based reasons. A diminished ability of an individual to control his or her actions will result in a concomitant reduction in the ability to influence such actions with punishments. Under the assumption that penalty resources are not limitless, this reduction of controllability should lead in a goal-rational system to the lowering of penalties. Assuming that the total amount of penalty resources is given, an increase in any one sector means a decrease in another sector. In this instance it would not be rational to sacrifice the same amount of resources for the prevention of an equal amount of harm, if the outcome is different (see in more detail, Lappi-Seppälä 1992a). The point is not to say that all value-based arguments in sentencing may be given a goal-rational—let alone crime-preventive—explanation at the legislative (aggregate) level but to show that it usually makes a lot of (goal-rational) sense (in an aggregate level) to follow the proportionality principle in the level of judicial application. Still, the tension between the protection of preventive aims and collective interests and the protection of individual rights remains. One cannot escape this tension and the need for balanced compromises in criminal justice simply by adopting one principle or by announcing that different principles are relevant at different stages of the criminal justice system. However, the latter point, made by the analytical philosophers (first of all by H. L. A. Hart [1968]) offers a valuable conceptual key in order to clarify the questions and to organize the arguments.

22. There is some similarity with the theory of "Interchangeability of Sanctions" by Morris and Tonry (1990). As the authors point out, all that the proportionality principle demands is a "rough equivalence" between the seriousness of the offense and the severity of the sanction. A choice can be made within these limits on other grounds without breaching the requirements of the proportionality principle. One has to admit that the equivalence between community service and imprisonment (one hour equals one day) may be "a bit more than rough." Still, the criticism against this lenient exchange rate has been quite mild. Evidently there was a kind of silent, collective agreement that the purpose was valuable enough in order to justify this slight deviation from the strict requirements of proportionality. The overall social benefits of community service (for both the offender and the society) in a way overrode the strict requirement that the intrusiveness of these sanctions

should be of exactly the same level with imprisonment. It also is interesting to note that in international comparisons (based on focus-group method), the Finnish judges rely more on community service than do the judges in England and California (see Takala 1997).

23. These legal principles have been deemed to be part of customary law and are considered part of the legal order even without the support of written law. The Swedish Criminal Code contains a provision that expresses this idea in connection with the use of imprisonment. According to chapter 30, section 4, "in choosing the sanction, the court shall especially pay heed to circumstances that suggest a less severe sanction than imprisonment."

24. There are no formal rules governing the order of these decisions. Since only terms of imprisonment not exceeding two years may be imposed conditionally, the length of the sentence may usually be determined first. However, both decisions are based on similar types of arguments and it is equally possible that the courts consider these two issues (both the length and the type of imprisonment) at the same time in what essentially amounts to an overall assessment.

25. Whether mitigation based, for example, on the old age or sickness of the offender really is a deviation from the principle of proportionality or "equality" depends much on the content given to these principles (and the concept of justice itself). Proportionality based on a broad (individualized) concept of justice might encompass also acts of equity and mercy under "proportionally just" sentences. Furthermore, from the point of view of the "principle of equal impact" (see Ashworth 1992a, p. 136), it would be perfectly correct to treat such a "deviation" as something that is required by the "principle of equality." A reasoned discussion of a "preferable sentencing model" would require a more careful definition (and justification) of basic concepts and principles than the present space allows.

26. The talk about "a" normal offense or punishment is, of course, a simplification. Instead of one normal offense it would be better to speak of several "typical offenses" and of the corresponding "zones of normal punishments" that have been used in these cases.

REFERENCES

Aho, Timo. 1997. "Land of Decreasing Prison Population." In *Prison Population in Europe and North America: Problems and Solutions*. Helsinki: Ministry of Justice, Department of Prison Administration.
Andenaes, Johs. 1974. *Punishment and Deterrence*. Ann Arbor: University of Michigan Press.
———. 1975. "General Prevention Revisited: Research and Policy Implications." *Journal of Criminal Law and Criminology* 66:338–65.
Anttila, Inkeri. 1971. "Conservative and Radical Criminal Policy in the Nordic Countries." In *Scandinavian Studies in Criminology*, vol. 3, edited by Nils Christie. London: Tavistock.
Anttila, Inkeri, and Patrik Törnudd. 1980. "Reasons for Punishment." In *Crime and Crime Control in Scandinavia, 1976–1980*, edited by Norman Bishop. Stockholm: Scandinavian Research Council for Criminology.
———. 1992. "The Dynamics of the Finnish Criminal Code Reform." In *Criminal Law Theory in Transition: Finnish and Comparative Perspectives*, edited by R. Lahti and K. Nuotio. Tampere: Finnish Lawyers' Publishing Company.
Ashworth, Andrew. 1992a. *Sentencing and Criminal Justice*. London: Weidenfeld and Nicolson.

————. 1992b. "Sentencing Reform Structures." In *Crime and Justice: A Review of Research*, vol. 16, edited by Michael Tonry. Chicago: University of Chicago Press.

Beyleveld, Deryck. 1980. *A Bibliography on General Deterrence Research*. Farnborough, England: Saxon House.

Bondeson, Ulla. 1989. *Prisoners in Prison Societes*. New Brunswick, N.J.: Transaction.

Canadian Sentencing Commission. 1987. *Sentencing Reform: A Canadian Approach*. Ottawa: Canadian Government Publishing Centre.

Christie, Nils. 1968. "Changes in Penal Values." In *Scandinavian Studies in Criminology*, volume 2, edited by Nils Christie. London: Tavistock.

————. 1993. *Crime Control as Industry*. New York: Routledge.

Council of Europe. 1987. *Disparities in Sentencing: Causes and Solutions—Reports Presented to the Eighth Criminological Colloquium (1987)*. Collected Studies in Criminological Research, vol. 26. Strasbourg: European Committee on Crime Problems.

Duff, Antony. 1996. "Penal Communications: Recent Work in the Philosophy of Punishment." In *Crime and Justice: A Review of Research*, vol. 20, edited by Michael Tonry. Chicago: University of Chicago Press.

Ekelöf, Per-Olof. 1942. *Straffet, Skandestandet Vitet*. Uppsala: A. B. Lundquist.

Feinberg, Joel. 1970. *Doing and Deserving*. Princeton, N.J.: Princeton University Press.

Greve, Vagn. 1995. "European Criminal Policy: Towards Universal Laws?" In *Towards Unversal Laws: Trends in National, European, and International Lawmaking*, edited by Nils Jareborg. Uppsala, Sweden: Iustus.

Grönfors, Martti. 1989. "Ideals and Reality in Community Mediation." In *Mediation and Criminal Justice*, edited by Martin Wright and Burt Galaway. London: Sage.

Hart, H. L. A. 1968. *Punishment and Responsibility*. Oxford: Oxford University Press.

Jareborg, Nils. 1988. *Essays in Criminal Law*. Uppsala, Sweden: Iustus.

————. 1992. *Straffrättsideologiska Fragment*. Uppsala, Sweden: Iustus.

————. 1995. "The Swedish Sentencing Reform." In *The Politics of Sentencing Reform*, edited by C. M. V. Clarkson and Rod Morgan. Oxford: Clarendon Press.

Kuhn, André. 1998. "Sanctions and Their Severity." In *Crime and Criminal Justice Systems in Europe and North America, 1990–1994*, edited by Kristiina Kangaspunta, Matti Joutsen, and Natalia Ollus. Helsinki: European Institute for Crime Prevention and Control.

Lahti, Raimo. 1977. "Criminal Sanctions in Finland: A System in Transition." *Scandinavian Studies in Law* 21:119–57.

————. 1985. "Current Trends in Criminal Policy in the Scandinavian Countries." In *Scandinavian Criminal Policy and Criminology, 1980–1985*, edited by Norman Bishop. Copenhagen: Scandinavian Research Council for Criminology.

————. 1993. "Recodifying the Finnish Criminal Code of 1889: Towards a More Efficient, Just, and Humane Criminal Law." *Israeli Law Review* 27:100–17.

Lappi-Seppälä, Tapio. 1990. "Sentencing Theory in Practice: Implementing the Notion of Normal Punishments in Finland." In *Scandinavian Criminal Policy and Criminology, 1985–1990*, edited by Norman Bishop. Stockholm: Scandinavian Research Council for Criminology.

————. 1992a. "Community Service and the Neo-Classical Framework of Penal Sanctions." In *Rapport fra Kontaktseminar om Samfundstjänste*. Reykjavik, Iceland: Scandinavian Research Council for Criminology.

————. 1992b. "Penal Policy and Sentencing Theory in Finland." *The Canadian Journal of Law and Jurisprudence* 5: 95–120.

————. 1995. "General Prevention: Hypotheses and Empirical Evidence." *Rapport fra NSfKs 37 Forskerseminar*. Arild, Sweden: Scandinavian Research Council for Criminology.

———. 1996. "Reparation in Criminal Law." In *Wiedergutmachung im Kriminalrecht*, edited by Albin Eser and Susanne Walther. Freiburg, Germany: Max-Planck-Institut für Ausländisches und Internationales Strefrecht.

———. 1998. *Regulating the Prison Population. Experiences from a Long-Term Policy in Finland.* Helsinki: National Research Institute of Legal Policy.

Lång, K. J. 1989. "Upplever Fängelsestraffet en Renässans." *Nordisk Tidskrift for Kriminalvidenskab* 76:83–94.

Mayhew, Pat, and Jan J. M. van Dijk. 1997. *Criminal Victimisation in Eleven Industrialized Countries.* The Hague: Dutch Ministry of Justice.

Ministry of Justice. Various years. *Prison Administration Statistics.* Helsinki: Ministry of Justice.

Morris, Norval, and Michael Tonry. 1990. *Between Prison and Probation: Intermediate Punishments in a Rational Sentencing System.* New York: Oxford University Press.

National Correctional Association, 1972. *The Correctional System, 1971.* Official Statistics of Sweden. Stockholm: National Correctional Association.

Proband, Stan. 1997. "Success in Finland in Reducing Prison Use." In *Sentencing Reform in Overcrowded Times*, edited by Michael Tonry and Kathleen Hatlestad. New York: Oxford University Press.

Schumann, Karl. 1989. *Positive Generalprävention.* Heidelberg, Germany: Müller.

Schünemann, Bernd, Andrew von Hirsch, and Nils Jareborg, eds. 1998. *Positive Generalprävention: Kritische Analysen im deutsch-englischen Dialog.* Uppsala-Symposium 1996. Heidelberg, Germany: C. F. Müller.

Snortum, John. 1990. "Drinking-Driving Compliance in Great Britain: The Role of Law as a 'Threat' and as a 'Moral Eye-Opener.' " *Journal of Criminal Justice* 18:479–99.

Statistics Finland. Various years. *Criminal Cases Tried by the Courts*, series XXIII B. Helsinki: Statistics Finland.

Takala, Jukka-Pekka. 1992. "Finland's Experiment with Community Service: How to Combine Mitigation, Quality Experience, and Fairness." *Rapport fra Kontaktseminar om Samfundstjänste.* Reykjavik, Iceland: Scandinavian Research Council for Criminology.

———. 1997. "Responses in Finland to Community Sanctions." In *Penological Esperanto and Sentencing Parochialism*, edited by Malcolm Davies, Jukka-Pekka Takala, and Jane Tyrer. Aldershot, England: Dartmouth.

Tarling, Roger. 1993. *Analysing Offending: Data, Models, and Interpretations.* London: Her Majesty's Stationery Office.

Träskman, Per-Ole. 1997. " 'Corpus juris': Ett Frestande eller ett Främmande Förslag till en Enhetlig Europeiska Rättsfär?" *Nordisk Tidskrift for Kriminalvidenskab* 84:262–77.

Tyler, Tom. 1990. *Why People Obey the Law.* New Haven, Conn.: Yale University Press.

Törnudd, Patrik. 1993. *Fifteen Years of Decreasing Prisoner Rates.* Helsinki: National Research Institute of Legal Policy.

———. 1996. *Facts, Values, and Visions: Essays in Criminology and Crime Policy.* Helsinki: National Research Institute of Legal Policy.

———. 1997. "Sentencing and Punishment in Finland." In *Sentencing Reform in Overcrowded Times*, edited by Michael Tonry and Kathleen Hatlestad. New York: Oxford University Press.

von Hirsch, Andrew. 1981. "Desert and Previous Convictions in Sentencing." *Minnesota Law Review* 65:591–634.

———. 1987. "Numeric Grids or Guiding Principles." In *The Sentencing Commission and Its Guidelines*, edited by Andrew von Hirsch, Kay Knapp, and Michael Tonry. Boston: Northeastern University Press.

————. 1993. *Censure and Sanctions.* Oxford: Clarendon Press.

von Hirsch, Andrew, Anthony E. Bottoms, Elizabeth Burney, and P.-O. Wikström. 1999. *Criminal Deterrence and Sentencing Severity: An Analysis of Recent Research.* Oxford: Hart Publishing.

von Hirsch, Andrew, and Nils Jareborg. 1989. "Sweden's Sentencing Statute Enacted." *Criminal Law Review* 275–82.

————. 1991. "Gauging Criminal Harm: A Living Standard Analysis." *Oxford Journal of Legal Studies* 11:1–38.

von Hofer, Hanns. 1997. *Nordic Criminal Statistics, 1950–1995.* Report 1997:2. Stockholm: Department of Criminology. Stockholm University.

Walker, Nigel, and Michou Argyle. 1964. "Does the Law Affect Moral Judgments?" *British Journal of Criminology* 4:570–81.

Sentencing and Punishment
in The Netherlands

The Dutch criminal justice system has long been noted for its mildness, with reference usually made to Holland's low imprisonment rate compared with those of other Western countries. In the early 1970s, the rate was around 20 per 100,000, but since then it has increased, at first gradually, but steeply since 1990. By 2000, Holland was incarcerating 90 per 100,000 of its inhabitants.

Comparison of the punitiveness of different countries from prison statistics is not an easy task. Both the prison population and its changes are affected by changes in prevalence and seriousness of offenses, police efficiency, the strictness of the law and judicial behavior, and the variety of modes of sentences available (Kuhn 1997). Nonetheless, imprisonment rates have risen faster in Holland since the mid-1980s than in any other European country (see table 4.1).

Sentencing policies, practices, and laws in Holland have changed considerably in the past twenty-five years. Relative to the increased crime rate, the number of prison sentences imposed held stable or even decreased. The average length of prison sentences, however, increased substantially. In 1970, nearly 13,000 prison sentences were imposed for a total of 2,100 detention years. By 1995, the number of prison sentences had doubled, and the number of detention years had increased by five times.

The Netherlands continues to observe a policy of confining only one prisoner to a cell, so the increasing number of detention years (see table 4.2) has required an increasing number of prison cells and a larger prison population.

For many this increase is remarkable and disturbing. That reaction is understandable when one looks only at the figures. Behind the figures, however, is a reality that differs considerably. The low numbers in the 1970s were partly misleading, because they camouflage a considerable difference between prison capacity and prison capacity needs. Offenders who were not in pretrial detention before trial and who were sentenced to imprisonment often were not sent im-

Table 4.1. European Prison Rates, 1985, 1990, 1995

Country	1985	1990	1995
Austria	120	90	85
Belgium	65	65	75
Denmark	65	60	65
England and Wales	90	90	100
Finland	80	60	60
France	75	85	95
Germany (West)	90	80	85
Italy	—	45	85
Netherlands	35	45	65
Norway	45	55	55
Portugal	90	90	125
Spain	60	75	105
Sweden	50	65	65

Source: Walmsley (1997).

mediately to prison but instead were placed on a waiting list and called to serve their sentences only when space became available.

Beginning in the mid-1970s, waiting-list backlogs increased, partly because of new legislation on pretrial detention, which reduced the number of pretrial detainees and in turn meant that fewer people served their sentences immediately after receiving them. Legislators assumed that the reduction in pretrial detention would lead to fewer prison sentences, but it did not. The Prison Department of the Ministry of Justice realized too late that prison population and capacity needs simply could not be reconciled. For a time, prison policies called for and caused a closing down of prisons.

Table 4.2. Average Number of Prisoners in the Netherlands, 1970–1997

Year	Prisoners	Year	Prisoners	Year	Prisoners
1970	2,644	1980	3,224	1990	6,481
1971	2,830	1981	3,486	1991	7,047
1972	2,774	1982	3,699	1992	7,317
1973	2,529	1983	3,971	1993	7,582
1974	—	1984	4,418	1994	8,285
1975	2,526	1985	4,608	1995	9,540
1976	2,866	1986	4,599	1996	10,690
1977	3,039	1987	4,883	1997	11,770
1978	—	1988	5,341		
1979	—	1989	6,027		

Source: Central Bureau of Statistics, various years.

Then, at the beginning of the 1980s, a construction program initiated to expand prison capacity led to an increase in capacity by 900 places. Despite this expansion, the backlog increased from 600 cells to 2,200 cells by 1990.

The largest expansion occurred in the early 1990s. Between 1994 and 1996, fourteen new prisons opened, and in 1999 capacity increased by nearly 3,500 places. By the beginning of 2000, there were approximately 16,300 cells. The dramatic expansion in prison capacity and incarceration rates is partly the result of criticism of the waiting-list policy.

Various memoranda and policy statements have emphasized the importance of efficient and effective implementation of prison sentences. The Prosecution Service's policy plan, "Criminal Law and Criminal Policy," criticized the delayed implementation of prison sentences for being in conflict with legal requirements (Ministerie van Justitie 1990). A proper implementation of sentences, they argued, is the cornerstone of reliable administration of criminal justice. The Committee on the Reconsideration of the Instruments for Law Enforcement also deplored the system of implementation of prison sentences or other judicial decisions involving deprivation of liberty (Commissie Heroverweging 1995).

The problems with the implementation of prison sentences concern three groups: offenders sentenced to imprisonment, mentally disturbed offenders, and illegal aliens. In 1995, a waiting list of more than 11,000 nonimplemented prison sentences accounted for more than 2,100 detention years.

Mentally disturbed offenders are being sentenced in increasing numbers under provisions calling for confinement in a penitentiary mental hospital ("entrustment orders"). The number of places in such hospitals is restricted. In many cases, the mental disturbance requires a lengthy stay. Recent delays in admission have coincided with a large increase in the number of entrustment orders. Early in 1995, there were one hundred persons under entrustment orders waiting implementation of the order. In mid-1998, there were more than two hundred.

Detention of illegal foreigners is a growing problem. Increased efforts to remove illegal foreigners and unsuccessful asylum-seekers require increased capacity. Illegal foreigners are detained in prison as an administrative measure in order to facilitate removal (van Kalmthout 1998). There are four such establishments in the Netherlands. Between 1988 and 1995, the number of illegals detained for removal grew from 2,000 to 9,600. Ten percent of the total prison capacity is now needed for detention of illegal foreigners and more capacity will be needed.

Because of the increased need for prison space, and in reaction to the policy plan and the committee report, the minister of justice announced that two tracks would be followed: to develop substitutes to imprisonment and further to expand prison capacity.

This had in effect been the policy since the early 1980s. Thereafter Dutch penal policies became harsher. Prison sentences became longer and the number of prison cells rose sharply. During the same period, however, the use of short-term imprisonment fell, fines became the preferred sentence, prosecutorial diversion grew rapidly, community sentences came into use, and new substitutes to custodial sentences were developed. This chapter gives an overview of those and other changes in Dutch sentencing policy since 1970.

I. Prosecutorial Diversion

Only a small percentage of crimes recorded by the police result in cases tried by a criminal court. Although the number of recorded crimes increased more than fivefold between 1970 and 1995, the number of tried cases only doubled (see table 4.3). In 1995 1.5 million crimes were brought to the notice of the police. An official report was made in 1.2 million cases. Of these, 210,000 cases were solved. The Prosecution Service made prosecution decisions in 260,000 cases. More than half (145,000 cases) were settled by the Prosecution Service, of which 30,000 were through dismissal for technicalities, 24,000 through a dismissal under the "expediency principle" (discussed below), 62,000 through negotiated dispositions called transactions (also discussed below), and the rest by other prosecutorial decisions. The remaining cases were tried by a criminal court and resulted in 130,500 sen-

Table 4.3. Registered Crimes and Their Disposition in the Netherlands, 1970–1995

Year	Registered Crimes	Cleared Up	Settled by Prosecution	Tried by Criminal Court	Non-prosecution, Total	Non-prosecution Due to Technicalities	Non-prosecution Due to Policy Considerations
1970	265.7	109.2	52.2	50.3	37.6		
1971	307.7	115.7	60.4	51.1	43.1		
1972	348.2	125.8	62.2	52.2	44.8		
1973	388.0	133.7	62.5	52.6	46.0		
1974	425.5	137.9	63.0	54.2	45.7		
1975	453.2	149.6	60.7	59.1	45.5		
1976	525.6	173.2	66.8	65.5	49.5		
1977	550.7	177.8	77.8	70.0	58.0		
1978	570.0	186.6	81.0	75.5	60.9		
1979	622.4	199.6	85.2	76.8	65.5		
1980	705.7	210.1	97.5	82.8	72.3	22.8	49.5
1981	812.1	234.6	109.3	83.8	78.7	24.6	54.1
1982	922.9	247.9	114.7	89.9	80.3	25.6	54.7
1983	986.3	257.7	133.3	85.9	82.1	26.4	55.7
1984	1,083.4	272.5	135.1	82.3	74.1	25.3	48.8
1985	1,093.7	262.8	137.0	83.8	74.8	26.5	48.3
1986	1,097.1	261.1	136.2	83.5	68.0	26.4	41.6
1987	1,129.5	266.6	135.1	83.2	66.7	29.2	37.5
1988	1,146.2	266.1	138.8	85.5	67.5	31.0	36.5
1989	1,159.6	266.5	142.5	85.6	69.0	31.5	37.5
1990	1,150.2	255.6	141.3	83.7	70.5	32.5	38.0
1991	1,181.8	238.1	—	—	—	—	—
1992	1,268.5	242.5	—	—	—	—	—
1993	1,272.3	237.7	161.8	85.0	58.1	28.1	30.0
1994	1,305.3	236.3	149.8	99.3	58.3	30.4	27.9
1995	1,230.7	210.6	145.1	102.3	55.4	30.8	24.6

Source: Central Bureau of Statistics, various years; Prosecution Service, various years.

Note: Figures are in thousands.

tences, of which 47,000 were fines, 47,000 prison sentences, 15,000 community service orders, and the rest other sanctions.

One important reason for the growing gap between the number of recorded crimes and the number of crimes tried by courts is that public expenditure for enforcement agencies has not kept pace with rising crime rates. The police have increasingly, because of resource considerations, set priorities in detecting and investigating cases. The effect has been falling percentages of cases cleared up. Between 1970 and 1995, the overall clearance rate fell from 41 percent to 18 percent.

A second reason why relatively few cases are tried by criminal courts is that, since the end of the 1960s, the Prosecution Service has settled more and more cases out of court. While this trend originally was driven by efforts to socialize, humanize, and rationalize the administration of criminal justice, the emphasis has shifted toward the goal of reducing case-processing pressures. One effect is that the Prosecution Service has been given steadily increasing adjudicatorial powers that formerly were exclusively within the domain of the judiciary. Two methods of settlement are commonly used: nonprosecution and the transaction.

A. Nonprosecution

Only the public prosecutors have authority to initiate criminal proceedings. Even when the Prosecution Service declines to prosecute, no other person or agency may do so. This monopoly does not require the Prosecution Service to prosecute every crime brought to its notice. The Prosecution Service may decide not to prosecute because, for lack of evidence or for technical considerations (technical or procedural waiver), a conviction is unlikely. In 1995, there were nearly 31,000 such cases. The prosecution may also decide not to prosecute under the expediency principle laid down in section 167 of the Code of Criminal Procedure (CCP), which authorizes waiver of prosecution "for reasons of public interest." Nonprosecution under the expediency principle has been declining from around 50,000 cases per year in the 1980s, but there were still nearly 25,000 such cases in 1995.

In addition, in appropriate cases the prosecutor may suspend prosecution conditionally. No explicit general or special conditions for suspended nonprosecution exist, but in practice the prosecutor imposes conditions similar to those attached to suspended sentences.

Until the late 1960s, discretionary power to waive prosecution was exercised on a very restricted scale. Thereafter, however, a remarkable change took place. Research on the effects of law enforcement, coupled with the limited resources of law enforcement agencies, made clear that it was impossible, undesirable, and in some circumstances counterproductive to prosecute all investigated offenses. The discretionary power not to prosecute for policy reasons began to be exercised more widely. To harmonize the use of this discretionary power, the Assembly of the Prosecutors General issued national prosecution guidelines (Tak 1986). Public prosecutors were directed to follow the guidelines except when special circumstances in an individual case were spelled out. Under the guidelines, a prosecutor could waive prosecution for reasons of public interest, if for example: (1) other than penal measures or sanctions are preferable or would be more effective (e.g., disciplinary, administrative, or civil measures); (2) prosecution would be disproportionate, unjust, or ineffective in relation to the nature of the offense (e.g., if the offense caused no harm and it was inexpedient to inflict punishment); (3) prosecution would be disproportionate, unjust, or ineffective for reasons related to the offender (e.g., age or health, rehabilitation prospects, first offender); (4) prosecution would be contrary to the interests of the state (e.g., for reasons of security, peace, and order, or if new applicable legislation has been introduced); (5) or prosecution would be contrary to the interests of the victim (e.g., compensation has already been paid) (Tak 1986).

In the early 1980s, the proportion of unconditional waivers was rather high. Approximately 28 percent of all cleared crimes were not further prosecuted for policy reasons. The rationale was that prosecution should not be automatic but should serve a concrete social objective. However, the 1985 criminal policy plan, *Society and Crime*, criticized such a high proportion of waivers on policy grounds (Ministerie van Justitie 1985). The Prosecution Service was instructed to reduce the number of unconditional waivers by making more frequent use of conditional waivers, reprimands, and transactions.

In conformity with the 1985 policy plan, and a 1990 policy plan, *Criminal Law and Criminal Policy*, the percentage of unconditional policy waivers dropped to only 4 percent in 1996 (Prosecution Service 1996). But because an increasing number of cases was either waived conditionally or settled out of court with a transaction, the decrease did not lead to an increase in the number of cases disposed in criminal court.

B. Transactions

The opportunity to settle criminal cases through a transaction has long existed. Transactions are a form of diversion in which offenders pay sums of money or fulfill one or more financial conditions in order to avoid further prosecution and a public trial.

Until 1983, transactions were reserved exclusively for infractions that are in principle punishable only with a fine. Following the recommendations of the Financial Penalties Committee, the Financial Penalties Act of 1983 expanded the scope of transactions to include more serious offenses (sec. 74, Penal Code [PC]).

The prosecutor before trial may propose one or more conditions in lieu of criminal proceedings for crimes that carry a statutory prison sentence of less than six years. Prosecution is in effect suspended, until such time as the conditions are met, after which the prosecution lapses.

A variety of conditions may be set: payment of a sum of money, not less than five guilders and not more than statutory maximum to the state; renunciation of title to objects that have been seized and are subject to forfeiture or confiscation; surrender of objects subject to forfeiture or confiscation or payment to the state of their assessed value; or payment in full to the state of a sum of money or transfer of objects seized to deprive the accused, in whole or in part, of gains acquired by means of or derived from the full or partial compensation for the damage caused by the offense.

Limitation of transactions to crimes carrying a statutory prison sentence exceeding six years is only a modest restriction. The overwhelming majority of crimes carry a maximum statutory prison sentence less than six years.

The prosecutors' broad powers to settle criminal cases by means of a transaction without the intervention of a court have been strongly criticized. The most important criticisms were that the increased transaction opportunities introduced the plea-bargaining system, represented a breach in the theory of the separation of powers, undermined the legal protections of the accused, favored certain social groups, and entrusted prosecutors with powers that should be reserved for the judiciary. Furthermore it was feared that with nearly 90 percent of all crimes brought within the sphere of the transaction, the public criminal trial, with its protections for the accused, would become the exception and not the rule.

Despite this criticism, the introduction of the broadened transaction was a great success. More than 30 percent of all crimes prosecuted by the Prosecution Service are now settled out of court by a transaction, in line with the 1990 criminal policy plan *Criminal Law and Criminal Policy*, which set as a target for 1995 that one-third of all prosecuted crimes be settled with a transaction (Prosecution Service 1996). According to the annual report of the Prosecution Service, in 1996 the average transaction amount was $440 U.S. (Prosecution Service 1996).

Transactions appear to meet important needs. They save the Prosecution Service and the offender time, energy, and money and protect the offender from stigmatization. Quite often, high transaction sums for environmental crimes committed by corporations are accepted in order to avoid negative publicity.

To minimize the risk of arbitrariness and lack of uniformity in application, the Assembly of Prosecutors-General has issued over the years a number of guidelines for the common crimes for which transactions are most frequently used, relating to the principles that need to be taken into consideration regarding transaction and prosecution (Steenhuis 1997). The guidelines, however, have not prevented considerable local variations in the frequency of application and in amounts, because the guidelines offer broad latitude (e.g., simple theft can result in a transaction between 100 and 750 guilders and for simple bicycle theft between 250 and 750 guilders; 2 guilders equals approximately one U.S. dollar).

Since 1993, police also may offer transactions for certain categories of crimes, notably shoplifting and drunken driving. The maximum authorized amount of a police transaction is 500 guilders (sec. 74c, PC). By contrast, the maximum authorized amount of a prosecutorial transaction is 1 million guilders.

II. Prison Reduction Policy

Dutch penal policy since the 1970s has been characterized by strong tendencies to reduce use of custodial sentences, to expand use of noncustodial sanctions in place of short-term imprisonment, to shorten effective terms of imprisonment, and to develop new noncustodial sanctions.

A series of substantive and procedural penal law reforms have been adopted. These include the reform of pretrial detention in 1973, passage of the Financial Penalties Act of 1983, reform of the suspended sentence in 1987, introduction of early release in 1989, the statutory introduction of the community service order in 1989, the introduction of other community sentences in the nineties, and experiments with use of electronic monitoring since 1995.

A. Pretrial Detention

The absolute number of pretrial detainees increased gradually during the fifties and sixties. Although the minister of justice (in 1953 and in 1965) issued directives to the prosecution service to limit use of pretrial detention to the most serious crimes, it was widely believed that pretrial detention was used inappropriately.

The decision to limit use of pretrial detention was based on several considerations. It infringes one of the most essential human rights—the right to liberty— before a court has established that a person has committed an offense. There were indications that pretrial detention often was used in effect as an anticipation of the prison sentence; pretrial detention increased the chances a prison sentence would be imposed. Pretrial detention may be more severe than a custodial sentence because the suspect has had no opportunity to prepare for loss of liberty; furthermore the place and manner of pretrial detention compare unfavorably with detention following sentence, and the suspect is uncertain how long he will be locked up.

A new law adopted in 1973 aimed to restrict the use of pretrial detention by establishing more restrictive criteria and by limiting its duration. Two statutory requirements must be met. The first concerns the kind of cases in which pretrial detention may be applied. The second deals with the grounds on which detention decisions must be based.

Under section 67 of the CCP, detention may be ordered if a serious suspicion exists that the offender committed an offense that meets one of several criteria: it carries a maximum penalty of not less than four years imprisonment or it is specifically designated (e.g., embezzlement, fraudulent misrepresentation, and threat) or it is potentially subject to imprisonment and the suspect does not have a fixed residence or regular place of abode in the Netherlands.

Section 67a of the CCP specifies when pretrial detention may be applied: if there is a danger that the suspect will abscond or if there is a serious concern for societal safety. A serious concern for societal safety exists if (1) the offense carries a statutory maximum sentence of at least twelve years' imprisonment and the legal order has been seriously shaken by the offense; (2) there is serious risk that the offender will commit a crime that carries a maximum statutory sentence not less than six years' imprisonment or by which the safety of the state or the health or safety of persons may be jeopardized or a general danger to property be created; (3) there is a serious suspicion that the offender has committed a property offense and will reoffend and less than five years have passed since he was sentenced to a deprivation or restriction of liberty or a community service order; or (4) it is necessary to detain the offender in order to establish the truth by methods other than through his own statements.

Other rules limit the length of pretrial detention. Pretrial detention may last up to one hundred days. After ten days, and every thirty days thereafter, the detention decision is reviewed by a criminal court. After one hundred days the prosecutor must present the case to the court or release the pretrial detainee. If the case is not ready for trial, which happens rarely, the trial may be adjourned. If the grounds for the application of pretrial detention remain valid, detention may be extended to a date sixty days in first instance. An automatic review by the court of the need to continue pretrial detention takes place at intervals of one month.

Three more general rules on the application of pretrial detention were formulated in the 1973 pretrial detention legislation. First, the full period of arrest and pretrial detention must be deducted from any term of imprisonment. Courts have no discretion in this respect (sec. 27 PC). Second, pretrial detention is not permitted if the offender is unlikely to be sentenced to imprisonment. Third, pretrial detention must end when it is likely that the expected actual term of imprisonment (taking the early release regulation into consideration) will last no longer than the pretrial detention already served (sec. 67a subsec. 3 CCP).

The court that remands the suspect in custody may suspend pretrial detention. The statutory condition is that the offender will not flee if the suspension is revoked or if he is sentenced to imprisonment. The court may impose other "special conditions." Sometimes these include the condition that the suspect admit himself to a clinic (e.g., for drug addicts). Checks on compliance with this condition, however, are not always very effective. In the great majority of cases, the court imposes conditions that restrict the freedom of the suspect to a lesser extent. Courts may impose bail as a guarantee that the conditions are observed but seldom do.

Table 4.4 shows the number of pretrial detainees at five-year intervals for 1970 to 1995. Since the early eighties, a lack of prison capacity has affected pretrial detention, because thousands of suspects for whom pretrial detention could be or was ordered were released by the Prosecution Service because space limits made detention impossible.

Inability to implement detention orders and delays in implementation of prison sentences are generally perceived as a serious defect in the administration of the Dutch criminal justice system. In order to ration detention space, (pretrial) detainees are divided into three categories (A, B, and C), depending on the seriousness of the alleged offense and the expected sentence (e.g., for A-cases, the expected prison sentence is greater than eighteen months; for B-cases, expected prison sentences range from nine to eighteen months). A-detainees have priority over B-detainees who have priority over C-detainees. When pretrial detention is ordered in an A-case and no cells are available, a C-detainee (or, if necessary, a B-detainee) is released. "A-plus" and "B-plus" categories have been introduced. An A-plus pretrial detainee may never be released to make room for another detainee (Richtlijn 1993).

Because space constraints became so pressing that even A-cases were released before remand (C-cases are now rare), it was further decided that, in "emergency

Table 4.4. Pretrial Detainees in the
Netherlands, 1970–1995, and Nonimplemented
Detention Orders, 1987–1997

Year	Pretrial Detainees	Nonimplemented
1970	7,048	
1975	6,586	
1980	8,502	
1985	11,875	
1987		2,187
1988		1,643
1989		1,549
1990	14,811	857
1991		1,204
1992		3,091
1993		4,340
1994		5,316
1995	3,288	4,200
1996		1,809
1997		910

Source: Tweede Kamer (1997).

cases," two pretrial detainees may be placed in one cell or a room not considered a cell may be used as such. This is a historic break with the golden "one prisoner, per cell" rule.

Table 4.4 also shows the number of nonimplemented detention orders for 1987–97. They peaked at more than four thousand per year in the mid-1990s. The number of nonimplemented orders led to a very critical report by the State Audit Committee in 1996 (Tweede Kamer 1997) and to a supplementary extension of the prison capacity. Since 1995 the number of nonimplemented detention orders has been decreasing because of the extension of prison capacity and adoption of a policy to release convicted prisoners who have only a small part of their sentence to serve in order to make room for pretrial detainees.

An increasing number of female remand prisoners have been released without detention. Recently, therefore, the capacity for female detainees has been extended.

Offenders whose pretrial detention order had not been implemented on average waited sixteen months after sentencing before serving their sentences: five months between release and trial and another eleven months before beginning the imposed prison sentence.

Almost half of the offenders whose pretrial detention order was implemented belonged to the A-category and 34 percent to the B-category. In 75 percent of the cases, the nonimplemented detention order was related to thefts by drug addicts,

10 percent concerned robberies and threats, 2.5 percent fraud and embezzlement, and 1.5 percent sexual offenses. The average prison sentence imposed on offenders whose pretrial detention order had not been implemented was eight months.

B. The Financial Penalties Act 1983

The fine is the last and formally the least severe of the principal sentences listed in Penal Code section 9. Originally intended only for infractions and minor crimes, it is now the most frequently imposed penalty for all crimes. Since passage of the 1983 Financial Penalties Act (sec. 23, subsec. 5 PC), all offenses, including those subject to life imprisonment, may be sentenced with a fine. The 1983 act established the principle that fines should be preferred over prison sentences (sec. 359 CCP) and requires the court to give special reasons whenever a custodial sentence is ordered instead of a fine.

The 1983 act was the final part of a major reform of the fines system that began in the mid-1970s with a goal of reducing the use of imprisonment. The changes were proposed by the Financial Penalties Committee, which was established in 1966 (van Kalmthout and Tak 1992). The reform was launched in 1976 by enactment of the Financial Penalties Enforcement Act. Its main purpose was to improve the enforcement of fines so that fines could function better as an alternative to short-term prison sentences. It introduced opportunities for paying fines in instalments, simplified the recovery procedures in cases of nonpayment, and reduced the maximum detention period on default.

The 1983 Financial Penalties Act was the next step. That act replaced the old fines system in which each offense carried its own statutory maximum fine with a simpler and more convenient system of fine categories. The minimum fine for all offenses is 5 guilders. The maximum fine depends on which of six fine categories a crime or infraction is placed in. The maxima are 500, 5,000, 10,000, 25,000, 100,000, and 1,000,000 guilders. Infractions come under the first three categories and crimes under the top five. Fines in the top category may be imposed only on corporate bodies and on individuals under a few special criminal laws, such as the Economic Offenses Act and the Narcotic Drug Offenses Act.

The old system of fixed sum fines was retained. Following the advice of the Financial Penalties Committee, day fines were rejected on theoretical and practical grounds. The act (sec. 24) urges the court when imposing a fine to take into account the financial position of the offender in order to arrive at sentence that will not disproportionately affect the offender in his or her income and capital. There must be proportionality between the crime and the fine and between the fine and the offender's ability to pay.

Implementation of fines and other financial penalties rests entirely with the Prosecution Service. If the convicted person does not pay the fine, its value may be recovered from the offender's property. If the Prosecution Service rejects recovery as an option, detention for default may be enforced; the default term is set by the court when imposing the original fine. In practice a conversion rate of 50 to 100 guilders per day of detention is usually applied.

The statutory minimum duration of default detention is one day, and the maximum is six months. A fine-default detainee will be released if he pays the fine while in prison. Because of the shortage of cell capacity, many fines go unpaid each year. The extra capacity needed annually for fine default detention was recently estimated at more than two hundred cells (Grapendaal and van der Heide 1997).

In order to reduce the need for prison capacity for fine-default detention, a more effective way to recover fines is needed. The aim of current policy is to recover 95 percent of the fines within a year after imposition (Ministerie van Justitie 1990). There are at present no alternatives to or substitutes for fine-default detention. This form of detention is not subject to current debate in penal policy.

C. The Suspended Sentence

The suspended sentence, conditional nonimplementation of a sentence, was introduced in 1915. Since its introduction, the governing regulations (secs. 14a-14k PC) have been radically revised a number of times, most recently in 1986 when the scope of application of the suspended sentence was greatly expanded.

The reform was inspired by a 1983 report of the Committee on Alternative Penal Sanctions and was strongly influenced by the need to reduce pressure on prison capacity (Commissie Alternatieve 1983). It responded to a long recognized need to make partial revocations of suspended sentences possible.

Since this act came into force on January 1, 1987, all fines and all prison sentences up to three years may be suspended. Prison sentences less than one year may be fully suspended, and prison sentences between one year and three years may be suspended for not more than one-third (sec. 14a PC).

The suspended sentence is always subject to the general condition that the convicted person must not reoffend during the probation period (sec. 14c PC). In addition, the court may impose one or more special conditions, including full or partial compensation for the damage caused by the offense, committal of the convicted person to an institution for treatment for a period of time not exceeding the period of probation, deposit of a sum of money as a security not exceeding the difference between the maximum statutory fine for the offense and the fine imposed, and special conditions with regard to the conduct of the convicted person.

The special conditions may not restrict the freedom to practice one's religion or personal beliefs or one's civil liberties (sec. 14c (3) PC). The suspended sentence is very widely applied. In recent years nearly 13 percent of all prison sentences have been partly suspended, and nearly half are fully suspended (see table 4.5).

The sharp rise in the number of suspended sentences in the 1980s resulted in an experiment with community service orders. Until formally introduced as a principal penalty in 1989, community service was usually imposed as a special condition attached to a suspended sentence.

Table 4.5. Prison Sentences and Fines in the Netherlands, 1970–1995

Year	Unsuspended Prison Sentence	Partly Suspended Prison Sentence	Suspended Prison Sentence	Fine
1970	8,407	4,547	10,151	20,789
1971	8,409	4,734	10,375	20,314
1972	9,612	4,747	11,054	20,573
1973	9,165	4,627	11,751	20,398
1974	—	—	—	—
1975	10,099	4,698	13,935	23,719
1976	10,973	4,966	15,621	26,307
1977	10,886	5,684	16,737	28,422
1978	9,469	5,356	15,909	34,967
1979	9,387	5,406	15,601	36,988
1980	9,261	6,108	16,509	40,084
1981	9,663	5,756	17,655	39,944
1982	10,171	6,133	19,652	41,967
1983	10,099	5,698	20,958	37,498
1984	10,010	5,456	21,056	31,349
1985	10,361	5,390	22,191	31,131
1986	9,282	4,988	20,870	30,372
1987	9,844	5,169	21,896	30,115
1988	10,404	5,359	23,592	29,850
1989	10,711	5,039	23,512	29,601
1990	10,051	4,582	19,875	27,861
1991	13,589	5,037	19,911	37,122
1992	14,195	4,420	17,792	34,829
1993	15,010	4,588	14,692	33,880
1994	19,372	4,810	17,147	39,231
1995	20,529	4,823	17,291	38,824

Source: Central Bureau of Statistics, various years.

The effectiveness and credibility of the suspended sentence depends upon enforcement compliance with the accompanying conditions. Formally, the Prosecution Service exercised control over compliance but in practice the Probation Service kept track of and advised the Prosecution Service and the court on the progress of the suspended sentence.

Compulsory probation supervision was abolished in 1973 because of pressure from the Probation Service, which argued that this task conflicted with its proper social work role. With the abolition of probation supervision, the judiciary's confidence in the special conditions plummeted and fewer special conditions were ordered. The decline in conditions was also influenced by criticism that special conditions were patronizing and highly invasive of privacy (Tak 1984).

Noncompliance with conditions may lead to revocation of the suspended sentence by the court on request of the public prosecutor. The court may decide partly to revoke the suspended sentence or to extend the probation period or to add or change the conditions (sec. 14f PC).

When the court considers revocation of a suspended sentence or part of it not exceeding six months, it may instead order community service (sec. 14g PC). Approximately 10 percent of all suspended sentences are revoked.

D. From Conditional to Early Release

Parole release, first introduced in 1886, was initially discretionary, but since 1987 has been automatic in most cases. Conditional release (parole) regulations were introduced in 1886. Prisoners were eligible for release after having served three-quarters of the sentence and at least three years of imprisonment. Today, release is required when prisoners have served specified fractions of their sentences.

Since 1915, prisoners have been eligible for conditional release after serving two-thirds of their sentence and at least nine months. The probation period lasted the longer of one year or the remaining unserved part of the sentence. The release decision was made by the prison administration (Ministry of Justice, Prison, and Probation Department) on advice from the Central Board for Probation. The decision was taken at the request of the local prison board on advice from the local probation council.

In addition to a mandatory general condition that the released prisoner not commit further offenses during the probation period and otherwise not behave badly, the administration could attach special conditions. Special conditions were related to the conduct of the released prisoner but were not further specified by rules. In practice the special condition mostly used was that the released person should accept special supervision by a probation officer.

The Prosecution Service was vested with rights to enforce compliance with the conditions and to seek revocation of the release. Breach of conditions was to be reported by the supervising probation officer.

In the sixties and seventies, the importance of the conditional release as a rehabilitative instrument decreased. This was partly a result of a decrease in the number of long prison sentences, which meant that the number of prisoners eligible for conditional release declined as well. In 1950, there were approximately 800, a number which by 1970 had declined to 340. Far more important, however, the professionalization of probation work and adoption of new probation work methods led to tensions between probation philosophy and the probation service's statutory task of postrelease supervision. The social work conception of the optimal relation between a probation officer and a client did not permit authoritarianism or compulsory supervision, which, however, formed basic parts of the statutory probation tasks. Because reporting on breaches of conditions did not fit with the professional ethos, such reporting was officially abolished in the early 1970s (Tak 1984).

Conditional release was no longer seen as a bonus for good behavior in prison or as an instrument of rehabilitation, and it became difficult for the Prison and Probation Administration to refuse to grant parole to an eligible prisoner. By 1973, more than 90 percent of those eligible for release were released.

Release was granted in most cases and refused only in very specific cases. A need was felt to create a way for a prisoner to appeal to a court when his or her request for release was denied. Since 1976, prisoners eligible for release can appeal to the special penitentiary chamber of the Arnhem Court of Appeal against a decision to reject, suspend, or revoke conditional release. The case law was very critical of the Prison and Probation Administration's release policies, and as a result the percentage of parole refusals fell from 11 percent in 1975 to 1 percent by 1986.

Conditional release had evolved from a privilege almost to an automatic right. Against this background, a committee was set up in 1980 to advise the minister of justice whether conditional release should be retained and, if so, whether the Penal Code should indicate that eligible prisoners have a right to be paroled.

The committee opposed automatic release. Although automatic release would save money, since the release procedure was time-consuming and very bureaucratic, and would save prisoners from uncertainty, it had serious drawbacks. With automatic release, there is a risk that courts will take the release into account when fixing the length of the sentence, lengthening the nominal sentences to ensure that the intended net sentence was served. Automatic release would mean that dangerous prisoners would be released. With automatic release, there is no incentive for good behavior for prisoners. Finally, automatic release would constitute a need for remission to be reserved for good conduct.

The committee's conclusion was that the conditional release regulations should be reformed. The Penal Code should not establish grounds for conditional release but establish grounds on which it should be refused. The committee advocated retaining the possibility of attaching special conditions in order to provide the released prisoner in order to make it possible for continuing probation contacts (Commissie Voorwaardelijke Invrijheidstelling 1982).

The government, however, preferring a system that would reduce the pressure on the prison system, eliminate red tape, and save money and time, introduced a system of automatic early release. The new release legislation (secs. 15–15d PC) came into force on January 1, 1987. Prisoners serving a sentence up to one year must be released after having served six months plus one-third of the remaining term. Prisoners serving a sentence of more than one year must be released after having served two-thirds.

There are a few narrow exceptions to the rule of automatic release. Early release may be postponed or refused when (1) because of mental disturbance the prisoner is serving his or her sentence in a mental hospital and the continuation of treatment is deemed necessary, (2) the prisoner is sentenced for an offense for which the statutory punishment is an imprisonment of four years or more, (3) the prisoner was guilty of very grave misconduct (e.g., a criminal offense for which pretrial detention would be allowed) after the commencement of serving of sentence, or (4) the prisoner, after the commencement of the serving of the sentence, escaped or attempted to do so.

The power to refuse or postpone early release rests not with the Prison and Probation Administration but with the penitentiary division of the Court of Appeal in Arnhem. It acts on the request of the public prosecutor attached to the court that imposed the prison sentence. The decision is made in a public trial at which the prisoner, assisted by counsel, may be heard. If the early release is postponed or refused, the penitentiary division fixes the date of release.

Since the new release regulations came into force, conditional release has ceased to exist in the Netherlands. Early release is final because it cannot be revoked. No conditions may be attached. Early release is thus no longer considered a restriction on liberty. It is an automatic sentence reduction with no rehabilitative aim and is intended solely as a means to reduce the pressure on the prison capacity (Tak 1989).

Recently, an interdepartmental task force considered proposals to make conditional release possible after serving half of the prison sentence. These changes would reduce prison capacity needs by more than four thousand prison places. The proposals were not supported because the task force feared that the adoption would lead to much more severe sentencing by courts, for crimes which now are sentenced with short prison sentences (Ministerie van Justitie 1997).

E. Community Sentences

Community sentences are increasingly used as substitutes for custodial sentences. There are various types. The oldest is the community service order (CSO) introduced in 1981. More recently implemented community sentences include training orders (*leerstraffen*) and combination orders (*combinatiestraf*). The latest developments are electronic monitoring devices and "penitentiary programs."

A community sentence may be imposed on juveniles and adults, particularly first offenders and offenders who have committed less serious crimes. For adults, a community sentence can be a substitute for a prison sentence of not more than six months. For juveniles, a community sentence may be a substitute for juvenile detention or a fine.

The community sentence may be imposed for any crime, without exception. In practice, however, courts do not impose community sentences for sexual offenses or firearms offenses. Community sentences are not imposed on offenders suffering from mental problems, drug addicts, recidivists, offenders who have previously breached a community service order, or persons without a fixed address.

The legal frameworks for community sentences vary considerably. The court may use a community sentence as a substitute for a custodial sentence or for a remand in custody or as a condition attached to a suspended sentence. The public prosecutor may use community sentence only for juvenile offenders as a condition attached to a conditional waiver (sec. 77f PC).

Community Service Orders

The development of community sentences started in the 1970s with the establishment in 1974 of the Committee on Alternative Penal Sanctions. This committee was set up to advise the government on new sentencing options. Resolution (76) 10 of the Committee of Ministers of the Council of Europe and the positive experiences in England (Pease 1985) and Scotland (McIvor 1995) with CSOs suggested their potential as a sentencing option. In 1979, the Committee on Alternative Penal Sanctions proposed a CSO experiment, which was initiated on February 1, 1981 (van Kalmthout and Tak 1992).

Ministerial guidelines directed that the experiments take place within the existing statutory framework. Therefore CSOs could be imposed by the Prosecution Service as a condition to a decision to waive prosecution or by the court as a condition attached to a decision to suspend a sentence. At the end of the experiment, statutory provisions governing use of CSOs for adult offenders were introduced in the Penal Code (secs. 22b–22j) in December 1987. Statutory provisions on use of CSOs for juvenile offenders followed in September 1995 (sec. 77m–77q PC).

The CSO for adult offenders is a distinct sentencing option and is considered a restriction of liberty less severe than the custodial sentence and more severe than a fine. A CSO may not exceed 240 hours. If less than 120 hours, the work must be completed within six months; otherwise within twelve months (sec. 22d PC). The criminal court may impose a CSO only if it would otherwise impose an unconditional prison sentence of six months or less, or a part-suspended prison sentence of which the unconditional part is six months or less (sec. 22b PC). Community service may not be used as an alternative to a suspended prison sentence, a fine, or a fine-default detention.

The court may impose community service only when there has been agreement from the accused that he is willing to carry out nonremunerated work of a type described in the proposal (sec. 22c PC). The accused's "compulsory consent" is a statutory requirement that addresses concerns about possible contravention of international conventions prohibiting forced labor. The judge must indicate the prison sentence for which community service is a substitute and specify the number of hours' work to be carried out, the period within which it must be completed, and the nature of the work (sec. 22d PC).

The Prosecution Service is responsible for overseeing CSOs, and information may be requested for this purpose from individuals and organizations involved in probation work (sec. 22e PC). When the Prosecution Service is satisfied that the work has been carried out properly, it must promptly notify the convicted person.

If the convicted person has not carried out the work properly, the Prosecution Service may request revocation of the CSO and imposition of the prison term indicated when the sentence was originally ordered. The judge must take into account work that has been properly carried out (sec. 22g PC). The Prosecution Service must make its revocation request within three months after the end of the completion period for the community service (sec. 22i PC).

The Probation Service is responsible for administering CSOs and coordinators have been appointed for each of the nineteen prosecutorial districts. The coordinator's job is to canvass for projects, maintain a project bank, maintain contacts with the project institutions, and write final reports. The coordinator decides on the nature of the work to be carried out, taking into account the offender's skills, education, and vocational training.

If the work requires team effort, the coordinator decides whether the offender fits. If the place or nature of work needs to be changed, the coordinator contacts the Prosecution Service, which has authority to make these changes. The convicted person is informed of the changes and may object within eight days to the sentencing court (sec. 22f PC).

Community service work must benefit the community. It can be with public bodies, such as the government or private organizations involved in health care, environmental protection, and social and cultural work. To discourage unfair competition with paid workers, regional review committees check that new regular workplaces are being used for community service.

No offenses are statutorily excluded from punishment with CSOs. Given the boundary of the six-month prison sentence, however, community service operates mainly for mid-level crimes and is seldom ordered for more serious offenses unless there are mitigating circumstances.

There are many advantages connected with community service. It eases pressure on the prison system, it is humane, and it has positive effects on rehabilitation of the offender. A further advantage is that the offender performs work that benefits society and helps repair the damage caused by his or her offense. Work that otherwise would not be done is carried out, and offenders serving community service sentences are slightly less likely to reoffend (Spaans 1994). A CSO does not carry the same negative side-effects as imprisonment, because the offender is not removed from his or her social environment and can perform community service in his or her leisure time. Also, unemployed offenders gain familiarity with regular work.

Has community service reduced the use of term imprisonment? Although a CSO may be imposed only when the court otherwise would impose a prison sentence of six months or less, CSOs substitute for noncustodial sentences as well. Recent research shows that 45 percent to 50 percent of CSOs substituted for short-term unconditional custodial sentences. Indications of net-widening were found in 30 percent to 45 percent of cases. These offenders had been sentenced to community service for offenses that were equally serious or less serious than those committed by most offenders sentenced to a suspended prison sentence. Net-widening was least common (28 percent) among offenders who received relatively long CSOs (151–240 hours) (Spaans 1995).

In this context it is remarkable that between 1985 and 1995, the relative share of short-term prison sentences among all sentences remained stable (± 18 percent), although the CSO share grew from 4 percent to 15 percent of all imposed sentences.

CSOs also function in relation to pardon. A pardon decision can be conditioned on performance of community service. In 1995, CSO conditions were attached to 605 pardon decisions.

The failure rate for CSOs imposed as a substitute for short-term imprisonment is 15 percent; for CSOs attached to a pardon decision, the failure rate is only 6 percent.

Training and Combination Orders

New community sentences were introduced in the early nineties that included training orders and combination orders. A training order requires the offender to learn specific behavioral skills or to be confronted with the consequences of his or her criminal behavior for the victim. Training orders are mainly imposed on juvenile offenders and on young adult offenders who, it is expected, are motivated to change their behavior by attending training courses or other activities aiming to improve communication or social skills.

Training orders are made for periods ranging from five meetings up to forty hours a week for three months or longer. Long-term intensive training orders may be imposed as a separate sentence only on adult offenders. Training orders are usually imposed in combination with a CSO or as a condition of a suspended sentence.

Community sentences are by far the most important sentences for juveniles. In 1995, both the CSO and the training order were introduced in the new juvenile criminal law. Community sentence is now imposed in 60 percent of all juvenile criminal cases. The CSO for juvenile offenders can be imposed by a court as a substitute to both youth detention and fines. The maximum number of hours is two hundred. The Prosecution Service can attach a CSO of forty hours maximum as a condition to a conditional waiver.

Electronic Monitoring

Electronic monitoring is the newest community sentence and might be given a statutory basis in the future. Electronic monitoring is a viable substitute for imprisonment or any other form of deprivation of liberty. This is the conclusion of an assessment of recent experiments with electronic monitoring in four jurisdictions (Spaans and Verwers 1997).

The aim was to determine whether electronic monitoring can serve as a substitute for imprisonment and other forms of detention. Electronic monitoring was used in the last phase of service of a prison sentence or in combination with a community sentence. By applying electronic monitoring in the last phase of the prison sentence, the stay in prison can be shortened. The combination of electronic monitoring with a community sentence can substitute for imprisonment between six and twelve months.

Candidates for electronic monitoring were proposed by the probation service, which was given supervision and control. Decisions to allow persons to serve their sentences through electronic monitoring was made by courts when combined with a community sentence and by the prison administration when it concerned the last phase of detention.

Between July 1995 and January 1997, 297 persons were candidates for electronic monitoring. Half were placed on electronic monitoring. They were sentenced for a range of crimes, including shoplifting, incest, kidnapping, and attempted murder or manslaughter.

The largest group were detained persons. They were serving prison sentences that averaged 28 months. The others were sentenced to CSOs of 240 hours plus a suspended prison sentence with electronic monitoring for 2 to 6 months. The electronic monitoring lasted an average of 3.5 months.

Those under electronic monitoring were obliged to follow a day program as specified by the Probation Service. In the hours the convict was required to be at home, he was electronically monitored. In cases of illegal absence, the probation officer contacted the monitored offender. This resulted in warnings or, for serious recidivism, in ending the monitoring.

Work is an essential element of the day program. Three-quarters of those under electronic monitoring worked in volunteer projects or professionally thirty-six hours a week. The rest received education or therapy or were kept busy with house-keeping.

Those who complied with the conditions were gradually granted extra free hours. The average number of free hours increased from thirteen hours a week in the beginning to twenty-two hours at the end. Most of the convicts complied with electronic monitoring without serious problems. Twenty had an official warning, because they either came home irregularly late or were irregularly absent. In ten cases, the electronic monitoring was stopped because of irregular absence. In two cases, electronic monitoring was stopped because of arrests for other offenses.

Those under electronic monitoring and their families perceived the monitoring as a serious sentence but not as punitive as imprisonment. Electronic monitoring was an appeal to responsibility and self-discipline. The strict day program constituted a serious restriction of freedom. Also the equipment used for electronic monitoring caused some restrictions (e.g., for sports). Positive elements prevailed, however. One could stay at home together with spouse and children and one could go to work.

During the experiments, courts seldom combined electronic monitoring with a CSO. The minister of justice, however, believed that electronic monitoring could substitute for prison sentences up to a maximum of one year, as expressed in the Ministry of Justice paper "Substitutie van Vrijheidsstraffen" (substitutes to imprisonment) (Ministerie van Justitie 1997).

The minister particularly urged consideration of the use of electronic monitoring for women and juveniles. If prison sentences imposed on women could be replaced by electronic monitoring, they could devote themselves to the daily education of their children in a natural environment.

Much is expected of electronic monitoring as a substitute for pretrial detention for juveniles. The advantage is that juveniles during the day can go to school and during the night are controlled. This will also reduce the pressure on the capacity of the youth prisons and reduce costs.

Penitentiary Programs

In 1998 a new Penitentiary Principles Act came into force. The act introduced the so-called penitentiary programs. Those programs start before the date of early release and have as their objective a smooth transition from prison to free society.

Electronic monitoring may be used to control the prisoner in the first phase of the penitentiary program.

Eligible prisoners will participate in a compulsory program of activities during the day when they will be electronically monitored. In the course of the program they receive more freedom, and eventually the electronic monitoring will cease. This fits with a rationale under which the detainee is gradually granted more personal responsibility.

Community Sentence Figures and Prospects

The number of community sentences increased rapidly from 1,972 in 1983 to over 25,000 in 1998 (see table 4.6). The target for 2000 is more than 30,000.

A bill is pending in Parliament that proposes to enhance the use of CSOs. The bill removes some restrictions on use of CSOs.

One restriction on CSOs is that the court may impose a CSO only if it would otherwise impose a short prison sentence. The proposal will make it possible to impose a CSO as a substitute for a fine as well. In case of noncompliance with the CSO imposed as a substitute for a fine, a fine default detention will take place. This seems counterproductive since community sentence is supposed to reduce the use of imprisonment and not to increase it through backdoor use of deprivation of liberty.

Table 4.6. Community Sentences in the Netherlands, 1981–1998

Year	Juveniles	Adults
1981	—	217
1982	—	917
1983	304	1,668
1984	780	2,431
1985	872	2,814
1986	1,398	3,419
1987	1,890	4,005
1988	2,160	4,913
1989	2,531	5,942
1990	2,776	6,626
1991	2,666	7,159
1992	3,248	8,585
1993	3,594	10,100
1994	3,979	12,171
1995	4,408	13,126
1996	6,452	15,589
1997*	7,925	15,896
1998*	9,800	16,142

Source: Verhagen 1999.

*Figures are provisional.

A further proposal is to extend training orders and combination orders to 480 hours, because training orders often last much longer than the CSOs (Tweede Kamer 1998).

Another proposal is to make a training order a principal penalty on its own. Until now, training orders have been used mainly as a condition for conditional waiver or for conditional suspension of pretrial detention or as a condition attached to a suspended prison sentence. Finally, the possibility will be introduced that the Prosecution Service may impose a training order of 120 hours maximum as a condition of an agreement to waive prosecution.

It is expected there will be 26,800 community sentences for adults and 6,000 for juveniles in 2000. There are, however, some problems. It will not be possible to extend regular project places on a large scale, nor will it be possible to place eligible offenders on an individual basis in projects. Therefore probation and after-care institutions are increasingly setting up self-governing group projects, in which work masters employed by these institutions are charged with the supervision of offenders serving community sentences. Furthermore, group projects are being developed with large-project providers such as landscape planning organizations (Wijn 1997).

III. Sentencing Practices

The Dutch judiciary is vested with wide discretion over sentencing. The few applicable statutory rules are expressed in general terms and do not limit the court in choices about the type and severity of sanctions in individual cases. The statutory framework for sanctions is very broad. The statutory minimum term of imprisonment is one day and applies to all crimes, regardless of the generic seriousness of the offense.

Maximum prison terms reflect the gravity of the worst possible cases. Few crimes are subject to life imprisonment, but instead of life-imprisonment a fixed-term sentence up to twenty years or a fine may be imposed.

The Penal Code provides restrictive rules on aggravating circumstances. Three circumstances may result in a more severe sentence: recidivism, concurrent offenses, and commission of an offense in the capacity of civil servant. In case of aggravating circumstances, the statutory maximum sentence may be increased by one-third.

Special aggravating circumstances are specified for a number of criminal offenses, which may result in a more severe sentence. This is true with offenses that are qualified by their consequences (e.g., assault resulting in the death of the injured person).

The Penal Code contains one general mitigating circumstance, tender age. Tender age results in the application of juvenile criminal law with a much lighter sanction system. The Penal Code also contains special mitigating circumstances related to pertinent offenses.

Consecutive prison sentences may not be imposed. When a suspect stands trial for multiple offenses, the court may impose a concurrent sentence, the maximum term of which may be one-third higher than the highest statutory maximum sentence for one of those offenses (sec. 5 PC). Cumulative fines may be imposed for any concurrent offenses. There is a limited possibility to combine various principal sentences. A prison sentence, if totally or partly suspended, may be combined with a fine.

The choice of sanctions lies with the court but is subject to procedural requirements concerning the reasons for the sentence. Section 359 (5) of the Code of Criminal Procedure requires that the verdict state the particular reasons why the sentence was imposed. The judge often will confine himself to boilerplate statements that the imposed sentence reflects the seriousness of the offense, the circumstances in which the criminal offense was committed, and the personality of the offender. This rationale, required by article 359 (5) CCP, is preprinted on the sentence form or flows easily from the word processor when conceiving the verdict.

Section 359 (6) CCP requires that, in a sentence involving a deprivation of liberty, the special reasons must be given that led to the choice of a custodial sentence, as well as the circumstances considered in determining the length of the sentence. The choice of a suspended sentence does not require provision of specific reasons. This requirement was incorporated in the CCP through the 1983 Financial Penalties Act.

Section 359 (7) CCP requires a statement of reasons when the court imposes a more severe sentence than the prosecution service requested. Section 359 (8) CCP requires reasons when the court denies the defendant's offer to perform community service.

Dutch criminal procedure provides for a two-step procedure in sentencing of adults (secs. 359 (5) and 359 (6) CCP). The first requires a decision on the amount of the punishment, which should be in proportion to the offender's blameworthiness and the seriousness of the offense.

The second requires a decision whether punishment should be a fine, a suspended sentence, or an enumerated sentence of imprisonment.

The aims of sentencing are retribution, special or general deterrence, reformation, protection of society, and reparation. The court is free to choose the aim it believes appropriate in each case. The chosen aim can often be deduced from the kind of sentence and the length of the sentence. Very often the court chooses for a combination of sentencing aims, but there are also many instances when one aim is emphasized. Examples include HR [Supreme Court] 26 August 1960, NJ [Dutch case law] 1960, 566: retribution ("that measures are not, unlike sentences, also beneficial to retribution of the criminal offense and are only aimed at the protection of public order and improvement of the offender"); HR 9 December 1986, NJ 1987, 540: general prevention ("that foreign criminals, like the defendant, should be deterred from providing for themselves by committing offenses in this country"); HR 12 November 1985, NJ 1986, 327: protection of society against the defendant ("In the imposition of a prison sentence, the reason that the court wanted to protect society maximally by doing so is not impermissible"); HR 15 July 1985, NJ 1986, 184: special prevention ("With a view to appropriate enforcement of norms, the court holds the opinion that no other sentence but deprivation of freedom shall be imposed").

The question arises to what extent the criminal liability of the offender puts a further limit to the severity of the sentence and to what extent the imposed sentence should be proportioned to the degree of criminal responsibility. The principle of "no criminal liability without blameworthiness" is part of Dutch penal law. It means that a defendant who is not responsible by reason of insanity cannot be punished and the case will be dismissed. But if the defendant is a danger to himself or herself or to others or to the general safety of persons or goods, the court must order that the defendant be admitted to a mental hospital under an entrustment order.

However, the principle of no criminal liability without blameworthiness does not mean that the sentence is fully determined by the offenders' blameworthiness or that a sentence that is disproportionate to the degree of blameworthiness is inappropriate. These sentences are determined not only by the degree of blameworthiness but also by factors such as protection of society from future risks presented by the offender, the seriousness of the offense committed, the effects of a serious offense in the legal order, and general and preventive effects (HR 15 July 1985, NJ 1986, 184). The Supreme Court has repeatedly accepted sentences in which a measure (e.g., an entrustment order) imposed because of diminished responsibility was combined with a very long prison sentence. Despite diminished responsibility, the court may impose a long-term prison sentence because it feels the need to keep the offender outside society for a long time in order to protect society (HR 6 December 1977, NJ 1979, 181; HR 12 November 1985, NJ 1986, 327).

Various personal factors may be reasons to adjust a sentence upwards or downwards. An upward adjustment may be justified by the defendant's noncooperation or by his negative attitude during the trial—for example, defendants who consequently deny having committed the crime or who try to evade a sentence by making false statements, defendants whose offenses were the result of offensive behavior, such as jealousy and hate, defendants who refused to cooperate in a psychiatric evaluation, or defendants who cannot understand that their behavior was wrong.

A downward adjustment may be predicated on a serious delay between the time when the offense was committed and the trial, by the defendant's voluntarily offering compensation for damages inflicted, by expressions of regret, by a lack of previous convictions, or by positive probation prospects.

A. Judicial Review of Sentencing

Sentences can be reviewed by an appellate court following an appeal by the defendant or the prosecutor. The appellate court has full discretion to determine a new sentence. Annually, 10 percent of (crime) cases dealt by the district court are followed by an appeal. On appeal, the appellate court retries the case in full. The district court is the appellate court for infractions (tried in the first instance by the subdistrict court). The court of appeal is the appellate court for crimes (tried in the first instance by the district court). The Supreme Court does not retry a case but only reviews the lawfulness of the judgment of the lower courts (subdistrict courts, district courts, and court of appeal) and the conduct of proceedings. It will quash a sentence in cases where the law has been improperly applied or the rules of due process and fair procedure have been violated (Tak 1999).

As a rule, appeal pays. Research on twenty thousand appealed cases in 1993, 1994, and 1995 showed that in 21.5 percent of these cases, the prison sentence set by the appellate court was similar to the sentence imposed in first instance. In 14.1 percent, the adjusted prison sentence was lower, and in 8 percent it was higher than the original prison sentence. In 51.8 percent of researched cases, the appeals court converted the prison sentence imposed by the district court into a suspended sentence or a CSO or, more rarely, into a fine (Engelhard 1997). The total number of prison days imposed by the trial courts was 1.8 million. Following appeal, this was reduced to 1.3 million prison days, a reduction of 1,370 prison years. Sentence reduction by the court is often a reward for good conduct during the time elapsed between the initial sentence and the appellate court session.

The Supreme Court also oversees sentencing, but review is restricted to the question whether adequate reasons have been provided to justify the sentence, according to the statutory requirements of section 359 CCP. The Supreme Court as a rule accepts as adequate explanation for a sentence the standard formula that the sentence is proportionate to the seriousness of the crime, the circumstances in which it was committed, and the personal circumstances of the suspect.

The Supreme Court does not accept the standard formula when there is an obvious discrepancy between the offense committed and the imposed sentence, for example, the seizure of a car worth 40,000 guilders for a criminal offense that carries a fine not exceeding 10,000 guilders (HR 13 June 1989, NJ 1990, 138); on appeal the sentence is augmented considerably without further reasoning, as when a suspended prison sentence imposed in the first instance is replaced by a determinate sentence (HR 2 April 1985, NJ 1985, 875); or the trial judge did not respond to credible, persuasive defense argument concerning the sentence (HR 1 November 1988, NJ 1989, 351).

B. Disparity in Sentencing

The absence of mandatory sentencing rules may contribute to the mild Dutch penal climate but it may also result in great disparity in sentencing. Disparity is a serious problem in the Netherlands and has long been a major concern. The appellate courts or the Supreme Court can undo extreme unjust sentences but neither can ever assure full equality in sentencing by lower courts.

Various proposals have been offered to improve equality in sentencing without severely restricting the judges' discretionary power to individualize the sentence. They range from the establishment of a special sentencing court, or a data bank on sentences, to sentencing checklists or sentencing guidelines, but none of those proposals has provided an effective solution to the problem.

For some offenses, there is less disparity in sentencing. This is not a coincidence, but is related to directives the Prosecution Service has issued on the prosecutors' sentencing proposals in the closing speech at trial. This applies to drunk driving, Social Security fraud, tax fraud, drug crimes, and some others. Those directives have a standardizing effect. Courts appear to give considerable weight to the sentence requested by the prosecutor. The directives are issued by the Assembly of the Prosecutors General, the body with responsibility for oversight of prosecution in the Netherlands. Individual prosecutors are in principle bound by these directives because of the hierarchical structure of the Prosecution Service, in which those lower in the hierarchy are obliged to respect instructions from superiors. This hierarchy is expressed in the law (sect. 5 Judicial Organization Act, and sect. 140 CCP). Courts, however, are not bound by these directives. Nor are they obliged to give reasons when they disregard the sentence recommendation and impose a harsher sentence on the defendant (HR 10 March 1992 NJ 1992, 593). In daily practice the directives are highly influential.

Although sentencing directives for prosecutors have been issued since the 1970s for many crimes, they have not had the desired or disparity-reducing effect. This is because the directives allow a wide range between the highest and lowest sentences to be requested, without indicating when a higher or lower sentence is appropriate. For example, the directive for simple bodily harm sets a fine of 250 guilders as the lowest sentence and a fine of 750 guilders as the highest.

There are also anomalies in the directives. Whether a weapon was used was very important in the directive on bodily harm, but use of a weapon played no role in the directive on use of violence.

Another reason sentencing directives were not an effective instrument against disparity in sentencing was that the directives left room for prosecutors in individual cases, without giving reasons, to deviate from them. As a result, in one jurisdiction a fine of 300 guilders for bicycle theft was requested by the public prosecutor and in another a fine of 1,250 guilders.

A project to develop comprehensive national prosecution guidelines was recently initiated (Steenhuis 1997). In this project, thirty-five new guidelines are being formulated that should lead to greater consistency in sentencing for the majority of crimes. The structure of the proposed new prosecutorial sentencing guidelines is very simple. For each crime a number of sentencing points is set, for example, bicycle theft, 10 points; burglary, 60 points; motor vehicle theft, 20 points; shoplifting, 4 points; destruction, 6 points; bodily harm, 7 points; threat, 8 points; insult 10 points; open or overt use of violence, 15 points; import or export of hard drugs, 30 points; burglary in a factory, 42 points. On account of special circumstances, the number of points can be higher or lower, for example, the use of weapons or victim injury lead to extra points. An attempted crime warrants a reduction of points. Recidivism increases the score by half. Multiple recidivism doubles the points.

Finally the points are converted into a sentence. Not all the points count equally for the sentence. A conversion system has been elaborated. Up to 180 points, every sentencing point counts. Between 181 to 540 points, each point counts as half a point, and above 541 points, each point counts as a quarter of a point.

Each point leads to a fine of 50 guilders or one day of imprisonment. Below 30 points, the public prosecutor need not go to trial and can resolve the case with a transaction or can propose a fine during the court session. Over 40 points, there will be an indictment and the prosecutor will request a prison sentence, or in appropriate cases, a CSO. Here is an example. Imagine a man is stopped for drunken driving. He refuses the breath-analysis order, insults the police officer, confesses that he has stolen a bike four times, and admits that he has been sentenced twice for bicycle theft. That leads to the following calculations: refusal of breath analysis, 10 points; insult to the police officer, 10 points; four times bicycle theft, 40 points. That he has been sentenced twice for bicycle theft doubles the points for the theft, yielding 100 points $(10+10+40+40)$. Because this is equivalent to less than six months (180 points), the public prosecutor will request a community service order of 150 hours.

Here is another example. A thief is caught red-handed and arrested. He confesses to 29 burglaries and 11 burglaries in factories. It is his first arrest. The number of points for 29 burglaries in houses (60 each) is 1,740 points. Eleven burglaries in factories $(11 \times 42$ points) equals 462 points, yielding 2,202 points, then, after conversion, 775 points, which means that the public prosecutor will request a prison sentence of 775 days.

The hope is that promulgation of the guidelines will lead to more uniform sentencing. Individual prosecutors may deviate from these guidelines but must give reasons for doing so. An advantage of this system is that it creates a common standard for the nineteen regional prosecution services. If one of them deviates very much from the national policy, monitoring data will make that evident.

IV. Crime Patterns

Between 1970 and 1984, the average annual increase in total recorded crimes was more than 10 percent. Since then it has been 2 percent (see table 4.7). In 1995 and 1996, the number of recorded crimes decreased 3 percent and 6 percent, respectively. Recorded crimes increased from 265,700 in 1970 to 1.3 million in 1994 and decreased to just under 1.2 million in 1996 (van den Berg 1997). Crime rates increased at an annual rate of 6 percent.

Relative to population aged 17–79 years old, the crime rate nearly quadrupled between 1970 and 1986. The peak year was 1994, when there were 10,350 recorded crimes per 100,000 people.

In 1970, 40 percent of all registered crimes were cleared by the police. In absolute figures, the number of cleared cases increased until 1984, but in later years the average clearance rate dropped, reaching 17.4 percent in 1996. In 1996, almost 12 percent of all registered property crimes were cleared. Three-quarters of all criminality consisted of property crimes.

There are four main categories of crimes, which constitute 98 percent of all recorded crimes: violent crimes, such as murder, homicide, rape, threat, assault, and robbery; property crimes, such as fraud, embezzlement, and theft; destruction (including crimes against public order); and traffic crimes, such as drunken driving and hit-and-run cases.

Violent crimes involve intentional violence threatening or violating a person's physical integrity. Between 1970 and 1996 the violent crime rate quadrupled (from 120 per 100,00 inhabitants in 1970 to 525 per 100,000 in 1996). While the total

Table 4.7. Recorded Crimes in the Netherlands and Rate per 100,000 Population Aged 12–79, 1970–1996

Year	Recorded Crimes	Rate per 100,000 People
1970	265,700	2,673
1975	453,200	4,246
1980	705,700	6,229
1985	1,093,700	9,168
1990	1,150,200	9,357
1995	1,230,700	9,651
1996	1,183,200	9,315

Source: van den Berg (1997).

number of crimes fell in 1995 and 1996, the number of violent crimes increased by 6 percent in 1996. The number of rapes and crimes against life were stable, but assaults, threats, and violent thefts increased. In 1996, 45 percent of violent crimes were assaults and 23 percent were robberies. Both percentages have been rather stable over the years.

Between 1970 and 1996, the number of property crimes per 100,000 inhabitants increased from 1,287 to 7,136. In 1995 and 1996 the number of property crimes, mainly bicycle theft and theft of or from cars, decreased annually by 8 percent. Because three-fourths of all criminality consists of property crimes, the overall decreases in 1995 and 1996 were a product of the decrease of property crimes.

The number of burglaries peaked in 1984 and 1994 but in the late 1990s was at the same level as in 1986. In 1996, the number of burglaries was twelve times as high as in 1970. The clearance rate fell to 11 percent in 1996. It was 19 percent in 1980.

There has been a gradual increase in crimes of vandalism and crimes against the public order, from 100 per 100,000 inhabitants in 1970 to more than 1,300 per 100,000 inhabitants in 1996. The average annual increase was 4 percent. The clearance rate was 27 percent in 1980 and dropped to 13 percent in 1996. Vandalism (144,000 cases) is by far the most important crime of this category (85 percent).

Between 1970 and 1996, the number of traffic crimes per 100,000 inhabitants increased from 254 to 780. In 1995 traffic crimes increased by 10 percent. In 1980, after the introduction of a new traffic code section on drunken driving, 50 percent of all traffic crimes consisted of drunken driving. Since 1992, it has been 30 percent. This decrease may be the result of less active enforcement by the police. In 1996, 62 percent of all traffic crimes were hit-and-run cases (in 1986, 30 percent).

The number of drug crimes increased between 1970 and 1996 from 442 to 6,600 (of which 1,300 were soft drugs cases and 5,300 were hard drugs cases).

Large-scale criminality is a problem of larger cities. The average rate of recorded crime for the whole of the Netherlands in 1996 was 9,315 per 100,000 inhabitants but in small communities (under 20,000 inhabitants), the average was 5,600. In larger towns (over 250,000 inhabitants), it was 16,000. In larger towns, the violent crime rate is four to five times higher than in smaller towns.

The number of juvenile suspects (12–17 years old) increased from 42,000 in 1980 to 51,000 in 1996 and the number of adult suspects from 152,000 to 179,300. The juvenile rate grew from 2,843 per 100,00 in 1980 to 4,665 per 100,000 in 1996. Per 100,000 adults, the figures were 1,704 in 1980 and 1,758 in 1996.

Although the larger majority of suspects are males, the number of female suspects is increasing more rapidly. The number of female juvenile suspects increased from 4,100 in 1980 to 6,800 in 1996 and the number of female adult suspects from 15,600 in 1980 to 24,800 in 1996. Per 100,000 juveniles, there were 561 female suspects in 1980 and 1,275 in 1996. Per 100,000 adults there were 313 female suspects in 1980 and 426 in 1996.

V. Sentencing Patterns

In the past fifteen years, there has been a constant need to increase prison capacity. Between 1980 and 1995, the total prison capacity increased from almost 3,900 cells to nearly 12,000. Recent governments have decided to further raise the total prison capacity in 2000 to more than 16,000. Table 4.8 shows Dutch prison capacity for adults, juveniles, and offenders needing psychiatric care between 1985 and 1997.

The present policy is to slow down this increase in prison capacity by increasing opportunities for the judiciary to impose various kinds of community sentences in lieu of prison sentences. In addition, a new crime prevention policy will be implemented, as will be the newly revised prosecutorial sentencing guidelines.

The permanent pressure on the prison capacity is caused by a variety of factors, including a rising crime rate, the increasing seriousness of criminality, and the more punitive penal climate. On average, the present prison population serves considerably longer sentences than in earlier years.

Recent research has examined the relative influence of changes in the average lengths of a prison sentence and the number of prison sentences on prison capacity needs, comparing 1995 with 1985 (Grapendaal, Groen, and van der Heide 1997). Since 1980 there has been a continual increase in the number of detention years imposed by courts, rising from 3,000 years in 1980 to 5,900 years in 1985 and 10,000 years in 1990.

For drug, violent, and property crimes, the likelihood of imprisonment increased significantly and the number of sentences longer than one year nearly tripled. Tables 4.9 and 4.10 show percentages of unsuspended prison sentences in 1985 and 1995 by offense category and the number of detention years related to sentences of various duration. Initially, the increase in imprisonment was caused mainly by increases in the average lengths of the prison sentences. The average sentence increased from 133 days in 1985 to 197 days in 1995. Until 1985, the increase was due to more severe sentences for drug crimes. After 1985, average prison sentences for other crimes increased as well, particularly for sexual crimes

Table 4.8. Prison Capacity for Adults, Juveniles, and Psychiatric Clinics in the Netherlands, 1985–1997

	Penitentiary Establishments		
Year	For Adults	For Juveniles	For the Implementation of Entrustment Orders in Psychiatric Clinics (TBS)
1985	4,827	667	402
1986	4,829	695	349
1987	5,170	707	358
1988	5,822	669	464
1989	6,240	691	470
1990	7,021	722	489
1991	7,650	802	528
1992	7,773	832	551
1993	8,151	846	578
1994	9,439	888	627
1995	10,249	1,045	650
1996	12,127	1,214	728
1997	12,579	1,413	873

Source: Gemert (1998).

(1985: 250 days; 1995: 501 days), violent crimes (1985: 280 days; 1995: 471 days), and crimes against public order (1985: 78; 1995: 161). The average prison sentences for drug crimes (1985: 401 days; 1995: 375 days) and property crimes (1985: 94 days; 1995: 91 days) decreased.

Between 1990 and 1995 the annual number of unsuspended and partly suspended prison sentences increased from 21,000 to almost 27,000. The total number of prison sentences (whether or not suspended) remained rather stable; the number of unsuspended prison sentences shows a strong increase. In 1990, the

Table 4.9. Percentage of Registered Crimes for Which Unsuspended Prison Sentences Were Imposed in the Netherlands, 1985 and 1995

Offense	1985	1995
Drug crimes	22%	34%
Violent crimes	16	21
Property crimes	13	18
Sexual crimes	18	17
Fire arms crimes	12	10
Crimes against public order	6	6
Traffic Act crimes	8	3
Economic crimes	—	1

Source: Grapendaal, Groen, and van der Heide (1997).

Table 4.10. Detention Years Imposed per Category of Prison Sentence, the Netherlands, 1985 and 1995

Prison Sentence Length	Number of Detention Years	
	1985	1995
Two weeks or less	133	149
Two weeks to one month	285	352
One to three months	881	1,362
Three to six months	1,111	1,615
Six to nine months	538	357
Nine to twelve months	439	947
One to two years	1,018	2,361
Two plus to four years	673	2,002
Four plus years	692	1,796

Source: Grapendaal, Groen, and van der Heide (1997).

proportion of unsuspended prison sentences to suspended prison sentences was 1: 1.5; in 1995 this ratio was 1:0.8. In particular for drug crimes, violent crimes, and property crimes, fewer suspended prison sentences were imposed.

Since 1990 the increases in average prison sentence length have slowed. Until 1990 the increase in average sentence length accounted for 82 percent of the increase in the total number of detention years and the increase in the number of sentences accounted for the other 18 percent. Between 1990 and 1995, these figures were 44 and 56 percent, respectively.

Why were there many more and much longer unsuspended prison sentences in 1995 than in 1985? There are at least five possible causes: criminal law reforms that increased the statutory maximum sentences; an increased willingness of the public to report crimes; changes in detection and investigation policies and expansion of the police force; changes in seriousness, amount, and kind of criminality; and a more punitive sentencing policy.

Interviews with representatives of the police, the Prosecution Service, the judiciary, and the bar revealed two primary causes. First, criminality, in particular violent criminality, became more serious between 1985 and 1995. Violent criminality leads to more severe sentences. Half of the increase of the number of detention years is attributable to more severe sentences for violent crimes (Grapendaal, Groen, and van der Heide 1997).

Second, judges and prosecutors became more punitive. Since 1985, the penal climate has become more punitive, at first slightly, and in the most recent years much more so. Courts are less likely to suspend prison sentences.

VI. Changed Prison Population Composition and Prison Regimes

Between 1970 and 1995, the composition of the prison population changed considerably (see table 4.11). In comparison with the 1970s, there are many different types of prisoners, serving much longer sentences, for different kinds of offenses.

Relatively little information is available on the nearly 30,000 people who enter and leave the Dutch penitentiaries each year. A study on the changes in prison population composition between 1977 and 1987 was published in 1989 (Verhagen 1989). The general trends during that period still seem to be valid (Verhagen 1997). In 1977, 16,570 prison sentences (including partly suspended) were imposed. The average was seventy days and in their aggregate they totaled to 3,175 prison years. Prison sentences were imposed for drug crimes (826 sentences), traffic crimes (6,762 sentences), and Penal Code crimes (8,982). For drug crimes, 450 detention years were imposed; for traffic crimes 292 prison years; and for Penal Code crimes, 2,433 detention years. Of every ten prison sentences, four were related to the Traffic Act, but sentences were so short that only one out of ten prisoners was a traffic offender; another was a drug offender and the remaining eight served sentences for Penal Code offenses. Of all prison sentences, 4.5 percent were long sentences, constituting 37 percent of the total number of detention years.

In 1987, 15,040 prison sentences were imposed. The average was 124 days. The total number of detention years was 5,321. The number of imposed prison sentences had decreased, but prison capacity needs increased 68 percent in ten years. Of all imposed prison sentences, 1,449 were under the Drugs Act, 2,662 under the Traffic Act, and 11,538 under the Penal Code. For the Drugs Act, there was a considerable increase and for the Traffic Act, a drastic decrease. Detention years under the Drugs Act totaled 1,318, under the Traffic Act 145, and under the Penal Code 3,858. One of every four detainees was serving a sentence for a drug crime; and one of every thirty for traffic crimes. In 1987, more than 10 percent of all prison sentences were long sentences. In 1977 one out of every seven prisoners was a drug addict; in 1987 it is one out of three. Since 1982 the number of the detention years imposed on female prisoners has gradually increased, from 99 years in 1982 to 219 years in 1987. Half of the total number of detention years were imposed for drug crimes (mainly drugs couriers). In 1977, forty-seven places were occupied by female prisoners and in 1987, two hundred places, which means the number of cells for female detainees quadrupled in ten years.

The changes in the prison population are reflected in changes in the prison system itself. The 1953 Principles of Prison Administration Act (PPA) formulates the task of the prison administration as follows: "While maintaining the nature of imprisonment, its implementation is to be made subservient to the preparation of the prisoner for his return into free society" (sec. 26 PPA).

Since this act came into operation in 1953, four so-called prison memoranda have been published. They indicate the changes in prison philosophy and regime policies in the past thirty years.

Table 4.11. Select Characteristics of the Prison Population in the Netherlands, 1970–1995

Characteristics	1970	1975	1980	1985	1990	1995
Prison sentences under 6 months (%)	15	—	—	—	—	25
Prison sentence in days (avg.)	59	61	96	133	152	197
Prison sentences among all sentences (%)	29	—	20	23	22	26
Detainees for Drugs Act offences (%)	—	—	—	—	19	17
Detainees for violent crimes (%)					34	36
Detainees younger than 25 years (%)	48	—	43	—	—	28
Detainees with psychiatric disturbances (%)	—	—	10	—	—	13
Addicted detainees (%)	—	14	—	35	48	—
Detainees born outside the Netherlands (%)	—	—	—	—	45	50

Source: Central Bureau of Statistics, various years; Tweede Kamer 1994; Verhagen 1985, 1997.

In the 1964 Prison Memorandum, the rehabilitative ideal was very much alive. The memorandum sets out several policy principles for the further development of the prison system. The most important are (1) the optimal security in the prison is minimal security; (2) the prison regime must be adapted to developments in free society; (3) the restriction of personal freedom of a prisoner must be in proportion with the need to fulfill the purpose of his or her detention; (4) the legal position of prisoners deserves statutory regulation; and (5) the professionalization of prison staff must be improved. High standards must be required of staff working in penal institutions (Tweede Kamer 1964).

After 1964 much effort was devoted to implementing these principles. Several open and half-open prisons were built. The National Prison Selection Center was set up to improve the selection of prisoners for the various penitentiary establishments. A prison building and renovation program was carried out to make prisons suitable to the implementation of these principles. Prison regimes changed. Visiting arrangements and facilities for exchanging letters were increased, as were opportunities to wear one's own clothes and keep personal belongings. Still no solution was found to the problem of purposeful prison work and prison wages.

In 1976, the Legal Status of Prisoners Act gave prisoners the right to lodge a complaint against decisions taken by prison governors concerning discipline and regime. The complaint would be put before a special committee, the so-called Complaints Committee, which formed part of the Prison Supervision Committee.

Professional prison staff were recruited from behavioral science and social work circles. Prison-officer training was reorganized to place more emphasis on their role as treatment agents and less on their role as guards, and group work and creative work were introduced.

These changes and improvements were applauded on all sides. Indeed, in the early 1970s there was, in the Netherlands, for a short while, such enthusiasm about the success of rehabilitation that it was felt that prison capacity (2,800 places in 1972) could be reduced by 500 places.

By the early 1970s, the composition and social background of the prison population had changed considerably. One-fifth of prisoners were foreigners. The liberal trends in society in the 1970s affected the prisons, making the inmates less manageable. The number of prisoners serving long-to-very-long sentences increased and the offenses for which prison sentences were imposed were increasingly violent offenses, drugs crimes, and drug-related crimes. These changes in combination with capacity problems and a financial crisis prompted the 1976 Prison Memorandum, in which some aspects of the policy principles of 1964 were reconsidered (Tweede Kamer 1976).

As time passed, scepticism developed about the rehabilitative ideal. Research had shown that differences in prison regimes had no effect upon recidivism. Serious doubts about the ability of prisons to reform prisoners before they leave prison were confirmed by these findings.

Due to this scepticism, the 1976 Prison Memorandum "expressed the idea that the requirement to rehabilitate should be less ambitious than formerly was the case. The idea that the prisoner can be made into a better person does not seem very realistic. Research has shown that imprisonment is not the most appropriate means of achieving this. The prison system must not turn back from its statutory duty to prepare prisoners for their return to the community, but expectations about changes in behavior and recidivism must not be attached to this" (Tweede Kamer 1976, p. 32).

The problems observed in the 1976 Prison Memorandum seem only to have increased when the third memorandum was presented in 1982. The total number of unsuspended and partly suspended prison sentences had risen from 12,946 in 1970 to 15,309 in 1980. In 1970, 89.8 percent of prison sentences were for less than six months; by 1980 that had fallen to 85.4 percent. Between 1970 and 1980, the number of prison sentences for more than one year had risen from 219 to 660 (Tweede Kamer 1982).

There was a serious shortage of prison capacity by the beginning of the 1980s. People sentenced to a short prison sentence had to wait years before they could serve their sentences. The number of sentenced prisoners awaiting admission to prison was growing at the rate of two hundred sentences a month. The number of prisoners who needed extra attention (long-term prisoners, foreign prisoners, prisoners of ethnic minorities, prisoners with psychiatric disturbances, and drug-addicted prisoners) also increased rapidly.

The wording of the new prison policy was very realistic. Efforts must be made, it said, to implement the prison sentence humanely. The damaging effects of imprisonment must be avoided, or at least minimized. Preparation for the prisoners' return to society must be effected by creating opportunities for work on personal development and by resolving any psychosocial problems.

The humane implementation of imprisonment was improved by decisions no longer to deny prisoners the right to vote, to allow prisoners to furnish their cells as they wished, to widen the possibilities for them to communicate by mail and to allow them to watch television in their cells.

Several changes in prison regimes had been effected in order to limit the damaging effects of imprisonment. Efforts were made to prevent the socialization of new inmates into the values of deviant and criminal subcultures. Prisoners were urged to take active part in programs in the prison. Furthermore, attempts were made to prevent prisoners from becoming drug addicted by setting up drug-free sections within a number of penitentiaries.

The most recent Prison Memorandum was issued in 1994. In Dutch it is called "Werkzame detentie," meaning both effective incapacitation and laborious or industrious detention (Parliament 1994). The main reason to develop a new prison policy was said to be the more serious nature of the prison population. An increasing number of prisoners were serving very long prison sentences, and there were more aggressive prisoners, prisoners with high escape-risk, and psychotic and drug-addicted prisoners.

There were also an increasing number of non-native prisoners who would be expelled from the country after their release. The number of nationalities, foreign languages, religions, and other such distinctions was growing every year. Another reason to reconsider the prison policy was the enormous extension of the penitentiary capacity since the previous prison memorandum.

What is the core of the present prison policy? The starting point is that a standard regime for all prisoners exists in which productive labor for twenty-six hours a week is a central element. The standard regime offers each prisoner a number of statutorily guaranteed activities, such as open-air visits, visits by family and friends, recreation, and sport.

The purpose of the standard regime is twofold: it leads to more constructive use of time spent in prison (reducing boredom and idleness), and it contributes to the integration of released prisoners in the society. Daily work to earn a living can have a beneficial effect on one's existence by teaching work discipline and how to structure the day around work.

A large majority of prisoners are subjected to the standard regime. A relatively small group qualify for special treatment that is more specifically directed towards promoting their integration into society after their release. In the closed prisons, there should be special facilities for drug addicts who want to break out of their drug-related criminal life style, prisoners with psychiatric disorders who require close supervision, and prisoners who want to improve their opportunities in society by means of education, occupational courses, and work-training programs. In the final phase of their sentence, prisoners may also qualify for placement in a penitentiary establishment with a regime that permits certain freedoms as part of the phased-detention process.

Some prisoners need extra attention because of the risk that they may try to escape or because they represent a threat to control in the penitentiary establishment. Two small top-security prisons have been constructed that house prisoners with a high escape-risk. For prisoners whose conduct causes additional problems in terms of control in the prisons, small units have been set up with a modified, rigidly structured regime (Tak 1999).

Dutch sentencing, sanctions, and prison policies have changed markedly since the early 1970s. Crime rates have grown and the prison population has at least kept pace, giving Holland the fastest rising population rate in Europe for the past fifteen years and an imprisonment rate that is no longer among the world's lowest.

New sanctions—community service, training orders, electronic monitoring, "penitentiary orders"—have proliferated and are in ever-increasing use. There is no basis for confident predictions that recent trends will continue or whether Holland will revert to the mild penal climates that characterized it for many years. The Dutch penal climate is still mild; one has only to look at the number of prisoners, and the way they are treated, the possibilities they have, and the money spent to support them psychologically and medically. I have been in prisons in many countries but never have I seen such a high level of care for prisoners as in the Netherlands. Furthermore, the penal climate is mild because the Netherlands has such a wide range of possibilities for avoiding imprisonment or reducing the length of sentences. It is not the penal climate that has changed but the societal climate—notably the increase of serious drug crimes and violence.

REFERENCES

Central Bureau of Statistics. Various Years. *Annual Prison Statistics*. The Hague: Sdu.
Commissie Alternatieve Strafrechtelijke Sancties. 1983. The Hague: Ministerie van Justitie.
Commissie Heroverweging Instrumentarium Rechtshandhaving. 1995. *Het recht ten uit-voergelegd: Oude en Nieuwe Instrumenten van Rechtshandhaving*. The Hague: Ministerie van Justitie.
Commissie Voorwaardelijke Invrijheidstelling. 1982. Rapport V.I., tenzij. The Hague: Ministerie van Justitie.
Engelhard, I. 1997. "Hoger Beroep in Strafzaken." *Kwartaalbericht Rechtsbescherming en Veiligheid*, 10.2. Voorburg: Centraal Bureau voor de Statistiek.
Grapendaal, M., and W. van der Heide. 1997. *Vier Substitutiescenario's voor Het Jaar 2001*. The Hague: Ministerie van Justitie.
Grapendaal, M., P. P. Groen, and W. van der Heide. 1997. *Duur en Volume: Ontwikkelingen van de Vrijheidsstraf tussen 1985 en 1995*. The Hague: Ministerie van Justitie.
Kuhn, André. 1997. "Prison Populations in Western Europe." In *Sentencing Reform in Overcrowded Times*, edited by Michael Tonry and Kathleen Hatlestad. New York: Oxford University Press.
McIvor, Gill. 1995. "CSOs Succeed in Scotland." In *Intermediate Sanctions in Overcrowded Times*, edited by Michael Tonry and Kathleen Hamilton. Boston: Northeastern University Press.
Ministerie van Justitie. 1985. *Samenleving en Criminaliteit: Een Beleidsplan voor de Komende jaren*. The Hague: Ministerie van Justitie.
———. 1990. *Strafrecht met beleid*. The Hague: Ministerie van Justitie.
———. 1997. "Substitutie van Vrijheidsstraffen." IBO-ronde 1996, report no. 8. The Hague: Ministerie van Justitie.
Tweede Kamer. 1964. *Het Nederlandse Gevangeniswezen*. Parliamentary Papers no. 7709. The Hague: Sdu.
———. 1976. *Beleidsvraagstukken Gevangeniswezen*. Parliamentary Papers no. 14102. The Hague: Sdu.
———. 1982. *Taak en Toekomstvan het Nederlandse Gevangeniswezen*. Parliamentary Papers no. 17539. The Hague: Sdu.
———. 1994. *Werkzame detentie*. Parliamentary Papers no. 22999. The Hague: Sdu.

———. 1997. *Heenzending en Tenuitvoerlegging van Straffen.* Parliamentary Papers no. 25630. The Hague: Sdu.

———. 1998. *Wetsvoorstel Taakstraffen.* Parliamentary Papers no. 26114. The Hague: Sdu.

Pease, Ken. 1985. "Community Service Orders." In *Crime and Justice: An Annual Review of Research*, vol. 6, edited by Michael Tonry and Norval Morris. Chicago: Chicago University of Press.

Prosecution Service. 1996. *Annual Report.* The Hague: Ministerie van Justitie.

Richtlijn Heenzendingen. 1993. *Staatscourant.* The Hogue: Sdu.

Spaans, E. C., 1994. *Appels en Peren. Een Onderzoek naar de Recidive van Dienstverleners en Kortgestraften.* Research and Documentation Centre Research and Policy Series no. 130. Arnhem: Gouda Quint.

———. 1995. *Werken of Zitten: De Toepassing van Werkstraffen en Korte Vrijheidsstraffen in 1992.* Arnhem: Gouda Quint bv.

Spaans, E. C., and C. Verwers. 1997. *Electronisch Toezicht in Nederland: Uitkomsten van het Experiment.* Research and Documentation Centre Research and Policy Series no. 164. The Hague: Ministerie van Justitie.

Steenhuis, D. W. 1997. "Nieuwe Richtlijnen Stap Naar Rechtsgelijkheid." *Opportuun* 4(3): 3–6.

Tak, P. J. P. 1984. "Two Processes of Change in Probation Activities in a Comparative Perspective." *Liverpool Law Review* 6:33–48.

———. 1986. "The Legal Scope of Non-Prosecution in Europe." HEUNI Publication Series no. 8. Helsinki: Government Printing Center.

———. 1989. "Concepts of Conditional Release in Western Europe." *Netherlands International Law Review* 1:19–49.

———. 1999. *The Operation and Organization of the Dutch Criminal Justice System.* WODC Reeks Onderzoek er Beleid no. 182. The Hague: Ministerie van Justitie.

van den Berg, W. 1997. "Geregistreerde Criminaliteit 1970–1996." *Kwartaalbericht Rechtsbescherming en Veiligheid*, 10.2. Voorburg: Centraal Bureau voor de Statistiek.

van Kalmthout, A.M. 1998. "De Tenuitvoerlegging van de Vreemdelingenbewaring: Kloon Voorlopige Hechtenis of Eigensoortie Maatregal." *Sancties* 5:18–27.

van Kalmthout, A. M., and Tak, P. J. P. 1992. *Sanctions Systems in the Member States of the Council of Europe. Deprivation of Liberty, Community Service and Other Substitutes.* Deventer: Kluwer International Publishers.

Verhagen, J. J. L. M. 1989. "Veranderingen in de Gedetineerden-Populatie in de Afgelopen tien Jaar." *Justitiele Verkenningen*, pp. 7–16.

———. 1997. "Verandernigen ni de justitiële nirichtingen." *Sancties* 4:229–40.

Walmsley, R. 1997. "Prison Population in Europe and North America." HEUNI papers no. 10. Helsinki: European Institute for Crime Prevention and Control.

Wijn, J. T. 1997. *Taastraffen, Stand van Zaken, Praktijk en Resultaten.* The Hague: Ministerie van Justitie.

Sentencing and Punishment in Germany

This chapter describes how sentencing policy in Germany has developed over the past thirty years and outlines its prospects for the future. I argue that, while some basic features of sentencing policy have remained unchanged over the years, Germany has made significant headway in the direction of rationality and parsimony of punishment, especially with respect to sentences implying incarceration. The trend of the present and the future seems, however, to revert to attitudes and practices of the past: severe sanctions have made a comeback, especially as a response to offenses regarded as a serious threat, such as drug offenses and organized crime.

A rough outline of the sentencing process may help in rendering what follows more comprehensible to readers not familiar with the German system. Several participants in the criminal justice system have a hand in sentencing. These include the legislature, the public prosecutor, the defendant, the trial court, and a special judicial body named Strafvollstreckungskammer (literally, "panel in charge of the execution of sentences"; see paras. 78a, 78b Code of Court Organization [CCO]).

Sentencing has traditionally been (and officially still is) the domain of the trial court. After a comprehensive trial at which issues of guilt and sentence are debated simultaneously, the court (in serious cases a mixed panel of professional and lay judges, in less serious cases a single professional judge) pronounces the verdict and—unless there is an acquittal—a fixed sentence. Most offenders receive fines only, a smaller group is given suspended prison sentences, and one of twelve convicted offenders (more exact figures follow) must immediately serve a prison sentence up to fifteen years, or a life sentence. The death penalty was abolished in 1949.

Authorized sentences are indicated individually for each offense in the Strafgesetzbuch (Penal Code [PC], dating originally from 1871 but since frequently amended), as well as in any other statute providing for criminal punishment.[1]

Statutory penalty ranges tend to be fairly broad, thus allowing significant leeway for judicial sentencing discretion. For example, nonaggravated larceny can be punished by a fine or by imprisonment between one month and five years (para. 242 PC),[2] the penalty range for nonaggravated robbery is six months to fifteen years (para. 249 PC), and a prison sentence between one and fifteen years can be imposed for rape (para. 177 sec. 2 PC). Murder carries a mandatory life sentence (para. 211 PC),[3] but the Federal Court of Appeals has nevertheless allowed imposition of a lesser penalty when the maximum penalty would be disproportionate in the light of mitigating circumstances (30 Entscheidungen des Bundesgerichtshofes in Strafsachen [BGHSt] 105 [1981]).[4] Overall, statutory sentence ranges in Germany give only a broad indication of the legislature's estimation of the relative seriousness of an offense and fail to offer significant guidance to the sentencing court for the resolution of individual cases.

The public prosecutor has no official sentencing authority but can influence sentencing in several ways. The prosecutor is generally duty bound to bring criminal charges whenever there is sufficient evidence of criminal conduct (para. 170, sec. 1 Code of Criminal Procedure [CCP]), and he or she cannot limit the court's jurisdiction to specific legal charges (para. 155, sec. 2 CCP);[5] but whenever the suspect has arguably committed two or more violations, the prosecutor can select one or more of the most serious offenses for trial and refrain from prosecuting the others (para. 154 CCP). More important, the prosecutor can, in misdemeanor cases, require the suspect to make restitution to the victim or to make a payment to charity or to the state in exchange for dropping criminal charges (para. 153a CCP).[6] This option, introduced in 1975, gives the prosecutor informal but, practically, highly relevant sentencing power. Finally, the prosecutor makes a sentencing recommendation at the end of the trial (para. 258, sec. 1 CCP) or suggests a specific sentence to the court in a written procedure (penal order; para. 409 CCP).

The defendant can informally influence sentence severity by making a confession or by otherwise cooperating with law enforcement. Although the Penal Code is silent on this issue, courts uniformly use leniency in sentencing to reward confessing or providing information on other suspects (*Leipziger Kommentar* 1995, sec. 46, n. 207; Grünwald 1987, p. 454; Schönke and Schröder 1997, sec. 46 n. 41a).[7]

Finally, the Strafvollstreckungskammer has the power to grant an early (conditional) release from prison when the offender has served two-thirds of the sentence; under special circumstances, release is possible even when only one-half of the sentence has been served (para. 57 PC). The most important criterion for early release is the "security interests of the public" (para. 57 sec. 1 no. 2 PC), that is, the risk of recidivism the offender poses. The Strafvollstreckungskammer is in most cases a single professional judge who decides after hearing the offender and the head of the institution in which he is serving the sentence (para. 454 CCP). Early release can be revoked whenever the offender commits a new offense or otherwise violates the conditions imposed on him (paras. 57, sec. 3, 56f PC).

Judicial sentencing decisions are subject to appellate review. The defendant as well as the public prosecutor can file an appeal if he or she is dissatisfied with the sentence imposed[8] or with a decision on suspension or early release. Courts of appeals tend to defer to the trial court's sentencing discretion, yet they require, in the trial court's written judgment, a fairly detailed explanation of the reasons for the sentence imposed. Courts of appeals sometimes cite an insufficient explanation of the judgment as grounds for reversal of the lower court's sentencing decision when it is in fact the excessive severity or leniency of the sentence that gives them cause for concern (see, e.g., *Leipziger Kommentar* 1994, sec. 46, nn. 326–35; Streng 1991, pp. 194–96).

The interplay of these various agencies makes for a complex system of sentencing. That German sentencing law places greater emphasis on "individualization" than on uniformity of sentences for similar offenses further adds to complexity and makes the outcome of the sentencing process in individual cases very difficult to predict.

I begin in section I by describing German sentencing law and policy as it was in 1968 (i.e., the year before the reforms initiated in the 1960s were implemented). Then in section II, I give an overview of sentencing options and the use being made of them in 1996. In conclusion, in section III, I take a glimpse into the future, attempting to evaluate currently visible trends and possible developments.

I. The State of the Art in 1968

When we look back at the theory and practice of sentencing in 1968, we see a concept based on ancient moralistic principles of retribution and deterrence and a heavy reliance on deprivation of liberty, predominantly in the form of short-term imprisonment, as the standard sanction even for common offenses such as theft and drunken driving (for a critical contemporary account of the situation, see Jescheck 1969, pp. 496–506).

Of all adults sentenced in 1968, 24 percent (more than 136,000 individuals) went to prison, the great majority of them for a period of less than nine months. Prison sentences were suspended for 13 percent of all sentenced offenders (Statistisches Bundesamt Reihe 9, 1970, p. 13). Under the law as it stood in 1968, prison sentences could be suspended only if the sentence did not exceed nine months and if the court trusted the offender to commit no further offense and to lead an "orderly" life. Suspension was impossible if the offender had, within the preceeding five years, received one or more prison sentences that, in combination, exceeded six months or if a suspended sentence had been imposed on him within that period (para. 23 PC, 1968 version). Even in the 1960s, the majority of sentenced offenders (63 percent in 1968) were fined. Fines were imposed as lump sums with a maximum of the then equivalent of US $3,000, or US $30,000 if the offense was committed for gain (para. 27, sec. 2 PC, 1968 version). If the offender failed to pay the fine, he had to serve a term of imprisonment to be fixed by the court in its discretion. On March 31, 1968, West German prisons held 44,000 convicted adult offenders, which is equivalent to a rate of 106 per 100,000 adults (Statistisches Bundesamt Reihe 9, 1970, p. 24).

II. The State of the Art in 1996

A. Imprisonment

When we look at the situation in 1996, twenty-eight years after the starting date of our time journey,[9] the number of persons sentenced to imprisonment has shrunk from more than 136,000 (in 1968) to fewer than 37,000, [10] and prison sentences make up only 5 percent of all court sentences. The great majority of offenders, 82 percent, receive fines and the remaining 12 percent get suspended prison sentences (Statistisches Bundesamt Reihe 3, 1997, pp. 44–45). The changes can be seen in table 5.1.

Optimists might be tempted to explain the reduction of prison sentences by citing a concomitant reduction in (serious) crime. Yet, between 1968 and 1996 both the number and the rate of nontraffic criminal offenses reported to the police rose threefold, the number of suspects identified by the police increased (though in a greater Germany) by approximately 130 percent, and the number of persons convicted of criminal offenses rose by 25 percent from 526,813 to 656,895. (see table 5.2).

Given the substantial increase in the numbers of suspects and convicted persons between 1968 and 1986, the soft curve of imprisonment rates in table 5.1, characterized by a sharp downward turn immediately after the impact of the reform and a slow upswing since 1976, may seem surprising. However, in the light of the "loss" of more than 100,000 sentences of imprisonment between 1968 and 1976, one might think the majority of prisons would have been converted into museums or university dormitories. But even in Germany, the iron rule applies that where there are prisons, there will be prisoners. Between 1968 and 1976, the number of adults in prison did decrease (from 42,122 to 31,592), but this curve declined to a much lesser degree than the massive decrease in custodial sentences imposed in the same period. And by 1996, the number of adults in prison on a given day just slightly exceeded the level it had reached twenty-eight years before.

Table 5.1. Sanctions Imposed in Germany, 1968–1996

Year	Adults Sentenced	Imprisonment Unsuspended	Thereof: Less Than 9 Months	Suspended Sentence	Fine	Convicted Adults in Prison (March 31)
1968	572,629	136,519	118,633	75,036	361,074	42,122
1976	587,815	35,371	19,004	59,196	492,561	31,592
1980	596,166	35,254	18,812	66,345	494,114	35,537
1990	613,713	35,526	17,874	68,574	512,343	34,799
1993	686,250	33,601	16,972	75,268	577,381	37,128
1996	682,844	36,874	18,031	84,452	561,238	43,475

Sources: Statistisches Bundesamt Reihe 9 (1970), pp. 13, 30; Reihe 1 (1996), pp. 24–25; Reihe 3 (1997), pp. 48–49; Reihe 4 (1977), p. 26; (1981), p. 21; (1991), p. 10; (1994), p. 36; (1997), p. 10.

Table 5.2. Crimes, Suspects, and Convictions in Germany, 1968–1996

Year	Criminal Nontraffic Offenses Recorded by the Police	Offense Rate (per 100,000)	Adult Suspects Identified by the Police	Adults Convicted in Criminal Court
1968	2,158,000	3,588	693,000	526,813
1976	3,063,000	4,980	790,000	543,059
1980	3,816,000	6,198	927,000	553,212
1990	4,455,000	7,108	1,084,000	590,707
1993	6,751,000*	8,337	1,548,000*	660,318
1996	6,648,000*	8,125	1,585,000*	656,895

Sources: Bundeskriminalamt 1997, p. 259; Statistisches Bundesamt Reihe 9 (1970), p. 13; Reihe 1 (1997), p. 16.

*Figure includes states of the former German Democratic Republic.

The development of German imprisonment rates thus runs counter to two plausible expectations: one would expect imprisonment rates to rise in consonance with crime rates; but, also, one would expect imprisonment rates to drop in consonance with rates of prison sentences. If, however, crime rates rise while rates of prison sentences decrease, the two curves may cancel each other out and produce the stalemate in imprisonment figures that German statistics bear out if viewed in long-term perspective.

Whereas the rise in crime rates between the 1960s and the 1990s has been a universal phenomenon in Western countries, it is natural to wonder how Germans managed to respond to this trend by a decrease rather than an increase in punitiveness. The reduction of prison sentences after 1968 was the result of a policy change brought about by legislation enacted in 1969 (Zweites Gesetz zur Reform des Strafrechts of July 4, 1969).[11] The new law was designed to limit the imposition of imprisonment strictly to cases so serious that a custodial sentence appeared inevitable. To achieve that goal, the reform law of 1969 combined several measures. First, prison sentences of less than one month were abolished altogether — fines were regarded as sufficient reaction to offenses of such low seriousness. Second, many petty offenses were decriminalized and turned into mere administrative infractions (*Ordnungswidrigkeiten*) punishable by fines only; most important in practice was the decriminalization of many traffic offenses,[12] but decriminalization also extended to a host of typical "public order" offenses, for example, making excessive noise in public, committing disturbing mischief (para. 360, no. 11 PC 1968 version), and throwing stones or dirt at persons, horses, or buildings (para. 366, no. 7 PC 1968 version). Third, the new version of the Penal Code strongly discouraged the imposition of sentences of less than six months: paragraph. 47, section. 1 PC requires courts to give specific reasons in writing for imposing short-term prison sentences,[13] and courts must provide additional justification if they refrain from suspending a sentence of less than one year.[14]

To a certain extent, the 1969 legislation was a typical product of 1960s rehabilitative optimism: long-term imprisonment was to be imposed only on those few offenders who were in need of long-term treatment, whereas the great majority were to be disciplined by a fine or treated in the community. However, the notion that short-term imprisonment should be restricted or even abolished because it does not serve any constructive purpose but only disrupts the offender's ties to society and provides him with a "school for crime" is not vintage 1960s but has a long tradition in German reform literature. One of the most forceful statements to this effect is contained in the great reformer Franz von Liszt's well-known Marburger Programm of 1882 (von Liszt 1883; for a modern assessment, see Müller-Dietz 1982; see also Weigend 1986, pp. 260–64). In a later article, von Liszt wrote: "Short-term imprisonment is not only useless. It does more harm to the legal system than the offender's total impunity would" (von Liszt 1889, p. 743). The reform movement of the 1960s was built on this nineteenth-century ideological foundation and when the legislation was introduced, it met little opposition (see Kürzinger 1984, pp. 1828–37; Schaeferdiek 1997, pp. 119–21; see also Gerken and Henningsen 1987, pp. 387–88).

Astonishingly, even the massive rise in crime after the 1960s did not lead to a demand for a general reevaluation of the policy choice in favor of noncustodial sentences. That courts were by law required primarily to rely on sanctions other than imprisonment for run-of-the-mill offenses indeed helped to soften the pressure a steadily increasing caseload exerted on the corrections system: as a comparison of the right-hand columns of tables 5.1 and 5.2 shows, the system was able to adjust to the substantial rise in convictions without need of more prison space in 1996 than in 1968. This may in turn have helped to create the impression that the threat of crime was "under control" and may thus have quelled political demands for a more repressive policy.

What remains to be explained is, first, the disproportionately modest *decrease* of imprisonment in the wake of the reform of 1969 with its great impact on sentencing law, and, second, the intermittent but persistent increase in prison population since the 1970s. Both phenomena are due to the fact that the decrease of custodial sentences in the 1970s was restricted almost exclusively to the segment of sentences below nine months. The total number of sentences above the nine month limit remained nearly stable in the period 1968–96, and the number of sentences of two years or more rose remarkably (see table 5.3). Whereas 4,744 offenders in 1976 received prison sentences of between two and fifteen years, these long-term sentences were imposed on 8,927 offenders in 1996, which reflects an increase of 88 percent. At first sight, it may be surprising that sentences of medium length (nine months to two years) did not increase but were used less often in 1996 than in 1976. This phenomenon is due to the fact that courts made increasing use of suspension: as table 5.1 shows, the number of prison sentences suspended rose from 59,196 to more than 84,000 between 1976 and 1996; this increase absorbed the increase in medium-term prison sentences that should have been expected in the light of rising numbers of convictions.

The trend toward more lengthy sentences cannot be traced to specific changes in legislation on sentencing. One explanation could be that convicted offenders have accumulated more serious prior records, thus subjecting themselves to more severe punishment. Yet there is little hard evidence to support this thesis: during

Table 5.3. Adult Prison Sentences (Not
Suspended), Germany, 1968–96, Selected Years

Year	9 Months–2 Years	2–15 Years
1968	17,116*	
1976	11,987	4,744
1980	11,559	5,102
1990	8,887	5,776
1993	9,407	7,261
1996	9,816	8,927

Sources: Statistisches Bundesamt Reihe 9 (1970), p. 13; Reihe 1
(1996) pp. 24–25; (1997), pp. 24–25.

*Statistics do not provide breakdown of sentences between 9
months and 5 years.

1986–96, the percentage of recidivists among convicted offenders did not change
significantly. In 1986 as well as in 1996, 20 percent of those convicted (of nontraffic offenses) had five or more prior convictions, and 10 percent (11 percent in
1986:) had three or four prior convictions (Statistisches Bundesamt Reihe 3, 1987,
p. 56; Reihe 1, 1997, p. 38). Another possible explanation is a change in the mix
of offenses adjudicated by the courts. Table 5.4 shows the changes, from 1986 to
1996, in the number of serious offenses adjudicated by criminal courts.

Whereas there was only a (noticeable but) modest increase in violent crime,
drug offenses more than doubled within a period of just ten years. Because drug
offenses carry heavy prison sentences under German law[15] and courts do not hes-
itate to implement the mandate of the law,[16] the rise in drug convictions goes a
long way to explain why German prisons are (again) filled to capacity and beyond.

B. Noncustodial Sentences

The 1969 legislation that effectively curtailed the use of short-term imprisonment
left open the question of how to deal with petty offenses and offenses of medium

Table 5.4. Convictions of Serious Crime (Adults) in Germany, 1986 and 1996.

Year	Homicide[1]	Rape[2]	Robbery[3]	Drug Offenses[4]
1986	579	1,306	3,097	12,754
1996[5]	668	1,402	3,878	28,361

Source: Statistisches Bundesamt Reihe 3 (1988), pp. 20–24, (1997), pp. 22–26; Reihe 1, (1997), p. 37.

[1]Includes murder and intentional manslaughter.
[2]Includes sexual coercion.
[3]Includes forcible theft and forcible extortion.
[4]Dealing with illicit drugs and importing illicit drugs.
[5]Figures relate exclusively to the states of (former) West Germany.

seriousness—an issue of special relevance in the light of a growing influx of suspects into the system. The additional input as well as the large number of offenders who had formerly received short prison sentences were absorbed by a combination of noncustodial, mostly monetary sanctions.

Fines

As had been intended by the 1969 reform legislation, fines are now imposed much more frequently than they were before. The former system had been criticized because the maximum amount of fines was insufficient as punishment for non-petty offenses and because lump-sum fines affected poor and affluent offenders unequally (Jescheck 1977, pp. 263–64; Tröndle 1974, pp. 548–50; Zipf 1974, pp. 522–24). The 1969 law aimed at solving these problems by introducing the day-fine system: according to paragraph 40, section 2 PC, fines are to be computed by multiplying two factors, one indicating the seriousness of the offense and the other indicating the offender's daily net income.[17]

Courts can thus—if they take the time to investigate the offender's economic situation—tailor the amount of the fine to the offender's financial means as well as to the seriousness of the offense. The field of application for fines was further enlarged by pushing the statutory maximum beyond the equivalent of US $2 million: the maximum number of day fines for a single offense is 360, and the maximum amount of 1 day fine is the equivalent of US $6,000 (para. 40, secs. 1, 2 PC).[18] Although German courts do not impose fines approaching the theoretical maximum,[19] fines have become the typical sanction for ubiquitous offenses such as larceny, small fraud, nonaggravated battery, and drunken driving; in 1996, 82 percent of all adults sanctioned in criminal court received only a fine (Statistisches Bundesamt Reihe 3, 1997, p. 44). And this is not even the whole story. Many of the petty offenses, in particular many traffic offenses, that were removed from the Penal Code in 1969, are now treated as administrative infractions and can also be sanctioned by fines.[20] The vast majority of penal and nonpenal transgressions are thus subject to monetary penalties. Seen from the traditional viewpoint, according to which only custodial and probationary sanctions are genuinely criminal, Germany has indeed undergone a massive process of depenalization and now has a system of social control of norm violations relying almost exclusively on economic sanctions.

Suspended Sentences

The increase in suspended sentences has made a further sizable reduction in the number of prisoners. The number of suspended sentences initially decreased after the 1969 reform law took effect, because short prison sentences (below six months), which formerly had been suspended, were now replaced by fines (see table 5.5). Yet by 1996, the number of suspensions again exceeded the 1968 figure, with an important difference: whereas the numbers of suspended prison sentences below one year were almost the same in 1968 and in 1996, in 1996 a significant portion of sentences in the one-to-two year bracket were suspended. The stability of the

Table 5.5. Prison Sentences and Suspended Sentences, Germany, 1968–1996

Year	Prison Sentences < 1 year		Prison Sentences 1–2 years	
	Not Suspended	Suspended	Not Suspended	Suspended
1968	na	75,036	na	—
1976	24,357	60,923	7,260	878
1980	23,936	67,332	6,880	1,546
1986	21,788	68,436	6,049	4,824
1990	21,853	63,734	5,064	5,971
1996	22,007	73,717	5,840	10,735

Sources: Statistisches Bundesamt Reihe (1970), p. 13; Reihe 1 (1997), pp. 24–25; Reihe 3 (1997), pp. 48–49.

relationship between unconditional and suspended prison sentences in the second column of table 5.5 (roughly three out of four offenders with sentences below one year receive a suspension) seems to reflect the courts' obedience to the legislative mandate. According to paragraph 56, section 1 PC, the court must suspend a prison sentence of up to one year whenever the offender can be expected to refrain from committing further criminal acts. What has changed remarkably since 1976 is the interpretation of paragraph 56, section 2 PC, which authorizes courts to suspend a sentence between one and two years only if the court finds "special circumstances" in the offense or in the personality of the offender,[21] especially if the offender has made restitution. What was originally understood as an exceptional act of clemency (see table 5.5: only 878 cases in 1976) has now become a routine disposition. In 1996, two of three prison sentences between one and two years were suspended.[22] As mentioned above, the expansion of suspended sentences has the beneficial effect of absorbing the increase in convictions for offenses of medium seriousness without overburdening the corrections system: the total number of persons receiving sentences between one and two years more than doubled from 1976 to 1996. Only by relying massively on suspensions were the courts able to avoid an additional influx of three thousand (in 1990) to nine thousand (in 1996) persons into the prison system.

Suspended sentences under German law to some extent resemble sentences of probation in the Anglo-American system. The court can calibrate the impact of a suspended sentence by imposing more or less onerous conditions. The offender might be required to do one or a combination of the following: pay a sum of money to the victim or a charitable organization or the state, report to the police at certain intervals, avoid contact with certain persons, or undergo treatment or rehabilitation (paras. 56b, 56c PC). The offender can also be required to cooperate with a probation officer, who is to support and at the same time to supervise his rehabilitation (para. 56d PC). If the offender commits a new offense or seriously violates the conditions of probation, the court can revoke suspension, which means that the offender must serve the original sentence of imprisonment (para. 56f PC). In 1991, 31 percent of those 16,000 adults who had been placed on supervision after receiving a suspended sentence had suspension revoked, in 84 percent of these cases because they had committed another criminal offense (Statistisches Bundesamt Reihe 5, 1994, pp. 20–21). The percentage of revocations has decreased over the years (41 percent in 1980, 37 percent in 1985, 31 percent in 1990; for earlier statistics, see Schöch 1992, C123; Eisenberg 1995, pp. 655–57).

A supplementary punishment of great practical relevance is the suspension of the offender's driving license (*Fahrverbot*) for a period of one to three months. This sanction is available whenever someone has (culpably) committed a criminal offense in connection with driving a motor vehicle (para. 44 PC). The purpose is to demonstrate to the offending driver the dangerousness of his conduct.

New Sanctions

Leaving special therapeutic measures apart, the arsenal of sanctions in 1968 was limited to imprisonment, probation, and fines. The intervening thirty years have seen an expansion and diversification of sanctions.

Warning with suspension. One new provision included in the 1969 reform package authorizes the court to suspend imposition of a fine of up to 180 day fines and to place the offender on probation, under similar conditions as for suspension of prison sentences (para. 59 PC). Courts have not embraced this new option with enthusiasm: in 1996, "warning with suspension of punishment" was applied in only 4,137 cases (Statistisches Bundesamt Reihe 3, 1996, p. 56; for an empirical study, see Scheel 1996). This is not a shining example of smart criminal legislation. Because it has no immediate negative impact on the offender, "warning with suspension of punishment" is not an adequate response to offenses of more than minimal seriousness, and the legislature has further limited its applicability to cases in which "special circumstances" indicate a necessity to refrain from imposing punishment on the offender (for a discussion of possible modifications of this sanction, see Schöch 1992, C90–C94; Weigend 1992, pp. 353–62; Neumayer-Wagner 1998, pp. 186–213).

Conditional dismissal. For dealing with cases of this kind, another option exists that requires neither a full-fledged trial nor a court judgment and is therefore greatly preferred by judges and prosecutors. This option is conditional dismissal of prosecution (para. 153a CCP), the introduction of which was also part of the reform legislation that took effect in 1975. Although there was no clear idea behind this new instrument except the wish to reduce the workload of criminal courts and to expand the area of depenalization (see the criticism by Dencker 1973; Schmidhäuser 1973; Fezer 1994, pp. 32–35; Pott 1996, pp. 90–126), prosecutors and courts alike were quick to embrace and broadly employ the new tool.

Table 5.6 shows the relevance of conditional dismissals in recent years.[23] Although the portion of conditional dismissals among all prosecutorial dispositions (6 percent) may appear small, in 1996 they constituted 17 percent of those cases that led to some form of sanctioning of a suspect. This disposition has become the sanction of choice for a wide range of minor offenses. Some prosecutor's offices have internal guidelines that prescribe conditional dismissal as the regular disposition for certain groups of cases—for example, shoplifting of nonvaluable goods by first-time offenders (for assessments of the practice, see Kunz 1980, pp. 69–94;

Table 5.6. Prosecutorial Dispositions, Cases with Known Suspects, in Germany, 1990 and 1996

	1990	1996
Dismissal for lack of evidence	774,712 (27%)	1,154,980 (27%)
Unconditional dismissal (para. 153)	428,427 (15%)	923,291 (21%)
Conditional dismissal (para. 153a)	177,983 (6%)	247,116 (6%)
Indictment or penal order	887,690 (31%)	1,206,840 (28%)
Other (e.g., referral, death of suspect)	607,278 (21%)	794,964 (18%)
Total	2,876,090 (100%)	4,327,191 (100%)*

Source: Statistisches Bundesamt Reihe 2 (1993), p. 94; (1997), p. 118.

*The number of cases has increased because of German reunification.

Hertwig 1982; Männlein 1992, pp. 37–51 sec., n–76). But conditional dismissal is being employed even in fairly serious cases as long as they are technically misdemeanors.[24] Cases in which white-collar offenders pay hundreds of thousands of German marks to "buy off" criminal prosecution are not unknown (Meinberg 1985, pp. 115–27). Conditional dismissal not only offers a convenient disposition for white-collar offenses, which are notoriously difficult to prove, but also has provided most welcome relief for the German criminal justice system in a time of rapidly growing case numbers: only by use of this tool was the system able to process and effectively sanction the 100 percent increase in suspects between 1976 and 1996 (see table 5.2).

Conditional dismissal is, at least in theory, not a criminal sanction (and is therefore not regulated in the Penal Code) but a procedural tool. Under German procedural law, the public prosecutor is generally required to file a formal accusation whenever there is sufficient evidence for conviction (para. 170, sec. 1 CCP). Under certain conditions listed in the Code of Criminal Procedure, the prosecutor can, however, refrain from prosecuting a misdemeanor (beginning with (para. 153 CCP).[25] Paragraph 153 CCP provides for this option whenever prosecution of a misdemeanor is not in the public interest and the suspect's guilt—if it were proved—is insignificant. Conditional dismissal (para. 153a, sec. 1) is a variant of this provision.[26] Even when there does initially exist a public interest in prosecution, the suspect can make this interest disappear by taking reparative action, especially by making a payment to the state, to a charitable organization, or to the victim of the offense.[27] The sum to be paid is not fixed or limited by statute but is left to the discretion of the public prosecutor. If the suspect accepts the proposed disposition and makes the required payment, the prosecutor is bound to dismiss the case and to refrain from prosecution (para. 153a, sec. 1, 4th sentence CCP). In more serious cases, the arrangement must be approved by the court (para. 153a, sec. 1, 6th sentence CCP), but overburdened courts are usually happy to give their consent.

Conditional dismissal has a number of features that make it attractive to all parties involved. The suspect avoids trial and judgment; he can even maintain his innocence because a confession is not a prerequisite for conditional dismissal. The prosecutor saves the time and effort necessary for accusation and trial, while justice and general prevention are served by the imposition of a financial payment as a response to the defendant's (suspected) guilt. That paragraph 153a CCP requires the suspect's cooperation and saves the prosecutor's office the effort of preparing for a trial leads to practices reminiscent of plea bargaining; in nonroutine cases, prosecutors often consult with the suspect (or the suspect's counsel) in advance of "imposing" a condition for dismissal in order to find out what amount the suspect may be willing to pay to avoid indictment and trial. Because conditional dismissal is often in the interest of the prosecutor's office, the defense does not have to accept the prosecutor's first offer but can try to get a better deal by pointing out the uncertainty of the outcome of a possible trial or by advancing grounds for clemency. Especially when the suspect is vulnerable to adverse publicity caused by a criminal trial, it is often the defense counsel who approaches the prosecutor early in the process to suggest an "amicable" resolution by conditional dismissal. As in plea bargaining, the quid pro quo character of conditional dismissal is not without its problems; prosecutors may offer attractive deals in cases where the evidence is weak and conviction unlikely, and even an innocent suspect may be tempted (or persuaded by counsel) to make a payment rather than take even the small risk of a conviction at trial. The voluntariness of the suspect's cooperation is thus somewhat doubtful in a fair (but unknown) number of cases (see Weigend 1984, pp. 26–31; Meinberg 1985, pp. 226–28).

Conditional dismissal is also possible *after* a formal accusation has been filed (para. 153a, sec. 2 CCP).[28] The same substantive requirements (no excessive guilt, dissolution of a public interest in prosecution) apply as for prosecutorial dismissal. However, it is the trial court that orders dismissal with the consent of the prosecutor and the defendant.[29] This option of a "belated" conditional dismissal was also introduced in 1975, probably on the assumption that filing of an indictment should not bar a reasonable resolution of less serious cases without a formal adjudication of guilt. Conditional dismissal after indictment has a lesser cost-saving effect but is a welcome option in legally or factually doubtful cases that have gone to trial because it allows both parties to "save face" and spares the court the effort of finding and justifying a verdict (see Ahrens 1978, pp. 156–66, showing that conditional dismissals in court occur most frequently when the relevant facts have not been fully cleared up and the defendant has confessed to some but not all elements of the offense).

Community service. A novel sanction that has gained increasing acceptance worldwide is community service. In Germany, a constitutional ban against forced labor except in prisons (Art. 12, sec. 3 Basic Law) has so far prevented wholesale adoption of community service as an independent criminal sanction. This option is nevertheless available as an alternative or supplementary sanction in various contexts.[30] Community service can be imposed as a condition of dismissal (para. 153a, sec. 1 CCP) or of probation (para. 56b, sec. 2 PC), and offenders unable or unwilling to pay a fine can report for community service instead of serving a jail term.[31] The Federal Constitutional Court has held these provisions to be constitutional because of the limited duration of the work requirement and because the offender has the option of avoiding community service by accepting an alternative sanction (74 Entscheidungen des Bundesverfassungsgerichts 102 [1987]; 83 Entscheidungen des Bundesverfassungsgerichts 119 [1990]; but see Köhler 1987). The practical relevance of community service is, however, quite limited. As a condition of probation or of conditional dismissal, community service is imposed in less than 1 percent of the relevant cases (Eisenberg 1995, p. 368). Programs that seek to replace jail for fine-defaulters by community service have so far managed to reach only 6 percent of defaulters (Feuerhelm 1991, p. 70). One explanation for this small percentage is that the great majority of those who initially fail to pay fines eventually come up with the required sum when faced with the prospect of jail. Only 11 percent actually serve an alternative jail sentence (Feuerhelm 1991, p. 76)—one of three truly penniless offenders may thus have been spared jail through the option of doing community service. One study based on data from 1987–88 found that the permission to do community service instead of jail had to be revoked in 31 percent of the cases, mostly because the offender had not appeared for work or had failed to complete the work hours imposed on him (Feuerhelm 1991, pp. 139–40).[32] The relatively high dropout rate is not surprising because offenders who fail to pay fines often also lack the discipline and stamina for regular work.

Restitution. The use of restitution to the victim as a criminal sanction reflects an international trend toward restorative justice, which favors an integrated response to crime over the traditional dichotomy between civil and criminal law. German scholars are divided on the theoretical persuasiveness of that approach. Some adhere to the traditional view that restitution cannot, for reasons of general deterrence, replace punishment (see Hirsch 1990, pp. 537–44; Loos 1993, pp. 52–54), others argue in favor of an integrated response to crime (see Frehsee 1987, pp. 120–39; Baumann et al. 1992, pp. 21–27; Sessar 1992, pp. 253–56; Walther 1999), and still others, who take an intermediate view, maintain that voluntary restitution can, under certain conditions, fulfill the traditional purposes of punishment by demonstrating to the offender (and the community) that breaking the law has negative consequences for which one has to take responsibility (Roxin 1987; Schöch 1992, C63–C66; Jescheck and Weigend 1996, p. 865; Meier 1996, pp. 438–39; Bannenberg and Uhlmann 1998, pp. 19–26). Despite these different views, there is little disagreement over the desirability of an expansion of opportunities for offenders and victims to achieve reconciliation or at least redress of material damages (for discussions of the practical aspects of victim-offender mediation, see Messmer and Otto 1992; Hering and Rössner 1993; Hassemer 1998). Until recently, German law and practice had little to offer in that regard. Like community service, restitution is available as a condition of probation (para. 56b, sec. 2, no. 1 PC) and of conditional dismissal (para. 153a, sec. 1 CCP) but is very rarely used in this context.[33] There exists, however, a growing interest in victim-offender reconciliation and in extrajudicial restitution programs. Such programs have developed in many communities, often concentrating on (but not limited to) nonviolent offenses committed by juveniles (see the overviews by Schreckling et al. 1991; Dölling and Henninger 1998; for an in-depth study of one project, see Pfeiffer 1997).

Victim-offender reconciliation programs mostly receive their cases from police or prosecutors' offices and work informally toward an amicable settlement between the parties, often by arranging personal meetings between the victim and the offender. If reconciliation has been achieved, prosecutors usually dismiss the case for lack of a public interest in prosecution (para. 153 CCP or para. 45 Jugendgerichtsgesetz [Juvenile Court Act]). There seems to be general agreement that victim-offender reconciliation is "a good idea," and the number of programs as well as the overall number of processed cases are growing;[34] yet many programs still suffer from a lack of case referrals.[35]

Recent legislation has explicitly recognized restitution as a ground for mitigation and in some cases for dispensing with punishment altogether. According to paragraph 46a PC, introduced in 1994, the court can mitigate the penalty or withhold imposition of a penalty of not more than one year's imprisonment if the offender has made efforts to achieve reconciliation with the victim and has compensated the victim in whole or in substantial part in pursuit of this goal, or if he has made a personal sacrifice in order to make restitution. The first alternative refers, somewhat obliquely, to participation in a victim-offender reconciliation program involving some element of personal encounter (see Kilchling 1996, pp. 311–12; Tröndle 1997, sec. 46a, n. 4; Rössner and Klaus 1998b, pp. 49–51). The second alternative requires only financial restitution but permits mitigation if the amount of restitution was so substantial that making the payment caused the offender some hardship. Courts are just beginning to interpret this new provision, trying to fend off offenders' claims for mitigation in cases in which there was only minimal restitution (see Bundesgerichtshof [Federal Court of Appeals] in 1995 Strafverteidiger 464; Bayerisches Oberstes Landesgericht [Bavarian High Court] in 1995 Strafverteidiger 367).

C. Rehabilitative and Security Measures

The multifaceted picture of—new and old—criminal sanctions is supplemented by rehabilitative and security measures (*Massnahmen der Besserung und Sicherung*). Rehabilitative measures include commitment to a psychiatric hospital (para. 63 PC) or to an institution for addicts (para. 64 PC), interdiction of practicing a certain trade or profession (para. 70 PC), and—in practice most relevant—revocation of the offender's driving license (para. 69 PC). The most onerous (and most criticized) measure is security detention (para. 66 PC). This measure consists purely of detention and does not have the purpose of treating or rehabilitating the offender.

Imposition of a measure does not presuppose a finding that the offender was blameworthy—many of those committed to psychiatric hospitals clearly are not guilty because of insanity—but only that he has unlawfully committed a criminal offense. Measures are exclusively geared toward the prevention of further crime by the individual concerned. They have been part of German criminal law—

though in different form—since the 1930s.[36] It should be noted that neither rehabilitative nor security measures are regarded as "civil"[37]—German law views them as criminal sanctions because their imposition invariably presupposes the commission of a criminal offense. There has been some debate about whether sanctioning nonculpable persons can be reconciled with the guilt principle (see Frisch 1990, pp. 352–70; Kaiser 1990; *Leipziger Kommentar* 1992, sec. 61, nn. 28–35; Köhler 1997, pp. 55–58). There seems to be widespread agreement about the general permissibility of rehabilitative measures: they do not imply—at least in theory—moral censure or reproach and thus are conceptually different from punishment (which presupposes blameworthiness). Imposition of rehabilitative measures is seen as a preventive measure substantively belonging to public security ("police") law but, for practical purposes, tied in with the investigation and adjudication of the criminal offense the offender is alleged to have committed (Jescheck and Weigend 1996, p. 803).[38] The integration of therapeutic measures into the criminal justice system offers another advantage: if an offender is liable for punishment and in need of a rehabilitative measure it is possible to submit him to the therapeutic measure first and to discount time spent in a therapeutic institution from the criminal sentence. This is indeed the preferred arrangement under German law (para. 67, secs. 1, 4 PC).

Security detention (para. 66 PC) presents a more difficult issue. This measure applies to multiple recidivists who present the risk of committing further serious offenses.[39] The offender is held in security detention after he has completed the prison term imposed for his most recent offense. The regular maximum duration of detention is ten years (para. 67d, sec. 3 PC). Yet if the offender's dangerousness is found to persist, he can be detained indefinitely.

Security detention has been criticized as violating the guilt principle: though a security measure by name, detention cannot easily be distinguished from punishment, and detainees in fact remain in the same prison in which they had served their prison terms (Weichert 1989, pp. 270–73; Streng 1991, p. 152; *Nomos-Kommentar* 1994, sec. 66 n. 33–39; see also *Leipziger Kommentar* 1992, sec. 66 n. 22a). It has been argued that security detention violates the dignity of the person (absolutely protected by Art. 1 Basic Law) because the measure treats the offender not as an autonomous person but as a dangerous object (Köhler 1997, p. 643). The Federal Constitutional Court has, however, rejected this argument, emphasizing the theoretical difference between punishment implying censure and morally neutral measures related only to dangerousness (2 Entscheidungen des Bundesverfassungsgerichts [1953] 118; see Kinzig 1996, pp. 39–46). Security detention can be seen as the dark side of the guilt principle: Germans are purists with respect to the proportionality of guilt and punishment and strongly disapprove of any penalty that exceeds—even for reasonable preventive purposes—what the individual offender deserves; yet they concede that there exist offenders who are not insane but are nevertheless eminently dangerous. It is for this group that the hybrid security detention has been designed (for a comprehensive study of the legal and empirical aspects of security detention, see Kinzig 1996; for another empirical study of detainees, see Kern 1997).

Courts make sparing use of security detention: in 1996, only 57 persons were sentenced to this measure (Statistisches Bundesamt Reihe 3, 1997, p. 72). Other measures are being imposed much more frequently. In 1996, 600 persons were criminally committed to psychiatric hospitals and 841 persons to institutions for addicts (Statistisches Bundesamt Reihe 3, 1997, pp. 72–73). Revocation of a driver's license — which the law provides as a regular sanction for common offenses such as driving under the influence of intoxicants or leaving the scene of an accident (para. 69, sec. 2 PC) — was by far the most frequently used measure (159,063 cases in 1996).

D. Confiscation and Forfeiture

Additional sanctions are aimed at depriving offenders of the proceeds of crime and of the means to commit further criminal acts. German law distinguishes between confiscation (of instruments used in the commission of or produced by an offense; para. 74 PC) and forfeiture (of the proceeds of crime; para. 73 PC). Weapons, cars, drugs, and counterfeit money are typical objects of confiscation, which can also extend to innocent third parties if the object concerned is dangerous to the public (para. 74, sec. 2, no. 2 PC). Forfeiture has the purpose of depriving the offender of illegal gains. Because of a change in the wording of the statute enacted in 1992, forfeiture now covers not only the net profit the offender has made but everything he has acquired by committing the offense.[40] With respect to designated offenses commonly related to organized crime, forfeiture extends to assets other than the proceeds of the offense of which the offender stands convicted if the court finds that the other assets also stem from criminal activity (para. 73d PC).[41] Despite this extension, proving the tainted source of assets still remains a practical problem. Another serious impediment is a provision (para. 73, sec. 1, 2d sentence PC) that excludes forfeiture whenever the victim has a claim for damages from the offender and execution of that claim might be affected by forfeiture. This caveat, though well-intended as a means to give victims' claims priority, effectively precludes forfeiture in many cases even if there exists only a theoretical possibility that victims' interests might be violated (see Eberbach 1987; *Systematischer Kommentar* 1992, sec. 73, n. 16). Because of these defects in the law, forfeiture is used to a lesser extent than the legislature had hoped: in 1996, forfeiture of proceeds of crime was ordered in only 807 cases (Statistisches Bundesamt Reihe 3, 1997, p. 69).[42]

E. Sentencing Rationales

German sentencing theory is complicated, conceptually murky, and of very limited practical relevance. As a result of the reform movement of the 1960s, a traditionally desert-based system has accommodated widespread demands for greater individualization and a more functional orientation toward preventive goals, in particular rehabilitation or, in German terminology, resocialization (see Tiedemann 1974, pp. 329–32; Kaiser 1996, pp. 986–93; for a critical assessment of the reform, see

Hirsch 1986, pp. 134–40). Neither German legal theory nor legislation has, however, embraced the rehabilitative ideal as wholeheartedly as some other legal systems have done. The seriousness of the offense and the offender's blameworthiness have always been regarded as the most important considerations in sentencing, especially as marking the upper limit of any criminal sanction (45 Entscheidungen des Bundesverfassungsgerichts 187 at 256–59 [1977] 20 BGHSt 264 at 266–267 [1965] Frisch 1987, pp. 361–73; Erhard 1992, pp. 91–100; Hirsch 1994, pp. 754–59).

The Penal Code's basic provision on sentencing is indicative of the compromise reached in 1969 between traditional retributivists and those who favor a stronger orientation toward preventive goals. Paragraph 46, sec. 1 reads: "The offender's blameworthiness is the basis of the determination of the penalty. The penalty's expected effects on the offender's future life in society shall be taken into consideration." Section 2 then lists several more specific sentencing criteria, including the offender's motives and goals, the consequences of the offense, the offender's prior life, and his conduct after the commission of the offense, in particular his efforts to achieve reconciliation with the victim. The code does not indicate what (relative) weight the sentencing court should accord each of the criteria listed, and the eclectic catalogue of sentencing factors in paragraph 46, section 2 PC fails to give clear guidance about the relevance of offense-based or offender-oriented considerations (cf. Frisch 1987, pp. 361–69; Streng 1991, pp. 173–74).

Various theoretical models attempt to explain the proper relationship between guilt-orientation and the preventive-rehabilitative function of sentencing (for overviews see, e.g., Hart-Hönig 1992, pp. 13–97; Müller-Dietz 1992; Neumann 1992; *Leipziger Kommentar* 1994, sec. 46, nn. 11–40; *Systematischer Kommentar* 1995, sec. 46, nn. 5–47; for a novel theory emphasizing the proximity between the offense descriptions and sentencing criteria, see Frisch 1993). The predominant theory starts from the assumption that the offender's desert should define and—in particular—limit the sanction. Desert is, however, not regarded as indicating a particular sentence but as precribing a fairly broad range ("Frame," or *Rahmen* in German terminology) within which the sentencer can choose a sentence; any sentence within that range comports with the principle of proportionality between guilt and punishment. Within the range of proportional penalties, the sentence is to be determined according to preventive needs. An early concise statement of this theory by the Federal Court of Appeals (7 BGHSt 28 at 32 [1954]) reads as follows:

> It cannot exactly be determined which penalty is proportionate to guilt. There exists a margin [*Spielraum*] that is limited at the bottom by the penalty already proportionate to guilt and at the top by the penalty still proportionate to guilt. The sentencing judge must not go beyond the upper limit. He must not impose a penalty that is so severe that he himself does not regard it as proportionate to guilt. But he can decide, in his discretion, how high he should reach within this margin. . . . If the sentencing judge selects, for reasons of general deterrence, the most severe among those guilt-proportionate penalties among which he can choose, there is no legal error.

As can be seen from this decision, the courts permit considerations of general deterrence to be included in fixing the sentence as long as the sentencing court remains within the limits set by the guilt principle (see also 24 BGHSt 40 at 44–47 [1970]; BGH in 1986 Neue Zeitschrift für Strafrecht 358; for a critical view, see Jescheck and Weigend 1996, pp. 881–82).

The application of suspended prison sentences is another example—at least in theory—for the interplay (or compromise) between retributive and preventive considerations. German law has not adopted the concept of probation as an independent sanction but interprets a sentence of "conditional freedom" (para. 56 PC) as suspension of the execution of a (fixed) prison sentence.[43] (There exists also the possibility of suspending execution only of the final portion of a prison sentence [para. 57 PC]—the equivalent of parole.) The basic sentence is hence to be determined on the basis of paragraph 46, section 1, first sentence PC, that is, on this basis, to the seriousness of the offense and the offender's blameworthiness. The decision about whether this sentence is to be immediately executed or suspended (i.e., the crucial in-out decision) depends, however, exclusively on preventive concerns, namely, the offender's risk of recidivism and the need for general prevention ("defense of the legal order") (para. 56, secs. 1 and 3 PC). In theory, this means that sentencing courts should first set the sentence without regard to the possibility of suspension, and only then—if, by chance, the sentence falls within the statutory two-year limit for suspension—consider the offender's chances of avoiding further crime if left at large (for a forceful statement in favor of this separation see *Systematischer Kommentar* 1995, sec. 46, nn. 33–40). Real-life courts, of course, do not make decisions in this manner. They treat a suspended prison sentence as a separate penalty of intermediate seriousness, often combining it with a fine in order to avoid the impression that the offender gets off free.[44]

In general, sentencing theory is not reflected in the courts' day-to-day decision making. The compromise formula of paragraph 46, section 1 PC in particular has remained without significant impact on actual sentencing practice.[45] Judicial sentencing, left without clear guidance from the legislature, is still dominated by a mild form of retributivism. The ideal of tailoring the sentence to the offender's individual blameworthiness and to his special preventive needs is largely being neglected in the face of pragmatic limitations: courts are, except in the occasional spectacular case, unable and unwilling to invest much time and effort into investigating and analyzing the defendant's personal history but tend to base their sentencing decisions on facts that are easy to establish—that is, the circumstances of the offense, the damage caused, and the defendant's prior convictions (Albrecht 1980, pp. 82–83; 1990, pp. 611–15; Oswald 1994, pp. 192–93; Kaiser 1996, pp. 947–48; for an in-depth empirical study see Albrecht 1994, pp. 329–86; for an English-language overview, see Weigend 1983, pp. 53–57). Even the defendant's income, though theoretically indispensable for the calculation of the day fine, is often "determined" by a rough estimate on the basis of information provided by the defendant (Albrecht 1980, pp. 79–81; 1994, pp. 436–37).

The facts found by the court at the trial need to be transformed into a specific sentence within the broad range provided by the Penal Code for each offense. Trial courts are guided in this operation by traditional standards and conventions that differ locally (Burgstaller 1989; Pfeiffer and Savelsberg 1989; Streng 1991, pp. 154–55; Albrecht 1994, pp. 204, 348–53; Eisenberg 1995, p. 493). The resulting moderate inequality of sentences is regarded with astonishing equanimity by practitioners and theorists (Giehring 1989, pp. 115–21; Albrecht 1994, pp. 492–94).

Appellate courts have full authority to review sentences as well as convictions. Until the 1960s, appellate courts pursued a hands-off policy, leaving sentencing to the trial courts' discretion unless there was blatant error apparent from the written judgment (cf. Frisch 1971, pp. 63–109). The modern trend goes in the opposite direction: appellate courts still pay lip service to sentencing discretion but in fact submit to strict scrutiny the lower courts' reasoning as well as the sentence itself (see 17 BGHSt 35 [1962]; 29 BGHSt 319 [1980]; for a comprehensive overview see Gribbohm in *Leipziger Kommentar* 1994, sec. 46, nn. 315–36). One study of judgments of the Federal Court of Appeals in criminal matters found that, in 1979–81, 42 percent of reversals concerned sentences and that the majority of reversals were based on errors in applying the substantive law (Riess 1982, pp. 51–52). Another study compared the outcome of cases in which reversal of the original judgment made resentencing necessary; it turned out that there was no net gain for defendants:[46] overall sentencing severity in cases of rape, robbery, and burglary remained almost equal in the "second round" of sentencing (Albrecht 1994, pp. 373–74).

III. The Road Ahead—Downhill?

I now take a furtive look into the crystal ball and attempt to divine the direction German sentencing policy might take in the future. I limit myself to pointing out two easily recognizable trends, diversification of sanctions and a marked tendency toward greater punitiveness.

A. Diversification

The safest bet is to predict a further diversification of criminal sanctions. Informal sanctions, such as conditional dismissal (para. 153a CCP), have already obtained an important position in the German sanctioning system and can be expected to expand further, given the present trend toward informality, simplification, and abbreviation of the criminal process (see Hamm 1994; Scheffler 1994; Weigend 1994) as well as toward "consensual" disposition of criminal cases. Although German law does not formally provide for guilty pleas or consent judgments, practice has developed functional equivalents: confessions are routinely rewarded by lenient sentences, and especially in complex cases courts are often willing to indicate in advance what sentence they might give if the defendant offered a confession, thus hoping to induce cooperation on the part of the defense (see 43 BGHSt 195 [1997] Schünemann 1990, 1993; Rönnau 1990; Weigend 1999). In this process of give-and-take, competent defense attorneys have as a valuable bargaining chip their right to present—almost without temporal limit—additional evidence; because courts cannot easily refuse such "offers of evidence" (cf. para. 244, sec. 3 CCP), this defense right has the potential of endlessly protracting the trial. A criminal process in which a culture of bargaining pervades can safely be expected to produce more variants of informal dispositions.

The movement toward expanding the role of restitution to the victim has recently been strengthened by introduction of paragraph 46a PC, which holds out to the offender the prospect of escaping punishment if he manages to reach a settlement with the victim. Given this chance, defense attorneys can be expected actively to pursue restitution and reconciliation with the victim. This development ties in with the procedural trend of avoiding formal prosecution and trial by promoting, in appropriate cases, various forms of victim-offender reconciliation. To what extent the movement toward expanding the position of the victim and to integrate the victim's claim for damages into the criminal process (see Weigend 1989, pp. 478–543; M. Kaiser 1992; Hamm 1995; Meier 1996; Pfeiffer 1997) will prevail over practitioners' dislike of computing and enforcing damage claims between private parties remains to be seen. Despite various efforts to bring it to life, the victim's option of attaching civil damage claims to criminal prosecution and to obtain a civil judgment in criminal court (paras. 403–6c CCP) has remained dead-letter law[47] (for a recent local attempt to revive the procedure, see Rössner and Klaus 1998a).

Community service is another sanction that can safely be predicted to expand. Even though high rates of unemployment make it politically difficult to introduce work programs for individuals unwilling to work, and even though both the pool of eligible defendants and the availability of suitable tasks are limited, the idea of replacing idle jail time by work for the community is highly attractive.[48] Several proposals to introduce community service as a primary sanction have been made, and it is only a matter of time until this sanction finds its way into the Penal Code (see Albrecht and Schädler 1987; Feuerhelm 1991; Jung 1992, pp. 165–81; Schöch 1992, C86–C88; for a critical assessment, see Weigend 1992, pp. 358–61). Experience with current programs involving community service in lieu of jail for fine-defaulters may help to define suitable groups of offenders and to provide the experienced staff necessary to organize such programs and to support offenders in fulfilling the work obligations imposed on them.

Another group of sanctions with good prospects are those that restrict offenders' ability to enjoy their time of leisure. A prominent example is the suspension of an offender's driving license. Current law limits this sanction to offenses committed in connection with the driving of a motor vehicle (para. 69, sec. 1 PC). One proposal would make temporary suspension of the right to drive a car applicable to all kinds of offenses (Schöch 1992, C116–C120). This proposal is based on the argument that the ability to drive a car is, in an eminently mobile society, a necessary prerequisite for the enjoyment of life; suspension is hence a smartly felt restriction, which cannot—like a fine—effectively be shifted to others. Obvious counterarguments are the lack of reliable enforceability of the interdiction—traffic controls are rare in Germany—and that suspension is inapplicable to offenders who do not have a driving license.

Restriction of personal freedom without the drawbacks of imprisonment is the idea behind another fashionable sanction, home arrest with electronic monitoring.

Introduction of this sanction, as an alternative to pretrial detention or short-term imprisonment, has increasingly been discussed in Germany, and experiments in Sweden, England, the United States, and the Netherlands have been followed with great interest (see Lindenberg 1992; Krahl 1997; Ostendorf 1997; Schlömer 1998). Until now, the arguments against "electronic chains" have prevailed. Electronic around-the-clock surveillance is seen by some writers as an unjustifiable invasion of human privacy and dignity (Dölling 1992, p. 286; Krahl 1997, p. 461; Ostendorf 1997, pp. 475–76), while others point out that in the German system, where most middle-of-the-road offenses are sanctioned by fines or probation, there is a lack of the typical clientele of electronically monitored home arrest: lower-middle-class offenders who would otherwise receive a short jail sentence. Despite widespread skepticism, the states of Berlin and Hamburg in 1997 filed a legislative proposal for the introduction of electronically monitored home arrest in lieu of the final portion of a prison sentence (Bundesratsdrucksache 698/97). This proposal was not further debated in Parliament, but discussions continue in a reform commission installed by the federal minister of justice in 1998 (see Schlömer 1998, p. 180). For those who do not reject electronic monitoring on principle but accept monitored home arrest as a lesser intrusion than prison, the main problem is to make certain that the introduction of this option does not lead to net-widening by extending to persons who would otherwise receive a non-custodial sanction (see Weigend 1992, p. 363).

The prospects of short-term imprisonment are more difficult to predict. As discussed above, the reform legislation of the 1960s succeeded in greatly reducing the portion of short prison sentences. Yet, on December 31, 1996, German correctional institutions held 9,867 convicted inmates with an expected stay of less than six months,[49] and in the course of the same year a total of 172,294 persons had entered prison for so short a time (Statistisches Bundesamt Reihe 4, 1997, p. 17). Only a very small portion of this amazingly high figure can be explained by the criminal courts' intentional reliance on short-term imprisonment: in 1996, only 9,896 persons received nonsuspended prison sentences of less than six months (Statistisches Bundesamt Reihe 3, 1997, p. 48). A much larger group (57,299 persons) entered prison because they had failed to pay a fine. Others had only a few more months to serve of a more extensive sentence because the Penal Code mandates time spent in pretrial dentention to be credited against a prison sentence (para. 51 PC);[50] and revocation of suspension caused yet another group of offenders to serve a short prison sentence or a short period left over from a longer sentence already served in part (paras. 57, 56f PC).

Academics have recently taken up the discussion whether the traditional consensus about the harmfulness of short-term imprisonment is in fact well-founded. Critics of this doctrine have argued that neighboring countries rely heavily on short-term imprisonment and have pointed out that a short prison sentence is in any event better than a longer one, given the lack of realistic prospects of rehabilitation by "treatment" in custody (Kunz 1986, pp. 198–205; Weigend 1986, pp. 264–67; Dolde and Rössner 1987; Kohlmann 1996, pp. 613–16). Yet legislative action in this area is unlikely. A return to the status quo before 1969 has no support and would indeed be irrational, and replacing longer prison sentences by shorter ones would run against the current trend of legislation.

B. Punitiveness

The progressive and optimistic trend toward individualizing and liberalizing the criminal law that characterized the reform movement of the 1960s may have come to an end. As in other countries, the lack of easily visible "improvements" in terms of reformed offenders and sinking crime figures has caused frustration and disappointment,[51] and the alleged rise of violent crime as well as of international organized crime have led to popular demands to "strengthen" the criminal law, in the vain hope of thereby reducing crime. One can observe several distinct developments that together make for a fairly clear trend toward greater punitiveness and a greater emphasis on the (individually and generally) deterrent quality of criminal law in general and of sentencing in particular.

Sentencing Theory

One remarkable development has occured in sentencing theory. The old controversy between retributivists and proponents of rehabilitation, which led to the uneasy compromise of paragraph 46 PC, has been superseded by the rise of a special German variant of general deterrence theory, something that can be called "affirmative general prevention." Today's most influential criminal law theorists proclaim the purpose of the criminal law to be the public reaffirmation of the validity of basic social norms that have been called into question by the offender's flagrant norm violation. Public reprobation and imposition of punishment is, according to this theory, a useful and necessary means to demonstrate the continued validity of the norm and to prevent imitation of the offender's conduct by others (Schünemann 1986, pp. 349–52; Streng 1989, pp. 286–97; Jakobs 1991, pp. 5–14; Frisch 1993, pp. 19–23; Jakobs 1995, pp. 843–49; Freund 1998, pp. 2–9; Müller-Tuckfeld 1998). Some writers have gone beyond this general explanation for the need to have and enforce criminal law and have tried to infer the necessary quantum of punishment in any individual case from the need to reaffirm the norm violated by the offender (Frisch 1987, pp. 386–88; Freund 1996, pp. 50–57). Because empirical social psychology is unable to determine the amount of punishment necessary to demonstrate, for example, the continued validity of the norm against theft after someone has stolen a ring from a jeweller's store or has embezzled $100,000 from a bank, the theory of "affirmative general prevention," if extended to sentencing, is forced to make normative judgments about the "necessary" penalty and thus returns to retributivism, though in the guise of modern sociology.[52] The importance of the new theory for criminal policy does not lie in the sentencing principles and standards it generates, because it does not generate any (see Lüderssen 1995, pp. 883–87), but in the fact that this theory regards as irrelevant the fate of the individual offender, whose only function, as in traditional deterrence theory, is to serve as an object for the edification of others (for criticism, see Hörnle and von Hirsch 1995, pp. 261–70; Köhler 1997, pp. 44–48; Roxin 1997, pp. 52–53). To the extent the currently prevalent explanation of criminal law brings its influence to bear on sentencing, we therefore have to expect a rougher climate of nonindividualistic and, in the last consequence, irrational sentencing.

Statutory Penalties

In recent years, whenever the German legislature produced new criminal law it almost invariably took the direction of expanding the ambit of prohibited conduct, raising penalties, or creating new ones. A few examples of this development should suffice. In its attempt to follow the international fashion of engaging in the combat against organized crime, the German legislature, in 1992, introduced a criminal prohibition of money laundering (para. 261 PC), as well as new provisions concerning the commission of larceny, receipt of stolen goods, and illegal gambling as a member of a criminal gang (paras. 244a, 260a, 284, sec. 3 PC). The legislature further created new sanctions specifically aimed at organized crime, that involved forfeiture of assets presumably stemming from other offenses (para. 73a PC) and a special fine the amount of which can reach the totality of the offender's assets (para. 43a PC). In 1994, penalties for assault and battery were generally increased.[53] As part of a broad legislative attack against corruption, the relevant criminal prohibitions (paras. 331–34 PC) were expanded and commercial corruption introduced into the Penal Code in 1997 (paras. 298–300 PC).

The most sweeping move toward greater repressiveness came in 1998 when the Act for the Reform of Criminal Law entered into force. There had been long-standing criticism of a discrepancy, in the German Penal Code, between the relatively stringent penalties for property offenses and the comparatively lenient attitude toward crimes against the person. The maximum penalty for simple battery (para. 223 PC) was three years' imprisonment, whereas simple larceny (para. 242 PC) was punishable by five years' imprisonment; the minimum penalty for aggravated robbery (para. 250 PC) was five years' imprisonment,[54] whereas a rapist could get off with six months in prison if there were extenuating circumstances (para. 177, sec. 2 PC); and an attempt to commit destruction of property (para. 303 PC) was punishable, whereas attempted battery was not. The legislature eliminated this discrepancy not by lowering the penalties for property crime but by drastically raising sentencing ranges for offenses involving violence. At the same time, several provisions of the Penal Code were reformulated to resolve differences of interpretation, almost always in favor of the more stringent alternative.[55]

Just to give a few examples of current sentencing ranges: murder (para. 211 PC) carries a mandatory life sentence, manslaughter (para. 212 PC), which is similar to second-degree murder, is punishable by five to fifteen years in prison or life imprisonment; the penalty range for aggravated battery (par. 224 PC) is six months to ten years, for nonaggravated rape (para. 177, sec. 2 PC) two to fifteen years, for aggravated robbery (para. 250) three to fifteen years, for burglary (para. 244, sec. 1, no. 3 PC) six months to ten years, and for dealing with significant quantities of prohibited drugs one to fifteen years (para. 29a Betäubungsmittelgesetz). Although German sentencing ranges may still be lower than those of many U.S. jurisdictions, they do not invite courts to be overly lenient, and the recent rise in maximum sentences is likely to lead to a significant overall increase in sentencing severity. It is true that German courts, whose discretion to determine a sentence within the broad limits of statutory sentence ranges is not limited by sentencing guidelines, tend to hand out sentences at the lower end of the statutory spectrum (see Albrecht 1994, pp. 287–91); yet their sentencing policies cannot remain unaffected by drastic upward expansions of sentencing ranges that raise the medium tariff of crime.

Crime statistics show that the level of serious crime has remained stable over the past decade in spite of the great social changes brought about by German unification and by the opening of borders toward Eastern Europe (Bundeskriminalamt 1998, p. 26). There is nevertheless a popular belief that serious crime has increased, and German courts have shown their willingness to respond to this misconception by imposing more lengthy sentences. By its latest "reform" efforts, the legislature has supported and further encouraged this trend, which will without doubt place great burdens on the prison system.

Suspended Sentences

The trend toward more severe sentences also threatens to counteract efforts to expand the use of suspended sentences. The reform law of 1969 set the upper limit of sentences subject to suspension at two years' imprisonment, and German courts, as we see in table 5.5, have made increasing use of suspended prison sentences in the range of one to two years. Criminologists, citing the example of several other European countries, have called for lifting the suspension borderline to three years (Dünkel 1983, pp. 1072–73; Schall 1990, pp. 345–49; Dölling 1992, pp. 277–78), yet legislative reforms in the direction of greater leniency do not seem to have good prospects in the present repressive climate.

The same is true for suspension of the final portion of a prison sentence ("parole"). Until April 1998, the Penal Code provided for early release after the offender had served two-thirds of his sentence if his prognosis was such that the court could responsibly test his ability to live in freedom without committing further offenses (para. 57, sec. 1 PC). Under special circumstances relating to the offense and the offender, early release was possible even when only one-half of the sentence had been served (para. 57, sec. 2 PC). Reform-minded writers had called for less restrictive rules on half-time release, which is used only in a minuscule portion of all theoretically eligible cases (Walter, Geiter, and Fischer 1989). Yet the "reform" legislation of 1998 went in the opposite direction by perceptibly tightening the conditions for early release. Courts, in determining parole eligibility, now are explicitly required to take the "safety interests of the public" into consideration (para. 57, sec. 1, no. 2 PC), and the "test" formula of the former law has been replaced by a new standard that requires the court to take full responsibility for the offender's release. Moreover, whenever the offender was convicted of a felony or of a designated misdemeanor causing or threatening bodily harm, the court cannot order his early release without having heard an expert witness on the issue of the offender's continued dangerousness (para. 454, secs. 2, 3 CCP). Taken together, these changes discourage courts from taking even slight risks in granting parole and will lead to a greater number of offenders remaining in prison for the full period of their sentence. This populistic trend toward greater "truth in sentencing" is counterproductive even in terms of crime prevention because it curtails the justice system's ability to support, control, and supervise a released person's first steps into freedom.

IV. Conclusion

If it is true that criminal policy develops in spiral form, there can be little doubt that we currently witness the beginning of a backward turn of the spiral. The aspirations toward a more rational and humane sentencing policy and the rehabilitative opitimism that were characteristic of the 1960s and early 1970s have been eroded by disillusionment, cynicism, and a populist response to the perceived pervasiveness of crime. In comparison with some other countries, sentencing policy in Germany is still moderate. This may be due, ironically, to the lack of clearcut, goal-oriented legislative standards—the vague, self-contradictory nature of the relevant legislation (see the discussion of para. 46 sec. 1 PC under section II E) in combination with broad statutory sentence ranges permits sentencing courts to adhere to their own traditions oriented toward equitability and pragmatism.

At this time, the most rational policy probably is to abstain from political activism in the area of sentencing, to study and record the success or failure of recent legislative measures, and to wait for the return of a more clement penological climate.

NOTES

1. One statute of great practical relevance is Gesetz über den Verkehr mit Betäubungsmitteln (Statute on the Traffic with Drugs) of 1994, which penalizes illicit dealing with drugs beginning with para. 29.

2. Prison sentences of two years or less can be suspended; para. 56 PC.

3. Murder is defined as an intentional killing aggravated by one or more designated factors regarding the offender's motive (e.g., greed, sexual satisfaction) or the manner in which the victim was killed (e.g., cruelty, surprise).

4. Moreover, parole is possible after a minimum of fifteen years of a life sentence has been served (para. 57a PC).

5. E.g., even if the prosecutor files an indictment for simple larceny the court can convict the defendant of robbery if it finds that he used violence in obtaining the goods.

6. For details, see section II.B.

7. A 1989 statute (Gesetz zur Änderung des Strafgesetzbuches, der Strafprozessordnung und des Versammlungsgesetzes und zur Einführung einer Kronzeugenregelung bei terroristischen Straftaten, arts. 4 and 5; Bundesgesetzblatt 1996 I, 58) provides for mitigation of sentence for offenders who have provided information on terroristic or organized crime.

8. Sentences can be—and frequently are—appealed from independently of the conviction (paras. 318, 344 CCP).

9. Despite German reunification, published official statistics for 1996 still apply only to (former) West Germany (Statistisches Bundesamt Reihe 3, 1997, p. 5). This is deplorable because it prevents us from seeing the complete picture of today's criminal justice in Germany, but it facilitates comparison with earlier data.

10. This figure does not include persons entering prison because of default in paying a fine or because of revocation of the suspension of a prison sentence.

11. This act, the Second Act to Reform the Criminal Law, which entered into force in 1975 (Bundesgesetzblatt 1975 I, p. 1), led to a total reform of the General Part of the Penal Code.

12. Driving under the influence of alcohol or drugs (paras. 315c, 316 PC) and driving without a license (para. 21 Strassenverkehrsgesetz [Road Traffic Act]) have remained criminal offenses.

13. Para. 47 sec. 1 PC limits prison sentences of less than six months to situations in which special circumstances relating to the offender or the offense make imposition of a custodial sentence indispensable for having an impact on the offender or for the defense of the legal order.

14. Para. 56 sec. 3 PC implicitly requires suspension of sentences of less than six months unless there is a substantial risk of recidivism. Sentences between six and twelve months must be suspended unless the offender poses a substantial risk of reoffending or the "defense of the legal order" (a synonym for an exceptionally strong public interest in general prevention) demands his immediate imprisonment (cf. Schönke and Schröder 1997, sec. 56, nn. 33–34).

15. Dealing in "not insignificant" quantities of illicit drugs is punishable by imprisonment between one and fifteen years (para. 29a Betäubungsmittelgesetz), and the minimum sentence is five years when the offender acts as a member of a gang that commercially deals in drugs (para. 30a Betäubungsmittelgesetz).

16. In 1996, 2,543 offenders convicted of drug offenses received prison sentences of more than two years (Statistisches Bundesamt Reihe 1, 1997, pp. 26–27). Drug offenders thus made up almost one-quarter of all offenders (8,927 in 1996; see table 5.3) receiving such sentences.

17. E.g., a typical first-time drunken driver is sanctioned by thirty day fines. The amount he has to pay equals the number of day fines (thirty) multiplied by his individual daily net income. It should be noted that the basis of determining the amount of one day fine is what the offender *earns*, not what he has to spare. For discussion of problems in setting the amount of a day fine in special cases (e.g., students, homemakers, unemployed persons), see Grebing 1976, pp. 1070–87; Jescheck and Weigend 1996, pp. 771–73; *Systematischer Kommentar* 1993, sec. 40, nn. 8–10).

18. If an offender is sentenced for more than one offense the number of day fines can be doubled to a maximum of 720 (para. 54, sec. 2 PC).

19. In 1996, only 5 percent of all fines imposed by criminal courts exceeded ninety day fines (Statistisches Bundesamt Reihe 3, 1997, p. 52). German law provides special legal tools for depriving offenders of illegal profits; see section II.D.

20. Details are regulated beginning with para. 17 Gesetz über Ordnungswidrigkeiten (Administrative Infractions Code).

21. Until 1986, para. 56 sec. 2 PC had required for suspension special circumstances in the offense *and* in the offender's personality (see *Leipziger Kommentar* 1994, sec. 56, n. 29). The slight change in the wording of the statute was meant (and understood) as an encouragement for courts to make more liberal use of suspension.

22. There is likely to be a link between the increasing use of "confession bargaining" in Germany since the mid-1980s and the rise in suspended sentences above one year: in

bargained cases of white-collar crime, the typical agreed-upon disposition is "two years suspended."

23. The overall portion of conditional dismissals has not changed significantly over the past ten years, but there are fairly strong regional differences in the frequency of its use, which ranges from 2 percent in Hamburg to 8 percent in Bavaria (see Eisenberg 1995, p. 369).

24. The dichotomy between *Verbrechen* (felonies) and *Vergehen* (misdemeanors) is different from what U.S. readers would expect. The Penal Code (para. 12 PC) defines *Verbrechen* as offenses with a minimum penalty of one year's imprisonment; all other offenses (e.g., larceny, burglary, forgery, extortion, and aggravated assault) are *Vergehen*. Offenses that belong to the *Verbrechen* category (e.g., murder, intentional manslaughter, rape, robbery, arson) statistically make up less than 2 percent of all offenses reported to the police (Bundeskriminalamt 1998, p. 28).

25. Examples are offenses committed abroad (para. 153c CCP) or offenses that the court would have legal authority to dismiss, e.g., because the offender made restitution to the victim (sec. 46a PC in connection with para. 153b CCP).

26. In para. 153a CCP, the "insignificant guilt" requirement has been lowered: dismissal is barred only if the suspect's guilt weighs so heavily that it is an obstacle to dismissal (see Fezer 1994, p. 35, who argues that this formulation in effect removes any seriousness-related restriction).

27. Para. 153a, sec. 1, no. 3 CCP also provides for the possibility of "otherwise providing for the common good," which is a synonym for community service; but this option is almost never used in practice (see Eisenberg 1995, p. 368).

28. In 1996, conditional dismissal in court occurred in 60,714 cases, i.e., in 8 percent of all cases scheduled for trial. By comparison, verdicts were returned in 52 percent of these cases (Statistisches Bundesamt Reihe 2, 1997, pp. 84, 94); the remaining cases were dismissed or otherwise disposed of.

29. The prosecutor does not have to give reasons for withholding consent, and the court cannot override his veto (Die Strafprozessordung und das Gerichtsverfassungsgesetz 1984). If, on the other hand, the parties agree on conditional dismissal, courts usually go along. The victim does not have a formal right to appeal conditional dismissal (see para. 172, sec. 2, 3d sentence CCP).

30. Federal legislation of 1986 created the option of community service but left its introduction to the states (Art. 293 Einführungsgesetz zum Strafgesetzbuch [Introductory act to the Penal Code]). By 1996, each state had enacted legislation providing for community service as an alternative to jail for fine-defaulters.

31. Under German law (para. 43 PC), persons who fail to pay day fines imposed on them must serve an equivalent number of days in jail, regardless of the reasons for nonpayment. Only if serving a jail sentence would create "undue hardship" on the offender will the jail sentence not be executed (para. 459f CCP; Schönke and Schröder 1997, sec. 43, n. 8, on the strict standards employed by the courts). This very strict rule is based on the theory that the offender's individual ability to pay is already taken into account in setting the amount of the day fine. Moreover, courts permit impecunious persons to pay fines in installments (para. 42 PC). About 6 percent of all offenders with fines eventually serve an alternative jail sentence (Schöch 1992, C124).

32. One day fine is converted into six work hours (see, e.g., para. 7, sec. 1 Verordnung über die Tilgung uneinbringlicher Geldstrafen durch freie Arbeit of the State of North Rhine—Westphalia of July 6, 1987).

33. One of the main reasons for practitioners' reluctance to make more frequent use of restitution as a sanction seems to be the relative difficulty of accurately determining the

amount due to the victim and of controlling whether the offender fulfills his obligations—payments to the state are much easier to monitor.

34. In 1995, there were 368 victim-offender reconciliation programs in existence (compared with 226 in 1992), which processed a total of 9,100 (compared with 5,100 in 1992) cases (Wandrey and Weitekamp 1998, pp. 130–31).

35. According to one study of forty-two selected victim-offender programs, these programs averaged only forty-three cases a year (Hartmann and Stroezel 1998, p. 154).

36. Although rehabilitative and security measures were first introduced in 1933, they are not typical Nazi law; their basic concept had been promoted for decades in an effort to avoid acquittal—without further consequences—of nonculpable but eminently dangerous persons (see *Leipziger Kommentar* 1992, sec. 61, nn. 1–12).

37. State law provides for civil commitment of persons who are, because of some mental defect, dangerous to others or to themselves (see, e.g., beginning with paras. 10 Gesetz über Hilfen und Schutzmassnahmen bei psychischen Krankheiten [Act on Support and Security Measures in Cases of Mental Disease] of North Rhine-Westphalia of December 2, 1969).

38. With respect to procedural law, the offender is better protected when he is adjudicated in a criminal process because the principle *in dubio pro reo* applies, and the requirements for imposing a measure must be established beyond a reasonable doubt.

39. The requirement of "recidivism" normally presupposes a prior nonsuspended prison sentence of at least two years. However, if an offender receives a prison sentence of three years or more for two felonies or for two offenses of aggravated assault or of sexual molestation of children, security detention can be ordered even without any prior conviction (para 66, sec. 3, 2d sentence PC).

40. For example, if the offender invests $1,000 in a fraudulent scheme and thereby induces the victim to pay him $2,000, forfeiture covers $2,000.

41. The Penal Code uses the term "if circumstances justify the assumption" that assets have been obtained through criminal activity. The Federal Court of Appeals has interpreted these words as requiring proof beyond a reasonable doubt (40 BGHSt 371 [1994]).

42. There is no equivalent in German law of "civil forfeiture."

43. As a consequence, if an offender violates the conditions of suspension there is no resentencing process but the offender must serve the prison sentence the court had originally fixed (para. 56f, sec. 1 PC).

44. Para. 56b, sec. 2 PC provides for the option of imposing payments to the victim, the state, or a charitable organization as a condition of suspension.

45. The normative requirements for sentencing do have an influence at the level of formally *justifying* sentences: courts must give reasons for penalties in the written judgment, and these reasons reflect legal requirements. A recent study (Albrecht 1994, pp. 408–27) shows that the substantive reasons trial courts give for sentences conform with the actual motives of their sentencing decisions; see below for appellate review of sentences.

46. Under German law, prosecutors as well as defendants can appeal sentences. If only the defendant files an appeal, the sentence cannot be increased (paras. 331, sec. 1, 358, sec. 2 CCP).

47. One of the reasons for the impracticality of this option seems to be criminal judges' unwillingness to immerse themselves in the intricacies of private damages law. The Code of Criminal Procedure offers criminal courts an easy way out by permitting dismissal of civil claims whenever their investigation would cause delay of the criminal process (para. 405, 2d sentence CCP).

48. An unresolved problem is the relationship between community service and imprisonment. Present law already provides the option of combining suspension of a prison sen-

tence with a work assignment (para. 56b, sec. 2 no. 3 PC). Introduction of community service as an independent sanction would thus only place a new label on an existing arrangement—unless one finds a feasible noncustodial backup sanction for those who wilfully fail to fulfill their work obligation.

49. Because on December 31 many prisoners are on furlough or have been released early, this figure is not representative of the average daily population of short-term prisoners. The figure cited in the text includes individuals detained as fine-defaulters.

50. Corrections statistics do not provide figures on the groups discussed in this part of the text.

51. The overall crime rate in (united) Germany has indeed decreased slightly since 1993 (1993: 8,337 reported offenses per 100,000 inhabitants; 1997: 8,031 offenses; Bundeskriminalamt 1998, p. 26), but this fact has hardly been noticed by the general public.

52. It is doubtful whether empirical social science can establish even the basic assumptions of "affirmative general prevention," i.e., that enforcing the criminal law promotes law-abiding behavior (see Schumann 1989; Bock 1991; Baurmann 1994).

53. The maximum penalty for simple battery (para. 223 PC) was raised from three years to five years, and a minimum penalty of three months' imprisonment was introduced for aggravated battery (para. 223a PC).

54. A robber who carried a toy gun to frighten his victim committed aggravated robbery (Bundesgerichtshof in 1976 *Neue Juristische Wochenschrift* 248).

55. E.g., larceny (para. 242 PC) and embezzlement (para. 246 PC) were redefined to cover the taking of goods with the intent to give them to another person, and exposure of a helpless person (para. 221 PC) was made to include cases in which there is no risk to the victim's life.

REFERENCES

Ahrens, Wilfried. 1978. *Die Einstellung in der Hauptverhandlung.* Göttingen: Schwartz.
Albrecht, Hans-Jörg. 1980. *Strafzumessung und Vollstreckung bei Geldstrafen.* Berlin: Duncker & Humblot.
Albrecht, H.-J., and W. Schödler. 1987. *Community Service, Travail d'Intérêt General, Dienstverlening, Gemeinnützige: A New Option in Punishing Offenders in Europe.* Freiburg: Max-Plauck-Institut.
———. 1990. "Strafzumessung bei schwerer Kriminalität im Vergleich." *Zeitschrift für die gesamte Strafrechtswissenschaft* 102:586–626.
———. 1994. *Strafzumessung bei schwerer Kriminalität.* Berlin: Duncker & Humblot.
Bannenberg, Britta, and Petra Uhlmann. 1998. "Die Konzeption des Täter-Opfer-Ausgleichs in Wissenschaft und Kriminalpolitik." In *Täter-Opfer-Ausgleich in Deutschland*, edited by Bundesministerium der Justiz. Bonn: Forum.
Baumann, Jürgen, et al. 1992. *Alternativ-Entwurf Wiedergutmachung.* Munich: Beck.
Baurmann, Michael. 1994. "Vorüberlegungen zu einer empirischen Theorie der positiven Generalprävention." *Goltdammer's Archiv für Strafrecht*, 368–84.
Bock, Michael. 1991. "Ideen und Schimären im Strafrecht: Rechtssoziologische Anmerkungen zur Dogmatik der positiven Generalprävention." *Zeitschrift für die gesamte Strafrechtswissenschaft* 103:636–56.
Bundeskriminalamt. 1997. *Polizeiliche Kriminalstatistik 1996.* Wiesbaden: Bundeskriminalamt.
———. 1998. *Polizeiliche Kriminalstatistik 1997.* Weisbaden: Bundeskriminalamt.

Burgstaller, Manfred. 1989. "Regionale Unterschiede der Strafzumessung in Österreich." In *Strafzumessung*, edited by Christian Pfeiffer and Margit Oswald. Stuttgart: Enke.

Dencker, Friedrich. 1973. "Die Bagatelldelikte im Entwurf eines EGStGB." *Juristenzeitung* 28:144–51.

Die Strafprozessordnung und das Gerichtsverfassungsgesetz. 1984. Edited by Reiss et al. Berlin: de Gruyter.

Dolde, Gabriele, and Dieter Rössner. 1987. "Auf dem Wege zu einer neuen Sanktion: Vollzug der Freiheitsstrafe als Freizeitstrafe." *Zeitschrift für die gesamte Strafrechtswissenschaft* 99:424–51.

Dölling, Dieter. 1992. "Die Weiterentwicklung der Sanktionen ohne Freiheitsentzug im deutschen Strafrecht." *Zeitschrift für die gesamte Strafrechtswissenschaft* 104:259–89.

Dölling, Dieter, and Susanne Henninger. 1998. "Sonstige empirische Untersuchungen zum TOA." In *Täter-Opfer-Ausgleich in Deutschland*, edited by Bundesministerium der Justiz. Bonn: Forum.

Dünkel, Frieder. 1983. "Rechtliche, rechtsvergleichende und kriminologische Probleme der Strafaussetzung zur Bewährung." *Zeitschrift für die gesamte Strafrechtswissenschaft* 95:1039–75.

Eberbach, Wolfram H. 1987. "Zwischen Sanktion und Prävention: Möglichkeiten der Gewinnabschöpfung nach dem StGB." *Neue Zeitschrift für Strafrecht* 7:486–92.

Eisenberg, Ulrich. 1995. *Kriminologie*. 4th ed. Cologne: Heymanns.

Erhard, Christopher. 1992. *Strafzumessung bei Vorbestraften unter dem Gesichtspunkt der Strafzumessungsschuld*. Berlin: Duncker & Humblot.

Feuerhelm, Wolfgang. 1991. *Gemeinnützige Arbeit als Alternative in der Geldstrafenvollstreckung*. Wiesbaden: Kriminologische Zentralstelle.

Fezer, Gerhard. 1994. "Vereinfachte Verfahren im Strafprozess." *Zeitschrift für die gesamte Strafrechtswissenschaft* 106:1–59.

Frehsee, Detlev. 1987. *Schadenswiedergutmachung als Instrument strafrechtlicher Sozialkontrolle*. Berlin: Duncker & Humblot.

Freund, Georg. 1996. "Zur Legitimationsfunktion des Zweckgedankens im gesamten Strafrechtssystem." In *Straftat, Strafzumessung und Strafprozess im gesamten Strafrechtssystem*, edited by Jürgen Wolter and Georg Freund. Heidelberg: Müller.

———. 1998. *Strafrecht: Allgemeiner Teil*. Berlin: Springer.

Frisch, Wolfgang. 1971. *Revisionsrechtliche Probleme der Strafzumessung*. Cologne: Heymanns.

———. 1987. "Gegenwärtiger Stand und Zukunftsperspektiven der Strafzumessungsdogmatik." *Zeitschrift für die gesamte Strafrechtswissenschaft* 99:349–88.

———. 1990. "Die Massregeln der Besserung und Sicherung im strafrechtlichen Rechtsfolgensystem." *Zeitschrift für die gesamte Strafrechtswissenschaft* 102:343–93.

———. 1993. "Straftatsystem und Strafzumessung." In *140 Jahre Goltdammer's Archiv für Strafrecht: Eine Würdigung zum 70. Geburtstag von Paul-Günter Pötz*, edited by Jürgen Wolter. Heidelberg: Decker.

Gerken, Ulrich, and Jörg Henningsen. 1987. "Ersetzung der Ersatzfreiheitsstrafe durch freie Arbeit." *Zeitschrift für Rechtspolitik* 20:386–90.

Giehring, Heinz. 1989. "Ungleichheiten in der Strafzumessungspraxis und die Strafzumessungslehre: Versuch einer Analyse aus der Sicht eines Strafrechtswissenschaftlers." In *Strafzumessung*, edited by Christian Pfeiffer and Margit Oswald. Stuttgart: Enke.

Grebing, Gerhardt. 1976. "Probleme der Tagessatz-Geldstrafe," *Zeitschrift für die gesamte Strafrechtswissenschaft* 88:1049–115.

Grünwald, Gerald. 1987. "Menschenrechte im Strafprozess," *Strafverteidiger* 7:453–57.

Hamm, Rainer. 1994. "Was wird aus der Hauptverhandlung nach Inkrafttreten des Verbrechensbekämpfungsgesetzes?" *Strafverteidiger* 14:456–59.

———. 1995. "Täter-Opfer-Ausgleich im Strafrecht." *Strafverteidiger* 15:491–96.

Hart-Hönig, Kai. 1992. *Gerechte und zweckmässige Strafzumessung.* Berlin: Duncker & Humblot.

Hartmann, Arthur, and Holger Stroezel. 1998. "Die Bundesweite TOA-Statistik." In *Täter-Opfer-Ausgleich in Deutschland*, edited by Bundesministerium der Justiz. Bonn: Forum.

Hassemer, Elke. 1998. "Praktische Erfahrungen mit dem Täter-Opfer-Ausgleich: Befunde und Konsequenzen." In *Täter-Opfer-Ausgleich in Deutschland*, edited by Bundesministerium der Justiz. Bonn: Forum.

Hering, Rainer-Dieter, and Dieter Rössner, eds. 1993. *Täter-Opfer-Ausgleich im Allgemeinen Strafrecht.* Bonn: Forum.

Hertwig, Volker. 1982. *Die Einstellung des Verfahrens wegen Geringfügigkeit.* Göttingen: Schwartz.

Hirsch, Hans Joachim. 1986. "Bilanz der Strafrechtsreform." In *Gedächtnisschrift für Hilde Kaufmann*, edited by Hans Joachim Hirsch, Günther Kaiser, and Helmut Marquardt. Berlin: de Gruyter.

———. 1990. "Wiedergutmachung des Schadens im Rahmen des materiellen Strafrechts." *Zeitschrift für die gesamte Strafrechtswissenschaft* 102:535–62.

———. 1994. "Das Schuldprinzip und seine Funktion im Strafrecht." *Zeitschrift für die gesamte Strafrechtswissenschaft* 106:746–65.

Hörnle, Tatjana, and Andrew von Hirsch. 1995. "Positive General-prävention und Tadel." *Goltdammer's Archiv für Strafrecht*, 261–82.

Jakobs, Günther. 1991. *Strafrecht: Allgemeiner Teil.* 2d ed. Berlin: de Gruyter.

———. 1995. "Das Strafrecht zwischen Funktionalismus und 'alteuropäischem' Prinzipiendenken." *Zeitschrift für die gesamte Strafrechtswissenschaft* 107:843–76.

Jescheck, Hans-Heinrich. 1969. *Lehrbuch des Strafrechts: Allgemeiner Teil.* 1st ed. Berlin: Duncker & Humblot.

———. 1977. "Die Geldstrafe in rechtsvergleichender Sicht." In *Kultur, Kriminalität, Strafrecht: Festschrift für Thomas Würtenberger*, edited by Rüdiger Herren, Diethelm Kienapfel, and Heinz Müller-Dietz. Berlin: Duncker & Humblot.

Jescheck, Hans-Heinrich, and Thomas Weigend. 1996. *Lehrbuch des Strafrechts: Allgemeiner Teil.* 5th ed. Berlin: Duncker & Humblot.

Jung, Heike. 1992. *Sanktionensysteme und Menschenrechte.* Bern: Haupt.

Kaiser, Günther. 1990. *Befinden sich die kriminalrechtlichen Massregeln in der Krise?* Heidelberg: Müller.

———. 1996. *Kriminologie.* 3d ed. Heidelberg: Müller.

Kaiser, Michael. 1992. *Die Stellung des Verletzten im Strafverfahren.* Freiburg: Max-Planck-Institut.

Kern, Johannes. 1997. *Brauchen wir die Sicherungsverwahrung?* Frankfurt am Main: Lang.

Kilchling, Michael. 1996. "Aktuelle Perspektiven für Täter-Opfer-Ausgleich und Wiedergutmachung im Erwachsenenstrafrecht." *Neue Zeitschrift für Strafrecht* 16:309–17.

Kinzig, Jörg. 1996. *Die Sicherungsverwahrung auf dem Prüfstand.* Freiburg: Max-Planck-Institut.

Köhler, Michael. 1987. "Zur Kritik an der Zwangsarbeitsstrafe." *Goltdammer's Archiv für strafrecht*, 145–61.

———. 1997. *Strafrecht: Allgemeiner Teil.* Berlin: Springer.

Kohlmann, Günter. 1996. "Vollstreckung kurzfristiger Freiheitsstrafen: Wirksames Mittel zur Bekämpfung von Kriminalität?" In *Festschrift für Otto Triffterer zum 65. Geburtstag*, edited by Kurt Schmoller. Vienna: Springer

Krahl, Matthias. 1997. "Der elektronisch überwachte Hausarrest." *Neue Zeitschrift für Straf-recht* 17: 457–61.

Kunz, Karl-Ludwig. 1980. *Die Einstellung wegen Geringfügigkeit durch die Staatsanwalts-chaft.* Königstein: Athenäum.

———. 1986. "Die kurzfristige Freiheitsstrafe und die Möglichkeiten ihres Ersatzes." *Schweizerische Zeitschrift für Strafrecht* 103:182–210.

Kürzinger, Josef. 1984. "Die Freiheitsstrafe und ihre Surrogate in der Bundesrepublik Deutschland." In *Die Freiheitsstrafe und ihre Surrogate im deutschen und ausländischen Recht,* edited by Hans-Heinrich Jescheck. Baden-Baden: Nomos.

Leipziger Kommentar zum Strafgesetzbuch. 1992, 1994. 1995. Edited by Burkhard Jähnke et al. Berlin: de Gruyter.

Lindenberg, Michael. 1992. *Überwindung der Mauern: Das elektronische Halsband.* Mu-nich: AGSPAK.

Loos, Fritz. 1993. "Zur Kritik des 'Alternativentwurfs Wiedergutmachung,' " *Zeitschrift für Rechtspolitik* 26:51–56.

Lüderssen, Klaus. 1995. "Das Strafrecht zwischen Funktionalismus und 'alteuropäischem' Prinzipiendenken." *Zeitschrift für die gesamte Strafrechtswissenschaft* 107:877–906.

Männlein, Ulrike. 1992. "Empirische und kriminalpolitische Aspekte zur Anwendung der Opportunitätsvorschriften §§ 153, 153a StPO durch die Staatsanwaltschaft." Ph.D. diss., University of Bielefeld.

Meier, Bernd-Dieter. 1996. "Täter-Opfer-Ausgleich und Wiedergutmachung im allgemei-nen Strafrecht." *Juristische Schulung* 36:436–42.

Meinberg, Volker. 1985. *Geringfügigkeitseinstellungen von Wirtschaftsstrafsachen.* Freiburg: Max-Planck-Institut.

Messmer, Heinz, and Hans-Uwe Otto, eds. 1992. *Restorative Justice on Trial.* Dordrecht: Kluwer.

Müller-Dietz, Heinz. 1982. "Das Marburger Programm aus der Sicht des Strafvollzugs." *Zeitschrift für die gesamte Strafrechtswissenschaft* 94:599–618.

———. 1992. "Strafzumessung und die Folgenorientierung." In *Festschrift für Günter Spendel,* edited by Manfred Seebode. Berlin: de Gruyter.

Müller-Tuckfeld, Jens-Christian. 1998. *Integrationsprävention.* Frankfurt am Main: Lang.

Neumann, Ulfrid. 1992. "Zur Bedeutung von Modellen in der Dogmatik des Strafzumes-sungsrechts." In *Festschrift füur Günter Spendel,* edited by Manfred Seebode. Berlin: de Gruyter.

Neumayer-Wagner, Eva-Maria. 1998. *Die Verwarnung mit Strafvorbehalt.* Berlin: Duncker & Humblot.

Nomos Kommentar zum Strafgesetzbuch. 1994. 1997. (loose-leaf). Edited by Ulfrid Neu-mann and Wolfgang Schild. Baden-Baden: Nomos.

Ostendorf, Heribert. 1997. "Die 'elektronische Fessel': Wunderwaffe im 'Kampf' gegen die Kriminalität?" *Zeitschrift für Rechtspolitik* 30:473–76.

Oswald, Margit E. 1994. *Psychologie des richterlichen Strafens.* Stuttgart: Enke.

Pfeiffer, Christian, ed. 1997. *Täter-Opfer-Ausgleich im Allgemeinen Strafrecht.* Baden-Baden: Nomos.

Pfeiffer, Christian, and Joachim J. Savelsberg. 1989. "Regionale und altersgruppenbezogene Unterschiede der Strafzumessung." In *Strafzumessung,* edited by Christian Pfeiffer and Margit Oswald. Stuttgart: Enke.

Pott, Christine. 1996. *Die Ausserkraftsetzung der Legalität durch das Opportunitätsdenken in den Vorschriften der §§ 154, 154a StPO.* Frankfurt am Main: Lang.

Riess, Peter. 1982. "Über Aufhebungsgründe in Revisionsentscheidungen des Bundesge-richtshofes." *Neue Zeitschrift für Strafrecht* 2:49–54.

Rönnau, Thomas. 1990. *Die Absprache im Strafprozess.* Baden-Baden: Nomos.

Rössner, Dieter, and Thomas Klaus. 1998a. "Dem Adhäsionsverfahren eine Chance!" *Zeitschrift für Rechtspolitik* 31:162–64.

———. 1998b. "Rechtsgrundlagen und Rechtspraxis." In *Täter-Opfer-Ausgleich in Deutschland,* edited by Bundesministerium der Justiz. Bonn: Forum.

Roxin, Claus. 1987. "Die Wiedergutmachung im System der Strafzwecke." In *Wiedergutmachung und Strafrecht,* edited by Heinz Schöch. Munich: Fink.

———. 1997. *Strafrecht. Allgemeiner Teil.* Vol 1. 3d ed. Munich: Beck.

Schaeferdiek, Sascha. 1997. *Die kurze Freiheitsstrafe im schwedischen und deutschen Strafrecht.* Berlin: Duncker & Humblot.

Schall, Hero. 1990. "Auf der Suche nach strafrechtlichen Modifikationen und Alternativen." In *Die 13: Bundestagung,* edited by Deutsche Bewährungshilfe e. V. Bonn: Forum.

Scheel, Jens. 1996. *Die Rechtswirklichkeit der Verwarnung mit Strafvorbehalt (§§ 59–59c StGB).* Göttingen: Cuvillier.

Scheffler, Uwe. 1994. "Kurzer Prozess mit rechtsstaatlichen Grundsätzen?" *Neue Juristische Wochenschrift* 47:2191–95.

Schlömer, Uwe. 1998. *Der elektronisch überwachte Hausarrest.* Frankfurt am Main: Lang.

Schmidhäuser, Eberhard. 1973. "Freikaufverfahren mit Strafcharakter im Strafprozess?" *Juristenzeitung* 28:529–36.

Schöch, Heinz. 1992. *Empfehlen sich Änderungen und Ergänzungen bei den strafrechtlichen Sanktionen ohne Freiheitsentzug? Gutachten C zum 59. Deutschen Juristentag Hannover 1992.* Munich: Beck.

Schönke, Adolf, and Horst Schröder. 1997. *Strafgesetzbuch: Kommentar.* 25th ed. Munich: Beck.

Schreckling, Jürgen, Erich Marks, Wolfgang Franzen, and Michael Wandrey. 1991. *Bestandsaufnahmen zur Praxis des Täter-Opfer-Ausgleichs in der Bundesrepublik Deutschland.* Bonn: Bundesministerium der Justiz.

Schumann, Karl F. 1989. *Positive General Prevention: Ergebnisse und Chancen der Forschung.* Heidelberg: C. F. Müller.

Schünemann, Bernd. 1986. "Die deutschsprachige Strafrechtswissenschaft nach der Strafrechtsreform im Spiegel des Leipziger Kommentars und des Wiener Kommentars." *Goltdammer's Archiv für Strafrecht,* 293–352.

———. 1990. *Absprachen im Strafverfahren? Grundlagen, Gegenstände, und Grenzen: Gutachten B zum 58—Deutschen Juristentag München 1990.* Munich: Beck.

———. 1993. "Wetterzeichen einer untergehenden Strafprozesskultur? Wider die falsche Prophetie des Absprachenelysiums." *Strafverteidiger* 13:657–63.

Sessar, Klaus. 1992. *Wiedergutmachen oder strafen.* Pfaffenweiler: Centaurus.

Statistisches Bundesamt Reihe 1. 1996. 1997. *Rechtspflege: Ausgewählte Zahlen für die Rechtspflege 1995, . . . 1996.* Stuttgart: Metzler Poeschel.

Statistisches Bundesamt Reihe 2. 1993. 1997. *Rechtspflege: Gerichte und Staatsanwaltschaften 1990, . . . 1995, . . . 1996.* Stuttgart: Metzler Poeschel.

Statistisches Bundesamt Reihe 3. 1987. 1988. 1996. 1997. *Rechtspflege: Strafverfolgung 1986, 1987, . . . 1995, . . . 1996.* Stuttgart: Kohlhammer (1987, 1988), Metzler Poeschel (1996, 1997).

Statistiches Bundesamt Reihe 4. 1977. 1981. 1991. 1994. 1997. *Rechtspflege: Strafvollzug 1976, . . . 1980, . . . 1990, . . . 1993, . . . 1996.* Stuttgart: Kohlhammer (1977, 1981), Metzler Poeschel (1991, 1994, 1997).

Statistiches Bundesamt Reihe 5. 1994. *Rechtspflege: Bewährungshilfe, 1991.* Stuttgart: Metzler Poeschel.

Statistisches Bundesamt Reihe 9. 1970. *Rechtspflege: Bevölkerung und Kultur, 1968.* Stuttgart: Kohlhammer.

Streng, Franz. 1989. "Schuld ohne Freiheit?" *Zeitschrift für die gesamte Strafrechtswissenschaft* 101:273–334.

———. 1991. *Strafrechtliche Sanktionen.* Stuttgart: Kohlhammer.

Systematischer Kommentar zum Strafgesetzbuch. 1992. 1993. 1995. (loose-leaf). Edited by Hans-Joachim Rudolphi, Eckhard Horn, and Hans-Ludwig Günther. Neuwied: Luchterhand.

Tiedemann, Klaus. 1974. "Die Fortentwicklung der Methoden und Mittel des Strafrechts unter besonderer Berücksichtigung der Entwicklung der Strafgesetzgebung." *Zeitschrift für die gesamte Strafrechtswissenschaft* 86:303–48.

Tröndle, Herbert. 1974. "Die Geldstrafe in der Praxis und Probleme ihrer Durchsetzung unter besonderer Berücksichtigung des Tagessatzsystems." *Zeitschrift für die gesamte Strafrechtswissenschaft* 86:545–94.

———. 1997. *Strafgesetzbuch und Nebengesetze.* 48th ed. Munich: Beck.

von Liszt, Franz. 1883. "Der Zweckgedanke im Strafrecht." *Zeitschrift für die gesamte Strafrechtswissenschaft* 3:1.

———. 1889. "Kriminalpolitische Aufgaben." *Zeitschrift für die gesamte Strafrechtswissenschaft* 9:737.

Walter, Michael, Helmut Geiter, and Wolfgang Fischer. 1989. "Halbstrafenaussetzung: Ein ungenütztes Institut zur Verkürzung der Freiheitsentzvges." *Neue Zeitschrift für Strafrecht* 9:405–17.

Walther, Susanne. 1999. "Was soll 'Strafe'?" *Zeitschrift für die gesamte Strafrechtswissenschaft* 111:123–43.

Wandrey, Michael, and Elmar G. M. Weitekamp. 1998. "Die organisatorische Umsetzung des Täter-Opfer-Ausgleichs in der Bundesrepublik Deutschland: Eine vorläufige Einschätzung der Entwicklung im Zeitraum von 1989 bis 1995." In *Täter-Opfer-Ausgleich in Deutschland,* edited by Bundesministerium der Justiz. Bonn: Forum.

Weichert, Thilo. 1989. "Sicherungsverwahrung: Verfassungsgemäss?" *Strafverteidiger* 9: 265–74.

Weigend, Thomas. 1983. "Sentencing in West Germany." In *Reform and Punishment,* edited by Michael Tonry and Franklin E. Zimring. Chicago: Chicago University Press.

———. 1984. "Strafzumessung durch den Staatsanwalt?" *Kriminologisches Journal* 16:8–38.

———. 1986. "Die kurze Freiheitsstrafe: Eine Sanktion mit Zukunft?" *Juristenzeitung* 41: 260–69.

———. 1989. *Deliktsopfer und Strafverfahren.* Berlin: Duncker & Humblot.

———. 1992. "Sanktionen ohne Freiheitsentzug," *Goltdammer's Archiv für Strafrecht,* 345–67.

———. 1994. "Empfehlen sich Änderungen des Strafverfahrensrechts mit dem Ziel, ohne Preisgabe rechtsstaatlicher Grundsätze den Strafprozess, insbesondere die Hauptverhandlung, zu beschleunigen?" In *Verhandlungen des 60. Deutschen Juristentages Münster 1994, vol.II/1,* edited by Ständige Deputation der Deutschen Juristentages, M 11–M 34. Munich: Beck.

———. 1999. "Eine Prozessordnung für abgesprochene Urteile?" *Neue Zeitschrift für Strafrecht* 19:57–63.

Zipf, Heinz. 1974. "Probleme der Neuregelung der Geldstrafe in Deutschland." *Zeitschrift für die gesamte Strafrechtswissenschaft* 86:513–44.

The Disassembly and Reassembly of U.S. Sentencing Practices

A process of recombination has been occurring in U.S. sentencing practices in the past three decades, in the sense that the foundational elements of punishment law and policy have undergone a kind of disassembly followed by a still-incomplete period of reassembly. In the important domain of the legal structures of punishment—the statutory and discretionary frameworks for sentencing decisions—the days are now gone in which every U.S. jurisdiction adhered to a similar approach. Since the mid-1970s, the United States has witnessed an unprecedented "sentencing reform movement" that has produced widespread and diverse structural experimentation among the nation's sentencing systems. Also, in terms of the numbers and severity of criminal punishments imposed, almost everything about the 1970s, 1980s, and 1990s has been dramatically different from the preceding decades of the 1940s, 1950s, and 1960s. Beginning in the early 1970s, the United States set out on a course of "punishment expansionism" that has entailed ever-increasing applications of all major forms of criminal sanctions. No resting place in the expansionist trend has yet appeared on the horizon. Finally, and in parallel with the upheavals in legal structure and systemic outputs, the theoretical fabric of U.S. sentencing had largely unraveled by the early 1970s and the process of finding new theoretical approaches has continued, without satisfactory completion, through the 1990s.

This chapter canvasses such recombinations in U.S. sentencing structures, outcomes, and theories during the current "expansionist" era that began in the early 1970s. Such tasks occupy sections I, II, and III. Section IV then reviews a handful of important issues in U.S. sentencing practice that have *not* changed markedly during the past thirty years but that remain important areas of concern in the coming years. These include the persistent and unaddressed tragedy of racial disproportionalities in sentencing in the United States, the failure to develop realistic theoretical goals for punishment decisions, the need to undertake comparative studies of diverse U.S. sentencing systems in operation, the painfully slow progress the United States has been making in the promotion of intermediate punishments, and the unmet challenges of prosecutorial discretion and plea bargaining within newly designed sentencing structures.

One preliminary caveat is needed. It is hard enough to compact three decades of complex national experience into a single book or chapter. The project is made more difficult, perhaps impossible, given the fact that there really is no such thing as "U.S. sentencing practice." Under the U.S. federal system, primary responsibility for criminal justice resides at the state level — and the states have varied greatly in their individual experiences of crime and their governmental responses to it. Much of the gross national data presented here, and the many sweeping authorial statements about U.S. attitudes and policy outlooks, merit a constant refrain of qualification and disclaimer. This chapter is written in the possibly misplaced belief that a satellite's eye view can yield insights of importance.

I. Punishment and Legal Structure: Changes in the Design of U.S. Sentencing Systems

One highly visible "recombination" in U.S. sentencing practices since 1970 has been occurring in the overarching legal structures that define who shall make punishment decisions, and the constraints of law and procedure that govern such decision-making. In the early 1970s, it was possible to say — without egregious oversimplification — that there was one ubiquitous U.S. design for the legal structure of punishment decisions: the indeterminate sentencing system (see Frankel 1973). In the intervening decades, however, indeterminacy has come under attack in many or most U.S. jurisdictions. In its place has arisen a patchwork of experimental approaches, none of which has yet gained a position of nationwide dominance (see Bureau of Justice Assistance 1996, 1997; National Center for State Courts 1997).

From the early twentieth century through the 1960s, the macro-components of indeterminate sentencing structures (if not their day-to-day micro-manifestations) were built on the idea that rehabilitation could be accomplished in large numbers of cases (Rothman 1980). Once that belief lost force in the 1970s, all the virtues of indeterminacy could be recast as vices. Why should legislatures have so little to say about criminal punishment if sensitive, individualized judgments were not really at issue? Why should judges possess nearly unconstrained sentencing authority, and how could it be defended against charges of gross arbitrariness, if no one believed in the efficacy of offender-based sanctioning? Why should parole boards, also vulnerable to sharp claims of caprice, be empowered to attempt the impossible — the detection of the mythical moment when rehabilitation had occurred? Why should the public, increasingly cynical about the criminal justice system, have to endure the disingenuousness of sentences that *sounded* impressive when pronounced, only to learn through repeated experience that "time served" was another matter?

For a combination of such reasons, and with a variety of results, indeterminate sentencing systems in many U.S. jurisdictions have given way since 1970 to an array of "determinate" sentencing reforms. All such reforms share a common feature. They seek to cabin, or even eliminate, the former reservoirs of case-by-case sentencing discretion held by trial judges and parole officials. In the place of such individualized sentencing authority, all determinate systems place new emphasis upon decision-making systemwide. In some instances this attack on case-specific discretion has been performed by statutory enactment; more often, in recent years, it has been advanced through sentencing guidelines created by sentencing commissions. The following sections outline the main structural innovations that have been attempted.

A. Statutory Determinacy

Beginning in the mid-1970s, a handful of states including Arizona, California, Colorado, Illinois, Indiana, and North Carolina modified their former indeterminate sentencing schemes to provide for greater specificity in authorized punishments as a matter of statutory command (Tonry 1996, p. 28). California adopted — and still follows—a "multiple-choice" approach under which each offense carries three potential punishments. For example, the current provision concerning first-degree burglary specifies that the sentencing options for the offense are "imprisonment in the state prison for two, four, or six years" (California Penal Code, Title 13, sec. 461, 1999). In the normal case, the trial judge is directed to impose the middle, or "presumptive," sentence laid out for each crime. As alternatives, the judge can select the "mitigated" or "aggravated" term, provided the judge can cite adequate reasons on the record. Once the court pronounces sentence in the California scheme, the stated judgment bears reasonable relation to the sentence actually served by the offender. Although prison terms are subject to discounts such as "good time," the determinate reform legislation abolished the parole board's authority to decide release dates.

Other statutory determinate sentencing reforms of the 1970s, such as those in Arizona, Colorado, Illinois, Indiana, and (for a few years) North Carolina, followed a somewhat different scheme. The criminal codes in such states were amended to set forth "ranges" of potential punishment for each offense, as opposed to the fixed integers in California law. Still, the overall plan was similar: typically these statutes provided a "presumptive" range for ordinary cases, with the bookends of "aggravated" and "mitigated" ranges available for unusual circumstances. Thus the judge was limited in punishment options (slightly or sharply, depending on the width of the ranges contained in the applicable statutes). A few states, such as Arizona, Illinois, and Indiana, joined California in the elimination of parole release (Bureau of Justice Assistance 1996, pp. 26–27).

The defining strength and weakness of statutory determinate reforms was that they relied on legislatures to choose specific penalties (or narrowed ranges of penalties) for specific crimes. Jurisdiction-wide uniformity in sentencing can be promoted in this way, but state legislatures do not have the time or expertise to ponder exact punishments with care. Nor do legislatures have the attention span needed to monitor their sentencing systems in operation, and to make periodic adjustments in the matrices of presumptive sentences. Indeed, most jurisdictions that enacted statutory determinate laws have found that their legislators tend to pass crazy-quilt amendments. In addition, legislative determinacy has proven a weak tool to manage prison population growth. The prison population in such states as California, Colorado, and North Carolina grew even more quickly under new determinate laws than before sentencing reforms were instituted. In part these developments can be attributed to changes in the political climates of individual states, but they led many to conclude that legislative determinacy was too blunt an instrument for the finely tuned decisions necessary for running a statewide sentencing system (Tonry 1996, p. 28).

B. Sentencing Commissions and Guidelines

In the late 1970s and early 1980s, several U.S. jurisdictions began to experiment with determinate sentencing reform based on the creation of a new administrative agency for sentencing policy: the permanent sentencing commission. The earliest commissions appeared in Minnesota, Pennsylvania, Florida, and Washington. By 1999, approximately twenty U.S. jurisdictions, including the federal system, had chartered such entities (as shown in table 6.1). It is fair to say that the commission-based approach became the most popular vehicle of sentencing reform in the last decade of the twentieth century. In that decade alone, new commissions were constituted in Arkansas, the District of Columbia, Kansas, Maryland, Massachusetts, Michigan, Missouri, North Carolina, Ohio, Oklahoma, South Carolina, Utah, and Virginia (see Frase 1995, p. 172; National Center for State Courts 1997). Preliminary study commissions are also at work in Alabama and Iowa. In contrast, no jurisdiction has adopted a statutorily based determinate structure since 1980 (Tonry 1996).

The sentencing commission was first proposed by Judge Marvin Frankel as a means to bring legal principles to bear on sentencing decisions in a uniform, rather than haphazard, way (Frankel 1972, 1973). Frankel's central concern was that discretionary actors such as judges and parole officials followed no rhyme or reason beyond their own personal instincts. He argued that no one would tolerate such "lawlessness" in litigation concerning a contract dispute or the repossession of a refrigerator. Punishment decisions, more important than much of the other routine business of the courts, were deserving of at least a comparable degree of care. Frankel therefore suggested that uniform standards for sentencing decisions be promulgated by a sentencing commission for application by courts throughout whole jurisdictions. (Later, "sentencing guidelines" became the term-of-art for such rules.) As with other areas of the law, Frankel urged that sentencing judges be required to explain their sentencing decisions on the record, subject to thoughtful appellate review.

For some people, Frankel's "rule-of-law" argument was sufficient by itself to win support for his suggestions of a sentencing commission and a new positive law of sentencing. In the decades following the early 1970s, however, other motivations (not all of them friendly to Frankel's original vision) have added to the trend toward proliferating commissions and guidelines. Speaking generally, these

Table 6.1. U.S. Sentencing Guidelines Systems as of June 1999

Jurisdiction	Effective Date	Features
Minnesota	May 1980	Presumptive guidelines for felonies; moderate appellate review; parole abolished; no guidelines for intermediate sanctions
Pennsylvania	July 1982	Presumptive guidelines for felonies and misdemeanors; minimal appellate review; parole retained; guidelines incorporate intermediate sanctions
Maryland	July 1983	Voluntary guidelines for felonies; no appellate review; parole retained; no guidelines for intermediate sanctions; legislature created permanent sentencing commission in 1998
Florida	October 1983	Guidelines repealed in 1997 and replaced with statutory presumptions for minimum sentences for felonies; appellate review for mitigated departures; parole abolished; no guidance regarding intermediate sanctions; sentencing commission abolished effective 1998
Washington	July 1984	Presumptive guidelines for felonies; moderate appellate review; parole abolished; no guidelines for intermediate sanctions; juvenile guidelines in use
Delaware	October 1987	Voluntary guidelines for felonies and misdemeanors; no appellate review; parole abolished in 1990; guidelines incorporate intermediate sanctions
Federal Courts	November 1987	Presumptive guidelines for felonies and misdemeanors; intensive appellate review; parole abolished; no guidelines for intermediate sanctions
Oregon	November 1989	Presumptive guidelines for felonies; moderate appellate review; parole abolished; guidelines incorporate intermediate sanctions
Tennessee	November 1989	Presumptive guidelines for felonies; moderate appellate review; parole retained; no guidelines for intermediate sanctions; sentencing commission abolished effective 1995
Kansas	July 1993	Presumptive guidelines for felonies; moderate appellate review; parole abolished; no guidelines for intermediate sanctions
Arkansas	January 1994	Voluntary guidelines for felonies; no appellate review; parole retained; guidelines incorporate intermediate sanctions; preliminary discussion of guidelines for juvenile cases
North Carolina	October 1994	Presumptive guidelines for felonies and misdemeanors; minimal appellate review; parole abolished; guidelines incorporate intermediate sanctions; dispositional grid for juvenile offenders to become effective July 1999
Virginia	January 1995	Voluntary guidelines for felonies; no appellate review; parole abolished; no guidelines for intermediate sanctions; study of juvenile sentencing under way
Ohio	July 1996	Presumptive narrative guidelines (no grid) for felonies; limited appellate review; parole abolished and replaced with judicial release mechanism; no guidelines for intermediate sanctions; structured sentencing for juveniles under consideration by legislature
Missouri	March 1997	Voluntary guidelines for felonies; no appellate review; parole retained; guidelines incorporate intermediate sanctions

Jurisdiction	Effective Date	Features
Utah	October 1998	Voluntary guidelines for felonies and selected misdemeanors (sex offenses); no appellate review; parole retained; no guidelines for intermediate sanctions; voluntary juvenile guidelines in use
Michigan	January 1999	Presumptive guidelines for felonies; appellate review authorized; parole restricted; guidelines incorporate intermediate sanctions
Alaska	Early 1980s	Judicially created "benchmark" guidelines for felonies; moderate appellate review; parole abolished for most felonies (retained for about one-third of all felonies); benchmarks do not address intermediate sanctions; no active sentencing commission
Massachusetts	Proposal Pending	Presumptive guidelines for felonies and misdemeanors; appellate review contemplated; parole to be retained; guidelines would incorporate intermediate sanctions
Oklahoma	Proposal Pending	Presumptive guidelines for felonies; appellate review contemplated; parole to be limited; guidelines would not incorporate intermediate sanctions
South Carolina	Proposal Pending	Voluntary guidelines for felonies and misdemeanors with potential sentence of one year or more; no appellate review contemplated; parole to be abolished for all felonies; guidelines would incorporate intermediate sanctions
Wisconsin	Proposal Pending	Voluntary guidelines for felonies; no appellate review contemplated; parole to be eliminated; guidelines would not incorporate intermediate sanctions; new permanent sentencing commission to be created
Washington, D.C.	Under Study	Temporary sentencing commission, scheduled to report to City Council in April 2000
Iowa	Under Study	Legislative commission to study sentencing reform, scheduled to report in January 2000
Alabama	Under Study	Study committee has requested that Alabama Judicial Study Commission create a permanent sentencing commission in 2000

Source: Information provided to author by state sentencing commissions.

have sprung from the discovery that sentencing commissions can pursue systemic objectives that formerly slipped through planners' fingers when judges and parole officials made policy decisions one case at a time.

Commissions have proven able, if so instructed, to restrain prison growth through the creation and monitoring of sentencing guidelines, assisted by computer projection models (Marvell 1995; Hunt 1999). Alternatively, they can predict and manage the contours of a pro-growth policy, if that is what is wanted (Tonry 1993). Although not a feature of Frankel's original scheme, sentencing commissions have attracted interest in part because they add a "resource management" capability to correctional planning. In the 1990s, states that have chartered commissions have frequently cited overcrowding and budgetary stress as primary factors in their decision to do so (Knapp 1993, pp. 686–89).

The constraint of prison growth has not been the sole motivation of commission-based reforms across the country. In some jurisdictions an agency of systemic competency was sought by policymakers who believed trial judges were too *lenient* when imposing sentences. Thus, in Pennsylvania, Virginia, and the federal system, commissions began their work with the resolution to increase aggregate sentence severity (although targeting some offenses more than others). In other places, such as Minnesota and Washington, commissions have operated for periods of years to restrain prison size, only to turn to a pro-growth course when asked to do so by their legislatures. In short, commissions have shown that they can be effective instruments of policy implementation, whether the prevailing impetus is one of lenity or severity.

This is not to say that the introduction of sentencing commissions has had no effect on the policymaking *process*. The commissions have added elements of predictability and manipulability to legislative decision-making about criminal punishments—and these new elements of the deliberative process have sometimes changed outcomes. For example, commissions are asked regularly to forecast the prison impact of proposals to amend guidelines or enact new sentencing legislation such as mandatory penalties or three-strikes laws. On occasion, sobering cost projections have dissuaded state legislatures from passing measures they might otherwise have enacted. Alternatively, the commissions' ability to calibrate sentences throughout the guidelines grid has created opportunities for legislative compromises combining the *increase* of sentences for offenses that the legislature most cares about (such as serious violent crimes) with *decreases* in sentences for other types of offenses (such as property and drug crimes). Legislatures have sometimes been grateful to be able to take dramatic action with respect to crimes that generate the highest public concern, and to do so without incurring the obligation of new prison construction. Without the commissions' ability to manipulate sentencing patterns line-by-line through offense categories, however, such trade-offs would be harder to engineer (see American Bar Association 1994, pp. 23–27).

For the reasons canvassed above, the idea of the sentencing commission has won favor with diverse constituencies, including those who promote law-and-order policies, those who think incarceration expansion has spun out of control, and those who simply want greater thoughtfulness and intentionality to guide the operation of sentencing systems on a macro level. The "resource management" capability of sentencing commissions is likely to remain a major selling point in the twenty-first century for jurisdictions that have not yet incorporated such entities, and a sustaining feature of existing commissions.

C. Mandatory Penalties

The "attack on case-specific discretion" has not always, since 1970, taken the form of reworkings of entire sentencing structures. It is much simpler, as a legislative matter, to create determinate sentencing laws that attach to one offense at a time. For example, some states have laws specifying that the penalty for aggravated murder must be a life term in prison without the possibility of parole. Such a provision is highly determinate in two senses. First, it removes the case-specific discretion of the trial judge to impose any sentence other than the mandatory penalty. Second, after the sentence is pronounced, the law removes any case-specific discretion on the part of the parole board to release the prisoner during his or her natural life.

A variation on this theme is the mandatory *minimum* penalty, which statutorily cuts off discretion to choose a sentence below, but not above, the stated minimum. For instance, a law might provide that, for a certain drug offense, the judge must impose a prison term of at least ten years. If the maximum authorized sentence under the statute is twenty years, the judge retains discretion to select a term between one decade and two but may not go lower than ten years. If the provision also restricts parole eligibility during the mandatory minimum prison term (which is a common device in such statutes), then the legislature has extinguished the parole board's release discretion for that duration, as well.

Since the 1970s, federal and state legislatures have enacted large numbers of mandatory penalty provisions, and the public popularity of such measures remains high. Such laws commonly apply to crimes involving serious violence, drugs, or firearms. Another species is keyed to criminal record: "habitual offender" laws have long been used to require heavier-than-normal sentences for criminals with substantial prior convictions. In the 1990s a potent variant of the habitual-offender approach appeared in the form of "three-strikes" laws. Congress and many states have now adopted such laws, which operate on a similar plan: upon conviction for a third "serious" felony (these are defined differently from place to place) the judge must sentence the offender to a life term of imprisonment without parole (Zimring 1996; see Dickey and Hollenhorst 1998).

Mandatory sentencing statutes have been adopted in jurisdictions that otherwise use indeterminate sentencing schemes, in jurisdictions that have followed the statutory determinacy approach, and in sentencing commission jurisdictions (Bureau of Justice Assistance 1996, pp. 26–27). In other words, U.S. legislatures have regarded mandatory penalties as a desirable means to produce zones of "hyper-determinacy" within every available structural environment. From a legislator's point of view, there is no more forceful way to express a policy judgment about what the sanction should be for a designated fact pattern. The motivating rationale is that every scenario of that type should result in an identical sentence, with perfect uniformity across offenders and zero discretion exercised by government officials (such as judges and parole boards) at the case level.

From the perspective of nonlegislative actors in the sentencing system, the wisdom and effectiveness of mandatory penalties are frequently challenged. In jurisdictions with sentencing commissions and guidelines, commissions often observe that mandatory penalties tend to be out of kilter with the scaling of offenses and punishments attempted by the guidelines. Moreover, since mandatory penalties cannot be altered short of legislative amendment, they are exempt from the commissions' ongoing processes of setting priorities and manipulating sentences to accommodate the realities of finite resources. For example, a jurisdiction that incarcerates large numbers of drug offenders for mandatory terms will have reduced flexibility to free up prison bed space for violent offenders. To the extent a sentencing commission is powerless to tilt the balance between drugs and violence in incarcerated populations, the jurisdiction has deprived itself of one advantage of having a commission in the first place.

On the ground level of individual sentences, trial judges are probably the most vocal critics of mandatory sentencing laws. Legislatures, when drafting such statutes, tend naturally to have unsympathetic offenders in mind—those criminals the public most fears and wants taken off the streets. On the case-specific level, in contrast, judges encounter offenders across a spectrum of blameworthiness and apparent dangerousness. Over time, many judges have accumulated experiences in which the mandatory penalty was far removed from their sense of justice in a given case (see Forer 1994; *United States v. Harris*, 154 F.3d 1082 [9th Cir.1998]). Usually on such occasions the judge follows the law against personal instincts, although some courts have found creative dodges to circumvent the statutes.[1]

The above complaints would carry less weight if mandatory penalty provisions actually achieved their objective of hyper-determinacy. There is overwhelming evidence, both recent and historical, that this does not occur. A recent survey by Michael Tonry (1996, chap. 5) charts the operation of such laws from England's Black Act in the eighteenth century and forward to a recent study by the U.S. Sentencing Commission (1991) during the Bush administration. Time and again, Tonry documents the tendencies of mandatory penalties to exacerbate rather than eliminate sentencing disparities, to create unintended bulges of discretion in prosecutors, to prompt nullification and avoidance strategies in courts and juries, to produce administrative bottlenecks (such as occur when large numbers of defendants refuse to plead guilty), and to fail in their goal of increasing the average severity of sentences.

One lesson of mandatory penalties may be that it is impossible to iron out all discretion at the case-specific level. Judges and parole officials may be taken out of the discretionary loop, but this still leaves prosecutors with unchecked power to file charges under the mandatory provision, to decline to do so, or to bargain down to less formidable charges (Reitz 1998). The U.S. Sentencing Commission study (1991) concludes that federal prosecutors have been selective in their use of mandatory laws and have pressed charges in only a fraction of the cases in which such laws apply. Usually, once such prosecutorial discretion is exercised, no remaining governmental decision-maker has authority to second-guess the decision. Thus the legislative vision of uniformity and hyper-determinacy can be disrupted by the eddies and currents of individual case processing.

Mandatory penalties have proliferated in all U.S. jurisdictions since 1970 despite the objections on grounds of policy and justice that have been leveled against them. In the absence of a change in the U.S. politics of law and order, widespread repeal or defanging of such statutes are unlikely events. It is probable that mandatory punishments will continue to exist as attempted pockets of hyper-determinacy within all varieties of sentencing structures, indeterminate and determinate.

D. The Staying Power of Indeterminacy

Although there have been impressive shifts in sentencing structure across the country in the past quarter century, a majority of U.S. jurisdictions continue to plow ahead with the high-discretion model of indeterminate sentencing for the bulk of their punishment decisions.[2] Some of these states have chartered sentencing commissions only to decide, ultimately, that they were not wanted on a permanent basis. Other states have not taken even such exploratory steps toward determinate reform. Jurisdictions that retain the traditional approach, and are not embarked upon the exploration of structural reform, include Connecticut, Hawaii, Idaho, Kentucky, Louisiana, Mississippi, Montana, Nebraska, New Hampshire, New Jersey, New Mexico, New York, North Dakota, Rhode Island, South Dakota, Texas, Vermont, West Virginia, and Wyoming (see Bureau of Justice Assistance 1996, pp. 26–27). In 2000, given the many permutations among "determinate" sentencing systems, it is fair to say that the traditional indeterminate structure remains the single most prevalent model of U.S. sentencing practice.

As under determinate regimes, indeterminacy can produce a wide range of sentencing patterns. In 1997, the state with the highest per capita incarceration rate in the country, Texas, built its prison populations out of indeterminate sentences. So did the state with the lowest incarceration rate, North Dakota (Bureau of Justice Statistics 1998c, table 2). Indeterminate states, compared with one another, have markedly different sentencing patterns for violent crime, drug crime, and property crime (Zimring and Hawkins 1991, chap. 5). Other observable outcomes, such as the racial composition of state prisons, are similarly divergent: indeterminate states achieve both high and comparatively low rates of racial disparity in sentenced populations (Blumstein 1993, table 3). There is, in short, no obvious correlation between the overarching structure that a jurisdiction chooses to erect for sentencing decisions and such things as the harshness, lenity, or distribution of punishments.

Still, large differences exist between traditional and "reformed" sentencing structures. Indeterminate systems produce their results without the benefit of generally applied legal principles, uniformity in sentences imposed, planning, predictability, and systemic oversight. Deliberate manipulations in sentencing patterns are difficult to engineer. Likewise, the policy judgments that underlie individual punishment decisions are unspecified. Sentencing judges need not concur with one another on whether the wealth of defendants (or any other aspect of the cases they hear) is an aggravating, mitigating, or impermissible factor in calculating appropriate penalties. Sentencing policy, writ small, is fashioned one judge at a time and one parole board at a time.

This state of affairs may have seemed appropriate in the heyday of rehabilitation theory, when the "diagnosis" and "treatment" of criminals were at issue. As noted, it is more difficult to explain the persistence of indeterminate structures in the post-rehabilitative era. What, one might ask, are the reasons that have supported such systems in the wake of Marvin Frankel's scathing—and unanswered—indictments (1972, 1973) of the indeterminate program? Two main explanations might be proffered for the staying power of indeterminacy: entrenchment of existing legal structures and their component bureaucracies; and the absence of a unified theory to replace the rehabilitative model as the foundation of system design.

Simple inertia favors the continuation of existing legal frameworks for sentencing in most jurisdictions. The switch from indeterminacy to determinacy involves study, effort, and risk. More important, it involves the relocation of sentencing authority in favor of some entities (such as a sentencing commission) and away from others (such as the parole board). Such changes are at least unfamiliar and, for agencies whose turf is threatened, can be highly unwelcome. As with any large reform project, an overhaul of the sentencing system is vulnerable to the expressed fear that "we might be worse off than before." In some jurisdictions judges and prosecutors have opposed proposals for sentencing guidelines — and vehement opposition from either constituency has proven the death knell of start-up commissions. In other states, influential judges and prosecutors have stood behind the idea of sentencing reform, and the statewide credibility of such leaders has contributed much to the ambitious undertaking of structural reform.[3]

An additional retarding factor in the current sentencing reform era, at least through the 1980s, has been the inaction of national law reform organizations with credibility and influence in state legislatures. The American Law Institute, whose prestigious Model Penal Code prompted a revolution in criminal code reform after its adoption in 1962, has never revisited its endorsement of indeterminate sentencing as formulated in the 1950s (American Law Institute 1985b, p. 10). Eighty percent of U.S. states have borrowed heavily from the Model Penal Code, including its sentencing provisions (American Law Institute 1985a, p. xi). No comparably authoritative law reform model has been designed for the emerging era of sentencing commissions and guidelines.

Other organizations, such as the American Bar Association, the National Conference of Commissioners on Uniform State Laws, and the National Council on Crime and Delinquency, issued aspirational reports on the structure of sentencing law in the 1970s — before any U.S. jurisdiction had adopted guidelines — and then fell silent through the 1980s (see Reitz and Reitz 1995, pp. 189–90). Indeed, the project of sentencing reform has proceeded largely at the state-by-state level, without the coordinating efforts of such national organizations. In 1993, the American Bar Association finally reentered the field with newly revised "Criminal Justice Standards for Sentencing" that rejected the model of indeterminacy and endorsed the state-sentencing-commission approach of jurisdictions such as Minnesota, Washington, and Oregon (American Bar Association 1994, p. xxi). Other organizations of stature, meanwhile, have remained dormant.

It would be unfair to attribute the residual vitality of indeterminate sentencing entirely to inertia or inattention. Many people continue to believe that the traditional approach is superior to newer reforms. And in a world that is lacking a vision of sentencing theory powerful and coherent enough to replace the eroded foundations of rehabilitation, there are understandable attractions to a process that is both indistinct on a systemic level and highly particularized to the individual case. An undoubted benefit of a nonregularized, high-discretionary system of sentencing is that it is capacious enough to include any and all theories of punishment. If one is uncertain about the best course to follow among contending theories of desert, incapacitation, deterrence, and, once in a while, rehabilitation, it may seem wise to keep all options open in every case (Packer 1968). Indeed, historian David Rothman has argued that this was one of the original allures of rehabilitation theory. Lacking any positive plan for crime reduction, the designers of indeterminate systems believed that unlimited inquiry into the facts of each case would yield productive conclusions (Rothman 1980). As Yogi Berra put it, "You can observe a lot just by watching."

A faith in induction, and the wisdom of judges, lends continuing support to the institution of high-discretion sentencing. Even among those who perceive the downsides of indeterminacy, there are some who take the view that the "cure" of sentencing guidelines is worse than the "disease" (Uelman 1992). The perceived excesses of some determinate laws, such as mandatory penalties and the labyrinthine provisions of the federal sentencing guidelines, are often cited as evidence that we are better off with the defects of discretion (Alschuler 1993; Forer 1994). There is force to the claim that a misconceived determinate scheme, enforceable across an entire jurisdiction, is worse than an indeterminate scheme, which yields a patchwork of good, bad, and indifferent outcomes. For reasons of momentum, attachment, and ambivalence about alternatives, indeterminate sentencing is not likely to disappear any time soon from the landscape of U.S. sentencing.

II. National Patterns of Punishment and Crime

Roughly overlapping the period of structural experimentation discussed in section I, there have been dramatic and continuous changes in the total quanta of punishments meted out by U.S. criminal justice systems.

A. Trends in the Use of Punishment

From the satellite's-eye view, no reconfiguration of nationwide policy stands out as distinctly as the three-decade growth trends in numbers of prisoners, jail inmates, probationers, parolees, and even death row inmates. Just as the past twenty-five to thirty years may be viewed as an experimental era in legal structures for punishment, they have also comprised an "expansionist" era in the use of all major forms of criminal sanctions. If the current expansionist period is driving toward a new steady state of punishment values, we have yet to discern what that new stasis will be.

Figures 6.1 and 6.2 depict some of the big-picture realities of punishment expansionism in the United States. Since 1970, the national incarceration rate (combining prisons and jails) has risen from 160 inmates per 100,000 general population to a 1997 level of 645 per 100,000 (Bureau of Justice Statistics 1998c, p. 1). The growth in confinement across this period has been especially rapid in the 1980s and 1990s. Incarceration rates increased by 51 per 100,000 through the 1970s, by 249 per 100,000 through the 1980s, and by 185 per 100,000 in the seven years from 1990 to 1997 (which yields a projected increase of 264 per 100,000 from 1990 to 2000). In raw numbers, there were 325,618 persons in prison

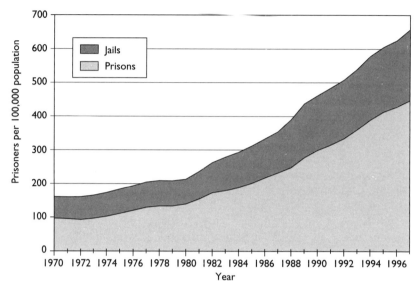

Figure 6.1. Incarceration rates in the United States, 1970–1997. *Sources*: Bureau of Justice Statistics (1997d, 1997e, 1998c, 1998d); Cahalan (1986).

or jail on a given day in the United States in 1970. By 1998 the one-day count had reached 1,825,400, and will likely reach 2 million by 2000. (Bureau of Justice Statistics 1999).

Similar growth patterns exist for the aggregate use of nonincarcerative sanctions. Despite gaps in the data, the long-term trends are unmistakable (see figure 6.2) There were a total (estimated) 603,794 probationers and parolees in 1970. By 1995, there were 3,796,703 — a more than sixfold increase. Corrected for population, the "probation-parole rate" in 1970 stood at about 294 per 100,000 general population; in 1995 that rate had swollen to 1,443 per 100,000 (see Bureau of the Census 1998, table 2). These numbers demonstrate an expanding U.S. investment in the use of nonprison punishments that parallels — and even outstrips — the long-term growth trends in confinement. While much of the recent commentary on U.S. sentencing patterns has been focused on the "prison boom," it is perhaps more accurate to say that there has been a "boom" in the application of *all* major categories of criminal sanctions in the United States in the past three decades.

The number of death sentences imposed by U.S. criminal courts has also been on the rise since the 1970s. Although the numbers are small in comparison with the other forms of punishment considered above, there were an average of 153 death sentences imposed per year through the 1970s, a yearly average of 263 such sentences through the 1980s, and, a yearly average of 290 from 1990 through 1997 (Bureau of Justice Statistics 1998a).[4] Despite the small numbers involved, and despite suspicions that capital punishment plays more of a symbolic than an instrumental role in U.S. criminal justice, the aggregate patterns of death penalty

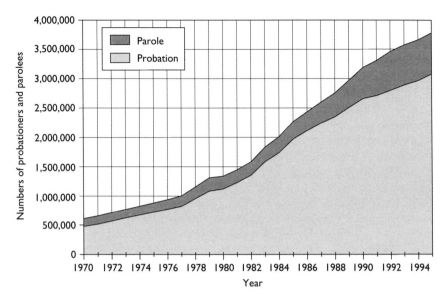

Figure 6.2. Estimated probation and parole populations in the United States, 1970–1995.
Sources: Bureau of Justice Statistics (1997e); Cahalan (1986).
Note: Values are estimated for years in which specific counts are not available.

administration are consistent with the general observation of U.S. punishment expansionism since the 1970s.

B. Crime Rates and Punishment

There has been no obvious correlation between changing sentencing patterns in the United States since 1970 and changes in crime rates (see Zimring and Hawkins 1991, chap. 5; Tonry 1998b). Whether one consults official crime records for the period, or victimization surveys, the measured rates of offending for the most serious crime categories (e.g., homicide, robbery, rape, aggravated assault) have increased over some multi-year periods and decreased in other periods — in seeming obliviousness to the steady drumbeat of punishment expansionism.

Two examples are given here. Figure 6.3 reproduces homicide statistics — the most accurate crime measure we possess — and provides a representative illustration of the up-down-up-down phenomenon in U.S. crime rates since 1970. To similar effect, figure 6.4 reports on two measurements of robbery rates from the early 1970s through 1997: the estimates of the National Crime Victims Survey and the FBI's compilations of reported offenses in the annual Uniform Crime Reports. Figure 6.3 and the twin measurements of Figure 6.4 tell a similar story in the following respect: the number of single-year observations in which homicide and robbery rates have gone up since 1970 is approximately equal to the number of single-year observations in which rates have gone down.[5]

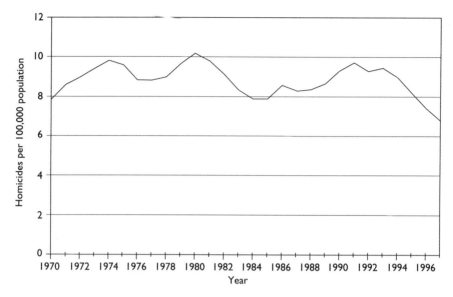

Figure 6.3. Homicide rates in the United States, 1970–1997. *Sources*: Federal Bureau of Investigation (1971–98).

The zigs and zags of figures 6.3 and 6.4 do not line up neatly with the steady growth trends in prison, jail, probation, and parole that are depicted in Figures 6.1 and 6.2. If punishment expansionism were a simple function of upsurges in crime, it is hard to account for the uninterrupted expansionist trends during multi-year periods in which crime rates have eased. Conversely, if punishment expansionism were an important retardant upon crime rates, the observed trendlessness in crime measures is a puzzle.

Of course, the present state of knowledge about the relationship between punishment and crime includes analyses far more sophisticated than these consultations of gross national statistics. Studies built upon varying methodologies have concluded (with a high degree of confidence) that incarceration growth does indeed yield crime reduction benefits—in both numbers of offenses and rates of offending (Zimring and Hawkins 1995; Reitz 1996a). With a lower degree of confidence, researchers have sought to quantify such effects. Two consistent findings emerged by the 1990s, commanding a scholarly consensus: the estimated crime avoidance effects of increased incarceration have been disproportionately small; and most of the offenses avoided through incarceration growth have been nonviolent rather than violent crimes.[6] Even one-time incapacitation enthusiast James Q. Wilson had conceded by 1994 that "very large increases in the prison population can produce only modest reductions in crime rates" (Wilson 1994, p. 38; cf. Wilson 1975, pp. 200–201).

In the past few years, the subject of the crime-reductive efficacy of carceral growth has been reopened in the United States. Between 1991 and 1998, national

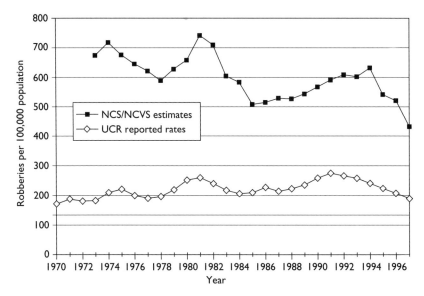

Figure 6.4. Robbery rates in the United States, 1970–1997.
Sources: Bureau of Justice Statistics (1997b, 1998b); supporting data at http://
www.ojp.usdoj.gov/bjs/glance/viotrd.txt; Federal Bureau of Investigation (1971–98).

homicide rates declined every year—and in some parts of the country the drop-offs were sharp and swift. Comparable, but not so dramatic, good news has come in falling rates of offending during the mid-to-late 1990s for other serious crimes such as armed robbery and sexual assault. These events, together with longer-term national declines in hard drug use and most property offenses, prompted novel and urgent questions about U.S. criminal justice policy: Why are U.S. crime rates now falling? After years of seeming futility, what are we now doing right?

One answer, posited by some, is that the long course of punishment expansionism in the United States, with particular stress on confinement growth, must be given a lion's share of the credit. This argument bears the burden of explaining why the first twenty years of punishment expansionism failed to achieve the impressive results now ascribed to the last seven. Such an explanation may be forthcoming, but the weight of criminological opinion has gravitated toward a cluster of alternative theories. These include changes in policing strategies (including a gamut of new approaches from "quality-of-life" policing to "zero-tolerance" policing to crime-mapping experiments), contractions in the urban crack markets (partly due to law enforcement efforts, partly due to lessening demand), reductions in the numbers of handguns carried illegally on the streets (thanks in part to gun-oriented policing initiatives, and in part to slowdowns and consolidation in the crack trade), a generally improving economy, temporary demographic lows in the numbers of crime-prone young males in the population, steady declines in the amount of alcohol consumed by Americans, and the optimistic theory that inner-city youths have learned positive lessons from the hard life experiences of their parents and older siblings (see Blumstein and Rosenfeld 1998; Fagan, Zimring, and Kim 1998; Parker and Cartmill 1998; Curtis 1998).

There is no one who can adjudicate definitively among these competing claims. It would be incautious to contend that punishment expansionism had *no* effect on crime rates between 1991 and 1998. On the other hand, given our very loose understanding of current crime patterns, it would be premature to conclude that the hard-won research consensus about the marginal benefits of incarceration growth should be cast aside.

A different question is whether recent declines in crime rates will affect future trends in the imposition of punishment in the United States. In the late 1990s, good news in the crime statistics did not herald a new phase of stagnating or declining confinement rates. There are murmurs that this may be beginning in some states (Marks 1998), but incarceration counts as late as 1998 showed continuing growth nationwide (Bureau of Justice Statistics 1999). One thing seems clear, however: a straight-line continuation of the past three decades' expansionism cannot continue far into the coming years without hitting a mathematical brick wall. The United States in 1999 had more than five times the inmate populations of twenty-five years ago. It is barely thinkable that another quintupling could occur between now and 2025, to yield a confinement count approaching 10 million. Moreover, as discussed in section IV, a mere doubling of current punishment rates overall, given the present racial demographics of prison, jail, probation, and parole, would place every young adult black male in some U.S. cities under the continuous jurisdiction of the criminal punishment system. Such specters are both physical and political impossibilities, one hopes. But it is only the fact that they have come into view that lends confidence to the prediction that the current expansionist era, in the short or middle term, must come to an end.

III. Changes in the Theoretical Underpinnings of Criminal Sanctions in America

A third major area of ferment, unrest, and lack of repose in U.S. sentencing practice has been in the domain of theory. Similar to the timelines of the changes in legal structure and punishment outcomes considered in sections I and II, this section takes note of destabilizing changes in the expressed goals of criminal punishment that first took root in the 1970s and ushered in an era of underarticulated punishment theory that continues with us today. Perhaps we indulge in a naïve fiction whenever we suppose that there might be an important relationship between stated philosophy and actual practice in criminal justice (see Garland 1990). However that may be, U.S. criminal justice since the 1970s has lacked even the illusory clarity of a widely voiced justification.

A. The Collapse of Rehabilitation Theory

Evidence of theoretical consensus is not unknown in U.S. criminal justice history. As late as 1970, all U.S. sentencing systems were built on the Progressive ideas that most criminal offenders could be rehabilitated and that this goal could best be accomplished through a system of individualized decisions about punishment. This approach took the legal form of "indeterminate sentencing" structures—so named because of the unpredictability of sentences they produced. Under indeterminacy, sentencing judges had discretion to choose sanctions from a wide range of options and were expected to tailor their sentences to the particular "correctional" needs of each offender. Unsurprisingly, penalties imposed tended to reflect the idiosyncrasies of the judge assigned to the case. No fixed rules governed courts' judgments (except that maximum statutory penalties could not be exceeded), there was no requirement that judges give reasons for their decisions, and no meaningful review of sentencing orders was available to the government or the defendant (see, generally, Frankel 1973). In cases of imprisonment, a parole board held further case-by-case authority to determine actual lengths of confinement. According to the theory of the day, the parole board was called upon to watch and discern when each prisoner had successfully been rehabilitated and could safely be returned to society. As with the initial sentence imposed by judges, parole-release decisions were essentially unguided by rule or principle, went unexplained on any official record, and were not appealable (Frankel 1973; Morris 1974).

To say that indeterminate sentencing systems were designed on a rehabilitative model is not to say, despite the good intentions of many people in the corrections field, that rehabilitation was pursued seriously or accomplished frequently. For one thing, most plausible programs to counsel or educate criminals are expensive, and U.S. legislatures have never shown great enthusiasm for major spending in the area. For another, few existing programs ever succeeded in producing widespread rehabilitation in offender populations. Such operational difficulties led to a fundamental irony: the large building blocks of the indeterminate sentencing system existed ostensibly in service of a treatment agenda, but no one could say with confidence how to perform that miracle on the ground level.

As the general justificatory aim of the sentencing structure, rehabilitation came crashing down in the 1970s. An influential empirical survey by Robert Martinson (1974), with the provocative title "What Works?" contributed to a new conventional belief that "Nothing works" where the rehabilitation of criminals is concerned. This sound-bite capsulation was a brusque simplification of Martinson's findings, which were discouraging on the whole, but which also found that a handful of programs had achieved modest improvements in the behavior of their clientele (see Lipton, Martinson, and Wilks 1975). Still, the message "heard" in the public and policy communities can be more significant than the message "delivered" in the academic literature.

For a number of reasons, the time was probably ripe for the idea that "Nothing works." Going into the 1970s, a number of societal currents had worn down patience with the rehabilitative experiment and were signaling widespread receptivity to alternative approaches. Reported crime rates, including homicide rates, had jumped sharply throughout the 1960s, and these alarming changes had coincided with a decade of slightly diminishing incarceration rates. In the same period, controversial defense-oriented rulings by the Supreme Court under Chief Justice Earl Warren had produced sentiment in some quarters that the legal system was "coddling criminals" and spawned an enduring public reaction against "lenient judges." Popular support for the death penalty, which had sputtered at submajority levels in the 1960s, soared to supermajority status during the next decade. For the first time in the nation's history, law and order became a national political issue in the presidential campaigns of the mid-1960s and early 1970s (Feeley and Sarat 1980).

Even for sophisticated policymakers, who understood that rehabilitation "Occasionally works," the intellectual and political climate of the 1970s made it difficult to maintain the posture that rehabilitation should continue to dictate the framework of *entire* sentencing systems. Instead, reformist objectives were demoted to a second order of priority, as in the following formulations: Such programs should be attempted, but only in conjunction with punishments imposed for other purposes (Packer 1968). They should be limited to convicts who volunteer to participate (Morris 1974). They should be pursued only for discrete subclasses of offenders who could be shown amenable to treatment (Frankel 1973). The crash in prominence of the treatment model had been stunning. As Albert Alschuler wrote in 1978, "That I and many other academics adhered in large part to this reformative viewpoint only a decade or so ago seems almost incredible to most of us today" (p. 552).

The fall of the rehabilitative ideal (Allen 1981) has had a powerful effect on U.S. sentencing law and practice. Perhaps most important, it created a policy vacuum that has yet to be filled. The past twenty-five years can be characterized as a period in which no single theoretical viewpoint has stood squarely behind the operation of U.S. sentencing structures — unless it has been the view that rehabilitation was *not* the way to go. James Q. Wilson, writing in 1975, captured well the emerging sentiments of moral judgmentalism and hard-nosed instrumentalism that would rush into the void.

> Wicked people exist. Nothing avails except to set them apart from innocent people. And many people, neither wicked nor innocent, but watchful, dissembling, and calculating of their opportunities, ponder our reaction to wickedness as a cue to what they might profitably do. We have trifled with the wicked, made sport of the innocent, and encouraged the calculators. Justice suffers, and so do we all. (Wilson 1975, p. 209)

As Wilson's statement suggests, the discrediting of reformative theory has had an interactive effect upon other extant sentencing policies. Once the softening tendency of rehabilitation theory is removed, the other mainstream goals of punishment can be pressed toward visions of increased severity. If it seems that criminals cannot be changed and have only themselves to blame for their behavior, then the most pivotal compunctions against harsh dispositions have been swept aside. There is no compelling argument against incapacitating as many offenders as the system can accommodate, for as long as possible; there is less to say in opposition to severe and even mandatory punishments in pursuit of increased marginal deterrence; and there are weaker moral claims to be marshaled against those whose retributive sense, driven by outrage at criminal behaviors, tells them that extremely harsh sentences are morally required (see Cullen and Gilbert 1982).

Widespread disillusionment with the treatment model has probably contributed to a number of developments in U.S. criminal justice since 1970. It has thrown criminal law into an ongoing crisis of justification and, by its remission, has helped fuel the upward spiral of U.S. prison sentences and other forms of punishment. It has also contributed to the era of structural experimentation in many U.S. jurisdictions. Rehabilitation theory's most visible effects in the world never took the form of armies of reformed offenders; rather, the theory's greatest impact was as the blueprint for indeterminate sentencing's procedures and institutions. The move of so many U.S. jurisdictions toward determinate sentencing reform must be viewed in this light. Somewhere in the workings of all the recombinatorial changes discussed in this chapter, the decline of the rehabilitative ideal has played a role.

B. The New Intolerance of Criminal Deviance

Increasingly in the wake of rehabilitation's decline, a broad-gauged intolerance toward criminal deviance of high and low seriousness can be observed across U.S. criminal justice systems—even if it is not always clear what theoretical bases have been driving the new intolerance. It might be said that the United States since the early 1970s has been living through a "punitive" era, one in which the operative theory has become "get tough on crime." Such colorful descriptives, however, are short on specifics about the identifiable goals of the new intolerance, or the hypothesized mechanisms for the accomplishment of those goals.

The substantive content of the new intolerance has been posited by some observers. For example, commentators have argued that incapacitation-oriented policy has filled the vacuum left by reformative theory (Zimring and Hawkins 1995), or that some version of retribution theory has become the new guiding light of U.S. punishment practices (von Hirsch 1993). There is only a modicum of truth to such categorical claims, however. Since the 1970s, throughout the many provinces of criminal justice, there has been spasmodic and overlapping interest in policies of incapacitation, retribution, and deterrence as well. Moreover, a new focus on community-based punishment theory has begun to assert prominence over older offense-and-offender-oriented theories.

One way to approach the new intolerance is to examine its manifestations. An obvious starting point is the massive incarceration expansion in the United States, and the fact that most of the expansion has caught up criminals at the lower end of the crime severity scale. As Zimring and Hawkins wrote in 1995:

> While much of the political rhetoric of incapacitation uses the imagery of violent crime, most sophisticated observers of the criminal justice system would acknowledge that the debate about prison expansion in the 1980s and 1990s is about burglars, automobile thieves, and minor property offenders, as well as the drug offenders previously discussed. (Zimring and Hawkins 1995, p. 165)

Zimring and Hawkins have also suggested that understandable fear about high levels of serious criminal violence has inspired an overbroad popular and policy reaction in the United States. When the average American thinks about a burglar coming through her window, she does not imagine the statistically probable un-armed teenager who rarely harms a victim; she pictures Willie Horton or some other media icon of lethal violence (Zimring and Hawkins 1998).

If there is an operative theory here, it is one of collapsing distinctions among categories of criminal offenders. To some degree, today's property offender may be viewed as a candidate for imprisonment on moral and utilitarian grounds be-cause he is seen *of a type* with the violent offender—or as someone likely to progress or diversify into violent crime (cf. Gottfredson and Hirschi 1990). Con-sistent with this view, burglary in many states is now classified statutorily as a violent crime for sentencing purposes and was included as a predicate felony for California's three-strikes law (Zimring 1996). For some legal purposes, the statis-tically probable nonviolent burglar is enveloped within the image of the statistically improbable violent burglar.

The new intolerance toward nonviolent crime, and the collapsed distinctions among different strata of criminality, are also evident in U.S. drug enforcement policy. In the latter 1980s and early 1990s, the growth in imprisonment rates for drug offenders was the single most important contributor to the U.S. incarceration explosion (Blumstein and Beck 1999). Especially in federal law, mandatory drug sentences of five, ten, and twenty years became fixtures of U.S. sentencing prac-tice—far outsizing the prison terms actually served in many jurisdictions for crimes of intentionally inflicted physical injury, sexual assault, and even homicide.

What may help explain the intensity of the U.S. War on Drugs in the past two decades is a readiness to associate all members of the criminal drug underworld with the worst representatives of the group. Drug crime is linked in the public mind with immorality and criminality of various kinds, including serious violent crime, even if no such connection has been proven in the case of an individual drug offender (see Bennett, DiIulio, and Walters 1996). A strong punitive stance against narcotics defendants will, in this view, have benefits that are pervasive even if they are hard to pinpoint.

The most recent manifestation of the new intolerance toward criminal deviance is the ongoing experiment in low-level law enforcement, expressed through changes in policing and prosecutorial practices that give emphasis to an attack on minor offenses, including the so-called quality of life offenses (see Kelling and Coles 1996; Livingston 1997). The theory here is that the disintegration of com-munities has provided hospitable breeding grounds for crimes at all severity lev-els—from the immediately visible transgressions of vandalism and outdoor drug markets all the way up to armed robbery and drive-by shootings. To combat this process of disintegration, the low-level enforcement strategy targets the most easily apparent symptoms of urban decay: the graffiti, the congregations of gang mem-bers, those who look suspiciously like drug dealers or prostitutes, the turnstile jumpers, the squeegee men, and the panhandlers. Ideally, there can be a "trickle-up" effect of such enforcement activities. Many suspected petty offenders, once arrested and searched, will turn out to be armed or wanted for arrest on other charges. Thus, crime prevention payoffs may travel up the ladder of crime seri-ousness.

Just as central to the low-level enforcement plan is the belief that an assertion of community standards, through quality-of-life policing, can incrementally promote an improved sense of social cohesion within blighted neighborhoods. Even community members who would never consider committing an offense, according to this theory, will gain confidence to take action against annoying and frightening law breakers in their locales. If such remediation can occur, even in stages, the prediction follows that there will be less crime at all levels of severity. Fewer violent crimes might ultimately result from continuous police efforts to maintain order, "kick ass," and clean up the streets (Wilson and Kelling 1982, p. 29; Skogan 1990, p. 75; Kelling and Coles 1996, pp. 24–25).

There is an uncertain logical leap here, between enforcement efforts dedicated to minor crimes and the eventual avoidance of major crimes. Still, the argument has resonated with many people since it was enunciated in 1982 as the "broken windows" thesis by James Q. Wilson and George Kelling. In some ways, the broken-windows approach is the standard bearer of the new intolerance. It provides a community-based rationale for a persistent law enforcement focus on all forms of criminal deviance and posits a relatedness between the most trivial and the most horrendous of offenses. The low-level enforcement strategy, in this understanding, departs from a focus on traditional principles of criminal punishment that relate directly to the offense and the offender. The goal of the law enforcement and punishment enterprise is now more diffuse and encompasses the notion that vigorous rehearsal and reinforcement of standards of societal conformity will seed larger commitments among community members to a law-abiding lifestyle.

It is clear from recent U.S. history that the low-level enforcement plan is politically viable (Harcourt 1998, p. 292), that it produces more work for the police and the courts (Rhode 1999), and that it coexists at times uncomfortably with the constitutional law of citizens' liberties from police interference (Livingston 1997). But does it reduce crime? Until recently, there was little evidence of such an effect, and the data in existence could support only an attitude of doubt (Livingston 1997; Harcourt 1998). The recent steep drop-offs in violent crime in major cities of the United States have stirred hopes, however, that we are seeing the rarest of all things: good results from criminal justice policy, deliberately effectuated. A new study of events in New York City by Jeffrey Fagan, Franklin Zimring, and June Kim (1998) concludes, without surrendering all skepticism, that the close timing overlap between changes in policing techniques and falling rates of violent crime suggests an authentic effect. Other observers, such as former New York Police Chief William Bratton, have been even quicker to declare a policy victory (Bratton and Knobler 1998).

In sum, one emerging paradigm in U.S. punishment theory, gathering steam in the 1980s and 1990s, is that of broad-gauged enforcement and punishment practices, aimed at an ever-widening spectrum of criminal conduct. This is something different from, or supplemental to, a belief that punishments for traditionally prosecuted behaviors should be increased. The new intolerance expands the net of law enforcement and punishment to reach behaviors that formerly would have gone overlooked. The theories driving such developments appear to have at least three identifiable features. First, they are based on a perception of increasing moral and utilitarian equivalence between offenders at the highest and lowest levels of crime severity, thus justifying punishment dispositions of offenders at the low end that more closely resemble dispositions at the high end. Second, they reveal a sense that the effort to rebuild whole communities requires increasingly aggressive law enforcement and punishment interventions and that the goal of community resuscitation is a proper consideration of sentencing policy, alongside considerations relating more directly to the offense and offender. Third, they presume that the moral and utilitarian ends of punishment in the intolerant era are not tempered by, and are certainly not subservient to, any view of the rehabilitative potential of individual offenders. The new intolerance thus entails a willingness to dispense hard treatment to the individual criminal in pursuit of its broader aims.

IV. Stalled and Emergent Issues in U.S. Sentencing Policy

This chapter's image of recombination—of a disassembly and reassembly of U.S. sentencing practices since 1970—suggests that pervasive and fundamental changes have been taking place in the way punishment is thought about and administered in the United States. The first three sections document such changes, on a large scale, in the areas of legal structure, punishment outcomes, and theory.

Alongside these instances of unfolding change, there are issues of high priority in U.S. punishment practice that have not been reconfigured in the 1970s, 1980s, and 1990s, which will demand attention in the coming years. The discussion that follows nominates five subjects for inclusion on such a list of concerns.

A. Racial Disparities in Punishment

Perhaps the most shocking realities of U.S. sentencing practice are those relating to the racial distribution of punishments. Throughout the period considered in this chapter, there have been heavy overrepresentations of African Americans within all sanctions categories for which data are available. Magnifying the impact of such racial disproportionalities, three decades of punishment expansionism have greatly increased the absolute numbers of persons subject to criminal sanctions. Thus, for example, close to 50 percent of U.S. incarceration growth since the early 1970s (about 700,000 inmates) has been extracted from African American communities that comprise only 12 percent of the nation's population.

In 1995, the combined incarceration rate (prison plus jail) of white males was 919 per 100,000 adult white males in the U.S. population. The black incarceration rate for the same year was a startling 6,926 per 100,000 adult black males (Bureau of Justice Statistics 1997e, table 6.12). A comparison of these two rates yields a "disproportionality ratio" of 7.54 to 1 (see Blumstein 1983, 1993). Since 1970, this ratio has been growing. Similar calculations yield black-white disproportionality ratios of 5.68 to 1 in 1970, 5.98 to 1 in 1980, 6.71 to 1 in 1985, and 7.47 to 1 in 1990 (based on Cahalan 1986; table 3–31 and table 4–15; Bureau of Justice Statistics 1997e, table 6.12).

Probation and parole populations likewise include an unexpected number of minority offenders, when measured against minority representation in the general population. In 1995, about 24 percent of state and federal probationers were black, and about 43 percent of state and federal parolees were black—compared with a baseline of about 12 percent of blacks in the general population (Bureau of Justice Statistics 1997e, tables 6.5, 6.52). The racial disproportionality in parole is not remarkably different from that seen in incarcerated populations, but the over-representation of blacks in probation counts is a much *smaller* overrepresentation than those observed in all other major categories of sanctions.[7]

In the capital punishment statistics, racial disparities among both sentenced and executed offenders are well known and have been long documented (see Kennedy 1997, pp. 312–26). As opposed to the trend for incarcerated populations, however, the racial disparities in death penalty administration have been diminishing in the past three decades. In the late 1960s and early 1970s there were slightly more blacks than whites on death row. The lines crossed in 1976, however, and white offenders have claimed a growing share of death row slots over the past twenty five years. At the end of 1996, blacks were 42 percent of all prisoners under sentence of death, down from 54 percent in 1970 (Bureau of Justice Statistics 1997a, table 5 and figure 2; Cahalan 1986, table 2–8). The 1996 figure, however, still represents a disproportionality ratio between blacks and whites in capital sentencing of more than a factor of six.

The fact that African Americans are overrepresented in all major categories of sentenced populations, and that the ratio of disproportionality in incarceration has been growing, means inevitably that punishment expansionism over the past three decades has taken an especially heavy toll on African American communities. Recent studies have quantified the omnipresence of criminal justice interventions in certain demographically and geographically discrete groups: on an average day in the mid-1990s, the Sentencing Project estimated that 30 percent of black males in the age group 18 to 29 were in prison, in jail, on probation, or on parole (Mauer and Huling 1995). These punishment effects have been particularly concentrated in urban areas. A similar calculation for the City of Baltimore estimated that the one-day total control rate for young black males was 56 percent, and 42 percent in Washington, D.C. (Miller 1996). In 1996, the U.S. Justice Department estimated that the likelihood of spending time in prison during one's lifetime was greater than one in four for African American males, compared with a one in twenty three chance for white males (Bureau of Justice Statistics 1997c).

Although some have argued that the racial demographics of punishment are conclusive evidence of a racist criminal justice system (Miller 1996), the picture is complex from both a statistical and policy viewpoint. However measured, rates of criminal offending among African American for many serious crime categories are much higher than comparable rates of offending among whites (Blumstein 1983, 1993; Tonry 1995). For the especially feared crimes of homicide and armed robbery in recent years, black rates of offending have been eight and ten times the white rate (Zimring and Hawkins 1998, chap. 5). For most crimes, with the glaring exception of drug offenses[8] and some property offenses, Blumstein (1983,

1993) has concluded that differential black imprisonment rates are explained almost entirely by differential rates of offending.

In addition, some policy advocates have taken the position that racial disproportionalities in punishment confer important benefits upon black communities and law-abiding black citizens. DiIulio (1994) argues that decent concern for African American crime victims should impel the United States toward still greater use of the prison sanction, despite (or because of) the fact that an increasing percentage of young black males would predictably be removed from their home communities. Kennedy (1997) expresses a related view that the *underenforcement* of criminal laws in African American neighborhoods has been more debilitating to the interests of black citizens than the discriminatory prosecution and punishment of black offenders.

No matter what view one takes of the causes and effects of the racial distribution of punishments in the United States, the aggregate statistics must be seen as warnings of serious dysfunctionality in U.S. society, in U.S. criminal justice, or both (see Tonry 1994). As the punishment enterprise has grown, the alarm bells have only become louder. Even so, at the turn of the new century, it is hard to maintain that the wrenching problems of race and criminal justice are in the process of being addressed in any systematic fashion. No national or comprehensive initiatives of any kind come to mind. Rather, in Michael Tonry's words, we remain in a period of "malign neglect" (Tonry 1995).

It seems clear that greater resources and creativity must be brought to bear on questions of race, crime, and punishment in the coming years. A straight-line continuation of current trends is not only unthinkable, it is mathematically impossible. A mere doubling of 1999s criminal justice control rate (which more than quadrupled in the preceding twenty-five years) would place *every* young adult African American male under the continuous jurisdiction of the criminal courts in some urban areas. This will never happen, of course, but we have yet to discover the means by which we will turn course from such a future of moral, political, and physical impossibility.

B. The Need for Realistic Theory and Evaluation

Although there have been signs of progress in the past several years, U.S. sentencing systems have not done nearly enough to incorporate sophisticated punishment policy into systemic design and evaluation. For example, theories of selective incapacitation have been debated in the criminological literature throughout the current era of sentencing commissions and guidelines (e.g., Wilson 1983, chap. 8; Zimring and Hawkins 1995, chap. 2). It was not until 1995, however, that the first sentencing commission (in the state of Virginia) made extensive use of this knowledge base to draft incapacitation-oriented guidelines targeted at high-rate recidivists (Kern 1995). Similarly, Norval Morris's theory of "limiting retributivism" has been in prominent circulation for many years (Morris 1974; Morris and Tonry 1990), but only recently has anyone argued that sentencing guidelines, such as those in force in Minnesota, can best be understood as operating along Morrisonian lines (Frase 1997). No jurisdiction to date has explicitly adopted a limiting retributive approach. Much newer ideas of "community justice" and "restorative justice" have in recent years gained considerable public attention, based on the appealing claims that criminal sanctions can be more responsive to the needs of offenders, victims, and whole communities, to repair the damage of criminal episodes (Braithwaite 1989; Clear 1999; but see Ashworth 1993). Such ideas have given shape to pilot programs in a few states, including Vermont and Wisconsin, but there is as yet no hint of jurisdiction-wide reform that incorporates such policies on a wide scale.

We do not know what the outcomes of such theoretical innovations will be, but the search for replacements for the cornerstone theory of rehabilitation is likely to demand experimentation along numerous dimensions. We should be glad that Virginia is "trying on" incapacitation theory for size; we should encourage Minnesota to ratify and refine its Morrisonian machinery; and we should watch the Pennsylvania guidelines with interest, since they incorporate yet another approach to sentencing policy, prescribing different substantive goals for different layers of the state guidelines grid (see section IV.C). Likewise, the new community-oriented innovations may begin to establish track records in practice that will merit emulation and expansion. All such experiments should be encouraged, even as they are scrutinized. The 1990s may foreshadow salutary trends in the future evolution of sentencing structures: the proliferation of efforts to mold punishment decisions to explicit goal-oriented criteria, and a concomitant recognition of the necessity to assess systemic performance against those stated goals.

Along the way, it will be crucial for sentencing commissions (or whoever holds systemwide authority over sentencing policy) to inject a healthy dose of reality into the engineering of sentencing structures. Rehabilitation lost public support not merely because it could seldom be achieved in practice but because the theory fell so far short of the overbroad claims that had been made for it. Similarly, deterrent and incapacitative programs, although currently in popular vogue, seem to yield only small (albeit real) reductions in crime in the community. As for the new community justice initiatives, it is possible they will prove even less realistic in their reformative ambitions than rehabilitation theory ever was.

The general point of importance is this. It is a recipe for poor systemic design, and for public and political dissatisfaction, to oversell the prospective utilitarian payoffs that may accompany changes in sentencing laws. Without deliberate efforts to inculcate an informed debate of punishment policy—one that appreciates that the criminal justice system operates at the margin of human behavior—even the best designed sentencing systems will perennially be vulnerable to the claim that "more needs to be done."

C. Exploration of System-Building Issues

A sentencing system, when examined as a whole, is one of the most complex and multilayered of all governmental bureaucracies (Zimring 1976). Instead of two or three relevant decision-makers, with power to influence the outcome of individual cases, the final sentence for any single offender might be determined through the collective input of legislators, sentencing commission members, police officers, prosecutors, probation officers, trial judges, appellate judges, correctional officials, and parole boards. It would not be unusual, in fact, in the "life history" of a single case of criminal punishment, for this entire cast of characters to be mobilized. Indeed, the list of relevant players only lengthens if we include nongovernmental input into sentencing decisions: the defendant himself, the defense attorney, and the victim all have potentially significant roles to play in the decision-making process (Reitz 1998).

Because sentencing guideline systems have not existed for very long, we are still in the rudimentary stages of understanding how the parts of such systems relate to the whole. Accordingly, deliberate changes in the workings of guideline systems are sometimes difficult to engineer. As sentencing commissions and guideline structures have increased in numbers and in time of operation, however, our knowledge about them has been growing steadily. Using the lens of comparative study of multiple systems, the store of supportable observations about guideline sentencing is now considerably greater than it was, say, ten years ago. And given the pace of reform at the state level, we can expect the coming decade to produce an even stronger current of new experience.

Comparative systemic study will be an increasingly powerful and important policy tool. It will assist in grappling with a variety of important questions. What is the most desirable allocation of sentencing discretion among legislatures, sentencing commissions, and trial courts, and how is it achieved? Why do some guideline systems appear to shift power to prosecutors more so than other systems? How can a jurisdiction deliberately encourage one result or the other? Which systems have proven particularly effective at managing prison population growth, and how did they do it? What is the desired role for the appellate judiciary in guideline structures, and how should the statutes and rules be arranged to encourage such appellate activity?

Projects directed to "design" questions of this kind have been undertaken in small numbers in the 1980s and 1990s, and will gain importance in coming years. New sentencing commissions, such as those in Massachusetts and Kansas, have benefited from cross-jurisdictional surveys during their start-up phases, before making recommendations about systemic design to their legislatures. The Pennsylvania commission, before reworking its guidelines in 1994, undertook a national study of other guideline states to discover ways in which Pennsylvania, one of the first guideline jurisdictions, may have fallen "behind the times" (Kramer and Kempinen 1995). In 1996, the Bureau of Justice Assistance issued the *National Assessment of Structured Sentencing*, which was one of the first attempts to compile comparative information about the sentencing systems of all fifty states. And the ABA, working from 1989 to 1994, issued its new edition of "Criminal Justice Standards for Sentencing" based heavily on a study of the structural models of up-and-running state systems (American Bar Association 1994).

Comparative analyses will be important both to advocates of the new determinate reform structures and to their skeptics and critics. For better or worse, we have no choice but to carry on parallel series of natural experiments in criminal punishment. Discontinuation, even temporarily, is not an option. One benefit of the present reform era has been the generation of a number of alternative legal structures for sentencing. As Justice Louis Brandeis famously hoped, the states are functioning well as "laboratories" for innovation (Reitz 1996b). The hard-won value of such experimentation, however, can only be harvested through watchful inter-jurisdictional study.

D. Slow Progress in the Use of Nonprison Sanctions

One of the great unsolved puzzles of the 1980s and 1990s is how to write sentencing guidelines for nonprison sanctions. Although there has been widespread agreement among policymakers and academics that creative exploitation of "intermediate punishments" (defined as those sanctions in-between the harshness of prison and the laxity of regular probation) would be a good idea in principle and might be the only realistic way to stem the tide of prison growth, no U.S. jurisdiction has yet implemented a systemwide program of intermediate punishments that has effectively diverted offender populations away from incarcerative sanctions (Morris and Tonry 1990; Tonry 1996, chap. 4).

A large part of the problem, in the view of experienced sentencing reformers such as Michael Tonry and Kay Knapp, is that the machinery of sentencing guidelines has not yet become fine-tuned enough to give structure to trial court decisions about intermediate sanctions (Tonry 1998a; Knapp 1993). The guidelines now in operation have proven useful for specifying the "in-out line" (i.e., the line between those offenders who should be confined and those who should not) and durations of confinement. It is a far more subtle undertaking, however, to prescribe the type and intensity of nonprison sanctions that include such things as intensive probation, community service, drug treatment, victim restitution, day fines, home confinement, forfeitures, and various forms of community treatment (American Bar Association 1994, pp. 85–94).

Promising experiments, still in their early stages, are under way in some states, including North Carolina and Pennsylvania. These may provide useful models for other jurisdictions in the years to come. The North Carolina Sentencing Commission devised a new "structured sentencing" grid in 1994 that layers intermediate punishments according to their level of intrusiveness. In a few of the grid's cells (that govern large numbers of the state's less serious cases), intermediate sanctions are the only option available to the judge. Since its effective date in 1994, the new law has pushed down North Carolina's confinement rate, following felony convictions, from 48 percent in 1993 to 34 percent in 1997 (Wright 1998, p. 12). An increased share of nonviolent offenders are now sentenced to intermediate punishments, and additional program slots were funded by the North Carolina legislature (Tonry 1998a, p. 211; Wright 1998, p. 12). However, because of offsetting increases in the penalties for violent offenders, the state's prison system has continued to grow over the same period. North Carolina's imprisonment rate from 1994 to 1997 increased by 15 percent—which was identical to the average increase among all other states for the same period (Bureau of Justice Statistics 1995, 1998d). Preliminarily, then, it can be said that North Carolina has succeeded in routing a greater number of offenders at the low-to-moderate levels of crime seriousness to intermediate punishments than had been the case under pre-guidelines practice. In addition, although the guidelines have not taken North Carolina off the course of prison growth experienced by other states, the guidelines have succeeded in reallocating the use of prison bed space toward longer sentences for the most serious offenders. Clearly, the state's new system will bear watching for its longer-term effects.

An intriguing experiment in Pennsylvania attempts to provide necessary links between sentencing theory and the choice of intermediate punishments. The state's current guideline matrix, designed in 1994 and updated in 1997, is divided into five zones.[9] For the most serious cases, incarceration is the only sentencing option. As one descends through the other guideline layers, however, "restrictive intermediate punishments" become available and, descending further, "restorative sanctions" are increasingly numerous among recommended sentences. Unique to the Pennsylvania system, each of the five zones of the guidelines grid is accompanied by narrative explanatory statements that set forth a changing hierarchy of sentencing purposes. At Level 5 (the most serious cases), retribution and incapacitation are dominant concerns. Moving downward to other levels, priorities of victim restitution, community service, and offender treatment become more prominent (see Kramer and Kempinen 1995; Tonry 1998a). The Pennsylvania framework might be called "three-dimensional" guidelines. They begin with a flat representation of the punishment menu on a familiar two-axis grid. This is then supplemented with narrative guidance that enriches the spare information contained in each guideline box. It is possible to find fault with the narrative instructions now in use in Pennsylvania (see Tonry 1998a); they are general and cryptic and give no case illustrations. Even so, the invention of the three-dimensional format is a large step forward, with much potential. Ultimately, some such mechanism will be needed to create a textured decision-making process for the full menu of sanctioning choices.

The North Carolina and Pennsylvania guidelines may not prove to be ideal models for other jurisdictions. Still, they stand as serious efforts, fashioned by people who have watched others try and fail, to address one of the highest-priority items on the current agenda of sentencing reform. In the coming years it will be incumbent upon policymakers to remain aware of, and learn from, such ongoing experiments.

E. The Unmet Challenges of Prosecutorial Discretion
   and Plea Bargaining

The sentencing reform era has made deep inroads, in many U.S. jurisdictions, into the discretionary powers formerly held by sentencing courts and the release authorities held by parole boards and correctional officials. The desirability of such emendations in discretionary power remains controversial. For instance, many critics of the federal sentencing guideline system charge that the federal law has gone too far in restricting the decisional latitude of district court judges (see Schulhofer 1992; Freed 1992). In the federal system, and in many states, some also doubt the wisdom of the abrogation of back-end release mechanisms, particularly in times of prison overcrowding when such safety valves may be among the few available tools for the emergency adjustment of incarcerated populations (Zimring 1976; Zimring and Hawkins 1991).

Putting such debates aside, there can be no doubt that the new U.S. sentencing structures have demonstrated that it is feasible to create powerful limitations on discretionary actors such as sentencing judges and parole boards—and that such constraints can be enforced. In contrast to this proven experience, however, very little has been attempted in any U.S. jurisdiction to confine the highly discretionary choices that comprise prosecutorial charging decisions and the plea bargaining decisions made by prosecutors and defense attorneys (see Walker 1993, chap. 4). Such discretionary inputs can bear enormous importance to the ultimate punishment imposed in particular cases. Indeed, in determinate sentencing structures, it is likely that the charges of conviction, together with any formal aggravating or mitigating circumstances to which the parties stipulate in advance, will determine for most cases what the approximate sentencing range will be. At least in the federal system, one often hears that the strict guidelines have greatly enlarged the sentencing powers of federal prosecutors, because the judge has very little to do once the relevant sentencing factors have been settled upon by the parties (e.g., Alschuler 1993).

Michael Tonry recently noted that, in contrast to prosecutors and police departments, judges and parole officials have borne the brunt of U.S. discretion-control initiatives since the 1970s. Tonry asks why this should be so and wonders whether it is coincidental that agents of law enforcement and prosecution have escaped the kind of legal controls that have been promulgated—sometimes with great ingenuity—for more objective decision-makers (Tonry 1998b). The provocative implication of Tonry's question is that the seemingly neutral project of sentencing reform has had a law enforcement bias.

I do not have an answer to Tonry's question, but I can offer some observations. In the 1970s, there was significant interest and concern surrounding issues of prosecutorial decision-making and the "back room" dynamics of plea bargaining. Indeed, in 1978, in the early stages of the sentencing reform movement, Albert Alschuler predicted that the limitation of judicial discretion through determinate sentencing laws would prove to be a windfall for prosecutorial power, unless equivalent means for the control of charging and plea bargaining decisions could be found (Alschuler 1978).

Jumping forward twenty years, the research base on prosecutorial discretion in determinate sentencing structures has barely advanced beyond Alschuler's early claims. Indeed, compared with the 1970s and early 1980s, the whole subjects of plea bargaining and prosecutorial discretion have inspired little scholarly interest, and even less empirical research. Why should this be so? One reason is that the realities of prosecutorial power under guideline systems have produced far less consternation than Alschuler forecast, in every guideline jurisdiction except the federal system (see Reitz 1998). Federal judges, frequently and loudly, have been heard to complain that their role under the current regime has been reduced, in many instances, to that of a rote functionary. It is the prosecutor, not the judge, we hear constantly from the federal system, who fixes punishment. The din of such complaints, however, has not been echoed in state guideline systems—by state sentencing judges or by anyone else. Such resounding non-utterances suggest that the dynamics of prosecutorial discretion under guidelines may be highly contingent, depending on other features of the overall sentencing system. If the evils projected by Alschuler have not occurred widely in the state guideline jurisdictions, this provides at least some explanation for the fact that state reformers have not focused their attention on the problem.

Still, our failure to invest in a better understanding of charging and plea bargaining discretions, and our failure to experiment with discretion controls in these areas, have deprived us of any clear sense of the complex decisions that take place behind closed doors in the new sentencing structures, and of the knowledge necessary to judge whether improvements in systemic operation could be within reach. Even if it appears likely that a shift of sentencing power to prosecutors has not occurred in state guideline systems, it remains probable that the *plea negotiation process* (involving the inputs of prosecutors and defense lawyers) has become more closely linked to punishment outcomes. This would be so, at any rate, if charge bargaining and fact bargaining now translate into predictable punishment consequences with regularity.[10] In a structure that operates in this fashion, the prosecutor's say-so counts for a great deal, of course—but only when the acquiescence of defense counsel can also be won. It takes two parties to conclude a plea agreement, and prosecutors have compelling interests to settle the majority of their cases and to reach accommodations with defense counsel that will accomplish this result (Scott and Stuntz 1992). Complaints about prosecutorial dominance, under such an analysis, are most likely to arise when a sentencing system has become more determinate than it used to be (thus enhancing the import of plea agreements)—and at the same time more punitive than it used to be in the penalties prescribed by statute or guidelines (thus enhancing prosecutors' bargaining position during plea negotiations). Defense lawyers are unlikely to conclude disadvantageous deals for their clients unless they are convinced that expected punishments, in the absence of deals, would be even worse.

At this point, however, our lack of empirical knowledge about the operation of most U.S. sentencing systems hobbles further analysis. We perceive that some systems work more smoothly than others, but we must draw upon theoretical models rather than data to explain why. We think that federal sentencing reform has exacerbated the problem of prosecutorial discretion over punishment, and that the state reforms have done better on this score, but we lack textured information about cross-jurisdictional differences. A host of important questions are therefore unanswerable. Have the states merely carried forward the pre-guidelines status quo of charging discretion and plea bargaining? Have they brought about modest or even substantial gains in the rationality of the guilty plea process? Are there areas of potential improvement in the regulation of charging and bargaining practices in the new systems that we are not exploiting simply because our eyes are closed to them?

More than twenty years after Alschuler's classic article, it appears that his dire predictions were largely correct for the federal guideline system but were off the mark for most or all of the state guideline systems. Nevertheless, Alschuler's article must also be remembered as directing our attention to a crucial, but little understood, stage of the case-processing march toward punishment. We would do well to rediscover that sense of importance today and to move toward an improved grasp upon the least visible decision points in the U.S. sentencing process.

V. Conclusion

U.S. sentencing practices since 1970 have seen greater changes than those in any other sector of U.S. criminal justice. This chapter argues that the leading edge of such changes was a failure of confidence in the institutions, theories, and outcomes of U.S. criminal punishment prior to 1970. The current era has been characterized by rejection of the sentencing practices of the 1940s, 1950s, and 1960s. This process of "disassembly" has in natural course lead to problems of "reassembly." If structural indeterminacy, rehabilitation, and stability in punishment are no longer the driving forces, what equivalent systemic cornerstones have taken their place?

This chapter argues also that the philosophical and structural components of the new era are still taking shape. We have seen continuous trends toward the increasing use and severity of criminal sanctions in the United States, and a spreading intolerance toward criminality at the low end of the gravity scale. Although many theoretical premises have contributed to these effects, the 1990s remain a decade of contestation among ideas of retribution, incapacitation, deterrence, and community-based utilitarianism. Similarly, in the legal structures that have been created for the dispensation of punishment, U.S. jurisdictions are notable for their diversity of approaches, much more so than for their similarities. The full recombination of U.S. sentencing practices, if it is to yield a new consensus of approach, lies somewhere in the future.

NOTES

1. For example, the California Supreme Court held that trial judges have statutory authority to dismiss charges brought under the state's three-strikes law. People v. Superior Court of San Diego County, 917 P.2d 628 (Cal. 1996).

2. Most or all indeterminate states have adopted mandatory penalty laws for selected offenses. Thus, there is probably no U.S. jurisdiction that follows a "pure" indeterminate program from top to bottom of the criminal code.

3. Such key proponents in their respective states have included Chief Justice Douglas Amdahl of the Minnesota Supreme Court; County Attorney Norman Maleng, King County, Seattle, Washington; District Attorney Michael Schrunk, Multnomah County, Portland, Oregon; and Judge Thomas Ross of the North Carolina Superior Court.

4. In the United States, judgments of death are far more commonplace than actual execution, although the pace of executions has also been rising since the 1970s (annual average of 0.3 executions in the 1970s; 11.7 in the 1980s; and 39.0 in the 1990s) (Bureau of Justice Statistics 1998a).

5. For a fuller discussion, including reference to crime statistics on homicide, robbery, rape, aggravated assault, and a variety of property crimes, see Tonry 1998b, pp. 12–16. Tonry observes "a general pattern of fluctuation" among rates of commission for all of these offenses from the early 1970s through the late 1990s (1998b, p. 12).

6. One study, performed for the National Academy of Sciences, estimated that the tripling of U.S. inmate populations between 1975 and 1989 had yielded marginal returns in the avoidance of violence. Cohen and Canelo-Cacho (1993) calculated that the relatively low U.S. incarceration rates of 1975 had been preventing 32.9 percent of potential violent episodes through incapacitation; the much higher incarceration rates in 1989 had improved estimated violent-crime avoidance only to 41.9 percent. There have probably been much larger gains in nonviolent-crime-prevention, however. A study by Zimring and Hawkins (1995, chap. 6) attempted to measure the effects of California's threefold increase in rates of confinement from 1981 to 1991. Under one formula (averaging the results of four crime-projection models), the authors estimated a total 15 percent reduction in California's crime rates owing to the state's tripling of incarceration rates. However, more than 90 percent of the estimated crime avoidance registered for the typically nonviolent offenses of burglary and larceny. Violent incidents such as homicides, rapes, and assaults were suppressed in much smaller numbers.

7. To my knowledge, the sharp differences in the racial disproportionalities evident in confinement and probation sanctions has not been explained (cf. Petersilia 1983, p. 28) (finding that African Americans convicted of felonies in California received sentences of probation in 67 percent of cases, while white felony offenders received probation in 71 percent of cases).

8. As Michael Tonry has argued, the increasing disproportionality ratios in incarceration since 1980 are closely linked to the U.S. War on Drugs. Both rates of arrest for drug offenses and the probability of incarceration following arrest grew markedly in the 1980s, and the largest impact by far was in black urban communities (Tonry 1995, pp. 81–123).

9. The 1994 iteration of the Pennsylvania guidelines had only four zones, but otherwise operated as described above.

10. We do not possess direct empirical data on this question within state systems, but we do know that the vast majority of state prosecutions are resolved by guilty plea and that state trial courts tend to follow sentencing guidelines in most of the cases that come before them. In the mass of cases, therefore, it seems reasonable to assume that the guilty plea brackets the expected sentencing outcomes.

REFERENCES

Allen, Francis A. 1981. *The Decline of the Rehabilitative Ideal: Penal Policy and Social Purpose.* New Haven, Conn.: Yale University Press.
Alschuler, Albert W. 1978. "Sentencing Reform and Prosecutorial Power: A Critique of Recent Proposals for 'Fixed' and 'Presumptive' Sentencing." *University of Pennsylvania Law Review* 126:550–77.
———. 1993. "The Failure of Sentencing Guidelines: A Plea for Less Aggregation." *University of Chicago Law Review* 58:901–51.
American Bar Association. 1994. *Standards for Criminal Justice, Sentencing.* Chicago: ABA Press.
American Law Institute. 1985a. *Model Penal Code and Commentaries.* Part 1. Philadelphia: American Law Institute.
———. 1985b. *Model Penal Code and Commentaries.* Part 2. Philadelphia: American Law Institute.
Ashworth, Andrew. 1993. "Some Doubts about Restorative Justice." *Criminal Law Forum* 4:277–99.
Bennett, William J., John J. DiIulio and John P. Walters. 1996. *Body Count: Moral Pov-*

erty and How to Win America's War against Crime and Drugs. New York: Simon & Schuster.

Blumstein, Alfred. 1983. "On the Racial Disproportionality of United States' Prison Populations." *Journal of Criminal Law and Criminology* 73:1259–81.

———. 1993. "Racial Disproportionality of U.S. Prison Populations Revisited." *University of Colorado Law Review* 64:743–60.

Blumstein, Alfred, and Allen Beck. 1999. "Population Growth in U.S. Prisons, 1980–1996." In *Prisons,* edited by Michael Tonry and Joan Petersilia. Vol. 26 of *Crime and Justice: A Review of Research,* edited by Michael Tonry. Chicago: University of Chicago Press.

Blumstein, Alfred, and Richard Rosenfeld. 1998. "Explaining Recent Trends in U.S. Homicide Rates." *Journal of Criminal Law and Criminology* 88:1175–216.

Braithwaite, John. 1989. *Crime, Shame, and Reintegration.* Cambridge: Cambridge University Press.

Bratton, William J., and Peter Knobler. 1998. *Turnaround: How America's Top Cop Reversed the Crime Epidemic.* New York: Random House.

Bureau of the Census. 1998. *Statistical Abstract of the United States.* Washington, D.C.: U.S. Government Printing Office.

Bureau of Justice Assistance. 1996. *National Assessment of Structured Sentencing.* Washington, D.C.: U.S. Government Printing Office.

———. 1997. *1996 National Survey of State Sentencing Structures.* Washington, D.C.: U.S. Government Printing Office.

Bureau of Justice Statistics. 1995. *Prisoners in 1994.* Washington, D.C.: U.S. Government Printing Office.

———. 1996. *Prison and Jail Inmates, 1995.* Washington, D.C.: U.S. Government Printing Office.

———. 1997a. *Capital Punishment 1996.* Washington, D.C.: U.S. Government Printing Office.

———. 1997b. *Criminal Victimization, 1973–95.* Washington, D.C.: Government Printing Office.

———. 1997c. *Lifetime Likelihood of Going to State or Federal Prison.* Washington, D.C.: U.S. Government Printing Office.

———. 1997d. *Prisoners in 1996.* Washington, D.C.: U.S. Government Printing Office.

———. 1997e. *Sourcebook of Criminal Justice Statistics 1996.* Washington, D.C.: U.S. Government Printing Office.

———. 1998a. *Capital Punishment 1997.* Washington, D.C.: U.S. Government Printing Office.

———. 1998b. *Criminal Victimization 1997: Changes 1996–97 with Trends 1993–97.* Washington, D.C.: U.S. Government Printing Office.

———. 1998c. *Prison and Jail Inmates at Midyear 1997.* Washington, D.C.: U.S. Government Printing Office.

———. 1998d. *Prisoners in 1997.* Washington, D.C.: U.S. Government Printing Office.

———. 1999. *Prisoners in 1998.* Washington, D.C.: U.S. Government Printing Office.

Cahalan, Margaret W. 1986. *Historical Corrections Statistics in the United States, 1850–1984.* Washington, D.C.: U.S. Government Printing Office.

Clear, Todd. 1999. *The Offender in the Community.* Belmont, Calif.: Wadsworth.

Cohen, Jacqueline, and José A. Canelo-Cacho. 1993. "Incarceration and Violent Crime: 1965–1988." In *Understanding and Preventing Violence,* vol. 4, *Consequences and Control,* edited by Albert J. Reiss Jr. and Jeffrey A. Roth, Washington, D.C.: National Academy Press.

Cullen, Francis T., and Karen E. Gilbert. 1982. *Reaffirming Rehabilitation.* Cincinnati, Ohio: Anderson.

Curtis, Richard. 1998. "The Improbable Transformation of Inner-City Neighborhoods: Crime, Violence, Drugs, and Youth in the 1990s." *Journal of Criminal Law and Criminology* 88:1233–76.

Dickey, Walter, and Pam Stiebs Hollenhorst. 1998. "Three-Strikes Laws: Massive Impact in California and Georgia, Little Elsewhere." *Overcrowded Times* 9(6):2–8.

DiIulio, John J., Jr. 1994. "The Question of Black Crime." *The Public Interest* 117:1–32.

Fagan, Jeffrey, Franklin E. Zimring, and June Kim. 1998. "Declining Homicide in New York City: A Tale of Two Trends." *Journal of Criminal Law and Criminology* 88:1277–323.

Federal Bureau of Investigation. 1971–98. *Crime in the United States: Uniform Crime Reports.* 28 vols. For 1970–97. Washington, D.C.: U.S. Government Printing Office.

Feeley, Malcolm M., and Austin D. Sarat. 1980. *The Policy Dilemma: Federal Crime Policy and the Law Enforcement Assistance Administration.* Minneapolis: University of Minnesota Press.

Forer, Lois G. 1994. *A Rage to Punish: The Unintended Consequences of Mandatory Sentencing.* New York: Norton.

Frankel, Marvin E. 1972. "Lawlessness in Sentencing." *University of Cincinnati Law Review* 41: 1–54.

———. 1973. *Criminal Sentences: Law without Order.* New York: Hill & Wang.

Frase, Richard S. 1995. "Sentencing Guidelines in Minnesota and Other American States: A Progress Report." In *The Politics of Sentencing Reform*, edited by C. M. V. Clarkson and Rod Morgan. Oxford: Clarendon Press.

———. 1997. "Sentencing Principles in Theory and Practice." In *Crime and Justice: A Review of Research*, vol. 22, edited by Michael Tonry. Chicago: University of Chicago Press.

Freed, Daniel J. 1992. "Federal Sentencing in the Wake of Guidelines: Unacceptable Limits on the Discretion of Sentencers." *Yale Law Journal* 101:1681–754.

Garland, David. 1990. *Punishment and Modern Society: A Study in Social Theory.* Chicago: University of Chicago Press.

Gottfredson, Don, and Travis Hirschi. 1990. *A General Theory of Crime.* Stanford: Stanford University Press.

Harcourt, Bernard E. 1998. "Reflecting on the Subject: A Critique of the Social Influence Conception of Deterrence, the Broken Windows Theory, and Order-Maintenance Policing New York Style." *Michigan Law Review* 97:291–389.

Hunt, Kim. 1999. "Sentencing Commissions as Centers for Policy Analysis and Research: Illustrations from the Budget Process." *Law and Policy* 20:465–89.

Kelling, George L., and Catherine M. Coles. 1996. *Fixing Broken Windows: Restoring Order and Reducing Crime in Our Communities.* New York: The Free Press.

Kennedy, Randall. 1997. *Race, Crime, and the Law.* New York: Pantheon Books.

Kern, Richard. 1995. "Sentencing Reform in Virginia." *Federal Sentencing Reporter* 8:84–88.

Knapp, Kay A. 1993. "Allocation of Discretion and Accountability within Sentencing Structures." *University of Colorado Law Review* 64:679–705.

Kramer, John, and Cynthia Kempinen. 1995. "The Reassessment and Remaking of Pennsylvania's Sentencing Guidelines." *Federal Sentencing Reporter* 8:74–79.

Lipton, Douglas S., Robert Martinson, and Judith Wilks, 1975. *Effectiveness of Correctional Treatment.* Springfield, Mass.: Praeger.

Livingston, Debra. 1997. "Police Discretion and the Quality of Life in Public Places: Courts, Communities, and the New Policing." *Columbia Law Review* 97:551–672.

Marks, Alexandra. 1998. "Signs of End to Decades-Long Prison Boom." *Christian Science Monitor*, October 27, p. 1.

Martinson, Robert. 1974. "What Works? Questions and Answers about Prison Reform." *The Public Interest* 35:22–54.

Marvel, Thomas B. 1995. "Sentencing Guidelines and Prison Population Growth." *Journal of Criminal Law and Criminology* 85:696–707.

Mauer, Marc, and Tracy Huling. 1995. *Young Black Americans and the Criminal Justice System, Five Years Later*. Washington, D.C.: The Sentencing Project.

Miller, Jerome G. 1996. *Search and Destroy: African-American Males in the Criminal Justice System*. New York: Cambridge University Press.

Morris, Norval. 1974. *The Future of Imprisonment*. Chicago: University of Chicago Press.

Morris, Norval, and Michael Tonry. 1990. *Between Prison and Probation: Intermediate Punishments in a Rational Sentencing System*. New York: Oxford University Press.

National Center for State Courts. 1997. *Sentencing Commission Profiles*. Williamsburg, V.: National Center for State Courts.

Packer, Herbert L. 1968. *The Limits of the Criminal Sanction*. Stanford: Stanford University Press.

Parker, Robert Nash, and Randi S. Cartmill. 1998. "Alcohol and Homicide in the United States 1934–1995; or, One Reason Why U.S. Rates of Violence May be Going Down." *Journal of Criminal Law and Criminology* 88:369–98.

Petersilia, Joan. 1983. *Racial Disparities in the Criminal Justice System*. Santa Monica, Calif.: Rand Corporation.

Reitz, Kevin R. 1996a. "The American Experiment: Crime Reduction through Prison Growth." *The European Journal on Criminal Policy and Research* 4–3:74–91.

———. 1996b. "The Federal Role in Sentencing Law and Policy." *The Annals of the American Academy of Political and Social Science* 543:116–29.

———. 1998. "Modeling Discretion in U.S. Sentencing Systems." *Law and Policy* 20:389–428.

Reitz, Kevin R., and Curtis R. Reitz. 1995. "Building a Sentencing Reform Agenda: The ABA's New Sentencing Standards." *Judicature* 78: 189–95.

Rhode, David. 1999. "A Glut of Minor Cases Swamps City's Courts." *New York Times*, February 2, p. 19A.

Rothman, David J. 1980. *Conscience and Convenience: The Asylum and Its Alternatives in Progressive America*. Boston: Little, Brown.

Schulhofer, Stephen J. 1992. "Assessing the Federal Sentencing Process: The Problem Is Uniformity, Not Disparity." *American Criminal Law Review* 29:833–73.

Scott, Robert E., and William J. Stuntz. 1992. "Plea Bargaining as Contract." *Yale Law Journal* 101: 1909–68.

Skogan, Wesley G. 1990. *Disorder and Decline: Crime and the Spiral of Decay in American Neighborhoods*. New York: Oxford University Press.

Tonry, Michael. 1993. "The Success of Judge Frankel's Sentencing Commission." *University of Colorado Law Review* 64: 713–22.

———. 1994. "Racial Disproportion in U.S. Prisons." *British Journal of Criminology* 34(special issue): 97–115.

———. 1995. *Malign Neglect: Race, Crime, and Punishment in America*. New York: Oxford University Press.

———. 1996. *Sentencing Matters*. New York: Oxford University Press.

———. 1998a. "Intermediate Sanctions in Sentencing Guidelines." In *Crime and Justice: A Review of Research*, vol. 23, edited by Michael Tonry. Chicago: University of Chicago Press.

————. 1998b. "Introduction: Crime and Punishment in America." In *The Handbook of Crime and Punishment*, edited by Michael Tonry. New York: Oxford University Press.

Uelman, Gerald F. 1992. "Federal Sentencing Guidelines: A Cure Worse Than the Disease." *American Criminal Law Review* 29:899–905.

U.S. Sentencing Commission. 1991. *Special Report to the Congress, Mandatory Minimum Penalties in the Federal Criminal Justice System*. Washington, D.C.: U.S. Sentencing Commission.

von Hirsch, Andrew. 1993. *Censure and Sanctions*. Oxford: Clarendon Press

Walker, Samuel. 1993. *Taming the System: The Control of Discretion in Criminal Justice, 1950–1990*. New York: Oxford University Press.

Wilson, James Q. 1975. *Thinking about Crime*. New York: Basic Books.

————. 1983. *Thinking about Crime*, Rev. ed. New York: Basic Books.

————. 1994. "Prisons in a Free Society." *Public Interest* 117:37–40.

Wilson, James Q., and George Kelling 1982. "Broken Windows: The Police and Neighborhood Safety." *Atlantic Monthly*, March, pp. 29–38.

Wright, Ronald F. 1998. "Flexibility in North Carolina Structured Sentencing, 1995–1997." *Overcrowded Times* 9(6):1, 11–15.

Zimring, Franklin E. 1976. "A Consumer's Guide to Sentencing Reform: Making the Punishment Fit the Crime. *Hastings Center Report* 6:13–17.

————. 1996. "Populism, Democratic Government, and the Decline of Expert Authority: Some Reflections on 'Three Strikes' in California." *Pacific Law Journal* 28: 243–56.

Zimring, Franklin E., and Gordon Hawkins. 1991. *The Scale of Imprisonment*. Chicago: University of Chicago Press.

————. 1995. *Incapacitation*. New York: Oxford University Press.

————. 1998. *Crime Is Not the Problem: Lethal Violence in America*. New York: Oxford University Press.

Comparative Perspectives on Sentencing Policy and Research

The chapters in this volume add to a rapidly growing English-language literature on sentencing laws and practices in Western countries and provide a rich source of data on the variety of approaches to common issues of sentencing policy faced by almost all modern nations. Although most of this literature is less than ten years old, it also provides instructive historical perspectives, revealing major changes that have occurred in several jurisdictions in just a few years.[1]

This chapter seeks to identify common issues and themes in Western sentencing and to emphasize some of the important similarities and differences in these systems. The common features include not only broadly similar sentencing purposes, procedures, and alternatives but also similar recent trends (e.g., toward increased severity, particularly for violent, sex, and drug offenders). These growing similarities make the remaining differences (e.g., limitations on sentencing discretion and severity; use of noncustodial sentencing alternatives) all the more interesting from the perspectives of research and law reform—international legal "transplants" are becoming increasingly viable, as potential "donor" and "recipient" systems become more compatible. Unfortunately, increasing similarity between sentencing systems makes it easier for bad practices to migrate across national boundaries; however, comparative research is also valuable for what it tells us *not to do* about crime and sentencing (chap. 1, this volume).

The chapter concludes with an assessment of the most important challenges confronting scholars of comparative sentencing, in the years ahead, in four key areas: developing a stronger international consensus on sentencing principles (especially *limiting* principles), expanding constitutional and international human rights limitations on sentencing, developing a true "comparative law of sentencing" (exploring why nations do or do not differ and "borrow" from one another), and improving the quality and comparability of data on sentencing and crime in Western countries.

I begin by stating my normative and methodological assumptions, because they underlie my assessments of what is "important" in the existing literature and in future research.[2] Scholars often describe or promote sentencing rules and practices as being more "rational," "fair," or "appropriate," without considering the normative premises that underlie these value judgments. In a field as value-laden as sentencing, it is important to openly recognize one's own values, and define one's terms, so that readers will know where the writer is coming from (and so that both readers and the writer can see the extent to which the writer's premises are shared by the public and by key policymakers and assess the difficulties of implementing the writer's views). Similarly, a brief initial statement of methodological assumptions and limitations helps to clarify and interpret the analysis and conclusions that follow.

Briefly stated: I believe that sentencing should endeavor to achieve the following goals, in the following order of priority:[3] first, proportionality to actual or potential harm and offender culpability—especially, avoiding undeservedly severe punishments; second, economic efficiency or "parsimony," at both systemic and case levels (preferring the least severe penalty that will adequately achieve other goals)—particularly in the use of custodial sentencing alternatives; third, crime-control effectiveness; and, fourth, victim and community satisfaction with sentencing processes and outcomes. These goals all rest on normative and practical considerations, and they tend to reinforce one another (for example, disproportionately severe penalties add little crime-control benefit, or are even counterproductive, and thus are also inefficient). I believe these goals and assumptions are similar to those adopted by most recent scholars of comparative sentencing (e.g., the other chapters in this volume; see also Ashworth 1995; Bottoms 1995; Davies 1996, pp. 197–98), and that they are also consistent with the better practices in a number of jurisdictions. Although my normative premises are clearly not shared by many citizens and their leaders, especially in the United States, I show later in this chapter that there is considerable common ground on these issues (even in the United States) and thus, some hope of achieving consensus and progress.

A sentencing scholar's subject matter and research methodology should also be clearly stated at the outset. In this chapter (and many of the previous studies cited), the topic of sentencing is broadly defined, to include not only the formal penalties imposed by judges upon conviction but also decisions before trial and after sentencing that are intended to serve similar punishment purposes (and that may have similar public and private effects). "Pre-adjudication sentencing" includes legislative decisions about the scope of the criminal law (criminalization) and authorized or required penalties, as well as police and prosecutorial decisions related to conditional and unconditional dismissal, pretrial diversion, charging, and nontrial disposition options (penal orders, "plea bargaining," etc.).[4] Post-adjudication sentencing includes probation and parole conditions that are added or modified by the court (and sometimes by nonjudicial authorities), probation revocation, prison "good-time" allowances and disciplinary measures, prison security and facility assignments and grants of temporary release; and parole release and revocation decisions.

This broad, "systemic" perspective (Albrecht 1995, p. 306) is not simply a valuable source of ideas for different ways of allocating sentencing authority; it is essential in order to understand how foreign systems operate and the variety of ways in which some systems have achieved low incarceration rates (Frase 1995b). Systemic analysis also helps avoid false comparisons between different jurisdictions (or within the same jurisdiction, at different times). For example: longer average prison terms and higher rates of custodial sentencing in one country (or period) may reflect higher rates of pretrial diversion and dismissal, which "siphon off" less serious cases; offense-specific comparisons improve, but do not eliminate, this source of non-comparability. These problems, and the major limitations of the currently available international sentencing data, are discussed more fully in section III. D.

I. The Globalization of Sentencing Policy: Similarities and Common Trends

In this section I examine the growing similarities in sentencing principles, laws, and practices in Western countries and some possible causes underlying this convergence. This discussion lays the foundation for an examination, in section II, of some of the most important differences that remain, particularly between the United States and other nations. In comparative research, similarities are just as important as differences; the many common features and trends in Western systems of sentencing suggest that nations have more and more to learn from each other's experience, in terms of both what to do and what not to do.

A. Broadly Similar Sentencing Purposes, Procedures, and Alternatives

Despite differences in language, laws, culture, and traditions, there is a substantial degree of similarity in the sentencing purposes, procedures, and alternatives currently employed in Western countries. Many Western countries have also experienced a similar evolution in penal theories since the late eighteenth century, beginning with the Classical School (emphasizing proportionality and deterrence), switching to a treatment-oriented "offender-instrumental" approach at the end of the nineteenth century, and recently returning to a mix of offense-based and risk-management approaches, with an ongoing struggle between prison-reductionists and prison-promoters (Davies 1996, pp. 156–69).

Principles of uniformity and retributive proportionality are now recognized to some extent in almost all systems, but sentences in these systems are also designed to prevent crime by means of deterrence, incapacitation, and rehabilitation. Reflecting these common purposes and principles, systems recognize very similar circumstances deemed to be "aggravating" and "mitigating" (see, e.g., chaps. 3 and 4, this volume). Some apparent differences in sentencing purposes are largely a matter of nomenclature: the Nordic and German concept of Indirect (or Positive) General Prevention (punishment as a means of strengthening social norms) (chaps. 3 and 5, this volume) is similar to what Anglo-American theorists call Denunciation or Norm-reinforcement (Greenawalt 1983, p. 1340; Davies 1996, pp. 192–93). Thus, the main differences between these systems involve questions of emphasis: in Finland, general prevention is strongly emphasized, and the more direct effects of punishment on crime (e.g., through general deterrence) are seen as very limited (chap. 3, this volume). In most other European countries, the goals of rehabilitation and reintegration of offenders seem to retain more importance than in the United States, at least to judge by sentencing literature and recent law reforms (although even in the United States, rehabilitation is alive and well).[5]

Sentencing procedures are also roughly similar, even in systems from different legal "families" (common law versus civil law), employing very different pretrial and trial criminal procedures. In most jurisdictions, prosecutors exercise substantial sentencing power by means of charging and diversion decisions (although this power is applied in very different ways and is sometimes exercised by the police).[6] In most jurisdictions, judges retain broad discretion in the sentencing of most cases, and parole or other administrative officials have substantial discretion to determine when and on what conditions prisoners will be released. This statement is true even for the United States, where "indeterminate" sentencing regimes are still much more common than binding sentencing guidelines, and "truth-in-sentencing" laws have only partially limited parole discretion (chap. 6, this volume).

Finally, the specific sentencing alternatives available at each "sentencing" stage are roughly similar in most jurisdictions. As illustrated by the chapters in this volume, such sentencing options include custody (which may be partly or entirely suspended); a fine (or day fine); probation supervision (in varying degrees of intensity, with or without treatment); and—in more and more systems—restitution, community service, various victim or community conferences, and home detention (with or without electronic monitoring) (see generally, chap. 8, this volume; Tonry and Hamilton 1995; Tonry and Hatlestad 1997).

In addition to (and perhaps partly because of) the broad similarities described above, there are a number common trends in contemporary sentencing policy and practice in Western countries. In the remainder of this section, I examine six of these trends—three of which have been identified by other authors, and three of which have not.

B. Populist Punitiveness (and the Decline
   of Nonpartisan Policy Elites)

In a 1995 essay, Anthony Bottoms identified a phenomenon he called "populist punitiveness"—politically driven penalty increases of the kind most evident in the "law-and-order" politics of the United States but which he also detected in some other countries (Bottoms 1995, p. 39; see also Morgan and Clarkson 1995, pp. 13, 15). In the past five years, it appears that this trend has continued, and become stronger; most of the countries of western Europe—even the formerly "mild" Netherlands—have experienced rising prison populations,[7] reflecting not just a harsher "societal climate" of increasing levels of violent crime (Council of Europe. 1995, pp. 182–87), but also a harsher "penal climate" (chap. 4, in this volume). Increasingly, sentencing severity has been championed by conservative politicians—or even moderate liberals, to avoid being labeled "soft on crime" (chap. 11, this volume; Kyvskaard 1998, p. 10).

One notable exception is Finland, which has been steadily scaling back its penalties to bring them in line with other Nordic countries (chap. 3, this volume, esp. table 3.3). Yet even in Finland, there are danger signs: increased competition in print and television markets has produced greater media attention to crime issues. If Finland has thus far resisted substantial politicization of crime issues, this may be because Finnish crime policy is still dominated by non-partisan policy elites (judges, academics, high-ranking civil servants, and other "experts") (chap. 3, this volume; Davies 1996, pp. 180–81). In other countries, increased media attention to crime has generated political pressures on legislators, executive officials, and judges to escalate penalties and has reduced the independence and influence of experts and professional elites (Junger-Tas 1998, p. 19). There is reason to believe this trend will continue in the future.

C. Bifurcation (Increasing Low-End Leniency
   and High-End Severity)

Closely related to Bottoms's theme of populist punitiveness is what he calls bifurcation, or the "twin-track" approach: governments simultaneously increase penalties in the most serious cases (especially for violent, sex, or drug crimes) and decrease penalties for the least serious offenders (Bottoms 1995, pp. 40–41). Bifurcation is one way to reconcile populist punitive pressures with budgetary and prison-capacity limitations—punitive pressures are greatest for the most serious crimes, both because the latter are of greater concern to the public and because the limited "visibility" of low-severity crimes and penalties allows leniency to escape sustained public and media attention. Thus, it is not too surprising to see recent evidence of bifurcation in many Western countries (Albrecht 1995, p. 307; Kensey and Tournier 1998, pp. 11–13; Kuhn 1999, pp. 12–15 [Switzerland, Greece, Portugal]; chaps. 1, 2, 4, and 5, this volume).

The one exception to this trend may be the United States; Anthony Bottoms felt that U.S. jurisdictions were willing to escalate severity across the board, "almost regardless of fiscal cost" (Bottoms 1995, p. 40); Kevin Reitz seems to agree, citing the recent increased enforcement of low-level, "quality-of-life" crimes ("zero-tolerance policing) as evidence of "the new intolerance" toward criminal deviance of all types (chap. 6, this volume). Yet despite the latter trend in the United States, there is still considerable evidence for increased low-end leniency, in the form of drug courts and other new and expanding diversion programs (Tonry 1999a). Also, several of the states that implemented sentencing guidelines have chosen to lower penalties for property offenders, in order to make room in prison for the increased penalties proposed to be given to violent offenders (Frase 1995a, p. 175).

The conflicting U.S. data point to an ambiguity in the "bifurcation" concept; in some countries, it may be that low-end offenders are being treated more "punitively" in the sense of facing increased risk of arrest and initial processing but that the resulting expansion of low-level "intake" generates even greater systemic pressures to dispose of these cases quickly and cheaply.

There seems to be little doubt, however, that many systems are increasing sentencing severity at the "high end," by imposing more and longer prison sentences (Kensey and Tournier 1998, pp. 11–13; chaps. 2, 4, and 5 this volume). In addition to issues of crime-control effectiveness and cost-benefit, there are important normative questions: does the growing gap between the most and the least severe penalties violate fundamental requirements of ordinal (i.e., relative) proportionality, for offenses of differing degrees of seriousness? (Cf. von Hirsch 1985, chap. 4; 1993, pp. 18–19) Or were the former penalty scales too compressed? Without more precise principles to guide these assessments (discussed in chap. 11, this volume), who can say?

Even if we were to conclude that "high-end" offenders are being treated unfairly, might such policies nevertheless be justifiable? Is it acceptable to sacrifice retributive justice in serious cases, to protect the "human rights" of crime victims, or simply to diffuse public pressure to escalate *all* penalties? At least one sentencing theorist has questioned whether we may "deal unjustly with a few so that we can persuade the legislature to deal more effectively and fairly with the many" (Morris 1974, p. 65). It is remarkable, but perhaps no coincidence, that jurisdictions that give the strongest overall emphasis to proportionality limits on sentencing severity (Australia, England, Finland, Germany, Minnesota, the Netherlands) have all recently wrestled with this moral dilemma and have chosen to permit the imposition of very long or indefinite incarceration, for certain highly dangerous offenders (Wasik 1995; Frase 1997b, pp. 408–9; see, generally, chaps. 1, 3–5, and 8, this volume).

D. Restorative Justice

A third theme noted by previous writers is the trend toward "justice in and for local communities and groups" (Albrecht 1995, p. 307; Bottoms 1995, pp. 34–38, 47–9; Tonry 1995b, p. 277). The tendency to give greater attention to the interests and input of crime victims, their families, and representatives of the community has recently grown much stronger in several countries (chaps. 1, 2, 5, and 8, this volume), and there is reason to believe that various forms of restorative justice will continue to thrive, at least in Western nations ("community" courts still have a bad reputation, in former communist countries; see chap. 8, this volume).

Victims' rights and remedies have great political appeal for the same reason that populist punitiveness does: more voters see themselves and their loved ones as actual or potential crime victims than as actual or potential criminal defendants.[8] Moreover, the factors in modern societies that are the source of the appeal of "community" justice seem likely to remain influential, or even grow stronger, in the years ahead. Such factors include the need for a sense of belonging, support, and identity, and the desire to return to a supposedly more peaceful, bygone era, when individuals trusted and were securely "embedded" in kinship and local community relations, religious cosmologies, and traditions (Bottoms 1995, pp. 46–47);

the practical or political need for the criminal process to reflect diverse views within a pluralistic society (Tonry 1995b, p. 277); and a preference for increased public participation, in lieu of lawyer- or official-dominated dispositions, and for negotiated settlements rather than winner-take-all decisions.

E. Substantial Growth in Drug Cases and Prisoners

Many Western nations have recently experienced substantial increases in drug-offense arrests, prosecutions, prison admissions, and prison durations, and these increases have been a major factor in the recent increases in prison populations observed in these countries (Larsson 1999, p. 11; chaps. 3 and 8, this volume). This pattern is true even in the Netherlands, which has long been known for its relatively tolerant, nonpunitive approach toward drug abuse (chap. 4, this volume).

Given the global consistency of this phenomenon, and its human and fiscal impact, there is clearly a compelling need for researchers and policymakers to achieve a better understanding of the causes of this trend, and the most effective ways to combat it. In particular, we need to know to what extent these changes reflect real increases in drug use and trafficking, and legitimate crime-control responses to these increases. In the United States, at least, it appears that the huge increase in drug cases and drug penalties reflected a politically motivated "war on drugs," rather than any increase in actual drug use or any reason to believe that increased punitiveness would have positive effects (Tonry 1995a, pp. 81–123). It also seems likely that, at least in some countries, much of the increase in sentencing severity was related to broader trends toward "populist punitiveness" and "bifurcation." Another specific cause of greater sentencing severity was the 1988 Vienna convention against drug trafficking, which adopted a strongly punitive (U.S. style) approach (chap. 8, this volume). Whatever the causes, the escalating penalties imposed on nonviolent drug offenders raise troubling issues of ordinal proportionality and highlight the importance of developing more precise standards and limitations on sentencing proportionality (see sections III. A and B, below).

F. Increased International "Borrowing" (Both Good and Bad)

While the U.S. continues to be skeptical of foreign ideas, other nations have a long tradition of studying and borrowing each other's laws.[9] Recent reports on sentencing reforms in Western countries suggest that the pace of borrowing may be accelerating. Day fines or their informal equivalent are now being used in most continental countries, and electronic monitoring has recently been widely adopted or proposed on the Continent (chap. 8, this volume).

Unfortunately, "bad" ideas have also spread across national boundaries — mandatory minimum penalties, three-strikes laws, and prison boot camps, although widely rejected by U.S. scholars and judges, have recently been adopted in England and Australia (chaps. 1 and 2, this volume). If borrowing, both good and bad, is indeed becoming more common, this probably reflects both the growing similarity of the world's sentencing systems, and the increasing accessibility of information about foreign practices.

G. Increasing Use of Noncriminal Laws and Procedures

Modern legal systems have several highly repressive measures that operate partially or entirely outside of the criminal and juvenile justice systems, and there is some evidence that the use of such "nonpenal" procedures may be increasing. The three most significant of these measures are procedures permitting seizure and forfeiture of alleged fruits and instrumentalities of crime (or, in some countries, seizure of *all* of an offender's property, whether crime-related or not) (chap. 8, this volume); "civil" commitment of sex offenders and dangerous mentally ill persons (Frase 1997b, p. 403; chaps. 1 and 3–5, this volume); and detention and deportation of noncitizens (Frase 1997a; chap. 4, this volume). The use of such measures is perhaps yet another aspect of the increasingly punitive "penal climate" in many nations, and the willingness to apply severe measures to certain offenders — particularly those with whom the average citizen feels little or no empathy. Since these measures are not officially intended to impose "punishment," they are generally not subject to criminal procedural safeguards; yet they pose substantial risks of government abuse and lack of uniformity and proportionality. Further research is needed on the extent to which these "civil" measures are being used to achieve sentencing purposes and the need for additional legal safeguards.

It should also be noted that many nations (but not all; see chap. 3, this volume) make broad use of "administrative penal laws," permitting the imposition of fines, loss of privileges, and other minor sanctions under very simplified, noncriminal procedures (Weigend 1988). This is yet another manifestation of the low-end "bifurcation" policy discussed above and raises similar issues of proportionality. It also underscores, again, the need to define "sentencing" broadly, to ensure that multi-jurisdictional studies are comparing "apples to apples" — the high volume of low-severity infractions can have a major statistical impact, depending on how many are included in the reported data.

H. Possible Causes of (and Cures for) These Trends

What explains the similarities and trends described above? We need to understand their causes in order more effectively to promote desirable trends and combat undesirable ones (or at least, prepare ourselves, if there is nothing we can do about them). A number of theories can be found in the recent international sentencing literature. In general, there are two basic reasons why similar practices might be found in different legal systems: they might have been transferred across national boundaries (i.e., imposed by, or borrowed from other countries); or they might have developed independently, reflecting a sort of "parallel evolution" in which similar problems faced by all modern societies produce similar solutions (chap. 8, this volume).

Some writers have suggested that parallel evolution is promoted by common aspects of modernity, politics, and sentencing theory in Western countries. Thus, an increased emphasis on equality and individual rights and responsibility results from a reduced sense of belonging to and trust in kinship and community ties, religious faith, and tradition (Bottoms 1995, p. 46); the decline in support for individualized, rehabilitation-centered sentencing results in reduced dominance by judges and other sentencing "experts" (Davies 1996, p. 189); increasing punitiveness results from the tendency of conservatives deliberately to exploit crime and sentencing for political gain (Tonry 1997b, p. 4). At the same time, conscious borrowing of foreign ideas has been greatly facilitated by increasingly widespread air travel and telecommunications, and the emergence of English as the dominant world language (Tonry 1997b, p. 10). Arie Freiberg combines several of the above theories and attributes the recent Australian adoption of several U.S. sentencing ideas to a mixture of parallel evolution, conscious borrowing, and overall U.S. hegemony (pervasive cultural, media, economic, and linguistic dominance) in the late twentieth century (chap. 1, this volume).

There are undoubtedly a great many causal factors at work, which interact in complex ways, and which are highly contingent on place and time. This is clearly a fertile field for future research in sentencing, law, and society. In addition to the factors listed above, research should consider the following additional common features of modern societies, which may contribute to parallel evolution (and especially, increased punitiveness, media attention to crime issues, and the decline of nonpartisan policy elites).

Crime and Arrest Rates

To the extent that there is more crime (and, especially, more violent and other very serious crime) in some jurisdictions, increasing rates of criminal prosecution and prison commitment are almost an inevitable consequence, and increased duration of prison terms is a natural (though not inevitable) social response. Although rates of reported crime (overall, and for most serious crimes other than drug offenses) declined in most European countries, in the mid-1990s (Ministère de l'Interieur 1998, pp. 36–40), most of these countries saw significant increases in violent crime rates between 1987 and 1993 (Council of Europe 1995, pp. 181–88). However, as discussed more fully in section III. D data on overall or violent crime rates do not allow us to make accurate comparisons of "sentencing severity" across jurisdictions (or over time, in a single jurisdiction); such comparisons require more precise and comparable data on the "seriousness" of cases eligible for pretrial or trial "sentencing" (e.g., the number of adults arrested or convicted, weighted by the seriousness of their offenses).

Public Perceptions

Even if crime rates are not rising, increased punitiveness can result from the perception that crime, or serious crime, is increasing, that criminals are being sentenced too leniently, or both. Studies in England, the United States, and other countries reveal that the average citizen generally overestimates the volume and seriousness of crime, almost always says that crime rates have been rising (whether or not they have), and generally underestimates the severity of sentences actually imposed (Roberts 1992, pp. 109–14; Hough and Roberts 1998). Recent studies also show that the public's attitudes and level of concern about crime are more likely to be based on the extent to which the media and politicians have recently chosen to emphasize crime issues, than on actual crime rates (Roberts 1992, pp. 116–17, 119–21; Beckett 1997). As a result of these factors, the public's concern about crime is subject to sudden, dramatic shifts, unrelated to any objective measure of crime. For example, the proportion of Gallup-poll respondents stating that crime or violence "is the most important problem facing this country today" varied between 1 and 6 percent from 1982 to 1992 and was 9 percent in 1993 but then jumped to 37 and 52 percent in January and August 1994 (Bureau of Justice Statistics 1998, table 2.1).

Improved System Efficiency

Information and other modern technologies also tend to cause prosecution and imprisonment rates to increase faster than crime rates, because such technologies make it easier for public authorities to identify suspects, find out if they are "wanted" or under supervision by other authorities, collect evidence against suspects and convicts (including evidence of drug use), and maintain (and share with other authorities) comprehensive records of a suspect's or defendant's prior convictions.

Public (Mis-)Information

The "information age" may affect sentencing severity in other ways. First, the more information the public has about how prosecutors, judges, and sentencing commissions make their decisions, the more pressure these actors will feel to make politically "safe" (more punitive) decisions (Zimring and Hawkins 1991, pp. 173–74). Second, the sheer mass of data available to the citizen—information overload—necessitates selectivity; this preference for *less* detail and analysis dovetails with the pervasive tendency of media newscasters, advertisers, and politicians to prefer "sound bites" and superficial descriptions of complex problems (Roberts 1992, pp. 117–19). The apparent increase in public awareness and "information" about public policy issues increases pressures toward direct democracy and weakens traditional representative democracy and deference to policy elites and experts; in some U.S. states, this process has led to increasingly severe criminal laws being adopted by citizen referendum (Tonry 1999b, p. 63).

The Need for New Dramas and Enemies

Increased U.S. public, media, and political attention to crime issues may also be, in part, a response to the end of the Cold War. The media are always in search of highly dramatic stories to tell, and studies in several countries have documented the strong media emphasis given to violent crimes in recent decades (Roberts 1992, p. 117). In the United States, there appears to have been a major further increase in media emphasis on crime issues (especially murder) since the early 1990s— except for 1996 (a presidential election year), crime stories were the most common television news topic in every year from 1993 to 1997 (Media Monitor 1994, 1998).

COMPARATIVE PERSPECTIVES 269

At about the same time, the public and politicians, especially in the United States, seem to have felt a need for new, internal enemies to replace the old, external ones. Perhaps humans have always defined themselves or their world in terms of some external enemy, or internal devils, personifying evil; increasingly, it seems, we demonize our criminals or declare war on them.[10]

Decreasing Social Solidarity

The tendency to demonize criminals is facilitated when criminals are seen as "different" from the political majority. When increasing numbers of offenders are noncitizens or are racial or ethnic minorities, whether due to increased immigration, poverty, racial bias, or racially selective policies such as America's Drug War (Tonry 1995a; Tonry 1997a), criminals are more likely to be viewed as "those people" and "their kids," not "us" and "our kids." A reduced sense of solidarity and empathy with criminal defendants makes it easier to impose harsh penalties on them, and even to imagine that some of them have "forfeited" their right to humane and fair treatment (chaps. 1 and 11, this volume).

Economic Restructuring

In some countries, increasingly punitive sentiments may also be promoted by the effects of global competition and domestic economic restructuring; stagnant wages, reduced job security and welfare benefits, and so on make citizens more angry and nervous and thus perhaps less tolerant of wrongdoing (Bottoms 1995, p. 47; Junger-Tas 1995, p. 298; Larsson 1999, p. 11). At the same time, major increases in incarceration rates may have been facilitated in some countries—notably, the United States—by rising overall societal affluence: with a booming economy and reduced military spending, it may have seemed that Americans could "afford" (at least, in a short-term view) to massively increase their incarceration rates.

Philosophical Trends

Worldwide trends in political and economic philosophy in the late twentieth century may also have contributed to more punitive attitudes. Increased belief in individual accountability (and reduced belief in social or governmental responsibility; Savelsberg 1994) may be linked to the seeming "triumph of capitalism" and calls for "less government," more "privatization," and free-market competition (Junger-Tas 1998, p. 19; chaps. 1, 3, and 8, this volume). Antigovernmental sentiments may also partially underlie support for restorative justice programs that give increased roles to victims, community groups, and nongovernmental organizations.

Competitive Severity

In some jurisdictions, increased punitiveness might also result from actual or perceived competition with neighboring jurisdictions, to avoid seeming to be the most lenient and therefore the most inviting place for criminals (Kelk, Koffman, and

Silvis 1993, p. 323; Kommer 1994, pp. 29–30). Such fears seem especially plausible with respect to drug dealers and other relatively rational, profit-maximizing, and readily mobile offenders. As with welfare policy, such sentencing "competition," in combination with increasing migration and more or less open borders, can cause a "race to the bottom" in terms of sound and humane public policy, and a leap-frog progression of penalty increases in adjoining jurisdictions.

I. Some Counterexamples, Opposing Factors, and Solutions

Lest the reader (and would-be researcher) conclude, from the sheer number of theories listed above, that increased punitiveness, severity-bifurcation, and the decline of expert policy elites are inevitable in modern societies, it is worth noting that a number of jurisdictions have maintained stable or even declining prison populations in the past fifteen years.[11] Prison populations were substantially reduced in Austria and Finland (chap. 3 and chap. 4, table 4.1, this volume); Denmark, France, Norway, and Japan have maintained fairly constant prison rates (or, at least, have avoided major permanent increases) (Kyvskaard 1998; Kensey and Tournier 1998; Larsson 1999; Hamai 1999); Germany substantially reduced its prison population in the 1970s (and later increases may have been largely the result of increased crime rates) (chap. 5, this volume); and throughout the 1980s, Minnesota maintained a constant level of custodial punishment relative both to felony caseloads and to adult arrest rates (Frase 1995a, pp. 193–95).

Whether these jurisdictions can maintain their moderate prison policies in the future remains to be seen, of course; but they (and other jurisdictions, hoping to emulate them) may be able to benefit from several countervailing factors and possible solutions to the problems previously identified.

Competitive Leniency

Regional "sentencing competition" can also produce a lowering of penalties, at least in some jurisdictions. For most types of crime, criminals do not cross borders or even know about the use of more lenient penalties elsewhere (or the penalties in their home jurisdiction). Moreover, increases in the frequency and quality of multi-jurisdictional comparisons may lead some countries to realize that they are wasting money on unnecessarily severe and expensive sanctions. Such comparisons — particularly with the three other Nordic countries — led Finland to substantially lower its imprisonment rate (which had been considered a national disgrace) (chap. 3, this volume); at the same time, careful comparative research has demonstrated that this major de-escalation of penalties caused little or no increase in Finnish crime rates.

Budget Limits and Processes

Eventually, budget limitations often force policymakers to slow or even reverse penalty increases (especially when the economic cycle turns down, or antitaxation sentiments rise). Although "bifurcation" can free up resources to permit increased high-end severity, there are limits to that strategy. This natural fiscal "brake" on punitive excess can be strongly encouraged by the simple expedient of creating public research and planning officials whose explicit duty is to provide precise estimates of future correctional costs — including the added costs of proposed penalty increases (and, if new funds are not available, the numbers of current prisoners who would have to be released, to make room for the inmates proposed to be held longer).[12] This "managerial" technique (Bottoms 1995, pp. 24–30) forces legislators and other politicians to accept financial responsibility for their punitive proposals, helps to avoid prison overcrowding, and allows policymakers to set priorities in the use of scarce and expensive prison resources. The technique has been used very successfully in Minnesota and a few other U.S. states with commission-based sentencing guidelines; indeed, this "resource management" goal is one of the main reasons why large numbers of states became interested in guidelines in the 1980s (Frase 1995a, pp. 175, 196–97).

It is important to stress that the management technique described above does not necessarily require the adoption of rigid sentencing guidelines — or, perhaps, any guidelines at all. As I have argued elsewhere (Frase 1997b), Minnesota's sentencing guidelines are very flexible (particularly since charging, plea bargaining, and probation conditions and revocations are almost completely unregulated); yet the prison-population projections prepared by the guidelines commission are quite accurate and are taken seriously by the legislature. As modeling and prediction technology improves, it may become possible to accurately forecast future inmate populations and correctional costs even in highly "indeterminate" sentencing regimes.

Human Rights Limitations

Domestic and international human rights principles will eventually be extended to protect defendants from substantive as well as procedural unfairness. The recent expansion in the procedural rights of criminal defendants, prompted by the European human rights convention, other international norms, and domestic constitutional laws suggests widespread support for the idea that governmental power must be strictly limited in criminal cases. As these procedural limitations become more and more widespread, it becomes increasingly absurd to suggest that legislatures and courts need not respect any limits whatsoever on the imposition and duration of custodial penalties.

Shifting Crime-Control Emphasis

There is reason to hope that improvements in police effectiveness may help take some of the political pressure off sentencing severity to achieve acceptable levels of crime prevention. Even very skeptical researchers now admit that new policing strategies in some U.S. cities might have contributed to the recent dramatic decreases in crime in those cities (chap. 6, in this volume). Some of these strategies, such as improved police-community relations, have relatively little impact on arrest and incarceration rates; other techniques (e.g., "zero-tolerance" policing) appear to have a substantial impact on low-end "punitiveness" (chap. 6, this volume). However, the latter change may have served only to reverse the low-end effects of previous "bifurcation" policies; nonetheless, moderately increased low-end severity may be preferable to (less unfair than) extreme high-end severity.

Restorative Justice

Victim-offender mediation, restitution, and community service programs and other forms of restorative justice can be successfully employed to counteract the recent tendency to demonize and dehumanize criminal defendants. Such programs tend to have a moderating effect on sentencing severity because they emphasize forward-looking, "healing" goals—reparation, forgiveness, victim-offender or community-offender reconciliation—and because the goal of maximizing the offender's ability to pay restitution or perform community service requires that the offender be released from custody. However, such sentence-moderating effects are not guaranteed. If restorative justice programs are captured by prosecutors, conservative politicians, or victims-rights groups emphasizing vindictive or "pay-back" sentiments, the result will probably be to maintain or even increase levels of sentencing severity.

II. *Vive la difference*: Modern Sentencing Systems Are (Still) Not All Alike

Despite all of the similarities and common trends discussed in the previous section, there are still several major differences in the sentencing systems of Western countries—and thus plenty of good ideas for them to borrow from one another, and bad ideas for them to avoid borrowing or independently developing.

A. Legal Limits on Sentencing Discretion

Although sentencing purposes are quite similar in all Western countries, and sentencing structures are broadly similar, there are several important differences. First, there are few legislatively imposed mandatory-minimum prison sentences outside the United States, and many of those that exist are either short (by U.S. standards) or not truly "mandatory" (chaps. 1, 2, and 5, this volume).[13] Second, all Western jurisdictions outside the United States retain parole-release discretion (although a few have partially adopted the U.S. concept of "truth-in-sentencing," by limiting or abolishing sentence-reductions for "good conduct" in prison [Tonry 1999b, pp. 59–61]).

Third, no jurisdiction outside the United States has adopted legally binding sentencing guidelines of the type found in U.S. federal and some state courts. Instead, other nations use more flexible means to limit sentencing disparities. In England, advisory, "guideline judgments" are issued by the Court of Appeal (which, since the end of 1999, has been assisted by the legislatively created Sentencing Advisory Panel (chap. 2, in this volume). Sentence appeals (by both the prosecution and the defense) are available in England, Australia, and most continental systems (Frase 1990, p. 682; chaps. 1 and 5, this volume). The Finnish and Swedish penal codes contain broad sentencing "principles." Dutch chief prosecutors have promulgated guidelines for their subordinates' sentencing recommendations—which are usually followed by courts (Tonry 1999b, p. 60; chap. 4, this volume). Dutch courts are required to state special reasons for imposing a prison sentence or for exceeding the prosecutor's sentence recommendation or for refusing a defendant's offer to perform community service (chap. 4, this volume). Finally, it seems likely that informal sentencing "guidelines" in the form of generally accepted norms or "tariffs" (Kelk, Koffman, and Silvis 1993, p. 327) exist in most systems, and that judges, with or without guidelines or tariffs, tend to base their sentencing decisions on a few salient, easily established facts (e.g., the nature and seriousness of the offense, and the defendant's prior record) (chap. 5, in this volume).

The scarcity of strict limits on sentencing discretion, outside of the United States, has sometimes been attributed to the more modest sentencing ranges and practices in these jurisdictions, or their less political, more official-dominated criminal justice systems (Tonry 1999b, p. 61). However, it may also be true that equality values are less strongly held in other countries, and that a certain amount of sentencing disparity (especially between a country's different regions) is tolerated (chap. 5, this volume). Such attitudes, combined with the retention of broad judicial and parole discretion, also help to explain why there appears to be little concern about possible abuses of prosecutorial discretion outside the United States—even in countries where, as in the United States, there are few formal limits on such discretion.

One further example of the broader sentencing discretion permitted outside the United States is the German treatment of young adults. Although offenders aged 18 to 20 are presumed to be fully responsible and are thus eligible for adult penalties, they may be (and very often are) prosecuted, adjudicated, and sentenced as if they were still juveniles. Indeed, 80 percent of young adults convicted or sex or property crimes, and almost all who are convicted of robbery or homicide, are sentenced this way (Albrecht 1995, p. 305). As for offenders less than 18 years old, discretion is both broader and narrower in Germany than in the United States: such offenders are handled only as juveniles and cannot be "waived" to adult court (which probably gives authorities more discretion to be selectively lenient, and less discretion to be punitive).

B. Legal Limits on the Severity of Sentences

Although judges and parole boards retain broad discretion in most Western sentencing systems (including the indeterminate sentencing regimes still found in most U.S. states), systems outside of the United States do place some significant limits on the severity of sentences. Capital punishment has been abolished, de jure or de facto, in all other Western nations and is strongly discouraged by an international human rights convention applicable throughout the world. In addition, European courts are beginning to recognize some limits on the use of sentences to life without parole (chap. 8, in this volume).

As for the length of prison sentences generally, some foreign jurisdictions apply important limitations rarely recognized in the United States. First, Australian courts impose strict limits on "real offense" sentence enhancement (chap. 1, this volume)—except for the immediate consequences of the charged act or omission, no enhancement or aggravation of sentence is permitted for more serious charges that were withdrawn or that ended in acquittal. Moreover, any aggravating circumstances that could have formed the basis for a more serious charge must be alleged and proven beyond a reasonable doubt; aggravating circumstances that could not have been separately charged must still be found by the sentencing judge to be proven beyond a reasonable doubt (failing which, they must be assumed not to exist).

These Australian rules go considerably beyond even the strictest U.S. limits on sentence enhancement. Under Minnesota's sentencing guidelines, for example, upward departure may not be based on aggravating facts that were chargeable as a separate offense, but sentences may be increased within the presumptive guidelines range without any requirement of reasoned findings, and departures above the presumptive range may be based on facts found only by a preponderance of the evidence (Frase 1993a, p. 288). The federal sentencing guidelines are even looser, since they not only authorize but require courts to increase the guidelines range based on certain uncharged facts (including acquitted-charge facts), which need only meet the preponderance-of-evidence standard (Frase 1993a, n. 29; United States v. Watts, 117 S. Ct. 633 (1997)). And of course, U.S. "indeterminate" sentencing systems (still the most common type) provide the broadest scope for permissive (but not required) enhancement—all the way up to the statutory maximum for the conviction offense, based only on a preponderance standard (McMillan v. Pennsylvania, 477 U.S. 79 (1986)), and including aggravating facts that could have been charged separately, or which were even dismissed or acquitted.

A second limitation on sentence enhancements, found in several systems outside the United States, relates to the use of consecutive sentences. Although some U.S. guidelines systems limit consecutive prison terms (Frase 1990, pp. 619–20), most U.S. states grant sentencing judges broad discretion to impose cumulative punishments for unrelated offenses (whether charged and convicted in a single trial or in separate trials)—up to the statutory maximum for each offense. But in Germany, consecutive sentences may not exceed a total of fifteen years and must also total less than the sum of the maximum terms allowed for each charge (Frase and Weigend 1995, p. 339). In the Netherlands, a defendant found guilty of multiple offenses can only receive an enhancement of up to one-third of the maximum allowed for the most serious offense (chap. 4, this volume); a similar rule also applies in Sweden (Jareborg 1995, p. 114). In France, no enhancement is allowed above the maximum authorized for the most serious offense, whether sentenced in a single trial or serially (Frase 1995b, p. 276).

Finally, some jurisdictions requires special justification to impose a custodial or other severe sentence. Dutch courts are required to state special reasons before imposing a prison sentence, exceeding the prosecutor's recommendation, or refusing a defendant's offer to perform community service (chapter 4, this volume).

C. Use of Non-Custodial Sentencing Alternatives

The chapters in this volume confirm the findings of previous studies, reporting widespread use of fines (especially day fines) and community service, even for relatively serious property crimes and mid-level assaults (Tonry and Hatlestad 1997; Tonry 1999b). In Germany, for example, fines are used for about a quarter of offenders sentenced for "aggravated theft" (including burglary), half of all drug offenders, and about 90 percent of offenders charged with simple theft, assault, and criminal damage (chap. 8, in this volume).

D. Frequency and Duration of Custodial Sanctions

Despite the recent increases in prison populations in a number of Western nations, there are still many countries that make extremely "parsimonious" use of custodial sanctions, while other nations go to the opposite extreme, producing very wide variations in incarceration rates. The member states of the Council of Europe have incarceration rates (per 100,000 population) ranging from a low of 16 (Cyprus) to a high of 694 (Russia) (chap. 10, this volume). Within the countries of Western Europe, the 1995 rates ranged from 55 (Norway) to 125 (Portugal) (chap. 4, this volume).

Perhaps even more surprising is the extent of variation in the use of custody among states within federal systems. As of December, 1998, U.S. states had incarceration rates (for inmates sentenced to more than one year) ranging from 117 (Minnesota) to 736 per 100,000 (Louisiana) (Bureau of Justice Statistics 1999b, table 2).[14] Australian states reported 1998 rates ranging from 49 (Capital Territory) to 335 (Northern Territory) (chap. 1, in this volume). In 1995, the provinces of Canada (which are subject to a single, nationwide penal code) had sentenced-prisoner rates ranging from 76 (Ontario) to 193 (Saskatchewan) (Sprott and Doob 1998, table 2).

The variations summarized above are also remarkably stable over time: out of thirteen European nations reporting, five of the six with the lowest incarceration rates in 1985 were still among the lowest six in 1995 (chap. 4, in this volume). The rank-order of all eight Australian states in 1998 was unchanged, or only one rank removed, from that state's position in 1987 (chap. 1, this volume). As for the United States, four of the five lowest-ranking states in 1980 (Maine, Minnesota, New Hampshire, and North Dakota) were still among the lowest five in 1998 (Bureau of Justice Statistics 1982, table 4; Bureau of Justice Statistics 1999b, table 2).[15]

Only some of these dramatic cross-jurisdictional variations are attributable to differences in the rates and seriousness of crime. As Michael Tonry points out in the introduction to this volume, recent international crime-victimization data suggest that high-custody nations like the United States do not have the highest crime rates across the board (although serious violent crime rates are higher). Moreover, studies comparing custody populations to criminal caseloads, or examining sentencing patterns by offense, have revealed substantial variations among Western nations in the use of custodial measures (Frase 1990, pp. 650–58; 1995b pp. 275–76; Young and Brown 1993, pp, 28–31; Kommer 1994, tables 3–5; Frase and Weigend 1995, pp. 347–48).

As discussed more fully in section III. D, further research is needed to specify the true extent of the variations in custodial sentencing for comparable cases. Such research should also examine in more detail the nature of noncustodial sanctions that are used in the more "parsimonious" systems, explore the ways in which these measures are viewed by citizens and officials, and assess the relationships over time between sentencing severity and crime rates. Such research will almost certainly reveal that nations have much to learn from one another's experiences with very different rates of incarceration: highly punitive nations will find (as Finland already has; chap. 3, this volume) that they could achieve acceptable crime-control results with much lower custody rates; "mild" and moderately punitive nations will gain further proof that the crime-control benefits of increased custody rates do not justify the greater costs and hardships they require.

E. Political and Media Influences on Sentencing

Although there are danger signs in several Western nations, it remains true that criminal justice issues in most European countries are still relatively nonpoliticized and unaffected by media-driven sensationalism: judges and prosecutors are largely career civil servants, not subject to short-term electoral pressures (Savelsberg 1994; Tonry 1999b),[16] and criminal justice policy is dominated by professional, academic, and bureaucratic elites. Future research should examine further the connections between politics, media attention, and sentencing severity and the ways in which nations can preserve democratic values and freedom of communication while containing pressures to escalate penalties above levels necessary for effective crime control (and above levels that the public really wants, or is willing to pay for). The clear lesson of research to date is that nations that still enjoy relatively nonpartisan and non-media-driven criminal justice systems should take steps to preserve these features.

As for other nations, the lessons of comparative research are more difficult to apply; it is easier to preserve traditions than to create or reestablish them, and it is especially difficult to change such fundamental institutions of government as elected judges and prosecutors. However, smaller changes are possible: merit assessment of judicial candidates; civil service protection and attractive salaries, for assistant prosecutors; and improved pre- and in-service training, for both judges and prosecutors (Frase 1990, pp. 559–67; Esterling 1999). There are also structural reforms that can help to maintain a balance between political accountability and parsimonious sentencing policy (and between short-term and long-term public interests). Several U.S. states have successfully employed legislatively created sentencing commissions, composed of public members and professionals, to design and implement punishment policy with some degree of insulation from direct electoral pressures (von Hirsch 1987, pp. 5–8; Frase 1993a, p. 282). As for the media and politicians, and their tendency to oversimplify or misuse information about crime and sentencing, the only solution is—more information: about the costs of proposed severity increases; their limited probable crime-control utility, and the availability of less costly alternatives. Again, this is an area where comparative research (both within and across national boundaries) can be critically important.

III. Where Do We Go From Here? Priorities for Future Comparative Research and Reform

A number of specific topics for future sentencing research and reform efforts have already been suggested. In this section, I identify several broader categories of comparative research and policy development that deserve particular priority. They address four critical challenges: the "sentencing theory gap;" the "international human rights gap," the "comparative law theory gap," and the "comparative data gap."

A. Developing an International Consensus on Sentencing Principles and Theory

Achieving some degree of consensus on basic punishment goals, limitations, and other normative issues is the first priority (chap. 11, this volume; Ashworth 1995, pp. 256–58). Without this, researchers, reformers, and sentencing policymakers cannot even agree on what is relevant and important (i.e., what to study and what to change) about different systems. The need to develop principles governing the maximum and minimum permissible sentencing severity would appear to be particularly great, in the light of the evidence of increasing populist punitiveness and sentencing bifurcation. Unfortunately, "the project of sentencing reform" (chap. 11, this volume) has failed, thus far, to produce a consensus view on principles and overall theory that can accommodate (as it must) all of the varied and conflicting sentencing goals and limitations that are recognized, to a greater or lesser extent, in almost all contemporary Western countries.

What are the prospects for developing such an international normative consensus? Recent comparative sentencing scholarship reveals not only general agreement on various crime-control purposes of punishment, and the most important aggravating and mitigating culpability and harm factors, but also broad acceptance of the overarching importance of the principles of proportionality and parsimony.[17] But how can all of these principles be reconciled so as to give appropriate consideration to both retributive and crime-control values, to offender- as well as offense-based criteria, and to the need for individualized justice as well as uniformity? How can Americans find their way out of the theoretical "void" (chap. 6, this volume) left by the collapse of the rehabilitative ideal? Finally, how should we go about defining global standards of ordinal and cardinal proportionality (the relative rank-ordering of crimes, and the absolute severity levels assigned to the most and least serious cases; see von Hirsch 1985, chap. 4), particularly in the light of the wide variations in sentencing severity found in different countries?

One approach to the problem of accommodating diverse sentencing aims is suggested by current practices in Germany, Sweden, Finland, and the Netherlands (Albrecht 1995, p. 306; Jareborg 1995, pp. 103–19; chaps. 3–5, this volume). In these systems, the overall severity ("penal value") of the punishment is based on the retributive value assigned to that particular crime (which courts may adjust, to take account of case-specific variations in culpability and harm). For each range of penal values, certain forms of punishment (e.g., custody, community service, or fines) are allowed. In choosing among these forms, courts may consider offender characteristics, crime-control goals, and other nonretributive factors, to arrive at the form or forms of punishment most appropriate for that case.[18] A somewhat similar two-step approach has also evolved under the Minnesota Sentencing Guidelines: prison-duration decisions are based only on presumptions (and, in departure cases, individual assessments) of harm and culpability (but also, as in Finland, Sweden, and the Netherlands, on the defendant's prior conviction record); prison "disposition" decisions (whether to stay or execute the prison term) are based primarily on presumptions (and, in departure cases, individual assessments) of the offender's "amenability to probation" or "unamenability to prison" (Frase 1997b, pp. 399–403).

As implemented in Sweden, Finland, Minnesota, and the Netherlands, the two-step approach places a high priority on avoiding disproportionately severe sentences, while granting courts greater flexibility in mitigating penalties and choosing among sanction types of roughly equal severity (Frase 1997b; Jareborg 1995, p. 108; chaps. 3 and 4, this volume).[19] The Australians, French, and Germans also appear to place much greater emphasis on avoiding sentences that are too severe than on avoiding sentences that are too lenient or on achieving a high degree of sentencing uniformity (Tomlinson 2000, pp. 8–14; chaps. 1 and 5, this volume). It thus appears that all of these jurisdictions subscribe more closely to a "limiting" retributive theory than to a more restrictive, "defining" retributivism (Morris 1974; Frase 1997b). The frequent use of suspended or conditional prison sentences in these countries (Frase 1995b, table 2; Kelk, Koffman, and Silvis 1993, pp. 329–30; chaps. 5 and 8, this volume) is also more consistent with a limiting retributive theory—the defendant is spared the full measure of his or her "deserved" but suspended prison sentence, provided that he or she complies with the court's conditions.

A flexible, limiting-retributive theory also appears to be more consistent with evolving world views on the priority of sentencing goals and values. Whereas disparity and just deserts were central issues in the comparative sentencing literature of the early 1990s (Kelk, Koffman and Silvis 1993; Morgan and Clarkson 1995; Tonry and Hatlestad 1997 [collecting articles published through 1995]), these considerations receive less emphasis in the chapters in this volume and in other recent scholarship. In most Western countries, there continues to be broad acceptance of official discretion and a willingness to trust judges and releasing authorities to make wise use of that discretion. Even in the United States, the values of uniformity and precise, just-deserts scaling seem to get less attention these days. In large part, I suspect, this is because such values were formerly promoted by politically liberal writers, who now realize that discretion (at all stages, and by all actors) more often mitigates than aggravates severity. Liberals may also feel that it is better to tolerate disparity for some offenders if the alternative, in the current political climate, would be a "leveling up" that imposes "uniform" severity for all (as happened recently in both Minnesota and Germany (Frase 1993a, p. 293, n. 51; chap. 5, this volume)).

The limiting retributive theory described above thus provides a basis for developing a consensus view of sentencing purposes and procedures that reflects current practices in many countries and strikes an appropriate balance between retributive values (especially maximum severity) and crime-control goals, while also promoting parsimony and efficiency and providing sufficient flexibility to incorporate victim and community participation, local values, and restorative remedies.

But what about proportionality itself? Can international standards and enforcement mechanisms be developed to limit across-the-board escalations in the penalty scale? If fifteen years in prison is usually the most severe penalty actually carried out in Germany, whereas the U.S. "top end" is likely to be death, life-without-parole, or at least thirty years in prison, what realistic prospects are there for global consensus on cardinal (absolute severity) proportionality principles? One approach to this problem would be to build on existing human rights principles, limiting the most severe physical punishments.

B. Expanding Constitutional and International
   Human Rights Protections

Domestic constitutional limitations and regional and international human rights conventions now grant substantial procedural protections to criminal defendants in most Western nations (Weissbrodt and Wolfrum 1997); they also place major limitations on corporal punishment and prison conditions, and (except in the United States) they forbid or strongly discourage capital punishment (chaps. 8–10, this volume). But these rapidly expanding, supra-legislative norms still fail seriously to address the problem of unnecessary or disproportionate custodial sentences. In the United States, which has the world's most extensive system of constitutional criminal procedure limitations, the federal constitution places almost no limits on very long prison terms (Harmelin v. Michigan, 501 U.S. 957 (1991)).[20] In Europe, expanding community law and the European human rights and torture conventions are beginning to have an effect on domestic criminal laws, sentences, and prison conditions, but progress has been slow (chaps. 9 and 10, this volume).

It is time for legal philosophers and reformers to plug this "human rights gap." Proportionality limitations on sentencing severity are closely related to human rights principles (Morris 1964; Bottoms 1995, p. 19).[21] Moreover, mere procedural guarantees are an inadequate safeguard against government oppression, at least in a system dominated by elected officials and mass media seemingly obsessed with issues of crime. Severe penalties not only directly result in loss of liberty and dignity, they also indirectly undermine procedural guarantees: defendants are pressured to waive their trial and other important procedural rights, to avoid the harshest penalties; at the same time, defense attorneys and sympathetic judges are tempted to distort or abuse procedural rules, in an attempt to indirectly attack excessive penalties.

Why don't constitutional and international norms regulate excessive prison sentences? The answer cannot simply be respect for national sovereignty, or a desire to leave legislatures free to tailor sentences to perceived crime-control needs; criminal procedural limitations also place major limits on state sovereignty and crime control efforts.

In particular, why is pretrial custody subject to so much stricter regulation? Is it simply because (some of) the unconvicted are "innocent" (or at least, legally presumed to be so) until proven guilty? Yet it would seem that guilty defendants should also be presumed eligible for the least onerous penalty, until the need for greater severity is proven, and that excessive punishment is just as unfair and oppressive as the imposition of liability on the innocent.[22] Moreover, excessive penalties violate widely held norms of ordinal and cardinal proportionality and threaten important crime-control goals that are closely related to ordinal proportionality—for example: denunciation (reinforcing individual and societal norms of relative crime seriousness) and marginal deterrence (giving offenders an incentive to "prefer" less harmful acts). Perhaps pretrial detention is more strongly discouraged because it jeopardizes the defendant's chances for an effective defense and a fair trial. Yet lengthy post-trial custody lasts far longer and often seriously damages or eliminates the defendant's chances of ever again leading a normal and productive life.

Thus, if constitutional and international human rights principles are to serve as an effective bulwark against government oppression, they must be extended beyond procedure and the more extreme, physical forms of sentence severity; such principles must be interpreted—or, if necessary, redrafted—so that they also place limits on the length of custodial terms. One way to do this would be to build on principles of proportionality and parsimony that are already recognized in a number of domestic sentencing systems (Frase 1997b), and on the principles of proportionality recognized in constitutional and human rights norms governing arrest and pretrial detention.[23] It will not be easy to define and implement precise limiting principles, given the different sentencing systems and traditions of nations around the world. But, of course, the same problem was faced, and overcome, in defining worldwide procedural norms. And, as noted, sentencing purposes and factors are not so different, in Western nations; indeed, there is probably more international agreement on sentencing principles than there was on procedural issues, when the drafters of international norms set out to develop standards that would apply in "adversary" as well as "inquisitorial" systems of criminal justice.

While the development of international sentencing norms of proportionality and parsimony will take time, a more immediate strategy to attack the excessive use of custody sentences is to strictly enforce international standards for prison conditions and programs (chap. 10, in this volume). Such enforcement not only improves the lives of prisoners and reduces the criminogenic consequences of incarceration but also raises the cost of incarceration (or, more precisely, forces governments to incur the true costs), thus discouraging unnecessary custody (Zimring and Hawkins 1991, p. 211).

Another way to improve sentencing decisions and indirectly discourage severe sentences (by raising their cost) would be to expand the notion—already applied in death-penalty proceedings and in pretrial and trial procedure (Frase 1997a, pp. 33–34)—that more severe potential consequences to the defendant's life, liberty, or reputation require more elaborate procedural safeguards. In particular, the minimal safeguards and one-size-fits-all-approach of U.S. sentencing law must change. The very low standards of sentencing due process required by the U.S. Supreme Court (Williams v. New York, 337 U.S. 241 (1949); McMillan v. Pennsylvania, 477 U.S. 79 (1986)) reflect outdated assumptions about the primacy of rehabilitation goals and the limited constraints of proportionality and uniformity.

C. Closing the Comparative Law Theory Gap

Comparative law scholars have thus far paid little attention to sentencing law and practice. Moreover, traditional comparative law theory (e.g., "adversarial" versus "inquisitorial" models) focuses mainly on procedural issues; such theory is of limited current utility even in that realm (Frase 1998) and may have even less value in explaining and predicting sentencing variations across state and national borders. Comparative and sentencing scholars need to start trying to understand why nations and states do or do not differ from one another, how sentencing practices change and migrate across national borders, and how foreign practices can be most successfully adopted (or avoided).

In particular, why are some countries (and some Australian, U.S., and Canadian states and provinces) so much more punitive than others, even when differences in crime rates are taken into account? Many scholars have pointed to differences in each system's "penal climate" or "culture" (Young and Brown 1993, pp. 40–44; Davies 1996, pp. 172–78). But what do these terms really mean? Where do such differences come from (especially within federal systems), and what explains major changes in punishment severity that occur, albeit infrequently, despite the pervasive and seemingly immutable constraints of national (or state) "culture"?

Documenting and explaining variations in sentencing practices in different jurisdictions and periods is clearly a rich subject for future research. The following is a very preliminary list of causal factors that should be investigated, particularly with respect to variations in sentencing severity:

1. *Traditional comparative law models and system types.* Are common law or "adversarial" systems generally more punitive than civil law or nonadversarial ("inquisitorial") systems? The chapters in this volume and other recent comparative sentencing literature suggest that this sort of distinction has fairly weak explanatory power by itself (although it may be correlated with stronger factors, such as the degree of politicization of criminal justice issues). For example, community service first began in the United States and England but then became much more

widely used in continental Europe (Tonry 1999b, pp. 56–57). Similarly, sentencing guidelines systems should have appeared in the supposedly more "hierarchical," rule-oriented, and less discretionary civil law systems (Frase 1998), which
have long given strong emphasis to proportionality values (Jescheck 1983, p. 484),
rather than in the United States.

2. *Geographic regions or nation "clusters."* Adjoining nations, and federal states, sharing strong historical and cultural ties, probably tend to adopt similar sentencing
   laws and practices (Zimring and Hawkins 1991, pp. 142–48, Tonry 1999b, p. 51).
   The Nordic countries provide one of the clearest examples of this phenomenon
   (Davies 1996, pp. 165–66; chap. 3, this volume). Nations and their former colonies are another example (chap. 1, this volume); so are states within a single
   federal system (although, as noted, there are still wide variations within such
   systems).

3. *Other political, economic, legal, historical, theoretical, and functional sentencing
   system "types."* There must be a large number of other factors underlying the wide
   variations in sentencing severity among and within Western nations.[24] In particular, what explains the extremes of mildness and punitiveness among Australian,
   Canadian, and U.S. states and provinces, and the substantial degree of stability
   in their rank-orderings, over time—despite the relatively similar "cultures" of these
   political subdivisions?

4. *Sentencing theory.* This does not seem like a strong factor. The primacy of rehabilitation goals was believed by some to have led to longer sentences, under the
   extremely indeterminate sentencing systems formerly used in some U.S. states
   (Morris 1974, p. 48). More recently, however, rehabilitation goals probably tend
   to mitigate severity (e.g., permitting downward departures from state and federal
   sentencing guidelines, for "amenable" offenders; Frase 1991). Similarly, retributive sentencing does not necessarily lead to either severe or mild sentencing. For
   example, both Minnesota and Kansas have "desert"-oriented guidelines, but Kansas has an incarceration rate almost three times as high (Bureau of Justice Statistics
   1999b, table 2).[25]

5. *Sentencing structures.* In the United States, jurisdictions with determinate and
   indeterminate sentencing systems display very wide and overlapping ranges in
   sentencing severity (chap. 6, this volume). Nevertheless, there is some evidence
   that sentencing guidelines can restrain the growth in prison populations, at least
   when their design and implementation are closely linked to available resources
   (Marvel 1995; Frase 1995a).

6. *Variations in actual or perceived crime levels and trends.* This factor seems likely
   to be related to variations in sentence severity (although the relationship is not
   nearly as strong as is often supposed; see the introduction to this volume).

7. *Degree of political or media (versus expert or elite) influence on crime policy.* This
   appears to be a very important factor.

8. *Degree of racial or ethnic diversity, or overall social "solidarity."* This is probably
   also an important factor.

9. *Nature and extent of social welfare programs.* Although this factor is likely to be
   closely associated with the "solidarity" factor mentioned above, social welfare programs can have several more direct effects on the nature and severity of sentences.[26] First, generous welfare benefits mean that most defendants have more
   disposable income with which to pay fines (Frase and Weigend 1995, p. 347). In
   contrast, most U.S. defendants have little to "give" but their labor and physical
   liberty. Second, meager training, educational, and welfare programs also cause

increased problems of "lesser eligibility"—moral or political objections to giving criminals social services that are not generally available to noncriminals (Morris and Tonry 1990, p. 122). Third, highly developed social welfare programs provide formal and informal social and community resources to control and support defendants who are allowed to remain at liberty. Fourth, inadequate social welfare programs are very likely correlated with, or a cause of, higher crime rates that, in turn, increase political pressures to maintain or further increase punitive sentencing. Finally, all of these processes reinforce one another, maintaining a vicious (or benign) circle of punitive (or mild) sentencing policy.

D. Closing the Comparative Data Gap

The projects suggested above will be difficult and time-consuming to implement. But there is much that can be done in the short run to lay the foundation for these projects. The most pressing need is to plug the "comparative data gap," by developing better and more comparable multi-jurisdictional statistics on sentencing and related aspects of criminal justice. Despite the substantial literature on sentencing in the United States and in many other Western countries, there are still some very elementary comparative questions that cannot be answered. A few examples follow.

Because of the absence of data on misdemeanor sentencing for the United States as a whole (or even for most states), it is not possible to estimate what proportion of U.S. offenders (or even what proportion of drunk drivers, thieves, or assaulters) receives a fine, community service, or an executed custody sentence.

The available data on U.S. felony sentencing (Bureau of Justice Statistics 1999a) are difficult to compare directly with foreign sentencing data, not only because of differences in offense definitions and grading (e.g., foreign offense categories such as larceny and assault include an unknown number of cases that would be classed as misdemeanors, in the United States), but also because of differences in typical offense behavior (e.g., proportion of robberies involving firearms) and offender characteristics (e.g., prior convictions). Differences in charging practices further complicate cross-jurisdictional comparisons (Frase 1990, pp. 653–54, 660). For instance, if one country has much higher rates of police or prosecutorial dismissal, diversion, or charge reduction for a particular offense such as rape or burglary, then convicted and sentenced "rape" or "burglary" cases in that country are likely to be more serious, and the average sentence will be more severe for that reason alone.

In the absence of comparable, offense-specific sentencing data, cross-jurisdictional comparisons of sentencing severity must be based on prisoner "stocks" (one-day counts; average daily populations) or "flow" data (e.g., annual admissions). Such data is fairly reliable, provided that it includes all inmates (in the United States: sentenced jail as well as state and federal prison populations), and provided further that steps are taken to control for variations in the extent to which sentences are "served" in pretrial detention.[27]

However, cross-jurisdictional comparison of prisoner stocks and flows is useless without some generally accepted "base" of comparison. The most frequently used base—the total population of each jurisdiction—controls for the size of countries but not for differences in the frequency or seriousness of crime. The best international crime data—victimization surveys—does not include some very important crimes (homicide, drug offenses), nor does it control for differences in the extent to which crimes are reported to the police and lead to the identification of a chargeable suspect. The latter problem (as well as the inability to separately measure crimes committed by adults) also limits the value of using crimes "known" to the police as an (adult-) imprisonment rate base.

The number of adult convictions in recent years, weighted by their seriousness, would seem to provide the best estimate of custody-sentence "eligibles" in any given jurisdiction. Again, however, there are no data on misdemeanor convictions for the United States as a whole (or even for many states); moreover, conviction data, even if broken down by offense categories, is subject to the problems of different offense definitions and charging practices, noted above.

Data on persons arrested or otherwise charged by the police are less subject to the latter problems and are reported widely, with detailed age and offense breakdowns. Thus, the best single rate base for multi-jurisdictional "imprisonment rate" comparisons appears to be the number of adults arrested in recent years, weighted by crime seriousness (Frase 1990, 1995a, 1995b; Frase and Weigend 1995). If this measure still seems unsatisfactory, then future researchers will have to agree upon some other standard method or methods for computing crime-adjusted measures of sentencing severity that are comparable across jurisdictions (and over time, in a single jurisdiction). Without such measures, it is not possible even to identify "lenient" and "severe" jurisdictions (and periods), which is the essential starting point for research into the causes of variation in sentencing severity.[28]

Given these problems, cross-jurisdictional sentencing comparisons cannot, for the foreseeable future, be based solely on sentencing or prisoner statistics but must also include interviews with judges and attorneys in each state or country—for example, posing a series of hypothetical cases of commonly occurring offenses with varying offense details, offender prior record, victim-offender relationship, evidentiary strength, and so on (Frase 1990, p. 660). So far, however, there are very few studies of this type.

For some, these concerns about data problems may seem unnecessary. It is tempting to think that we already "know" the answers to most of the comparative sentencing questions listed above. But until concrete, apples-with-apples data is available, skeptical U.S. citizens and their leaders will continue to ignore foreign comparisons, and observers both in and outside of the United States may misunderstand the true nature and extent of variations in sentencing between jurisdictions and over time within jurisdictions.

The quality of international victimization and police crime data has improved considerably, in recent years; comparable sentencing and other criminal justice data is also becoming available for the countries of Europe (chap. 8, this volume; Council of Europe 1995). The next step is to improve the comparability of sentencing data for other Western countries, while continuing to improve comparative crime data. The latter statistical need is critically important; without it, data showing greater leniency in a particular state or country might suggest that the lenient jurisdiction is "out of line," threatening public safety. Accurate and comparable crime data can show that it is the extremely punitive jurisdictions that are out of line, wasting scarce public resources. Chapter 3 in this volume provides an excellent example of analysis that combines comparative sentencing and crime data in this manner. On the other hand, if accurate crime and sentencing data suggest that a particular type of sentencing severity has substantial public safety benefits, the public and officials will be able to make more informed decisions about the costs and benefits of that sentencing strategy.

IV. Conclusion

Sentencing rules and practices vary considerably among Western countries (and even between states and provinces within some of them), yet there are major similarities as well. Moreover, the similarities seem to be growing, as information, travel, and language barriers diminish and modern societies increasingly confront very similar problems. The remaining differences suggest that modern jurisdictions have much to learn from one another's experiences — both what to do and what not to do. The increasing similarities suggest that comparative research and policy analysis are becoming more and more feasible; modern systems now appear to form a continuum of options on any given policy issue (e.g., severity, uniformity and proportionality, range of sanction alternatives employed), and systems at any point on the continuum can use the experiences of other places (and times) to help them decide whether to shift their policy in one direction or the other.

The diverse patterns of similarity and difference across jurisdictions provide rich veins of material for researchers to mine, and strong incentives for them to work toward the consensus on normative principles, and the improvements in data and methods, that such comparative research requires. Consensus on principles and better data and methods for cross-jurisdictional research will also facilitate more accurate comparison of sentencing practices in political subdivisions within countries, and in a single jurisdiction at different times; the normative, data, and methodological problems posed by such "domestic" and historical "comparative" research are not unlike those that arise in foreign comparative research. But domestic and historical comparisons have the advantage of confronting fewer actual (or perceived) barriers of "culture" — that vague seemingly immutable nemesis of foreign comparativism. Historical studies may also help to show that, in a broader temporal perspective, domestic and foreign systems are even more similar — if "America's today could be other countries' tomorrow" (Tonry 1997a, p. 3), then America's yesterday may be other countries' today. Like cross-jurisdictional comparisons, historical studies are a useful source of new ideas; such "old ideas" not only illustrate different approaches that could be (and once were) adopted in a given jurisdiction, they also have a way of coming back periodically, even when we do not recognize them as "reruns."

Of course, cultural differences between foreign and domestic jurisdictions remain important. Even with improved theory, data, and methods, there will still be major barriers to "importing" foreign concepts and practices — especially in the United States, which freely imports consumer goods but tends to view itself as primarily an exporter of ideas in the realms of government and public policy.

However, comparative research and policy analysis are also valuable in teaching countries about serious mistakes that have been made elsewhere, and it may be easier to prevent undesirable imports than it is to facilitate desirable ones. Sentencing is certainly one area in which the United States has a great deal to teach the rest of the world about *what not to do*; if foreign countries can avoid some of the mistakes we have made, then perhaps America's recent experiment with massive overincarceration will not have been entirely in vain.[29] Again, the growing similarity of the world's legal systems makes it increasingly likely that bad sentencing ideas in one country will eventually appear in others; at the same time, this similarity makes it possible for comparative scholars to identify the common trends in modern societies that have led to undesirable sentencing policies — and to address the early symptoms of these political maladies in their own country, before they attain their full virulence.

Jurisdictions outside the United States will undoubtedly also continue to learn positive lessons from one anothers' sentencing ideas and practices. These jurisdictions, especially in Europe, will also probably continue to develop supra-national norms applicable not only to criminal procedure but also to criminal penalties. As the recent experience in the United States (and in any number of dictatorships, throughout history) demonstrates, governments can oppress their citizens by means of harsh penalties as well as by unfair procedures; constitutional and human rights protections can and must be applied to control excessive custodial sentences.

Although the United States was once a world leader in defining and implementing higher standards of criminal due process, it has not kept pace with international developments in this area (Frase 1997a). But with more and better comparative sentencing data, and expanding international human rights standards, there is reason to hope that Americans will eventually heed foreign lessons — if not to avoid international criticism for our totalitarian sentencing systems, then at least out of a concern for budget limitations and financial waste.

NOTES

1. For an earlier historical account, see Mannheim 1958.

2. Normative issues are addressed at greater length in section III.A of this chapter and also in chapter 11, this volume. Some important methodological issues are further addressed in section III.D.

3. These views are developed in more detail in Morris 1974 and Frase 1997b.

4. In Australia, this broader definition is apparently already in use — pretrial diversion is deemed to be an "intermediate sanction" (chap. 1, this volume).

5. Almost half of respondents in national surveys cite rehabilitation as the most important goal of imprisonment, compared with 15 percent for "punishment," and 33 percent for "crime prevention/deterrence" (Bureau of Justice Statistics 1998, table 2.53). Even Minnesota, with its emphasis on "just deserts" principles, also gives strong emphasis to offender-characteristics such as "amenability to probation" (Frase 1997b).

6. In England, fifteen years after the creation of the Crown Prosecution Service, the police still control most pretrial diversion ("cautioning") decisions (chap. 2, this volume). In Germany, prosecutors impose fines by conditional dismissal or penal order, subject to

little or no court review (chap. 5, this volume). French prosecutors lack both the conditional dismissal and postfiling *nolle prosequi* powers and have less control over the content of penal orders but decline a high proportion of matters outright (Frase 1990, 1995b, 1999). U.S. prosecutors exercise most of their "sentencing" power by means of plea bargaining, whereas these practices are less important (but still present) in Germany (Frase and Weigend 1995) and in France (Frase 1990, 1995b, 1999).

7. See chapter 4, this volume, table 4.1 (nine out of thirteen European countries had rising population-based incarceration rates between 1990 and 1995; eight of twelve countries reporting data for 1985 had higher rates in 1995). Prison populations have also been rising in Australia (chap. 1, this volume) and Canada (Manson 1997) (and, of course, have risen most dramatically in the United States; chap. 6, this volume).

8. This is one of several results predicted by "public choice" theory—politicians respond most consistently to the expressed or assumed preferences of the people whom they believe are most likely to vote. See, generally, Dripps 1993.

9. For some historical examples of criminal law and sentencing reforms modeled after foreign practices, see chaps. 1 and 8, this volume; Jescheck 1983.

10. As the philosopher Friedrich Nietzsche (1966, p. 81) put it: "Under peaceful conditions, a warlike man sets upon himself." (I am indebted to my colleague Rob Weidner for bringing this quotation to my attention.)

11. For examples of major reductions in prison populations earlier in the twentieth century, see Mannheim 1958; Zimring and Hawkins 1991, pp. 8–9.

12. Of course, to the extent that proposed penalty increases will be largely or entirely paid for many years in the future, prison-need forecasts must be combined with normative arguments for "intergenerational equity"—each generation should pay for its own "desert" and public safety measures (and especially, its own political gimmicks).

13. Minnesota also has several such "non-mandatory mandatories" (Frase 1993a, p. 287); such penal "faux amis," like their linguistic counterparts, are one of the well-known hazards of comparative research.

14. When jail and other short-term prisoners are included, the U.S. rates are higher, and the variation among the states is even wider: in 1994, these total custody rates ranged from 127 (North Dakota) to 899 (Louisiana) (Kuhn 1996b, table 2).

15. See also Zimring and Hawkins 1991, pp. 144, 151 (reporting stable rank-ordering of U.S. states and regions in earlier—and even longer—periods). However, the seemingly stable rank-ordering of prison rates per population may mask important changes in some jurisdictions. For example, Minnesota's per-population rank changed only slightly between 1980 and 1990 (going from third lowest to second lowest), and both Minnesota and national inmate populations increased substantially. But a very different picture emerges when inmate populations are compared to crime rates (total prison and jail inmates per weighted adult arrest (violent index-crime arrests multiplied by ten). By this measure, Minnesota's custodial severity remained constant between 1980 and 1990, while the national rate increased by 80 percent (Frase 1995a, p. 194).

16. Even in Europe, however, some observers are concerned that prosecutors are subject to political pressures from high-level executive branch officials (Jung 1998, p. 214).

17. The principles of proportionality and parsimony seem to be given particularly great weight in Australia (chap. 1, this volume) and Minnesota (Frase 1997b).

18. For a description of a similar concept of interchangeability of sanction types, designed to match sentencing goals to the needs of individual cases, see Morris and Tonry 1990.

19. The sanction equivalencies used in some of these systems suggest very loose standards of "equality." For example, an hour of community service (CS) in Finland is deemed

equivalent to one day in custody, which is admittedly "more lenient than prima facie required" (by penal value assessments) (chap. 3, this volume). Similarly, in the Netherlands the maximum CS order is 240 hours, which, when compared with the maximum custody term of six months in CS-eligible cases, works out to an equivalency of 1.33 CS hours per day of custody (chap. 4, this volume). A very different conception of "equivalency" (and of the punitive "meaning" of different sanctions) is reflected in typical U.S. exchange rates, requiring one to three *days* of CS per day of custody (Tonry 1999b, p. 58).

20. A few lower courts have recognized proportionality limits under state constitutions, see, e.g., In re: Lynch, 8 Cal. 3d 410 (1972). See also State v. Bartlett, 830 P.2d 823 (Ariz. 1992) (distinguishing *Harmelin* and holding sentence of forty years without possibility of parole was so disproportionate as to violate the Eighth Amendment of the U.S. Constitution).

21. As noted in section I.E, however, international conventions are not invariably a source of greater parsimony and humanity; the 1988 Vienna convention against drug trafficking appears to have contributed to *greater* sentencing severity.

22. This argument finds support in Australian rules, requiring aggravating sentencing factors to be proven beyond a reasonable doubt (Section II. B, above).

23. See, e.g., U.S. Constitution, Amend. IV, VIII; International Covenant on Civil and Political Rights, Art. 9; [European] Convention for the Protection of Human Rights and Fundamental Freedoms, Art. 5; Frase 1990, pp. 605–6; Frase and Weigend 1995, pp. 326–29. A few U.S. Supreme Court cases have implied that the Fourth Amendment ban on "unreasonable" searches and seizures imposes a general requirement of proportionality between investigative measures and crime seriousness. See, e.g., Tennessee v. Garner, 471 U.S. 1 (1985) (use of deadly force to arrest an unarmed burglary suspect was an unreasonable seizure, even if the failure to shoot would allow the suspect to escape); Welsh v. Wisconsin, 466 U.S. 740 (1984) (warrantless home entry to arrest for first-offense drunk driving—a "civil," fine-only violation—constituted an unreasonable search, even if the need to test the suspect's alcohol level would have constituted "exigent circumstances," justifying the entry in a more serious case).

24. For a summary of research on the relationship between unemployment rates and prison rates, see Young and Brown 1993, pp. 35–38.

25. Kansas's crime rates are higher but not by enough to account for the three-fold difference in prison rates. In 1997, Kansas's violent index crime rate was 21 percent higher than Minnesota's, its property index crime rate was 2 percent higher, and its total index crime rate was 3 percent higher (Federal Bureau of Investigation 1998, table 5).

26. See also Young and Brown 1993, pp. 41–43, reporting on attempts to correlate income inequality and incarceration rates, across jurisdictions.

27. Because of the common practice of granting sentencing credit for time served in pretrial detention, many defendants serve some or even all of their custody sentence prior to being convicted and may thus spend little or no time as a "sentenced" prisoner. If this practice is more common in some jurisdictions than in others, it may seriously distort sentencing comparisons based on "sentenced" prisoner stocks (Frase 1990, pp. 652, 658). Another problem with comparisons based on inmate stocks is that some jurisdictions do not define an inmate as "sentenced" until the time for appeal has expired, whereas other jurisdictions use a broader definition (Young and Brown 1993, pp. 10–11). One way to eliminate both of these problems is to include all inmates, whether convicted or not—in effect, counting pretrial detention as a "sentence." Comparisons based on sentenced prisoner admissions ("flow") are somewhat less subject to the two problems described above. However, flow data measures only the frequency of custody sentences, whereas inmate-stock data takes account of both the frequency and average duration of custody terms. Flow

data is also subject to major cross-jurisdictional variations in counting rules (Young and Brown 1993, p. 14).

28. Some comparative sentencing scholars have wondered whether "punitiveness" measures should distinguish between custodial frequency (or "breadth") and duration (or "intensity")—in other words, is a society that imposes a small number of very long custody sentences more punitive than one that imposes a large number of short sentences (Young and Brown 1993, pp. 14–16)? I tend to agree with those who have argued that every day in prison is harmful (and costly), no matter how the days are distributed; thus, prison "stock" data (which reflects both frequency and duration of custodial terms) is the best single measure of relative punitiveness (Kuhn 1996a, p. 4). If jurisdictions A and B have the same prison stock, but A has a higher frequency of custodial sentences and B has a higher average duration, then the two jurisdictions are equally "punitive." If jurisdictions A and B impose the same average duration, but A's frequency is higher, then A is "more punitive." And if A and B have same custodial frequency, but A's average duration is higher; then again, A is "more punitive." Of course, the distribution of custodial sanctions may raise other problems, not only of racial and other forms of discrimination, but also of proportionality. A jurisdiction with high custodial frequency but low average duration is likely to have a fairly "compressed" range of custody terms, which may fail to achieve desired retributive, denunciatory, and deterrent "spacing" of sanctions. A jurisdiction with low custodial frequency but very high average duration risks the opposite problem—too great a range between the most and least severe sanctions.

29. Cf. von Hirsch et al. 1999, for an example of research drawing skeptical conclusions from America's recent experience with greatly increased imprisonment rates.

REFERENCES

Albrecht, Hans-Jörg. 1995. "Sentencing in the Federal Republic of Germany." *Federal Sentencing Reporter* 7:305–7.

Ashworth, Andrew J. 1995. "Reflections on the Role of the Sentencing Scholar." In *The Politics of Sentencing Reform*, edited by and C. M. V. Clarkson and Rod Morgan. Oxford: Clarendon Press.

Beckett, Katherine. 1997. "Political Preoccupation with Crime Leads, Not Follows, Public Opinion." *Overcrowded Times* 8(5):1, 8–11.

Bottoms, Anthony. 1995. "The Philosophy and Politics of Punishment and Sentencing."

In *The Politics of Sentencing Reform*, edited by and Rod Morgan C. M. V. Clarkson. Oxford: Clarendon Press.

Bureau of Justice Statistics. 1982. *Prisoners in State and Federal Institutions on December 31, 1980.* Washington, D.C.: U.S. Government Printing Office.

———. 1998. *Sourcebook of Criminal Justice Statistics, 1997.* Washington, D.C: U.S. Government Printing Office.

———. 1999a. *Felony Sentences in State Courts, 1996.* Washington, D.C.: U.S. Government Printing Office.

———. 1999b. *Prisoners in 1998.* Washington: U.S. Government Printing Office.

Council of Europe. 1995. *European Sourcebook of Crime and Criminal Justice Statistics, Draft Model.* Strasbourg: Council of Europe.

Davies, Malcolm. 1996. "Penological Esperanto and Sentencing Parochialism: Convergence and Divergence in Sentencing Policy." In *Penological Esperanto and Sentencing Parochialism: A Comparative Study of the Search for Non-Prison Punishments*, edited by Malcolm Davies, Jukka-Pekka Takala, and Jane Tyre." Aldershot: Dartmouth.

Dripps, Donald A. 1993. "Criminal Procedure, Footnote Four, and the Theory of Public Choice; or, Why Don't Legislatures Give a Damn about the Rights of the Accused?" *Syracuse Law Review* 44:1079–1101.

Esterling, Kevin. 1999. "Judicial Accountability the Right Way: Official Performance Evaluations Help the Electorate as well as the Bench." *Judicature* 82:206–15.

Federal Bureau of Investigation. 1998. *Crime in the United States: Uniform Crime Reports 1997*. Washington, D.C.: U.S. Government Printing Office.

Frase, Richard S. 1990. "Comparative Criminal Justice as a Guide to American Law Reform: How Do the French Do It, How Can We Find Out, and Why Should We Care?" *California Law Review* 78:539–683.

———. 1991. "Defendant Amenability to Treatment or Probation as a Basis for Departure under the Minnesota and Federal Sentencing Guidelines." *Federal Sentencing Reporter* 3:328–33.

———. 1993a. "Implementing Commission-Based Sentencing Guidelines: The Lessons of the First Ten Years in Minnesota." *Cornell Journal of Law and Public Policy* 2:279–337.

———. 1993b. "Sentencing Guidelines in the States: Lessons for State and Federal Reformers." *Federal Sentencing Reporter* 6:123–28.

———. 1995a. "Sentencing Guidelines in Minnesota and Other American States: A Progress Report." In *The Politics of Sentencing Reform*, edited by C. M. V. Clarkson and Rod Morgan. Oxford: Clarendon Press.

———. 1995b. "Sentencing Laws and Practices in France." *Federal Sentencing Reporter* 7:275–80.

———. 1997a. "Fair Trial Standards in the United States of America." In *The Right to a Fair Trial*, edited by David Weissbrodt and Rüdiger Wolfrum New York: Springer.

———. 1997b. "Sentencing Principles in Theory and Practice." In *Crime and Justice: A Review of Research*, vol. 22, edited by Michael Tonry. Chicago: University of Chicago Press.

———. 1998. "Comparative Criminal Justice Policy, in Theory and in Practice." In *Comparative Criminal Justice Systems: From Diversity to Rapprochement. Vol. 17 in Nouvelles Etudes Pénales*, pp. 109–21. Toulouse, France: Eres.

———. 1999. "France." In *Criminal Procedure: A Worldwide Study*, edited by Craig Bradley. Durham, N.C.: Carolina Academic Press.

Frase, Richard S., and Thomas Weigend. 1995. "German Criminal Justice As a Guide to American Law Reform: Similar Problems, Better Solutions?" *Boston College International and Comparative Law Review* 18:317–60.

Greenawalt, Kent. 1983. "Punishment." In *Encyclopedia of Crime and Justice*, pp. 336–46. New York: Macmillan.

Hamai, Koichi. 1999. "Prison Population in Japan Stable for Thirty Years." *Overcrowded Times* 10(1):1, 14–19.

Hough, Michael, and Julian Roberts. 1998. "English Believe Sentences Soft and Crime Rising." *Overcrowded Times* 9(1):1, 12–15.

Jareborg, Nils. 1995. "The Swedish Sentencing Reform." In *The Politics of Sentencing Reform*, edited by C. M. V. Clarkson and Rod Morgan. Oxford: Clarendon Press.

Jescheck, Hans-Heinrich. 1983. "Criminal Law Reform: Continental Europe." In *Encyclopedia of Crime and Justice*, pp. 484–90. New York: Macmillan.

Jung, Heike. 1998. " 'L'état et moi': Some Reflections on the Relationship between the Criminal Law and the State." *European Journal of Crime, Criminal Law, and Criminal Justice* 6:208–15.

Junger-Tas, Josine. 1995. "Sentencing in the Netherlands: Context and Policy." *Federal Sentencing Reporter* 7(6):293–99.

———. 1998. "Dutch Penal Policies Changing Direction." *Overcrowded Times* 9(5):1, 14–20.

Kelk, Constantijn, Lawrence Koffman, and Jos Silvis. 1993. "Sentencing Practice, Policy, and Discretion." In *Criminal Justice in Europe: A Comparative Study*, edited by Phil Fennel, Christopher Harding, Nico Jörg, and Bert Swart. Oxford: Clarendon Press.

Kensey, Annie, and Pierre Tournier. 1998. "French Prison Numbers Stable since 1988, but Populations Changing." *Overcrowded Times* 9(4):1, 10–16.

Kommer, Max. 1994. "Punitiveness in Europe: A Comparison." *European Journal on Criminal Policy and Research* 2:29–43.

Kuhn, André. 1996a. "Imprisonment Trends in Western Europe." *Overcrowded Times* 7(1): 1, 4–9.

———. 1996b. "Incarceration Rates: Europe versus USA." *European Journal on Criminal Policy and Research* 4(3):46–73.

———. 1999. "Incarveration Rates across the World." *Overcrowded Times* 10(2):1, 12–20.

Kyvsgaard, Britta. 1998. "Penal Sanctions and the Use of Imprisonment in Denmark." *Overcrowded Times* 9(6): 1, 9–10.

Larsson, Paul. 1999. "Norway Prison Use Up Slightly, Community Penalties Lots." *Overcrowded Times* 10(1): 1, 11–13.

Mannheim, Hermann. 1958. "Comparative Sentencing Practice." *Law and Contemporary Problems* 23: 557–82.

Manson, Alan. 1997. "The Structure of the Canadian Sentencing System." *Federal Sentencing Reporter* 9: 235–38.

Marvel, Thomas B. 1995. "Sentencing Guidelines and Prison Population Growth." *Journal of Criminal Law and Criminology* 85: 696–707.

Media Monitor. 1994. "Crime Down, Media Crime Coverage Up." *Overcrowded Times* 6(2): 7.

———. 1998. "Crime Regains Top Spot in Television News Coverage in 1997." *Overcrowded Times* 9(2): 4.

Ministère de l'Interieur. 1998. *Aspects de la criminalité et de la délinquance constatées en France en 1997*. Paris: La Documentation Française.

Morgan, Rod, and Chris Clarkson. 1995. "The Politics of Sentencing Reform." In *The Politics of Sentencing Reform*, edited by C. M. V. Clarkson and Rod Morgan. Oxford: Clarendon Press.

Morris, Norval. 1964. "Penal Sanctions and Human Rights." In *Studies in Criminal Law*, edited by Norval Morris and Colin Howard. Oxford: Clarendon Press.

———. 1974. *The Future of Imprisonment*. Chicago: University of Chicago Press.

Morris, Norval, and Michael Tonry. 1990. *Between Prison and Probation: Intermediate Punishments in a Rational Sentencing System*. New York: Oxford University Press.

Nietzsche, Friedrich. 1966. *Beyond Good and Evil*. New York: Vintage Books.

Roberts, Julian. 1992. "Public Opinion, Crime, and Criminal Justice." *Crime and Justice: A Review of Research*, vol. 16, edited by Michael Tonry. Chicago: University of Chicago Press.

Savelsberg, Joachim. 1994. "Knowledge, Domination, and Punishment." *American Journal of Sociology* 99:911–43.

Sprott, Jane B. and Anthony N. Doob. 1998. "Imprisonment Rates in Canada: One Law, Ten Outcomes." *Overcrowded Times* 9(4): 1, 6–9.

Tomlinson, Edward A. 2000. "Translator's Preface." In *The French Penal Code of 1994*. Littleton, Color. : Rothman.

Tonry, Michael. 1995a. *Malign Neglect: Race, Crime, and Punishment in America*. New York: Oxford University Press.

———. 1995b. "Sentencing Reform across National Boundaries." In *The Politics of Sentencing Reform*, edited by C. M. V. Clarkson and Rod Morgan. Oxford: Clarendon Press

———. 1997a. "Ethnicity, Crime, and Immigration." In *Ethnicity, Crime, and Immigration: Comparative and Cross-National Perspectives*, edited by Michael Tonry. Chicago: University of Chicago Press.

———. 1997b. "Sentencing Reform." In *Sentencing Reform in Overcrowded Times*, edited by Michael Tonry and Kathleen Hatlestad. New York: Oxford University Press.

———. 1999a. "Fragmentation in American Sentencing and Corrections Policies." Washington, D.C.: National Institute of Justice, U.S. Department of Justice.

———. 1999b. "Parochialism in U.S. Sentencing Policy." *Crime and Delinquency* 45: 48–65.

Tonry, Michael, and Kate Hamilton, eds. 1995. *Intermediate Sanctions in Overcrowded Times*. Boston: Northeastern University Press.

Tonry, Michael, and Kathleen Hatlestad. 1997. *Sentencing Reform in Overcrowded Times: A Comparative Perspective*. New York: Oxford University Press.

von Hirsch, Andrew. 1985. *Past or Future Crimes: Deservedness and Dangerousness in the Sentencing of Criminals*. New Brunswick, N.J.: Rutgers University Press.

———. 1987. "The Sentencing Commission's Functions." In *The Sentencing Commission and Its Guidelines*, edited by Andrew von Hirsch, Kay Knapp, and Michael Tonry. Boston: Northeastern University Press.

———. 1993. *Censure and Sanctions*. Oxford: Clarendon Press.

von Hirsch, Andrew, Anthony E. Bottoms, Elizabeth Burney, and P.-O. Wikström. 1999. *Criminal Deterrence and Sentence Severity: An Analysis of Recent Research*. Oxford: Hart Publishing.

Wasik, Martin. 1995. "England's Longer-Than-Normal Sentences for Violent and Sexual Offenders." *Federal Sentencing Reporter* 7: 284–87.

Weigend, Thomas. 1988. "The Legal and Practical Problems Posed by the Difference between Criminal Law and Administrative Penal Law." *Revue Internationale de Droit Pénal*. 59: 67–93.

Weissbrodt, David, and Rüdiger Wolfrum, eds. 1997. *The Right to a Fair Trial*. New York: Springer.

Young, Warren, and Mark Brown. 1993. "Cross-National Comparisons of Imprisonment." In *Crime and Justice: A Review of Research*, vol. 17, edited by Michael Tonry. Chicago: University of Chicago Press.

Zimring, Franklin E., and Gordon Hawkins. 1991. *The Scale of Imprisonment*. Chicago: University of Chicago Press.

Post-Adjudication Dispositions in Comparative Perspective

Post-adjudication dispositions include sentencing, enforcement of sanctions, and corrections. A cross-sectional look at post-adjudication dispositions may promote understanding of trends in sanctions systems, how and why certain types of penalties spread, what forces operate when new sanctions are adopted, and how criminal sanctions are implemented and to what end. The last of these deserves particular attention because sanctions such as imprisonment, fines, and community service may operate differently in relation to links between policymaking and implementation.

It is common to hear that broad international trends can be observed in the reform systems of criminal sanctions. However, it is less likely that there are common trends in sanctions practice than in discussions of sentencing, sanctions, and corrections. A 1997 collection of essays dealing with trends in criminal law, for example, assumes a broad common trend in criminal sanctions (Tiedemann 1997). This trend is seen in the abolition and marginalization of short prison terms and in the introduction of substitutes such as community service, weekend imprisonment, and fines. Note is taken of the abolition of traditional shaming penalties and of new concerns to interdict professional activities or the revocation of professional licenses in cases of serious economic crimes. Finally, new conceptions of corporate liability and corporate penalties are identified as common elements in changing systems of criminal sanctions.

However, the changes are more apparent than real. Certainly, use of short-term imprisonment has been sharply reduced in Germany and Austria. But, in the rest of Europe, short-term imprisonment is used as often today as before. Even in Austria and Germany, many more offenders are sentenced to imprisonment (conditional and unconditional) of less than six months than to one year or more. Day fines have succeeded in replacing imprisonment in various western European countries, but that trend came to a stop some ten years ago. Community service has been introduced in various European countries, as have weekend imprisonment, electronic monitoring, and restitution. However, the backbones of sanction systems in Europe remain the fine, suspended sentences and probation, and imprisonment. Outside Europe and some other regions, the death penalty and corporal punishment remain widely available and accepted.

What can be observed is an emphasis on particular countries and information. One recent claim that the United States is the "world model for penal policy" was based on two insignificant events: a statement made by a British Home Secretary (calling for the introduction of curfews, which — in his view — had been applied successfully in Missouri) and calls for tougher sentencing laws in Queensland and New South Wales (Snider 1998). Garland (1996) describes "strategies of crime control in contemporary Britain and elsewhere," plainly treating "elsewhere" as consisting of Australia and the United States; after conceding that the British trends he describes most probably operate also in Australia and in North America, he adds another, "and elsewhere, too." The "model-monger" hypothesis suggested by Braithwaite (1994) is another example that receives its strength solely from looking at Australia, Canada, and the United States and forgetting about the "elsewhere."

There may be ways to observe or characterize changing systems of sanctions. There may be transfers of sentencing and punishment policies across national boundaries, from one system or jurisdiction to another one or from a group of countries to another. There may be also processes that drive different countries in similar social, economic, or political circumstances toward the same solutions. Such processes may include active selection of problems. Pressure and incentives may, moreover, play a role in joining particular types of punishment policies.

Certainly, there are also limits to transfers of criminal sanctions and methods of corrections, that can be explained by reference to history, culture, or inertia. Criminal sanctions are not merely factual consequences of norm violation but themselves represent norms and are therefore not easily transplanted into another social system. This normative core of criminal sanctions is where processes of legitimation are located and explains why many systems continue jointly to adduce rehabilitation, deterrence, proportionality, and justice as sentencing goals. Other variables that might explain why systems differ in their receptivity to innovations concern the role of professionalism in criminal justice personnel and relationships between crime policies and general politics.

I. Criminal Sanctions and Social Change

This chapter draws on information from ongoing research on developments in the criminal law in Europe (e.g., Eser and Huber 1985, 1988, 1990, 1994, 1997). It crudely summarizes statutory changes and reform processes in various European countries and attempts to portray what has been and is going on in relation to criminal sanctions. Several conclusions can be drawn. First, at least in Europe, change seems to be slow and unpredictable. Second, in some instances, new penalties have been introduced where for years before there were firm commitments not to introduce those very penalties. Third, changes in Europe are not very dramatic. As has been stated recently with respect to the new Swedish sentencing law: it is revolutionary and leaves everything as it was (Arnholm 1997).

The dramatic changes are better seen when looking not at short periods or the past decade but at centuries. This is where we see socioeconomic and political changes affecting sanction systems and their implementation. These include transition from ubiquitous use of corporal punishment and the death penalty to the modern prison, the transition from prison as the regular standard punishment to alternatives such as the fine, probation, suspended sentences, and other intermediate penalties and, most recently, attempts to shift the focus from punishment to mediation and reparation. These shifts demonstrate enormous changes in sanction systems and underlying philosophies and point toward the potential for further change. Associated with these trends are changes in explanations of crime and deviance and of the sanctions themselves. Theoretical work has gone beyond mere description and has attempted to explain basic changes, making use of concepts of social, economic, cultural, and political change. Civilization theory, as developed by Elias (1976) and adapted to criminological theories and penal law doctrine, points toward shifts from external controls on human behavior to internal controls and thus to the increasing potential to reduce sanction severity. Rusche and Kirchheimer (1973) emphasize the relationship between labor markets and changes in labor markets and the use of imprisonment. Foucault (1977) stresses the roles of prisons and other carceral institutions in socializing individuals into conformity with the needs of the modern state.

A. Theories of Changes in Sanction Systems

Criminal justice systems must deal with new kinds of offenses and offenders. Sanctioning systems must therefore adapt to contemporary needs. Long-term trends, displaying steadily declining levels of severity, have been explained by a growing awareness for humanity.[1] There is still ample evidence from debates about criminal law reforms that "making criminal sanctions more humane" can be a powerful argument in the political arena. But, such an approach does no more than suggest changes in the motives for punishment that themselves have to be explained. The stability of punishment hypothesis, for example, assumes that the level of punishment meted out in any society in the long run is due to an essentially stable societal demand for punishment.[2] Stability of punishment may be explained on the basis of normative theory and theories of prevention, as elaborated by the German sociologist Popitz in a study (1968) of the links between the preventive potential of criminal sanctions and deficits in public knowledge about the actual levels of punishment. This theory assumes that an ideal amount of punishment exists that contributes efficiently to social integration and is subject to a self-regulating process that corrects deviations. However, as Zimring and Hawkins (1994) point out, current developments in the United States do not support the hypothesis of punishment as a homeostatic process (though it may be unsound to suggest an "open-ended potential for prison population increase"). For Europe, though, the theory might still be valid.

Changes in sanctioning have also been explained as a mere function of the number of offenders detected, convicted, and hence punished. Changes in punishment levels then would amount to linear correlates to changes in crime. However, most studies on sentences, imprisonment, and sentencing in Europe and North America point to two findings. First, sentencing of drug offenders has been a primary cause for the increases in the use of imprisonment (and in particular long-term imprisonment) since the 1970s (Pavarini 1994; Zimring and Hawkins 1994). Second, the penal climate in general may change in relation to perceptions of what kinds of offenses do and do not deserve tough responses.

B. Pessimistic and Optimistic Explanations

Levels of punishment severity have changed significantly over the centuries and are still changing (Grebring 1978; Heinz 1981). To explain these trends, two theoretical options are available, one basically optimistic, the other pessimistic (Popper 1984). The pessimistic interpretation has been elaborated by the abolitionist approach (van Dijk 1989). Here, the trends are not interpreted as displaying a gradual and even linear decrease in sanction severity. Instead, the shifts from corporal punishment to imprisonment, and from imprisonment to community penalties, are seen as intensifications of social control and more efficient forms of exerting power (Foucault 1977; Bianchi and van Swaaningen 1986). Changes in systems and in use of sanctions therefore reflect processes of creation and stabilization of power.

Elias's theory of civilization (1976) opposes the pessimistic theories. Elias proposes that social and cultural developments in European societies are linked to a process of replacement of external types of behavioral control in favor of internal controls. The course of these changes correlates with a steady long-term decrease in violence in society. The emergence of internal controls and the decrease in human violence are due to a process of differentiation and intensification of human interactions that in turn produce increasing levels of dependence and interdependence experienced by individuals. With these changes, individual violence increasingly becomes counterproductive and irrational. Similarly, there is a steadily decreasing need for resort to methods of forced compliance with basic social norms (van Dijk 1989).

On the basis of this theory, conditions can be observed that account for developments in criminal sanctions to date and can serve as guidelines for future directions. First, modern societies have achieved considerable changes in conditions of social integration, characterized by dramatic increases in the dependence of individuals on various social institutions and administrative agencies, with the welfare state pointing to a particular European standard (that still exists) (Krüger 1994). Second, there has been a dramatic increase in the efficiency of formal social control systems. Major parts of the male population in modern societies are processed at least once through the criminal justice system. It is estimated that between 30 and 40 percent of young male adults will be punished at least once before reaching age 24 (Keske 1979; Kaiser 1988; Villmow and Stephan 1983). Cohort research indicates that 7 percent of cohort members have contact with the police by age 14 because of criminal offenses (Karger and Sutterer 1988). The reach of penal systems becomes even clearer when taking into account administrative fines and other noncriminal punishments.

These conditions have to be considered when deciding how severe criminal punishments should be and what directions sanction systems should take. Research on deterrence and prevention of criminal behavior instructs that, if control itself becomes tight and more efficient, the severity of punishment can be decreased without losses for deterrence and prevention. However, as a result of dependence in modern societies, the vulnerability of offenders who are exposed to punishment increases, too. These questions are being discussed in Scandinavian countries, as for example, with regards to the question of how long prison sentences should be. The significant question under conditions of modern societies, therefore, is not how many offenders must be punished but how many of those offenders who are in principle subject to criminal punishment should be punished, and what types of punishment should be applied? The preventive results of criminal penalties cannot be conceived merely as linear correlates of the number of offenders punished; too much punishment may be counterproductive in terms of crime prevention (Popitz 1968; Kaiser 1988). However, current trends point not only to the growth of interdependence but also to emergence of new precarious populations for whom strategies of physical control are rapidly developing.

C. New Precarious Groups

In many Western countries, illicit drugs and drug users rank among the preeminent problems. In post-socialist countries, too, drug problems are moving up the political agenda (Tobolska-Rydz 1986; Weigend 1988; Levai 1990). The drug problem is an example of the spread of social problems, and the spread of certain types of criminal sanctions. Participants in black markets always have been treated as rational offenders. Until the 1960s, the concept of the professional offender prevailed. Since then the model of the organized criminal, closely associated with subcultures of crime, deviance, and illicit services, has been stripped of the subcultural elements and has evolved into the model of the rational offender driven by financial motives and behaving like an ordinary economic actor distinguishable only by the illegality of the economic activity. For this type of "adventure capitalism," a particular set of criminal penalties emerged that was justified in terms of prevention and incapacitation. Forfeiture and confiscation have become prominent responses to black market phenomena. However, the major difference between criminal organizations and legal organizations engaging in illegal (economic) activities is that corporations may be punished. Corporate liability is receiving attention, and it is widely acknowledged that the organization itself and not those individuals acting on its behalf should be the primary target of sentencing and criminal penalties (Heine 1995).

Drug users were assigned a particular status by criminal law and sanctions systems. Especially in the 1970s, addicts and users were often understood in terms of the sickness model. Responses for addicted individuals were introduced that mixed punishment and treatment far more than had been done for alcohol-dependent offenders. But, more recently, new concern for drug users is expressed in the legislation of some Western countries (Office of National Drug Control Policy 1989; Albrecht 1991; Bernat de Celis 1992), and in most other countries such concerns are voiced and receive at least some support (Katholnigg 1990). This new interest is based on the recognition that drugs are dangerous only if people are willing to use them. The same argument can be observed in other fields, such as possession of child pornography. Drug markets depend on demand, so the argument goes, and those who support the markets by expressing demand for their products are not merely victims of dangerous substances but are also responsible for the dangers that arise from the supply of drugs. According to a recent U.S. National Drug Control Strategy, they are members of an international criminal enterprise (Albrecht 1995).

D. Challenges of Modern Societies with Respect to Criminal Sanctions and Their Implementation

Contemporary criminal justice systems must deal with new kinds of crime and with traditional crimes that are newly important. Mass delinquency ranks high in placing new strains on criminal justice systems. Likewise, organized crime, transnational and cross-border crimes, and new economic and environmental crimes are on policy agendas (Farkas 1993). Sensitive crimes such as hate crimes, sexual violence, terrorism, and drug crimes continue to provoke debates.

Mass crimes have led to capacity problems and have contributed to significant trends toward simplification and streamlining of criminal law and procedure. Organized, economic, and other types of rational crime have generated an ongoing search for measures to improve clearance rates and to overcome problems of evidence and have become a central concern in most countries. This is especially true for so-called victimless crimes. These changes have contributed to the emergence of proactive policing with increased use of undercover police, new investigative technologies, and a conceptualization of crime as a network of relationships among individuals. These developments can blur the line between investigations triggered by reasonable suspicion that a crime has been committed, and investigations that take place without previous individualized suspicion.

Certain types of complex economic, environmental, and transnational crimes place new and hitherto unknown demands on the procedural, legal, and technological expertise of criminal prosecution and criminal courts. Finally, costs of criminal justice have increased dramatically. New types of offenders partly linked to new crime phenomena—for example, the rational offender, the minority offender, and criminal organizations or corporate criminals—must be considered. With such offenders the basic rehabilitation and reintegration approach of the 1960s and 1970s, focused on individuals, has come under pressure. Socioeconomic changes in modern societies also create new demands. Societies in transition undergo major changes with black markets and the shadow economy representing new social and economic frameworks and producing new precarious groups from which and for whom crime policy and criminal justice reform has to be developed. Victims came back into the picture, including concern for their needs and expectations in terms of compensation and restitution. In addition, the community's role in crime control and private sector roles in crime control, justice administration, and corrections have become issues.

In summary: crime has become a mass phenomenon while the complexity of certain types of crimes has increased. The first development results from opportunity- and risk-structures in modern societies that make crime ubiquitous (in particular for youth). The use of criminal law in complex environments has created a need for criminal justice systems to develop correspondingly complex structures. Interdependency of criminal law and its implementation with other legal and administrative systems thus is another major complication. The complex criminal law interferes in other systems (economy, commerce, or environment) where organized interests provide for conditions of implementation very different from those found in traditional criminal law fields.

The basic question is what role criminal law should play in organizing risk management in modern societies. Modern criminal law relies essentially on the concept of "endangering offenses," a concept widely used in European criminal legislation to ensure traffic safety, a proper natural environment, the well-being of the economy, public health, internal security, and ultimately feelings of safety. The focus switches from the results of human behavior to risks attributable to human behavior, and modern criminal laws become part of risk management. Easily portrayable interests or values traditionally protected by criminal law (such as life and property) in certain fields have been exchanged for abstract interests (public health) that lack any meaningful profile (at least in the context of criminal law). With risk management and the concept of endangering offenses come mechanisms that influence the types of sanctions used. Endangering offenses and punishments for creating unacceptable risks have several consequences.

First, there is convergence between sanctions or sanctions severity for intentional and for negligent behavior. Second, endangering offenses are frequently linked to organizational behavior and thus demand concepts that acknowledge corporate liability rather than focus on individual liability. The need is created for criminal penalties adapted to the particular conditions of law-breaking emerging from organizational contexts.

Third, sanctions and sentencing become intertwined with administrative laws and thus become dependent on goals and interests conceived and developed by other agencies. Drug offenses, environmental offenses, and some economic offenses are not completely defined by legislative bodies but are shaped by discretionary decision-making within the ministries of health or interior, or an administrative authority competent to add to the lists of drugs annexed to drug laws or to prescribe conditions under which criminal offenses can be established.

The primary problem here concerns conflicts of goals, which seem inevitable and may be easily demonstrated when contrasting a legalist perspective on environmental or drug problems (aiming at detection, conviction, and sentencing of offenders) with an administrative or public health perspective (aiming at improving the quality of the environment or of health or minimizing health risks). One consequence, for example, is the intertwining of treatment and therapy with criminal penalties for drug addicts. The relationship between therapy and criminal sanction comes up in various forms, although the most widely used seems to be attaching treatment conditions to a suspended prison sentence, postponement of prosecution, or sentencing.

E. International Crime Control and the Development of
International Standards

So far, I have discussed developments that affect sanction systems from within
countries. Various international and extranational developments are also important
(see chaps. 9 and 10, this volume).

Demands for Uniform Crime Legislation

Sanction systems are shaped partly by international demands. Countries from eastern Europe provide a good example. With transition into modern societies, eastern
European countries continue to try to achieve full integration into international
legal and control systems that have been developed in Western industrialized
countries. These efforts are simultaneously part of the transitional process itself
and a mechanism to shape and promote transition. With efforts to become part
of international crime control structures comes the need for uniform criminal
legislation and minimum requirements for sanction systems. For example, the
1988 UN Convention against Illicit Traffic in Narcotic Drugs and Psychotropic
Substances contains explicit obligations in the creation of uniform criminal law
and in demands for uniform criminal penalties. The international drug control
system and Western drug policies go far beyond mere drug offenses and also target
related problems of organized crime, corruption, and illegal profits. These problems have fueled demands for wider powers for law enforcement agencies in Western countries. These reforms focus on organized crime. Criminal law changes aim
at strengthening forfeiture rules, penalizing money laundering, streamlining international police cooperation, and penetrating private space or other systems (for
example, the financial system). Eastern European countries have adopted the 1988
UN Convention, although specific patterns of drug law legislation, such as crim-
inalizing drug use, were not immediate consequences (Musil, Valkova, and Cisarova 1994).

European Conventions

The integration of transitional countries into international and European covenants, conventions, and treaties has had considerable effect on types of sanctions
and their implementation (Walmsley 1996; Zimmermann 1992). Transitional
countries must take account of the European Convention for the Protection of
Human Rights and Fundamental Freedoms, The European Convention for the
Prevention of Torture and Inhuman or Degrading Treatment or Punishment, and
the European Prison Rules (Morgan 1993).

Integration into European legal and economic structures was sought by the
transitional countries and has been implemented within a short period (as can be
shown in the rapid entry of central and eastern European nations into the Council
of Europe, and the adoption and ratification of numerous European Conventions)
(Wilkitzki 1995). Legal changes introduced in most central and eastern European
countries have concentrated on the improvement of protection of human rights.

The European convention against torture and other types of degrading and inhumane punishment has received particular attention (Morgan and Evans 1994; chap. 10, in this volume). With the Anti-Torture Convention, a significant step was made for the control of the implementation of the relevant principles of the European Convention on Human Rights, as well as the European Prison Rules (European Committee on Crime Problems 1994). The Torture Convention became a powerful instrument (Evans and Morgan 1992). Broad approaches are used to control and prevent inhuman and degrading punishment and treatment, in terms not only of monitoring but also of elucidating conditions indicative of degrading and inhuman punishment (Kaiser 1991).

F. Commercialization, Privatization, and the Penal-Industrial Complex

Cost-benefit considerations and low criminal justice budgets focus attention on privatization, in particular for pretrial detention facilities and prisons. Privatization will play a role in eastern European countries, too, although the legacy of the past, as in many western European countries, includes a firm belief in the public nature of criminal corrections. The trend toward privatization, and its labeling as "commercialization" of criminal justice, may be conceptualized as an alternative to reprivatization of criminal justice from the perspective of community participation (Jung 1993). The privatization issue triggers basic questions concerning the state monopoly of power. Privatization represents a response to the criticism that the state cannot implement criminal sanctions cost-efficiently. But responses can point in different directions. One direction is to view the private sector as being the community, which can handle crime problems itself. The other is the model of the free market and its potential for providing rational solutions (Jung 1993). However, the main pressures for privatization are rising prison populations, a general commitment to "rolling back the state," and the view that expansion of prison capacity can be done more efficiently by contracting out, reducing costs, and increasing managerial controls (Kinkade and Leone 1992).

Three fields of prison privatization can be differentiated: labor, funding of construction, and operation of facilities (Mullen, Chabotar, and Cartow 1985). Privatization has gone furthest in the United States, Australia, and England, with private corporations constructing and offering prison facilities.

Privatization has also received attention in Europe (McDonald 1994). The debate will continue although the approaches (for example, those implemented in France and in England) differ from those adopted in North America and Australia. A common trigger in Europe seems to be detention of illegal immigrants (McDonald 1994). Private operation of institutions for adjudicated and sentenced individuals is well-known in juvenile criminal justice and the history of adult prisons (McDonald 1994). But the basic reason to involve the private sector with juvenile corrections was related not to a cost-benefit theory but to the principle of subsidiarity; education (as the primary goal of juvenile justice) was thought to be better implemented by private and charitable institutions designed for that and related purposes than by prison managers.

In my view, privatization may be justified if prison administrators make use of the private sector for construction or renting of prison facilities, and for medical or other services. However, limits should preclude transfer of adjudicated and sentenced offenders to privately operated facilities and cessation of the state of major responsibilities for supervision and care. A cautious approach is advisable, since the question whether privatization reduces costs seems to be open (McDonald 1994).

Privatization has been seen as an expression of the emergence of a "correctional-commercial complex" (Lilly and Knepper 1992) or a "penal-industrial complex" that threatens to develop powerful new lobbies for tougher sentencing. However, there is no empirical evidence for such hypotheses. Imprisonment rates at least in Europe are driven by penal control of illicit drugs and immigrants, not by lobbyists.

II. Developments in Sanctions Systems

Change in sentencing and sanctions systems is slow, and the causes of change are many. Nonetheless, perceptible trends can be documented.

A. The Death Penalty

Hood's work (1996) on the death penalty reveals considerable changes during the past three decades. He noted in 1996 an increasing movement toward abolition. Abolition certainly has accelerated in eastern Europe where the death penalty was a standard penalty for the most serious crimes throughout the 1960s, 1970s, and 1980s. Western Europe — particularly under the auspices of the Council of Europe — became a death penalty–free zone in the early 1980s (see European Convention on Human Rights, Protocol 6), but strong support for it is still voiced in some eastern European countries (Buchala 1993; Gruev 1993; Schittenhelm 1993; Walmsley 1996). The debate seems to represent an important symbolic point in transitions in criminal justice policies. In Hungary, the death penalty was set aside when the Constitutional Court ruled that it is a disproportionate and inhumane punishment (Nagy 1993). In the Czech Republic and in Romania, the death penalty was abolished in 1990 (Musil, Valkova, and Cisarova 1994; Walmsley 1996). The new criminal code in Poland also provides for abolition (Buchala 1993). In Russia, an amendment of April 29, 1993, made young offenders, female offenders, and those over 65 years old ineligible for the death penalty (Schittenhelm 1994). However, death sentences are still imposed in Russia, Belarus, and the Ukraine.

Nonetheless, some countries have reinstated the death penalty or resumed executions (Hood 1996). The driving force — at least in some regions — is the search for increasingly tougher responses to drug trafficking. Chinese policy insists firmly on retaining the death penalty, although the subject is controversial (Xin-Liang 1998). The conflicts and debates are comparable to those in other countries. China has adopted the position that current social, political, and economic conditions do not permit abolition of the death penalty (Xuan 1987). However, voices can be heard calling for restrictive application (Kaminski 1978; Amnesty International 1979; Xuan 1987; Lenz and Heuser 1995).

The Chinese government made its firm official support for the death penalty clear in the reservations it expressed when signing the International Covenant on Civil and Political Rights in September 1998. The reservations are comparable to those expressed by the United States when ratifying the International Covenant in 1992 (Hood 1998). The People's Republic noted that in the current stage of social and economic development the death penalty cannot be abolished and that the restrictions of Article 7 proscribing the use of cruel, unusual, and degrading punishments cannot be understood as prohibiting imposition and enforcement of the death penalty.

China's position is based on utilitarian considerations, moral considerations, and social attitudes (Shutong 1987). Arguments emphasize the goals of incapacitation, general deterrence, and positive general prevention (Hood 1996), as well as reduction in the risk that victims will take the law into their own hands (Xuan 1987). Official statements associate abolition with increases in crime, threats to public safety, and deterioration of the public's belief in the rule of law (Xuan 1987). Similar reservations by the United States (Schabas 1997), however, were judged by the United Nations Committee of Human Rights to be incompatible with the goals of the International Covenant (Hood 1998).

B. Life Imprisonment

Life imprisonment is the response in Europe to the most serious crimes, in particular murder (Gruev 1993; Tubex and Snacken 1995). That policy raises the questions of how long life imprisonment should be and under what conditions parole should be granted, if at all. There are no clear-cut trends. The French Parliament recently enacted a new criminal code that provides for life imprisonment without parole. In England and Wales, life imprisonment has received new attention in the context of drug trafficking and violent and sexual offenses. Norway and Portugal, by contrast, have abolished life imprisonment. The German Constitutional Court has held (with some exceptions, in particular for dangerous offenders) that life imprisonment must include the possibility of release. In Slovenia, where the death penalty was abolished, the maximum term of imprisonment is twenty years (Bavcon 1993). The debate over life imprisonment centers on the prohibition of cruel and unusual, or inhumane or degrading, forms of punishment and includes questions of proportionality and individualization (Buchala 1993).

In Germany, the Constitutional Court has addressed whether life imprisonment is constitutional (BverfGE 45, p. 187). Although the Court has held that life imprisonment for murder is proportionate to the harm caused and therefore constitutional, important limitations have been set. First, statutory criteria for life imprisonment must define the types of murder that deserve a life sentence, without taking into account any other factors otherwise considered in sentencing (and so contradict or eliminate the recognized principle that the sentence should be individualized to the offender's circumstances).

However, the Constitutional Court has held that life imprisonment must be scrutinized for possible violations of the principle of the dignity of mankind, and that the basic principle requires that an individual not be deprived of all hope of leading a meaningful life. Thus, life prisoners must at some point have the possibility of release and reintegration into society. In effect, the Court held that legislation must establish the minimum time to be served, and the conditions under which a life prisoner may apply for parole. However, the Court acknowledged that dangerous individuals exist for whom release will not be possible. But, in all other cases, rehabilitative opportunities must be offered and the possibility of parole had to be introduced.

As a result, the German Parliament amended the Criminal Code; section 57a allows for parole in a case of life imprisonment after fifteen years under the condition that the prisoner not present a continuing threat to society. Later decisions of the Constitutional Court addressed the question of how life imprisonment and parole must be implemented, with the practical effect that life imprisonment was restricted to a small group of dangerous offenders. For the others, two kinds of long-term imprisonment—fifteen years for "ordinary" murder and twenty years and up for "aggravated" murder—have been established (BverfGE, NeueJuristische Wochenschrift 1992, p. 2947). In the eastern European countries, a range of fifteen to twenty-five years' effective imprisonment seems to be considered sufficient and proportional for the most serious offenses (Farkas 1993; Bavcon 1993; Buchala 1993).

During the 1990s, various European countries held debates on how to respond to dangerous offenders generally and dangerous sexual offenders particularly. Two approaches emerged. In Germany, Austria, and Switzerland, the principle of guilt determines the proportionate sentence and prevents dangerousness from being taken into account in sentencing decisions. However, a "two-track" system of criminal punishment (responding to guilt) and preventive-incapacitative measures (responding to dangerousness) allows for the imposition of an additional incapacitative (indeterminate) sentence if dangerousness can be established (and other requirements are fulfilled).

The second approach relies on imprisonment alone, allowing either for discretionary life imprisonment (as introduced in England and Wales in the Criminal Justice Act 1991) or for extended prison sentences in case of dangerousness (or as a simple response to recidivism) (Kinzig 1997). Dangerousness usually is closely associated with mental illness and therefore points to (indeterminate) detention in psychiatric hospitals as a consequence of criminal or civil commitment orders in cases of mentally ill offenders. Civil and criminal detention orders may well serve as functional equivalents to life imprisonment and long prison sentences (without providing the same legal safeguards concerning imposition, detention regimes, and parole).

C. Prison Sentences

Ordinary prison sentences have recently received particular attention because of the large increase in prison populations in some European countries. Research on criminal law developments in Europe (e.g., Eser and Huber 1994, 1997) dem-onstrate significant differences between countries in the use of criminal sanctions and distinct preferences for certain punishment strategies and penalties. Choices made decades ago determine to what degree short-term imprisonment is used as a standard penalty and how long prison sentences should be in general. There is wide divergence within Europe in the details of imprisonment practices (see table 8.1).

Correctional institutions since the 1950s have been given an important role in modifying prison sentences through parole and significant differentiation among types of imprisonment. Prison differentiation has led to forms of imprisonment (Parvarini 1994) that vary by the degree of restrictions placed on prisoners and the availability of leaves and admission to furlough programs (King 1994). The roots of prison differentiation are found in the correctional systems themselves and in the search for alternatives to imprisonment. Within the correctional systems, dif-ferentiation of prison regimes and parole became elements of the rehabilitative approach. The search for alternatives led in some jurisdictions to alternative dis-positions within the correctional system itself.

Since the 1970s, changes have occurred in some countries in the roles of the correctional system. This was a consequence partly of implementing determinate sentencing laws and "truth in sentencing" policies and partly of changes that brought the judiciary more deeply into the correctional process and gave judges increased control over correctional differentiation (or different prison regimes).

With determinate sentencing and truth-in-sentencing policies (mainly in the United States) has come a strong push toward the abolition of parole. However, in many places, despite the abolition of parole, other mechanisms for reduction of prison sentences (e.g., good-time reductions) remained operative. Research on the effects of these changes provides mixed results. Some determinate sentencing laws do not seem to have contributed to prison population growth but seem partly to have moderated the upward trend in imprisonment (Marvell and Moody 1997). Increased lengths of stay that contribute to increases in prison populations concern exceptional cases. Judges seem often to respond to truth in sentencing by reducing prison sentences (at least in certain categories of crime) (Wood 1997).

Prison differentiation has in many places led to stand-alone penalties or substi-tutes for imprisonment employed by the judiciary. Weekend imprisonment, semi-liberty, and the like fall between full imprisonment and community sanctions.

In many countries, serious attempts have been made to reduce the use of long prison terms, often by the use of partly suspended sentences (Kuhn 1993). How-ever, partial suspension is not a new sanction. As early as 1929, it was introduced in the Netherlands. Denmark followed in 1961, Belgium in 1964, France in 1970, and Austria in 1988. In other countries, including Switzerland and Germany, partly suspended sentences have occasionally been discussed but have not been included in law reforms. In Austria, partly suspended sentences have been avail-able since 1988, but it is not clear whether they merely replaced fully suspended sentences.[3]

Table 8.1. Characteristics of Prison Sentences and Prison Populations in Europe

Country	1991			1993	
	Prison Sentences	Prison Sentences per 100,000	Percentage over 1 Year	Prisoner Rate per 100,000	Prison Admissions per 100,000
Germany	37,171	58	40	81	149
Belgium	na	na	na	72	194
Denmark	14,671	285	6	71	na
Spain	na	na	na	115	181
Finland	11,533	230	11	62	196
France	92,383	162	17	86	155
Italy	100,289	175	25	89	157
Norway	4,597	108	20	60	271
Holland	19,243	128	11	51	187
England and Wales	61,249	120	34	89	na
Sweden	13,422	155	17	66	na
Switzerland	12,190	177	9	81	na

Source: Council of Europe 1996.

D. Day Fines

Finland first introduced a day-fine system in 1921 (see Jescheck and Grebing 1978). The primary reason lay in the rapidly declining value of money. Compared to summary fines, day fines can easily be adjusted to changes in the economy brought about by inflation or recession. Nevertheless, with the exception of some South American countries, Finland, Sweden, and Denmark were the only countries to introduce a day-fine system during the first half of the twentieth century. Italy, Germany, the Netherlands, Austria, and Switzerland made substantial revisions in the penal codes during the 1920s and 1930s but did not adopt day fines. The concept generated substantial controversy in all three Scandinavian countries, and was far from being unanimously supported.[4]

Subsequently, the Federal Republic of Germany and Austria introduced day-fine systems in 1975 (Grebing 1982), followed by Hungary in 1978 (Nagy 1993), and France and Portugal in 1983 (Spaniol 1985; Hünerfeld 1983). Most recently, a system of unit fines was introduced in England and Wales at the end of 1992 (Gibson 1990; Wasik and Taylor 1991) but was not successful. Six months after the system went into effect, the Home Office announced a preliminary suspension of those provisions and quietly repealed the legislation (Moxon 1997). The new French Criminal Code, in force since March 1994, has expanded the scope of day fines, which had previously been narrow (Ministère de la Justice 1993). Proposed revisions to the penal codes of Switzerland (Schultz 1987; Heine and Spalinger 1988) and Poland[5] include recommendations for the introduction of day-fine systems.

By contrast, the current draft of a proposed penal code in Belgium retains the concept of summary fines (Legros 1985), thereby suggesting that the trend toward extended use of day fines is not inexorable. Other European countries, including the Netherlands, Norway, Italy, and Iceland have not incorporated day fines into their criminal justice systems and are not considering abolition of summary fines. But at the same time, fines per se continue to play a major role in the sentencing practices of these countries. Some jurisdictions in the United States[6] have experimented with day fines (Hillsman and Greene 1987; McDonald 1992). Evaluations so far have been mixed, but day fines have been portrayed as a promising penalty in a recent report to the U.S. Congress on crime-prevention programs (MacKenzie 1997).

Other suggestions have been made regarding use of criminal fines. For example, in the 1960s, a group of German law professors drafted a model penal code (Baumann 1969), which introduced the concept of the "installment fine," a model that combines day fines with mandatory installment payments. The aim was to deprive the offender, for a fixed time, of all the income that the offender could spare, thereby relegating the offender's income to a subsistence level. It was hoped that an installment fine would amount to something like "partial imprisonment" or "restricted liberty," since offenders would be deprived of resources necessary for mobility. This proposal was rejected in the Federal Republic of Germany and was not picked up in other European countries.

The Dutch Commission on Monetary Penalties attempted to improve the fixed-sum fine systems by proposing fine categories for offenses, each with a different upper limit (see van Kalmthout and Tak 1992). The upper limits would be adjusted according to the seriousness of offenses. There would be a general provision requiring the adjustment of the amount of the fine within each offense-specific range, according to the financial circumstances of the offender. The proposal was approved by Dutch legislation (see Waling and van Kalmthout 1988). Otherwise, virtually all criminal justice systems that still use the fixed-sum fine have adopted provisions requiring consideration of the financial situation and income of the offender when determining the total amount.

The fundamental difference between summary and day fines is to be found in the two-step process peculiar to day-fine systems. The first is a decision regarding the number of day fines. This should reflect the seriousness of the offense. The second is a decision regarding the size of a one-day-fine unit. This should be adjusted or determined according to the economic and financial circumstances of the offender.

Rationales

Fines play a major role in sentencing in virtually all Western industrialized countries. Fines as a proportion of all sentences meted out by criminal courts in Western European countries varied between 30 percent and 85 percent at the end of the 1980s and in the early 1990s.[7] Differences in fine use are not dependent on whether a day-fine system has been adopted. Rather, the differences result from variations in the extent to which the criminal justice systems vary in the emphasis placed on sentencing options other than fines, for example, suspended sentences, probation, and community service.

The reasons for the introduction of day-fine systems in Austria and the Federal Republic of Germany during the 1970s, and in France and Portugal during the 1980s, are diverse. There is also variation in the arguments in countries considering or experimenting with day-fine systems. There are several distinct, though not mutually exclusive, positions.

First, day fines, unlike fixed-sum fines, are assessed to satisfy the need for both equal and proportionate punishment. Day fines, at least in theory, may be adjusted to the individual financial circumstances of the offender. Although fines often have been viewed as an inexpensive and feasible alternative to prison sentences, negative attitudes toward their use have persisted. Critics have stressed that fines enable the better-off offender to buy his or her way out of the system while the poor offender often eventually serves time in prison because of a default due to inability to pay.

A second argument stresses that acceptance of fines and of the criminal justice system can be increased by making the process of assessing fines more visible. Day fines can provide public evidence that differences in each offender's means and assets are taken into account.

Third, day-fine systems can permit wide extension of the scope of fines, thereby restricting the use of prison sentences to offenders for whom imprisonment is seen as a last resort. Consequently, day fines help concentrate criminal justice resources on the small group of most serious offenders.

Fourth, day fines are congruent with contemporary views that emphasize a shift in sentencing away from rehabilitation and treatment and toward proportionality. Since the seriousness of the offense should be the basic determinant of the number of day fines, that number can readily be related to the length of time in prison or length of time on probation or periods of community service. Thus, the day fine can serve as a common denominator for different types of penalties and the deprivation or pain associated with each.

Fifth, day fines lead to increased rationality in sentencing because the judge first must decide the number of day fines in proportion to the seriousness of the offense, the harm caused, and the culpability of the offender and then must adjust the level of the day fine to the financial circumstances of the offender. Theoretically, inequities are less likely to occur than with fixed-sum fines and uncontrolled discretion. The decision-making process may be reviewed more easily than with fixed-sum fines.

Finally, a less important argument, the day-fine system provides for a clear method of converting fines into default imprisonment. Regardless of the offender's level of income, failure to pay should result in a similar number of days of imprisonment, assuming that the offense is of equal seriousness.

Several arguments against day-fine systems have been noted. First, day-fine systems are said to put too much emphasis on the financial circumstances of the offender, thereby leading to what has been called an "over-dimensionalization" of offenders' financial capacity, while other factors affecting proportionate punishments are underweighed.

Second, there are problems of implementation and the feasibility of ascertaining the income and financial circumstances of the offender. This is crucial, since virtually all advantages attributed to the day-fine system depend on reliable and valid information about an offender's financial and income status.

Third, it is argued that judges could deliberately avoid the two-step decision process by continuing to impose the equivalent of fixed-sum fines that they then divide into the number of day fines and day-fine levels. Judges might do this for reasons of convenience, or simply because the day-fine system appears too complicated. This argument was offered by the French Commission on Law Reform in the 1970s.

Consideration needs to be given to the punitive impact of a fine. A fine should affect the offender's standard of living and reduce consumption levels. Consequently, the fine requires individual adjustment if this punitive impact is to be achieved and if fines are to be more than a mere nuisance. However, as with other penalties, fines must be related to the harm done and the culpability of the offender. An analogy may be made to adjustment of prison sentences according to needs or characteristics of different groups of offenders. Open prison settings, work furloughs, controlled liberty, or semi-imprisonment, for example, represent efforts to adjust imprisonment to the needs and characteristics of individual offenders. This occurs not only in terms of the length of imprisonment but also in terms of the degree of restriction of liberty. Day fines in theory are better suited to adjusting the punitive impact to the offender and the penalty according to the harm done.

Scope

In general, the day-fine system applies to all fines imposed by criminal courts. France is an exception. Day fines there are used primarily as a substitute for imprisonment, while ordinary fines are for fixed sums. Thus, the use of day fines is drastically restricted in practice.

In France, day fines are used in approximately 1 percent of all sentences. In other criminal justice systems, certain types of monetary penalties are excluded. Thus, in Denmark, and sometimes in Sweden, fines imposed in summary proceedings are for fixed sums.

In Germany, fines imposed as a condition of dismissal by the public prosecutor's office, or as a condition of suspension of a prison sentence, are determined summarily and are not subject to the day-fine procedure. This is mainly for administrative convenience. Since such cases concern only petty offenses, the day-fine system is regarded as an obstacle to streamlined procedures. In Austria and Germany, petty misdemeanors have to a large extent been decriminalized and are treated as "administrative offenses." These offenses carry as penalties only noncriminal (administrative) fines based on statutory tariffs.[8]

The scope of day fines is usually defined in the penal code sections that describe offenses and assign types and ranges of penalties. Statutorily, most offenses may be punished by a fine. Only the most serious are excluded. There are substantial differences between countries in upper limits. In Scandinavian countries, day fines are limited to a maximum of 120 days (in Denmark, 60 days). The upper limit in Germany, Austria, and France is 360 days. The draft Swiss Criminal Code contemplates an upper day-fine level of 360 days. Although these differences might suggest that the scope of day fines is larger than in Scandinavia, this is not necessarily true. Day fines of more than 180 units are extremely rare in Germany and Austria. Moreover, the scope of day fines depends on the general level of punishment. Whereas, for example, the average prison sentence in Germany, Austria, and France is long, approximately six months, average sentences in Scandinavian countries are comparatively low (two to three months). That fines in Germany and Austria represent a large proportion of penalties, slightly more than 80 percent of sentences, is not due to the greater number of day fines permitted but to differences in assessment of the benefits of short-term imprisonment, and the introduction of other noninstitutional punishment options. The Scandinavian countries continue to use short-term imprisonment on a large scale, especially in the cases of drunken driving and other traffic offenses. Penal law reforms in Germany and Austria contain binding rules regarding the choice of the penalty. In both countries, the day fine has priority over any prison sentence of less than six months, unless exceptional circumstances concerning the offender, the offense, or both indicate the need for a different type of sentence. Such sentences should be predicated on a need for individual or general deterrence and general prevention. In all instances, courts must justify sentences of less than six months; therefore, the courts may be reluctant to resort to short-term imprisonment.

Studies of the use of day fines show that they are used as penalties for a wide range of offenses, adjusted or determined according to the economic and financial circumstances of the offender. Day fines play a significant role in Germany in punishing traditional crimes and traffic offenses; it is also evident that fines routinely are used for petty crimes see table 8.2). However, in 1996 one of four aggravated thefts was followed by a fine and approximately half of all drug offenders received fines.

German research shows that day fines are used regularly as a substitute for prison sentences of up to six months. Thus, the fine is the typical punishment not only for traffic offenses but also for more traditional crimes such as theft, larceny, burglary, fraud, assault, and drug offenses (Albrecht 1980; Janssen 1993). More

Table 8.2. The Share of Fines in Germany (%), 1968–1996

Offense	1968	1982	1990	1996
Assault	77	85	85	84
Theft	74	86	86	85
Aggravated theft	20	22	23	26
Fraud	52	71	78	81
Criminal damage	85	95	94	95
Drug offenses	43	40	49	50
Drunken driving	66	93	95	90

Sources: Statistisches Bundesamt, various years.

recently, the emergence of environmental crimes has created another field for the application of day fines, although there is heated discussion whether the response to these crimes should not be immediate imprisonment.

The Size of the Day-Fine Unit

Determining the number of days to serve as the basis for a day fine does not attract much attention since sentencing is subject to general rules. However, determination of the size of a day-fine unit reveals important variations and is the subject of ongoing debates.

Several points must be addressed. First, which part of income should be covered by the day fine? Second, what factors should be taken into account when determining the offender's financial status or income? Third, how should income levels and financial circumstances be ascertained? Fourth, how should economically marginal groups be treated (students, the unemployed, offenders relying on Social Security, pensioners, institutionalized offenders, or, in general, offenders dependent on maintenance payments and not integrated into the labor force)? These issues, of course, arise not only in day-fine systems, but in any system making wide use of fines. Limits on the size of one day-fine unit are usually set in countries' penal codes.

Variation is greater in upper limits (see table 8.3). While all day-fine systems allow for comparable minimum amounts—in U.S. currency ranging between $1.00 and $2.00—upper limits vary much more. Germany provides a maximum of 10,000 DM per day, approximately US $6,500. Other systems are more moderate, ranging from approximately $155 to $350 per day. In practice, day fines of more than 100 DM (US $55) are extremely rare in Germany. Only 0.2 percent of all day fine units were greater than 100 DM in 1996.

The upper limits have been much debated in Germany, with many legal scholars arguing that the principle of proportionality of punishment would be violated by fines of this size even if someone with an income of that size had committed a crime. Take the example of drunken driving, where, depending on other factors, the number of day-fine units generally falls between thirty days and sixty days; the maximum difference in the total amount of the fine would be almost 300,000 DM (US $170,000). This point has been noted in Swiss Draft Penal Code, where a maximum of 1,000 Swiss francs, approximately US $600, is considered sufficient.

With respect to lower limits, there is continuing debate whether these are too low to be taken seriously. However, considering that the majority of offenders come from the lower socioeconomic strata of society, or from marginal groups, it seems reasonable to keep those limits rather low. So far, efforts to increase lower limits have not succeeded.

Examination of the justifications used to determine the size of a day-fine unit reveals two basic approaches. The first looks to the principle of "strict economy," the other to the principle of net income. The choice concerns the part of income that should be considered. According to the principle of strict economy, the offender should be deprived of that amount of money that is left daily when expenses are drastically restricted to very basic needs.[9] The principle of net income is more

Table 8.3. Minimum and Maximum Number of Day-Fine Units and Unit Sizes

	Min. No. of Units	Max. No. of Units	Min. Size of Unit	Max. Size of Unit
Austria	2	360	20 ÖS	3000 ÖS
Denmark	1	60	2 kroner	—
Finland	1	120	—	—
France	1	360	—	2000 FF
Germany	5	360	2 DM	10,000 DM
Hungary	10	180	50 forint	1,000 forint
Portugal	10	300	100 escudos	10,000 escudos
Sweden	30	150	30 kroner	1,000 kroner
Poland	10	360	10 zloty	2,000 zloty
Spain	1	720	100 pesetas	20,000 pesetas
Switzerland*	2	360	5 SF	1000 SF

*Draft criminal codes.

aggressive, suggesting that the day fine should be the offender's total daily income after taxes. This would include first subtracting those expenses usually accepted by tax authorities as decreasing taxable income.

The net-income principle is in force only in Germany. Since the courts also have to take into account personal and other financial circumstances when determining the amount of a day-fine unit, the rigidity of the net-income principle is softened. In practice, therefore, there appears to be little difference between it and the principle of strict economy.

The second point concerns factors taken into account when determining the financial status or income of the offender. In all day-fine systems, the starting point is the offender's earnings or income. This determination is independent of the origin of the income and includes employment, pensions, maintenance payments, social welfare, unemployment benefits, stipends, interest earned on investments, and so forth. Issues of morality regarding the source of the income may not be raised, in most European systems, as a basis for excluding income from consideration. Thus, for example, income derived from prostitution, whether full-time or supplemental, may serve as a basis for fixing the level of the day-fine unit.

Disagreements exist over what other resources should be taken into account in order to increase the level of the day-fine unit. In general, the practice has been to refrain from taking other than substantial assets into account, although statutes typically would allow this to be done. Only the Swedish Public Prosecutors' Office has set precise rules determining what can be used to increase day-fine levels. In other jurisdictions the issue remains open.

Since most offenders do not own considerable assets, the more important issue is what expenses or obligations should be taken into account in order to lower or decrease the day fine. Liability for maintenance and maintenance payments is one factor accepted in every day-fine system. Calculation of the size of maintenance varies. In Scandinavian countries, a fixed proportion of income is deducted for every dependent person. Thus, 20 percent is deducted for a wife or a husband who is not employed and 10 percent for each dependent child. In Germany and Austria, judges are bound by superior court rulings and must take into account standard maintenance rates that are fixed annually in the civil court system responsible for civil maintenance law suits.

Opinions vary about whether other debts or permanent financial obligations should be considered. In general, a restrictive approach is favored. Swedish courts accept debts as a reason for decreasing the level of day fines only if they represent an exceptional burden. In Germany and Austria, only those obligations that correspond to rational and plausible economic behavior should be taken into account. This would include, for example, debts resulting from the purchase of an apartment or a house but would exclude payments for a luxury automobile. Other more general debts would be excluded.

Most recently, in continental countries, discussion centers on compensation and reparation resulting from the crime, and the needs of the victim. As part of the general movement toward better treatment of victims, the idea that fine levels should be adjusted to take account of victim compensation and reparation is receiving growing support. Norway has introduced legislation to give compensation priority over enforcement of fines (Husabo and Strandbakken 1997).

Marginal groups present serious problems for any fine system. Technically, there should not be much of a problem in basing day-fine units on offenders' income from Social Security payments, pensions, or maintenance payments. The modest lower limits of day-fine units should allow for adjustment to such low levels of income. Nevertheless, several problems arise.

First, in cases where the offender is dependent on Social Security, the state provides resources thought to represent a minimum level of maintenance. Part of these resources, then, are taken away by another agency of the state under the day-fine system. A policy inconsistency is raised in attempting to keep people slightly above a subsistence level by maintenance payments and then pushing them below that level with a day fine. This problem may be resolved by always resorting to the minimum level for a day fine or, better still, by providing alternatives for these groups of offenders.

German and Finnish laws provide for the possibility of taking into account not only earned income but income the offender could earn if employed and capable of working. This is problematic since such a rule would require the judge to decide on employment opportunities and the acceptability of certain lifestyles. These are decisions that should not fall within the scope of the law.

Earnings from criminal activities, for example, drug money or income resulting from theft may not be included when determining the day-fine unit. This often would be precluded anyway by the present trend toward confiscation of drug money.

Investigation of Finances

Another crucial issue concerns acquisition of reliable financial information. Mathematical precision is not required, but basic information is essential. This has not been a big problem in Scandinavian countries, where the police, public prosecutor, and courts have free and unrestricted access to any information known to tax authorities. In other European countries, tax authorities may not disclose information except for the purpose of prosecuting tax offenses; the problem arises of how to ascertain financial information by other means.

In systems using day fines, income and financial circumstances have become part of the routine police interrogation. Although in practice all systems rely heavily on the offender's declaration of income, assets, debts, and maintenance liabilities, authorities may use standard investigative procedures to provide evidence. Witnesses may be examined or the offender's premises may be searched. However, as these procedures may often be thought too intrusive given the gravity of the offense, or economically unfeasible, the German and Austrian penal codes provide for estimation of the offender's income and financial capacity. In practice, information on the offender's professional status and standard of living are considered sufficient and provide reasonably accurate estimates in most cases. Some cases, however, for example, involving professions where income variation is large, do pose problems (Albrecht 1981). Encounters with these types of offender are rare.

There has been disagreement whether day-fine levels should be adjusted to changes in income or employment after conviction. All systems, except Austria, attempt to cope with this problem by granting installment payments or extending the payment schedule.

Enforcement

Enforcement practices vary, primarily in relation to the use of default imprisonment. The conversion rate between day fines and default imprisonment, statutorily fixed in all systems, varies, with one or two day fines corresponding to one day of default imprisonment. However, differences in the percentage of fines resulting in (partial or complete) default imprisonment are large, varying from practically zero in Sweden to approximately 5 percent in Germany (Albrecht 1981; Janssen 1993). This is due principally to differences in legal requirements governing conversion. In Sweden, this decision is at the discretion of the criminal justice system. In Germany, it is quasi-automatic.

In the early 1980s, fine defaults became more prevalent, partly as a result of increasing unemployment (Moxon 1983). To alleviate this problem, community service was made an option to imprisonment for defaulters in Germany. Currently, six hours of community service equals one day fine.

Evaluations of use of community service rather than imprisonment has yielded positive results (Albrecht and Schädler 1987, 1988). Experiments with day fines in England showed a positive impact on enforcement, with fewer defaults and imprisonments for default compared with traditional summary fines (Moxon 1991).

E. Community Participation

There is increased interest in many countries in the role of the community in systems of sanctions and their implementation. Much of this interest focuses on alternatives to imprisonment as a means to reduce recidivism and stigmatization attributed to the prison system. Community participation has also been credited with advantages said to be inherent in informal and extrajudicial procedures, including cost reductions and increased community responsibility for coping with crime problems.

The formerly socialist countries of eastern Europe offered a widely known approach to community participation (Eser 1993). With systems of "comrade courts," "conflict resolution commissions," "conciliation boards," or "community courts," the community perspective was introduced. The theoretical and ideological rationales were drawn from the concept of direct popular participation in justice administration and from Marxist forecasts of the ultimate disappearance of the state (Krapac 1995). These theoretical foundations have parallels in abolitionist perspectives, but in practice community participation was used to extend and intensify social control. During the 1960s and 1970s, small-scale crimes and small conflicts were subject to extra-judicial dispute settlements and small-scale sanctions (fines, admonitions, etc.). Evaluations of such approaches suggested major deficiencies, such as their being controlled by "activists," being loyal to the government, offering weak procedural guarantees, and being characterized by poor selection of staff (Krapac 1995). This is why attitudes toward community participation and extra-judicial control are today not positive. The new Slovenian procedural code, for example, completely eliminated referrals to conciliation boards (a procedural option of the former Yugoslavian criminal procedure) and adopted a system of prosecutor-based exemptions from mandatory prosecution (Krapac 1995). The new moves toward legalism and the rule of law have created tendencies to distrust informality and extra-judicial proceedings, while rising crime rates and safety concerns are said to lead to demands for retributive justice (Krapac 1995).

F. Strengthening the Roles of Victims

Reparation, restitution, compensation, victim-offender mediation, and reconciliation have received increased attention in many countries. International standards concerning the role and position of the victim have emerged. The UN Declaration of Basic Principles of Justice for Victims of Crime and Abuse of Power[10] and the Council of Europe's recommendations on the position of the victim within the framework of criminal law and criminal procedure and on assistance to victims and the prevention of victimization express new concern for crime victims and enunciate policies designed to recognize the victim in the sanctioning system. Restitution and victim-offender reconciliation alternatives to traditional criminal penalties are sought, and procedural alternatives to the criminal process are envisaged.

Although numerous experiments with restitution and mediation have been carried out (including in transitional countries)[11] and reparation and compensation have been introduced as sole sanctions in some systems (particularly for juvenile delinquents), many questions remain (Albrecht 1990; Ashworth 1993). One is why did restitution receive so much attention in the 1980s, and how does that relate to policy developments in the first half of the 1990s? The perspective of the victim has to be taken into consideration. It has been claimed that victims of crime are marginalized in the criminal process. Formulating criminal procedures and penalties with reference to the offender corresponded with prevailing legal theory, since prevention pursued through individual or general deterrence, rehabilitation, or incapacitation was the main goal of the criminal law and sanctions. When evidence on the effects of rehabilitation and deterrence cast doubt on their effectiveness, a vacuum was left behind that could be filled with new goals, including restitution and victim compensation. Cost-benefit considerations also argue for introducing pretrial restitution as an alternative for regular proceedings and penalties.

A range of different models of restitution has emerged. Countries in transition, particularly, have taken up restitution and mediation. Differences are visible in terms of the goals and the concept of restitution, and the location of restitution in criminal procedure. One model of restitution locates it outside the justice system and aspires to replace criminal law and procedure at large. This type of "restorative justice" is built into mediation schemes such as that introduced in Norway in 1991 in the law on conflict resolution commissions (Husabo and Strandbakken 1997). Restitution may also be used as a condition for dismissing a case or withholding a verdict of guilt and punishment (Buchala 1993). Restitution may be combined with probation or may be used as a condition for the suspension of a prison sentence. Restitution is sometimes used as a sole sanction (compensation). Finally, restitution may be located in the correctional system and used as a condition of parole.

G. Confiscation and Forfeiture

Anti-money-laundering and confiscation measures have received increased attention and led to the development of a new track of criminal sanctions. Ambitions to prevent profiting from organized crime, especially drug trafficking, have led in North America and in many European countries to passage of legislation facilitating seizure, freezing, and forfeiture of crime proceeds (Levi 1995; Weigend and Wrobel 1996). Transitional countries have particular need of such laws because their less developed administrative controls on financial and banking systems make them especially vulnerable to money laundering. The Council of Europe's Convention on Money Laundering guidelines, issued by the European Commission, oblige member states to enact legislation forbidding money laundering and to establish systems of control to enhance capacity for identifying, freezing, and confiscating crime money. The 1988 UN Convention against Illicit Traffic in Narcotic Drugs and Psychotropic Substances also emphasizes the need to crack down on illegal profits and to control money laundering. All member states of the European Union have taken action against money laundering and have intensified their efforts to confiscate and forfeit the proceeds of crime (Kilchling 1997).

Money-laundering and confiscation legislation must be analyzed within a broader scope that aims at control of the flow of money, especially in the context of banking transactions. Policing financial transactions is not an end in itself but is linked to a wide range of policy goals, among which forfeiture of illegal gains and deterrence of organized crime play major roles. Illegal profits from drug trafficking have been a core issue (Meyer, Dessecker, and Smettan 1989). Interest in strengthening control over the flow of money and interest in confiscation of crime proceeds arose primarily within the context of drug trafficking and related problems at the beginning of the 1980s (Pachmann 1985) but has been extended to profits generated by other criminal enterprises and organizations (Gilmore 1992). Organized crime has become rhetorically important in the debates on money laundering and criminal profits (in the United States, Germany, the Netherlands, and Italy, organized crime has been prominent in policy debates since the 1980s, while other European countries have not placed organized crime that explicitly on their political and research agendas). Legislative bodies have been very active in adjusting legal frameworks to the needs identified by advocates of confiscation and forfeiture. Confiscation and forfeiture of criminal proceeds now seem to represent the most powerful weapons available in the fight against drug trafficking and other types of organized crime.[12] The traditional responses such as imprisonment and fines alone are said to be ineffective, the better alternative being to follow the money trail (Pieth 1990; Savona 1992). Within one decade, most European countries have amended criminal codes and procedural laws in order to facilitate seizure and forfeiture of ill-gotten gains (Meyer Dessecker, and Smettan 1989).

The international framework built up during the 1980s has to be taken into account (Keyser-Ringnalda 1992; Pieth 1990; Commonwealth Secretariat 1991). The first major international effort was the 1988 UN Convention against Illicit Traffic in Narcotic Drugs and Psychotropic Substances.[13] Article 5, paragraph 1 provides: "Each party shall adopt measures as may be necessary to enable confiscation of proceeds derived from offenses established in accordance with article 3, para. 1, or property the value of which corresponds to that of such proceeds; to ensure the effectiveness of confiscation procedures, and to enable international cooperation in confiscation matters either by giving effect to a confiscation order of a requesting party or by issuing on request its own confiscation orders." Priority is given to mutual assistance in identifying, finding, and seizing suspicious property. Article 3 obliges treaty members to enact legislation making various money-laundering activities criminal offenses, separately addressing transfer and disguise activities, as well as purchase, possession and use of assets. The September 1990 Council of Europe 'Convention on Laundering, Search, Seizure and Confiscation of the Proceeds of Crime' is of particular significance. It is a joint initiative of the Council of Europe and the European Community (EC). It takes the UN Convention of 1988 into consideration, but its scope is much broader, not restricted to drug trafficking (Council of Europe 1991), and it extends to other serious criminal offenses likely to be committed within a context of criminal enterprises. It does not carry the title "European Convention" because other nations that participated in its drafting (e.g., the United States, Canada, Australia) are encouraged to join. The main purpose is to facilitate identification, seizure, and confiscation of proceeds of crimes generating large profits. Parties are obliged to enact legislation authorizing freezing, seizure, and final confiscation. Money laundering must be made a criminal offense and assistance with respect to confiscation must be granted to requesting parties.

Another European treaty that references drug trafficking and confiscation came out of the "Schengen Agreement" (1985) and the "Schengen Convention" (1990), which have been accepted by several EC countries (including Germany). The most important aim concerns harmonization of criminal law in EC countries (especially drug laws and laws on firearms) and establishing a general framework for police cooperation in Europe and laying a groundwork for a system of unified European police. Article 71 of the Schengen Convention obliges parties to make all types of narcotics trafficking criminal offenses. Article 72 expresses the need to establish measures to seize and confiscate drug-trafficking proceeds. The EC directive on money laundering[14] obliges EC countries to enact legislation that complies with guidelines on money laundering and, more important, to establish a system of control over banks, financial institutions, and commerce with identification, documentation, and reporting duties.[15]

The international (and European) community have adopted an approach to illicit drugs that is based upon criminal law and does not take into account alternative drug policies (Albrecht and van Kalmthout 1989). Although most European countries have either signed the international conventions or will do so, skeptical voices are still heard and consensus will not be easy to achieve below the abstract level of the international treaties (Rüter 1993).

In comparative analysis of forfeiture and money-laundering control systems, several models must be included that incorporate considerable differences. In principle, all these models threaten serious infringements on civil rights. Ironically, some of the transitional eastern European countries have eliminated confiscation rules once aimed at deterrence and expropriation from their legal systems.

Among the confiscation models that have received considerable attention are the U.S. federal statutes on forfeiture and the English Drug Trafficking Act 1986 (and the Criminal Justice Act 1993). These were among the first jurisdictions to introduce forfeiture legislation that addresses issues perceived to obstruct attempts to combat drug trafficking through tough confiscation policies. These concern such matters as whether the net profits or the gross receipts or proceeds of crime should be subject to confiscation and what evidence must be provided to link assets with criminal offenses. One central and controversial issue is whether burdens of proof can be reversed, with the property owner being required to prove assets are unrelated to criminal activity. The 1988 UN convention dealt with this gingerly, urging parties to the treaty to consider whether it would be possible to introduce reversal of the burden of proof in case of forfeiture of suspect assets.

The United States was among the first countries to push for efficient confiscation legislation as a tool to attack drug trafficking and organized crime. Confiscation has become a major tool in the War on Drugs. The key statutes are the Comprehensive Drug Abuse Act of 1986 and the Racketeer Influenced Corrupt Organizations (RICO) statute. The U.S. federal law distinguishes between civil and criminal forfeiture. Civil forfeiture is much more important as it is not predicated on filing of criminal charges or on convictions, is characterized by simplified and efficient procedures (e.g., reversed burdens of proof), and generates more than $1 billion a year in seized assets.

The English system formerly was similar to that of standard European legislation in this field. Under the powers of the Criminal Courts Act 1973, any property in the possession of an offender at the time of apprehension that was used or intended to be used in the commission of any offense could be forfeited (Zander 1989). These powers were significantly changed in 1987 when the Drug Trafficking Offenses Act 1986 went into force. Although, initially the 1986 law was restricted to drug-trafficking offenses, it has been extended to other types of crimes. If the court finds that the offender has benefited from drug trafficking, the second decision concerns the value of these proceeds. The 1986 law reduced the burden of proof below the reasonable doubt standard. If the court decides that the offender profited from drug trafficking, it may base the forfeiture decision on assumptions about the origins of the assets.

French drug laws formerly allowed for forfeiture of drugs, the instruments used to produce drugs, and profits linked to a specific drug offense. However, under Law No. 87-1157, which took effect in 1988, criminal courts may order confiscation of the total property of an offender found guilty of drug trafficking (especially import, export, or production of controlled drugs) (Detzkies 1989). This type of general confiscation was not new but had been confined to certain types of political criminal offenses such as treason. Section 629 of the Code of Public Health now provides that in drug-trafficking cases the court may order confiscation of all or part of the property of the offender. The confiscation order is at the court's discretion and represents a "complementary penalty." Because the general confiscation order is punitive, critics argue that general confiscation does not correspond with the personal character of punishment and violates the principle of individual guilt.

Still another model has been introduced in Germany (Dreher and Tröndle 1993). In 1992 the federal Parliament introduced two forfeiture penalties for use in combating organized crime. These measures combine features of the French model and reversed burdens of proof used in England and the United States. The principle of net profits was eliminated and replaced with the principle of crime proceeds. The new sanctions are confiscation of property ("Vermögensstrafe," sec. 43a G.C.C.) and extended forfeiture of crime proceeds ("erweiterter Verfall," sec. 73d G.C.C.). If certain requirements are satisfied, the court may order confiscation of an amount up to the value of all of the offenders' assets and property. The total value of the offender's property may be estimated. No distinction is made between property from illegal sources and from legal sources. The court must also determine a period of substitute imprisonment if the confiscated money cannot be collected. Substitute imprisonment may range from one month to two years. Confiscation is subject to the general principles of sentencing (sec. 46, German Criminal Code), which require that penalties correspond with individual guilt expressed in the offense. Thus, a prison sentence added to confiscation may not exceed the punishment deserved for the proven offense. If confiscation is ordered, repercussions on the length of prison sentences have to be considered. With confiscation, problems embedded in the requirement of ascertaining the criminal origins of proceeds faded away. It is no longer necessary to establish links between certain property and specified criminal offense.

With "extended forfeiture," the court may order forfeiture of assets or property independent of individual guilt, if an offense provides for this measure and if the assumption is justified that the assets or property were proceeds of criminal offenses. Extended forfeiture is mandatory and is based on a link between a criminal offense and assets of the offender. But with extended forfeiture, the burden of proof is reduced. Proof beyond a reasonable doubt is not required with respect to the criminal offense from which it is assumed that the property or assets originated (although it is not yet clear upon what facts the assumption may be based and how convincing such facts must be in order to justify the assumption).

H. Intermediate Punishments

Faced with rising crime rates and increasing numbers of adjudicated and sentenced offenders, virtually all criminal justice systems since the 1970s have searched for effective, affordable noncustodial sanctions other than fines and conditional discharges.

A widespread international trend has emerged to introduce a range of sanctions intermediate between imprisonment and minor penalties such as small summary fines, cautions, and discharges. Sentences such as community service, compensation orders, and probation or suspended prison sentences with such conditions as fines, compensation, or mediation are being considered in many countries. In addition, restrictive community sentences, such as house arrest and various forms of electronic monitoring, are increasingly discussed, have received wide adoption in the United States, and have recently been implemented in some European countries. Some sanctions, such as probation, suspended prison sentences, community service, restitution, compensation orders, and mediation are still linked to the aim of rehabilitation of the offender; electronic monitoring aims to achieve tight supervision at a minimum of costs (Landreville 1999).

There are many arguments for intermediate sanctions. They are said to be a better alternative to imprisonment at least as efficient in preventing individual relapse in crime. Furthermore, a critical feature of prison sentences—separation of the offender from his or her immediate environment and with that the risk of destroying the bonds between offender and society and accelerating movement into a criminal career—is avoided. It can also be argued that public participation in implementation of community sanctions improves the criminal justice system as a whole by increasing public confidence, while facilitating the social integration of offenders.

Implementation of intermediate sanctions is dependent on the availability of probation services or similar bodies that provide particular services, such as counseling, and supervise and enforce conditions. Particular structures of implementation are needed if intermediate sanctions are to demonstrate to the public and to the judiciary that punishment is implemented seriously (Walmsley 1996). Efforts to establish such structures face problems of resources (Walmsley 1996). However, investments should pay off in the long run, as imprisonment meeting human rights standards will always be the more expensive option.

One intermediate sanction that should be ranked high is suspension of prison sentences. Probation is similar. Their origins can be found in rehabilitative ideas, and both are carried out in the community. Suspended sentences have played a major role, falling between fines and imprisonment. However, the suspended sentence has gradually moved away from the rehabilitative goal and has been transformed into a punitive sanction by the requirement that additional conditions be fulfilled or by its being combined with other penalties such as compensation or community service.

Community service is another intermediate sanction that has received considerable interest since the early 1980s. It can easily be incorporated into systems of criminal sanctions because, like day fines, its measurement in time units makes comparisons with imprisonment straightforward. Community service is easily built into sentencing schemes that take time to be served as a point of departure. Community service has been introduced in various European countries, including Holland, England and Wales, Scotland, Norway, and France (Husabo and Strandbakken 1997). Elsewhere, including Germany, community service may not be imposed as the sole criminal penalty in adult criminal law but is available as a condition to a suspended prison sentence or as a substitute for fine-default imprisonment.

Possible constraints on the use of community service are found in international conventions and national constitutions on forced labor outside the prison context. Requiring consent of the offender to a community service order is seen as a way to avoid infringement of this provision. Whether this is an adequate solution to the problem has been doubted, but in practice community service is accepted virtually everywhere when consented to by the offender. Sanction systems in those European countries where community service is a sole sanction set minimum and maximum numbers of hours to be imposed, maximums between 240 and 360 hours being the norm.

New technologies in criminal penalties are exemplified by electronic monitoring. It has been available in the United States since the mid-1980s. European countries have been reluctant to add electronic controls to their systems of sanctions, but recent developments point to growing acceptance (Bishop 1995).

Since 1990, electronic monitoring has come to Europe. England and Wales (Pease 1985), Sweden (Bishop 1995), and The Netherlands (Ministry of Justice 1996) were among the first to explore use of electronic monitoring as a main penalty and as an alternative to pretrial detention. After some experimentation in those countries, electronic monitoring (essentially a form of house arrest or home detention) moved onto the agenda in 1996 and 1997 in virtually all other European countries. Several German states (including Berlin and Hamburg) (Lindenberg 1997), Swiss cantons, Belgium (Ministere de la Justice 1997), and France (la Commission des Lois du Senat 1996) are considering introducing electronic monitoring. In most proposals, the focus is on replacement of short-term imprisonment, most of the arguments in favor being based on problems of prison overcrowding and costs. In Holland, the prison sentence of less than six months is to be replaced.

Electronic monitoring is also used in the control of prisoners released after lengthy periods of imprisonment (combined with other elements, such as participation in training programs) and as an alternative for shorter prison sentences (combining electronic monitoring and community service). In Sweden, prison sentences of up to three months are targeted. There, electronic monitoring is part of intensive probation supervision.

It is doubtful, however, whether electronic monitoring will ever play a significant role in penal dispositions. Doubts arise from the difficulty of identifying suitable groups of offenders. The interest arises from heavy concern for rising costs and the potential simultaneously to demonstrate cost-benefit concerns and modernity, to symbolize politicians' concern for tough crime control and supervision.

What seems of paramount importance is the need for clear and rational conversion rates among the various penalties in a system of criminal sanctions. Intermediate and community-based sanctions must be related to financial and custodial sanctions and made comparable on one or several dimensions. This is one of the weakest points in many recent innovations. It is not self-evident when a prison sentence of, for example, one year can be replaced by a community sanction of 240 hours, when each failure to work hours can be substituted for by imprisonment on default. One year's imprisonment, originally replaced by 240 hours community service, will on default be replaced by a prison sentence of no more than 120 days.

There are two dimensions on which various penalties can be compared. The first is the time an offender is subject to a criminal penalty. The second is the intensity of restrictions. Creating plausible and persuasive systems for translating sanctions from one to another is an important step in the development of intermediate sanctions. These could be elaborated in administrative guidelines.

Research on the implementation of intermediate sanctions suggests that they can successfully replace imprisonment. In most places in Europe, there are clear priorities in their use. Day fines and summary fines are used most widely. Probation and suspended sentences and combinations follow. Compensation and restitution and community service rank low on the list, although some community service and compensation are comparatively widely used in some countries. Most systems use compensation and community service as attachments to suspended prison sentences and probation or at the end of the enforcement process.

Post-adjudication dispositions of criminal cases in every country are being influenced by international developments and by examples of experiences in other countries. This is to be expected. The world is becoming smaller, crime problems confront every government, and communication steadily becomes faster and easier. Although differing cultural attitudes and historical experiences will long sustain significant differences in sentencing practices and sanctions systems, convergences are likely. International conventions on such things as drug trafficking, money laundering, and organized crime provide external pressures for convergence. Information on effective practices elsewhere, exemplified by community service, electronic monitoring, conditional dismissal policies, and day fines, create internal pressures for convergence.

How different national criminal justice systems will be from one another one hundred years from now cannot confidently be predicted. However, the major changes in most countries over the past one or two centuries provide a solid basis for predicting that sentencing practices and sanctioning systems of the twenty-first century will be very different from those we know today.

NOTES

1. See Exner 1931 for the development of sanctions in Germany after 1945, pointing besides leniency and humanity also to the topics of economy and efficiency of criminal penalties.

2. This can be traced back to Durkheim 1977. The assumption has been subject to tests in the 1970s and 1980s. See Blumstein and Cohen 1973; Greenberg 1977; Biles, 1982, Moitra 1987.

3. Suspended sentences made up some 50 percent of all prison sentences in 1975 in Austria, their share (including partly suspended sentences) was up to 70 percent in 1993.

4. For a review of the use of fines in Europe also see Casale 1981. A general overview of sanction systems is provided by van Kalmthout and Tak 1992.

5. The new draft criminal code of Poland contains the day-fine system, see Buchala 1993, p. 275 (the draft provides for a range of 14 to 360 day-fine units).

6. For a review of the use of fines in the United States, see Hillsman, Sichel, and Mahoney 1984; see also Zamist 1986.

7. In the Federal Republic of Germany the proportion of fines amounted to 84 percent in 1991; a similar proportion can be noted for Austria; in France the share of fines was 31 percent in 1991.

8. The administrative fine is fixed by administrative bodies or police but may be subject to a review by ordinary courts upon the offender's request.

9. See, e.g., the Swedish method to establish the size of a day fine. Here, the gross income of the year prior to the conviction is taken and then income tax, living costs, and the costs involved in earning the income are deducted; Thornstedt 1974.

10. Adopted by the Resolution A/Res/40/34, General Assembly 1985; see also Joutsen, 1991, p. 768.

11. See, e.g., Joutsen 1991; Krapac 1995.

12. See Tullis 1991, p. 133, quoting voices assuming that asset-forfeiture policies are the ultimate solution to international drug trafficking.

13. The Federal Republic of Germany has ratified the UN Convention of January 1989.

14. Council Directive of June 10, 1991, on the prevention of the use of the financial system for the purpose of money laundering.

15. See in this respect the German law on tracing proceeds from serious crimes (Geldwäschegesetz) of July 2, 1993 (Bundesratsdrucksache 456/93).

REFERENCES

Albrecht, H. -J. 1980a. "Die Geldstrafe im Prozess strafrechtlicher Sanktionierung." In *Empirische Kriminologie* edited by Forschungsgruppe Kriminologie. Freiburg: Max-Planck-Institut.

————. 1980b. *Strafzumessung und Vollstreckung bei Geldstrafen.* Berlin: Duncker & Humblot.

————. 1981. "Alternativen zur Freiheitsstrafe: Das Beispiel Geldstrafe." *Monatsschrift für Kriminologie und Strafrechtsreform* 64:265–78.

————. 1990. "Kriminologische Aspekte der Wiedergutmachung: Theoretische Grundlagen und empirische Befunde." In *Neue Wege der Wiedergutmachung im Strafrecht,* edited by A. Eser, G. Kaiser, and K. Madlener. Freiburg: Max-Planck-Institut.

————. 1991. "Suchtgiftgesetzgebung im internationalen Vergleich." In *Forensia Jahrbuch* 2. Berlin: Springer.

————. 1995. "Drug Policies and National Plans to Combat Drug Trafficking and Drug Abuse: A Comparative Analysis of Policies of Co-ordination and Co-Operation." In *Policies and Strategies to Combat Drugs in Europe,* edited by G. Estievenart. Amsterdam: Dordrecht Nijhoff.

Albrecht, H. -J., and A. van Kalmthout, eds. 1989. *Drug Policies in Western Europe.* Freiburg: Max-Planck-Institut.

Albrecht, H. -J., and W. Schädler, eds. 1987. *Community Service, Travail d' Intérêt General, Dienstverlening, Gemeinnützige Arbeit: A New Option in Punishing Offenders in Europe.* Freiburg: Max-Planck-Institut.

————. 1988. "Die gemeinnützige Arbeit auf dem Wege zu einer eigenständigen Sanktion?" *Zeitschrift für Rechtspolitik* 21:278–83.

Amnesty International. 1979. *Die Todesstrafe.* Hamburg: Amnesty International.

Arnholm, M., ed. 1997. *The System of Administrative and Penal Sanctions in Sweden.* Uppsala: Swedish Society for European Criminal Law.

Ashworth, A. 1993. "Some Doubts about Restorative Justice." *Criminal Law Forum* 4:277–99.

Baumann, J., et al. 1969. *Alternativentwurf eines Strafgesetzbuches.* 2d edition. Tübingen: Beck.

Bavcon, L. 1993. "Stand und Tendenzen der Strafrechtsreform in Slowenien." In *Von totalitärem zu rechtsstaatlichem Strafrecht: Kriminalpolitische Reformtendenzen im Strafrecht osteuropäischer Länder,* edited by A. Eser, G. Kaiser, and E. Weigend, E. Freiburg: Max-Planck-Institut.

Bernat de Celis, J. 1992. *Fallait-il créer un délit d'usage illicite de stupéfiant?* Paris: Centre de Recherches Sociologiques sur le Droit et les Inst. Pénales.

Bianchi, H., and R. van Swaaningen, eds. 1986. *Abolitionism: Towards a Non-Repressive Approach to Crime.* Amsterdam: Free University Press.

Biles, D. 1982. "Crime and Imprisonment: An Australian Time Series Analysis." *Australian and New Zealand Journal of Criminology* 15:133–53

Bishop, N. 1995. "Le Controle intensif par surveillance electronique: Un Substitut suedois à l'emprisonnement." *Bulletin d' information penologique* 19/20: 8–9.

Blumstein, A., and J. Cohen. 1973. "A Theory of the Stability of Punishment." *Journal of Criminal Law and Criminology* 64:198–207.

Braithwaite, J. 1994. "A Sociology of Modelling and the Politics of Empowerment." *British Journal of Sociology* 45:445–79.

Buchala, K. 1993. "Arten und Reform punitiver und nicht-punitiver Sanktionen im polnischen Strafrecht." In *Von totalitärem zu rechtsstaatlichem Strafrecht: Kriminalpolitische Reformtendenzen im Strafrecht osteuropäischer Länder,* edited by A. Eser, G. Kaiser, and E. Weigend. Freiburg: Max-Planck-Institut.

Casale, S. S. C. 1981. *Fines in Europe: A Study of the Use of Fines in Selected European Countries with Empirical Research on the Problems of Fine Enforcement.* London: Vera Institute of Justice.

Commission des Lois du Sénat. 1996. *Propositions de loi de Mr. Guy Cabenel*. Report no. 3. Paris: Sénat.

Commonwealth Secretariat. 1991. *Basic Documents on International Efforts to Combat Money Laundering*. Cambridge: Grotius.

Council of Europe. 1991. *Explanatory Report on the Convention on Laundering, Search, Seizure, and Confiscation of the Proceeds from Crime*. Strasbourg: Council of Europe.

———. 1996. *Prison Information Bulletin, 1994–1995*. Strasbourg: Council of Europe.

Detzkies, J. 1989. "Landesbericht Frankreich." In *Gewinnabschöpfung bei Betäubungsmitteldelikten*, edited by J. Meyer, A. Dessecker, and J. R. Smettan. Wiesbaden: Bundeskriminalamt Wiesbaden.

Dreher, E., and H. Tröndle. 1993. *Strafgesetzbuch. Kommentar*. 46th ed. Munich: Beck.

Durkheim, E. 1977. *Über die Teilung der sozialen Arbeit*. Frankfurt: Suhrkamp.

Elias, N. 1976. *Über den Prozess der Zivilisation*. 2 vols. Frankfurt: Suhrkamp.

Eser, A. 1993. "Gesellschaftsgerichte." In *Kleines Kriminologisches Wörterbuch*, 3d ed., edited by G. Kaiser, H.-J. Kerner, F. Sack, and H. Schellhoss. Heidelberg: C. F. Müller Juristischer Verlag.

Eser, A. and B. Huber, eds. 1985. *Strafrechtsentwicklung in Europa: Landesberichte 1982/1984 über Gesetzgebung, Rechtsprechung und Literatur*. Freiburg: Max-Planck-Institut.

———. 1988. *Strafrechtsentwicklung in Europa: Landesberichte 1984/1986 über Gesetzgebung, Rechtsprechung und Literatur*. Freiburg: Max-Planck-Institut.

———. 1990. *Strafrechtsentwicklung in Europa: Landesberichte 1986/1988 über Gesetzgebung, Rechtsprechung und Literatur*. Freiburg: Max-Planck-Institut.

———. 1994. *Strafrechtsentwicklung in Europa: Landesberichte 1989/1992 über Gesetzgebung, Rechtsprechung und Literatur*. Freiburg: Max-Planck-Institut.

———. 1997. *Strafrechtsentwicklung in Europa: Landesberichte 1993/1996 über Gesetzgebung, Rechtsprechung und Literatur*. Freiburg: Max-Planck-Institut.

European Committee on Crime Problems. 1994. *Results of the Survey into the Application of the European Prison Rules in the Member States of the Council of Europe*. Strasbourg: Council of Europe.

Evans, M., and R. Morgan. 1992. "The European Convention for the Prevention of Torture: Operational Practice." *The International and Comparative Law Quarterly* 41:590–614.

Exner, F. 1931. *Studien über die Strafzumessungspraxis der deutschen Gerichte*. Leipzig: E. Wiegandt Verlagsbuchhandlung.

Farkas, A. 1993. "Stand und Tendenzen der Strafrechtsreform in Ungarn." In *Von totalitärem zu rechtsstaatlichem Strafrecht: Kriminalpolitische Reformtendenzen im Strafrecht osteuropäischer Länder*, edited by A. Eser, G. Kaiser, and E. Weigend. Freiburg: Max-Planck-Institut.

Foucault, M. 1977. *Überwachen und Strafen*. Frankfurt: Suhrkamp.

Garland, D. 1996. "The Limits of the Sovereign State: Strategies of Crime Control in Contemporary Society." *British Journal of Criminology* 36:445–71.

Gibson, B. 1990. *Unit Fines*. Winchester: Waterside Press.

Gilmore, W. C. 1992. "International Efforts to Combat Money Laundering." *Commonwealth Law Bulletin* 18:1129–42.

Grebing, G. 1978. "Landesbericht Bundesrepublik Deutschland." In *Die Geldstrafe im deutschen und ausländischen Recht*, edited by H.-H. Jescheck and G. Grebing. Baden-Baden: Nomos.

———. 1982. "The Fine in Comparative Law: A Survey of Twenty-one Countries." Institute of Criminology Occasional Papers no. 9. Cambridge: Institute of Criminology.

Greenberg, D. 1977. "The Dynamics of Oscillatory Punishment Processes." *Journal of Criminal Law and Criminology* 68:643–51.

Gruev, L. 1993. "Arten und Reform punitiver und nicht-punitiver Sanktionen in Bulgarien." In *Von totalitärem zu rechtsstaatlichem Strafrecht: Kriminalpolitische Reformtendenzen im Strafrecht osteuropäischer Länder*, edited by A. Eser, G. Kaiser, and E. Weigend. Freiburg: Max-Planck-Institut.

Heine, G. 1995. *Die strafrechtliche Verantwortlichkeit von Unternehmen: Von individuellem Fehlverhalten zu kollektiven Fehlentwicklungen, insbesondere bei Grossrisiken.* Baden-Baden: Nomos.

Heine, G., and B. Spalinger. 1988. "Landesbericht Schweiz." In *Strafrechtsentwicklung in Europa*, vol. 2, edited by A. Eser, and B. Huber. Freiburg: Max-Planck-Institut.

Heinz, W. 1981. "Entwicklung, Stand und Struktur der Strafzumessungspraxis: Eine Übersicht über die nach allgemeinem Straf-recht verhängten Hauptstrafen von 1882 bis 1979." *Monatsschrift für Kriminologie und Strafrechtsreform* 64:148–73.

Hillsman, S. T., and J. A. Greene. 1987. *Improving the Use and Administration of Criminal Fines: A Report of the Richmond County Criminal Court Day-Fine Planning Project.* New York: Vera Institute of Justice.

Hillsman, S. T., J. L. Sichel, and B. Mahoney. 1984. *Fines in Sentencing: A Study of the Use of Fines as a Criminal Sanction.* Washington, D.C.: National Institute of Justice.

Hood, R. 1996. *The Death Penalty: A World-Wide Perspective.* New York: Oxford University Press.

———. 1998. "Capital Punishment." In *The Handbook of Crime and Punishment*, edited by Michael Tonry. New York: Oxford University Press.

Hünerfeld, P. 1983. "Neues Strafrecht in Portugal." *Juristenzeitung* 7:673–75.

Husabo, E. J., and A. Strandbakken. 1997. In *Strafrechtsentwicklung in Europa*, edited by A. Eser and B. Huber. Freiburg: Max-Planck-Institute.

Janssen, H. 1993. *Die Praxis der Geldstrafenvollstreckung.* Frankfurt: Peter Lang.

Jescheck, H.-H., and G. Grebing, eds. 1978. *Die Geldstrafe im deutschen und ausländischen Recht.* Baden-Baden: Nomos.

Joutsen, M. 1991. "Changing Victim Policy: International Dimensions." In *Victims and Criminal Justice*, vol. 52/2, edited by G. Kaiser, H. Kury, and H.-J. Albrecht. Freiburg: Max-Planck Institute.

Jung, H. 1993. "Private Verbrechenskontrolle." In *Kleines Kriminologisches Wörterbuch*, 3d ed., edited by G. Kaiser. Heidelberg: Müller.

Kaiser, G. 1988. *Kriminologie. Ein Lehrbuch.* 2d ed. Heidelberg: Müller.

———. 1991. "Die Europäische Antifolterkonvention als Bestandteil internationalen Strafverfahrens- und Strafvollzugsrechts: Vorgeschichte, Ausgangspunkte und Bedeutung." *Schweizerische Zeitschrift für Strafrecht* 108:213–31.

Kaminski, G. 1978. "Menschenrechte in China." *Ludwig Boltzmann Institut für China- und Südostasienforschung* 8:61–63.

Karger, T., and P. Sutterer, P. 1988. "Cohort Study on the Development of Police-Recorded Criminality and Criminal Sanctioning." Part 2, "On Longitudinal Research and First Results from the Freiburg Cohort Study." In *Crime and Criminal Justice*, edited by G. Kaiser and I. Geissler. Freiburg: Max-Planck Institute.

Katholnigg, O. 1990. "Ist die Entkriminalisierung von Betäubungsmittelkonsumenten mit scharfen Massnahmen zur Eindämmung der Betäubungsmittelnachfrage vereinbar?" *Goldammers'Archiv für Strafrecht* 137:193–200.

Keske, M. 1979. "Der Anteil der Bestraften in der Bevölkerung." *Monatsschrift für Kriminologie und Strafrechtsreform* 62:257–72.

Keyser-Ringnalda, F. 1992. "European Integration with regard to the Confiscation of the Proceeds of Crime. *European Law Review* 17:499–515.

Kilchling, M. 1997. "Comparative Perspectives on Forfeiture Legislation in Europe and the United States." *European Journal of Crime, Criminal Law, and Criminal Justice* 5: 342–61.

King, R. D. 1994. "Russian Prisons after Perestroika." *British Journal of Criminology* 34:62–82.

Kinkade, P. T., and M. C. Leone. 1992. "Issues and Answers: Prison Administrators' Responses to Controversies Surrounding Privatization." *The Prison Journal* 72:57–68.

Kinzig, J. 1997. "Preventive Measures for Dangerous Recidivists." *European Journal of Crime, Criminal Law, and Criminal Justice* 5:27–57.

Krapac, D. 1995. "The Position of the Victim in Criminal Justice: A Restrained Central and Eastern European Perspective on the Victim-Offender Mediation." *European Journal of Crime, Criminal Law, and Criminal Justice* 3:230–40.

Krüger, J. 1994. "Sozialstrukturelle Modernisierung: Stabilisierung oder Destruierung des Wohlfahrtsstaats." *Soziale Probleme* 5:5–30.

Kuhn, A. 1993. "Le Sursis partiel: Un Moyen de lutter contre les longues peines?" *Schweizerische Zeitschrift für Strafrecht* 113:173–96.

Landreville, P. 1999. "La Surveillance électronique des délinquants: Un Marché en expansion." *Déviance et Société* 23:105–21.

Legros, R. 1985. *Avant-Projet de Code Penal.* Brussels: Moniteur Belge.

Lenz, K.-F., and R. Heuser. 1995. *Strafrechtsentwicklung in Japan und der Volksrepublik China.* Freiburg: Max-Planck Institut.

Levai, M. 1990. "Drogenprobleme und Drogenkriminalität in den 70er und 80er Jahren." *Monatsschrift für Kriminologie und Strafrechtsreform* 73:90–104.

Levi, M. 1995. "Incriminating Disclosures: An Evaluation of Money Laundering Regulation in England and Wales." *European Journal of Crime, Criminal Law, and Criminal Justice* 3:202–17.

Lilly, J. R., and P. Knepper. 1992. "An International Perspective on the Privatisation of Corrections." *Howard Journal* 31:174–91.

Lindenberg, M. 1997. *Ware Strafe, elektronische Überwachung und die Kommerzialisierung strafrechtlicher Kontrolle.* Munich: AG-SPAK Bucher.

MacKenzie, D. L. 1997. "Criminal Justice and Crime Prevention." In *Preventing Crime: What Works, What Doesn't, What's Promising—A Report to the United States Congress,* edited by L. W. Sherman. Washington, D.C.: U.S. Department of Justice.

Marvell, T. B., and C. E. Moody. 1997. "Determinate Sentencing and Abolishing Parole: The Long-Term Impacts on Prisons and Crime." *Criminology* 35:107–28.

McDonald, D. C. 1994. "Public Imprisonment by Private Means: The Re-Emergence of Private Prisons and Jails in the United States, the United Kingdom, and Australia." *British Journal of Criminology* 34:29–48.

————, ed. 1992. *Day Fines in American Courts: The Staten Island and Milwaukee Experiments.* Washington, D.C.: National Institute of Justice.

Meyer, J., A. Dessecker, and J. R. Smettan, eds. 1989. *Gewinnabschöpfung bei Betäubungsmitteldelikten: Eine rechtsvergleichende und kriminologische Untersuchung.* Wiesbaden: BKA-Forschungsreihe.

Ministère de la Justice. 1993. "Circulaire generale presentant les dispositions du nouveau code de procédure penal." *Journal Officiel de la Republique Française* 125:1687.

Ministère de la Justice. 1997. "Elektronisch Toezicht." Circulaire Mo 1680/ix, November 27, 1997. Brussels.

Ministry of Justice. 1996. *Electronic Monitoring.* The Hague: National Agency of Correctional Institutions.

Moitra, S. 1987. *Crimes and Punishments.* Freiburg: Max-Planck-Institut.

Morgan, R. 1993. "Convention Improves European Prisons." *Overcrowded Times* 4:1, 5–7.

Morgan, R., and M. Evans. 1994. "Inspecting Prisons: The View from Strasbourg." *British Journal of Criminology* 34:141–59.

Moxon, D. 1983. *Fine Default: Unemployment and the Use of Imprisonment.* Research Bulletin No. 16, Home Office Research and Planning Unit. London: Home Office.

————. 1991. *Developments in Fines and Fine Enforcement.* Research Bulletin, Home Office Research and Planning Unit. London: Home Office.

————. 1997. "England Abandons Unit Fines." In *Sentencing Reform in Overcrowded Times,* edited by M. Tonry and K. Hatlestad. New York: Oxford University Press.

Mullen, J., K. Chabotar, and D. Cartow, D. 1985. *The Privatization of Corrections.* Washington, D.C.: National Institute of Justice.

Musil, J., H. Valkova, and D. Cisarova. 1994. "Tschecheslowakei." In *Strafrechtsentwicklung in Europa: Landesberichte 1989/1992 über Gesetzgebung, Rechtsprechung und Literatur,* edited by A. Eser and B. Huber. Freiburg: Max-Planck Institut.

Nagy, F. 1993. "Arten und Reform punitiver und nicht-punitiver Sanktionen in Ungarn." In *Von Totalitärem zu rechtsstaatlichem Strafrecht: Kriminalpolitische Reformtendenzen im Strafrecht osteuropäischer Länder,* edited by A. Eser, G. Kaiser, and E. Weigend. Freiburg: Max-Planck-Institut.

Office of National Drug Control Policy. 1989. *Review of the National Drug Control Strategy.* Washington, D.C.: Office of National Drug Control Policy.

Pachmann, C. 1985. "Gigantisches illegales und internationales Finanznetz." *Kriminalistik* 85: 182–89.

Pavarini, M. 1994. "The New Penology and Politics in Crisis: The Italian Case." *British Journal of Criminology* 34:49–61.

Pease, Ken. 1985. "Community Service Orders." In *Crime and Justice: A Review of Research,* vol. 6, edited by Michael Tonry and Norval Morris. Chicago: University of Chicago Press.

Pieth, M. 1990. "Gewinnabschöpfung bei Betäubungsmitteldelikten." *Strafverteidiger* 558–62.

Popitz, H. 1968. *Über die Präventivwirkung des Nichtwissens.* Tübingen: Mohr, Dunkelziffer.

Popper, K. R. 1984. *Auf der Suche nach einer besseren Welt.* Munich: Piper.

Rusche, G., and O. Kirchheimer. 1973. *Strafvollzug und Sozialstruktur.* Frankfurt: Europäische Verlagsanstat.

Rüter, C. F. 1993. Harmonie trotz Dissonanz: Gedanken zur Erhaltung eines funktionsfähigen Strafrechts im grenzenlosen Europa. *Zeitschrift für die Gesamte Strafrechtswissenschaft* 105:30–47.

Savona, E. U. 1992. "The Organized Crime/Drug Connection: National and International Perspectives." In *Drugs, Law, and the State,* edited by H. H. Traver and M. S. Gaylord. Hong Kong: Hong Kong University Press.

Schabas, W. A., ed. 1997. *The International Sourcebook on Capital Punishment.* Boston: Northeastern University Press.

Schittenhelm, U. 1993. "Diskussionsbericht." In *Von totalitärem zu rechtsstaatlichem Strafrecht. Kriminalpolitische Reformtendenzen im Strafrecht osteuropäischer Länder,* edited by A. Eser, G. Kaiser, and E. Weigend. Freiburg: Max-Planck-Institut.

———. 1994. "Russland." In *Strafrechtsentwicklung in Europa: Landesberichte 1989/1992 über Gesetzgebung Rechtsprechung und Literatur*, edited by A. Eser and B. Huber. Freiburg: Max-Plank-Institut.

Schultz, H. 1987. *Bericht und Vorentwurf zur Revision des Allgemeinen Teils des Schweizerischen Strafgesetzbuchs*. Bern: Verlag Stämpfli and Cie AG.

Shutong, Yu. 1987. "Le Système de la Peine Capitale Dans le Droit Pénal Chinois." *Revue International de Droit Pénal* 58:689–98.

Snider, L. 1998. "Towards Safer Societies: Punishment, Masculinities and Violence against Women." *British Journal of Criminology* 38:1–39.

Spaniol, M. 1985. "Landesbericht Frankreich." In *Strafrechtsentwicklung in Europa. Landesberichte 1982/1984 über Gesetzgebung, Rechtsprechung und Literatur*, edited by A. Eser and B. Huber. Freiburg: Max-Planck Institut.

Statistisches Bundesamt. Various years. *Rechtspflege: Strafverfolgung*, various years. Stuttgart: Kohlhammer/Metzler Poeschel.

Thornstedt, H. 1974. "Skandinavische Erfahrungen mit dem Tagesbussensystem." *Zeitschrift für die Gesamte Strafrechtswissenschaft* 86:595–613.

Tiedemann, K. 1997. "Die Europäisierung des Strafrechts." In *Die Europäisierung der mitgliedstaatlichen Rechtsordnungen in der Europäischen Union*, edited by K. F. Kreuzer, D. H. Scheving, and U. Sieber. Baden-Baden: Nomos.

Tobolska-Rydz, H. 1986 "Problems of Drug Abuse and Preventive Measures in Poland." *Bulletin on Narcotics* 38:99–104.

Tubex, H., and S. Snacken. 1995. "L'Évolution des longues peines: Aperçu international et analyse des causes." *Déviance et Société* 19:103–26.

Tullis, L. 1991. *Handbook of Research on the Illicit Drug Trade: Socioeconomic and Political Consequences*. New York: Greenwood Press.

van Dijk, J. J. M. 1989. "Strafsanktionen und Zivilisationsprozess." *Monatsschrift für Kriminologie und Strafrechtsreform* 72:437–50.

van Kalmthout, A., and P. Tak. 1992. *Sanctions Systems in the Member States of the Council of Europe: Deprivation of Liberty, Community Service, and Other Substitutes*. Boston: Kluwer.

Villmow, B., and E. Stephan. 1983. *Jugendkriminalität in einer Gemeinde*. Freiburg: Max-Planck-Institut.

Waling, C., and A. van Kalmthout. 1988. "Landesbericht Niederlande." In *Strafrechtsentwicklung in Europa: Landesberichte 1984/1986 über Gesetzgebung, Rechtsprechung und Literatur* edited by A. Eser and B. Huber. Freiburg: Max-Planck-Institut.

Walmsley, R. 1996. *Prison Systems in Central and Eastern Europe: Progress, Problems, and the International Standards*. Helsinki: European Institute for Crime Prevention and Control.

Wasik, M., and R. D. Taylor. 1991. *Criminal Justice Act 1991*. London: Blackstone.

Weigend, E. 1988. "Landesbericht Polen." In *Strafrechtsentwicklung in Europa: Landesberichte 1984/1986 über Gesetzgebung, Rechtsprechung und Literatur:* edited by A. Eser and B. Huber. Freiburg: Max-Planck-Institut.

Weigend, E., and W. Wrobel. 1996. "Geldwäsche im polnischen Strafrecht." *Zeitschrift für die Gesamte Strafrechtswissenschaft* 108:416–28.

Wilkitzki, P. 1995. "On Judicial Mutual Assistance in Criminal Matters between the States of Western and Eastern Europe." *European Journal of Crime Policy and Research* 3:91–98.

Wood, P. B. 1997. "Mississippi's Ongoing Experience with Truth-in-Sentencing." *Association for Correctional Research and Information Management Newsletter* 15:1,6.

Xin-Liang, Chen. 1998. "The Death Penalty." In *The United Nations' Standards and China's Legal System of Criminal Justice,* edited by G. Chen and D. Purifangting. Peking: Talü Chubanshe.

Xuan, Gao Ming. 1987. "A Brief Dissertation on the Death Penalty in the Criminal Law of the People's Republic of China." *Revue International de Droit Pénal* 58:399–405.

Zamist, I. 1986. *Fines in Sentencing: An Empirical Study of Fine Use, Collection, and Enforcement in New York City Courts.* New York: VERA Institute of Justice.

Zander, M. 1989. *Confiscation and Forfeiture Law: English and American Comparisons.* London: The Police Foundation.

Zimmermann, A. 1992. "Erste praktische Erfahrungen mit dem Europäischen Überein-kommen zur Verhütung von Folter." *Neue Zeitschrift für Strafrecht* 12:318–320.

Zimring, F. E., and G. Hawkins. 1994. "The Growth of Imprisonment in California." *British Journal of Criminology* 34:83–96.

International Standards for Sentencing and Punishment

Decisions about sentencing and punishment of criminal offenders and issues of substantive criminal law more generally, have traditionally been within the sovereignty of each nation state. This is not true anymore. International standards for criminal justice are common and cover areas that have no international dimension.

International standards or limits for domestic criminal justice systems are often located in general human rights instruments and discussed under "international human rights law," which regulates states' responsibility toward their own citizens (Ratner 1998). "International criminal law" is usually defined to include treaty-based cooperation in police investigation and transfer of offenders, procedures, and prisoners; treaty-based regulation of transnational or transborder crime; and control and prosecution of war crimes, genocide, and crimes against humanity (Dugard and van den Wyngaert 1996).

Several United Nations conventions and all regional human rights conventions include articles about core areas of criminal law: criminal investigation, procedural requirements for charges and criminal trials, limits on criminalization and punishment, and standards for implementation of punishments. Aspects of arrest, other police powers, pretrial detention, fair trial or due process requirements, prohibited forms of punishments, and prison conditions, for example, are regulated internationally, although forms of regulation, control measures, enforcement systems, and their efficiency vary. The main human rights instruments that include criminal justice standards are the United Nations' Universal Declaration of Human Rights, the International Covenant on Civil and Political Rights (UN), the European Convention for the Protection of Human Rights and Fundamental Freedoms (Council of Europe), the American Convention on Human Rights (Organization of American States), the African Charter on Human and Peoples' Rights (Organization of African Unity), the Convention against Torture and Other Cruel, Inhuman or Degrading Treatment or Punishment (UN) and the European Convention for the Prevention of Torture and Inhuman or Degrading Treatment or Punishment (Council of Europe).

Instruments that focus on a specific topic also impose international standards for sentencing and criminal laws. The United Nations and regional bodies, the Council of Europe, for example, have passed standard minimum rules or guidelines for use of the death penalty, treatment of prisoners, noncustodial community sanctions, sentencing laws and structures, management of criminal justice, administration of juvenile justice, protection for detained juveniles, and prevention of juvenile delinquency (Clark 1994). However, these instruments are not binding treaties and lack enforcement systems (Clark 1995).

Provisions of these two types of international instruments that set standards or limits for national sentencing laws and punishments, are discussed in this chapter. Some matters, however, are excluded. First, the essay does not examine international fair trial standards, which determine procedural limits for investigation and prosecution of crimes. There already exists a sizable literature about international fair trial requirements and they are probably the most researched area of the European Convention on Human Rights (e.g., Ashworth 1999; van Dijk and van Hoof 1998; Weissbrodt and Wolfrum 1997). Second, international efforts to prevent torture or other inhuman or degrading treatment, including such topics as conditions in pretrial custody and prisons as well as prisoners' rights, are discussed separately in this volume, in chapter 10. Third, the focus tends to be on the European system, although reference is made to the relevant UN conventions and U.S. practices. This is because standards related to sentencing or substantive criminal law are almost identical in different human rights instruments, but protective mechanisms and their effectiveness vary significantly. There is little doubt that the European Convention on Human Rights has the most effective protections system as well as the most developed caselaw.

The European Court of Human Rights has examined all core issues of sentencing and punishments: what must be criminalized by national laws, what may not be criminalized, what forms of punishments are prohibited, and how much to punish. For example, it has ruled that certain actions should be criminalized, or at least prohibited effectively. Any corporal punishment of children that leaves visible bruises, swelling, or marks is unacceptable and excessive punishment should constitute a criminal offense and be charged. Marital rape should be defined as a criminal offense and criminal laws should not exclude protection for any groups of people. The Court has ruled that mandatory life imprisonment is allowed for adult offenders, but not for juvenile offenders. If the life sentence is discretionary, there should be a regular review of possible release. Sentences that are clearly disproportionate to the offense might constitute inhuman or degrading punishment under the European Convention. The Court of Justice, the judicial body of the European Union, has used proportionality as a guiding principle and held that the punishment in a particular case must be proportionate to the severity of the offense and to punishments imposed for comparable crimes in the same country and other member states.

The idea that imprisonment should be used only as the last resort is expressed in several international recommendations. There is global pressure to abolish capital punishment and consensus that it cannot be imposed for juvenile, pregnant, or insane offenders or for other than the most serious crimes. Member states of the Council of Europe refuse to extradite offenders unless the receiving state guarantees that the death penalty will not be imposed.

These are only examples of the issues that are discussed in this chapter. The first section briefly introduces the main human rights instruments, the rights protected by them, and their enforcement mechanisms. Before moving to the substantive regulation of sentencing, the second section sketches the system of protection under the European Convention on Human Rights. Then, the third section focuses on the limits and standards for sentencing laws and punishments, and the last section presents conclusions.

I. Sentencing and Punishments in the Main International Human Rights Documents

International human rights instruments vary by levels of regulation, binding effects, and systems of enforcement. United Nations documents are global and open for ratification by all nations. Regional documents affect countries in certain regions. Declarations, recommendations, resolutions, and such are merely suggestions or guidelines without binding obligations or enforcement systems. They are passed by international organizations, for example, the General Assembly of the United Nations or the Committee of Ministers of the Council of Europe, and require no special acknowledgment by the member states of the organization. Conventions, covenants, and treaties require ratification by individual states and are, at least in principle, binding after they have entered into force in the states, although the extent to which this is true depends on the law of the particular country. They often establish special mechanisms and bodies to control states' compliance, although the forms and powers of enforcement vary. There are basically two kinds of enforcement bodies. A commission or committee may accept reports or claims but does not have final, binding jurisdiction over member states. A court functions as a judicial body, accepts applications of alleged violations, holds oral hearings, and gives final decisions. The control mechanisms can be triggered in a variety of ways: country self-reporting to a committee; complaints by other states, and sometimes also by individuals, to a committee; investigative country visits by a committee; and applications to a court by other states, and sometimes also by individuals.

A. United Nations Human Rights Instruments

The Universal Declaration of Human Rights, adopted by the General Assembly of the United Nations in 1948, was the first global instrument to define fundamental human rights and to promote their protection. Although not intended to establish binding international norms, it has served as a model and inspiration for other United Nations and regional instruments, and its influence cannot be overestimated. For example, the European Convention on Human Rights, drafted two years later, relies heavily on the Universal Declaration.

The Universal Declaration established the foundation for international standards for criminal justice and sentencing, and norms expressed more recently in other international conventions have changed little in content. The declaration defines the five basic rights that are included in later instruments: freedom from torture or cruel, inhuman, or degrading treatment or punishment; freedom from arbitrary arrest or detention; the right to fair and public trial; the right to be presumed innocent in criminal charges; and prohibition of retroactive criminal law (see Appendix 9.A). However, since the declaration does not impose binding obligations on states and lacks any control mechanism, there has been little opportunity to develop the content of the rights under the Declaration. Without a special body or referral or claims procedures, there is no case law or authoritative interpretation that can give more concrete meaning to the abstract rights.

The International Covenant on Civil and Political Rights (Civil Rights Covenant) was adopted by the United Nations General Assembly in 1966 and entered into force in 1976 following the thirty-fifth ratification by a member state, but its drafting began as early as 1947. Compared to the Universal Declaration, the covenant addresses procedural rights related to arrest, pretrial detention, and criminal trial in much more detail. In contrast, articles related to substantive criminal law are almost identical to those in the declaration, with two exceptions. First, the Civil Rights Covenant includes absolute limits on the death penalty: it may be imposed only for the most serious crimes, it may not be imposed for crimes committed by children under 18 years, and it may not be carried out on pregnant women (Article 6). Second, the covenant requires that changes in criminal law (between the commitment of crime and sentencing) that benefit the defendant must be applied retroactively (Article 15; see Appendix 9.A).

The covenant assigned responsibility for state compliance to the Human Rights Committee. States are obliged to give periodic reports about their efforts to enhance protection and recognition of the rights guaranteed; the committee expresses its opinion about state compliance in "concluding observations" and may also issue "general comments" about the covenant's implementation. An optional protocol established an individual right to petition to the committee and to claim state violations of protected rights. The committee gives its opinion on alleged violations in "views." Although the committee has been able to create something akin to a specialized jurisprudence, its comments have received little attention outside a small circle of human rights advocates and are seldom subject to research. This is understandable since the committee jurisprudence can be characterized as soft or weak law with no means of enforcement. The case of the United States serves as an example of this.

When the United States ratified the Civil Rights Covenant in 1992, it made several reservations that undermined the essence of the Covenant. The most significant was the declaration that the first twenty-seven articles are not self-executing, which means that they require implementation by congressional legislation. Other reservations mean that the United States committed to the covenant only as far as it is in compliance with U.S. criminal law. For example, the United States reserved the right to impose capital punishment on any person and to treat juveniles as adults; declared itself bound to the prohibition of cruel, inhuman or degrading treatment or punishment only to the extent that these terms are inter-preted the same as the prohibition of cruel or unusual punishment in the Eight Amendment to the U.S. Constitution; and declined to accept application of crim-inal law retroactively for the benefit of the defendant. Eleven European countries objected to the U.S. reservations and the Human Rights Committee found that most were incompatible with the purpose of the covenant (e.g., Heffernan 1996; Newman and Weissbrodt 1996). However, the international criticism has had no effect on the United States and the Human Rights Committee has no enforcement power. The United States has not ratified the optional protocol and thus does not acknowledge the individual right to initiate claims procedure at the Human Rights Committee, which is a further indication of U.S. reluctance to accept international control in the areas of human rights or criminal law.

B. Regional Human Rights Instruments

The European Convention for the Protection of Human Rights and Fundamental Freedoms (1950) was the first regional human rights instrument. When it entered into force in 1953, the more modern human rights conceptions concerning civil, social, economical, and cultural rights had not yet been fully developed. As a result, the European Convention has a short and simple list of protected rights that falls short in comparison with other more recent instruments. The European Convention was also the first to establish a system of enforcement. It created two independent bodies, the European Commission of Human Rights and the Euro-pean Court of Human Rights, for this purpose. Unlike the level of substantive protection, the level of procedural protection is still after forty-five years one of the most effective of all human rights instruments. Articles related to punishment and substantive criminal law are nearly identical with the Universal Declaration of Human Rights (see Appendix 9.A), but fair trial and other procedural rights are regulated in much more detail. This difference is evident in other human rights instruments as well: rights concerning arrest, pretrial detention, and fair trial tend to be much more clearly and concretely defined than those concerning forms of punishments, criteria for proportionate sentences, or prohibited scope of crimin-alizations. The difference is reflected also in academic writing, which tends to concentrate on rights in criminal procedure (e.g., Ovey 1998). More important, procedural rights are typically defined positively as a right to something, for ex-ample, a right to trial within reasonable time, a right to be informed promptly about the nature and cause of charges, and a right to have adequate time and facilities for preparation of defense. However, standards for criminal sentencing and punishments are typically defined negatively as freedom from something, for example, a right not to be subject to torture or inhuman or degrading treatment or punishment. Thus, all human rights instruments lack positive criteria or defi-nitions for humane and proportionate punishments; they merely prohibit or limit punishments that can be considered inhuman or degrading.

Regional systems for protection of human rights operate also in America and Africa. The American Convention on Human Rights (1969) entered into force in 1978 and the African Charter on Human and Peoples' Rights (1981) in 1986. The

United States has signed but not ratified the American Convention. The American Convention is implemented by the Inter-American Commission and Court of Human Rights and thus resembles the European system (Mower 1991). The African Convention is based on state-initiated reports and claims presented to the African Commission on Human and Peoples' Rights (see, for example, Ankumah 1996; Bassiouni and Motala 1995).

There are striking differences, however, in the quantity and quality of decisions in the three regional systems. The European Court and Commission have produced significant, detailed, and often well-reasoned case law similar to jurisprudence of national constitutional or supreme courts. The focus has been on analysis and development of the content and meaning of the protected rights. In contrast to the mostly stable political and social milieu of western Europe, the American and African systems have operated in climates in which principles of legality and rule of law have regularly been ignored and political power has often been maintained by gross and widespread human rights violations. The Inter-American and African bodies have been preoccupied with matters of fact and evidence in situations where there is no question about violations if the facts can be proven. In cases of arbitrary arrest and imprisonment, torture and brutality, and enforced disappearance and killings, there is seldom need for analyses of the content of the protected rights (see Davidson 1997).

The Inter-American Court handles significantly fewer cases than the European Court. For a long time, states were reluctant to recognize its jurisdiction and the Inter-American Commission seldom referred cases—it took eight years before the Inter-American Court received its first contentious case. Most people agree that the most effective and important tools of the Inter-American Convention are on-site country visits by the commission, not the application procedure to the court (Davidson 1997; Newman and Weissbrodt 1996).

II. The European System for Protection of Human Rights

The Council of Europe was established by ten countries in 1949 to "achieve a greater unity between its Members for the purpose of safeguarding and realising the ideals and principles which are their common heritage and facilitating their economic and social progress."[1] For the first forty years, the Council of Europe remained a western European institution, but since the dramatic political changes in Europe that began in 1989, it has become the main political tool for cooperation with countries from central and eastern Europe. All the member states are required to ratify the European Convention on Human Rights, and at the end of 1999, it was in force in forty-one European countries.[2]

The effective procedures at the European Commission of Human Rights[3] and the European Court of Human Rights[4] distinguish the European Convention from other human rights instruments; the European Convention accepts applications from any person or group of individuals whose rights have allegedly been violated by a state party (Jacobs and White 1996; van Dijk and van Hoof 1998). The first fifteen articles identify individual rights. The rest deal with procedural or technical matters. The convention has been amended or altered by eleven protocols, of which Protocols 1, 4, 6, and 7 added new rights and the rest made procedural changes (see Appendix 9.B, which summarizes the rights protected).

Until October 1998 the role of the European Commission of Human Rights was to examine the admissibility of all state or individual applications. After observations were received from the respondent government and applicant, it made a decision on the question of admissibility, provided a report on the facts and merits of an admissible case, and gave an opinion on whether the European Convention was violated. The final decision was made by the Court of Human Rights or the Committee of Ministers, which is a political body of the Council of Europe.[5] Without a request by the Commission, the respondent state, the applicant's state, or the applicant, the case was automatically decided by the Committee of Ministers (Gomien, Harris, and Zwaak 1996). By Protocol 11, the Commission and the Court were replaced in November 1998 by a new full-time court that handles questions of admissibility and merits in all cases. The much-criticized quasi-judicial role of the Committee of Ministers was abolished (see, for more details, Cameron 1995; Reid 1998).[6]

While the number of member states and awareness of the protection system have increased, so also have the number of applications and the number of admitted applications. Admissions in 1997 made up 17 percent of the total admitted applications since 1955. By the end of 1997, the European Commission of Human Rights had opened provisional files in 117,169 cases, registered 39,047 cases, and declared 4,161 cases admissible (10.7 percent of registered cases admitted). In 1997 alone, the Commission opened provisional files in 12,469 cases, of which 4,750 applications were registered and 703 declared admissible (14.8 percent of registered cases admitted; see the Council of Europe's human rights Web page at www.dhdirhr.coe.fr). However, the majority of applications did not reach the Commission. Petitions were placed in a "provisional file," from which the secretary to the Commission selected those that could be registered and finally screened out those registered cases that did not deserve consideration by the Commission.

In principle, the European Court of Human Rights does not have general authority to examine claims that domestic courts have made an error of law or fact in their decisions, unless the error potentially violates a right protected by the European Convention. Thus, the Court lacks competence routinely to review the correctness of national judgments (Gomien, Harris, and Zwaak 1996). The convention covers only violations by a state party, and therefore applications against private people or institutions are not admissible. However, there are situations when a government may in practice be held responsible for a private action within its territory. The convention imposes not only negative obligations to not violate human rights but also positive obligations to ensure a legal system that effectively protects them. States may be found in breach of the convention if national laws do not give adequate protection against violations or do not provide effective remedies in case of violations (Harris, O'Boyle, and Warbrick 1995; van Dijk and van Hoof 1998). At least twice a government has been held responsible when national criminal laws did not provide effective protection for two vulnerable groups, children and mentally disabled persons (A. v. United Kingdom, X. and Y. v. the Netherlands; discussed in section II.A).

Because of the nature of human rights law and broad interpretation methods, the European Court of Human Rights exercises wide discretion and freedom in its decision-making (de Blois 1994). The character of human rights law — principles rather than strict legal rules — includes a dimension of political judgment when individual rights are balanced against state interests. The terms that describe human rights are typically general and abstract and sometimes also ambiguous, uncertain, or vague. Concepts allow broad latitude for interpretation and, at least in the European context, most cases tend to be "hard" in the sense that application of law to the facts is not self-evident (Reid 1998). The Court has emphasized that all provisions of the European Convention must be applied "as to make its safeguards practical and effective" and "to be consistent with the general spirit of the Convention" (e.g., Soering, v. United Kingdom, Judgment of 7 July 1989, Series A, No. 161, para. 87). The Court uses the so-called sociological or evolutionary interpretation method and has ruled that changes in common moral values (e.g., regarding homosexuality, abortion, or illegitimacy of children) or penal policies of the member states are relevant factors in decision-making (Matscher 1993). In *Tyrer*, the Court acknowledged that the European Convention is a living instrument that must be interpreted in the light of present-day conditions (*Tyrer v. United Kingdom*, Judgment of 25 April 1978, Series A, No. 26). In *Dudgeon*, the Court banned criminalization of consensual adult homosexual relations because "there is now a better understanding, and in consequence, an increased tolerance, of homosexual behaviour" (*Dudgeon v. United Kingdom*, Judgment of 22 October 1981, Series A, No. 45, para. 60). By interpretation, the Court has also broadened the textual or common meaning of the concepts of "criminal charge" and "criminal penalty" to include procedures related to administrative traffic and competition rule violations and sanctions of forfeiture and customs laws.

III. Standards and Limits for Sentencing Laws and Punishments

Although provisions directly regulating sentencing and punishment are scarce in human rights instruments, a variety of relevant matters has been addressed by enforcement bodies. The most developed core area includes regulation of the death penalty, corporal punishments, life sentence, and penalties for juveniles. The European Court of Human Rights has some case law about types of offenses that must be punished and behavior that may not be punished. Then there is a large gray area, which may raise human rights concerns but has seldom been an issue in applications to human rights bodies. The gray zone includes other penalties, often defined as civil by national laws, like forfeiture, disenfranchisement, and other civil disabilities, and proportionality requirements for punishments.

A. What Must Be Punished?

Although the European Court and Commission of Human Rights have repeatedly emphasized the sovereignty of member states in the area of criminal law — the European Convention leaves the states free to designate as a criminal offence an act or omission — they have also made it clear that the sovereignty to create crimes is not absolute. Since the convention protects many basic civil and political free-doms, such as rights to private and family life; freedom of thought, conscience, and religion; freedom of expression; freedom of assembly and association; and free movement of persons, it takes little effort to envision situations in which national criminal provisions could prohibit citizens from exercising these basic freedoms. Criminalization of political opinions and organizations, religious views and oper-ation of churches, sexual orientation and practices, and lifestyles, personalities, or sole moral issues, are obvious possibilities. However, not only is the influence of the convention negative in the sense that certain types of criminalizations are not acceptable, it is also positive in the sense that certain actions must be criminalized. Member states are obliged to provide effective protection against human rights violations and sometimes the only sufficient means is the criminal law. Unlike situations where national criminal laws may overcriminalize behavior, one cannot easily imagine situations where national criminal laws fall short and undercrimin-alize behavior, but there are some examples.

In *A. v. United Kingdom*, English law allowed parents to use corporal punish-ment on their children if the punishment was moderate and reasonable in the circumstances (Application No. 25599/94, Judgment of 23 September 1998, Re-ports 1998-VI). Based on this parental discretion of moderate corporal discipline, an English jury acquitted a stepfather who had regularly beaten his 9-year-old stepson with a garden cane. The applicant asked the Commission and the Court to find two things: that the stepson was subjected to degrading treatment and punishment (Article 3) and that the United Kingdom was responsible for the action.

The Commission had little difficulty in finding that strokes with a garden cane that left visible bruises for several days amounted to degrading treatment. This was true even though the punishment was given privately at home and lacked any public character; for example, it was not administered by a school or other public authorities. The U.K. government argued that the Commission could not review the correctness of national judgments and that it was up to national courts to determine whether the punishment was indeed executed and whether it was more than moderate and reasonable. The Commission recognized that the United King-dom could not be held directly responsible for the acts of the stepfather or the verdict of the jury. However, it was responsible for ensuring a legal system that gives adequate protection against all forms of physical ill-treatment of children, who are especially vulnerable and incapable of protecting themselves. Unani-mously, the Commission held that the English criminal law failed to provide such protection and found a violation of Article 3 (*A. v. United Kingdom*, Application no. 25599/94, Report of 18 September 1997). The Court merely affirmed this decision in a short judgment, since the English government accepted its respon-sibility and acknowledged that national law failed to protect children adequately (*A. v. United Kingdom*, Judgment of 23 September 1998, paras. 18 and 33).

The UN Convention on the Rights of the Child (U.N. Doc. A/44/49 [1989]) entered into force in 1990. It protects children from all forms of physical or mental violence, injury or abuse, and neglect. Children's physical integrity is absolute: any corporal punishment as a means of discipline, whether used in schools or homes and whether considered mild, moderate, or severe, is prohibited. The Committee on the Rights of the Child, a body established to monitor states' compliance, has repeatedly stated that any corporal punishment is incompatible with the convention and recalled national legislation to ban corporal punishment within the family (Hodgkin and Newell 1998). However, thus far only a few states have done so. Sweden was the first one in 1979, followed by Finland, Denmark, Norway, Austria, Cyprus, and Italy (see Bitensky 1998). Finland's Supreme Court upheld a criminal conviction for petty assault in a case where a stepfather pulled a child's hair and slightly slapped her. The Court ruled that parents or guardians have no right to use physical punishments (KKO 1993:151, Decision of the Highest Court of Finland; available at http://www.finlex.edita.fi/oiktap/fkko.html in Finnish).

The European Court of Human Rights required effective protection by criminal law earlier in the case of *X. and Y. v. the Netherlands* (Judgment of 26 March 1985, Series A, No. 91), in which a mentally disabled girl and her father were unable to institute criminal proceedings against the girl's sexual assaulter, since Dutch law requires a complaint by the victim of crime in person, and in this case she lacked the capacity to make one. The Dutch government tried to argue that civil procedures and remedies were available and provided adequate protection. However, the European Court held that civil law was not enough: "Effective deterrence is indispensable in this area and it can be achieved only by criminal-law provisions; indeed, it is by such provisions that the matter is normally regulated" (para. 27). Exclusion of a group of especially vulnerable persons from an otherwise comprehensive system of criminal protection was not acceptable and the Court found a breach of Article 8 (right to respect for private life).

Effective protection by criminal law was also an issue, at least indirectly, in *S. W. v. United Kingdom* (Judgment of 22 November 1995, Series A, No. 355-B). Traditionally, English law did not consider a rape by a husband as a crime, since the old common-law doctrine held that consent to sexual intercourse was inherent in marriage. The statutory law did not distinguish between wives or other women, but the marital exception (with some limited exceptions) was based on common law and respected by courts. By the time of S. W.'s offense, it was unclear whether the marital immunity doctrine was still part of English law. The facts of the case were complicated, but basically S. W. argued that criminal law was applied to him retroactively since the House of Lords declared the marital immunity doctrine abolished only after he had raped his wife.

S. W. claimed a violation of Article 7, which requires that criminal law must fulfill the principles of legality and certainty of law (*nullum crimen sine lege and nulla poena sine lege*). Crimes and punishments must be prescribed by law; criminal provisions and punishments cannot be applied retroactively; criminal provisions must be precise and foreseeable; and criminal law cannot be extended by analogy to the detriment of the defendant. The requirements for precise and foreseeable criminal law were expressed for the first time in *Sunday Times v. United Kingdom,* in which the European Court held that citizens should be able to have an indication how legal rules are applied in a given case (Judgment of 26 April 1979, Series A, No. 30). Criminal norms must be precise enough to enable citizens, with appropriate advice, to judge their conduct and foresee consequences of their acts.

The facts of the S. W. case were as follows: On September 17, 1990, the Law Commission recommended that the marital immunity doctrine should be abolished by legislation. On September 18, 1990, S. W. forced his wife to have sexual intercourse, and later all domestic courts rejected the marital immunity defense and found him guilty of rape. The Crown Court in the S. W. decision on April 19, 1991, referred to another domestic case, R. v. R., where for the first time in the English history a court ruled that the marital immunity was abolished. The case R. v. R. was decided in the Crown Court on July 30, 1990, in the Court of Appeal on March 14, 1991, and in the House of Lords on October 23, 1991. In its decision, the House of Lords stated that the general principle that a husband cannot rape his wife no longer existed in the law of England and Wales.

Based on these facts, it appears the marital immunity doctrine was not yet effectively abolished in English law when S. W. committed his offense. Only a day before the alleged crime, the Law Commission called for legislation to abolish the doctrine. Less than two months before S. W.'s offense, a Crown Court in R. v. R. rejected the marital immunity doctrine, but this unpublished decision could hardly be considered as a precedent at the time of S.W.'s offense. The Court of Appeal and House of Lords affirmed the judgment in R. v. R. only after S.W.'s offense. Based on these facts, it does not seem reasonable to expect that S. W. could have foreseen or known that the marital immunity doctrine was in fact abolished by the time of his offense.

That a husband may not be held criminally liable for raping his wife is detestable and unacceptable. However, one could argue that it is the government's responsibility clearly to define the limits for criminal liability, and the offender should not be held responsible when the scope of criminal liability is uncertain or ambiguous. The European Court of Human Rights did not follow this line of argumentation.

The Court did not explain why the marital immunity defense did not constitute an essential element of rape. Second, the Court did not explain why the abolition of marital immunity doctrine was not applied retroactively to S.W. Third, the Court did not explain how the abolition could have been foreseen or known by ordinary citizens. Instead, the Court merely concluded, "This evolution has reached a stage where judicial recognition of the absence of immunity had become a reasonably foreseeable development of the law" (S. W. v. United Kingdom, para. 43/41). This conclusion was offered even though the Court was provided several examples of English court decisions where marital immunity defense had been successful in rapes that had been committed after S. W.'s offense.

Although the Court does not express it clearly, its main argument appears to be based on the requirement of effective protection by criminal law. The Court is in effect saying that rape of any woman, by any man, must be punished by criminal law. Therefore it was able to ignore or at least not give full potential, for the general prohibition of retroactive criminal law: "The essentially debasing character of rape is so manifest that the result . . . cannot be said to be at variance with the object and purpose of Article 7 of the Convention. . . . What is more, the abandonment of the unacceptable idea of a husband being immune against prosecution for rape of his wife was in conformity not only with a civilised concept of marriage but also, and above all, with the fundamental objectives of the Convention, the very essence of which is respect for human dignity and human freedom" (*S. W. v. United Kingdom*, para. 44/42).

However, there is a crucial difference between S. W. and the two other cases concerning effective protection by criminal law discussed before, *A. v. United Kingdom* and *X. and Y. v. the Netherlands*. In them, the victim of crime claimed that the government did not provide effective protection, and the decisions by the European bodies did not affect any rights of the offender. The European Commission and Court declared that the national criminal laws were inadequate and should be corrected. In the case of S. W., the offender claimed that the government violated his basic human rights. The European Court stated that as a rapist he did not deserve full protection against retroactive application of the criminal law, but it failed to address the essential problem: the U.K. government had failed to provide adequate protection to married women by criminal law; therefore the government should have been held responsible, not the offender. In fact, the Court in S. W. balanced two different human rights against each other, determined that one was superior (women's right to protection of their physical integrity) and that the inferior (offenders' right not to be subject to retroactive criminal law) could be violated.

B. What Must Not Be Punished?

The European bodies have received several claims that national criminal provisions prohibit citizens from exercising their protected rights. Typically the question has been about the right to privacy or civil and political freedoms of thought, conscience, religion, expression, assembly, association, and movement (see Bengoetxea and Jung 1991). However, articles describing these privacy and freedoms rights (Articles 8–11) include also certain clauses that allow national discretion and restrictions that are necessary in democratic societies and prescribed by national laws. This so-called margin of appreciation doctrine acknowledges that certain civil and political rights are not absolute, that their content may vary within certain limits from state to state, and that there is no shared European consensus of their meaning (see Yourow 1996).

National restrictions to freedoms articles are acceptable if they are necessary to ensure public safety, protection of health or morals, protection of the rights and freedoms of others, or other comparable values. The European Court of Human Rights has ruled that there must be a reasonable relationship between the nature and severity of the restrictions and the public goals that are enhanced by them. However, the Court has also held that national authorities are often in a better position than the international judges to assess the need for restrictions and better equipped to balance the governmental needs with individual freedoms (Yourow 1996). This said, it is hardly a surprise that in only a few cases has the Court found that a national criminal provision violated the right to privacy or one of the civil and political freedoms.

The best known is *Dudgeon*, in which the applicant claimed that the criminal law provision of Northern Ireland that punished sexual practices between consenting adult males violated his right to private life, since he had been investigated, although not charged or convicted, for the offense (*Dudgeon v. United Kingdom*, Judgment of 22 October 1981, Series A, No. 45). The government argued that the criminal provision was necessary to protect the health and morals of the Northern Ireland society. There was significant public support both for and against criminalization of consensual homosexual conduct, although it was not clear which was the majority view of the Northern Irish. Even though the European Court of Human Rights acknowledged the more conservative and religious nature of the Northern Ireland society, it did not agree that there was a pressing social need to penalize homosexuality in order to protect national morals. The Court emphasized the changing attitudes of the public and its increased tolerance of homosexual behavior in other European countries that no longer criminalized homosexual practices. In balancing governmental needs and individual rights, the Court stated, "On the issue of proportionality, the Court considers that such justifications as there are for retaining the law in force unamended are outweighed by the detrimental effects which the very existence of the legislative provisions in question can have on the life of a person of homosexual orientation" (para 60).

The Court concluded that Dudgeon had suffered and continued to suffer an unjustified interference with his right to respect for his private life. Later in *Norris v. Ireland* (Judgment of 26 October 1988, Series A, No. 142), the Court held that criminalization of adult homosexual conduct violated the right to private life, regardless whether the person had been subject to any police investigation or prosecution. This decision was affirmed in a case against Cyprus (*Modinos v. Cyprus*, Judgment of 22 April 1993, Series A, No. 259).

Five years after *Dudgeon*, the U.S. Supreme Court held criminalization of homosexual practices constitutional in a five-to-four decision in *Bowers v. Hardwick*, 478 U.S. 186 (1986). The line of argumentation was the exact opposite of that of the European Court of Human Rights. First, the U.S. Supreme Court declined to recognize that the question concerned the right to privacy. Instead, it turned the question around and stated that it was about "a fundamental right upon homosexuals to engage in sodomy" (p. 190), which was not protected by the U.S. Constitution. Second, the Court emphasized the ancient tradition to penalize sodomy and did not acknowledge any societal change in the attitudes toward homosexuality. In a concurring opinion, Chief Justice Burger stated: "Condemnation of those [homosexual] practices is firmly rooted in Judeo-Christian moral and ethical standards. . . . To hold that the act of homosexual sodomy is somehow protected as a fundamental right would be to cast aside millennia of moral teaching" (pp. 196–97). Some U.S. states differ on the matter, and consensual homosexual sodomy laws have been held unconstitutional by some state supreme courts.

For decades, the European Commission of Human Rights approved the setting of a higher minimum age of consent (often 21 years) for homosexual than for heterosexual sexual relations. In *Sutherland v. the United Kingdom*, the commission departed from its previous case law (Application No. 25186/94, Report of 1 July 1997). It held that modern developments in the majority of member states and in medical opinion did not justify discriminatory age limits, which in England at that time were 16 years for heterosexual and 18 years for male homosexual relations.

The European Court of Human Rights has also examined state limits to interfere, by criminal law, in cases in which individuals harm their own welfare. In the case *Laskey, Jaggard, and Brown v. United Kingdom*, the applicants were involved in a group that participated in voluntary sado-masochistic sexual practices (Judgment of 20 January 1997, Reports 1997-I). The acts had been conducted in private for pleasure, none of the injuries had required medical care, and no complaints had made to the police. However, the group had recruited new members, specially equipped rooms for action, and shot videos that were distributed among the members. The applicants were convicted for criminal assault and their sentences were reduced from six to three months on appeal. The Court of Human Rights stated that the levels of harm and violence that can be tolerated among consenting adults were in the first instance within national discretion. Since the reduced penalties were proportionate, they did not violate the right to respect for private life (Article 8).

A number of cases have dealt with freedom of expression, when persons have been convicted in national courts because of their writings, art, films, or broadcasting. In the majority of cases, the European Court of Human Rights has recognized primary national discretion to determine needs, forms, and limits to interfere with these freedoms. For example, in *Handyside v. United Kingdom* (Judgment of 7 December 1976, Series A, No. 24) and *Müller v. Switzerland* (Judgment of 24 May 1988, Series A, No. 133), it was left to English and Swiss courts to decide whether a children's book or paintings in a exhibition were obscene.

However, the Court has also found violations. In *Jersild v. Denmark* (Judgment of 23 September 1994, Series A, No. 298), the applicant was a journalist who made a documentary about a group of racist youth, which was broadcast on Danish television. The film included an interview of three teenagers, who made extremely derogatory and racist remarks about blacks and immigrants. They were convicted in a criminal trial for publicly making statements that were threatening, insulting, or degrading a group of persons on account of their race, color, or national ethnic or origin. The applicant was convicted of aiding and abetting them. The Court of Human Rights emphasized the role of the free press and found a violation of freedom of expression: "The punishment of a journalist for assisting in the dissemination of statements made by another person in an interview would seriously hamper the contribution of the press to discussion of matters of public interest and should not be envisaged unless there are particularly strong reasons for doing so" (para 35).

The Court has underlined several times that true religious pluralism is an inherent part of a democratic society. In *Manoussakis and Others v. Greece* (Judgment of 26 September 1996, Reports 1996-IV), the Court disapproved Greek administrative requirements that imposed prohibitive conditions on certain non-Orthodox religious movements, particularly on Jehovah's Witnesses. The applicants had failed to meet the administrative requirements and had been convicted for operating a place of worship without prior authorization and sentenced to three months' imprisonment (convertible into fiscal penalty) and a fine. The criminal conviction was held in violation of applicants' freedom of religion by the Court.

C. How to Punish?

International standards limit or prevent the use of certain types of punishments, and the death penalty is the most discussed and researched. It is regulated in all major human rights instruments and several optional protocols require its abolition. All major human rights instruments also include an article that prohibits torture or other inhuman or degrading treatment or punishment. However, only the European human rights bodies have examined this article's potential influence on other punishments than the death penalty, and on proportionality requirements for sentences. Criminal penalties hardly ever extend to *inhuman* treatment or punishment, which by the definition of the European Court of Human Rights covers situations where severe physical or mental suffering is deliberately caused without appropriate justification. However, some criminal penalties may amount to *degrading* treatment or punishment, which the Court has defined as an action that grossly humiliates a person or drives him or her to act against his or her conscience or will. The humiliation must exceed an acceptable level but need not cause severe or long-lasting physical or psychological effects (e.g., Addo and Grief 1995; Duffy 1983). International standards for types of punishments include limits on the use of the death penalty, corporal punishment, life sentence, and other sanctions (e.g., forfeiture, civil disabilities).

Promotion of Community Sanctions

Several researchers have identified an international movement toward a more just and proportionate system of punishments that is a part of increased global attention to human rights. The goals include greater proportionality and consistency in sentencing, wider use of moderate and short prison sentences, increased use of noncustodial and community penalties, development of mediation and victim assistance programs, and stricter legislative guidance for sentencing judges (e.g., Jung 1993). However, at the same time, there is increased intolerance and punitiveness regarding certain crimes, especially drug, sex, and violent offenses, organized crime, and white-collar crime (e.g., Kaiser 1996). In 1992, the Council of Europe adopted a recommendation, "Consistency in Sentencing,"[7] which promotes humane goals: "Sentencing rationales should be consistent with modern and humane crime policies, in particular in respect of reducing the use of imprisonment, expanding the use of community sanctions and measures, pursuing policies of decriminalisation, using measures of diversion such as mediation, and of ensuring compensation of victims" (Council of Europe 1993, Article A.6, p. 6; see, for more details, Ashworth 1994). The recommendation underlines that custodial sentences should be regarded as the last alternative and imposed only when the seriousness of the offense would make any other sentence clearly inadequate. Use of community sanctions instead of imprisonment was encouraged, and a recommendation for general European rules on community sanctions and measures was passed by the Council of Europe (Council of Europe 1994.)

The General Assembly of the United Nations passed a resolution, Standard Minimum Rules for the Administration of Juvenile Justice, in 1985 (the Beijing Rules, U.N. Doc. A/40/53 [1985]). The rules restricted the use of custodial sentences to cases of serious violent crimes or persistence in committing other serious crimes. Since "little or no difference has been found in terms of the success of institutionalization as compared to non-institutionalization" and since "the negative effects [of institutionalization] are certainly more acute for juveniles than for adults," the rules limited custodial sentences to cases where they are absolutely necessary (Beijing Rules, commentary to Rule 19.1).

The United Nations Standard Minimum Rules for Non-Custodial Measures (the Tokyo Rules, U.N. Doc. A/45/49 [1990]), passed by a General Assembly resolution in 1990, is the most detailed international document to promote the use of community sanctions. The rules recall that all criminal justice systems should provide a wide range of noncustodial sanctions from pretrial to postsentencing dispositions, that unnecessary use of imprisonment must be avoided, that offenders should be dealt with in the community and formal proceedings or trials should be avoided as far as possible, that greater community involvement in the management of criminal justice should be encouraged, and that the increased use of community sanctions should be part of the movement toward depenalization and decriminalization, not toward increased control of offenders.

These rules and recommendations are unknown to many practitioners and academics, and uncited in most research. Although unfortunate, this is understandable since the rules have no binding effect and are quite general. Many people accept their message in its abstract form: prison sentences should be avoided and community sentences promoted. However, problems arise when details are discussed. What kinds of crimes should be characterized as violent or serious crimes, how many previous convictions show persistence in committing crimes, should minor crimes be counted as previous convictions, and how should the penal values of fines, community service, suspended prison sentence, supervised probation, and imprisonment be ranked and compared? Should one day of imprisonment be equivalent to one hour or one day of community service, or some other amount? As long as these kinds of concrete problems are not addressed or discussed in the recommendations, they are likely to remain general declarations of principles with little influence on practices.

The Death Penalty

Capital punishment is linked to two universally recognized human rights, the right to life and the protection against cruel, inhuman, or degrading punishments. Worldwide, the change is clearly toward abolition of the death penalty: the number of countries that have abolished the death penalty in peacetime increased from 23 in 1965 to 73 in 1996. Another 13 countries use the death penalty only for exceptional crimes committed during war and 24 countries have not executed any person for the past ten years or more. This means that more than half of the member states of the UN have abolished capital punishment by law or de facto (105 abolitionists vs. 89 retentionists; Amnesty International 1999). In 1998, at least 1,625 prisoners were executed in 37 countries and 3,899 persons were sentenced to death in 78 countries. Amnesty International (1999) reports that the majority of known executions in 1998 took place in four countries: China (1,067), the Democratic Republic of Congo (over 100), the United States (68), and Iran (66). However, confirmed figures for China, Congo, and Iran are widely believed to be lower than the true ones and hundreds of executions were also reported in Iraq, but Amnesty International was unable to obtain confirmation of them.

While the majority of the world is abandoning the death penalty, the United States is moving in the opposite direction with such countries as the Philippines, Papua New Guinea, and Gambia that have reinstated the death penalty or increased its use (see Hood 1998, p. 742). In the United States, only twelve states and the District of Columbia have remained abolitionist. Furthermore, the Violent Crime Control and Law Enforcement Act of 1994 reintroduced a federal capital punishment, which means, among other things, that the death penalty may be imposed in federal courts for a crime that was committed in a state jurisdiction that does not recognize the death penalty. In 1998, nineteen persons were awaiting execution of federal capital punishment (Bureau of Justice Statistics 1999). Between 1996 and 1997, the number of executions in the United States increased by 65 percent from forty-five to seventy-four—half of the 1997 executions occurred in Texas (Bureau of Justice Statistics 1998). The number of executions decreased slightly in 1998 to sixty-eight but increased to ninety-eight in 1999 (see Death Penalty Information Center Web page at http://www.essential.org/dpic/dpic.html). The last time this many persons were executed in the United States was in the early 1950s.

Although the international trend is to abolish the death penalty, it cannot yet be said that abolition would be a customary norm of international law. Customary international norms emerge when there is evidence of a widespread general acceptance of a practice that is recognized as a law. A customary international norm is binding on all states regardless of whether they have ratified any of the treaties the norm is based on or otherwise recognized it (Hodgkinson and Rutherford 1996). The International Covenant on Civil and Political Rights and the European and American Conventions on Human Rights include optional protocols that require abolishment of the death penalty. The new members of the Council of Europe are expected to ratify Protocol 6, which entered into force in 1985 and was the first international instrument to abolish capital punishment. The protocol is in force in thirty-five member states and signed by an additional four member states. Albania and Turkey have not taken any action.[8] For example, Protocol 6 entered into force in Croatia, Macedonia, and Moldova in 1997, in Estonia and Greece in 1998, in Belgium, Bulgaria, Latvia, Lithuania, and the United Kingdom in 1999, and in Cyprus in 2000. Russia and Ukraine signed the protocol in 1997, Poland and Georgia in 1999 (see Council of Europe's Web page at www.coe.fr/eng/legaltxt/treaties.htm).

However, so far none of the courts or bodies attached to global or regional human rights instruments has held that the death penalty violates the right to life or constitutes cruel, inhuman, or degrading punishment. Even though the prohibition of the death penalty has not yet ripened to the level of a customary international norm, it can be argued that certain restrictions in its application have attained the status of customary law (Schabas 1997). These restrictions are based on the major human rights instruments and the United Nations resolution "Safeguards Guaranteeing Protection of the Rights of Those Facing the Death Penalty," adopted by the Economic and Social Council in 1984 (U.N. Doc. E/1984/84 [1984]; see also Amnesty International 1998a).

First, capital punishment may be imposed only for the most serious crimes. The U.N. Safeguards define the concept of most serious crimes as "intentional crimes with lethal or other extremely grave consequences" (Article 1), which is interpreted to imply that the crimes should in their typical forms be life-threatening and that their very likely consequence is death (Schabas 1997). Many countries violate this customary norm when the death penalty may be imposed for such crimes as drug trafficking, espionage, treason, kidnapping, or rape.

Second, capital punishment may not be applied retroactively to crimes for which it was not prescribed as a punishment by law at the time of commission. In addition, if changes that benefit the offender are made between the commission of crime and sentencing trial, these changes must be applied retroactively in favor of the offender. As mentioned before, the United States made a reservation concerning this principle when it ratified the UN Covenant on Civil and Political Rights. Hood reports that four U.S. states raised the minimum age for imposing the death penalty in 1987 but did not apply the higher age limit to those offenders who were already on the death row (Hood 1996).

Third, capital punishment may not be imposed on juvenile offenders who were under 18 years old when they committed their crime. Amnesty International reports that eighty-three of the eighty-nine retentionist countries respect this customary norm. All the remaining six countries (Iran, Nigeria, Pakistan, Saudi Arabia, the United States, and Yemen) have executed juveniles during the 1990s, the United States leading with nine executions (Amnesty International 1998b).

In the United States, the age limit for capital punishment is 16 years in twelve states, 17 in four states, and not statutorily specified in eight states. Thus, only fourteen states and the federal system comply with the international age limit of 18 years (Bureau of Justice Statistics 1999). The U.S. Supreme Court has held that the death penalty may not be imposed on juveniles who were 15 years or younger at the time of the offense (*Thompson v. Oklahoma*, 487 U.S. 815 [1988]) but may be imposed to 16- and 17-year-old juveniles (*Stanford v. Kentucky* and *Wilkins v. Missouri*, 492 U.S. 361 [1989]; see more details in Bedau 1997; Heffernan 1996). In his dissenting opinion in *Stanford*, Justice William Brennan concluded, "Within the world community, the imposition of the death penalty for juvenile crimes appears to be overwhelmingly disapproved" (p. 390) and supported his view by citing legislation and practices in other countries, human rights treaties, and opinions of respected organizations (e.g., the American Bar Association, the American Law Institute). At the end of 1997, at least seventy-two juveniles who were under 18 when they committed their offenses were on death row in the United States (Bureau of Justice Statistics 1999).

In his 1998 report on his visit to the United States, the UN Special Rappoteur on Extrajudical, Summary, or Arbitrary Executions stated, among other things, that the use of the death penalty against juvenile offenders violates international law and should be abolished. In response, the chair of the Senate Foreign Relations Committee urged the U.S. government to "reverse all cooperation with this absurd UN charade," the U.S. Ambassador to the UN said that the report would only "gather dust," and the Republican National Committee chairman called for further withholding of payment of U.S. debts to the UN until the report was "formally withdrawn and apologized for" (citations from Amnesty International 1998c, p. 8).

Fourth, capital punishment may not be imposed on mentally incompetent or insane persons, and most countries comply with this customary norm. The U.S. Supreme Court has held that insane prisoners cannot be executed (*Ford v. Wainwright*, 477 U.S. 399 [1986]), but the majority of U.S. states have not statutorily barred their execution. Furthermore, the Supreme Court decided later that mentally retarded persons were not categorically exempt from execution and upheld the death penalty for an offender with an IQ of 50 to 63, a mental age that of a 6½-year-old, and an ability to function that of a 9-year-old; who had organic brain damage and was moderately retarded; and who had been subject to significant physical and emotional abuse as a child (*Penry v. Lyngauh*, 492 U.S. 302 [1989]).

Fifth, capital punishments may not be imposed on pregnant women or on new mothers. Only a few countries have exempted women as a whole from the death penalty. For example, according to the Death Penalty Information Center, forty-seven women in the United States were on death row in June 1999, and for the first time since 1984 two women were executed in 1998 (Death Penalty Information Center Web page at http://www.essential.org/dpic/dpic.html).

Methods of execution are not regulated by the human rights instruments, although the UN Safeguards require that capital punishment be carried out in a way that inflicts the least possible suffering. This safeguard is violated regularly all over the world, since the most common methods of execution in most countries are hanging or shooting. Some Arabic countries allow stoning to death. In the United States, the predominant method of execution is lethal injection, although eleven states allow electrocution, five gas chamber, three hanging, and three firing squad (Bureau of Justice Statistics 1999). The U.S. Supreme Court has not ruled on the methods of execution since 1890, when it considered electrocution constitutional. Challenges have been more common in lower federal courts, but their decisions are inconsistent. For example, the Ninth Circuit held hanging constitutional (*Cambell v. Wood*, 18 F.3d 662 [9th Cir. 1994]) but later found execution by lethal gas unconstitutional (*Fierro v. Gomez*, 77 F.3d 301[9th Cir. 1996]). A district court in Washington state held hanging unconstitutional (*Rupe v. Wood*, 863 F. Supp. 1307 [W. D. Wash. 1994]; the Fourth Circuit found execution by lethal gas constitutional (*Hunt v. Nuth*, 57 F.3d 1327 [4th Cir. 1995]) (see, for more details, Beard 1997).

The UN Human Rights Committee is the only international body that has considered methods of execution. In *Ng v. Canada*, the committee ruled that Canada should not extradite the applicant to the United States, where he was subject to execution by gas asphyxiation, which "may cause prolonged suffering and agony and does not result in a death as swiftly as possible, as asphyxiation by cyanide gas may take over 10 minutes" (Communication no. 469/1991, U.N. Doc. CCPR/C/49/D/469/1991 [1994], para 16.3.) However, this decision was little help for Chitat Ng, whom Canada had already extradited to the United States, thus ignoring a specific request from the committee's Special Rapporteur not to extradite him before the committee had an opportunity to give its final opinion.

Although all member states of the Council of Europe are expected to abolish the death penalty, or at least not to carry out capital sentences, the European Court of Human Rights has refused to rule that the death penalty constitutes inhuman or degrading punishment under Article 3. Despite the western European consensus that the death penalty is against the essential principles of humanity, the Court decided that adoption of Protocol 6 (abolishing the death penalty) in 1983 showed that it was not considered prohibited by the convention itself. However, the Court has held that certain factors together in the administration of capital punishment may amount to inhuman or degrading treatment.

In the notorious *Soering* case, an 18-year-old German man killed his girlfriend's parents in the state of Virginia (*Soering v. the United Kingdom*, Judgment of 7 July 1989, Series A, No. 161). The two teenagers planned the murder together and fled to Europe. They were apprehended in England and asked by the United States to be returned to Virginia to face the criminal trial (see, for more details, Breitenmoser and Wilms 1990; Lillich 1991). The questions in the European Court of Human Rights were whether the European Convention protected against extradition to a third country where the applicant might be subject to inhuman or degrading treatment, and whether the death row phenomenon and some other factors together could be considered as inhuman or degrading treatment. The Court answered the affirmative to the both questions. First, it stated that it would be against the underlying values, spirit, and intent of the convention to surrender a person to a country where he or she would be at risk of inhuman or degrading treatment or punishment (changing the previous view of the Commission that an uncertain possibility or risk of the death row phenomenon did not amount to a violation, *Kirkwood v. United Kingdom* [1984], 37 DR 158). Second, the Court listed factors under which the death penalty may amount to a breach of Article 3, such as the manner in which the death penalty is imposed or executed, the personal circumstances of the offender, the death penalty's disproportionality to the gravity of the offense, and conditions of detention while awaiting execution. In *Soering*, the special circumstances that together amounted to a violation were the length of incarceration on death row (on average six to eight years), the very controlled and restricted prison conditions, applicant's young age (18 years), and his reduced mental capacity at the time of the offense. Later, the prosecutor of the state of Virginia guaranteed that he would not seek the death penalty, and Jens Soering was extradited from England to the United States.

The U.S. federal and state courts have declined to hold that long delays in execution may constitute cruel or unusual punishment. For example, sixteen, seventeen, and twenty-one years on death row have not been considered cruel or unusual, and the U.S. Supreme Court has regularly denied certiorari in death row cases. The U.S. courts argue that the whole death row phenomenon is caused by inmates who take advantage of the generous appeals system, and they should not be able to benefit from unsuccessfully pursuing their constitutional rights (see Bell 1996). In *Soering*, the European Court of Human Rights acknowledged that this is largely true but nevertheless stated that "it is equally part of human nature that the person will cling to life by exploiting those safeguards to the full" (at para. 106).

The UN Human Rights Committee has also developed a rule that the length of detention on death row itself does not amount to inhuman or degrading treatment, since "the cruelty of the death row phenomenon is first and foremost a function of the permissibility of capital punishment under the Covenant" (*Johnson v. Jamaica*, Communication no. 588/1994, U.N. Doc. CCPR/C/56/D/588/1994 [1996], para 8.4). Only if the conditions on death row are more restrictive or brutal than normally expected, may it constitute inhuman or degrading treatment. This was the case in *Daley v. Jamaica*, where the applicant had been assaulted repeatedly by other inmates and lacked sanitation, light, ventilation, and bedding (Communication no. 750/1997, U.N. Doc. CCPR/C/63/D/750/1997 [3 August 1998]). For example, almost sixteen years on death row in Trinidad and Tobago before the sentence was commuted to life sentence was not considered inhuman or degrading (six of sixteen committee members dissented (*Bickaroo v. Trinidad and Tobago*, Communication no. 555/1993, U.N. Doc. CCPR/C/61/D/555/1993 [29 October 1997]).

The current member states of the Council of Europe allow extradition to a retentionist country if the receiving government guarantees that the death penalty will not be imposed. However, Canada, where the death penalty for ordinary crimes was abolished in 1976, has extradited suspect criminals to face the death penalty in the United States without such guarantees. The UN Human Rights Committee has held that although Canada itself has abolished the death penalty, the International Covenant on Civil and Political Rights does not require that Canada should refuse to extradite or seek assurance that the death penalty will not be imposed (*Chiat Ng v. Canada*, Communication no. 469/1991, U.N. Doc. CCPR/C/49/D/469/1991 [1994]; *Kindler v. Canada*, Communication no. 470/1991, U.N. Doc. CCPR/C/48/D/470/1991 [1993]). Some European countries (for example, Italy and Portugal) refuse to extradite suspects under any circumstances if capital punishment may be imposed, regardless of any promises by the receiving state. A diplomatic conflict emerged among Turkey, Italy, and Germany in the end of 1998, when Italy refused to extradite the Kurdish leader Abdullah Öcalan to Turkey because he may be subject to the death penalty, and the German government refused to initiate criminal charges against him because it feared protests by the large German Kurdish population (e.g., *New York Times*, November 17, 1998).

Corporal Punishment

Judicial corporal punishment has been considered inhumane and unacceptable in most Western societies for decades but is used regularly in many other countries, especially in Islamic nations. Corporal criminal penalties are not directly prohibited or mentioned in the major human rights instruments or conventions preventing torture. If they are prohibited, it is because they fall under the general definition of inhuman or degrading punishment. However, the UN Convention on the Rights of the Child and Standard Minimum Rules for the Administration of Juvenile Justice expressly ban judicial corporal punishment on juveniles.

Corporal punishments may amount to torture, which by the UN Torture Convention means "any act by which severe pain or suffering, whether physical or mental, is intentionally inflicted on a person for . . . punishing him for an act he . . . has committed" (Convention against Torture and Other Cruel, Inhuman, or Degrading Treatment or Punishment, Article I.1). The UN Human Rights Committee has stated that prohibition of torture and inhuman or degrading punishments must extend to corporal punishment, including excessive chastisement as a punishment of crime and as a disciplinary measure at schools or medical facilities. The committee emphasized that children, students, and patients are particular groups protected (General Comment 20, U.N. Doc. HRI/GEN/1/Rev.1 at 30 [1994]).

Corporal criminal punishments are abolished in western Europe, and the only case by the European Court of Human Rights was about a sentence of birching in the Isle of Man, an independent part of the United Kingdom with its own government and legislative, judicial, and administrative bodies. In *Tyrer*, a 15-year-old boy was sentenced to corporal punishment for assaulting his schoolmate (*Tyrer v. United Kingdom*, Judgment of 25 April 1978, Series A, No. 26). The punishment was administered in a police station where he was held by two policemen while a third gave him threes strokes of birch on bare buttocks; afterwards his skin was sore but not cut by the strokes. The Court held that the severity of punishment did not amount to torture or inhuman punishment but issued a strong decision against any forms of judicial corporal punishments because of their inherent humiliating and degrading nature. The Court emphasized that judicial corporal punishment is institutionalized violence exercised by the state. It treats a person as an object in the power of state authorities and therefore violates the very nature of the Article 3—protection of a person's dignity and physical integrity.

In the United States, no jurisdiction allows corporal punishment as a criminal penalty, although one might claim that some aspects of boot camps come close to it. Legislation authorizing punishment of juvenile offenders by hitting with a wooden paddle was introduced in several states (including California, Louisiana, Missouri, Ohio, and Texas) during the 1990s, but none of the proposals succeeded (see Bloom 1995).

In cases related to corporal punishment at state or private schools, the European Court of Human Rights refused to hold that corporal punishment in itself, regardless of severity or forms of administration, is degrading (all cases have been against the United Kingdom, see e.g., Swart and Young 1995; Dickson 1997). In *Campbell and Cosans*, applicants claimed that the Scottish state school system, in which corporal punishment was used regularly as a disciplinary measure, violated the Convention (*Campbell and Cosans v. United Kingdom*, Judgment of 25 February 1982, Series A, No. 48). The Court held that although a system of corporal punishment may cause "a certain degree of apprehension," the humiliation or debasement inherent in the system did not attain a minimum level of severity (para 27). The Commission and the Court tend to compare the circumstances of each case to those in *Tyrer*, and if they do not amount close to similar severity and humiliation, there is no violation.

In *Warwick*, the European Commission of Human Rights found the hand caning and injury of a 16-year-old girl by a male teacher, in the presence of another male teacher, a breach of Article 3 (*Warwick v. United Kingdom* [1986], 60 DR 5). Similarly, there was a violation in a case where a 15-year-old boy was caned four times through his pants by a headmaster, who took several steps back before striking to generate more force in the strikes (*Y. v. United Kingdom*, Judgment of 8 October 1991, Series A, No. 247-A). However, the Court did not find a violation when the headmaster of a private boarding school whacked a 7-year-old boy three times through his shorts with a rubber-soled gym shoe (*Costello-Roberts v. United Kingdom*, Judgment of 25 March 1993, Series A, No. 247-C). Although there were some concerns about the automatic nature of the punishment and the three-day wait before its imposition, the Court held that the requirement of minimum level of severity was not met in this case. A rough measure for severity is that the punishment leave visible bruises, marks, or swelling. Dissenting members of the Commission and the Court thought that corporal punishment at schools could never be necessary or acceptable in a democratic society; if it did not amount to degrading treatment, it was at least against the right to respect for private life guaranteed in Article 8.

The United Kingdom prohibited corporal punishment in public schools in 1986, while most western European countries had abolished it decades ago. About half of the U.S. states allow corporal punishment in public schools, where students are not protected against cruel or unusual punishments, since the U.S. Supreme Court held in 1977 that the Eighth Amendment applies only to criminal punishments (*Ingraham v. Wright*, 430 U.S. 651 [1977]). Later, federal appeals courts have held that children are protected constitutionally against excessive corporal punishments at schools by substantive due process requirements but have often created vicious standards for violations, which are similar to those used in police brutality cases.

> The substantive due process inquiry in school corporal punishment cases must be whether the force applied caused injury so severe, was so disproportionate to the need presented, and was so inspired by malice or sadism rather than a merely careless or unwise excess of zeal that it amounted to a brutal and inhumane abuse of official

power literally shocking to the conscience. (*Hall v. Tawney*, 621 F.2d 607 [4th Cir. 1980], p. 613)

In practice, the standard has meant that "a child in public school will have to be severely beaten before a court will consider that child's constitutional claim" (Parkinson 1994, p. 289). Kids have been severely battered because they forgot to bring in their homework, were humming in the boys' bathroom, snickered, spoke Spanish at recess, or puffed their cheeks when playing the clarinet, and this was constitutional. Kids have been spanked with a wooden paddle on their buttocks seven times, held upside down by their ankles and hit in the front of the legs with a wooden paddle, and pierced in an arm with a straight pin, and this was constitutional. Kids have suffered severe bruising and pain, broken arm, broken nose, possible permanent back and spine injuries, and permanent scars, and this was constitutional. Kids have been hospitalized, missed days of school, and been subject to child abuse according to welfare authorities, and this was constitutional (see Parkinson 1994).

The UN Convention on the Rights of the Child prohibits any forms of physical punishment or violence on children. The Committee on the Rights of the Child has criticized legal provisions that attempt to draw a line between acceptable and unacceptable forms of corporal punishment (Hodgkin and Newell 1998). The committee considers the ban absolute: there should be no justifications or excuses, no cases where corporal punishment could be declared reasonable. The convention is ratified by nearly two hundred countries, but not by the United States.

Life Sentences

Since the Council of Europe countries have abolished the death penalty, life imprisonment is used instead for the most serious crimes. However, the forms and length of life imprisonment vary. Mandatory life sentences are determined by law as the only applicable sentence. Discretionary life sentences can be imposed at the discretion of the trial judge. Mandatory life sentences are usually final in the sense that there is no regular release mechanism or right to parole; discretionary life sentences are usually considered as a hybrid of prevention and punishment— after the punitive period has expired, the question of release must be addressed regularly.

No single form is predominant in Europe, and there are conflicting developments under way. France introduced a new life imprisonment without parole; a proposal in Finland would establish a general release mechanism. Norway and Portugal have abolished life imprisonment. The German Constitutional Court has held that it would be inhumane to deny offenders any hope of returning back to the normal society, unless they are dangerous and pose a risk for the public safety (see chap. 8, this volume; van Zyl Smit 1992). Some countries restrict the use of life imprisonment to murder (e.g., Finland), but many allow it for other serious violent, sexual, or drug crimes as well (e.g., England). Life imprisonment in some countries is typically shorter than fixed prison sentences in other countries (e.g., in Finland, life inmates are usually pardoned after serving eleven to thirteen years).

The European Court of Human Rights has never ruled that life imprisonment without parole would constitute inhuman or degrading punishment when used for adult offenders. However, it held in *Weeks* that discretionary life sentences must include a mechanism to examine release from prison. The Court held that the intention of the indeterminate life sentence was to guarantee a continuing security measure in the interest of government. The grounds for this form of deprivation of liberty are likely to change, and therefore, after the punitive period has expired, the offender must be entitled regularly to challenge the continuance of imprisonment (*Weeks v. United Kingdom*, Judgment of 2 March 1987, Series A, No. 114). The release process must meet the requirements of Article 5(4) and guarantee a right to participate in an oral hearing, present testimony, cross-examine witnesses, and obtain legal representation (*Thynne, Wilson, and Gunnell v. United Kingdom*, Judgment of 25 October 1990, Series A, No. 190; see also Richardson 1991). Based on these decisions, the United Kingdom changed the discretionary life sentence system in 1991 so that the tariff sentence is fixed by a judge in a court hearing. After the tariff has expired the prisoner is entitled to a regular review of release by the Parole Board in a hearing that meets the requirements of Article 5(4).

Later in *Wynne*, the Court upheld the distinction between discretionary and mandatory life sentences and stated that in the case of mandatory life sentences, all requirements by the Convention are met by the original trial and appeal procedures (*Wynne v. United Kingdom*, Judgment of 18 July 1994, Series A, No. 294-A).

The distinction between mandatory and discretionary, or wholly punitive and at least partly preventive sentences, has potential to evolve under the European Convention. In *Mansell*, the applicant claimed that he was entitled to an oral hearing by the Parole Board, meeting the requirements of Article 5(4), since he was convicted to a longer than normal prison sentence for preventive reasons (*Mansell v. United Kingdom*, Application no. 32072/96, Decision 2 July 1997). As a sexual offender, he received a 5-year-sentence instead of the otherwise appropriate sentence of 2.5 years, based on the provisions in the U.K. Criminal Justice Act 1991. He argued being in the same position as discretionary life prisoners whose sentence consist of a punitive part and a preventive part and whose release must be considered regularly in an oral hearing. Although the European Commission of Human Rights recognized the distinction between punitive and preventive sentences, it emphasized the distinction between indeterminate and determinate sentences. Since the original sentence was a fixed sentence of 5 years, the Commission considered it different from discretionary life sentences or indeterminate sentences, the length of which is open and typically depends on the personal development of the offender. Thus, the Commission declared the application inadmissible.

Many countries that impose mandatory life imprisonment for adults do not allow it for juveniles, since automatic life-time deprivation of liberty for juveniles who have not reached their full maturity and capacity is too severe a punishment. Some countries, like Finland, do not allow even discretionary life sentences for juvenile offenders. The UN Convention on the Rights of the Child explicitly prohibits life imprisonment for juveniles who were under 18 when they committed the crime, unless there is a regular possibility of release (Article 37). It is the only international human rights instrument to include such a provision.

However, the European Court of Human Rights has implied that a mandatory life sentence for juveniles without possibility for parole may be considered inhuman or degrading punishment (*Hussain v. United Kingdom*, Judgment of 21 February 1996, Reports 1996-I). The "Detention during Her Majesty's pleasure," English life imprisonment automatically imposed for all juveniles who committed a murder when under 18, was considered discretionary by the Court. It held that there must be a regular review of release when the punitive tariff has expired, since young persons' personality and attitudes develop when they grow older, and not to take into account maturation would mean that they have forfeited their liberty for the rest of their lives, which may constitute inhuman or degrading punishment (see also *Singh v. United Kingdom*, Judgment of 21 February 1996, Reports 1996-I). In 1997, the United Kingdom added a regular review of release by the Parole Board in the detention during Her Majesty's pleasure. However, the punitive tariff sentence is still determined by the secretary of state, a representative of the executive, instead of a court.

In the United States, over twenty states allow mandatory life sentences without parole for juvenile offenders who are 15 years old. For example, in *Harris v. Wright*, the 9th Circuit held that these sentences are consistent with evolving standards of decency and not rejected by U.S. culture and laws (*Harris v. Wright*, 93 F.3d 581 [9th Cir. 1996]; see also Harvard Law Review 1997a). The U.S. Supreme Court has never reviewed the effect of juvenile status on Eighth Amendment considerations in other than capital punishment cases.

The European Court of Human Rights considered complex and fundamental issues of juvenile criminal justice systems in two cases (*T. v. United Kingdom*, Application no. 24724/94, Judgment of 16 December 1999; *V. v. United Kingdom*, Application no. 24888/94, Judgment of 16 December 1999). They are based on the internationally famous English case of two 10-year-old boys who in 1993 murdered a 2-year-old, James Bulger. The applicants argued that several aspects of their criminal trial had violated the European Convention on Human Rights, including criminal liability of children who are only 10 years old, public trial in an adult court for 11-year-old children, high publicity that jeopardized fair-trial guarantees, a tariff sentence that was imposed by the secretary of state rather than by an impartial court, and a disproportionate tariff sentence of fifteen years that constituted inhuman punishment.

The Court basically agreed that applicants' procedural rights had been violated but refused to acknowledge that these violations amounted to inhuman or degrading treatment or punishment (Article 3). The Court did not find a shared European practice in setting the minimum age of criminal responsibility although only Cyprus, Ireland, Switzerland, Liechtenstein, Scotland, and England and Wales use criminal justice system procedures for acts of children younger than 13 years. Therefore, the relatively low minimum age for criminal liability in itself did not constitute inhuman or degrading punishment. Likewise, the Court held that the highly publicized trial in an adult court, "even if there is evidence that proceedings such as those applied to the applicant could be expected to have a harmful effect on an eleven-year-old child" (para. 77), did not violate Article 3. However, the Court recognized that criminal trials need to take full account of children's age and intellectual and emotional capacities and to find ways to ensure their ability to understand and participate in the proceedings. The English trial had been unable to provide such effective participation, and the Court found a violation of the right to a fair trial (Article 6).

Applicants' tariff sentence for the detention during Her Majesty's pleasure was initially set at fifteen years by the secretary of state in 1994. This decision was quashed by the House of Lords in 1997 and since then no new tariff had been set—the applicants had served six years at the time of the European Court's judgment. Although the Court confirmed its previous view that an indeterminate life sentence for juvenile offenders in itself does not violate the Convention, there were several other problems. Decisions on the sentence tariff amount to exercise of sentencing power and need to be determined by an independent court (violation of Article 6). Although the six years served by the applicants did not constitute inhuman or degrading punishment, the failure to set the tariff deprived them of their right to a periodic review of the indefinite detention by a judicial body (violation of Article 5).

Other Penalties

National criminal laws typically include sanctions that are regularly imposed in connection to criminal proceedings but are not necessarily considered as criminal penalties by them. Forfeiture, cancellation of driving license, and cancellation of other professional licenses are the most common; more unusual are notification of release or registers for special criminals (often sex offenders), loss of voting rights or citizenship, and restrictions in the rights to receive social services, welfare benefits, or certain governmental or other jobs.

The European human rights bodies have established an autonomous concept of "criminal penalty" and "criminal charge." They are not bound by the national legal definitions but remain free to go beyond appearances and assess the true nature and effects of procedures and measures. For example, procedures related to administrative traffic violations, competition rule violations, price-control regulations, and tax-evasion penalties have been considered criminal, although they were characterized as civil or administrative by national laws.

In *Welch v. United Kingdom*, the Court held that a forfeiture based on the English Drug Trafficking Offences Act 1986 was a criminal penalty and could not be applied retroactively (Judgment of 9 February 1995, Series A, No. 307-A). The applicant was arrested on November 1986 for smuggling large quantities of cannabis and convicted on August 1988. The forfeiture order was based on the 1986 act that entered into force on January 1987. The Court considered the forfeiture as a criminal punishment because of its broad scope—all property passing through the offender's hands over a six-year period were assumed the fruit of drug trafficking unless proved otherwise. In addition, confiscation was not limited to actual enrichment or profit; judges had a wide discretion in determining the amount of confiscation order, and default of payment may have resulted in imprisonment.

Later in 1996 (*Jamil v. France*, Judgment of 8 June 1995, Series A, No. 320) and 1998 (*Soumare v. France*, Application no. 23824/94, Judgment of 24 August 1998, Reports 1998–VI), the Court held that customs fines are criminal penalties if the default may result in imprisonment. In both cases, the customs fines were related to smuggling of drugs, their amount was equivalent to the value of the imported drugs, and their purpose was determined deterrent. In *Jamil*, the Court held that customs fines could not be applied retroactively; in *Soumare* it held that the procedural rights in case of deprivation of liberty apply to imprisonment in default of customs fines.

When the European Court of Human Rights considers forfeiture or customs fines as a criminal penalty, it means that all the procedural and material safeguards that apply in criminal cases should be met. Fair trial requirements should be respected, and in Europe forfeiture is typically ordered in a criminal procedure and based on a crime conviction. Therefore, the rights are the same as in a criminal case and include the right to a public hearing, to be presumed innocent, and to have a counsel. Also, the burden of proof is typically on the government, although the European Convention does not prohibit a reversed burden on the defendant or strict criminal liability. The situation is very different in the United States, where civil forfeiture is the most commonly used form of forfeiture. No criminal conviction is required, the property owner must prove that the property was not connected to crime, and the property is regularly forfeited in a written procedure in the absence of the owner (Tonry 1997).

In many European countries nonpayment of criminal fines, forfeiture orders, or community charges (often related to taxes) may result in imprisonment. Replacement of fiscal obligations with imprisonment following default is not against the convention, provided that the procedure complies with pretrial detention standards and fair trial requirements of Articles 5 and 6 (e.g., *Benham v. United Kingdom*, Judgment of 10 June 1996, Reports 1996-III).

The United Kingdom introduced a sex-offender registration requirement in the Sex Offenders Act 1997. Offenders must inform the police of their address and possible changes within fourteen days; registration is indefinite to those who are sentenced for thirty months imprisonment or more; and a failure to comply with the requirements is a criminal offense punishable up to six months. Both the Commission (*Ibbotson v. United Kingdom*, Application no. 40146/98, Decision of 21 October 1998) and the Court (*Adamson v. the United Kingdom*, Application no. 42293/98, Decision on Admissibility 26 January 1999) have held that the sex-offender registration cannot be considered a criminal penalty. It operates separately from the ordinary sentencing procedures, does not require any other action than submitting information, and lacks procedures or implementation measures. In *Adamson*, the Court considered the interference with applicant's private and family life necessary in a democratic society and proportionate for the aim pursued. It declined to find evidence that the applicant was at particular risk of any public humiliation or attack because of the registration. However, the Commission recognized in *Ibbotson* that registration information had been made available to the public and local campaigns mounted against sex offenders, but it did not consider these factors relevant.

A few Western countries restrict the right to vote for convicted offenders, but only if the crime was connected to abusing or violating electoral or other political rights. In other cases, most Western countries allow and encourage prison inmates to vote and use their democratic rights (for example, Denmark, Finland, France, German, Netherlands, Norway, and Sweden). The situation is strikingly different in the United States, which currently denies the right to vote for an estimated 3.9 million Americans convicted of a felony. Only four states do not disenfranchise convicted felons (Maine, Massachusetts, Utah, and Vermont). Twelve states deprive their right to vote for life (Alabama, Arizona [second felony], Delaware, Florida, Iowa, Kentucky, Maryland [second felony], Mississippi, Nevada, New Mexico, Virginia, and Wyoming). Thirty-one states and the District of Columbia disenfranchise felons while they are in prison, and often also felons on parole or probation (see Sentencing Project 1998; Fellner and Mauer 1998).

The major human rights instruments protect the right to participate in government directly or through representatives and the right to vote in public elections. The UN Human Rights Committee has stated that restrictions to the right to vote should be objective and reasonable. It has called for abolishing disenfranchisement as a criminal punishment and emphasized that if it is used, the period of deprivation should be proportionate to the offense and the sentence (General Comment 25 [57], U.N. Doc. CCPR/C/21/Rev.1/Add.7 [1996]).

It is understandable that previous criminal convictions restrict employment chances and, if the information is made available for employers, are considered in hiring workers. However, it is unusual to have broad statutory limitations for employing former convicts, and I have not heard that such restrictions are a common practice in western Europe, where the basic principle is that criminal penalties should be the only consequence of a crime. When offenders have served their criminal sentences, they have fulfilled their responsibilities toward society and should not face other formal sanctions. It is also unheard of that they would be denied social services, welfare, housing, educational benefits, or other public services that are regularly available for other citizens. These kind of restrictions may also raise questions about human rights violations. The International Covenant on Economic, Social, and Cultural Rights (UN) and the European Social Charter (Council of Europe), for example, protect every person's right to work, to an adequate standard of living (including food, clothing, and housing), and to Social Security and welfare, and education.

So-called civil disabilities as a consequence of felony conviction are widely used in the United States. Most states impose restrictions on ex-felons to hold public offices or other governmental employment, but also a broad variety of other jobs or occupational licenses may be denied, including, for example, accountant, architect, barber, insurance agency, dentist, engineer, nurse, psychologist, and teacher (see U.S. Department of Justice, Office of the Pardon Attorney 1996). Convicted felons are denied public employment for their life in six states (Alabama, Delaware, Iowa, Mississippi, Rhode Island, and South Carolina). Four states impose "civil death" on persons who are sentenced to life imprisonment (Idaho, Mississippi, New York, and Rhode Island). This means forfeiture of most civil rights, such as the right to vote, to make contracts, and sue or to be sued (see Oliveras, Burton, and Cullen 1996).

The U.S. laws that deny federal benefits for drug offenders are especially disturbing. According to the Anti-Drug Abuse Act of 1988, courts may deny drug traffickers' eligibility permanently and drug possessors' eligibility up to five years for any federally provided or funded grant, contract, loan, professional license, or commercial license, including, for example, student loans. However, retirement, welfare, Social Security, health, housing, and other such benefits were excluded from the restrictions. This changed in 1996, when the Personal Responsibility and Work Opportunity Reconciliation Act (Welfare Act) introduced a mandatory non-eligibility of any felony drug offender to federally funded cash assistance or food stamps (see Carey 1998; Godsoe 1998; Harvard Law Review 1997b). The ban is for life. For example, cultivation of a single plant of marijuana is a felony in most of the states as well as selling any amount of any drugs. The only programs that are excluded are emergency medical care, noncash disaster relief, immunizations, prenatal care, job training, and drug treatment. States may choose to grant federally funded benefits, but only by specific statutes, which are unlikely to be proposed or passed in the current political climate. In addition, the 1996 Welfare Act authorizes states to test welfare recipients for drugs and sanction those who test positive (see Carey 1998).

D. How Much to Punish?

Sentencing theories and rationales influence the types of punishments and length of sentences in use in different countries. Understanding about the essence of different sentencing theories vary, but the most persistent is the dichotomy of consequentialist (utilitarian, teleological) and desert-based (retributivist, deontological) theories. Consequential theories propose that punishments ought to achieve a certain goal in order to be justified; desert-based theories propose that punishments be proportionate to the offense and offender's culpability (e.g., von Hirsch and Ashworth 1998). Consequentialists, however, disagree on the goals for sentencing, which typically are contradictory and may include incapacitation, prevention (individual and general deterrence), rehabilitation, enhancement of public safety, or restoration of relationships. Desert-based theorists agree that there must be a justifiable goal for *the system of punishments* (i.e., general deterrence) but believe that *individual sentences* can never be justified by utilitarian goals. Consequentialist sentencing systems are much more common than just desert systems, and only a few sentencing systems are based solely on proportionality values — Finland introduced the first one in 1975.

The difficulty of obtaining an agreement on a single sentencing theory or a set of sentencing rationales is evident from the Council of Europe recommendation "Consistency in Sentencing," which failed to prefer or suggest any particular sentencing rationale (Asworth 1994; Killias 1994). However, the recommendation suggests that, whatever the rationales, they should be clearly articulated, the primary rationale should be identified, and they should be consistent with the goals of reducing the use of imprisonment and increasing the use of community sanctions, decriminalization, and mediation (Council of Europe 1993; see Appendix 9.C).

Most sentencing systems are based on some type of proportionality requirement, although the principle of proportionality has different meanings in different systems. In most countries it is used as a limiting principle against grossly excessive and disproportionate punishments (a position often associated with Norval Morris; see Frase 1997). However, in the just-desert systems it is the guiding principle of individual sentencing: the sentence in a particular case should be proportionate to the offense and offender's culpability. Ideally, *ordinal proportionality* (ranking of crimes) provides equality when persons convicted of comparable crimes receive comparable punishments and *cardinal proportionality* provides proportionate sentences when the appropriate level of punishments for each rank are determined (see, e.g., Ashworth 1995; von Hirsch 1998).

In the Council of Europe recommendation, Consistency in Sentencing, proportionality is used as a limiting standard: "Whatever rationales for sentencing are declared, disproportionality between the seriousness of the offence and the sentence should be avoided" (Article A.4). However, the recommendation also recognizes the value of ordinal proportionality and proposes a national grading of all sanctions by relative severity in order to promote the use of intermediate sanctions and to prevent net-widening effect (the tendency to use an alternative sentence instead of another noncustodial sentence). The UN Standard Minimum Rules for the Administration of Juvenile Justice emphasize the well-being of the juvenile and the principle of proportionality as the two most important objectives of the juvenile justice system (Article 5.1). However, the requirement of proportionality is understood as a principle that would take account of both the gravity of the offense and the individual circumstances of the offender (social status, family situation, and harm caused are mentioned as examples). This seems peculiar for those who associate proportionality with desert-based sentencing. Nonetheless, the rules appear to call for individualized juvenile sentencing that may take into account various personal circumstances, but in which excessive rehabilitative efforts are limited by overall proportionality requirements.

The European Convention on Human Rights

The European Commission of Human Rights and the Court have never referred to the Council of Europe's recommendation Consistency in Sentencing or held that a disproportionate sentence violated the convention. It is clear that the European bodies lack the competence and tools to analyze proportionality requirements in detail (see Kelk, Koffman, and Silvis 1995). First, they are limited by the nature of Article 3, which prohibits only inhuman or degrading punishments. A sentence that seems unnecessarily severe does not amount to inhuman or degrading punishment unless it is grossly or clearly disproportionate to the gravity of the offense. Second, because sentencing rationales and severity of punishments vary significantly in the member states, the European bodies are unable to establish a commonly agreed-upon ranking of crimes and appropriate sentences.

The European Commission of Human Rights has several times pointed out that the Convention does not include any article that would provide "a general right to call into question the length of a sentence imposed by a competent court" (*X. v. United Kingdom* [1974], 1 DR 54; *Nelson v. United Kingdom* [1986], 49 DR 170). However, it has also recognized, although in quite weak terms, that a disproportionate sentence in certain circumstances may constitute a breach of Article 3. It has stated, for example, that "an exceptionally harsh punishment for a trivial offence might raise a question under Article 3" and "that factors such as those invoked by the applicant could in exceptional cases be relevant under Article" 3 (*X. v. United Kingdom* [1973], 43 Coll. 160, and *X. v. Germany* [1976], 6 DR 127, respectively). For example, the Commission did not find any indication that a four-year prison sentence for arson (*X. v. United Kingdom* [1974], 1 DR 54) or five years for robbery (*X. v. United Kingdom* [1973], 43 Coll. 160) could possibly constitute inhuman or degrading punishment. Most would agree that these sentences appear not to be grossly disproportionate to the offenses. However, the Commission's conclusions would probably be different in more extreme cases.

Although proportionality of criminal penalties has not yet been an issue at the Court of Human Rights, it has made reference that a disproportionate sentence may violate Article 3. For example, the Court gave the following description of the *Weeks* case: Mr. Weeks was convicted of armed robbery and, aged only 17, was sentenced to life imprisonment, the severest sentence known to English law. . . . Armed with a starting pistol loaded with blank cartridges, he had entered a pet shop and stolen 35 pence. . . . Later the same day, he had telephoned the police to announce that he would give himself up. It emerged from the evidence that he had committed the robbery because he owed his mother £3. What otherwise would appear a "terrible" sentence in relation to these pathetic circumstances was seen by the trial judge and the Court of appeal as appropriate in the light of the purpose intended to be achieved [indeterminate sentence for his own and the public's protection] (*Weeks v. United Kingdom*, Judgment of 2 March 1987, Series A, No. 114, para 46).

The Court continued that "if it had not been for the specific reasons advanced for the sentence imposed, one could have serious doubts as to its compatibility with Article 3 of the Convention, which prohibits, inter alia, inhuman punishment" (para. 47).

However, in addition to Article 3, proportionality of sentences may become an issue under the articles that protect the right to privacy and civil and political freedoms of thought, conscience, religion, expression, assembly, association, and movement (Articles 8–11). National restrictions to these freedoms are allowed, but there must be a reasonable relationship between the nature and severity of the restrictions and the public goals that are enhanced by them. If the restrictions include criminal penalties, they should be proportionate to the offense and the public good that is ensured. Under the privacy and freedoms articles, the Court is not restricted to examine whether a sentence is grossly disproportionate to the offense; it can consider whether the sentence is actually proportionate to the offense.

For example, in *Janowski v. Poland*, the applicant had been convicted of insulting public guards and thus being in contempt of Polish legal order (Application No. 25716/94, Judgment of 21 January 1999, not yet published). He argued that he had used his freedom of expression and only criticized the guards without using defamatory words. The district court had sentenced him to eight months' suspended prison sentence and fines and ordered a payment of court costs and a sum to charitable institutions. On appeal, the prison sentence and payment to charitable institutions were quashed. The European Court of Human Rights held that the governmental interference was within the national discretion and proportionate, mainly because the prison sentence had been overruled in the appeals court: "In this connection, it is noteworthy that the applicant's sentence was substantially reduced on appeal and, most significantly, his prison sentence was quashed" (*Janowski v. Poland*, para 35).

Similarly in *Laskey, Jaggard, and Brown v. United Kingdom* (Judgment of 20 January 1997, Reports 1997-I), discussed in section III.B, the European Court of Human Rights emphasized that prison sentences reduced from six to three months for sado-masochistic sexual practices (assaults causing actual bodily harm) were proportionate and therefore did not violate the right to respect for private life (Article 8). The initial prison sentences ranged from one to three years.

The Council of Europe recommendation "Consistency in Sentencing" reveals a serious concern about mechanical and mandatory application of sentencing laws. It speaks against mandatory minimum laws that do not allow judges to reduce the sentence below the minimum in special circumstances (Article B.2; Council of Europe 1993, p. 25). It also suggests that previous convictions should not be used mechanically as an aggravating factor against the defendant at any stage of the criminal justice system (Article D.1). Although previous convictions are relevant in sentencing, the punishment should always be proportionate to the current offense (Article D.2). The explanatory memorandum for the recommendation also points out that a disproportionate sentence, even though within the statutory maximum, might be contrary to Article 3 of the European Convention (Council of Europe 1993, p. 19).

U.S.-style mandatory minimum laws or three-or two-strikes laws are not used in Europe, which partly explains why the European Commission and Court have not had occasion thus far to examine proportionality issues in cases where the sentence seems clearly too severe in relation to the offense or is primarily based on previous convictions. This may change, however, since England in 1997 became the first country in Europe to introduce mandatory minimum laws. The Crime (Sentences) Act 1997 requires a life sentence for a second serious violent or sexual offense, a seven-year prison sentence for a third drug dealing offense, and a three-year prison sentence for a third offense of domestic burglary, unless there are "exceptional circumstances" (mandatory life) or the sentence would be "unjust in all the circumstances" (drug dealing and domestic burglary) (see chap. 2, this volume; Thomas 1998).

Compared with U.S. three-or two-strikes laws, the English mandatory sentencing laws are still mild. For example, in Washington, the third strike of most serious offenses results in a life sentence without parole. In California, any felony counts as the third strike because only the first two convictions need to be from a list of more serious offenses (including robbery, assault, arson, burglary, and promotion of prostitution). Thus, a minor theft or marijuana possession may result in a life sentence, although with a possibility for parole after twenty-five years of imprisonment. A second strike of any felony, if the offender has one prior conviction from the list of more serious offenses, automatically means that the otherwise applicable term of sentence must be doubled (see Clark, Austin, and Henry 1997; Shichor and Sechrest 1996). In Michigan, the sentence for first conviction of possession of drugs (650 grams or more) was life imprisonment without parole, which according to the U.S. Supreme Court did not constitute cruel or unusual punishment (five-to-four decision; *Harmelin v. Michigan*, 501 U.S. 957 [1991]; see also Mun 1992). Two of the justices believed that the Eight Amendment does not protect against disproportionate prison sentences; three thought that the narrow proportionality requirement was not violated since the sentence was not grossly disproportionate to the crime. After severe criticism and citizen activity, the Michigan law was changed in 1998 to include eligibility for parole after fifteen to twenty years of imprisonment.

A recent decision of the Court of Appeal in England (*Wijs*, 20 May 1998) gives an idea how differently drug offenders are punished in Europe. The Court of Appeal suggested the following guidelines for importing or supplying amphetamine (see *Criminal Law Review* 1998, Case and Comment, pp. 587–88):

1. Up to 500 grams: up to 2 years imprisonment,
2. More than 500 grams but less than 2.5 kilos: 2–4 years,
3. More than 2.5 kilos but less than 10 kilos: 4–7 years,
4. More than 10 but less than 15 kilos: 7–10 years,
5. More than 15 kilos: upwards of 10 years, subject to the statutory maximum of 14 years

Earlier, the Court of Appeal recommended that the sentence for possessing 25,000 dosage units or more LSD should in an ordinary case be ten years or more. For possessing 250,000 dosage units or more the sentence should be fourteen years or more (*Hurley* [1998] 1 Cr.App.R.(S.) 299; *Criminal Law Review* 1997, Case and Comment, pp. 840–41.)

Both the European Commission and Court of Human Rights have considered the fairness of taking aggravating and mitigating factors into account in sentencing. The influence of prior criminal behavior has been challenged under Article 6(2), according to which "everyone charged with a criminal offence shall be presumed innocent until proved guilty according to law." In *Engel*, a military supreme court had taken into account as an aggravating factor applicants' participation in a forbidden publication, for which they had not been prosecuted or convicted. The Court refused to see a connection between Article 6(2) and sentencing: "As its wording shows, it deals only with the proof of guilt and not with the kind or level of punishment" (*Engel v. the Netherlands*, Judgment of 8 June 1976, Series A,

No. 22, para. 90). The Commission has followed the Court's interpretation that the presumption of innocence is a procedural, not a substantive right, and held that the European convention does not prevent considering an individual's personality as an aggravating factor in sentencing. In this case, the previous conviction was reversed on appeal, sent back to retrial but not pursued further (*X. v. Germany* [1976], 6 DR 129).

While aggravating factors are categorically exempt from consideration, the Commission has stated that mitigating factors might be relevant under Article 3. However, it applied the margin of appreciation doctrine in *R.M. v. United Kingdom*, where it held that a decision not to take into account AIDS as an mitigating factor in sentencing was not unreasonable and that the question of early release could be left to the discretion of the Home Office. Applicant's life expectancy was between twelve and twenty-four months, but the English court refused to consider this circumstance as a mitigating factor and sentenced him to prison for 3.5 years ([1994], 77 DR 98).

The European Convention requires that relevant aggravated factors be included in the prosecutor's charge, Article 6(3). In *De Salvador Torres v. Spain*, the commission found a violation because the applicant had not been formally notified about the aggravating circumstance that led to a heavier sentence (Judgment of 24 October 1996, Reports 1996-V). However, the Court held that the aggravating factor — the public nature of applicant's position — was an intrinsic element of the original charge of embezzlement of public funds and hence known to the applicant from the beginning of the proceedings. However, the Court's reasoning appears to be flawed since knowledge of one's public position does not necessarily include knowledge that it may be used as the aggravating factor in a lesser charge.

The Council of Europe recommendation "Consistency in Sentencing" requires that time spent in custody before trial or appeal should be counted toward the sentence. This right was acknowledged by the European Commission of Human Rights for the first time, although without mentioning the recommendation, in *P.L. v. France* (Judgment of 2 April 1997, Reports 1997-II). After the applicant had been detained for over a year, all orders and decisions concerning his crimes and detention were declared null and void because of a technical defect. Later, he was detained again for the same crimes, charged, and convicted, but the national courts refused to count the first detention against the final sentence since it was "in law deemed never to have taken place" (para. 20). After the Commission found a violation of the applicant's right to liberty, he was granted a pardon by the president of France (equivalent of the period of detention) and the European Court of Human Rights struck the case from its list.

So far, all applications claiming a right for parole or conditional release from prison have been declared inadmissible by the commission. It has held that the European Convention does not include a right to be released on parole, which is primarily a matter for national discretion. However, the commission has stated that discriminatory treatment in parole policy, for example based on sex, age, race, or AIDS, would constitute a violation of Article 14 in conjunction of Article 5 (e.g., *Grice v. United Kingdom* [1994], 77 DR 90; *B. v. United Kingdom* [1995], 45 DR 41). The commission did not find a breach in *Nelson*, where the question involved different treatment of adult and juvenile offenders in Scotland. Juveniles were not eligible for early release because of good conduct, but adult offenders were (*Nelson v. United Kingdom* [1986], 49 DR 170).

The European Union

Although the legal character and influence of the European Union[9] is very different from the international human rights instruments, it is discussed briefly since the Court of Justice, the judicial body of the European Community, has been very straightforward in its decisions about proportionality of criminal sentences. This may seem peculiar because the community has no competence to define criminal conduct or to impose criminal penalties (e.g., Dine 1993; Hartley 1981). Also, it lacks authority to require that member states impose criminal penalties to ensure effective application of community law (Guldenmund, Harding, and Sherlock 1995; Schutte 1991). However, if a member state chooses to use criminal penalties in the implementation of community law, these national criminal provisions become subject to the scrutiny of the community (Salazar 1996; Sevenster 1992). Furthermore, national criminal laws that are not directly related to the enforcement of community law may still be in conflict with it, if they jeopardize the exercise of freedoms guaranteed by the community or otherwise violate directly effective provisions of community law (Baker 1998; Delmas-Marty 1998; Müller-Graff 1998).

Private citizens or legal persons cannot sue a member state before the Court of Justice, but they may challenge a state action in national courts, which then may refer the matter to the Court of Justice for preliminary ruling. As a result, national courts may refer questions about the scope and interpretation of criminal law as well as about type and proportionality of penalties to the Court of Justice. The Court has held that, "[a]lthough in principle criminal legislation and the rules of criminal procedure are matters for which the member states are responsible, it does not follow that this branch of the law cannot be affected by Community law" (para. 19). In this instance, the question was about using a breath analysis test in a drunk driving charge, which became a community law issue under a directive regulating technical standards and requirements for certain equipment (*Lemmens*, Case C-226/97, [1998] All ER 604).

In the vast majority of cases, community law does not provide or require any sanctions, and the member states are free to adopt any penalties they find suitable. However, they are obliged actively to enforce community law, and the Court of Justice clarified the standards for effective domestic enforcement in a case against Greece (*Greece*, Case 68/88, [1989] ECR 2965). It was established that a fraud against the community was accomplished with the assistance of Greek civil servants and that a number of officials had provided false documents and statements during the investigation by the European Commission. Despite these findings, Greece failed to initiate any judicial or administrative proceedings against the responsible individuals. The Court of Justice held that domestic sanctions must be "effective" in practice, "proportionate," and "dissuasive." It created the principle of nondiscrimination, which requires that breaches of community law must be prohibited and sanctioned under the same conditions as similar breaches of national law. The principle covers the type of procedure (civil, criminal, or administrative), questions of substantive law (definitions of obligations or scope of prohibited actions; severity of penalties), and investigation practices (violations of community law must be investigated with the same diligence as analogous violations of national law).

The Court of Justice has considered proportionality of criminal sentences in several cases. It has clearly expressed that the proportionality requirement does not only work as a limiting principle against grossly excessive and disproportionate sentences. It has explicitly used proportionality as a guiding principle and ruled that the punishment in a particular case must be proportionate to comparable crimes in the same country and other members states (ordinal proportionality) as well as to the severity of the offense (cardinal proportionality). Three cases serve as an example.

In *Pieck*, a Dutch citizen failed to obtain a residence permit (with a declarative effect) after staying more than six months in the United Kingdom (Case 157/79, [1980] ECR 2171). The English penalties for such an overstay of leave were a fine up to £200 or imprisonment up to six months, and possible deportation. The Court held that deportation in this case jeopardized the very essence of free movement of workers and was "certainly incompatible" with community law. Imprisonment was considered a disproportionate penalty, when compared with minor offenses by nationals and the severity of the offense—a failure to comply with administrative formalities.

In *Messner*, Italian law required that workers from other member states register their presence within three days of the entry; the penalty for violation was a fine up to 400,000 lire or imprisonment up to three months (Case C-265/8, [1989] ECR 4209). Again, the Court of Justice held that imprisonment was a disproportionate penalty for a failure to obey an administrative formality. A fine could be compatible with community law only if it was set at a level comparable to those for minor national offenses. However, the Court found the whole criminal provision unreasonable since the three-day period for a declaration of residence was unnecessarily short to provide sufficient time to travel from the frontier to the final destination and to inquire about administrative formalities.

In *Skanavi*, the question was about a failure to exchange a valid foreign driving license for a German one, an omission punishable by a fine or imprisonment up to one year (Case C-193/94, [1996] CMLR 372). The national requirement of exchange was allowed by community law at that time, before the complete harmonization of driving licence laws in 1996. However, the right to drive was based directly on community law, and the exchange of driving licenses was merely considered evidence of it. The German law, however, treated the failure to exchange a member state driving license to a German one as driving without any valid license. The Court of Justice ruled that any criminal punishment was disproportionate to the severity of the omission and that it could not be defined as a criminal offense.

The requirement of equal treatment between violations of European Union law and national law and its effects on proportionality consideration of sentences has been developed further in two cases about taxation of imported goods. In *Drexl*,

Italian law attached different control systems and penalties for similar offenses; a failure to pay value-added tax on imports and on domestic transactions (Case 299/86, [1988] ECR 1213). A failure to pay value-added tax on imports was treated as a customs offense and smuggling, subject to imprisonment and forfeiture. A failure to pay value-added tax on domestic transactions was characterized as an administrative offense subject to administrative fines. The Court of Justice held that there were no differences between the offenses that could justify these manifestly disproportionate penalties.

In *Klattner*, Greek law attached the same penalty for different offenses; a failure to pay tax on temporary and permanent (smuggling) importation of a vehicle (Case C-389/95, [1997] CMLR 1301). The Advocate General held in his opinion that the assimilation of temporary and permanent importation violated the principle of equality, since the intention of the offender and the severity of the offense were not comparable. The Court did not rule on this matter, since the whole basis of the criminal provision was incompatible with community law (importation of a second vehicle had to be tax-free under community law).

VI. Concluding Remarks

There is a striking difference between the international regulation of the procedures by which crimes are investigated and charged and the regulation of the punishments that may be imposed. Much more effort and detail has been put into requirements and standards for the criminal process than for its outcomes. All the major human rights instruments lack a framework or theory for punishments and lack provisions about purposes of punishments in general, goals for certain types of punishments, definitions or requirements for humane punishments, rationales for sentencing, or principles for sentencing decisions. The only provision in the human rights instruments with a judicial body and case law is the prohibition of torture or other inhuman or degrading punishments. The death penalty is an exception to the nonregulation, and its use is in several documents either abolished or explicitly limited to the most serious crimes and prohibited for juveniles or pregnant or mentally insane persons.

More detailed international recommendations, declarations, and guidelines about criminal sentencing exist, but they are not considered binding, have gained little publicity, and have had little effect on national practices.

Most of the more detailed international standards concerns juvenile offenders and the death penalty. It is a customary international norm that juveniles under 18 at the time of their offense cannot be sentenced to the death penalty. There is also strong support for the view that they may not be sentenced to mandatory life imprisonment or corporal punishment. The Convention on the Rights of the Child goes furthest when it prohibits any type or level of corporal punishment on children, including parental discipline. Regrettably, the European Court of Human Rights has held that reasonable or mild corporal punishment is allowed at schools and homes. However, it has also ruled that excessive corporal discipline must be not only criminalized but also prosecuted and punished in order to give effective protection to children.

Since "torture" and "inhuman or degrading punishment" by nature encompass only grossly or clearly inappropriate and unacceptable sentencing decisions and sanctions, most applications in these matters have been considered unwarranted by international human rights bodies. Unless the interpretation of the concept of inhuman or degrading punishment is radically altered, significant change is unlikely. Nevertheless, the case law of the European Court of Human Rights has evolved, and it has lately found human rights violations in questions related to substantive criminal law, sentencing, and punishments. Although the Court seems to lack effective tools, since these questions are scarcely addressed by the European Convention, it has been able to give some strong decisions. This is a recent development of the late 1980s and 1990s.

The Court found in 1998 that England violated the European Convention in a case where a stepfather who had regularly beaten his stepson was acquitted in a criminal trial. In 1995, it gave a strong opinion that marital rape should be criminalized in a civilized society and declined to acknowledge that abolition of marital immunity doctrine was applied retroactively. This is atypical, since the Court generally avoids giving general advice or statements on problematic practices unless there is a violation of the convention. In 1989, it held that conditions and length of stay on death row may constitute inhuman or degrading punishment and prohibit extradition to a retentionist country—a view not shared by the UN Human Rights Committee or most countries outside Europe. It ruled in 1987 that discretionary life imprisonment must include a regular review of possible release, fulfilling the fair trial requirements for criminal procedures, and in 1996 that juveniles cannot be sentenced to mandatory life imprisonment. In 1999, the Court affirmed criminal liability at age 10 but held that a highly publicized trial in an adult court at age 11 violated fair trial requirements. The Court has also expanded the fair trial requirements for criminal procedure to apply to cases that were civil or administrative under national laws, for example, traffic violations, forfeiture orders, and customs fines.

Then there is a large gray area of matters related to sentencing and punishments that likely raises human rights concerns but is rarely discussed in the literature or addressed by human rights bodies. Registration of particular offenders, disenfranchisement, and other civil disabilities are in wide use in the United States, and no doubt elsewhere. Sweeping authorization to deprive ex-offenders of their right to vote, restrict their ability to obtain jobs and occupational licences, or deny them social services or welfare benefits might be considered inhuman or degrading punishment. More likely these restrictions violate the right to vote in public elections, the right to work, and the right to an adequate standard for living, Social Security and welfare, and education, protected, for example, by the International Covenant on Civil and Political Rights, the International Covenant on Economic, Social, and Cultural Rights, and the European Social Charter.

Proportionality requirements for criminal sentences is another gray zone. Some international recommendations, although nonbinding, clearly prohibit disproportionate sentences, but no human rights body has thus far ruled that a disproportionate sentence constitutes inhuman or degrading punishment. Although not a human rights body, the Court of Justice of the European Union has shown that enforceable international control of national sentencing practices is possible, but few are aware of its decisions in this area. In fact, when most member states accept proportionality only as a limiting principle for excessive punishments, the Court of Justice has enforced it as a guiding principle for determining appropriate punishments. It has ruled that the sentence in a particular case must be proportionate to the severity of the offense and to sentences imposed for comparable crimes in the same state and other members states as well. For example, it has held that a failure to comply with administrative formalities may not be punished by imprisonment and, in some cases, may not be defined as a criminal offense.

The limits of existing human rights instruments make it difficult for their enforcement bodies to take a more influential role in questions related to criminal sentencing and punishments. Innovative interpretation is unlikely to bring substantial change, and it might be better to begin discussions about the needs and forms for international control in this area. Are more authoritative standards and control desirable? Is a human rights system the best way to enforce implementation in national level? Should additional protocols about sentencing and punishments be added to the main human rights instruments? The European human rights system has shown its efficiency in regulating the investigation and prosecution of criminal charges, but it is still curious how the procedure became more important than its outcomes.

APPENDIX 9.A. ARTICLES RELATED TO SUBSTANTIVE CRIMINAL LAW AND SENTENCING IN MAJOR HUMAN RIGHTS INSTRUMENTS

Universal Declaration of Human Rights (1948)

Article 5   No one shall be subjected to torture or to cruel, inhuman or degrading treatment or punishment.

Article 9   No one shall be subjected to arbitrary arrest, detention or exile.

Article 10   Everyone is entitled in full equality to a fair and public hearing by an independent and impartial tribunal, in the determination of his rights and obligations and of any criminal charge against him.

Article 11.1   Everyone charged with a penal offence has the right to be presumed innocent until proved guilty according to law in a public trial at which he has had all the guarantees necessary for his defence.

Article 11.2   No one shall be held guilty of any penal offence on account of any act or omission which did not constitute a penal offence, under national or international law, at the time when it was committed. Nor shall a heavier penalty be imposed than the one that was applicable at the time the penal offence was committed.

International Covenant on Civil and Political Rights (1966)

Article 6.2   In countries which have not abolished the death penalty, sentence of death may be imposed only for the most serious crimes in accordance with the law in force at the time of the commission of the crime and not contrary to the provisions of the present Covenant and to the

Convention on the Prevention and Punishment of the Crime of Genocide. This penalty can only be carried out pursuant to a final judgement rendered by a competent court.

Article 6.4   Anyone sentenced to death shall have the right to seek pardon or commutation of the sentence. Amnesty, pardon or commutation of the sentence of death may be granted in all cases.

Article 6.5   Sentence of death shall not be imposed for crimes committed by persons below eighteen years of age and shall not be carried out on pregnant women.

Article 7   No one shall be subjected to torture or to cruel, inhuman or degrading treatment or punishment. In particular, no one shall be subjected without his free consent to medical or scientific experimentation.

Article 15.1   No one shall be held guilty of any criminal offence on account of any act or omission which did not constitute a criminal offence, under national or international law, at the time when it was committed. Nor shall a heavier penalty be imposed than the one that was applicable at the time when the criminal offence was committed. If subsequent to the commission of the offence, provision is made by law for the imposition of a lighter penalty, the offender shall benefit thereby.

[European] Convention for the Protection of Human Rights and Fundamental Freedoms (1950)

Article 2.1   Everyone's right to life shall be protected by law. No one shall be deprived of his life intentionally save in the execution of a sentence of a court following his conviction of a crime for which this penalty is provided by law.

Article 3   No one shall be subjected to torture or to inhuman or degrading treatment or punishment.

Article 6.2   Everyone charged with a criminal offence shall be presumed innocent until proved guilty according to law.

Article 7   No one shall be held guilty of any criminal offence on account of any act or omission which did not constitute a criminal offence under national or international law at the time when it was committed. Nor shall a heavier penalty be imposed than the one that was applicable at the time the criminal offence was committed.

American Convention on Human Rights (1969)

Article 4.2   In countries that have not abolished the death penalty, it may be imposed only for the most serious crimes and pursuant to a final judgment rendered by a competent court and in accordance with a law establishing such punishment, enacted prior to the commission of the crime. The application of such punishment shall not be extended to crimes to which it does not presently apply.

Article 4.3   The death penalty shall not be reestablished in states that have abolished it.

Article 4.4   In no case shall capital punishment be inflicted for political offenses or related common crimes.

Article 4.5   Capital punishment shall not be imposed upon persons who, at the time the crime was committed, were under 18 years of age or over 70 years of age; nor shall it be applied to pregnant women.

Article 5.2   No one shall be subjected to torture or to cruel, inhuman, or degrading punishment or treatment. All persons deprived of their liberty shall be treated with respect for the inherent dignity of the human person.

Article 5.6   Punishments consisting of deprivation of liberty shall have as an essential aim the reform and social readaptation of the prisoners.

Article 9   No one shall be convicted of any act or omission that did not constitute criminal offense, under the applicable law, at the time it was committed. A heavier penalty shall not be imposed than the one that was applicable at the time the criminal offense was committed. If subsequent to the commission of the offense the law provides for the imposition of a lighter punishment, the guilty person shall benefit therefrom.

African Charter on Human and Peoples' Rights (1981)

Article 5   Every individual shall have the right to the respect of the dignity inherent in a human being and to the recognition of his legal status. All forms of exploitation and degradation of man particularly slavery, slave trade, torture, cruel, inhuman or degrading punishment and treatment shall be prohibited.

Article 7.2   No one may be condemned for an act or omission which did not constitute a legally punishable offence at the time it was committed. No penalty may be inflicted for an offence for which no provision was made at the time it was committed. Punishment is personal and can be imposed only on the offender.

APPENDIX 9.B. SUMMARY OF THE RIGHTS PROTECTED BY THE EUROPEAN CONVENTION ON HUMAN RIGHTS

Article 2   The right to life
Article 3   Freedom from torture or other inhuman or degrading treatment or punishment
Article 4   Freedom from slavery, servitude, or compulsory labor
Article 5   The right to liberty and security of person
Article 6   The right to a fair and public trial within a reasonable time
Article 7   Freedom from retroactive effect of criminal law
Article 8   The right to respect for private and family life, home, and correspondence
Article 9   Freedom of thought, conscience, and religion
Article 10   Freedom of expression
Article 11   Freedom of assembly and association
Article 12   The right to marry and found a family
Article 13   The right to an effective national remedy in case of violation of the Convention
Article 14   Freedom from discrimination in respect for protected rights

Protocol no. 1   Protection of property, the right to education, and the right to free elections

Protocol no. 4   Prohibition of imprisonment for contractual breach, freedom of movement, and prohibition of collective expulsion of aliens

Protocol no. 6   Abolition of the death penalty

Protocol no. 7   Safeguards for expulsion procedures, the right for appeal in criminal matters, compensation in criminal matters, prohibition of double jeopardy, equality between spouses

APPENDIX 9.C. SELECTED PROVISIONS OF THE COUNCIL OF EUROPE RECOMMENDATION NO. R (92) 17: CONSISTENCY IN SENTENCING

A.1   The legislator, or other competent authorities where constitutional principles and legal traditions so allow, should endeavour to declare the rationales for sentencing.

A.4   Whatever rationales for sentencing are declared, disproportionality between the seriousness of the offence and the sentence should be avoided.

A.6   Sentencing rationales should be consistent with modern and humane crime policies, in particular in respect of reducing the use of imprisonment, expanding the use of community sanctions and measures, pursuing policies of decriminalisation, using measures of diversion such as mediation, and of ensuring the compensation of victims.

B.2   The range of available sentences for an offence should not be so wide to afford little guidance to courts on its relative seriousness. States should therefore consider the grading of offences into degrees of seriousness, provided, however, that minimum penalties, where applicable, do not prevent the court from taking account of particular circumstances in the individual case.

B.5.a   Custodial sentences should be regarded as a sanction of last resort, and should therefore be imposed only in cases where, taking due account of other relevant circumstances, the seriousness of the offence would make any other sentence clearly inadequate.

D.1   Previous convictions should not, at any stage in the criminal justice system, be used mechanically as a factor working against the defendant.

D.2   Although it may be justifiable to take account of the offender's previous criminal record within the declared rationales for sentencing, the sentence should be kept in proportion to the seriousness of the current offence(s).

G   In principle, time spent in custody before trial or before appeal shall count towards the sentence. There should be a coherent policy with regard to time spent in custody abroad.

NOTES

1. Article 1, Statute of the Council of Europe. The original ten state parties were Belgium, Denmark, France, Ireland, Italy, Luxembourg, the Netherlands, Norway, Sweden, and the United Kingdom.

2. The other thirty-one member states in addition to the ten original ones are Albania, Andorra, Austria, Bulgaria, Croatia, Cyprus, Czech Republic, Estonia, Finland, Georgia,

Germany, Greece, Hungary, Iceland, Latvia, Liechtenstein, Lithuania, Malta, Moldova, Poland, Portugal, Romania, Russian Federation, San Marino, Slovakia, Slovenia, Spain, Switzerland, Ukraine, Turkey, and the former Yugoslav Republic of Macedonia.

3. The European Commission of Human Rights has a member from each state party of the European Convention; members are elected for six years by the Committee of Ministers of the Council of Europe and sit in their individual capacity.

4. The European Court of Human Rights has a judge from each state party of the European Convention; judges are elected by the Parliamentary Assembly of the Council of Europe.

5. The Committee of Ministers consists of the foreign ministers of the members states of the Council of Europe. Normally it used to endorse the Commission's opinion of violation without further investigation or adversary procedure.

6. Decisions and reports by the Commission and judgments and decisions by the Court can be obtained from the Council of Europe's Web page (www.dhdirhr.coe.fr) by using the Hudoc database.

7. Previously in 1974, the European Committee on Crime Problems published a report, "Sentencing," which documents differences in sanctions and sentencing policies among member states (Council of Europe 1974). The Eighth Criminological Colloquium, "Disparities in Sentencing: Causes and Solutions," proposed a working group to examine general sentencing principles and systematization of sentencing decisions (Council of Europe 1989). The work of the Select Committee of Experts on Sentencing was the basis for the "Consistency in Sentencing" recommendation (Council of Europe 1993).

8. The protocol is in force in Andorra, Austria, Belgium, Bulgaria, Croatia, Czech Republic, Denmark, Estonia, Finland, France, Germany, Greece, Hungary, Iceland, Ireland, Italy, Latvia, Liechtenstein, Lithuania, Luxembourg, Macedonia, Malta, Moldova, the Netherlands, Norway, Portugal, Romania, San Marino, Slovakia, Slovenia, Spain, Sweden, Switzerland, and the United Kingdom. It is signed by Cyprus, Germany, Poland, Russia, and Ukraine. Albania and Turkey have not taken any action.

9. The European Union is based on three pillars: (1) the European Community, the European Coal and Steel Community, and the European Atomic Energy Community; (2) the common foreign and security policy; and (3) police and judicial cooperation in criminal matters. The Court of Justice has primary jurisdiction only in the first pillar and also European Union law exists only in the first pillar. Although this is changing, it is still a custom to refer to the European Community in discussing the decisions of the Court of Justice or binding laws of the European Union. In this chapter, the concept of community is used. Currently the member states of the European Community are Belgium, France, Germany, Italy, Luxembourg, the Netherlands, the United Kingdom, Spain, Denmark, Portugal, Ireland, Greece, Austria, Sweden, and Finland.

REFERENCES

Addo, M., and N. Grief. 1995. "Is There a Policy Behind the Decisions and Judgments Relating to Article 3 of the European Convention on Human Rights?" *European Law Review* 20:178–93.
Amnesty International. 1998a. "International Standards on the Death Penalty." Report ACT 50/10/98. Available at www.amnesty.org/ailib/aipub/1998/ACT/A5001098.htm.
———. 1998b. "Juveniles and the Death Penalty: Executions Worldwide since 1990." Available at www.amnesty.org/ailib/aipub/1998/ACT/A5001198.htm.

————. 1998c. "On the Wrong Side of History: Children and the Death Penalty in the USA." Available at www.amnestyusa.org/rightsforall/juvenile/dp.htm.

————. 1999. "The Death Penalty Worldwide: Developments in 1998." Report ACT 50/04/99. Available at www.amnesty.org/ailib/aipub/1999/ACT/A5000499.htm.

Ankumah, E. 1996. *The African Commission on Human and Peoples' Rights.* The Hague: Kluwer Law International.

Ashworth, A. 1994. "Towards European Sentencing Standards." *European Journal on Criminal Policy and Research* 2:7–11.

————. 1995. 2d ed. *Sentencing and Criminal Justice.* London: Butterworths.

Baker, E. 1998. "Taking European Criminal Law Seriously." *Criminal Law Review,* 361–77.

Bassiouni, M. C., and Z. Motala, eds. 1995. *The Protection of Human Rights in African Criminal Proceedings.* Dordrecht: Kluwer.

Bedau, H. 1997. *The Death Penalty in America.* New York: Oxford University Press.

Bell, A. A. 1996. "McKenzie v. Day: Is Twenty Years on Death Row Cruel and Unusual Punishment? *Golden Gate University Law Review* 26:41–72.

Bengoetxea, J., and H. Jung. 1991. "Towards a European Criminal Jurisprudence? The Justification of Criminal Law by the Strasbourg Court." *Legal Studies* 3:239–80.

Bitensky, S. H. 1998. "Spare the Rod, Embrace Our Humanity: Toward a New Legal Regime Prohibiting Corporal Punishment of Children." *University of Michigan Journal of Law* 31:353–474.

Bloom, S. 1995. "Spare the Rod, Spoil the Child? A Legal Framework for Recent Corporal Punishment Proposals." *Golden Gate University Law Review* 25:361–89.

Breitenmoser, S., and G. Wilms. 1990. "Human Rights v. Extradition: The Soering Case." *Michigan Journal of International Law* 11:845–86.

Bureau of Justice Statistics. 1998. *Capital Punishment 1997.* Washington, D.C.: U.S. Government Printing Office.

————. 1999. *Capital Punishment 1998.* Washington, D.C.: U.S. Government Printing Office.

Cameron, I. 1995. "Protocol 11 to the European Convention on Human Rights: The European Court of Human Rights as a Constitutional Court?" *Yearbook of European Law* 15:219–60.

Carey, C. 1998. "Crafting a Challenge to the Practice of Drug Testing Welfare Recipients: Federal Welfare Reform and State Responses as the Most Recent Chapter in the War on Drugs." *Buffalo Law Review* 46:281–345.

Clark, J., J. Austin, and A. Henry. 1997. *"Three Strikes and You're Out": A Review of State Legislation.* Washington, D.C: National Institute of Justice.

Clark, R. 1994. *The United Nations Crime Prevention and Criminal Justice Program.* Philadelphia: University of Pennsylvania Press.

————. 1995. "United Nations Standards and Norms in Crime Prevention and Criminal Justice." *Transnational Law and Contemporary Problems* 5:287–306.

Council of Europe. 1974. *Sentencing.* Strasbourg: Council of Europe.

————. 1989. *Disparities in Sentencing: Causes and Solutions.* Collected Studies in Criminological Research vol. 26. Strasbourg: Council of Europe.

————. 1993. *Consistency in Sentencing.* Recommendation no. R (92) 17. Strasbourg: Council of Europe.

————. 1994. *European Rules on Community Sanctions and Measures.* Recommendation no. R (92) 16. Strasbourg: Council of Europe.

Davidson, Scott. 1997. *The Inter-American Human Rights System.* Aldershot: Dartmouth.

de Blois, M. 1994. "The Fundamental Freedom of the European Court of Human Rights." In *The Dynamics of the Protection of Human Rights in Europe*, edited by R. Lawson and M. de Blois. Dordrecht: Kluwer.

Delmas-Marty, Mireille. 1998. "The European Union and Penal Law." *European Law Journal* 4:87–115.

Dickson, B., ed. 1997. *Human Rights and the European Convention: The Effects of the Convention on the United Kingdom and Ireland*. London: Sweet & Maxwell.

Dine, J. 1993. "European Community Criminal Law?" *Criminal Law Review*, 246–54.

Duffy, P. J. 1983. "Article 3 of the European Convention on Human Rights." *International and Comparative Law Quarterly* 32:316–46.

Dugard, J., and C. van den Wyngaert. 1996. *International Criminal Law and Procedure*. Aldershot: Dartmouth.

Fellner, Jamie, and Marc Mauer. 1999. "Nearly 4 Million Americans Denied Vote Because of Felony Convictions." *Overcrowded Times* 9(5): 1, 6–13.

Frase, R. S. 1997. "Sentencing Principles in Theory and Practice." In *Crime and Justice: A Review of Research*, vol. 22, edited by Michael Tonry. Chicago: University of Chicago Press.

Godsoe, Cynthia. 1998. "The Ban on Welfare for Felony Drug Offenders: Giving a New Meaning to 'Life Sentence.' " *Berkeley Women's Law Journal* 13:257–67.

Gomien, D., D. Harris, and L. Zwaak. 1996. *Law and Practice of the European Convention on Human Rights and the European Social Charter*. Strasbourg: Council of Europe.

Guldenmund, R., C. Harding, and A. Sherlock. 1995. "The European Community and Criminal Law." In *Criminal Justice in Europe: A Comparative Study*, edited by P. Fennell, C. Harding, N. Jorg, and B. Swart. Oxford: Clarendon Press.

Harris, D. J., M. O'Boyle, and C. Warbrick. 1995. *Law of the European Convention on Human Rights*. London: Butterworths.

Hartley, T. C. 1981. "The Impact of European Community Law on the Criminal Process." *Criminal Law Review*, 75–85.

Harvard Law Review. 1997a. "Recent Case: Eight Amendment—Juvenile Sentencing." *Harvard Law Review* 110:1185–90.

———. 1997b. "Recent Legislation: Welfare Reform." *Harvard Law Review* 110:983–88.

Heffernan, D. 1996. "Comment: America the Cruel and Unusual? An Analysis of the Eighth Amendment under International Law." *Catholic University Law Review* 45:481–560.

Hodgkin, R., and P. Newell. 1998. *Implementation Handbook for the Convention on the Rights of the Child*. Geneva: United Nations Children Fund.

Hodgkinson, P., and A. Rutherford. 1996. *Capital Punishment: Global Issues and Perspectives*. Winchester: Waterside Press.

Hood, R. 1996. *The Death Penalty: A World-Wide Perspective*. New York: Oxford University Press.

———. 1998. "Capital Punishment." In *The Handbook of Crime and Punishment*, edited by Michael Tonry. New York: Oxford University Press.

Human Rights Watch. 1999. *Human Rights Watch World Report 1999*. Available at http://www.hrw.org/worldreport99.

Jacobs, F., and R. White. 1996. *The European Convention on Human Rights*. Oxford: Clarendon Press.

Jung, H. 1993. "Criminal Justice: A European Perspective." *Criminal Law Review* 237–45.

Kaiser, G. 1996. "Crime Policy from a West European Perspective." *European Journal on Criminal Policy and Research* 5:58–71.

Kelk, C., L. Koffman, and J. Silvis. 1995. "Sentencing Practice, Policy, and Discretion." In *Criminal Justice in Europe: A Comparative Study*, edited by P. Fennell, C. Harding, N. Jörg, and B. Swart. Oxford: Clarendon Press.

Killias, M. 1994. "Sentencing Reform: From Rhetorics to Reducing Sentencing Disparity." *European Journal on Criminal Policy and Research* 2 (1):19–28.

Lillich, R. 1991. "The Soering Case." *American Journal of International Law* 85: 128–49.

Matscher, F. 1993. "Methods of Interpretation of the Convention." In *The European System for the Protection of Human Rights*, edited by R. Macdonald, F. Matscher, and H. Petzold. Dordrecht: Kluwer.

Mower, G. 1991. *Regional Human Rights: A Comparative Study of the West European and Inter-American Systems*. Westport, Conn.: Greenwood Press.

Müller-Graff, P.-C. 1998. "The European Treaty Framework and the Criminal Law: EC Competences in Criminal Law." In *Crime Sans Frontières: International and European Legal Approaches*, edited by P. Cullen and W. Gilmore. Edinburgh: Edinburgh University Press.

Mun, A. 1992. "Mandatory Life Sentences without Parole Found Constitutionally Permissible for Cocaine Possession." *Washington Law Review* 67:713–30.

Newman, F., and D. Weissbrodt. 1996. *International Human Rights: Law, Policy, and Process*. Cincinnati, Ohio: Anderson.

Olivares, K. M., V. S. Burton, and F. C. Cullen. 1996. "The Collateral Consequences of a Felony Conviction: A National Study of State Legal Codes ten Years Later." *Federal Probation* 60:10–16.

Ovey, C. 1998. "The European Convention on Human Rights and the Criminal Lawyer: An Introduction." *Criminal Law Review*, 4–15.

Parkinson, J. 1994. "Federal Court Treatment of Corporal Punishment in Public Schools: Jurisprudence That Is Literally Shocking to the Conscience." *South Dakota Law Review* 39:276–311.

Ratner, R. 1998. "The Schizophrenias of International Criminal law." *Texas International Law Journal* 33: 237–56.

Reid, K. 1998. *A Practitioner's Guide to the European Convention on Human Rights*. London: Sweet & Maxwell.

Richardson, G. 1991. "Discretionary Life Sentences and the European Convention on Human Rights." *Public Law*, 34–40.

Salazar, L. 1996. "The European Community and Criminal Law: An Obstacle Course." In *What Kind of Criminal Policy for Europe?* edited by M. Delmas-Marty and M. Summers. The Hague: Kluwer.

Schabas, W. 1997. *The Abolition of the Death Penalty in International Law*. New York: Cambridge University Press.

Schutte, J. 1991. "The European Market of 1993: Test for a Regional Model of Supranational Criminal Justice or of Interregional Cooperation in Criminal Law." *Criminal Law Forum* 3:55–83.

The Sentencing Project. 1998. "Losing the Vote: The Impact of Felony Disenfranchisement Laws in the United States." Washington, D.C.: The Sentencing Project.

Sevenster, H. 1992. "Criminal Law and EC Law." *Common Market Law Review* 29:29–70.

Shichor, D., and D. Sechrest, eds. 1996. *Three Strikes and You're Out: Vengeance as Public Policy*. Thousand Oaks, Calif.: Sage.

Swart, B., and J. Young. 1995. "The European Convention on Human Rights and Criminal Justice in the Netherlands and the United Kingdom." In *Criminal Justice in Europe: A Comparative Study*, edited by P. Fennell, C. Harding, N. Jorg, and B. Swart. London. Oxford: Clarendon Press.

Thomas, D. A. 1998. "The Crime (Sentences) Act 1997." *Criminal Law Review*, 83–92.

Tonry, Michael. 1997. "Forfeiture Laws, Practices, and Controversies in the US." *European Journal of Crime, Criminal Law, and Criminal Justice* 5:294–307.

U.S. Department of Justice, Office of the Pardon Attorney. 1996. "Civil Disabilities of Convicted Felons: A State-by-State Survey." Washington, D.C: Office of the Pardon Attorney.

van Dijk, P, and G. J. H. van Hoof. 1998. 3d ed. *Theory and Practice of the European Convention on Human Rights*. The Hague: Kluwer Law International.

van Zyl Smit, D. 1992. "Is Life Imprisonment Constitutional? The German Experience." *Public Law*, 263–278.

von Hirsch, A. 1998. "Penal Theories." In *The Handbook of Crime and Punishment*, edited by Michael Tonry. New York: Oxford University Press.

von Hirsch, A., and A. Ashworth, eds. 1998. *Principled Sentencing: Readings on Theory and Policy*. 2d ed. Oxford: Hart Publishing.

Weissbrodt, D., and R. Wolfrum, eds. 1997. *The Right to a Fair Trial*. New York: Springer.

Yourow, H. C. 1996. *The Margin of Appreciation Doctrine in the Dynamics of European Human Rights Jurisprudence*. Dordrecht: Kluwer.

International Controls on Sentencing and Punishment

International human rights law as yet impinges on domestic sentencing policy to a very limited extent. Following a brief outline of the international human rights law framework, this chapter explores three lines of limited influence, actual or potential. First is the degree to which international human rights mechanisms provide models for sentencing policy and do, or might, take responsibility for sentencing in certain situations overlapping with domestic responsibilities. I consider the International War Crimes Tribunal for the former Yugoslavia and the shortly-to-be-established International Criminal Court. The second line of inquiry is the degree to which international human rights law serves directly to limit the range and application of penalties domestically. Here I focus on efforts to restrain the use of capital punishment. Third is the degree to which international human rights law indirectly constrains the domestic use made of certain sentences, principally incarceration, by setting standards to be met in the execution of sentences. Here I concentrate on the working of the European Convention for the Prevention of Torture and Inhuman or Degrading Treatment or Punishment.

This chapter moves from the general to the particular. It begins with a brief survey of the international mechanisms that might conceivably exercise influence on sentencing policy and thereafter considers those mechanisms in relation to each of the above possible lines of influence. At the close I consider, using domestic case studies, how international standards regarding what has in most states become the most widely used criminal sanction—imprisonment—are, within the Council of Europe, being brought to bear on local practice.

The overall tone of this chapter might appear to be one of skepticism and pessimism. Although international human rights law appears to exercise little influence on sentencing policy with regard to the type of penalties imposed or the severity of their application, the relevant international mechanisms are mostly in their infancies. It seems likely that peace-keeping and conflict control efforts, the processes of globalization, in particular the increased mobility of people for the purposes of employment and leisure, and the corresponding pressures that extradition procedures be backed up by common understandings and protections will gradually whittle away the sovereignty that states have previously assumed in the area of sentencing and penal policies.

I. The International Framework

The starting point must be the 1948 Universal Declaration of Human Rights (UDHR), in particular Articles 3 (the right to life, liberty, and security of person), 5 (no torture, cruel, inhuman, or degrading treatment or punishment), 9 (no arbitrary arrest, detention, or exile) and 10 (fair and public hearings by an independent and impartial tribunal). I concentrate largely on Article 5 with regard to both substantive standards and the development of international oversight and enforcement mechanisms.

Because the UDHR was intended to be "a common standard of achievement for all peoples and all nations" rather than a source of legal obligation, two consequences followed its passage. First, a state would become subject to an obligation covered by any provision in the UDHR only if it subsequently chose to become a party to a legal instrument subsequently drafted. Second, because it did not oblige any state to do anything; no mechanisms were originally established through which the UDHR standards could be enforced. Since 1948, however, several treaties have been established, both internationally and regionally, to give force to UDHR standards and the UN has developed several Charter-based mechanisms to oversee the human rights records of all member states. These Charter- and treaty-based mechanisms now constitute a web of bewildering complexity.

In the Charter-based sphere, for example, the UN Commission of Human Rights is enabled publicly to debate and investigate alleged abuses of human rights taking place as a matter of state policy, mandate working groups or special rapporteurs, or request the UN secretary-general to examine the human rights situation in any number of countries, debate their reports, and adopt resolutions. The third procedure was used in 1985 to establish the Special Rapporteur on Torture.

Of particular note is the Human Rights Committee (HRC) established in 1966 by the UN-sponsored International Covenant on Civil and Political Rights (ICCPR), which as of December 31, 1997, had been ratified by 140 states. This committee oversees the implementation of the obligations assumed by those states that become a party to the covenant. All states party to it are obliged to submit reports to the HRC on the measures they have adopted to give effect to the rights contained in the covenant, and the process of examining these reports provides an opportunity for rigorous scrutiny of particular situations. The HRC now makes "concluding observations" that highlight matters of particular concern and include recommendations.

The regional human rights organizations, like the UN, have devised systems and structures to achieve investigation and oversight. I concentrate here on those in Europe, where development has been greatest.

Thus, with respect to UDHR Article 5, the prohibition of torture and inhuman or degrading treatment or punishment has passed into the body of customary international law and, as such, applies to all states irrespective of whether they have become a party to an international instrument (Rodley 1987; Meron 1989). The general obligation is mirrored in Article 3 of the European Convention for the Protection of Human Rights and Fundamental Freedoms (1950), Article 5.2 of the American Convention on Human Rights (1969), Article 5 of the African Charter on Human and Peoples' Rights (1981), and Article 7 of the ICCPR. This last complements the prohibition of torture and inhuman and degrading treatment with the provision in Article 10(1) that "All persons deprived of their liberty shall be treated with humanity and with respect for the inherent dignity of the human person." Furthermore, in 1992 the HRC updated its General Comments on Article 10 and drew attention to the relevance of the various UN codes—the UN Standard Minimum Rules for the Treatment of Prisoners (1955), the UN Standard Minimum Rules for the Administration of Juvenile Justice (the Beijing Rules, 1985), the Body of Principles for the Protection of All Persons under Any Form of Detention or Imprisonment (1988), and the Basic Principles for the Treatment of Prisoners (1990)—which, while not legally binding, were thereby given an enhanced status.

We might begin with a brief consideration of the International Criminal Tribunal for the Prosecution of Persons Responsible for Serious Violations of International Humanitarian Law Committed in the Territory of Former Yugoslavia since 1991 (ICTY). The tribunal is arguably relevant for the following reasons. First, it is an international tribunal established by statute adopted by UN Security Council Resolution (No. 827; May 25, 1993). Second, it has been established specifically to deal with grave human rights violations (crimes against humanity, violations of the laws and customs of war and genocide). Third, it undoubtedly provides a model for the shortly-to-be-established International Criminal Court and could provide a model for sentencing for domestic criminal law systems. Fourth, because the ICTY deals, as does the parallel body established for Rwanda, with grave offenses that could also be tried domestically, there is need to ensure that there is a measure of concordance between the procedures adopted and penalties imposed by the relevant international and domestic tribunals. Rwanda, for example, has the death penalty but the international tribunal for Rwanda does not: it was widely hoped that Rwanda would agree to commute capital sentences in order that there not be gross disparity between the sentences that might be imposed in the Rwandan courts and those imposed in the international tribunal. Unfortunately, this has not happened. In April 1998 the Rwandan authorities executed in public, by firing squad, twenty-two persons convicted of genocide in the Rwandan domestic courts despite pleas from UN officials that they not do so.

This process of alignment is little developed, however. For example, the Statute and Rules of Procedure that govern the work of the ICTY provide limited guidance on sentencing as opposed to proceedings generally. Moreover, because the tribunal has been established in order to deal with a narrow range of extremely grave offenses, the tribunal is of limited application as an exemplar. The ICTY has, for example, no discretion to pass a sentence other than imprisonment—given the gravity of the offenses involved the absence of power to impose the death sentence is of significance—though any sentence of imprisonment passed can be of any determinate length or for life (Article 24(1)). In deciding the period of imprisonment following conviction the tribunal shall take into account such factors as the gravity of the offense and the individual circumstances of the convicted person (Article 24(2)). Both the defense and prosecution may submit any relevant information to help the court determine the appropriate sentence (Rules of Procedure and Evidence, IT/32/Rev.14, December 1998) and in determining sentence the court shall also consider such factors as any aggravating circumstances, any mitigating circumstances including substantial cooperation with the prosecutor by the convicted person before or after conviction, the general practice regarding prison sentences in the courts of the former Yugoslavia, and the extent to which any penalty imposed by a court of any state on the convicted person for the same act has already been served, as referred to in Article 10(3) of the statute (Rules of Procedure 101(B)).

The tribunal may impose consecutive or concurrent sentences in the case of multiple sentences and credit is to be given for any period spent in pretrial custody. Sentence is to be pronounced publicly and is subject to both appeal and review should relevant new facts come to light (Rules of Procedure 101(C-E), 107–18, 119–25).

But there is no statement of sentencing purpose, and scrutiny of the tribunal's judgments so far reveals that there are few relevant precedents in international criminal law to guide it. The tribunal has concluded that the relevant case law indicates that penalties should be directed to general deterrence and retribution and that this is broadly consistent with the declarations of UN Security Council members when establishing the tribunal: success by the tribunal in bringing to book grave human rights violators would undermine perceptions about the impunity of the guilty and thus dampen desire for vengeance. Furthermore, it would deter the perpetration of further crimes. The tribunal has justified its sentencing decisions thus:

> The International Tribunal sees public reprobation and stigmatization by the international community, which would thereby express its indignation over heinous crimes and denounce the perpetrators, as one of the essential functions of a prison sentence for a crime against humanity. In addition, thwarting impunity even to a limited extent would contribute to appeasement and give the chance to the people who were sorely afflicted to mourn those among them who had been unjustly killed. (Sentencing Judgment in *Drazen Erdomovic* [29 November 1996], paras. 58–59)

There is evidence of a degree of confusion in the proceedings before the tribunal about the meaning of offenses and their relative seriousness. Thus the first case leading to imposition of sentence by the tribunal was successfully appealed on the grounds that the accused did not fully understand, and had not adequately been advised regarding, the charge of *crime against humanity* to which he had pled guilty. The defendant was retried and fresh pleas were taken. Pleading guilty now to an *offense against the laws and customs of war* as opposed to a crime against humanity—though the nature of his actions were found to be substantially the same as those established during the first trial—his sentence was reduced from ten to five years' imprisonment.[1] It is not clear whether crimes against humanity (which extend from murder, extermination, and enslavement to persecution on political, racial, or religious grounds) are more serious than war crimes (which extend from wilful killing, torture, or inhuman treatment through various property-related offenses such as the seizure, destruction, or wilful damage of public institutions to the plunder of public or private property) or whether one category can be understood to subsume the other (Statute of the International Tribunal, Articles 2, 3, and 5). There is certainly no guidance, other than the availability of imprisonment alone, about what sentences are appropriate for what offenses set out in the statute.

In a later judgment the tribunal focused on the sentencing practices of the courts in the former Yugoslavia on the grounds that "international law has not developed a sentencing pattern of its own and must rely on domestic jurisdictions for its guidance (Sentencing Judgment in *Zejnil Delalic et al.* [16 November 1998], 408). But this process has been far from straightforward, not least because the courts of the former Yugoslavia had recourse to the death penalty, which the ICTY does not. The tribunal has decided that the law and practice of domestic courts is a point of reference but is not binding. In the case of *Delalic* and others the tribunal discussed a variety of sentencing objectives — retribution, public protection, incapacitation and deterrence — before concluding that deterrence is "probably the most important factor in the assessment of appropriate sentences for violations of international humanitarian law." The court passed a sentence of twenty year's imprisonment on one of the accused, five years longer than the maximum available in the former Yugoslavia.

There appears to be insufficient detail in the statute and rules of procedure of the ICTY to safeguard the court against inconsistency in sentencing and the Statute for the International Criminal Court (adopted July 17, 1998) provides only the bare minimum regarding penalties and sentencing. The International Court is to have available to it powers to impose imprisonment up to thirty years or life (but not the death penalty), fines, and forfeiture of proceeds, property, or assets derived directly or indirectly from the crime (Article 77(1) and (2)). Moreover, in determining sentence "the Court shall, in accordance with the Rules of Procedure and Evidence, take into account such factors as the gravity of the crime and the individual circumstances of the convicted person" (Article 78(1)). There is a substantial sentencing policy lacuna here, which the rules of procedure, currently being drafted,[2] may or may not adequately fill.

This is a topic on which more detailed guidance is provided by the recommendation adopted by the Council of Europe's Committee of Ministers, "Consistency in Sentencing" (Council of Europe 1993), a document which is analyzed in some detail in chapter 9, this volume. The recommendation arose out of the deliberations of a committee of experts and comprises sections covering rationales for sentencing, penalty structure, aggravating and mitigating circumstances, previous convictions, the giving of reasons for sentences, and so on. Of particular interest is the discussion in the accompanying explanatory memorandum regarding "warranted" and "unwarranted disparity." The committee came quickly to agree in paragraph 13 that "consistency of approach" should be the appropriate goal, not "arithmetical consistency of outcomes"—a project linked to the sentencing guideline systems operating in some U.S. jurisdictions. Whereas "warranted disparity" means properly treating like cases alike and different cases differently according to a clear statement of sentencing rationales, "unwarranted disparity" means:

> differences in sentencing which result from variable approaches which do not form part of the (professed) sentencing policy of the jurisdiction—for example, variations stemming from personal views, local or regional traditions which are perpetuated without being justified, or variations influenced by the mass media. (para. 8)

Thus competent authorities are advised to declare their rationales for sentencing, and, where different rationales may conflict, indicate ways of establishing possible priorities; declare wherever possible a primary rationale for classes of offenses or offenders; and avoid disproportionality between the seriousness of the offense and the sentence (Council of Europe 1993, Appendix A(1–4)). The committee failed, however, to recommend any particular sentencing rationale and its deliberations have had no discernible influence: "Consistency in Sentencing" is at present little known and so far almost uncited.

Further, though the Council of Europe has adopted a clear policy of restraint in the use of imprisonment—which "Consistency in Sentencing" implicitly endorses—the variations in the use of custody within Council of Europe member states and the general trend toward increased reliance on custody in Europe suggests strongly that little influence is being exercised on the policies of member states (Council of Europe 1998; Evans and Morgan 1998, chap. 9). The adoption of fortress-Europe policies in relation to immigration, fears about organized crime, and Europe-wide pressures to adopt more repressive policies against the trafficking and consumption of illegal drugs are combining to make European criminal justice systems more punitive (Sim, Ruggiero, and Ryan 1995). Though comparison of crude incarceration rates in relation to aggregate population is not the ideal guide to relative levels of punitiveness (Pease 1994), the size of the incarceration rate differences within the Council of Europe area (which now includes most of the former Warsaw Pact states) cannot plausibly be explained by factors other than relative punitiveness. The differences in incarceration rates within the Council of Europe area are now significantly greater than those exhibited between states within the United States. They range from 26 and 33 per 100,000 (Cyprus and Slovenia, respectively) to 392 and 694 per 100,000 (the Ukraine and Russian Federation, respectively). This is a topic to which I return in section III.

II. Restraining the Use or Application of Penalties

By far the most controversial and telling illustration of the limited impact of international human rights law on the use of particular penalties is that provided by capital punishment. The UN has conducted a vigorous campaign for abolition for over half a century and yet, as we move into the new millennium, member states, including the most powerful nation on earth, resist the call and, indeed, resort increasingly to the sanction.[3]

In furtherance of its interpretation of Article 3 of the UDHR, the UN has made its objective the progressive restriction in the number of offenses for which capital punishment might be imposed with a view to the eventual abolition of the penalty. This objective has been insistently reflected in various resolutions of the UN General Assembly and the Second Optional Protocol to the ICCPR (which, in Article 6, allows for retention of the death penalty), adopted in 1989, which affirms that the abolition of the death penalty contributes to the enhancement of human dignity and the progressive development of human rights in general. Yet reviews conducted on behalf of the UN make it abundantly clear that the death penalty persists and that the issue whether it can legitimately be used is not resolved and shows no sign of being resolved.

According to the most recent evidence the cumulative movement towards restriction and abolition of the death penalty has not been universal. Western Europe is completely abolitionist, de facto if not de jure, and those former Warsaw Pact countries that have either joined, or applied to join, the Council of Europe have signaled their intention to become abolitionist.[4] By contrast the Middle Eastern and North African states are mostly committed retentionists that have extended the scope of the death penalty and continue to execute offenders, in some instances in greatly increased numbers. The growing influence of Islamic law is a major factor here and several representatives of Islamic states have stated their position in unequivocal terms before the UN: use of the death penalty for the most heinous crimes is a cardinal principle and their divine right. They will brook no interference from the imperialist West. Yet the imperialist West is itself divided. The United States and several Caribbean states have in recent years moved dramatically against abolition.[5] By contrast, South America is now almost completely abolitionist. Elsewhere — in Sub-Saharan Africa and Asia — there is no clear pattern of opinion or practice. Support for the death penalty therefore makes strange bedfellows — from the United States to China, the Sudan to Singapore.

Capital punishment has recently been reintroduced in several countries and in others executions have been carried out where the death penalty had for some time been in abeyance. Moreover, in some parts of the world the death penalty has been extended to crimes not directly associated with homicide (Hood 1996, para. 90). With respect to the "Safeguards Guaranteeing Protection of the Rights of Those Facing the Death Penalty" adopted by the UN Economic and Social Council (ECOSOC) in 1984, it is, for example, questionable whether retentionist countries are applying the penalty only to "the most serious crimes, it being understood that their scope should not go beyond intentional crimes with lethal or other extremely grave consequences" (ECOSOC Resolution 1884/50, Safeguard 1). In most retentionist countries capital punishment is available for certain offenses against the state and though this sometimes means limitation to waging war against the state, elsewhere it encompasses a wide range of what Hood has generically termed "political offenses" such as treason (Hood 1996, para 92). In China, for example, the death penalty is applicable to a wide range of economic offenses said to involve "undermining the economy."

The penalty has been introduced retroactively in several countries, including, for example, Israel for crimes committed during the Nazi period (ECOSOC Resolution 1884/50, Safeguard 2). The penalty is available in many countries and in recent years has been used for categories of persons excluded by UN Safeguard 3. The U.S. Supreme Court, for example, has ruled that it is a matter for state legislatures whether the death penalty shall be available for persons aged 16 or 17 years at the time of the offense, and at the end of 1994 only twenty five of the thirty-eight retentionist U.S. states had determined that the minimum age for death penalty liability should be 18 years in accordance with UN Safeguard 3 (Hood 1996, paras. 85–89). In the United States, thirty-six persons who were aged under 18 years at the time of their offense were executed between 1990 and 1995, and there were a further forty-two such persons on death row in twelve states in 1995 (Hood 1996, para. 137). Moreover, though the majority of U.S. states have pro-visions—statutory, common law, case law, or executive clemency—designed to ensure that the mentally incompetent are not executed, the available evidence does not inspire confidence that, contrary to the terms of UN Safeguard 3, they will not be and are not being executed (Hood 1996, paras. 149–50).

Most states, though by no means all, claim that the UN Safeguards regarding the protection of the innocent (clear and convincing evidence), fair trials (proce-dures at least equal to those contained in ICCPR Article 14), right of appeal (including, after 1989, provision for mandatory appeal), right to seek a pardon or commutation of sentence, and delay of execution pending the outcome of legal proceedings are covered by their domestic provisions. But there is a good deal of doubt about these assurances. In the United States, for example, there remains considerable uncertainty over whether the use of relatively inexperienced counsel working on meager pay rates in many capital cases adequately satisfies the require-ment that defendants in capital cases receive "effective assistance of counsel" (Hood 1996, paras. 159–64), and in some countries executions are being carried out while appeals are pending.

Finally, and a bridgehead to the next section, it is questionable whether capital punishments are carried out in a manner so as to inflict the minimum possible suffering (ECOSOC, Safeguard 9). The U.S. Supreme Court has deprecated lengthy delays in executing sentences but has not held that, for example, a 1992 Utah case of eighteen years on death row before execution or a 1994 Arkansas case of nineteen years on death row before commutation to life imprisonment is "cruel and unusual punishment" (Hood 1996, para. 196). In Japan, a prisoner was executed in 1993 after spending twenty-three years on death row in conditions described by Amnesty International as "inhuman and degrading." There is abun-dant evidence that conditions for death row prisoners are in many jurisdictions impoverished if not inhuman and degrading. Yet not all courts have followed the example of the European Court in *Soering v. United Kingdom,* in which it was decided that extradition to face the death sentence in Virginia would be a breach of the European Convention on Human Rights Article 3 because his inevitably long wait on death row, and the conditions prevailing there, would amount to inhuman and degrading punishment. The Canadian Supreme Court ruled in *Kindler* that the defendant could be extradited to Pennsylvania, where he faced capital punishment because, although the wait might be long ("The death row phenomenon and the psychological stress inherent in it cannot be dismissed lightly"), "it pales by comparison with the death penalty. Moreover a defendant is never required to pursue the delay of appellate remedies." In *Kindler* the Court distinguished its decision from that in *Soering* on the grounds of the age and mental state of the applicant and the different conditions prevailing on death row in Pennsylvania. In another case involving extradition to face the death penalty, the HRC distinguished its decision in *Ng v. Canada* on the grounds that the mode of execution in the state concerned was gas asphyxiation, which it declared to be a violation of Article 7 of the ICCPR. Finally, in *Pratt and Morgan v. AG of Jamaica* the Privy Council held that prolonged delay in administering a death sentence — in this instance nearly fourteen years — amounted to inhuman treatment irrespective of the circumstances of the delay. Despite the similar wording of the relevant standards, very different interpretations compete with each other.

Hood concludes his review of the UN Safeguards with the statement that "very few retentionist countries have put in place a systematic means for ensuring that all persons in the criminal justice system, including defendants and their legal representatives, are made familiar with the ECOSOC" provisions and that "more still needs to be done to ensure that the formalities of both the substantive law and legal procedures are translated invariably into the realities of enforced rights for citizens under the threat of the death penalty" (Hood 1996, paras. 202–3).

The European Convention on Human Rights Article 3 excludes the death penalty and has made it, and abolition, the subject of the Sixth Protocol (1983). But Article 3 has also been used to outlaw the use of judicial corporal punishment. The leading case is *Tyrer v. United Kingdom*, in which the applicant had, as a 15-year-old, been birched on the order of the court in the Isle of Man following his plea of guilty to the charge of assault, occasioning actual bodily harm to a senior pupil at his school. The European Commission of Human Rights did not think that corporal punishment as practiced in the Isle of Man constituted torture or inhuman and degrading treatment or punishment "as understood in its previous jurisprudence or by any ordinary understanding of those terms" but accepted that "[j]udicial birching humiliates and disgraces the offender and can therefore be said to be degrading treatment or punishment."[6] It was the nature of the practice rather than its effects in the particular case that was decisive.[7]

Self-evidently all forms of punishment carry a degree of humiliation and for many analysts that is part of the purpose of the exercise. Thus the European Court of Human Rights pointed out that "it would be absurd to hold that judicial punishment generally, by reason of its usual and perhaps almost inevitable element of humiliation, is 'degrading' within the meaning of Article 3." Nevertheless the Court went on to confirm that

> The humiliation or debasement involved must attain a particular level and must in any event be other than the usual element of humiliation [inherent in judicial punishment]. The assessment is in the nature of things, relative: it depends on all the circumstances of the case and, in particular, on the nature and context of the punishment itself and the manner of its execution.[8]

The Court concluded on the facts of the case that the required degree of severity had been reached. This was an institutionalized infliction of violence, compounded by an aura of official proceedings administered by strangers (police officers).

The Court's approach in *Tyrer* has not commanded the support of all commentators and was the subject of a powerfully argued dissent that suggested that the Court had been swayed more by opinions about the undesirability of corporal punishment than by the degrading aspects of its use (see Feldman 1993, pp. 132–34; Evans and Morgan 1998, chap. 3). Yet, whether Article 3 was used in this case "as a vehicle of indirect penal reform, for which it was not intended,"[9] the judgment has had an influence beyond Europe.[10] It has reinforced the general movement towards the abolition of judicial corporal punishment.

The European Court has not been faced with more severe corporal punishments of the sort that are widely used in some jurisdictions outside Europe. But these matters have been considered by the HRC. The committee interprets the prohibition in Article 7 of the ICCPR "to extend to corporal punishment, including excessive chastisement ordered as a punishment for a crime or as an educative or disciplinary measure."[11] Thus, it goes scarcely without saying that when the committee is faced with evidence of more draconian punishments being used—much as, for example, judicial mutilation, severe flogging, and the like in the Sudan—it declares unequivocally that these penalties are inconsistent with both Articles 7 and 10 and should be abolished.[12]

III. Standard Setting Regarding Incarceration

The use of custody, whatever standards are applied in custodial institutions, is relatively costly compared with alternative methods of incapacitation or sanction. In the United States the use of imprisonment is estimated to cost twenty-six times as much per offender per year as probation (Donziger 1996, pp. 190–92). In the United Kingdom the comparable figure is estimated to be ten.[13] The relative cost of imprisonment almost certainly depends on the proportionate use of custody as a sanction by the courts, as well as on the quality of life provided for prisoners, however. First, to the extent that custody is reserved for a small proportion of offenders—those who have committed serious offenses and those who are alleged to represent a threat to community safety and are serving long sentences—a relatively high security quotient is likely to be maintained. Whether achieved architecturally, through the use of technology or the provision of a high staff-to-prisoner ratio, the costs of imprisonment vary largely in accordance with the level of security provided. Second, there are custodial economies of scale. Jurisdictions with the lowest incarceration rates tend to provide smaller than average custodial institutions and vice versa. It follows that the marginal cost savings from cutting prison populations are generally recognized to be substantially below average costs and this is likely to remain so even if the reduction permits the closing of institutions.

Nevertheless, it is the overall quality of life provided for prisoners—the amount of space provided per prisoner, their access to facilities, and the range of programs provided for them—that most affects average costs and the cost of imprisonment relative to community-based sentences. It follows that the extent to which governments feel bound by high custodial standards set by international bodies may indirectly shape sentencing practice.

The body that has taken furthest forward the detailed question of custodial conditions is the European Committee for the Prevention of Torture and Inhuman or Degrading Treatment or Punishment (CPT), established in 1989 under the convention of the same name. Though the CPT has encountered practices that it has described as torture, and though the committee has devoted a substantial part of its energy to recommending safeguards that might prevent torture or serious ill-treatment of a physical nature from taking place particularly in police stations, a good part of the committee's work has been devoted to preventing inhuman and degrading treatment, particularly in prisons.[14] Moreover, the committee concluded early in its life that the various bodies of jurisprudence and standards that it might use as a source of guidance[15]—a "wealth of material" that included the jurisprudence of the HRC and the European Convention on Human Rights, the UN Standard Minimum Rules for the Treatment of Prisoners, the European Prison Rules, and so on—"no clear guidance can be drawn from it for the purpose of dealing with specific situations encountered by the Committee."[16]

Because the CPT is not a judicial body and because its purpose is prevention rather than resolution ("conflict avoidance" rather than "conflict solution"), the function of the committee is not to establish whether there has been a breach of the European Convention on Human Rights Article 3, and thus it has no obligation to define the key terms—*torture* and *inhuman and degrading*—in Article 3 and has not done so except by example. The CPT maintains that it is concerned with the future rather than the past.

This is the theory. Yet the reality is somewhat different. In reality what the majority of readers of CPT reports most want to know is whether the committee has, during the course of its visits to member states, found evidence of torture or inhuman or degrading treatment. And to the extent that the committee has employed those terms, how have they used them? What practices have the committee discovered that they judge to be torture? What procedures or custodial conditions have they concluded are inhuman or degrading? In asking these questions, senior officials are mindful of more than the international reputations of the custodial systems for which they are responsible. For to the extent that the CPT finds torture or inhuman or degrading treatment, one response to the finding may be—and under certain circumstances is likely to be—that like-situated detainees will petition the Human Rights Commission in Strasbourg to test the proposition that there has indeed been a breach of Article 3. This consequence can never be far from the minds of the CPT and its secretariat, bodies quite separate from the European Commission of Human Rights and the Court, but nevertheless part of the Council of Europe and housed in the same human rights building in Strasbourg as the Commission and the Court. For, as the secretary to the CPT has made clear, there is in reality a two-way relationship between the CPT and the Commission and Court. The decisions of the latter guide the CPT and the findings of the CPT may both stimulate petitions to the Commission and the Court and on occasion may directly influence the decisions of the Commission and the Court. In a recent finding of the Commission about whether conditions in a Belgian psychiatric hospital amounted to inhuman and degrading treatment, both the majority and minority reports cited the facts established by the CPT and the interpretation by the committee of their meaning (*Aerts v. Belgium*). For these reasons it is important to consider how the CPT has used the key terms from Article 3. I concentrate on use of inhuman and degrading treatment or punishment.

A. Use of the Key Terms

The CPT has never used the terms *inhuman* and *degrading* to refer to physical or psychological ill-treatment but has reserved these terms almost exclusively to describe aspects of custodial living conditions. It would seem, therefore, that the CPT is using the terms *torture* and *inhuman and degrading* to refer to different forms of ill-treatment—that is, to use the terms in a "branched" manner, as opposed to the largely "linear" usage of the European Human-Rights Commission and the Court.[17] Whereas the latter view inhuman and degrading treatment and torture as different points along a continuum, or in a hierarchy, of severity,[18] the CPT appears to be reserving the terms for different types of ill-treatment more or less closely linked. *Torture* is almost exclusively used to refer to physical ill-treatment employed instrumentally by the police. *Inhuman and degrading*, used either separately or together, the committee has reserved for forms of environmental ill-treatment—mostly the conditions in which groups of prisoners are housed—where the instrumental element, at least in individual terms, is lacking or obscure. The words *inhuman* and *degrading* are sometimes used separately in situations where the ill-treatment appears to fall short of that which is inhuman and degrading, and environmental ill-treatment falling short of the inhuman *or* the degrading, and well below that which is deemed inhuman *and* degrading, may be said to be unacceptable, or it is sometimes said that they could be considered to be inhuman and degrading.

The committee has also adopted a cumulative view of *inhuman or degrading* (not unlike the "totality of conditions" approach employed by U.S. federal courts in prisoner's rights) so that conditions that might in themselves not be considered inhuman or degrading become so when combined with others.[19] Thus the combination of overcrowding, lack of integral sanitation, almost unalleviated cellular confinement, and lack of outdoor exercise have on several occasions been judged to amount to inhuman and degrading treatment.[20] However, the committee has also emphasized that physical overcrowding can be so acute as to amount to inhuman and degrading treatment in its own right[21] and on at least one occasion the committee has found it to be so.[22] Furthermore, there is a suggestion that breach of the general duty of care (interprisoner violence and intimidation, and so on) that all custodial authorities owe to their charges—a duty to which the committee attaches particular importance—may combine with physical and social custodial conditions to constitute inhuman and degrading conditions.[23]

The committee has sometimes employed the words *degrading* or *inhuman* separately, though it has not always been clear whether any significance can be attached to this distinction in terms of the degree of environmental ill-treatment. In one instance the committee has made itself very clear. In its second general report the CPT emphasized that it did "not like" the practice of "slopping out"[24] but later hardened this opinion by unequivocally asserting that the practice is "degrading" not just for the persons having to discharge their human waste in the presence, without privacy, of other prisoners in a confined living space but "degrading" for the prison staff who have to supervise the subsequent "slopping out."[25] Other custodial conditions have been described as "inhuman," for example, some overcrowded, unhygienic, dilapidated, and poorly equipped accommodation,[26] or confinement in very small, dark, and unventilated cells without the possibility of outdoor exercise.[27] It is not clear whether the CPT has intended the words *inhuman* and *degrading* to have distinct meanings in these contexts.

Despite the cumulative approach taken by the CPT to prison conditions it is nonetheless possible to identify discrete standards recommended by the committee and to attempt to compare those adopted by other human rights bodies. Thus I briefly consider the jurisprudence of the HRC and the European Convention on Human Rights relating to custodial conditions.

As noted, the ICCPR, unlike the European Convention, complements the prohibition of torture and ill treatment with Article 10(1). This goes further than Article 3 of the convention, which, like Article 7 of the ICCPR, protects the individual from ill treatment at the hands of the state. Article 10(1) obliges the state to adhere to minimum standards of humane treatment. This is a positive obligation[28] and "cannot be dependent on the material resources available in the State party."[29] Any situation that amounts to a violation of Article 7 will, in a custodial context, necessarily imply a violation of Article 10(1). But the converse does not apply. Thus if it is assumed that the limits of "inhuman and degrading" treatment under Article 3 of the European Convention are conterminous with the limits of the similarly worded Article 7 of the ICCPR, one can infer that there are circumstances that give rise to responsibility under the ICCPR but not under the convention. It is also possible, however, to see in Article 10(1) an alternative basis for a finding of a violation that might otherwise have fallen within an expansive interpretation of inhuman and degrading treatment. Certainly, most of the individual communications that have led to findings of a violation of Article 10(1) seem capable of being fairly described as "inhuman or degrading treatment or punishment" and might have been so but for Article 10(1). For example a string of cases confirmed conditions in the "Libertad" prison in Uruguay to be "inhumane."[30] One judgment cited the following abuses:

> harassment and persecution by the guards, the regime of arbitrary prohibitions and unnecessary torments; the combination of solitude and isolation on the one hand and the fact of being constantly watched, listened to and followed by microphones and through peepholes on the other hand; the lack of contact with families, aggravated by worries about the difficulties, experiences and pressures exerted on their families; the cruel conditions in the punishment wing in which a prisoner might be detained for up to 90 days at a time;[31] the breakdown of physical and mental health through malnutrition, lack of sunshine and exercise, as well as nervous problems created by tension and ill-treatment.

Among the specific prison conditions recorded were very small cells shared by two detainees for twenty-three hours a day,[32] prisoners being prevented from taking exercise at other times, prisoners being forbidden to lie on their beds from 6.30 A.M. to 9.00 P.M., and being allowed visits of only forty-five minutes' duration every two months.[33] It is virtually impossible to discern any meaningful difference between those cases in which the HRC found that conditions violated Article 10(1) and those in which they violated Article 7, as is evident from those instances in which the committee found violations of both articles without distinguishing between them.[34] It is sufficient to note here that over a period of time it appears that the threshold at which conditions qualify for dual censure has been lowered somewhat.[35]

To the extent that it is possible to provide a rough guide to the HRC's approach it might be that conditions of detention tend to fall for consideration under Article 10 unless there is evidence to suggest that conditions or regime features were part of a deliberate attempt to undermine the personality of the individual concerned and could therefore be considered ancillary to a principal purpose of inhumanity and degradation, rather than indicating a generalized lack of respect for the individual in question.[36] It is clear that there is an almost limitless array of factors that may need to be taken into consideration when determining whether the conditions in which a person is detained are inhumane for the purposes of the convention. This, it seems, has been recognized by the HRC. In its latest General Comment on Article 10 the committee chose not to explore the practical consequences of this obligation in detail. Rather, it invited states "to indicate in their reports to what extent they are applying the relevant UN standards applicable to the treatment of prisoners."[37]

The absence within the European Convention on Human Rights of an obligation equivalent to Article 10(1) of the ICCPR has not prevented the development of a jurisprudence relating to conditions of detention. However, it has arguably acted as a restraining factor and that jurisprudence is not well developed.

In the leading *Greek* case, for example, where conditions of detention were considered to be in breach of Article 3, the Commission relied on a complicated combination of factors that included, in a police station: severe overcrowding; incommunicado detention for up to thirty days; no access to open air, limited light, no exercise, and, most critically, prolonged duration of detention in such conditions—in excess of thirty days in many cases (including one of up to nine months).[38] In the prisons the conditions included gross overcrowding, no heating in winter, no hot water, limited access to sanitation, poor dental care, and severe restrictions to family contact.[39] The emphasis placed upon their cumulative impact makes its virtually impossible to determine whether any particular factor had a critical impact on this finding or to construct a set of benchmarks against which to measure the acceptability of particular conditions.[40] It does, however, provide an important indication of those aspects of detention that can fall for evaluation under Article 3 and in relation to which the CPT can legitimately be expected to develop standards as part of its preventive function. Subsequent cases have confirmed that the conditions of detention can give rise to violations of Article 3 but have done little to clarify when this is likely to be true.[41]

Assessment turns on the particular circumstances of cases and there is a reluctance by the European Commission and the Court to characterize general conditions of detention[42] as inhuman or degrading, even in circumstances where the CPT has expressed its opinion that this is so. In *Delazarus v. United Kingdom*[43] the applicant, a sentenced prisoner in Wandsworth Prison, was held in solitary confinement for fourteen weeks pending a disciplinary hearing. During that time, he was kept in his cell with no integral sanitation for twenty-three hours a day. The Commission accepted that overcrowding, a lack of regime activities, and an absence of sanitary facilities could combine to produce a violation of Article 3 — a combination of conditions so described by the CPT following their visit to Wandsworth Prison in 1990 — but decided that the application was inadmissible since the applicant could not complain of overcrowding and the very fact of being in solitary confinement mitigated the impact of the lack of proper sanitation. The same issues were also raised in *Raphaie v. the United Kingdom.* [44]

The principal contribution of the CPT to the development of standards concerning custodial conditions lies not so much in the committee's identification of aspects deserving critical scrutiny but rather in the degree of specificity that it brings to its tasks. The fact that the work of the CPT revolves entirely around visits means that the committee is brought face to face with custodial conditions. This has inevitably led the committee to move beyond the generality of the UN Standard Minimum Rules for the Treatment of Prisoners and the European Prison Rules. The process is best considered by way of illustration.

B. Case Study: Overcrowding

Consider the question of overcrowding — the related issues of cell size and occupancy level. The UN Standard Minimum Rules are premised upon the belief that single occupancy of cells is the ideal.[45] Although this belief is now widely regarded as outmoded,[46] it is reflected also in the European Prison Rules: "Prisoners shall normally be lodged during the night in individual cells except in cases where it is considered that there are advantages in sharing accommodation with other prisoners."[47] The CPT has not taken a view on this issue[48] but instead has chosen to focus on the levels of occupancy relative to the size of the cell or dormitory. Overcrowding is relevant to the CPT's mandate both because it affects the overall quality of life in an establishment and because, in the committee's opinion, it "might be such as to be in itself inhuman or degrading from a physical standpoint."[49] A prison population in excess of the official capacity, though never ideal, is not necessarily unacceptable.[50]

In the report on its first visit to the United Kingdom, the committee described as "outrageous" the situation in Leeds Prison, where up to three prisoners were held in cells of 8.6 square meters.[51] Single cells of 6 square meters have been described as "rather small" but acceptable if a significant portion of the day is spent out of the cell.[52] Cells of 4 square meters and smaller are considered to be altogether unacceptable, irrespective of their use.[53] Further, the committee seems to have adopted a toleration threshold of around 9 square meters for two-person cells,[54] below which conditions are considered "cramped."[55] Cells of 7 square meters should hold no more than one prisoner.[56]

A reasonably good indication of CPT thinking is given in the report on the first periodic visit to Slovakia, in which it was noted that Bratislava Prison[57] in theory had three types of cell: two-person (approximately 9–10 square meters), three-person (about 12 square meters) and four-person (16–17 square meters). Although the committee considered these living spaces to be "restricted," the measurements appear to be an acceptable baseline. When the occupancy levels of such cells increase, however, they become "unacceptable."[58]

In general, the CPT considers large-scale dormitory-style prison accommodation to be unsatisfactory, even if not overcrowded, because of the increased lack of privacy and risk of violence.[59] However, the committee has said that cells of 21 square meters are acceptable for five prisoners,[60] cells of 25 square meters "should accommodate an absolute maximum of six prisoners,"[61] and "a dormitory of 60 square meters should never be used to accommodate more than twelve prisoners and one of 35 square meters more than seven."[62] Once again, the toleration threshold appears to be somewhat lower, and the Slovak report, acknowledging that the Leopoldov Prison represents only "a limited amount of living space," indicates broad tolerance of the following official occupancy levels at the prison:

> cells measuring 11–22 square meters—up to three prisoners: cells measuring 21–29 square meters—six or seven prisoners; cells measuring 25–38 square meters—eight or nine prisoners; cells measuring 31–35 square meters—ten prisoners; cells measuring approximately 40 square meters—twelve prisoners; and cells measuring 51 square meters—sixteen prisoners.[63]

C. Case Study: Custodial Regimes for Untried Prisoners

The UN Standard Minimum Rules stipulate that "every prisoner who is not employed in outdoor work shall have at least one hour of suitable exercise in the open air daily if the weather permits."[64] This specific provision is endorsed in the European Prison Rules and elaborated with a general statement covering physical fitness, adequate exercise, and recreational opportunities generally.[65] Moreover, both the UN and the European rules have a good deal to say about work and education and recreational programs. All prisoners shall be required to work; subject to their physical and mental fitness, they shall be "actively employed for a normal working day," "the organization and methods of work . . . shall resemble as closely as possible those of similar work outside institutions," "provision shall be made for the further education of all prisoners capable of profiting thereby," and so on.[66] Unfortunately these generalized ideals scarcely accord with the realities of prison life in many countries where there is little employment for prisoners, or where the work provided finds little or no comparison in the community.

The CPT is focused on the bottom line. "All prisoners without exception (including those undergoing cellular confinement as a punishment) should be offered the possibility to take outdoor exercise daily," and it is "axiomatic that outdoor exercise facilities should be reasonably spacious and whenever possible offer shelter from inclement weather."[67] In individual country reports even this level of generality has been fined down. Thus, where the CPT has encountered very small exercise pens the committee has recommended that they be improved immediately. All "exercise areas should be sufficiently large to allow prisoners to exert themselves physically," a criterion which, for example, compartments of 15 square meters have not satisfied.[68]

Moreover, the CPT goes beyond recognition that "a satisfactory program of activities (work, education, sport, etc.) is of crucial importance for the well being of prisoners."[69] For example, the committee has paid particular attention to regimes for remand prisoners, that group of prisoners who are generally subject, despite the legal and ethical imperatives that would seem logically to flow from the presumption of innocence, to be held in the most restrictive and impoverished prison conditions (Morgan 1993; United Nations 1994). The committee recognizes that it is not possible to offer as well developed a program of activities for remand prisoners as for sentenced prisoners. Nevertheless, the committee takes the view that "the aim should be to ensure that remand prisoners spend a reasonable part of the day (8 hours or more) outside their cells, engaged in purposeful activities of a varied nature (work, preferably with vocational value, education; sport; recreation/association)."[70] Sentenced prisoners should enjoy an even more favorable regime, in the sense that the activities offered should be geared more closely to the particular needs of the prisoner concerned.

The committee's approach to regimes for remand prisoners is well illustrated by its response to two situations encountered in several European countries: the use of police stations for prolonged periods on remand and restrictions placed or authorized by the courts on remand regimes.

All criminal justice systems provide, following initial police custody and pending charges being laid or suspects being brought before a court, for the remand in custody of persons awaiting trial. Remands in custody may be for a few days but are more typically for several weeks or months and, in some countries, can last for a year or more. Such custody is normally in a prison, as the European Prision Rules assume it should be, and this assumption no doubt informed the CPT's thinking when it accepted that short-term custody in a police station would probably involve physical conditions of a lower standard than those to be found in, and expected of, prisons designed for prolonged custody.[71] The problem is that police stations, though seldom designed for prolonged custody, are in some jurisdictions routinely or occasionally used for that purpose. The CPT has encountered police stations being used to accommodate remand and administrative detainees[72] and might well find them being used for sentenced prisoners.[73] This practice the CPT has repeatedly deplored, the physical standards and facilities to be met being those required for pretrial custody in prisons, physical standards and facilities that no police station is ever likely to be able to meet. Where prisoners are remanded to police custody they are typically confined to their cells practically throughout the twenty-four hours with little or no possibility of exercise, outdoor or indoor, and provided with no opportunity for work or recreation. Wherever such conditions have been encountered the CPT has emphasized that the use of police stations is not appropriate for long-term custody and has recommended that in the event of the authorities deciding that it is unrealistic to provide the facilities and regime in police stations that the CPT considers appropriate, then the continued use of police accommodation should cease.[74]

The question of remand regime restrictions has arisen most prominently out of CPT visits to Denmark, Norway, and Sweden, where it is relatively common for pretrial prisoners to be, on the authority of the court, and, as a consequence, to some extent at the discretion of prosecutors (and directly or indirectly the investigating police), prohibited from or limited in their contacts with fellow prisoners and other persons (whether through visits, telephone calls, or correspondence) or even in their access to television, the radio, and newspapers and magazines. Such restrictions are legally justified in Scandinavia by the need to safeguard evidence or to prevent collusion or intimidation. During visits to Scandinavia the CPT has encountered examples of pretrial prisoners subject to total restrictions of this nature (though still able to be visited by their lawyers) for prolonged periods, and the committee has found some evidence to support claims that such treatment has had to adverse mental health consequences.[75] The committee has been unequivocally critical of prolonged isolation but has stopped short of describing instances of it as "psychological torture" despite evidence of the police using restrictions to exert pressure on suspects to cooperate and despite its being clear from prisoners' testimonies that, whether or not restrictions are partly or wholly designed and applied to achieve cooperation, this is certainly the consequence.[76] The furthest that the CPT has so far been prepared to go is to say that "solitary confinement can, in certain circumstances, amount to inhuman and degrading treatment" and that therefore it should be "as short as possible."[77]

To ensure that resort to restrictions on prisoners' contacts be used parsimoniously the CPT has recommended that the following principles be followed and procedural safeguards adopted:

1. that the use and prolongation of solitary confinement be "resorted to only in exceptional circumstances," be "strictly limited to the requirements of the case,"[78] and be "proportional to the needs of the criminal investigation concerned";[79]
2. that each particular restriction be authorized by a court, the reasons recorded in writing, and "unless the requirements of the investigation dictate otherwise, the prisoner [be] informed of those reasons";[80]
3. that the imposition of restrictions, and the justification for their continued application, be regularly reviewed by the court;[81] and
4. "that prisoners subject to restrictions have an effective right of appeal to a Court or another independent body in respect of particular restrictions applied by a public prosecutor."[82]

It follows that restrictions though legally justified may nevertheless have harmful consequences. The CPT has accordingly recommended the following safeguard and compensating principle designed to reduce the likelihood of that outcome:

1. Whenever a prisoner subject to restrictions (or a prison officer on the prisoner's behalf) requests an examination by a medical doctor, that the doctor be called without delay to carry out an examination and the results of that examination, including an account of the prisoner's physical and mental condition as well as, if need be, the foreseeable consequences of prolonged isolation, be set out in a written statement to be forwarded to the competent authorities.[83]

2. "Any prisoner subject to restrictions for an extended period is offered activities in addition to outside exercise and guaranteed appropriate human contact."[84]

This means that even though pretrial prisoners may legitimately be prevented from having contact with fellow prisoners and may not be allowed to receive visits or telephone calls either generally or from specific persons, they should be provided with human contact with staff through out-of-cell activities specially designed to compensate for the lack of mainstream interprisoner association. In this sort of detailed respect the CPT has come to grips with the day-to-day realities of custodial practice much more closely than do the UN codes and other instruments, [85] and the early evidence suggests that the CPT intervention is prompting reviews of practice in the Scandinavian states.

D. The Influence of the CPT

The immediacy of visits may have led the CPT to develop highly specific responses to the practical custodial conditions the committee encounters but it has also reduced the general impact of the committee's work. Since the standards are developed in relation to specific institutions visited, it is sometimes difficult to separate points of general application from points of detail that partly or wholly relate to the custodial location in question. This problem is exacerbated by the sheer number and complexity of the interrelating factors often involved. Sometimes this means that the work of the committee is more geared to the problems of the particular places visited than to the problems within the system as a whole. As a consequence, CPT reports can be seen as having two elements: the restatement of primary standards, pitched at a level of generality not far removed from that set out in the nonbinding codes and rules (the UN Standard Minimum Rules and so on), and a series of institution-specific recommendations that reflect the CPT's perception of the shortcomings of the visited place.

The CPT has been in operation for a decade, yet it is too early to gauge how great an impact it is having on the domestic policies of state parties.[86] Though most of the original parties to the European Convention for the Prevention of Torture from western Europe have been visited several times, recent signatories in eastern Europe are still in the process of receiving their first visits or have yet to respond to first-visit CPT reports. If criminal justice reform takes many years to be achieved following scandal or fiscal crisis and inquiry within a purely domestic setting—and that is the typical pattern—then we should expect a much longer gestation period when the stimulus is an external nonjudicial human rights body based in Strasbourg without sanctions and about which little is as yet known. At this stage the most that can be said is as follows:

- The CPT is generally taken seriously by state parties insofar as the reports are published, and though the quality of government responses varies, CPT recommendations and requests for information are for the most part responded to in detail
- Urgent CPT recommendations that prisoner accommodation not be further used, or recommendations that the quality of accommodation be improved, are mostly

responded to positively and there is already some evidence from follow-up visits and reports that living conditions have often improved
- Recommendations that there be structural change (for example, that "fundamental safeguards"—such as the provision of legal advice from the outset of custody in police stations—be met) are encountering a good deal of overt resistance

It should be remembered also that the CPT has begun life during an inauspicious period. In the past decade the incarceration rate in most of the countries in the Council of Europe has risen, there is an increased emphasis on security in prisons, and the proportions of prisoners comprising foreign nationals has grown. Because prison building has lagged behind this surge in prison numbers, overcrowding has increased and this factor, combined with a raised security quotient, has depressed the quality of life available for many prisoners (see Council of Europe 1998, table. 1; Stern 1998; Evans and Morgan 1998, chap. 9). Whatever improvements the CPT has been able to achieve, the custody tide is at present arguably moving in the opposite direction. Yet without the intervention of the CPT the situation would almost certainly be worse and, to the extent that the committee is able to persuade governments to adopt higher custodial standards, the relative cost of incarcerating offenders will grow and fiscal crisis and the search for cheaper, more humane, and more effective sanctions will come that much the sooner. What is not yet clear is the degree to which the jurisprudence of the European Human Rights Commission and the Court regarding to Article 3 will be dragged forward in the wake of what all observers are agreed is the more precise and radical "jurisprudence" of the CPT (Murdoch 1994, 1999).

IV. Conclusion

By the time this book is published, the establishment of a permanent international criminal court is likely to be within sight. In 1989 the European Convention for the Prevention of Torture and Inhuman or Degrading Treatment or Punishment, which was originally envisaged by western European states as an example to the rest of the world of how sovereign states might allow an international body to peer behind the customarily secret curtain of state-imposed custody, came into operation. Today the CPT, the committee created by the convention, is a more or less accepted part of the European human rights infrastructure—a Europe that has since expanded to the Sea of Japan and now incorporates the Warsaw Pact states, to whom the original concept was thought of only as an exemplar. Although international human rights law as yet impinges little on the sentencing policies of sovereign states, international mechanisms, as part of the process of globalization to which all states are increasingly subject, are growing apace and we should anticipate some convergence in the currency of sentencing theory and practice. This does not necessarily mean consensus regarding the use made of particular penalties—such as the death penalty—which continue to attract sharply divided symbolic loyalties and objections. But it probably does mean greater conformity in the employment of customary penalties—such as imprisonment—for serious crimes and the adoption of common criminal justice and penal procedures that will have fiscal implications for penality.

ACKNOWLEDGMENTS

I am grateful to my colleague and research collaborator Malcolm Evans, Professor of International Law at the University of Bristol, for his assistance in preparing this chapter. Without his advice I would not have pursued several of the lines of argument that I have pursued. To the extent that there are errors of fact and judgment they are entirely mine. But if, as a nonlawyer, I have managed to avoid major howlers, the credit should almost certainly go to Malcolm Evans.

NOTES

1. Sentencing Judgment in *Drazen Erdomovic* (March 5, 1998). See also separate opinions of Judge Shahabuddeen (March 5, 1998) and Judge Li (October 7, 1997).

2. There is time enough for this to be done well. It is doubtful that the Court will come into operation for at least five years, sixty ratifications being required before that happens.

3. See, for example, the Message from Mary Robinson, UN High Commissioner for Human Rights, on March 23, 1998, expressing concern regarding the execution by lethal injection of Karla Faye Tucker in Texas and emphasizing the UN view that abolition of the death penalty reflects the argument that life itself is the most fundamental of human rights. Note also the Virginia state authorities' refusal to stay the execution of Angel Breard in April 1998 following the order of the International Court of Justice (*Paraguay v. United States*, April 9, 1998) pending an investigation of the claim by the government of Paraguay that the Vienna Convention on Consular Relations had been breached when the defendant was arrested, charged, and sentenced.

4. This is now required of applicants for membership, though it has to be doubted whether all the undertakings given can be taken at face value. Russia, for example, has increased its rate of executions since joining the Council of Europe.

5. In October 1997 Jamaica denounced the Optional Protocol to the ICCPR, thereby withdrawing the right of individual petition to the UN Human Rights Committee. The purpose, following judgment in *Pratt and Morgan*, was clearly to shorten the appellate process for death row prisoners and thereby allow the government of Jamaica to pursue its stated wish to resume executions (see Schiffrin 1998, pp. 563–68). In May 1998 Trinidad and Tobago took a similar step by becoming the first-ever state to withdraw from the American Convention on Human Rights.

6. *Tyrer v. United Kingdom*, Comm. Rep. 14 December 1976, paras. 32 and 35.

7. This is confirmed by the Commission's principal delegate in the case (Kellberg 1991).

8. *Tyrer v. United Kingdom*, Judgment, 25 April 1978, Series. A, No. 26, para 30.

9. Ibid., Separate Opinion of Judge Fitzmaurice, para. 14.

10. For example, the penalty has been held to inhuman and degrading and thus contrary to the Constitution of Zimbabwe. See Bradley 1991, pp. 481–84.

11. HRC Gen. Com. 20, HRI/Gen/1/Rev.2, 29 March 1996.

12. HRC, *Concluding Observations, Sudan*, CCPR/C/79/Add.85, 19 November 1997.

13. House of Commons Home Affairs Committee 1998, paras. 2 and 22.

14. The committee is mandated to consider custody on the authority of the state in any place. For a general study of the origins and work of the CPT, see Evans and Morgan 1998.

15. The CPT is not bound by the jurisprudence of the European Commission or Court of Human Rights.

16. CPT (1991) *1st General Report on the CPT's Activities 1990*, CPT/Inf(91)3 (Strasbourg: Council of Europe). All references to CPT publications henceforward cite only the year of publication, the date of the visit (where applicable, with reference to country reports), and the Council of Europe reference number.

17. For a full discussion of this issue, see Rodley 1987, pp. 63–70; Evans and Morgan 1998.

18. This theory has not been fully reflected in the court's practice. See Evans and Morgan 1998, chap. 3.

19. For an account that may reflect the committee's thinking, see Cassese 1996, pp. 48–49; Evans and Morgan 1998, chap. 6.

20. See CPT (1992) *2nd General Report 1991*, CPT/Inf(92)3, para. 50; CPT (1993) *France Visit 1991*, CPT/Inf(93)2, paras 93–102; CPT (1995) *Italy Visit 1992*, CPT/Inf(95)1, para 77; CPT (1996) *Portugal Visit 1995*, CPT/Inf(96)31, para 95; CPT (1991) *UK Visit 1990*, CPT/Inf(91)15, para. 57.

21. CPT (1992) *2nd General Report 1991*, CPT/Inf(92)3, para. 46.

22. CPT (1996) *Spain Visit 1994*, CPT/Inf(96)9, paras. 113–14.

23. CPT (1996) *Portugal Visit 1995*, CPT/Inf(96)31, paras. 94–5.

24. CPT (1992) *2nd General Report 1991*, CPT/Inf(92)3, para. 49.

25. CPT (1995) *Ireland Visit 1993*, CPT/Inf(95)14, para. 100; see also Cassese 1996, pp. 49–50.

26. CPT (1994) *Greece Visit 1993*, CPT/Inf(94)20, para. 76.

27. CPT (1997) *Bulgaria Visit 1995*, CPT/Inf(97)1, paras. 109–10.

28. Gen. Com. 21 (44), para. 2.

29. Ibid., para. 3.

30. E.g., *Cámpora Schweizer v. Uruguay*, Comm. no. 66/1980 (12 October 1982) 2 *SD* 90, para. 11; *Estrella v. Uruguay*, Comm. no. 74/1980 (29 March 1983) 2 *SD* 93; *Bequio v. Uruguay*, Comm. no. 88/1981 (29 March 1983), 2 *SD* 118; *Nieto v. Uruguay*, Comm. no. 92/1981 (25 July 1983) 2 *SD* 126; *Cabreira de Estradet v. Uruguay*, Comm. no. 105/1981 (21 July 1983) 2 *SD* 133; *Acosta v. Uruguay*, Comm. no. 110/1981 (29 March 1984) 2 *SD* 148; *Lluberas v. Uruguay*, Comm. no. 123/1982 (6 April 1984) 2 *SD* 155; *Conteris v. Uruguay*, Comm. no. 139/1983 (17 July 1985) 2 *SD* 168; *Cariboni v. Uruguay*, Comm. no. 159/1983 (27 October 1987) 2 *SD* 189. See also *Gilboa v. Uruguay*, Comm. no. 147/1983 (1 Nov 1985) 2 *SD* 176 for similar conditions at female prisons and *Voituret v. Uruguay*, Comm. no. 109/1981 (10 April 1984) 2 *SD* 146 (holding of a women in solitary confinement in a cell with virtually no artificial light for six months in violation of Article 10(1)).

31. This wing, known as "La Isla," comprised "small cells without windows, where artificial light is left on 24 hours a day." See *Bequio v. Uruguay*, Comm. no. 88/1981 (29 March 1983), 2 *SD* 118, para. 10.3, where the HRC was of the view that Uruguay had violated both Article 7 and Article 10(1) in holding the applicant in these cells for one month.

32. In *Nieto v. Uruguay*, Comm. no. 92/1981 (25 July 1983) 2 *SD* 126, para. 1.7, these were recorded to be 2 mm. by 3.5 mm.

33. *Estrella v. Uruguay*, Comm. no. 74/1980 (29 March 1983) 2 *SD* 93, paras. 1.10–1.16.

34. E.g. *Portorreal v. Dominican Republic*, Comm. no. 188/1984 (5 Nov 1987) 2 *SD* 214, paras. 2.2 and 11. The HRC was of the view that the applicant had been "subjected to inhuman and degrading treatment and to lack of respect for his inherent human dignity during his detention" in violation of Articles 7 and 10(1) following his being held for fifty hours in a cell 20 by 5 mm., holding in the region of 125 persons, in which "owing to lack of space some detainee had to sit on excrement." See also *Marais v. Madagascar*, Comm. no. 49/1979 (24 March 1983) 2 *SD* 82 (solitary confinement in police cell measuring 2mm. by 1m. for 20 months); *Wight v. Madagascar*, Comm. no. 115/1982 (1 April 1985) 2 *SD* 151 (including solitary confinement in cell measuring 2mm. by 1.5mm. for 3.5 months, chained to the floor with minimal food and clothing); *Muteba v. Zaire*, Comm. no. 124/1982 (24 July 1984) 2 *SD* 158; *Herrera v. Colombia*, Comm. no. 161/1983 (2 Nov 1987) 2 *SD* 192; *Jijon v. Eucador*, Comm. no. 277/1988 (26 March 1992), A/47/40, Annex IX-I.

35. E.g. *Conteris v. Uruguay*, Comm. no. 139/1983 (17 July 1985) 2 *SD* 168, at para. 10, finding a violation of Article 7 "because of severe ill treatment . . . suffered during the first three months of detention and the harsh and, at times, degrading conditions of his detention since then."

36. This might explain why the Human Rights Committee was of the view in *Griffin v. Spain* that holding the applicant for a period of seven months in the following conditions in Melilla Prison violated Article 10(1), but made no mention of Article 7 *(Griffin v. Spain*, Comm. no. 493/1992 (4 April 1995), CCPR/C/57/1, p. 52, at para. 3.1.).

37. This is presumably an error: detainees must have been intended, given the inclusion of the Principles of Detention in the following list.

38. Comm. Rep., 5 November 1969 (1969) 12 *ECHR Yb.* 186 at 468–80. Where similarly severe conditions were endured for shorter periods, the Commission did not find a violation of Article 3: e.g. 4th floor of Bouboulinas Street Police Station and at the security police headquarters in Pireaus (at 480–81).

39. Ibid., at 489.

40. A similar observation can be made with regard to the recent finding of the European Commission in *Tekin v. Turkey*, Comm. Rep., 17 April 1997, in which it was found that the applicant had been "kept in a cold and dark cell, blindfolded and treated in a way which left wounds and bruises on his body in connection with his interrogation." It was concluded that "the conditions of detention and the treatment to which the applicant was subjected constituted at least inhuman and degrading treatment within the meaning of Article 3 of the Convention" (at paras. 214, 215). Here the difficulty is exacerbated by the linkage with physical ill treatment. It is unlikely that the conditions of detention were considered as being "at least" inhuman or degrading.

41. In *Cyprus v. Turkey*, for example, the European Commission concluded that "withholding of an adequate supply of food and drinking water and of adequate medical treatment" amounted to "inhuman treatment" *(Cyprus v. Turkey*, App. nos. 5780/74 and 6950/75, Comm. Rep., 10 July 1976, at para. 405, 4 *EHRR* 482 at 541).

42. When more specific conditions—such as solitary confinement with a degree of sensory isolation—have been involved, both the Commission and the Court have been reluctant to find a breach of Article 3. As Rodley (1987, p. 232 has put it: "the task of balancing humane treatment with exceptional security needs is a difficult one, but it seems that, for the Commission, the balance can tilt a long way towards security concerns before article 3 comes into play."

43. *Delazarus v. United Kingdom*, App. no. 17525/90, Comm. Dec., 16 Feb 1993.

44. *Raphaie v. United Kingdom*, App. No. 20035/92, Comm. Dec., 3 December 1993.

45. UN Standard Minimum Rules for the Treatment of Prisoners, Rule 9(1).

46. See, for example, Prison Reform International 1995, p. 60, and Cassese 1996, pp. 27–28.

47. European Prison Rule 14(1).

48. It does, however, incline toward single occupancy as the most desirable option. See, e.g., Denmark 1, paras. 39–40.

49. CPT (1996) *Spain Visit 1991*, CPT/Inf(96)9, para. 117; CPT (1992) *2nd General Report 1991*, CPT/Inf(92)3, para. 46.

50. CPT (1991) *Austria Visit 1990*, CPT/Inf(92)10, para. 33.

51. CPT (1991) *United Kingdom Visit 1990*, CPT/Inf(91)16, para. 39.

52. CPT (1992) *Sweden Visit 1991*, CPT/Inf(92)4, paras. 46, 73 (Kumla Remand Centre).

53. CPT (1993) *Finland Visit 1992*, CPT/Inf(92)8, para. 81; and CPT (1996) *Hungary Visit 1994*, CPT/Inf(96)5, paras. 93, 97 where cubicles of 1.2 mm.[2] in a reception unit at Budapest Remand Prison were condemned outright.

54. CPT (1996) *Spain Visit 1991*, CPT/Inf(96)9, para 126; CPT (1995) *Ireland Visit 1993*, CPT/Inf(95)14, para. 78; CPT (1996) *Spain Visit 1991*, CPT/Inf(96)9, para. 113, where 10 mm.[2] for two inmates was described as "just about adequate" and CPT (1996) *Austria Visit 1994*, CPT/Inf(96)28, para. 103, where the CPT stressed that "cells of about 10m[2]—even when fitted with a partitioned lavatory—are not of an ideal size for double occupancy." Cf. CPT (1994) *Greece Visit 1993*, CPT/Inf(94)20, para. 109, where the committee urged that cells of 9.5mm.[2] should hold no more that three prisoners and "serious efforts" be made to reduce this to two.

55. CPT (1994) *United Kingdom Visit 1993*, CPT/Inf(94)17, para. 119.

56. CPT (1996) *Hungary Visit 1994*, CPT/Inf(96)5, para. 97. The committee had found instances of as many as four in a cell of this size in the Budapest Central Remand Prison and up to six in cells of 14 mm.[2] (para. 91). But cf. CPT (1996) *Slovenia Visit 1995*, CPT/Inf(96)18, para. 63, where the dual occupancy of such cells was considered "cramped" rather than unacceptable.

57. CPT (1997) *Slovakia Visit 1995*, CPT/Inf(97)2, para. 75.

58. In fact, the CPT noted that in Bratislava Prison, "two-person cells often had three or four occupants, three-person cells four occupants and four person cells six occupants" (ibid).

59. CPT (1996) *Spain Visit 1991*, CPT/Inf(96)9, para. 122.

60. CPT (1994) *Greece Visit 1993*, CPT/Inf(94)20, para. 117—although it was made clear that a maximum of four would be preferable.

61. CPT (1996) *Austria Visit 1994*, CPT/Inf(96)28, para. 66.

62. CPT (1996) *Slovenia Visit 1995*, CPT/Inf(96)18, para. 63.

63. CPT (1997) *Slovakia Visit 1995*, CPT/Inf(97)2, para. 86. Once again, however, actual occupancy rates were in excess of the official levels, and fourteen beds were noted in a nine person units of 35 mm.[2], which was considered "quite unacceptable" (para. 87).

64. UN Standard Minimum Rules for the Treatment of Prisoners 21(1).

65. European Prison Rules 83–86.

66. UN Standard Minimum Rules for the Treatment of Prisoners 71, 72, 77.

67. CPT (1992) *2nd General Report 1991*, CPT/Inf(92)3, para. 48.

68. CPT (1992) *Sweden Visit 1991*, CPT/Inf(92)4, paras. 50–53.

69. Ibid., para. 47.

70. CPT (1996) *Hungary Visit 1994*, CPT/Inf(96)5, para. 97; CPT (1996) *Slovenia Visit*

1995, CPT/Inf(96)18, para. 71. Also CPT (1992) *2nd General Report 1991*, CPT/Inf(92)3, para. 47.

71. CPT (1992) *2nd General Report 1991*, CPT/Inf(92)3, para. 42.

72. See, for example, CPT (1997) *Bulgaria Visit 1995*, CPT/Inf(97)1, paras. 46–64; CPT (1993) *Finland Visit 1992*, CPT/Inf(93)8, paras. 52–53; CPT (1996) *United Kingdom Visit 1994*, CPT/Inf(96)11, paras. 18–23.

73. Following a prison officers' industrial dispute in England and Wales and the emergency passage of the Imprisonment (Temporary Provisions) Act 1980, it became possible for any category of "Home Office" prisoner (including the convicted and sentenced) to be housed temporarily in police stations designated for the purpose. Throughout the 1980s this was regularly done to a significant degree.

74. See CPT (1993) *Finland Visit 1992*, CPT/Inf(93)8, para. 25.

75. CPT (1991) *Denmark Visit 1990*, CPT/Inf(91)12, para. 25; CPT (1997) *Norway Visit 1996*, CPT/Inf(97)11, para. 29.

76. CPT (1991) *Denmark Visit 1990*, CPT/Inf(91)12, para. 60; CPT (1997) *Norway Visit 1996*, CPT/Inf(97)11, para. 34.

77. CPT (1992) *2nd General Report 1991*, CPT/Inf(92)3, para. 56.

78. CPT (1991) *Denmark Visit 1990*, CPT/Inf(91)12, para. 29.

79. CPT (1995) *Sweden Visit 1994*, CPT/Inf(95)5, para. 27.

80. That is, they should not be the decisions of police officers or prosecutors (ibid.).

81. It is not clear how frequently the CPT considers it necessary for reviews to take place. In Denmark they must be at least every eight weeks (CPT (1991) *Denmark Visit 1990*, CPT/Inf(91)12, Appendix 2, para. 11) and in Sweden at least every two weeks (CPT (1995) *Sweden Visit 1994*, CPT/Inf(95)5, para. 25), neither of which intervals did the CPT criticize or recommend be changed.

82. In Sweden the use of restrictions is generally authorized by the court but the particular restrictions imposed lie at the discretion of the prosecutor in the particular case (CPT (1995) *Sweden Visit 1994*, CPT/Inf(95)5, paras. 25–7).

83. CPT (1991) *Denmark Visit 1990*, CPT/Inf(91)12, para. 29. Interestingly, this specific recommendation is not included in the general digest of medical standards in prisons in the CPT's third general report. The recommendation is nevertheless repeated the following year in CPT (1994) *Norway Visit 1993*, CPT/Inf(94)11, para. 65.

84. CPT (1994) *Norway Visit 1993*, CPT/Inf(94)11, para. 65; CPT (1995) *Sweden Visit 1994*, CPT/Inf(95)5, paras. 19–20.

85. For a detailed review of those codes with respect to pretrial detention, see United Nations 1994.

86. For a collection of essays on this issue, see Morgan and Evans 1999.

REFERENCES

Bradley, A. W. 1991. "Inhuman or Degrading Punishment? Judicial Whipping in Zimbabwe." *Public Law*, 481–84.

Cassese, N. 1996. *Inhuman States: Imprisonment, Detention, and Torture in Europe Today.* Cambridge: Polity Press.

Council of Europe. 1993. *Consistency in Sentencing.* Recommendation no R(92) 17. Strasbourg: Council of Europe.

———. 1998. *Penological Information Bulletin No. 21.* Strasbourg: Council of Europe.

Donziger, R., ed. 1996. *The Real War on Crime: The Report of the National Criminal Justice Commission.* New York: Harper.

Evans, M., and R. Morgan. 1998. *Preventing Torture: A Study of the European Convention for the Prevention of Torture and Inhuman or Degrading Treatment or Punishment*. Oxford: Clarendon Press.

Feldman, D. 1993. *Civil Liberties and Human Rights in England and Wales*. Oxford: Clarendon Press.

Hood, R. 1996. *The Death Penalty: A World-Wide Perspective*. New York: Oxford University Press.

House of Commons Home Affairs Committee, 1998. *Alternatives to Prison Sentences*, 481-I. London: Her Majesty's Stationery Office.

Kellberg, L. 1991. "The Case-Law of the European Commission of Human Rights." In *The International Fight Against Torture*, edited by N. Cassese. Baden-Baden: Nomos.

Meron, T. 1989. *Human Rights and Humanitarian Norms as Customary Law*. Oxford: Clarendon Press.

Morgan, R. 1993. "An Awkward Anomaly: Remand Prisoners." In *Following Woolf: Reform Through Riot*, edited by E. Player and M. Jenkins. London: Routledge.

Morgan, R., and M. Evans, eds. 1999. *Protecting Prisoners: The Standards of the European Committee for the Prevention of Torture in Context*. Oxford: Clarendon Press.

Murdoch, J. 1994. "The Work of the Council of Europe's Torture Committee." *European Journal of International Law* 5(2): 220.

———. 1999. "CPT Standards within the Context of the Council of Europe." In *Protecting Prisoners: The Standards of the European Committee for the Prevention of Torture in Context*, edited by R. Morgan and M. Evans. Oxford: Clarendon Press.

Pease, K. 1994. "Cross-National Imprisonment Rates: Limitations of Method and Possible Conclusions." In *Prisons in Context*, edited by R. D. King and M. Maguire. Oxford: Oxford University Press.

Rodley, N. 1987. *The Treatment of Prisoners under International Law*. Oxford: Clarendon Press.

Shiffrin, N. 1998. "Jamaica Withdraws the Right of Individual Petition under the International Covenant on Civil and Political Rights." *American Journal of International Law* 92(3):563–68.

Sim, J., V. Ruggiero, and M. Ryan. 1995. "Punishment in Europe: Perceptions and Commonalities." In *Western European Penal Systems: A Critical Anatomy*, edited by V. Ruggerio, M. Ryan, and J. Sim. London: Sage.

Stern, V. 1998. *A Sin against the Future: Imprisonment in the World*. Harmondsworth: Penguin.

United Nations. 1994. *Human Rights and Pre-Trial Detention: A Handbook of International Standards Relating to Pre-Trial Detention*. New York: United Nations.

The Project of Sentencing Reform

T he contributors to this volume, whatever their disagreements over the partic-
ulars of sentencing policy, seem united in their support of what might be called
the "project of sentencing reform." An agenda for such a project was set forth over
two-and-a-half decades ago and continues to influence our own thinking today.[1]
It has, to my mind, the following three main elements: a principled approach to
sentencing, parsimony, and fairness.

A principled approach to sentencing. The project of sentencing reform supports
a *principled* approach to sentencing. Sentencing reform, it is assumed, should be
guided by a coherent set of aims or principles.

A principled approach does not require that there be a single, exclusive penal
purpose. Several aims may properly be pursued, so long as there are explicit norms
concerning their interrelationship. A desert rationale gives primacy to notions of
penal censure and to proportionality of punishment to crime seriousness. Within
a desert framework, however, other penal purposes may properly be taken into
account, to the extent this is consistent with proportionality requirements.[2] Norval
Morris's "limiting retributivism" operates with two penal goals rather than one:
desert and crime prevention. Desert sets the limits for the permissible sentence,
within which crime prevention goals (including rehabilitation) may be pursued
(Morris 1982, chap. 5). Having the sentence depend on two main aims may be
consistent with the reform project, provided that the theory can help account for
the relationship between those aims.

This principled approach rules out primarily intuitive approaches to sentencing—such as the notion adopted in some Australian jurisdictions that a good
sentence should be the product of an "intuitive synthesis" among different goals.[3]
It also rules out the ad hoc adoption of differing sentencing goals for various
different kinds of cases: that the drug offender should get a deterrent sentence, the
repeat burglar an incapacitative one, and the shoplifter a rehabilitative one, and
so forth. True, Morris and Tonry (1990, p. 104) speak of "purposes at sentence,"

405

whereby the court may adopt different aims for different kinds of cases; this choice, however, is constrained within their basic principles of limiting retributivism. The repeat burglar's incapacitative sentence, for example, may not exceed the upper desert limits for offenses of this degree of seriousness.

Parsimony. A second major element in the project of sentencing reform is an emphasis on *parsimony* in punishment. Parsimony, properly understood, does not involve the adoption of a particular sentencing rationale, be it one of desert or of crimeprevention (see von Hirsch 1984, pp. 1105–07). It is, instead, a principle of self-restraint: of preferring milder penal impositions, in the interest of reducing the extent to which convicted offenders' lives are disrupted. Either a desert-oriented or a more preventively-oriented theory can be implemented with greater or less parsimony. Parsimony does, however, call for adoption of principles that explicitly set limits on permissible punishment. A purely functionalist sentencing theory, which permits whatever severity would "work" best, is not likely to be parsimonious.

Parsimony is based on certain normative grounds. These grounds include, first, that convicted defendants are assumed to have continued human status and continuing membership in the legal and moral community; and as such, are entitled to concern for their welfare and dignity. Second these grounds include that punishment—involving as it does the censure of the offender and the purposeful infliction of deprivations on him or her—is something painful and potentially humiliating; and imprisonment particularly so. Such impositions, if they must be inflicted at all, need to be imposed with restraint.

The emphasis on principle is reinforced by parsimony concerns. If convicts are to be regarded as human and if their dignity and welfare are important—and if punishment is so painful—then the imposition of penal sanctions needs to be supported by strong and principled reasons. Someone's intuition, or someone's unsupported preference for some penal aim in a particular kind of case, is not a good enough reason for treating another person (the convicted defendant) badly.

Fairness. A third element in the project of sentencing reform is an idea of fairness: that the sentence should visit a fair and proportionate sanction on the offender. Debate exists about the criteria for proportionality.[4] Notwithstanding such divergences of view, however, there is agreement that proportionality should be an important, not just a marginal, constraint; and that disproportionate sentences should be impermissible—irrespective of their possible crime-preventive effects. This concern with the justice of sentences depends also on the assumption of convicted offenders' having continued membership in the moral and legal community.

I. Role of Rationale

The project of sentencing reform gives much importance, as noted, to the choice of a guiding sentencing rationale. This raises the question of what the proper role of a sanctioning rationale should be in fashioning sentencing policy.

A. Rationale versus Form of Guidelines or Guidance

It is important, first, to bear in mind the distinction between a sentencing rationale, and the legal norms designed to implement it. Within a given rationale, there remains considerable flexibility concerning what form these legal norms should take and how much residual discretion they should permit. A desert rationale, for example, may be implemented through detailed numerical sentencing guidelines (such as Oregon's),[5] or else through statutory statements of sentencing principles (such as those used in Sweden)[6] that leave the development of the actual sentencing tariff to the judiciary. What the rationale points to is the emphasis on proportionality and offense seriousness; how much detail should be provided depends, in part, on how much the judiciary in a particular jurisdiction may be expected to be willing to cooperate in implementing a policy of proportionate sanctions.[7]

In the U.S. debate, unfortunately, this distinction between the sentencing rationale and legal norms for implementation is sometimes overlooked. In the 1970s, critics of the rehabilitative ideal focused on the injustices of California's (since repealed) indeterminate sentence. But rehabilitative sentences are not necessarily best achieved through the kind of wide indeterminacy California permitted (indeed, the old California system, through its wide discretion, permitted judges to take into account all kinds of aims other than rehabilitation). More recently, some critics of the desert rationale have emphasized the apparent rigidities of Minnesota's guidelines (Tonry 1994).[8] But, there exists a considerable degree of choice, within this rationale, concerning how much discretion to allow. Generally formulated statutory principles such as Sweden's, for example, offer judges more leeway in deciding the sentencing tariff than Minnesota- or Oregon-style numerical sentencing grids do.

A sentencing rationale is capable of providing assistance in developing a system of sentencing guidance—particularly, by pointing to what characteristics of the offender or his or her offense should be given primary emphasis in sentencing decisions. But a particular system of guidelines, or of statutory sentencing principles, can always be subjected to criticism from the viewpoint of how well it implements a given rationale. With the Minnesota guidelines, for example, there has been some debate about which rationale the guidelines principally reflect;[9] and about how well the guidelines implement a given rationale, say, that of desert.[10] This kind of analysis can be done only if the rationale, and the legal guidance scheme, are kept conceptually separate.

B. How Much Help Can a Rationale Provide?

A sentencing rationale can only point sentencing policy in a given direction. It can suggest what kind of offender or offense characteristics should be given primacy, what their comparative emphasis should be, and why so. (A rationale can, for example, be suggestive about the relative weight to be given the seriousness of the current crime compared with that given the defendant's criminal record—see section II.) A sentencing rationale can give some guidance on the scaling of penalties, relative to one another. It might tell one *something*, but not a great deal, about the magnitudes and anchoring points of a penalty scale.[11] But a sentencing theory can do little more than that: it is not pregnant with a ready-made tariff of penalties. Critiques of desert theory that point to the imprecision of desert judgments (see Walker 1991, chap. 12), and similar critiques addressed to other theories, suffer from misplaced expectations of what a penal theory can accomplish.

There is also likely to be some inevitable "slippage" in the implementation of any sentencing theory into workable practical norms for sentencers. Standards that grade punishments according to the seriousness of crimes will have to lump together some distinguishable cases, because legal rules are capable of no more than a certain degree of refinement.[12] Moreover, no jurisdiction is likely to implement any sentencing theory in its pure form: compromises with other aims are inevitable, as part of the political process.[13] When analyzing a set of sentencing standards, one may ask whether and to what extent it *substantially* fulfills a given rationale for sentencing; but the "fit" between theory and practice cannot be expected to be perfect.

C. What Importance Does "Disparity" Have?

The U.S. debate over sentencing has taken a wrong turn, I think, in its preoccupation with equality of sentence. It is seldom that equality of treatment should be seen as an end in itself. Indeed, what constitutes sentencing "disparity" depends on the aims to be achieved. How problematic is it that offenders convicted of the same kind of crime get unequal punishments? On a deterrent or incapacitative rationale, this might not be a cause for much concern: what would matter, instead, is whether the sentencing policy *on average* intimidates potential offenders more efficiently, or restrains dangerous ones better. On a rationale emphasizing proportionality, unexplained differences in sentence would be more problematic. But variations in the sentences for a given category of offense would be permissible (indeed, would not be considered disparities at all), where these reflect differences in the harm or culpability of the conduct in the particular circumstances. The significance of disparity thus depends on the choice of sentencing rationale.

II. Desert versus Limiting Retributivism

In using rationales in order to develop guidelines (or other forms of legal guidance) for sentencing, it is important to understand those rationales' operational differences: to what extent, and at what points, do they really point to different results? For some rationales, the differences are readily apparent. A desert rationale, for example, relies primarily on the seriousness of the current crime and gives only limited weight to prior convictions (see von Hirsch and Ashworth 1998, pp. 191–97). A selective-incapacitation rationale, however, gives primary weight to the criminal record—including not only past convictions but also past arrests not leading to conviction (see, more fully, von Hirsch 1985, chap. 11).

The two rationales to which several chapters in this volume refer are "just deserts" and "limiting retributivism." As the latter view was originally formulated by Norval Morris, the differences between it and desert-based conceptions seemed quite large. Limiting retributivism apparently made use of the seriousness of the current offense only to set rather broad limits on the permissible sanction, within which the sentence in the individual case would be set on other (including predictive) grounds. Recent discussions by advocates of limiting retributivism, however, have hinted at significant changes—ones that would lead to results somewhat more congruent (although by no means entirely so) to those yielded by a desert model.

First, Morris in his initial formulations treated the desert limits as being based in community sentiment: sentences are not to exceed *what is seen by current popular mores* as excessive (Morris 1974, pp. 74–76).[14] The difficulty with such a formulation, however, is that it provides scant restraint: even quite draconian sanctions could be permissible, if current community sentiment were to support them (see Zimring and Hawkins 1995, pp. 64–67). However, Michael Tonry (1994) has recently rejected the community-mores definition and opts for desert-based maximum penalties derived from similar normative principles as those of desert theorists.

Second, advocates of limiting retributivism are more chary of predictions of dangerousness than appears at first impression. Norval Morris and Marc Miller (1985) assert that such predictions may be employed to fix the sentence anywhere within the applicable desert limits. Given the breadth of those limits on their formulation, this could have made predictive judgments a major (indeed, possibly the primary) determinant of the sentence. In a seemingly technical qualification, however, these authors assert that permissible predictive judgments must rely on factors *other than* the seriousness of crime or the offender's criminal record.[15] But since the latter factor, the criminal record, is ordinarily the main basis for predictive judgments, this sharply restricts the scope of those judgments. The authors do not explain their reasons for adding this qualification, but it seems to reflect their discomfort at a sentencing system resting chiefly on risk predictions.

Third, advocates of limiting retributivism appear to be reconsidering their views regarding lower desert limits on permissible punishment. Although Morris sometimes speaks of there being lower (as well as upper) desert limits on permissible punishments, he does not articulate how these might be set. Tonry, in a 1994 essay, asserts that there should be no lower limits based on desert. But in the absence of such lower desert limits, there remains the question of what grounds would sustain *any* quantum of sentence at all. One possibility would be incapacitation: offenders should be given sentences suited to their degree of risk, within applicable upper desert limits. However, this effectively would make incapacitation the primary determinant of the sentence: burglars might be imprisoned more frequently than armed robbers, if their risks of recidivism are higher. The desert limit would merely ensure that burglars could not actually serve as long as the robbers *might* serve, were the latter imprisoned for the maximum permissible period.

In a National Institute of Justice publication on sentencing guidelines, Tonry (1997) seemingly changes position and opts for lower offense-based limits. A sentencing-guidelines system, he suggests, might have six severity bands (in his terminology, "zones of discretion"), based on the seriousness of the offenses involved. Substitutions among unequally severe penalties may be made within a given band, but not outside of it. This would ensure that serious crimes ordinarily received significant sentences and that there would be an approximate ordering of penalties according to offense gravity. But it seems to involve acceptance of the idea of desert-based lower bounds on penalties. Richard Frase (1997, p. 383), also an advocate of limiting retributivism, explicitly accepts the idea of desert-based lower bounds, which would be ordinally scaled in the same manner as the upper desert limits.

The upshot could be a scheme that has greater similarities to a desert model than Morris's early formulations. Crime seriousness (at least, in ordinary cases) would receive substantial weight in determining the penalty. Yet there still might be significant differences from desert theory. Greater freedom might still exist to make interchanges among unequally severe penalties. The lower desert limits might be more permeable — to allow consideration, for example, of mitigating factors that do not directly relate to offense gravity but nevertheless suggest merit on the part of the defendant (Tonry 1994).[16] In assessing how much greater freedom this model allows, however, the possibilities of limited modifications of the desert model would also need to be considered. These might, for example, permit modest deviations from the parity requirements of desert (see, more fully, von Hirsch 1993, pp. 54–56).[17]

III. Obstacles to the Sentencing Reform Project

It should be evident from the other chapters in this volume, surveying reform efforts in various jurisdictions, that the sentencing-reform project is not easily accomplished; some formidable obstacles stand in the way.

A. Discretionary Sentencing

One obstacle is the discretionary ethos for sentencing. Each case, according to this perspective, is unique; all sentencing aims have relevance; the judge, using personal experience on the bench, should apply aims of his or her choosing to the "unique" facts of the case, using his or her intuition or common sense. What is notable about this approach is not that it involves elements of discretion, for virtually any workable sentencing scheme must have such elements. It is, rather, that sentencing should *primarily* be a matter for judicial discretion. Illustrative of this approach is the doctrine used (until quite recently) by the English Court of Appeal for determining whether an offense is sufficiently serious to warrant imprisonment. Seriousness, the Court opined in several cases, should depend on the hypothetical view of "right-thinking members of the public," and (in the Court's words) resembles the elephant in that it can be recognized without need for further definition.[18]

Taken literally, such claims are absurd. Were every situation coming before the courts incomparably different, law itself would be impossible because it necessarily involves classification. If judges' intuitions were so reliable, we would rely generally on *khadi* justice in our judicial system, and legal standards and precedents would have no role. Why, then, this insistence on unfettered judicial sentencing power in the area of sentencing?

According to one explanation, the faith in wide discretion stems from the rehabilitative ideal: the judge is seen as a kind of healer, who fits his or her "treatment" to the needs of the offender. Rehabilitation, however, is no longer widely regarded as constituting the primary aim of sentencing. And even a rehabilitative approach would call for sentencing standards—if for no other purpose, in order to ensure that sentencing judges pursue that aim, and not others of their own choosing.

Another explanation has been that judges do not wish to part with sentencing discretion because this would diminish their power. Concerns about maintaining judicial power have not, however, hindered the development of standards in other areas of law. The probate judge is required to distribute the decedent's property to his legal heirs, according to the terms of his will or the rules of intestate succession. There is no talk of recognizing elephants there, nor of assigning the property to the heir whom the judge believes to possess the greatest personal merit.

The discretionary approach is better understood, perhaps, as one in which penal purposes serve not so much as principles designed to provide rational support and guidance for the choice of sentence, as *aspirations* to be expressed through the sentence. When a defendant is sentenced to extra time in prison "for deterrence," for example, it is not necessarily supposed that such a sentence will in fact have added deterrent impact. The extra time, instead, symbolizes a desideratum: that it would be a good thing were criminal defendants to be better deterred. The judge, here, is deemed to be the authoritative presence, whose role in sentence is to give ritual expression to such aspirations.

Seen in this light, discretionary sentencing becomes comprehensible. Why is every case "different"? And why are all the aims of sentence deemed relevant, notwithstanding their potential for leading to conflicting results? It is because this allows varying aspirations to be given ritual expression through the sentence. The sentencer thus can, depending on the character of the case, express that we *want* the sentence to achieve this or that desirable aim, whether it be rehabilitative, deterrent, incapacitative, or desert-orientated.

What is wrong with such an approach? Since it is so difficult to know what sentencing policy would best prevent crime, why not have the sentence express what we *wish* the sentence should accomplish? Even a wholly discretionary sentencing system is capable of achieving a modicum of deterrent and incapacitative effects, and principled sentencing may not achieve much more law-enforcement efficiency (see, e.g., von Hirsch 1985, chap. 15). A modern society has many other rituals that express its various aspirations. Why not the sentence?

The difficulty is, of course, that sentencing is done at the offender's expense. The infringement of the defendant's liberties that the sentence imposes calls for a justification going beyond the expression of supposed community aspirations. Consider the practice, prevalent in English courts today, of imposing added punishment for crimes that become more prevalent (see Ashworth and von Hirsch 1997, pp. 191–92). The purported rationale for the practice is deterrence: the enhanced sentence's intimidating effects will help reduce the incidence of the conduct. But because of the extra pain thus inflicted on offenders, this practice calls for justification. There would need to be evidence that such a deterrence strategy has significant chances of success—evidence largely lacking today (see von Hirsch et al. 1999). There would also need to be convincing argument why it is fair—or at least, not patently unfair—to add to an offender's punishment not because his crime is any more harmful or culpable but because other persons (over whom he has no control) are committing it more often. But entering into such arguments is precisely what the discretionary approach avoids. The English courts have not been willing to consider what evidence there is, if any, of any marginal deterrent utility of exemplary sentences; and they have not addressed the fairness of such sentences.

Some penologists speak of "denunciation" as a possible purpose of sentencing (see Walker 1991, pp. 29–33). Why should not the sentence, under the discretionary approach, be seen as a means through which disapprobation can officially be expressed of the convicted offender and his conduct? The problem here lies in the character of the denunciatory message. Punishment has a legitimate censuring function: of visiting blame upon the perpetrator for his conduct. Since the blame is being conveyed through penal hard treatment, the severity of that treatment should fairly reflect the conduct's degree of blameworthiness (i.e., its seriousness). This is, indeed, the basis for the principle of proportionality (see von Hirsch 1993, chap. 2).

Unfortunately, "denunciation" goes beyond this notion of censure, directed at an offender seen as an agent capable of moral deliberation. In the discretionary sentence, it may include any expression of disapproval of the deplorable state of affairs wrought by crime. Through raising sentences when a crime has become more frequent, for example, the courts might indeed be giving vent to "denunciation," in the sense of conveying on behalf of the community their indignation over a recent rise in the crime rate, and their aspirations to halting that rise. But if these phenomena cannot properly be attributed to the fault of the defendant, then the moral justification of the extra punishment is called into question.

I sometimes wonder whether recently fashionable notions of restorative justice share these problematic features. In the literature of restorative justice, the aims are extremely hazy. It is said that the sentence should resolve the "conflict" between offender and victim. But crimes are different from disputes (the criminal ordinarily makes no claim of being entitled to what he takes), so what "dispute" is there to be resolved? The sentence is supposed also to "restore" the bonds of community, frayed through the offense; but it is not explained how this aim can be accomplished.[19] Much emphasis is placed, instead, on the modalities of the decision process—on participation by offenders, victims, and community representatives. Such participative decision-making, which is to remain largely discretionary, is said to lead to greater satisfaction among the participants than a criminal trial (see, e.g., Braithwaite 1998). One is tempted to suspect that what is chiefly involved is a changed ritual, in which the judge no longer officiates, and others (victims, representatives of the public) express, through a discretionary disposition, varying aspirations on the community's supposed behalf.

B. Law-and-Order

Another major obstacle to sentencing reform in recent years has been "law-and-order." This, unfortunately, will be apparent to the reader from perusing the national surveys in this volume. Sentencing reforms are blocked or repealed, and harsh penalties adopted, to reflect posturing stances of toughness on crime. "Populist punitiveness," as Anthony Bottoms (1995) terms it, comes to shape sentencing policy in many jurisdictions.

Law-and-order approaches involve not only sharp increases in penalties but also escalated rhetoric concerning crime and criminals. Convicted criminals are to be subjected to drastic sanctions, in view of their supposed depravity and status as moral outlaws.

Having discussed law and order at greater length elsewhere (von Hirsch and Ashworth 1998, chap. 9), let me simply point out here that it involves rejection of the sentencing-reform project. The advocacy of harsh sentences is inconsistent with the principle of parsimony. And the assumption underlying parsimony, that offenders are human beings entitled to proper respect and concern, is rejected as well. The law-and-order approach tends to utilize what Arie Freiberg (chap. 1, this volume) characterizes as "forfeiture": convicted offenders are deemed to have excluded themselves from the body politic and have forfeited any claims to be treated as citizens entitled to even a minimum of respect. In one version of law and order, offenders are to be subjected to degrading penalties as an expression of community indignation at their crimes (Kahan 1996). Because the offender is granted no moral standing, such penal responses may disregard the degree of blameworthiness of the offender's conduct, as well as any claims he might have to dignified treatment; what counts, instead, is giving vent to respectable citizens' animus at criminals and their behavior.

The sentencing-reform project's emphasis on substantive penal goals is also rejected. Proportionality of sentence is jettisoned, because the sanctions recommended by law and order proponents tend to be quite disproportionate to the gravity of the offense or to the penalties for other offenses. A notorious example is California's three-strikes law, according to which two convictions for burglary and a third conviction for a lesser offense suffices for near-lifetime imprisonment. In a substantial number of recent cases under this statute, the third "strike" was a conviction for marijuana possession (Dickey and Hollenhorst 1998).

Notwithstanding rhetorical claims that "prison works" and suchlike, there is also little serious interest in crime-prevention effects; symptomatic of this, proposals for new harsh measures are almost never accompanied by any serious efforts to estimate the likely crime-preventive effects. Thus, the former British Home Secretary, Michael Howard, when introducing his version of three strikes (providing for substantial mandatory sentences for third-time burglars and drug dealers)[20], asserted in his accompanying White Paper that these measures would reduce the rates of burglary and drug dealing by 20 percent (Home Office 1996, pp. 54–55). The figure was pulled out the air, however, with no supporting evidence offered whatever.

Sometimes, it is asserted (notwithstanding this seeming lack of concern with actual preventive effects) that law and order "works" anyway, because sharply increased sentences do reduce crime rates. Thus Charles Murray (1997) calls attention to the fact that, during recent decades, rates of imprisonment has been rising in the United States while crime rates have been falling; whereas in England, the reverse has been occurring. This is his basis for asserting that tougher sentencing policies (especially more reliance on sentences of imprisonment) prevent crime more effectively. Murray's purported evidence, however, is unpersuasive: his figures on rates of imprisonment fail to distinguish the severity of punishment (which is what is at issue in sentencing policy) from an offender's likelihood of conviction if he commits an offense (which is a matter of the effectiveness of police and prosecution strategies). More careful studies by David Farrington and his colleagues of crime and punishment patterns in these two countries over the past fifteen years disclose that while likelihood of conviction shows significant negative statistical correlations with crime rates, the severity of punishments generally does not.[21] An analysis of recent deterrence studies, conducted by other researchers from the Institute of Criminology at Cambridge, concludes also that there is little or no reliable evidence that raising penalty levels generally enhances deterrent effects (von Hirsch et al. 1999).

If law-and-order approaches are not well suited for reducing crime, what other functions might they serve? Their primary function, it appears, is to mobilize and exploit popular resentment at crime or criminals—a strategy that can, in certain political environments, be a way to garner political support.[22] In England, for example, Michael Howard's campaign that "prison works" became a useful unifying theme for an otherwise divided Conservative Party. Once introduced into political discourse, law and order also has a tendency to spread. In the late 1990s, for example, several European parties of the moderate left endorsed surprisingly repressive penal policies. At least in part, the strategy seems to be one of seeking protection from vulnerability to attacks for being "soft" on crime.

Where law and order dominates the debate on crime, sentencing reform of the kind I am speaking of becomes very difficult to accomplish. A notable example is the U.S. federal sentencing guidelines. Congress passed legislation in the mid-1980s creating a U.S. sentencing commission to write guidelines for sentences in federal cases. By the time the Reagan-appointed members of the commission were drafting its standards, law and order had become a much-emphasized theme for the administration and Congress. A study by Anthony Doob (1995) shows the results. The federal sentencing guidelines adopt no particular penal philosophy and show no consistent substantive approach. There is, however, one clear (and clearly intended) effect of the guidelines: large increases in penalty levels.

It has sometimes been suggested that sentencing-reform efforts are themselves the cause of law-and-order responses: explicit general standards for sentencing give right-wing politicians an easy opportunity to escalate penalties (see Rothman 1995). However, law and order has a multiplicity of forms: where no sentencing guidelines exist, penalties can be escalated through the adoption of mandatory minimum sentences, or through putting pressure on judges to raise their sentences.[23] What is true, however, is that where law-and-order pressures are strong, it will be difficult to develop a set of sentencing standards properly.

Law-and-order pressures, where great enough, can also force reformers into strange postures, in order to try to alleviate "get tough" measures' worst features. For example: the U.S. Sentencing Commission's federal sentencing guidelines prescribe incarceration in almost all cells in the sentencing grid, save for those with the lowest offense rankings. To permit greater use of noncustodial sanctions, a first-offender exception has been suggested—permitting such sanctions to be used on all offenders save for those who are especially dangerous or whose crimes are particularly serious (Tonry 1992). The enabling statute authorizes the commission to make such an exception, so that the commission could reduce first-offender penalties without having to go back to Congress. On the merits, such a "reform" seems hard to defend: giving the presence or absence of a criminal record so much weight clearly does not comport with a desert model and probably does not comport with limiting retributivism either.[24] The proposal was designed simply as a pragmatic step for helping to alleviate somewhat the federal guidelines' unwonted harshness. Perhaps, steps of this kind might sometimes be helpful. But then, reformers should be aware of, and make explicit, what they are doing: conducting emergency surgery to soften the worst effects of a bad scheme. Such remedial steps should not be presented, or seen, as models for sentencing reform.

IV. Conclusions

This chapter has five main themes.

First, sentencing reformers have had some impressive successes over recent years—for example, the sentencing guidelines of Oregon and Minnesota, and the statutory sentencing regulation schemes of Sweden and Finland. And even where reform efforts have been less effective in altering actual sentencing policies, as in England, they have contributed a great deal to stimulating and clarifying thinking about sentencing.

Notwithstanding divergencies of theory and strategy, the various reform efforts discussed in this volume seem to share certain common assumptions. These assumptions, taken together, undergird what I term here the project of sentencing reform. The assumptions are that *sentencing reform should be guided by a coherent set of aims or principles; sanctions should be* parsimoniously *imposed, and sentencing policy should visit fair and proportionate sanctions.* Within these assumptions, there is room for divergence (e.g., on whether proportionality requires only the setting of certain limits on permissible punishments, or more specific requirements); nevertheless, it is understood that fairness to convicted offenders should be an important and not just a marginal concern. Underlying this triad of assumptions are certain deeper normative postulates—the most notable being that convicted offenders should be assumed to have continued human status.

Second, the sentencing-reform project's emphasis on principle means that having a consistent sentencing rationale is important. I make certain suggestions about what role a sentencing rationale is and is not able to perform. A rationale is a set of mutually consistent principles that can point the general directions for legal schemes of sentencing guidance. It can suggest, for example, what factors should be given emphasis in sentencing decisions, and what their relative weight should be. But a rationale is not the same thing as an actual sentencing tariff and can go only a certain distance in suggesting how such a tariff should be constituted. Indeed, an important role of a rationale is to provide a norm for evaluating proposed systems of legal sentencing guidance.

Third, among sentencing reformers, there has been considerable discussion on what the guiding sentencing rationale should be. Particularly lively has been the debate over the relative merits of "just-deserts" and "limiting-retributivist" theories. This debate has stimulated thought on both sides, and helped clarify ideas. But sometimes, it has led to unnecessary rhetoric, involving an overstatement of the differences.[25]

Desert theory and limiting retributivism have evolved over the past two decades, developing certain common features—ones I sketch in this chapter. Limiting-retributivists, for example, now appear to endorse substantial, desert-based upper and lower bounds on permissible punishments. This gives the seriousness of the offense increased weight in the sentence, thus bringing the limiting-retributivist approach into somewhat greater congruence with desert-based perspectives. The fact that a single set of sentencing guidelines, Minnesota's, is said by a desert theorist to be strongly influenced by desert principles (von Hirsch, 1987, chap. 5) and yet is said by a limiting-retributivist to reflect that latter view (Frase 1997) suggests that the theories cannot be utterly unreconcilable. The similarities should not be overstated: there are still ample differences between the two theories. But the elements of commonality should continue to be explored.

Fourth, a major obstacle to sentencing reform in many jurisdictions has been the insistence on preserving wide judicial discretion. Sometimes, this insistence has been based on sound practical reasons. In a jurisdiction where law-and-order pressures are extremely strong, for example, it may simply be impractical to formulate schemes of sentencing guidance without incurring the risk of escalating sentencing levels unduly. But sentencing reform often is resisted by a discretionary sentencing ethos, and that is more problematical: it treats sentencing as a hortatory or denunciatory institution, the aim of which is to express (at the convicted offender's expense) various aspirations on the community's supposed behalf. A judge thus may, for example, impose extra punishment "for deterrence," as a way of expressing the aspiration that potential offenders should be better deterred. If the sentenced offender's human status is taken seriously, however, better reasons are needed for visiting a sentence's penal deprivations on him.

Fifth, another major obstacle to reform is law-and-order pressures. The law-and-order ethos, I suggest, operates according to quite a different logic than that of the sentencing-reform project. Get-tough-on-crime advocacy, ordinarily, does not provide reasons why harsh penalties would work better or be more just; what counts, instead, is the expression through the sentence of loathing of convicted criminals—a class deemed largely undeserving of the concern and respect due other human beings. The real opponent of sentence reform of the kind discussed in this volume, we should thus bear in mind, is not another reformer who happens to favor a somewhat different theory of punishment or a somewhat different strategy for guiding sentence; he is, rather, the person who thinks that harsh penalties are justifiable because offenders are not good enough to be treated fairly and humanely at all.

ACKNOWLEDGMENTS

The author is grateful to Andrew Ashworth, Richard Frase, and Michael Tonry for their comments.

NOTES

1. See, e.g., Frankel 1973; Morris 1974; and von Hirsch 1976. Of course, this has by no means been the first movement in reform of sentencing. For an interesting sketch of earlier efforts, see Radzinowicz 1999. The project of which I am speaking, however, represents the current generation of liberal reform efforts.

2. Since the principle of proportionality addresses only the deserved *severity* of punishment, crime-preventive goals (say, rehabilitation) may be considered when choosing among penalties of approximately comparable severity (see von Hirsch 1993, chap. 7).

3. See, chap. 1, in this volume. See also, the notion of "existential conversation" reportedly used by judges in Austria to decide sentence; Tonry 1996, p. 179.

4. See discussion in section II of this chapter.

5. For an analysis of Oregon's guidelines, see von Hirsch 1995.

6. For discussion of the Swedish system, see von Hirsch and Ashworth 1998, pp. 240–52, and Jareborg 1995. For the comparative merits of numerical guidelines and statutory-sentencing principles, see von Hirsch, Knapp, and Tonry 1987, chap. 3.

7. Both Sweden and England adopted the statutory-principles approach to adopting a policy of proportionate sentences — with Sweden passing its statute in 1988 and England in 1991. Sweden appears to have had considerable success in inducing judges to take proportionality concerns into account in their sentencing judgments (see Jareborg 1995), but England has been much less successful, with the judiciary watering down or disregarding important requirements of its 1991 sentencing statute, such as the requirement that the conduct be serious before a custodial sentence is imposed (see Ashworth and von Hirsch 1997, and n. 18 below). In part, these differences may be attributable to the more careful drafting of the Swedish statute. But they seem attributable also to differences in judicial outlook. The Swedish judiciary has a tradition of taking statutory formulations of policy seriously, and of examining and relying upon the legislative history of such provisions. The English judiciary has no such traditions and is strongly committed to discretionary sentencing.

8. The supposed "rigidity" of Minnesota's guidelines also is questionable. For discussion of the elements of flexibility in these standards, see Frase 1993, pp. 13–23.

9. Compare von Hirsch (1994) with Frase (1994) on the question of the extent to which Minnesota's guidelines reflect a desert rationale.

10. For an analysis and critique of Minnesota's and Oregon's guidelines from a desert perspective, see von Hirsch 1995.

11. For a discussion of the magnitude of a penalty scale on a desert rationale, see von Hirsch 1993, chap. 5.

12. See von Hirsch 1993, pp. 104–05 in response to Tonry's (1994) criticisms of desert theory, based on the supposed "aggregative" character of Minnesota's guidelines.

13. Sweden, for example, has included in its sentencing statute a provision that permits deterrent sentences for certain types of crime, such as drinking and driving. See more fully, von Hirsch 1987, p. 754.

14. John Monahan (1982) also prefers for such a consensus approach to setting desert limits and suggests a procedure for determining the consensus that is designed to rule out "outlying" views.

15. This qualification is put in rather technical language by the authors (Morris and Miller 1985, p. 37), to wit: "The base expectancy rate of violence for the criminal predicted as dangerous must be shown by reliable evidence to be substantially higher than the base expectancy rate of another criminal with a closely similar criminal record and convicted of a closely similar crime but not predicted as unusually dangerous, before the greater dangerousness of the former may be relied upon to intensify or extend his punishment."

16. As an example of such grounds, Tonry (1994) describes the offender from a deprived social background who has succeeded in obtaining steady employment; but see von Hirsch 1993, pp. 109–10. To the extent such factors are admissible, they might be characterized as "quasi-retributive"; see von Hirsch 1994, pp. 46–48.

17. This desert-derived hybrid scheme should be usefully compared with the scaling principles Richard Frase develops on the basis of an analysis of Minnesota's guidelines. See Frase 1997, pp. 407–22.

18. For the relevant cases, see Ashworth and von Hirsch 1997, p. 187. This "right-thinking members of the public" doctrine was used to interpret sec. 1(2)(b) of the Criminal Justice Act 1991, which required that crimes be serious before a custodial sentence could be invoked. By making the determination of seriousness almost wholly a discretionary matter, this doctrine largely vitiated the act's limitation on use of custody. The doctrine has quite recently been overruled, and the Court has stated that the decision to invoke imprisonment should be based on a number of factors—including especially the harm done by the offense and the character of the defendant's intentions. See *Howells*, reported in [1998] *Criminal Law Review* 836–39. Even this case, however, gives only a very limited degree guidance to sentencers.

19. For the pros and cons of restorative justice, see von Hirsch and Ashworth 1998, chap. 7. In some versions, however, discretionary restorative-justice dispositions are supposed to be constrained by some outer limits of proportionality. In others, such dispositions are available only for certain lesser offenses; see von Hirsch and Ashworth 1998, chap. 7.

20. Howard's "three strikes" provisions were embodied in the 1997 Crime (Sentences) Act, legislation that passed immediately before the dissolution of the Conservative government in spring 1997. He did not have time before dissolution to put the statute's provisions into effect, but his Labour successor, Jack Straw, has taken that step. Straw implemented the act's seven-year minimum sentence for a third drug-dealing offense shortly after he took office and implemented the three-year minimum for third burglary convictions in January 1999.

21. See Farrington, Langan, and Wikström 1994; Langan and Farrington 1998. These authors use three measures of severity in their calculations: likelihood of imprisonment given conviction, duration of sentence, and duration of actual confinement.

22. For more on these political functions of law and order, see von Hirsch and Ashworth 1998, chap. 9.

23. California's three-strikes law adopted in 1994 is a notable example of the use of mandatory minimums to raise sentence levels. Michael Howard's law-and-order rhetoric during his 1993–97 term of office helped induce English judges to raise sentence levels

considerably, even though his mandatory minimum sentences were enacted only in 1997 and put into effect after he left office (see n. 20).

24. Such heavy emphasis on the prior criminal record would be inconsistent with a desert rationale, given that rationale's primary orientation to the seriousness of the current crime. Such an emphasis—by creating large differentials between the punishments of first and repeat offenders—may also breach the desert-based limits of "limiting retributivism."

25. Examples of such rhetoric are recent assertions by limiting-retributivists that desert theory is in substantial part responsible for the rise in sentencing levels in the United States (Tonry 1995) or that desert theory largely precludes the use of noncustodial penalties (Tonry 1998, p. 206).

REFERENCES

Ashworth, Andrew, and Andrew von Hirsch. 1997. "Recognising Elephants: The Problem of the Custody Threshold." *Criminal Law Review*, 187–200.

Bottoms, Anthony. 1995. "The Philosophy and Politics of Punishment and Sentencing." In *The Politics of Sentencing Reform*, edited by C. M. V. Clarkson and Rod Morgan. Oxford: Clarendon University Press.

Braithwaite, John. 1998. "Restorative Justice." In *The Handbook of Crime and Punishment*, edited by Michael Tonry. New York: Oxford University Press.

Dickey, Walter, and Pam Stiebs Hollenhorst. 1998. "Three-Strikes Laws: Massive Impact in California and Georgia, Little Elsewhere." *Overcrowded Times* 9(6):2–8.

Doob, Anthony. 1995. "The United States Sentencing Commission Guidelines: If You Don't Know Where You're Going You Might Not Get There." In *The Politics of Sentencing Reform*, edited by C. M. V Clarkson and Rod Morgan. Oxford: Clarendon Press.

Farrington, D. P., P. A. Langan, and P.-O. Wikström. 1994. "Changes in Crime and Punishment in America, England, and Sweden between the 1980s and 1990s." *Studies in Crime Prevention* 3: 104–31.

Frankel, Marvin. 1973. *Criminal Sentences: Law without Order*. New York: Hill & Wang.

Frase, Richard S. 1993. "The Uncertain Future of Sentencing Guidelines." *Law and Inequality* 12:1–42.

———. 1994. "Purposes of Punishment under the Minnesota Guidelines." *Criminal Justice Ethics* 13:11–20.

———. 1997. "Sentencing Principles in Theory and Practice." In *Crime and Justice: A Review of Research*, vol. 22, edited by Michael Tonry. Chicago: University of Chicago Press.

Home Office. 1996. *Protecting the Public*. Cm 3190. London: Her Majesty's Stationery Office.

Jareborg, Nils. 1995. "The Swedish Sentencing Reform." In *The Politics of Sentencing Reform*, edited by C. M. V. Clarkson and Rod Morgan. Oxford: Clarendon Press.

Kahan, Dan. 1996. "What Do Alternative Sanctions Mean?" *University of Chicago Law Review* 63:591–653.

Langan, P. A., and D. P. Farrington. 1998. *Crime and Justice in the United States and England and Wales, 1981–96*. Washington, D.C.: Bureau of Justice Statistics.

Monahan, John. 1982. "The Case for Prediction in the Modified Desert Model for Criminal Sentencing." *International Journal of Law and Psychology* 5:103–13.

Morris, Norval. 1974. *The Future of Imprisonment*. Chicago: University of Chicago Press.

———. 1982. *Madness and the Criminal Law*. Chicago: University of Chicago Press.

Morris, Norval, and Marc Miller. 1985. "Predictions of Dangerousness." In *Crime And Justice: An Annual Review of Research*, vol. 6, edited by Michael Tonry. Chicago: University of Chicago Press.

Morris, Norval, and Michael Tonry. 1990. *Between Prison and Probation: Intermediate Punishments in a Rational Sentencing System*. New York: Oxford University Press.

Murray, Charles. 1997. *Does Prison Work?* London: Institute of Economic Affairs.

Radzinowicz, Leon. 1999. *Adventures in Criminology*. London: Routledge.

Rothman, David. 1995. "More of the Same: American Criminal Justice Policies in the 1990s." In *Punishment and Social Control*, edited by Thomas Blomberg and Stanley Cohen. New York: de Gruyter.

Tonry, M. 1992. "Salvaging the Sentencing Guidelines in Seven Easy Steps." *Federal Sentencing Reporter*, May–June, 355–59.

———. 1994. "Proportionality, Interchangeability, and Intermediate Punishments." In *Penal Theory and Penal Practice*, edited by R. Dobash, R. Dobash, R. A. Duff, and Sandra Marshall. Manchester: Manchester University Press.

———. 1995. *Malign Neglect: Race, Crime, and Punishment in America*. New York: Oxford University Press

———. 1996. *Sentencing Matters*. New York: Oxford University Press.

———. 1997. *Intermediate Sanctions in Sentencing Guidelines*. Washington D.C.: National Institute of Justice.

———. 1998. "Intermediate Sanctions in Sentencing Guidelines." In *Crime and Justice: A Review of Research*, vol. 23, edited by Michael Tonry. Chicago: University of Chicago Press.

von Hirsch, Andrew. 1976. *Doing Justice: The Choice of Punishments*. New York: Hill & Wang.

———. 1984. "Equality, 'Anisonomy,' and Justice." *Michigan Law Review* 82:1093–112.

———. 1985. *Past or Future Crimes*. New Brunswick, N.J.: Rutgers University Press.

———. 1987. "Guiding Principles for Sentencing: The Proposed Swedish Law." *Criminal Law Review*, 746–55.

———. 1993. *Censure and Sanctions*. Oxford: Clarendon Press.

———. 1994. "Sentencing Guidelines and Penal Aims in Minnesota." *Criminal Justice Ethics* 13:39–49.

———. 1995. "Proportionality and Parsimony in American Sentencing Guidelines: The Minnesota and Oregon Standards." In *The Politics of Sentencing Reform*, edited by C. M. V Clarkson and Rod Morgan. Oxford: Clarendon Press.

von Hirsch, Andrew, and Andrew Ashworth, eds. 1998. *Principled Sentencing: Readings in Theory and Policy*. 2d ed. Oxford: Hart Publishing.

von Hirsch, A., A. E. Bottoms, E. Burney, and P.-O. Wikström. 1999. *Criminal Deterrence and Sentence Severity: An Analysis of Recent Research*. Oxford: Hart Publishing.

von Hirsch, A., K. Knapp, and M. Tonry. 1987. *The Sentencing Commission and Its Guidelines*. Boston: Northeastern University Press.

Walker, Nigel. 1991. *Why Punish?* Oxford: Oxford University Press.

Zimring, Franklin, and Gordon Hawkins. 1995. *Incapacitation*. New York: Oxford University Press.

Index

Mississippi, 231, 359, 360. *See also* United States

Missouri, 225, 226, 294, 352. *See also* United States

mitigation: and AIDS, 365; in Australia, 51; and court discretion, 279; and culpability, 128–29; in England and Wales, 73–74; in Finland, 128–35, 147n.25; in Germany, 189, 201, 212n.7; and human rights, 364–65; and ICTY, 381; and just deserts model, 410; and meritorious conduct, 129; in Netherlands, 172; and proportionality in sentencing, 278; and sentencing generally, 261; in United States, 224, 231

Modinos v. Cyprus, 343

Moldova, 347, 374n.2, 374n.8

money laundering, 316–17

Montana, 231. *See also* United States

morality and punishment, 109–10, 123, 144nn.6–8, 145n.12

Morgan, Neil, 36, 42

Morgan, Rod, 379–417

Morris, Norval, 35, 38, 45–46, 146–47n.22, 246, 287n.18, 405–6, 409, 410

Müller v. Switzerland, 344

murder. *See* violent crime

Murray, Charles, 414

Muteba v. Zaire, 401n.34

mutilation, 388

Nazis, 385–86

Nebraska, 231. *See also* United States

Nelson v. United Kingdom, 362, 365–66

Netherlands: and aggravating factors, 172; aims of sentencing in, 173; appellate system in, 174–75; automatic release in, 165; and blameworthiness, 174; civil servant offenses in, 172; cleared-up crimes in, 155, 156, 177; combination orders in, 166, 169; community sentences in, 153, 166–72; community service in, 4, 166–69, 171, 186; consecutive prison sentences in, 172–73; and Council of Europe, 373n.1; crime rates in, 3, 151, 177–79; day fines in, 306–7; disparity in sentencing in, 175–77; drug offenses in, 161, 175, 176, 178–79, 182, 184, 186; drunk driving in,

175, 178; early release in, 164–66; electronic monitoring in, 166, 169–70, 171, 186, 208, 321; Financial Penalties Act of 1983, 156, 158, 161–62, 173; fines in, 153, 155, 163, 167, 173, 176–77, 306–7; foreign prisoners in, 153, 184; human rights protections in, 367; imprisonment rates in, 4, 9, 17, 18, 20, 104, 151–53, 262–63, 306; juvenile offenders in, 166, 169, 172, 179; life imprisonment in, 172; mandatory sentencing in, 175; mentally disturbed offenders in, 153, 165, 166, 184, 185; mitigating circumstances in, 172; nonprosecution in, 155–56; organized crime in, 317; parole in, 164–66; partly suspended sentences in, 305; penitentiary programs in, 170–71, 186; pretrial detention in, 152–53, 158–61, 160; prison capacity in, 151–53, 159, 179–80, 184; prison conditions in, 151; Prison Memorandums in, 183–85; prison population composition in, 182–86; prison reduction policy in, 157–72; property crimes in, 169, 177–78; and proportionality, 174, 264, 278; prosecutorial discretion in, 153–57, 176–77; and Protocol 6, 374n.8; recidivism in, 166, 172, 184; rehabilitation in, 183; resource considerations in, 155; restorative justice in, 173; sentence enhancement in, 274–75; sentencing policies in, 22–23, 151–86; sentencing statistics in, 171, 180–82; and society safety concern, 158–59; suspended sentences in, 155, 162–64, 305; training orders in, 166, 169, 186; and transactions, 154, 156–57; victimization rates in, 13; violent crime in, 177–81, 263; voting rights of criminals in, 184, 359

Nevada, 359

New Hampshire, 231, 275. *See also* United States

New Jersey, 231. *See also* United States

New Mexico, 231, 359. *See also* United States

New South Wales: imprisonment rates in, 48; judicial discretion in, 35; mediation in, 45; preventive detention in, 40–41;

overcrowding in, 5, 20, 35–36, 228;
privatization of prisons in, 52, 301;
probation in, 30, 234, 236, 245; property
crimes in, 12, 17, 235, 242; and
proportionality, 25, 264, 288n.20,
288n.23, 407; prosecutorial discretion
in, 223, 230, 250–53; public perception
of crime rates in, 267–69; punishment
attitudes in, 233–38, 295; and
punitiveness, 16, 18, 262; "quality-of-
life" criminal justice in, 237, 242, 263;
racial disproportionality in sentencing
in, 222, 231, 238, 244–46, 254nn.7–8;
rehabilitation in, 223, 232, 233, 238–41,
286n.5; restorative justice in, 247;
retribution in, 241; sentencing
commissions in, 225–28, 230, 231, 232;
"sentencing guidelines" in, 5, 136, 138,
225–28, 233, 246–49, 274, 407, 415;
sentencing policies in, 6, 15, 18–23, 25,
32–33, 222–53, 273, 278; sentencing
reform in, 222–24; statutory determinacy
in, 224–25; three-strikes laws in, 6, 15,
16, 21, 229, 242, 253n.1, 363–64, 413;
truth in sentencing in, 15, 53–54, 272,
305; victimization rates in, 13; violent
crime in, 9, 10, 12–14, 17, 21, 228–29,
231, 236, 237, 241–43, 245, 249, 276;
voting rights of criminals in, 359; as
world model for penal policy, 294;
"zero-tolerance" policing in, 237, 263,
271–72
United States v. Harris, 230
unit fines, 71–72
Universal Declaration of Human Rights
  (UDHR), 333–35, 370, 380–81
Uppsala School, 109, 144n.6
Uruguay, 400nn.30–33
Utah, 225, 227, 359, 386. *See also* United
States

Vermont, 231, 359. *See also* United States
victims: mentally disabled victims, 340;
  rights of, 44, 315–16; study of, 12–13;
  victimization rates, 13; victim-offender
  reconciliation, 200–201, 207, 215n.34.
  See also specific countries and crimes
Victoria: appellate review in, 31, 37; crime
  rates in, 50; imprisonment rates in, 48,
  51; mediation in, 45; privatization of

prisons in, 52, 53; restitution in, 34–35;
  Sentencing Alternatives Committee in,
  31; "serious offenders" in, 39–40;
  suspended sentences in, 47–48; victim
  rights in, 44. *See also* Australia
violent crime: in Australia, 39–42, 56n.1,
  56n.5, 57n.12; and bifurcation, 263–64;
  in England and Wales, 14, 79, 80–81;
  and fines, 310; in Finland, 101; in
  Germany, 12, 194, 210–11, 212n.3,
  212n.5, 214n.24, 216n.54; international
  sentencing perspective on, 259; and life
  sentences, 354, 364; in Netherlands,
  169, 177–81, 263; trends in, 9–14; in
  United States, 9, 10, 12, 13–14, 17, 21,
  228–29, 231, 236, 237, 241–43, 245,
  249, 276. *See also* sexual offenses
Virginia, 15, 225, 226, 228, 246, 250, 359,
  386, 399n.3. *See also* United States
Voituret v. Uruguay, 400n.30
Von Hirsch, Andrew, 15, 20, 38, 88n.23,
  405–17
Von Liszt, Franz, 193
voting rights of criminals, 184, 357, 359,
  369
V. v. United Kingdom, 356

Wackenhut Corrections Corporation of
  America, 52
Wagga Wagga experiment, 45
Wales. *See* England and Wales
Walker, Nigel, 41, 110
War Crimes Tribunal for former
  Yugoslavia, 379
war, offenses against laws and customs of,
  382–83
Warren, Earl, 239–40
Warwick v. United Kingdom, 353
Washington, D.C., 225, 227. *See also*
  United States
Washington state, 22, 225, 226, 227. *See
  also* United States
Weeks v. United Kingdom, 355, 362
Weidner, Rob, 287n.10
Weigand, Thomas, 188–218
Welch v. United Kingdom, 357–58
West Virginia, 231. *See also* United
  States
White Paper, 70, 71, 72, 78
Wight v. Madagascar, 401n.34